THE GAY&
LESBIAN
LITERARY
COMPANION

THE GAY& LESBIAN LITERARY COMPANION

Sharon Malinowski and Christa Brelin

Malcolm Boyd, Consulting Editor

DETROIT   WASHINGTON, D.C.   LONDON

THE GAY & LESBIAN LITERARY COMPANION

Published by Visible Ink Press™
a division of Gale Research Inc.
835 Penobscot Building
Detroit, MI 48226–4094

Visible Ink Press is a trademark of Gale Research Inc.

Most Visible Ink Press books are available at special quantity discounts when purchased in bulk by corporations, organizations, or groups. Customized printings, special imprints, messages, and excerpts can be produced to meet your needs. For more information, contact Special Markets Manager, Visible Ink Press, 835 Penobscot Bldg., Detroit, MI 48226. Or call 1–800–776–6265.

Design by Mary Krzewinski

ISBN 0–7876–0033–4

Contents

v

Foreword

Reality and Conscience in Gay and Lesbian Literature

by Malcolm Boyd

I remember fondly and with deep gratitude when, as a youth and later a closeted gay man, I was awakened, stirred, and shaken by my first reading experiences in what was then a trickle instead of a flood of lesbian and gay literature.

My introduction to a beckoning gay world occurred when I was in junior high school. Each Saturday morning I returned a dozen books to the public library and checked out an equal number of new titles. Here, I encountered a new continent of experience. I didn't deliberately seek out gay and lesbian literature but I was amazingly intuitive.

Later, I was far more perceptive when Dag Hammarskjold's gay identity leapt out at me from between the lines of *Markings*. And shortly I encountered three gay men who helped me find myself. Like the Marschallin in *Der Rosenkavalier*, each held a mirror. I stole a look.

There was Tom in the Tennessee Williams play *The Glass Menagerie*: "I would have stopped, but I was pursued by something." (I wondered: How did Williams know my story?)

There was a lover saying goodbye in James Baldwin's novel *Giovanni's Room*: "I felt that I was drowning in his eyes." (I realized I had drowned that way too.)

There was a young screenwriter in Christopher Isherwood's novel *Prater Violet*: "The need to get back into the dark, into the bed, into the warm naked embrace ... The pain of hunger beneath everything." (That need expressed by Isherwood was also mine.)

Now I realize it's our task as gay and lesbian writers to help other people like ourselves find themselves. And we need to help heterosexual people find and know us. We also need to fulfill our own needs. But what is our place in the world as gay and lesbian writers?

Although gays and lesbians now have a recognizable place, and though our ethnicity stands with that of other minorities, we still occupy an insecure place in mainstream culture. We are always in jeopardy. Our nonconformity and diversity make us suspect. In one moment we may appear indispensable; in the next we may be fired, unpopular, even in danger.

Gay books have increased by leaps and bounds. We are on the cutting edge as lesbians and gay men who are writers. We have stories to tell. The extraordinary outpouring of our books is the vehicle of our stories. Yet as theologian Carter Heyward pointed out, there are no solos. Ours is a collective experience rooted in archetypes.

As I wrote in *Take Off the Masks*, our collective story is not unlike that of the Passover Seder, the observance based on the story of the Exodus in the Bible. First there is slavery. This is followed by a courageous and impassioned refusal to remain victims and prisoners of hatred and rejection. Facing down our Pharaohs becomes a third step. Many of us have experienced a fourth stage in a long wandering in the wilderness: searching for identity, relationship, trying to find roots. This is one of the richest sources of our literature. Finally, in our collective experience we come to arrival: roots, home, a sense of meaning, community, a promise of fulfillment, and life-affirming connections with other lesbian and gay people.

I feel I'm correct to say we wish neither to be confined within a ghetto nor be assimilated. I believe we need to retain our sharp particularity and, at the same time, occupy our place in the world. So our experience can never be characterized simplistically under a label of "either/or." Ours is a "both/and" existence. Our sexual orientation, coupled with the nature of our cultural and spiritual journey, makes us different.

Our journey has been our common teacher. Out of our lesbian and gay journey come our stories, our histories and herstories. Their individual focus inescapably opens up to a wider, broader view. This is because the particular epitomizes universal expression. So we become bearers of words of universal meaning.

The gay artist is often one who provokes wrath and censorship. A true writer or artist cannot live in isolation. He or she cannot look the other way when an attempt is made—as in the United States at the present time—to control art, suppress it, harness it to serve a utilitarian purpose. This reduces art or literature to an acceptable common denominator, and kills it.

AIDS has laid its hand on the gay community and elicited a response of sorrow and rage, survival and love. A true writer feels, cares, wishes to communicate, and expresses a willingness to enter into the dark night of the soul—his or her own, someone else's, even that of a people, or nation, or culture.

Often we are told, as writers, to listen to our muse. I have found it far more demanding and nurturing to listen to my conscience. In 1961 I was asked to join one of the early Freedom Rides in the Deep South, to ride with other unarmed people pledged to nonviolence in an effort to change laws of racial segregation. Martin Luther King, Jr., instructed us in nonviolence. I learned that it is not a tactic, but a way of life. I remember how scared I was. But after sitting all night in a dark room pondering the matter, I knew I had either to go on the Freedom Ride or die spiritually as a person, and therefore as a writer. I have no regrets; I became fully alive. In due time out of the experience came four strong dramatic sketches, often performed in various parts of the United States, and a book. Creativity was linked to life. An irony is that the dramatic sketches were later banned by a frightened, insecure television station after they were filmed, and my books were angrily burned as a form of censure after I'd come out of the closet as a gay man.

Our conscience says, "This is reality. This is you in reality. Do it. Become it. Then act it out, dance it, compose it, paint it, write it." The gay or lesbian writer's pact with conscience is his or her pact with humanity and a commitment to life itself.

Introduction

The Gay & Lesbian Literary Companion gathers the writings and biographies of 45 of literature's most talented and influential writers. The writers themselves are lesbian, gay, bisexual, heterosexual—or perhaps choose none of these terms. Their stories, plays, poems, and essays examine those themes that literature has always addressed—the myriad expressions of love, the relations of friends and family, the despair and hope, shame and dignity, and trials and joys inherent in being human. In particular, these writers have illuminated these universal themes through the light of homosexual relationships. Sometimes the references are subtle or covert, as Virginia Woolf points out in her examination of the simple sentence "Chloe liked Olivia" in *A Room of One's Own;* other times the message is bold and clear, as was Radclyffe Hall's initially banned, now celebrated novel *The Well of Loneliness.* Sometimes the relationships are analyzed philosophically and with much melancholy, as James Baldwin does in *Giovanni's Room;* other times flippantly (like Quentin Crisp in *The Naked Civil Servant*) or laughing with amusement amidst the sadness, which David Feinberg accomplishes with finesse in his tribute to a failed romance, "Breaking Up with Roger."

The *Companion* celebrates the influence of homosexual themes—and homosexual writers—on the literary canon. Often these themes have been overlooked or pointedly ignored, as was the case when Baldwin's *Giovanni's Room* was first published in 1956; more often the authors were vilified as unhealthy or criminal and their books banned as pornographic, as the famous trials of Oscar Wilde and banishment of Hall's *Well of Loneliness* can attest. During the first half of the 20th century most overtly gay and lesbian writings occupied the realm of pornography, and most managed to achieve publication only when their protagonists suffered unhappy endings—the suicide of one lover, perhaps, and the conversion of the other. Patricia Highsmith, already a successful mystery writer, achieved a breakthrough of sorts in 1952 when her novel *The Price of Salt* was released, featuring a hopeful ending for the lesbian couple and a pseudonym for the author—Highsmith wrote as Claire Morgan. The fact that Highsmith re-released the book, through Naiad

Press, under her own name in 1984, that *The Well of Loneliness* is now considered a literary classic, that the bisexual content of *Giovanni's Room* is recognized instead of ignored, testifies to how much acceptance gay and lesbian love—and literature—has achieved during this century.

Manuel Puig's novel *Kiss of the Spider Woman* won Oscar-winning recognition as a major motion picture; Virginia Woolf's *Orlando*, Jane Rule's *Desert of the Heart*, and David Leavitt's *Lost Language of the Cranes* have been filmed as well. Larry Kramer's drama dealing with the struggle against AIDS, *The Normal Heart*, was widely lauded for its frankness, and Tony Kushner's Broadway play *Angels in America: Millennium Approaches* received the 1993 Pulitzer Prize. Armistead Maupin's *Tales of the City*, originally serialized in the *San Francisco Chronicle*, became a highly popular television mini-series; Randy Shilts is universally praised for his journalistic excellence in such books as *And the Band Played On: Politics, People and the AIDS Epidemic* and *Conduct Unbecoming: Lesbians and Gays in the U.S. Military*; and classic literary giants like James Baldwin, Gertrude Stein, and Oscar Wilde continue to be read with new understanding. Certainly, gay and lesbian acceptance, like its literature, has come far.

Just as certainly, it has a long way to go. Before the civil rights era, during the formation of the gay rights movement, and throughout today's debates over military service, legal protection, and society's alternate rejection and acceptance of gays and lesbians, writers like the ones represented in the *Companion* have persistently documented their experiences and perspectives on these issues. In Patricia Highsmith's *The Price of Salt*, published in 1952, a woman loses custody of her daughter when her ex-husband presents evidence of her lesbianism. Two other stories reprinted in this volume, Jane Rule's "His Nor Hers" and Ann Allen Shockley's "A Birthday Remembered," both published during the 1980s, also address the threat of gay parents losing custody of their children solely because of the parents' sexual orientation. Fortunately, such occurrences are less automatic today; regrettably, they still happen.

The modern gay rights movement has done much to affect laws and court rulings, like those involving child custody, as well as societal perceptions. The germination of the movement is symbolized by the rebellion at Stonewall Inn in June of 1969, when patrons and staff members of a Greenwich Village gay bar fought off police for two nights after a violent raid on the club. The riot signaled the beginning of a serious resistance to such routine treatment and has become a rallying point for gay unity and action.

And the gay community has remained unified, even through inevitable internal debates. When evidence began to accumulate on the impact of AIDS during the mid-1980s, the community split for a time on responses to the disease and the people it afflicted. Was AIDS, in fact, a gay disease? Should its impact on the gay male population be reported, denied, quelled with medical care or life-style changes? In his book *And the Band Played On*, Randy Shilts describes this initial division as well as the support that gays, lesbians, and other compassionate members of society have ultimately provided to AIDS victims and to the research, medical, and educational facilities that combat the disease.

Other debates continue over such issues as "outing" prominent individuals, the publishing of pornography versus the threat of censorship, and the service of lesbians and gays in the military. Battles are won and lost: Many businesses and cities have adopted domestic partnership policies as well as ordinances that prohibit discrimination based on sexual orientation. Some states, however, have passed laws and amendments that specifically exclude homosexuals from legal protection. The struggle continues.

In his foreword to this *Companion*, noted theologian and writer Malcolm Boyd invites us to accompany him through his own journey through lesbian and gay history and its literature. Later in this book, in his autobiography and passages from *Take Off the Masks*, he describes his own awakening and urges other gay and lesbian writers to affirm their commitment to the literature and, as he writes, "to life itself." The authors profiled in the *Companion* have contributed, through their writing and their example, to our literary and cultural awakening. They are by no means alone; from a list of more than one thousand, an advisory board of gay and lesbian literary scholars (to whom we are eminently grateful and thank more fully in the **Acknowledgments**) helped narrow the list to 200 writers. This list was further narrowed to the 45 authors portrayed in the *Companion*. By representing such popular contemporary writers as Rita Mae Brown and David Leavitt, as well as historic figures like Oscar Wilde and Radclyffe Hall; by including examples of the poetry of Adrienne Rich and Gertrude Stein along with the dramas of Larry Kramer and Tony Kushner, the essays of Mary Daly and Andrea Dworkin, the autobiographies of Marie-Claire Blais and Joseph Hansen, and the novels and stories of Marion Zimmer Bradley, Jewelle Gomez, Audre Lorde, Paul Monette, Gore Vidal, Edmund White, and many others, we strove to present a representative selection of writers of lesbian and gay literature.

Here you'll learn more about these authors' lives and become acquainted with new favorites, read a sample of their writings, and find complete lists of their published works. In the **Sources** chapter at the end of the book you'll find references to further information about these writers, and the **Index** will guide you to specific authors and their works covered in this volume. Ahead is an exciting literary journey; let *The Gay & Lesbian Literary Companion* accompany you.

Sharon Malinowski
Christa Brelin

 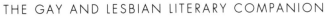

Acknowledgments

We gratefully acknowledge the advisory board members for their generous expertise and valuable suggestions in helping us select the writers included in *The Gay & Lesbian Literary Companion:* Cal Gough of the Atlanta-Fulton Public Library in Atlanta, Georgia; Roland C. Hansen of the John M. Flaxman Library at the School of the Art Institute of Chicago; Jane Jurgens of the Northeastern Illinois University Library in Chicago; Marie J. Kuda; H. Robert Malinowsky of the University of Illinois at Chicago; Adam L. Schiff of the California Academy of Science in San Francisco; David Streeter of the Pomona Public Library in Pomona, California; and Suzy Taraba.

Several talented and knowledgeable writers contributed the biographies: Karl Beckson, SDiane A. Bogus, Bradley Boney, Malcolm Boyd, Michael Broder, Michael Bronski, Jayne Relaford Brown, Paul Christensen, Andrea R. Cumpston, Carmen Embry, Jeff Hill, Jane Jurgens, Jim Kepner, Lucille Kerr, Marie J. Kuda, Michael Lutes, Pamela J. Olano, Kevin Ray, Robert B. Marks Ridinger, Pamela S. Shelton, Jeanette Smith, Deborah A. Stanley, Dayana Stetco, Claude J. Summers, and Dawn Thompson.

For editorial contributions ranging from research to typing to proofreading, thank you Shelly Andrews, Charles A. Beaubien, Julie Carnegie, Dean D. Dauphinais, Susan Knoppow, Toni Kovac, Marie J. MacNee, Neil R. Schlager, and Pamela L. Shelton. For persistent and patient acquisition of photo and text permissions, we are grateful to Margaret Chamberlain and Kim Smilay. And for all the lovely flowers, thank you Pamela Ann McIntosh.

Credits

The editors wish to thank the copyright holders of the literary excerpts and photographs included in this volume and the permissions managers of many publishing companies and photograph sources for assisting us in securing reprint rights. We are also grateful to the staffs of the Detroit Public Library, the Library of Congress, the University of Detroit Mercy Library, Wayne State University Purdy/Kresge Library Complex, and the University of Michigan Libraries for making their resources available to us. Following is a list of the copyright holders who have granted us permission to reprint material in this volume. Every effort has been made to trace copyright, but if omissions have been made, please let us know.

Photographs appearing in *The Gay & Lesbian Literary Companion* were received from the following sources:

AP/Wide World Photos: **pp. 2, 24, 32, 82, 87, 108, 161, 193, 257, 294, 304, 306, 362, 364, 427, 463, 500, 537**; Photograph by June Arnold: **p. 14**; UPI/Bettmann Newsphotos: **pp. 26, 225, 288, 354, 496**; Photograph by Marc Drolet, Montreal: **p. 36**; Copyright © Jerry Bauer: **pp. 56, 100, 158, 229, 310, 410, 460**; Copyright © Rollie McKenna: **p. 65**; Photograph by Robert E. Clark: **p. 71**; Hulton Deutsch Collection Ltd: **pp. 121, 223, 350, 356, 532**; Copyright © 1978 Gail Bryan: **p. 127**; Photograph by Gene Bagnato: **pp. 166, 509**; Photograph by Maureen Kely, courtesy of Katherine V. Forrest: **p. 184**; The Bettmann Archive: **p. 192**; Photograph by Layle Silbert: **pp. 195, 314, 424, 448**; Photograph by Val Wilmer, courtesy of Jewelle Gomez: **p. 202**; The Granger Collection, New York: **pp. 222, 446, 488, 489, 492, 522, 526, 540**; Archive Photos/Copyright © 1991 Horst Tappe: **p. 254**; Drawing by Don Bachardy: **p. 286**; Copyright © Alan Reininger/Contact Images: **p. 298**; Photograph by Robert Giard: **p. 334**; Photograph by David Perry: **p. 340**; Photograph by Mary Vazquez, courtesy of Lesléa Newman: **p. 370**; Photograph by Tee Corrine: **p. 432**; Photograph by Betty Fairbank: **p. 437**; Photograph by Julia Scher, courtesy of Routledge: **p. 452**; Springer/Bettmann Film Archive: **p. 498**; Copyright © Archive Photos: **p. 520**.

THE GAY & LESBIAN LITERARY COMPANION

DOROTHY
ALLISON

WITH THE PUBLICATION of her first novel, *Bastard Out of Carolina*, in 1992, Dorothy E. Allison moved from relative small press obscurity to near national acclaim as a writer. Although she has written for feminist, lesbian, and gay newspapers, periodicals, and presses for almost two decades, Allison—like many other gay and lesbian writers—never received much attention from the mainstream media. What was surprising about the mainstream acceptance of *Bastard Out of Carolina* was that while the book does not deal specifically with lesbianism (a topic that is present in almost all of Allison's other writings), it explores in detail domestic, personal, psychic, and sexual violence from a specifically lesbian-feminist, and to some degree, sadomasochistic point of view. It is Allison's depictions of interpersonal violence—and especially her frank and troubling analysis of how it is intrinsic to family life and personal identity—that many readers have found disturbing in her work.

Born in 1949 to a poor white family in Greenville, South Carolina, Allison grew up in an abusive but loving family. It is from this experience that she has drawn most of the material for her fiction. During and after her college years she was active in a variety of feminist projects involving battered women, child care, and women's health. It was during this time—and with these political roots—that she began writing poems and short stories. Much of Allison's writing is an attempt to understand her own abusive upbringing and the effect it had upon her life. At the same time she is completely honest about her own sexual desires and how crucial her sexuality is for her emotional and psychic survival.

In 1983 Allison published a book of poetry, *The Women Who Hate Me*. (This was updated and re-released in 1991 under the title *The Women Who Hate Me: Poetry 1980–1990*.) It was here that Allison began to detail not only her love and sexual desire for women, but also how this placed her at odds with some segments of the feminist movement. While some more mainstream feminists spoke against promiscuous sexuality, sadomasochism, and butch/femme role playing, Allison explored these very ideas in her life and her work. In an interview with *Advocate*, she spoke about those years: "I felt like a spy. During the daytime I was a

Essay by
MICHAEL BRONSKI

1

Dorothy Allison moved from relative small press obscurity to near national acclaim as a writer with the publication of her first novel, *Bastard Out of Carolina*, in 1992.

nice, lean lesbian-feminist living in a collective; at night I was a subterranean slut." In the book's title poem, Allison writes, "The women who hate me cut me / as men can't. Men don't count. / I can handle men. Never expected better / of any man anyway."

This tension between a responsible feminist analysis of sexual freedom and an anti-sexual prejudice within a segment of the mainstream feminist movement has always fueled Allison's commitment to her writing and her politics. In 1982, feminist anti-pornography advocates picketed Allison, who was speaking at a symposium on sexuality at Barnard College. "The worst accusation though," she claims in the *Advocate* interview, "was that I was guilty of child sexual abuse because of the writing I was doing." At the time, Allison was beginning to publish the stories that would eventually appear in her 1988 collection *Trash*. These harsh, funny, emotional stories about growing up poor, socially despised, and abused also include some graphic depictions of sexuality and numerous indications that Allison was, as she put it, "addicted to violence."

The themes of personal and sexual violence in *Trash* reappear in *Bastard Out of Carolina*. Allison's fiction, like that of lesbian writers Blanche McCrary Boyd and Rita Mae Brown, is closely tied to her Southern roots. But unlike Boyd, who writes from an upper-middle-class perspective, or Brown, who usually presents a somewhat sentimental view of Southern life, Allison illuminates the hard, uncertain lives of the urban and rural poor. Allison's characters are, in common parlance, trash. *Bastard Out of Carolina* tells the story of Bone, a young girl who deeply loves, and is loved by, her mother and who is physically and sexually abused by her stepfather. The emotional tension of the book arises from the fact that Bone's mother knows about this abuse but does nothing about it, thus on some level condoning the violence.

Allison understands the potential problems with this sort of material and has explicitly communicated the way in which she approached the novel. She told *Advocate*, "I wanted to write a book about a girl in a working class environment who loves her family and is smart and power-

American novelist, poet, and author of short stories.

Born: Greenville, South Carolina, April 11, 1949.

Partnerships: Companion of Alix Layman; one child.

Education: Florida Presbyterian College, St. Petersburg, B.A. 1971; New School for Social Research, New York, M.A. (anthropology).

Recipient: Lambda Literary awards for *Trash*, 1988; National Book Award nomination and Bay Area Book Reviewers Association prize for fiction for *Bastard Out of Carolina*, 1992.

Address: P.O. Box 14474, San Francisco, California 94114, U.S.A.

Agent: Frances Goldin, 305 East 11th Street, New York, New York 10003, U.S.A.

---

ful. I hate victim portraits. And I hate the pornography of victimization. Half of the incest books or family violence books sell on sexual voyeurism…. It's very hard not to titillate when you're working with this kind of material, because American culture is consumed with it." What makes *Bastard Out of Carolina* so powerful is that Allison does not attempt to present her material through any lens other than simple emotional realism. She avoids sentimentality and exploitation—the narrative's emotional quality is more than enough to grip and move us—and she feels that to do otherwise would be to betray not only her fiction but her life as well.

In her story "Her Body, Mine, and His," published in Mark Thompson's *Leatherfolk: Radical Sex, People, Politics, and Practice* in 1991, Allison describes in graphic detail a physically exhausting, tremendously powerful sexual encounter. She then writes: "I have been told that lesbians don't do this. Perhaps we are not lesbians? She is a woman. I am a woman. But maybe we are aliens? Is what we do together a lesbian act?" Much of Allison's work attempts to define an honest lesbian sexuality that takes into consideration desire, lust, past history, violence, need, class, politics, and love. Allison's prose and poetry—even when it talks about past or current violence—is an attempt to understand and redefine a whole host of physical experiences in light of the transformative power of sexuality. Later in "Her Body, Mine, and His," she writes, "The holy act of sex, my sex, done in your name, done for the only, the best reason. Because we want it." Sexuality in *Trash* and *Bastard Out of Carolina* is an instrument of self-love and salvation, a way to overcome past terrors and hurts, a way to see the present and the future. As Allison explains in the preface to *Trash:* "I write stories. I write fiction. I put on the page a third look at what I've seen in life—the condensed and reinvented experience of a cross-eyed working class lesbian, addicted to violence, language and hope, who has made the decision to live, is determined to live, on the page and on the street, for me and mine."

BASTARD OUT OF CAROLINA

Excerpt reprinted from *Bastard Out of Carolina,* Plume, copyright 1992 by Dorothy Allison.

The spring Mama married Glen Waddell, there were thunderstorms every afternoon and rolling clouds that hung around the foothills north and west to the Smokies. The moon came up with a ghostly halo almost every night, and there was a blue shimmer on the horizon at sunset. "An't no time to be marrying," Granny announced. "Or planting or building nothing."

"You sure, now, Anney?" Earle must have asked Mama twice before he drove her down to the courthouse in his pickup truck to meet Glen and get the license. It seemed he just couldn't take her ready smile for an answer, even though he agreed to be best man after Glen's brother had refused the honor. He asked her one more time before he let her out of the truck. "You're worse than Granny," Anney told him. "Don't you want to see me settled down and happy?" He gave it up and kissed her out the door.

Granny wasn't surprised when she heard that Great-Grandma Shirley had turned down her invitation to the wedding dinner Aunt Alma organized. The Eustis aunts, Marvella and Maybelle, the ones who insisted they could tell the future from their beans, also skipped the dinner, though Marvella was polite about it. "I know he loves Anney," Marvella told Alma when she came by to collect flowers from their garden. "And sometimes love can change everything."

Maybelle was not so generous. "Yeah, Glen loves Anney. He loves her like a gambler loves a fast racehorse or a desperate man loves whiskey. That kind of love eats a man up. I don't trust that boy, don't want our Anney marrying him."

"But Anney loves Glen," Alma told Maybelle impatiently. "That's the thing you ought to be thinking about. She needs him, needs him like a starving woman needs meat between her teeth, and I an't gonna let nobody take this away from her. Come on, Maybelle, you know there an't no way to say what's gonna happen between a man and a woman. That an't our business anyway, that's theirs."

Alma took Maybelle's hands between her own. "We just got to stand behind our girl, do everything we can to make sure she don't get hurt again."

"Oh, Lord." Maybelle shook her head. "I don't want to fight you, Alma. And maybe you're right. I know how lonely Anney's been. I know." She pulled her hands free, tucked some loose gray hairs up in the bun at the back of her neck, and turned to her sister. "We got to think about this, Marvella. We got to think hard about our girl."

They did what they could. The sisters sent Mama a wedding present, a love knot Marvella had made using some of her own hair, after Maybelle had cut little notches in their rabbits' ears under a new moon, adding the blood to the knot. She set the rabbits loose, and then the two of them tore up half a dozen rows of their beans and buried honeycomb in a piece of lace tablecloth where the beans had flourished. The note with the love knot told Mama that she should keep it under the mattress of the new bed Glen had bought, but Mama sniffed the blood and dried hair, and shook her head over the thing. She couldn't quite bring herself to throw it away, but she put it in one of her flower pots out in the utility room where Glen wouldn't find it stinking up their house.

* * *

Reese and I hated the honeymoon. We both thought we would get to go. For weeks before the wedding Mama kept telling us that this was a marriage of all of us, that we were taking Glen as our daddy at the same time she was taking him as a husband. She and Alma had even sewed us up little lace veils to wear as we walked ahead of her at the wedding, Reese carrying flowers while I carried the rings. But Mama and Glen left halfway through Aunt Alma's dinner, with only one quick kiss goodbye.

"Why don't we get to go?" Reese kept demanding while everybody laughed at her. I got so mad I hid in Alma's sewing room and cried myself to sleep in her rocker. When I woke up I was on her daybed with a quilt across me and the house quiet. I got Alma's picture album out and climbed into the rocker. The new pictures from the picnic were at the back. There were half a dozen snapshots of Reese and me, alone, together, and with Granny or Earle. There was only one good one of Glen and Mama, only one in which you could see her smile and his eyes. In most of them, Mama's head was bent so that only her chin showed, or Glen's face was turned away so that you saw only the pale line of his neck and ear under his new haircut. Because of that, perhaps, the good picture was even more startling.

Everything in that picture was clear, sharp, in focus, the contrast so strong you could trace the lines where sunlight sheared off and shade began. There was a blush on Mama's cheek like the shadow of a bird, polka dots on her seersucker blouse, a raised nap on her dark calf-length skirt, and a fine part in her brushed-back blond hair. Mama was beautiful in it, no question, though there was a puffiness under her eyes and a tightness in the muscles of her neck that made her chin stick out. But her smile was full, her eyes clear, and you could see right into her, see how gentle she was in the way her neck angled as she looked past Glen to Reese and me, the way her hands lay open on her lap, the fingers slightly bent as if they were ready to catch the sunlight.

Beside Mama, Glen was half in shadow with his head turned to the side, but the light shone on his smile, his cheek, his strong hands and slender frame. The smile was determined, tight, forceful, the eyes brilliant in the camera lens, gleaming in the sun's glare, the shoulders tense and hunched forward a little, one arm extended to hold Mama close, reaching around her from where he sat to her left. You could not tell a thing about Glen from that picture, except that he was a good-looking man, strong and happy to be holding his woman. Mama's eyes were soft with old hurt and new hope; Glen's eyes told nothing. The man's image was as flat and empty as a sheet of tin in the sun, throwing back heat and light, but no details—not one clear line of who he really was behind those eyes.

I tried to imagine what it would be like to live with him once the honeymoon was past. I looked at the picture again and remembered the day of the picnic, the way he kept pulling Mama back against him, his hands cupped over her belly possessively. I had heard Alma tease Mama the day before the wedding that she better hurry up and get married before she started showing. Mama had gotten all upset, demanding to know how Alma had found out she was pregnant. I wondered if she had told Glen yet.

"Come on, girls." Glen's voice when he called Reese and me for the picture had had a loud impatient note I had never heard before. I'd come back around Earle's truck at a walk and looked into his face carefully. Yes, he knew. He was so pleased with himself, he looked swollen with satisfaction under that terrible haircut. Mama had said he wanted her to have his son, and it looked to me like he was sure he had it on the way.

I sat in that rocker with those pictures until morning woke the house and Aunt Alma came to check on me. I ran my fingers over Reese's baby smile on one, traced Earle's dark hair on another, examined just how far Granny's chin pushed out under her lower lip, and looked back to my own face in each to see how the camera had seen me—my eyes like Mama's eyes, darker but open as hers, my smile fiercer and wider than Reese's, and my body in motion across Alma's yard like an animal leaping into the air.

* * *

Novels

Bastard Out of Carolina, 1992.
Cavedweller, in press.

Short Stories

Trash, 1988.
"A Lesbian Appetite," in *Women On Women*, edited by Joan Nestle and Naomi Holoch, 1990.
"Private Rituals," in *High Risk*, edited by Amy Shoulder and Ira Silverberg, 1991.
"Her Body, Mine, and His," in *Leatherfolk: Radical Sex, People,*

Politics, and Practice, edited by Mark Thompson, 1991.

Poetry

The Women Who Hate Me, 1983; as *The Women Who Hate Me: Poetry, 1980–1990*, 1991.

Other

"I Am Working on My Charm," in *Conditions: Six*, 1980.
"The Billie Jean King Thing," in *New York Native*, May 18–31, 1981.
"Confrontation: Black/White," in *Building Feminist Theory: Essays from*

"*Quest*," edited by Charlotte Bunch and others, 1981.
Skin (essays), 1993.

Recordings

Keynote address for OutWrite '92: Lesbian and Gay Writers Conference, Boston, March 20, 1992.

Adaptations

Bastard Out of Carolina (audiocassette), 1993.
Bastard Out of Carolina has been optioned for film.

Glen was like a boy about the baby, grinning and boasting and putting his palms flat on Mama's stomach every chance he could to feel his son kick. His son—he never even entertained the notion Mama might deliver a girl. No, this would be his boy, Glen was sure. He bought a crib and a new layette set on time payments, put them in their bedroom, and filled the crib with toys a boy baby would love. "My boy's gonna look like the best of me and Anney," he told everyone insistently, as if by saying it often enough he could make it so. He even went out to Aunt Maybelle and Aunt Marvella's house with a gift of sweet corn for the rabbits, just so he could look into their eyes when he said "a boy" and hear them say it back to him when they took the corn.

"They said it was a boy," he told Earle later over pinto beans and cornbread at Aunt Ruth's house—the first evidence he'd ever given that he believed in the Eustis aunts' claim to women's magic. He was bursting with pride.

"Well, goddam, Glen. Congratulations." Earle kept his face carefully neutral.

"Never come between a man and his ambitions," he told Uncle Beau after Glen had gone. "Glen ever gets the notion that anybody messed up his chance of getting a boy child out of Anney, and he's gonna go plumb crazy."

"A man should never put his ambition in a woman's belly." Beau didn't like Glen much at all, couldn't, he admitted, since he never trusted a man who didn't drink, and Glen was as close to a teetotaler as the family had ever seen. Beau spit out the side of his mouth. "Serve him right if she gave him another girl."

Uncle Nevil harrumphed, pouring them each a short glass of his home stock. Nevil never wasted words when he could grunt, or a grunt when he could move his hands. He was supposed to be the quietest man in Greenville County, and his wife, Fay, was said to be the fattest woman. "The two of them are more like furniture than anything," Granny had once said. "Just taking up space and shedding dust like a chifforobe or a couch." Nevil and Fay had heard her and in their quiet way refused to be in the same room with her ever again. It complicated family gatherings, but not too much. As Aunt Alma told everybody, Nevil wasn't any great loss to conversation anyway.

It was a surprise, then, when Nevil sipped his whiskey, lifted his head, and spoke so clearly he could be heard out on the porch. "Me, I'm hoping Anney does give him a son, half a dozen sons while she's at it. That Glen's got something about him. I almost like him, but the boy could turn like whiskey in a bad barrel, and I'm hoping he don't. Anney's had enough trouble in her life." He sipped again and shut his mouth back to its usual flat line.

Earle and Beau stared at him, unsure whether to laugh or curse, but finally they dropped their glances into their cups. It was true enough, they both agreed. Anney deserved an end to trouble in her life.

* * *

The night Mama went into labor, Glen packed the Pontiac with blankets and Cokes for Reese and me, and parked out in the hospital lot to wait. He'd been warned it was going to take a while for the baby to come, and when he couldn't stand pacing the halls anymore, he came down to smoke cigarettes and listen to music on the car radio while Reese and I napped in the backseat. At some point well before dawn, when it was still dark and cold, he reached across the seat to tug my shoulder and pull me up front with him. He gave me some Coke and half a Baby Ruth and told me he'd been in to check a little earlier and Mama was doing fine.

"Fine." I blinked at him and nodded, unsure what I was supposed to do or say. He smoked fiercely, exhaling out the top of the window where he'd opened it just a few inches, and talking to me like I was a grown-up. "I know she's worried," he said. "She thinks if it's a girl, I won't love it. But it will be our baby, and if it's a girl, we can make another soon enough. I'll have my son. Anney and I will have our boy. I know it. I know."

He talked on, whispering quietly, sometimes so softly I could not understand him. I pulled my blanket around me and watched the sprinkling of stars visible just over the tall fir trees at the edge of the lot. The song playing low on the radio was a Kitty Wells tune that Mama liked. I rocked my head to the music and watched the night. I was thinking about the baby Mama was having, wondering what it might be like, if maybe it wouldn't be a girl. What were they going to name it? Glen Junior, if it was a boy? They had never said. Mama thought it was unlucky to choose a name for a baby till it was born.

Glen put his hand on my neck, and the stars seemed to wink at me. I wasn't used to him touching me, so I hugged my blanket and held still. He slid out from behind the steering wheel a little and pulled me up on his lap. He started humming to the music, shifting me a little on his thighs. I turned my face up to look into his eyes. There were only a few lights on in the parking lot, but the red and yellow dials on the radio shone on his face. He smiled, and for the first time I saw the smile in his eyes as plain as the one on his mouth. He pushed my skirt to the side and slid his left hand down between my legs, up against my cotton panties. He began to rock me then, between his stomach and his wrist, his fingers fumbling at his britches.

It made me afraid, his big hand between my legs and his eyes glittering in the dim light. He started talking again, telling me Mama was going to be all right, that he loved me, that we were all going to be so happy. Happy. His hand was hard, the ridge of his wristbone pushing in and hurting me. I looked straight ahead through the windshield, too afraid to cry, or shake, or wiggle, too afraid to move at all.

He kept saying, "It's gonna be all right." He kept rocking me, breathing through his mouth and staring straight ahead. I could see his reflection in the windshield. Dawn began to filter through the trees, making everything bright and cold. His hand dug in further. He was holding himself in his fingers. I knew what it was under his hand. I'd seen my cousins naked, laughing, shaking their things and joking, but this was a mystery, scary and hard. His sweat running down his arms to my skin smelled strong and nasty. He grunted, squeezed my thighs between his arm and his legs. His chin pressed down on my head and his hips pushed up at the same time. He was hurting me, hurting me!

I sobbed once, and he dropped back down and let go of me. I bit my lips and held still. He brought his hand up to wipe it on the blanket, and I could smell something strange and bitter on his fingers. I pulled away, and that made him laugh. He kept laughing as he scrubbed his fingers against the blanket. Then he lifted me slightly, turning me so he could look into my face. The light was gray and pearly, the air wet and marble-cold, Glen's face the only thing pink and warm in sight. He smiled at me again, but this time the smile was not in his eyes. His eyes had gone dark and empty again, and my insides started to shake with fear.

He wrapped the blanket around me tight and put me back with Reese in the nest of blankets and pillows he'd built up so many hours ago. I hunched my shoulders against the seat and watched Glen's head in the gray light, his short hairs bristly and stiff. He lit another cigarette and started humming again. He looked back once and I quickly closed my eyes, then was too afraid to open them again. His hum went on in time to the soft radio music, and the smell of Pall Malls began to soothe me. I didn't know I was falling asleep until I woke up in the bright gray light of full morning.

Glen was gone, the car still and cold. There was an ache between my legs, but I wasn't afraid in the daylight. I sat up and looked out on gray clouds and dew-drenched fir branches. The asphalt looked wet and dark. There were a few nurses going in and out the emergency-room doors, talking in low mumbly tones. I breathed through my mouth and watched as more and more people drove into the lot, wondering if I had dreamed that whole early-morning scene. I kept squeezing my thighs together, feeling the soreness, and trying to imagine how I could have bruised myself if it had been a dream.

When Glen came out of the emergency room, the doors swung back like a shot in the morning air. His face was rigid, his legs stiff, his hands clamped together in front of him, twisting and twisting. I looked into that face and knew it had not been a dream. I pulled Reese up against me, ignoring her soft protesting cry. Glen climbed in the car and slammed the door so hard Reese woke up with a jerk. She twisted her head like a baby bird, looking from me to Glen's neck and back again. We sat still, waiting.

He said, "Your mama's gonna be all right." He paused.

"But she an't gonna have no more babies." He put his hands on the steering wheel, leaned forward, pushed his mouth against his fingers.

He said, "My baby's dead. My boy. My boy."

I wrapped my arms around Reese and held on, while in the front seat, Glen just sobbed and cried.

* * *

After Mama got home from the hospital, her sisters came around to see us every day. Aunt Ruth had been in the hospital with what Granny called female trouble only a few weeks before, and still wasn't well enough to do much but sit with Mama for an hour or two and hold her hand, but she called every morning. Aunt Alma practically moved in and took over, making Mama stay in bed, doing all the cooking, and fixing beef and bean stew. "To put some iron back in your blood, honey," she said.

Aunt Raylene showed up in her overalls and low boots to clean the house from one end to the other, going so far as to make Reese and me help her move furniture out in the yard for the sun to warm it. When she went in to change the sheets on Mama's bed, she lifted Mama easily and carried her out to sit on the couch in the fresh air. Everyone stepped around Glen like he was another chair or table, occasionally giving him a quick hug or squeeze on the shoulder. He didn't respond, just shifted from the table to the porch when Raylene started sweeping. When Nevil and Earle came over, he stood out in the yard with them and drank until his shoulders started to go up and down in fierce suppressed sobs and they looked away to spare him being embarrassed.

I watched him closely, staying out in the yard as much as I could, squatting down in the bushes where I hoped no one could see me. I put my chin on my knees and hugged myself into a tight curled ball. Mama's face had been so pale when they brought her home, her eyes enormous and unblinking. She had barely looked at me when I tried to climb up in her lap, just bit her lips and let Aunt Alma pull me away. I cried until Aunt Raylene took me out in her truck and rocked me to sleep with a damp washcloth on my eyes.

"Your mama's gonna need a little time," she told me. "Then she's gonna need you more than she ever has. When a woman loses a baby, she needs to know that her other babies are well and happy. You be happy for her, Bone. You let your Mama know you are happy so she can heal her heart."

They did name him Glen Junior, Reese told me. She had heard Aunt Ruth and Aunt Alma talking. They had buried the baby in the big Boatwright plot Great-grandma Shirley owned, with the four boys Granny had lost and Ruth's stillborn girls and Alma's first boy. Glen had wanted a plot of his own but had no money to buy one, and that seemed to be the thing that finally broke his grief and turned it to rage. His face was swollen with crying and gray with no sleep. He found a house over by the JC Penney mill near the railroad tracks and came home to announce we were moving. Aunt Alma was outraged he'd take us so far away, but Mama just nodded and asked Raylene to help her pack.

"It'll be all right," she told Reese and me.

Glen put his arms around Mama and glared at Aunt Alma. "We don't need nobody else," he whispered. "We'll do just fine on our own."

JUNE ARNOLD

JUNE DAVIS ARNOLD had a unique vision of a world where it was possible for women to exert control over their own destinies. Her work as a novelist, feminist, and publisher contributed to the dissemination of that ideal. The women in her novels come together, draw support from one another, and gird their loins to do battle with the controlling order that oppresses them. As cofounders of Daughters, Inc., in 1973, Arnold and her partner, attorney Parke Bowman, put their theories of empowerment into practice. Together with Bertha Harris—novelist and coauthor of *The Joy of Lesbian Sex*—and feminist political guru Charlotte Bunch, Arnold and Bowman set out to take on the establishment presses that gave little attention to women's work.

Essay by
MARIE J. KUDA

Arnold's success in writing and publishing came after some 40 years of varied life experiences. She lived most of her childhood in Houston, Texas, and after a period at Vassar from 1943 to 1944, she took two literature degrees from Rice University. After being married and divorced, Arnold and her four children moved to Greenwich Village, where she wrote her first novel, *Applesauce*, published by McGraw-Hill in 1967. The author's political concerns became evident as she undertook her writing career; in response to a query from *Contemporary Authors* in the 1970s, she listed her politics as "Feminist" and her religion as "Women." With her lover, Bowman, she moved to Plainfield, Vermont, where they started their feminist publishing venture in the early 1970s. Daughters, Inc., published five titles annually from 1973 through 1978, including three by Arnold: *The Cook and the Carpenter*, under Arnold's pseudonym, Carpenter; *Sister Gin*; and a reprint of *Applesauce*. Arnold also contributed to a number of periodicals, including the *Village Voice*, *Quest*, *Amazon Quarterly*, the *Houston Post*, *Plexus*, and *Sister Courage*. Since Arnold's death in 1982, excerpts of her work have appeared in several anthologies, and the novel *Baby Houston* was published in 1987.

Generally held to be her most popular work, *Sister Gin* was an immediate success, due in no little part to an excerpt that appeared in a special "Sexuality" issue of *Amazon Quarterly*. The chapter in which the aging, slightly deaf Mamie Carter and the menopausal Su engage in sen-

suous sex was hailed as a *tour de force* by lesbians, feminists, and octogenarians. In *Sister Gin* Arnold dealt with the then-timely feminist issues of alcoholism, race, and obesity, treating them with insight and humor.

Arnold's fiction has generally been labeled "experimental" and "lesbian." *Applesauce* features an androgynous character that experiences life from both male and female perspectives, and has been compared more than once to Virginia Woolf's *Orlando*. The book was largely ignored by lesbians, however, until its later reprint from Daughters, Inc. *The Cook and the Carpenter*, on the other hand, made an immediate impact on the lesbian-feminist community. The book featured a commune of people with neutral names, and the author's creation of the neutral pronouns "na" and "nam" allowed free exploration and testing of preconceptions about roles and class in society. Copies of the book were passed around discussion groups, and Arnold's name became rapidly known in the lesbian subculture of the early 1970s.

In June Arnold's vision of the world, women could exert control over their own destinies by coming together, drawing support from one another, and girding their loins to do battle with the controlling order that oppressed them.

Included in the first offering of titles from Daughters, Inc., was Rita Mae Brown's *Rubyfruit Jungle* as well as *The Cook and the Carpenter*, and both quickly established the reputation of the press. *Rubyfruit Jungle* eclipsed the popularity of almost every lesbian novel that had ever been published; the book sold 90,000 copies in 11 printings. With this kind of success, it was inevitable that the mainstream entertainment industry would attempt to capitalize on the book's appeal. By 1976 Daughters, Inc., was besieged by the establishment with offers for paperback and movie rights for the book. As reported by Lois Gould in the *New York Times Magazine*, Brown was in favor of the sale while others at Daughters, Inc., were uncertain about the feminist ramifications of the movie deal. The eventual sale of the film rights at a seven-figure price was perceived by some in the feminist community as a compromise of the small press's principles.

In spite of the income and attention created by *Rubyfruit Jungle*, Arnold believed in the necessity of a strong, independent women's communications network. She had envisioned presses, publishers, book-

American novelist. Also wrote as Carpenter.

Born: Greenville, South Carolina, October 27, 1926. Raised in Houston, Texas.

Partnerships: Married (and divorced), four children; companion of Parke Bowman.

Education: Vassar College, 1943–44; Rice University, B.A. 1948, M.A. 1958.

Died: March 11, 1982.

sellers, magazines, writers, and women consumers linked by a media under their own control. In an article she wrote for *Quest*, Arnold noted that the "words of earlier feminists were lost because they were the property of male publishers who easily avoided reprinting them." She outlined the reasons writers should publish with feminist presses, stressing, "It is vital that we spend the energy of our imaginations and criticisms building feminist institutions that women will gain from both in money and skills." She foresaw that the establishment presses "will publish some of us—the least threatening, the most saleable, the most easily controlled or a few who cannot be ignored."

Arnold and Daughters, Inc., initiated a conference of women that she hoped would be instrumental in advancing such a women's network. In late summer of 1976 about 130 women representing more than 80 presses, publishers, journals, and bookstores met for seven days in a dry, hot Nebraska Campfire Girls campground. The majority of those attending the conference were lesbian, and most took to heart the various lessons learned in workshops and by networking with one another at the event. In the years since that first Women in Print conference, economics and politics have taken their toll among the participants, but the survivors are journals and presses that have allowed lesbian-feminist publishing to reach a readership that numbers in the millions. Despite this success, it is more than an exercise in fantasy to speculate on the quality and direction lesbian-feminist book publishing would have taken had not Arnold been forced to withdraw and do battle with cancer.

She and Bowman returned to Texas, where Arnold worked on a novel about her mother. *Baby Houston* was published posthumously to positive reviews. Philip Lopate, author of *The Rug Merchant*, declared in a dust jacket blurb that the book was "simply the best novel ever written about Houston." Jane Marcus in the *Women's Review of Books* called it "the novel of the year," and added that "the portrait it paints of a mother and two daughters in Houston between 1939 and 1964 is as bitter and as sweet as a good margarita."

The underground demand for *Sister Gin*, widely circulated in Xeroxed fragments among women's studies classes and readers of lesbian erotica, resulted in a 1989 reprint of the work now dubbed a feminist classic. Bonnie Zimmerman in *Safe Sea of Women* (a title drawn from *Sister Gin*) praises Arnold as an experimental writer and cites her as one of few lesbians writing political fiction in the 1970s. She also notes Arnold's impact as a publisher and calls attention to the fact that of the small group of politically-aware writers of lesbian material, all—including Arnold, Elana Nachman, Monique Wittig, and Rita Mae Brown—were published by Daughters, Inc.

SISTER GIN

Excerpt reprinted from *Sister Gin*, Daughters, Inc., copyright 1975 by June Arnold.

With a late September sunset of lavender-gold behind her and the smell of fish and seawater making her hungry all over, Sue stepped into the inside of her love's house for the first time. The flat straw rug made the soles of her feet ache through sandals and long to be kissed. Mamie Carter kissed her on the cheek after the custom. Seizing that proximate cheek's smell with her nostrils, Su inhaled her reward and knew better than to kiss back.

They sat on the back porch and watched the sun set over Wrightsville Sound, on that old weathered porch of an old two-story beach house where Mamie Carter had spent her summers as a child (and subsequently her children and then her grandchildren), one of the few houses to withstand all the hurricanes—sat listening to the leftover summer sounds of children's water games and deploring the increasing number of motored boats each season replacing the elegant sails. The martini threw a skin over Su's brain wiping out the city as they sat in the gentle decay of the day, the house softly decaying behind them, the summer itself mature and used and gracefully marked, letting out its last few days with the dignity of a menopausal woman releasing her last few eggs, knowing that they were for form only, that the season was over but there was no hurry about slipping over into the next, it will come in its season and here, these my last are as worthy as my first.

Su felt ashamed that she had been afraid ... of Mamie Carter who was as legal in all her tentacles as old Wilmington itself; of her own passion which, here on this clan-protected porch, could be sublimated into charm as if she were a real member of that impeccable clan.

Shaking her olive free from its gregarious ice, Su heard Mamie Carter's voice off her left ear asking her to fetch them each a refill,

THE GAY AND LESBIAN LITERARY COMPANION

because Captain wasn't here, because she was alone, expecting no one but Su this evening. Su took each glass in a grip firm enough to break them—someone could still drop in, would come visit, seeing the lights, her car, could drop by for hours yet, this being the tradition of the beach, the gregariousness of ice and an island.

* * *

They talked of the town's recent rapes and the bizarre circumstance of the two rapists' being laid out, tied to a board, one on the steps of the old folks' home, one in the front yard of the councilman who pulled the largest vote and was therefore mayor. Both rapists were white, short-haired, in their middle thirties, and were found nether-naked and tied outstretched to a piece of plywood in the shape of an x. Since the first rape had been of a sixty-five-year-old woman of color, it was thought that the first man's punishment was the work of a Black Klan group. The rapist had hysterically insisted that the old woman sent five old women spirits after him but no one paid him any mind. The second rape victim had been a junior high-school girl, forced at stranglehold to suck off her attacker; since she was white and since in this case too the rapist had babbled of five grannies who, though masked, had white hands, some of the townspeople wondered if there were witches still afoot.

"Posh," Mamie Carter said. "What kind of talk is that? Black Klans and witches. Next thing they'll say the freebooters are back haunting the Cape Fear."

"What do you think?" Su asked.

"I think the rapists are getting a big fuss made over them. They're not the victims."

"Do you think it was really … women who did it?"

"*Old* women?" Mamie Carter's black eyes glinted with laughter. She stood up. "You know, I can't wear flat-heel shoes any more," she said, looking at her medium-heeled sandals below white sharkskin slacks. "I wore high heels so long my Achilles' tendon is permanently shortened."

"Do you?"

Su followed her strong slightly-humped back into the house. "These slacks are from before the war. Would you feel bad if a real shark had given his skin for them?"

The inside of the house was dark after the bright twilight reflections of the porch. Mamie Carter led Su to the kitchen and flicked on the light.

"You've painted it yellow!" Su remembered to speak loud. "Yellow is my favorite color."

"Mine too." Mamie Carter's smile was a caress. "Have you ever thought of wearing a bright yellow wig? Now don't try to talk to me while I'm fixing dinner. You know I can't hear you when my back is turned."

* * *

"Now that streak there," Mamie Carter said, nodding at a white swath across the middle of the dining room table, "was made by the yankees. They came to my grandmother's house and took everything they could. Since they didn't have any way to carry off the table, the yankee officer sent to the kitchen for some vinegar and poured it across there. It won't come off. Have some more shrimp, Su." Mamie Carter wiped her mouth delicately and smiled. "Old tables tell old tales."

"Mamie Carter," Su said, her fingers holding the ancient heavy lace of her napkin, her other fingers resting on the heavy stem of the goldleaf wine glass, her eyes staring at that bright elfin face leaning toward her through the candlelight. "I've never eaten such delicious shrimp."

"It wasn't too hot, was it?" Mamie Carter had cooked the tiny North Carolina shrimp with sour cream, wine, onions, mushrooms, and a lot of cayenne. "I don't taste anything without cayenne any more. Besides, it's the only way I can keep my grandchildren from eating every meal with me."

"It made all other shrimp seem bland, diluted, incomplete, wan, and colorless. Unworthy of notice." All unmarked tables, unlined faces, modern clothes, new napkins, streamlined wine glasses, all young or middle-aged things were thrown into a heap of inconsequentiality which, like herself, Su felt to be unfinished, unseasoned, green and smooth and callow. "I think I am in love with you, Mamie Carter."

The bright elfin face smiled broadly and did not answer.

Had she heard? In this pocket of the past, within dark wood and the dark saltiness of a September tide coming in and the faint rust smell of old screens and occasional sound of wind flapping the awnings, Su felt herself suddenly dead. She doubted that she had spoken. She had been switched into afterlife where words did not need to be spoken. She had left her amorphous dully-young fifty-year-old body behind and drifted through the definite world of the dead, the epitomized grave, the capsule of self which carried in its concentrate all the love she had ever sought. Mamie Carter did not need to hear; she would know.

A spare hand marbled with a bulging network of veins reached for Su's. "I know."

"Of course you do," Su said, laughing, unable to move her own hand caught in a cave beneath that perfect antique one.

"I've known for a while."

"Of course you have!" Su's smile was as stiff as her body balanced off the touch of that hand. "I should have known you'd know."

* * *

"Mamie Carter?" She held that final face taut on a thread of sight. Her hand closed across the silk bones that were Mamie Carter's hand, curled up-reaching on a free patch of sheet in the middle of a Queen Anne bed. Memory was already claiming the sight of her dimpled flesh, infinite dimples winking in their softness, skin so old it had lost all abrasives, rid itself of everything that can shield the body against the world; skin vulnerable, nonresilient, soft forever—Su's fingers had to resist the longing to take some of that flesh and mold it.

"Yes, perfect?"

Su sunk her face into the ageless curve of her love's shoulder and smothered a giggle. "There is one extraordinary thing about us that I have to say, even here on these romantic rainswept sheets, even at the risk of hearing your 'posh'... your silk is matched only by our exquisite ability to prolong swallowing, our mutual toothlessness allowing for such a long balance on the tip of flavor: I just never imagined that the delights of age would include the fact of endlessly drawnout orgasms. Did you always know?"

"You like it, too?"

"Without leaving us with a mouthful of cotton wadding. Without wearing down flavor. Without diminishment. With the loss of nothing at all, in fact, except fear."

"I always thought, if old age could be beautiful, life would hold no more terrors. Now if you'll stop talking a minute, Su, I want to get up and put on my negligee."

Mamie Carter swung her legs out of sight, turned her beautiful back, and slipped into a charcoal-red robe—really slipped, but then she had had sixty years' practice. Su saw in her mind her coveted breasts, bound flat to her chest when she was in her twenties to produce a flapper fashion, hanging now from the base of the breastbone like soft toys, too small to rest a head upon, fit for a hand to cuddle very gently like the floppy ears of a puppy.

Memory moved her hand to Mamie Carter's belly—skin white as milk, finely pucked like sugar-sprinkled clabber; memory dropped her hand to Mamie Carter's sparse hair curling like steel—there was strength

Novels

Applesauce, 1967.
The Cook and the Carpenter (as Carpenter), 1973.
Sister Gin (one chapter originally pub- lished in *Amazon Quarterly* 3:2, 1975), 1975; with afterword by Jane Marcus, 1989.
Baby Houston, introduction by Beverly Lowry, 1987.

Other

"Feminist Presses and Feminist Politics," in *Quest: A Feminist Quarterly*, summer 1976, 18–26.

between her legs and no dough there where the flesh was fluid enough to slip away from the bone and leave that tensed grain hard as granite and her upright violent part like an animal nose against Su's palm. The impact of memory bruised. Su said, to the back that could not hear, "Don't you dare die, Mamie Carter Wilkerson."

Now, as Su was feeling wicked lying in bed while Mamie Carter sat up in her little armchair with the rose-colored skirt, a flash began in a tiny prickling over her upper skin. Last night, just as she had reached to kiss Mamie Carter the second time, reached toward those lips as to a dandelion, she had felt this same beginning prickle and a tear had dropped down each cheek, prewetting the flash with despair.

"You're flashing, Su," Mamie Carter had said.

Tears streamed as if they would flood out the flash and Su had said helplessly, "Why now? Why why why *now?*"

"Why not now?" Mamie Carter had said gently, laying Su back down on the bed, circling her shoulder, stroking her cheek and neck and breasts. "Why not now?" she had said, kissing the shame from Su's flushed lips, sliding her cheek over the sweat of Su's doubly-wet cheek and slippery forehead. Her arm had reached through Su's legs and she had held her in an infant curve, whispering again, "Why not now?" as Su slipped down into the abandon of hotly wetting herself and the flash had raged, burst, and slowly subsided.

Now, lying wickedly in bed, Su ducked under the prickles and welcomed the flash which centered her whole extraordinary body in a fever of change.

"What about Bettina?" Mamie Carter said and Bettina's voice echoed in the room, her blue quilted robe accusing.

I'll always love you, Bettina had said twenty years ago, when always had been forever. Now, with always cut in half, it seemed she had exchanged her mobility for a foundation of quicksand which would suck the house in after it. But still Bettina said it, and even now the words made her feel safe inside their sucking sound.

"*I'll* always love you, Su," Mamie Carter said with a small dry laugh like a kick. "Now Bettina's old enough to know better than to compare her 'always' with mine ... certainly old enough to know better than that and I naturally know exactly how old she is since her mother and I had our daughters the same month." Mamie Carter held Su's flailing head. "When I say always, perfect, it's an underbid."

"Mamie," Su said to feel the impertinence of using that bare name. "Did you really fall in love with me?"

"No. I just wanted to get you in bed where I could hear you."

* * *

"Now you sit among the yellow and read the paper. I'll fix breakfast," Su said, wishing Mamie Carter were fragile so she could perch her on the breakfast table in a vase. Her hand met an upper arm as muscular as her own.

"That's yesterday's paper."

"Well, I didn't read it. I was out all day. Doesn't news keep?"

"You didn't read the paper yesterday?"

Su put coffee on to perk and squeezed two glasses of orange juice as if this kitchen were her own. "Why, what's in the paper? How do you like your eggs?"

"Quietly in the icebox."

A bumping along the boardwalk and cry of *o-cree! o-cree! fresh tomatoes and o-o-o-creeeee!* came into the morning. Su sat down with a temporary cup of instant coffee and pulled the paper over. "What's in the paper?"

"What we were talking about last night. There."

BOUND SOCIALITE LEFT ON CORNWALLIS STEPS

Clayton Everett Eagle III, Wilmington socialite, was found tied to a board early this morning by a fish merchant, Rowland Livers. Mr. Livers called the police, who reached the scene at approximately seven o'clock.

Mr. Eagle, who declined to comment, was apparently the victim of the same person or persons responsible for similar incidents in the past month. He was tied, partially nude, to a piece of plywood and had been placed in the side yard by the steps leading up to the Cornwallis house sometime early this morning.

The most puzzling clue was a note pinned to his shirt reading, *Shirley Temples Emeritae*. When a reporter asked the police if this might indicate that the gang responsible included some members of the fair sex, Lieutenant Francis Colleton, who described himself as an amateur Shakesperian, replied, "If fair is foul and foul is fair."

The question still unanswered is the reason for Mr. Eagle's pillorying. The previous victims of the gang had been an alleged rapist and an alleged sodomite. The choice of the Cornwallis house might be connected to the fact that Mr. Eagle recently moved to this area from New England.

"Isn't he related to you?" Su asked.

"Connected. Or was. He's kin only to Lucifer."

"Who do you think …?" A non–North Carolinian herself by birth, Su felt the reflex of an outsider who would never be able to say *ho-oose* (house) giving the word its full Chaucerian diphthong like a native. Although she was not a yankee, she wondered if Clayton Eagle had gotten himself labelled "outside agitator" and prepared to draw in her liberal skirts against this Temple gang.

"Now that's just damned nonsense, Su. We're not still fighting the War Between the States here. You know we'd already voted not to secede, but when they opened fire on our cousins, then we had to. South Carolina was family—we weren't even separated until 1729. No, I think Mr. Eagle has more to answer for than his misfortune of a birthplace. The Temple Gang. I like that."

* * *

Driving back across the causeway that separated land from land, Su threw her words wide so they could skip across the gray glass of Wrightsville Sound: "Change of life by definition refers to the future; one life is finishing therefore another life must be beginning. The menopausal armies mass on the brink of every city and suburb; everything that was is over and there is nothing left there to keep our sights lowered. See the rifles raised? This army doesn't travel on its uterus any more. Bettina, you must see that to stay back in that young section with you when I can reach out to age itself, lust after a final different dry silken life and so much grace and elegance from all that knowledge of days…. There is no more beautiful word in the language than withered."

JAMES BALDWIN

RENOWNED NOVELIST and essayist James Arthur Baldwin bore articulate witness to the unhappy consequences of American racial strife. His
writing career began in the last years of legislated segregation; his fame as
a social observer grew in tandem with the civil rights movement as he
mirrored the aspirations, disappointments, and coping strategies of blacks
in a hostile society. In the novels, plays, and essays he wrote during the
turbulent decades of the 1950s and 1960s, Baldwin explored the psychological implications of racism for both the oppressed and the oppressor.
Works such as *Notes of a Native Son* and *Nobody Knows My Name*
acquainted wide audiences with his highly personal observations and his
sense of urgency in the face of rising black unrest.

Essay by
PAMELA S. SHELTON

Baldwin's own story is as compelling as that of the characters he
created within his novels. The oldest of nine children, he was raised in
Harlem by his stepfather, an evangelical preacher who struggled to support a large family from whom he demanded excessively rigorous religious
behavior. As a youth, Baldwin found time away from caring for his
younger siblings to read and write; he was an excellent student who
sought escape from the increased abusiveness of his stepfather through
literature, movies, and the theatre. At the age of 14, he underwent a dramatic religious conversion. Partly in response to his nascent sexuality and
partly as a further buffer against the ever-present temptations of drugs
and crime, Baldwin began a junior ministry at the Fireside Pentecostal
Assembly. After three years, however, he lost the desire to preach as he
began to question African Americans' acceptance of the Christian tenets
that had, in his estimation, been used to enslave them.

After graduating from high school in 1942, Baldwin took a job at a
railroad site in nearby New Jersey to help support his family; mental
instability had incapacitated his stepfather. There he was confronted
daily with racism, discrimination, and the debilitating regulations of segregation. Following his stepfather's death in 1946, Baldwin determined to
make writing his sole profession. Tired of grappling with the overt racism
then prevalent in New York City, as well as with the growing awareness
of his own homosexuality, he began to find the social tenor of the United

23

James Baldwin in his Saint Paul de Vence house in 1983, four years before his death there of cancer.

States increasingly stifling. Despite the fact that such prestigious periodicals as the *Nation, New Leader,* and *Commentary* had begun to accept his essays and short stories for publication, in 1948, at the age of 24, Baldwin moved to Paris. He lived in France, on and off, for the remainder of his life.

"Once I found myself on the other side of the ocean," Baldwin told the *New York Times,* "I could see where I came from very clearly, and I could see that I carried myself, which is my home, with me. You can never escape that. I am the grandson of a slave, and I am a writer. I must deal with both." Through some difficult financial and emotional periods, Baldwin undertook a process of self-realization that included both an acceptance of his heritage and an admittance of his bisexuality. Europe gave the young author many things: a broader perspective from which to view his own identity, the love affair with Lucien Happersberger that would dominate his later fiction, and a burst of creative energy. Baldwin composed a wealth of essays, beginning with 1953's *Autobiographical Notes.* Concurrently published were novels, such as *Go Tell It on the Mountain,* and the play *The Amen Corner,* the first of Baldwin's works to explore both race and sexuality freely.

THE GAY AND LESBIAN LITERARY COMPANION

American civil rights activist, novelist, short story writer, playwright, poet, and essayist.

Born: New York City, August 2, 1924.

Education: DeWitt Clinton High School, New York City, 1942.

Career: Youth minister at Fireside Pentecostal Assembly, New York City, 1938–42; variously employed as a handyman, dishwasher, and waiter in New York City, and in defense work in Belle Meade, New Jersey, 1942–46. Lecturer on racial issues at universities in the United States and Europe, 1957–87. Director of play, *Fortune and Men's Eyes*, in Istanbul, Turkey, 1970, and film, *The Inheritance*, 1973. Contributor of book reviews and essays to periodicals, including *Harper's, Nation, Esquire, Playboy, Partisan Review, Mademoiselle*, and *New Yorker*.

Memberships: Member of Congress on Racial Equality national advisory board, American Academy and Institute of Arts and Letters, Authors League, International PEN, Dramatists Guild, Actors' Studio, National Committee for a Sane Nuclear Policy.

Recipient: Eugene F. Saxton fellowship, 1945; Rosenwald fellowship, 1948; Guggenheim fellowship, 1954; National Institute of Arts and Letters grant for literature, 1956; Ford Foundation grant, 1959; National Conference of Christians and Jews Brotherhood Award, 1962, for *Nobody Knows My Name: More Notes of a Native Son*; George Polk Memorial Award, 1963, for magazine articles; Foreign Drama Critics Award, 1964, for *Blues for Mister Charlie*; D.Litt. from the University of British Columbia, Vancouver, 1964; National Association of Independent Schools Award, 1964, for *The Fire Next Time*; American Book Award nomination, 1980, for *Just Above My Head*; named Commander of the Legion of Honor (France), 1986.

Died: In St. Paul de Vence, France, of stomach cancer, December 1, 1987.

Many critics view Baldwin's nonfiction as his most significant contribution to American literature. His essays probed beyond problems of white versus black, uncovering the essential issues of personal identity and self-determination. But racial unrest was not the only topic of controversy that Baldwin addressed through his writing. In fictional works, such as *Go Tell It on the Mountain* and 1956's *Giovanni's Room*, his bold introduction of homosexual themes provided Baldwin with another vehicle for the exploration of prejudice. "By insisting on honest explorations of gay and bisexual themes in his novels," notes Emmanuel S. Nelson in *Contemporary Gay American Novelists*, "Baldwin made a sharp break from the African-American literary conventions; through a radical departure from tradition, he helped create the space for a generation of young African-American gay writers who succeeded him. Long before the Stonewall Riots of 1969 helped liberate the gay literary imagination in the United States, Baldwin boldly made his sexuality a vital part of the vision he projected in his art. He was, in the finest sense of the word, a revolutionary."

Because Baldwin's fiction contains interracial love affairs—both homosexual and heterosexual—he came under attack from the writers of the Black Arts Movement who called for a literature exclusively by and

Noted social commentator James Baldwin in his thirties.

for blacks. Eldridge Cleaver, in his book *Soul on Ice*, accused Baldwin of a hatred of blacks and "a shameful, fanatical fawning" love of whites. Baldwin refused to be pigeonholed by reverse racism—he referred to himself as an "American writer" as opposed to a "black writer" and continued to confront the issues facing a multi-racial society. What Cleaver and others saw as complicity with whites, Baldwin defended as his personal attempt to alter the violent and oppressive environment faced by minorities. The masked homophobia of the Black Arts Movement found its reflection in the mainstream media's critical response to much of Baldwin's fiction: sometimes a reviewer's response was a violent denunciation of a work's homosexual theme, but more often such themes were discreetly overlooked and answered with silence. As Nelson asserts: "[The critics'] silence is not merely a result of blindness but a carefully defined political posture. It is a strategy of enforcing invisibility; it is a way of denying the significance of Baldwin's sexual identity and the gay content of his work."

It was Baldwin's stature as a champion of the black cause that enabled him to weather such cool and evasive critical reception. As James Levin notes in *The Gay Novel in America*, "Baldwin could write about homosexuality because his literary reputation had been confirmed and because those who wished to support him as a black writer refrained from attacking him on what seemed to be an extraneous or possibly detrimental issue." His fiction continued to explore the "full weight and complexity" of the individual in a society prone to callousness and categorization; love, both sexual and spiritual, continued to be the essential component of Baldwin's characters' quests for self-realization. John W. Aldridge observes in the *Saturday Review* that sexual love "emerges in [Baldwin's] novels as a kind of universal anodyne for the disease of racial separatism, as a means not only of achieving personal identity but also of transcending false categories of color and gender." Homosexual encounters were, for Baldwin, a principal means to achieve important revelations. Typically, some reviewers chose to see Baldwin's use of gay protagonists in this manner as merely a literary device: a human being whose acceptance of his own deviant nature made him uniquely capable of giving love unconditionally.

Baldwin died in 1987, a victim of cancer. The publication of his collected essays, *The Price of the Ticket: Collected Nonfiction, 1948–1985*,

THE GAY AND LESBIAN LITERARY COMPANION

and his subsequent death sparked reassessments of his career and comments on the quality of his lasting legacy. In a posthumous profile for the *Washington Post*, Juan Williams wrote: "The success of Baldwin's effort as the witness is evidenced time and again by the people, black and white, gay and straight, famous and anonymous, whose humanity he unveiled in his writings. America and the literary world are far richer for his witness. The proof of a shared humanity across the divides of race, class and more is the testament that the preacher's son, James Arthur Baldwin, has left us."

GIOVANNI'S ROOM

I repent now—for all the good it does—one particular lie among the many lies I've told, told, lived, and believed. This is the lie which I told to Giovanni but never succeeded in making him believe, that I had never slept with a boy before. I had. I had decided that I never would again. There is something fantastic in the spectacle I now present to myself of having run so far, so hard, across the ocean even, only to find myself brought up short once more before the bulldog in my own backyard—the yard, in the meantime, having grown smaller and the bulldog bigger.

I have not thought of that boy—Joey—for many years; but I see him quite clearly tonight. It was several years ago. I was still in my teens, he was about my age, give or take a year. He was a very nice boy, too, very quick and dark, and always laughing. For a while he was my best friend. Later, the idea that such a person *could* have been my best friend was proof of some horrifying taint in me. So I forgot him. But I see him very well tonight.

It was in the summer, there was no school. His parents had gone someplace for the weekend and I was spending the weekend at his house, which was near Coney Island, in Brooklyn. We lived in Brooklyn too, in those days, but in a better neighborhood than Joey's. I think we had been lying around the beach, swimming a little and watching the near-naked girls pass, whistling at them and laughing. I am sure that if any of the girls we whistled at that day had shown any signs of responding, the ocean would not have been deep enough to drown our shame and terror. But the girls, no doubt, had some intimation of this, possibly from the way we whistled, and they ignored us. As the sun was setting we started up the boardwalk towards his house, with our wet bathing trunks on under our trousers.

Excerpt reprinted from *Giovanni's Room*, Doubleday, copyright 1956 by James Baldwin.

And I think it began in the shower. I know that I felt something—as we were horsing around in that small, steamy room, stinging each other with wet towels—which I had not felt before, which mysteriously, and yet aimlessly, included him. I remember in myself a heavy reluctance to get dressed: I blamed it on the heat. But we did get dressed, sort of, and we ate cold things out of his icebox and drank a lot of beer. We must have gone to the movies. I can't think of any other reason for our going out and I remember walking down the dark, tropical Brooklyn streets with heat coming up from the pavements and banging from the walls of houses with enough force to kill a man, with all the world's grownups, it seemed, sitting shrill and dishevelled on the stoops and all the world's children on the sidewalks or in the gutters or hanging from fire escapes, with my arm around Joey's shoulder. I was proud, I think, because his head came just below my ear. We were walking along and Joey was making dirty wisecracks and we were laughing. Odd to remember, for the first time in so long, how good I felt that night, how fond of Joey.

When we came back along those streets it was quiet; we were quiet too. We were very quiet in the apartment and sleepily got undressed in Joey's bedroom and went to bed. I fell asleep—for quite a while, I think. But I woke up to find the light on and Joey examining the pillow with great, ferocious care.

"What's the matter?"

"I think a bedbug bit me."

"You slob. You got bedbugs?"

"I think one bit me."

"You ever have a bedbug bite you before?"

"No."

"Well, go back to sleep. You're dreaming."

He looked at me with his mouth open and his dark eyes very big. It was as though he had just discovered that I was an expert on bedbugs. I laughed and grabbed his head as I had done God knows how many times before, when I was playing with him or when he had annoyed me. But this time when I touched him something happened in him and in me which made this touch different from any touch either of us had ever known. And he did not resist, as he usually did, but lay where I had pulled him, against my chest. And I realized that my heart was beating in an awful way and that Joey was trembling against me and the light in the room was very bright and hot. I started to move and to make some kind of joke but Joey mumbled something and I put my head down to hear. Joey raised his head as I lowered mine and we kissed, as it were, by accident. Then, for the first time in my life, I was really aware of another per-

Novels

Go Tell It on the Mountain, 1953.
Giovanni's Room, 1956.
Another Country, 1962.
Tell Me How Long the Train's Been Gone, 1968.
If Beale Street Could Talk, 1974.
Just Above My Head, 1979.
Harlem Quartet, 1987.

Short Stories

Going to Meet the Man, 1965.
Contributor, American Negro Short Stories, 1966.
"Just Above My Head," in The Faber Book of Gay Short Fiction, edited by Edmund White, 1991.

Plays

The Amen Corner, produced Washington, D.C., 1955; on Broadway, 1965.
Giovanni's Room, based on author's novel; produced New York, 1957.
Blues for Mister Charlie, produced on Broadway, 1964.
One Day, When I Was Lost: A Scenario (screenplay; based on The Autobiography of Malcolm X by Alex Haley), 1972.
A Deed for the King of Spain, produced New York, 1974.
The Welcome Table, 1987.

Nonfiction

Autobiographical Notes, 1953.
Notes of a Native Son, 1955.
Nobody Knows My Name: More Notes of a Native Son, 1961.
The Fire Next Time, 1963.
Nothing Personal, photographs by Richard Avedon, 1964.
Black Anti-Semitism and Jewish Racism, with others, 1969.
Menschenwuerde und Gerechtigkeit (essays delivered at the fourth assembly of the World Council of Churches), with Kenneth Kaunda, edited by Carl Ordung, 1969.
A Rap on Race, transcribed conversation with Margaret Mead, 1971.
No Name in the Street (essays), 1972.
Cesar: Compressions d'or, with Françoise Giroud, 1973.
A Dialogue, transcribed conversation with Nikki Giovanni, 1973.
The Devil Finds Work, 1976.
Harlem, U.S.A.: The Story of a City within a City, with others, edited by John Henrik Clarke, 1976.
The Evidence of Things Not Seen, 1985.
The Price of the Ticket: Collected Nonfiction, 1948–1985, 1985.
Perspectives: Angles on African Art, with others, edited by Michael J. Weber, 1987.

Other

"Mass Culture and the Creative Artist: Some Personal Notes," in Culture for the Millions, 1959.
Author of introduction, To Be Young, Gifted, and Black by Lorraine Hansberry, 1970.
Little Man, Little Man: A Story of Childhood (children's book), with Yoran Cazac, 1976.
"In Search of a Basis for Mutual Understanding and Racial Harmony," in The Nature of a Humane Society, edited by H. Ober Hess, 1976–77.
Jimmy's Blues: Selected Poems, 1983.
Author of introduction, The Chasm: The Life and Death of a Great Experiment in Ghetto Education by Robert Campbell, 1986.
Author of introduction, Duties, Pleasures, and Conflicts: Essays in Struggle by Michael Thelwell, 1987.
Conversations with James Baldwin, edited by Fred L. Standley and Louis H. Pratt, 1989.

Adaptations

The Amen Corner was adapted as a musical stage play by Garry Sherman, Peter Udell, and Philip Rose, and produced on Broadway, 1983.
Go Tell It on the Mountain was dramatized on "American Playhouse," Public Broadcasting System, 1985.

---

son's body, of another person's smell. We had our arms around each other. It was like holding in my hand some rare, exhausted, nearly doomed bird which I had miraculously happened to find. I was very frightened; I am sure he was frightened too, and we shut our eyes. To remember it so clearly, so painfully tonight tells me that I have never for an instant truly forgotten it. I feel in myself now a faint, a dreadful stirring of what so overwhelmingly stirred in me then, great thirsty heat, and trembling, and tenderness so painful I thought my heart would burst. But out of this astounding, intolerable pain came joy; we gave each other joy that night. It seemed, then, that a lifetime would not be long enough for me to act with Joey the act of love.

But that lifetime was short, was bounded by that night—it ended in the morning. I awoke while Joey was still sleeping, curled like a baby on his side, toward me. He looked like a baby, his mouth half open, his cheek flushed, his curly hair darkening the pillow and half hiding his damp round forehead and his long eyelashes glinting slightly in the summer sun. We were both naked and the sheet we had used as a cover was tangled around our feet. Joey's body was brown, was sweaty, the most beautiful creation I had ever seen till then. I would have touched him to wake him up but something stopped me. I was suddenly afraid. Perhaps it was because he looked so innocent lying there, with such perfect trust; perhaps it was because he was so much smaller than me; my own body suddenly seemed gross and crushing and the desire which was rising in me seemed monstrous. But, above all, I was suddenly afraid. It was borne in on me: *But Joey is a boy.* I saw suddenly the power in his thighs, in his arms, and in his loosely curled fists. The power and the promise and the mystery of that body made me suddenly afraid. That body suddenly seemed the black opening of a cavern in which I would be tortured till madness came, in which I would lose my manhood. Precisely, I wanted to know that mystery and feel that power and have that promise fulfilled through me. The sweat on my back grew cold. I was ashamed. The very bed, in its sweet disorder, testified to vileness. I wondered what Joey's mother would say when she saw the sheets. Then I thought of my father, who had no one in the world but me, my mother having died when I was little. A cavern opened in my mind, black, full of rumor, suggestion, of half-heard, half-forgotten, half-understood stories, full of dirty words. I thought I saw my future in that cavern. I was afraid. I could have cried, cried for shame and terror, cried for not understanding how this could have happened to me, how this could have happened *in* me. And I made my decision. I got out of bed and took a shower and was dressed and had breakfast ready when Joey woke up.

I did not tell him my decision; that would have broken my will. I did not wait to have breakfast with him but only drank some coffee and made an excuse to go home. I knew the excuse did not fool Joey; but he did not know how to protest or insist; he did not know that this was all he needed to have done. Then I, who had seen him that summer nearly every day till then, no longer went to see him. He did not come to see me. I would have been very happy to see him if he had, but the manner of my leave-taking had begun a constriction, which neither of us knew how to arrest. When I finally did see him, more or less by accident, near the end of the summer, I made up a long and totally untrue story about a girl I was going with and when school began again I picked up with a rougher, older crowd and was very nasty to Joey. And the sadder this made him, the nastier I became. He moved away at last, out of the neighborhood, away from our school, and I never saw him again.

I began, perhaps, to be lonely that summer and began, that summer, the flight which has brought me to this darkening window.

And yet—when one begins to search for the crucial, the definitive moment, the moment which changed all others, one finds oneself pressing, in great pain, through a maze of false signals and abruptly locking doors. My flight may, indeed, have begun that summer—which does not tell me where to find the germ of the dilemma which resolved itself, that summer, into flight. Of course, it is somewhere before me, locked in that reflection I am watching in the window as the night comes down outside. It is trapped in the room with me, always has been, and always will be, and it is yet more foreign to me than those foreign hills outside....

For I am—or I was—one of those people who pride themselves on their willpower, on their ability to make a decision and carry it through. This virtue, like most virtues, is ambiguity itself. People who believe that they are strong-willed and the masters of their destiny can only continue to believe this by becoming specialists in self-deception. Their decisions are not really decisions at all—a real decision makes one humble, one knows that it is at the mercy of more things than can be named—but elaborate systems of evasion, of illusion, designed to make themselves and the world appear to be what they and the world are not. This is certainly what my decision, made so long ago in Joey's bed, came to. I had decided to allow no room in the universe for something which shamed and frightened me. I succeeded very well—by not looking at the universe, by not looking at myself, by remaining, in effect, in constant motion. Even constant motion, of course, does not prevent an occasional mysterious drag, a drop, like an airplane hitting an air pocket. And there were a number of those, all drunken, all sordid, one very frightening such drop while I was in the Army which involved a fairy who was later court-martialed out. The panic his punishment caused in me was as close as I ever came to facing in myself the terrors I sometimes saw clouding another man's eyes.

What happened was that, all unconscious of what this ennui meant, I wearied of the motion, wearied of the joyless seas of alcohol, wearied of the blunt, bluff, hearty, and totally meaningless friendships, wearied of wandering through the forests of desperate women, wearied of the work, which fed me only in the most brutally literal sense. Perhaps, as we say in America, I wanted to find myself. This is an interesting phrase, not current as far as I know in the language of any other people, which certainly does not mean what it says but betrays a nagging suspicion that

"Perhaps, as we say in America, I wanted to find myself.... I think now that if I had had any intimation that the self I was going to find would turn out to be only the same self from which I had spent so much time in flight, I would have stayed at home."

something has been misplaced. I think now that if I had had any intimation that the self I was going to find would turn out to be only the same self from which I had spent so much time in flight, I would have stayed at home. But, again, I think I knew, at the very bottom of my heart, exactly what I was doing when I took the boat for France.

MARIE-CLAIRE BLAIS

ONE OF THE MOST PROMINENT and internationally recognized writers of Québec's "Quiet Revolution," Marie-Claire Blais has consistently depicted characters who hold a marginal place in society: the poor and the dispossessed, children, the physically and mentally ill, criminals, gays, lesbians, and artists are rebels who transgress and thus permit a questioning of the rules of conventional society. They live in a world that is dark and alienating; pain, anguish, and despair are commonplace. For Blais, the task of a writer in this world is to bear witness to the suffering of humanity. Art in any form is a means of salvation, of healing the wounds inflicted by an oppressive society. And the most consistent wound experienced by her characters, especially those who are gay and lesbian, is a split between mind and body. Blais writes the body: its pain and its pleasure. Her sensual imagery is embedded in the long, flowing sentences that have become her trademark. Her writing oscillates between the "not quite realism" of many women writers and the lyrical, existential, and surreal.

Blais's first novel, *La Belle Bête* (*Mad Shadows*), received mixed reviews; lauded by liberal critics, it was strongly criticized by more conservative elements of the literary institution. In an effort to escape artistic and social repression, Blais left Québec and lived for more than 15 years in Paris and the United States, where she was "discovered" by well-known literary critic Edmund Wilson. Wilson also introduced her to painter Mary Meigs, and a relationship ensued that, according to Meigs's autobiography, *Lily Briscoe: A Self-Portrait*, underwent almost as many variations as those depicted in Blais's novels.

The appearance of *Une Saison dans la vie d'Emmanuel* (*A Season in the Life of Emmanuel*) in 1965 established Blais as a literary "genius." An attack on the hypocrisy and oppressive nature of the institutions of the traditional family and the Catholic church, this novel focuses primarily on children as society's outcasts. The sexual explorations of these children, as yet uninhibited by heterosexual convention, permit Blais's first explicit literary treatment of homosexuality, albeit in the form of fantasy, metaphor, and symbol. This novel also establishes a link, which becomes

Essay by
DAWN THOMPSON

35

Marie-Claire Blais in 1985.

a major theme in her subsequent work, between homosexuality and art, as the protagonist is censored both for his sexual and his literary activities.

Many of Blais's subsequent works include homosexual characters: *L'Insoumise* (*The Fugitive*) depicts a father who must deal with the (mistaken) suspicion that his son is gay, as well as the unrequited love of the son's male friend; *Les Manuscrits de Pauline Archange* (*The Manuscripts of Pauline Archange*) is similar to *Une Saison dans la vie d'Emmanuel* in its focus on a child protagonist's precocity both literary and (bi)sexual. In 1976 Blais collaborated with a group of Québec feminists to produce *La Nef des sorcières* (*A Clash of Symbols*), in which she portrayed a lesbian. *Visions d'Anna* (*Anna's World*) includes a lesbian character who is depicted as an independent and nurturing young woman despite her family's lack of understanding and acceptance.

Blais has written three novels that focus almost exclusively on gay and lesbian characters, and each can be seen as a further development of both her artistic vision and her political stance.

Le Loup (*The Wolf*) is a confessional novel in which a young gay pianist, Sébastien, recounts his sexual experiences. A study of desire, seduction, and sensuality, the novel explores how each new lover attempts to possess Sébastien in order to fill his own emptiness. Sébastien in turn sees himself as a Christ figure; he chooses partners who are incapable of returning his love, in an attempt to redeem them. In a violent inversion of Christian imagery, he depicts his exploits as acts of charity and redemption, but physical rather than spiritual: "carnal pity" and "sensual commiseration." Despite jealousies and emotional abuse, Sébastien continues his search for beauty in love—for it is only beauty, that of love and of art, that offers even the smallest hope for salvation, even if that salvation is only a momentary easing of the pain of existence.

The most fascinating aspect of this novel is its structure: a musical arrangement as a fugue in four parts, each focusing more or less on one lover, with memories of and dialogues with the others returning in counterpoint and harmony. Sébastien's description of his most recent lover also pertains to the novel as a whole: "a fugue woven of conflicts, torments and perpetual change." And as Victor Tremblay has pointed out in his study of this work, the musical and sexual imagery combine with that of food to produce perhaps the most sensual of all of Blais's novels.

THE GAY AND LESBIAN LITERARY COMPANION

Le Loup concludes with an idylic dream of self-acceptance, acceptance by family, and a revision of the traditional family by offering alternatives within the gay community. Characters attempt to succeed at homosexual "open marriages" and long-term "ménages à trois"; although jealousy hinders these attempts, the novel is open-ended; like a fugue, it is open to further variations.

The publication of *Les Nuits de l'Underground* (*Nights of the Underground*) coincided with Blais's return to Québec with Mary Meigs to live. Centered on a lesbian club in Montréal, the Underground, this novel is basically an extremely lyrical and complex "coming out" story. Geneviève Aurès, a Québécoise sculptor living with a man in Paris despite her attraction to women, returns to Québec for an exhibition and falls in love with Lali Dorman, a woman who stands out from the others in the club in her acceptance of her sexuality and her refusal to try to "pass" for straight. The two become lovers for a short time. Upon her return to Paris, Geneviève is finally able to leave her male partner. As expected, Lali soon moves on to other lovers and Geneviève meets Françoise, an older woman who has led a closeted double life and who is now very ill. Through Geneviève's new-found self-acceptance, Françoise also finds a new joy in life and recovers, both sexually and physically.

Throughout much of the novel, Québec's freezing winter is contrasted with scenes in the warm and steamy bar, which offer elegant and humorous vignettes of solidarity: a mixture of races, classes and what the narrator describes as a "tangled underbrush of … various languages" and dialects. The novel concludes in spring, as the bar patrons come out into the sunshine to mix with artists, both gay and straight, in a new restaurant, and to begin a housing project that promises to integrate them into the larger community.

As in *Le Loup*, it is art that gives meaning to suffering in this subterranean world of society's outcasts. Geneviève's obsession for Lali "began as for a work of art," and as she finds herself unable to possess Lali, nor to liberate her from the pain of her past, she finally creates a bust of Lali. This act, which universalizes the beauty of a woman and the artist's love for that woman, frees Geneviève from her obsession.

Blais's latest novel, *L'Ange de la solitude*, begins in a lesbian community, depicting a group of young artists who live together in a commune. Structured around a rudimentary plot involving the disappearance and eventual death of one of the women, the narrative follows each of these women as she drifts through her own alienated psychological, artistic and romantic travels, until the tragedy brings them together to form a family.

These three novels have in common a mixture of lyricism and didacticism as they explore the difficulties involved in being gay or lesbian in a homophobic society. From *Le Loup* to *L'Ange de la solitude* there is a decreasing interest in structural experimentation and plot and the development of an increasingly more explicit political program. Christian imagery is gradually replaced by a more open and accepting spirituality. The diversity and complexity of gay and lesbian relationships is explored in increasing detail, as are alternatives to the traditional heterosexual family. Finally, in all three of these novels, Blais examines and rejects rigid gender roles: gay men in *Le Loup* and lesbian women in *Les Nuits de l'Underground* are described as both warrior-like and maternal in their love-making. The two lesbian novels depict characters who take on masculine names, refer to each other as "brothers," and are both sons and daughters to their parents. Blais repeatedly depicts sexual ambiguity as beautiful: Geneviève describes Françoise as "at once masculinely handsome and seductively feminine." This gender-bending is one instance of the profound humanism of all of Marie-Claire Blais's work, as she attempts to reach through the suffering in order to create a world in which the individual is free, both corporally and spiritually.

AUTOBIOGRAPHY, 1986

Reprinted from *Contemporary Authors Autobiography Series*, volume 4, copyright 1986 by Gale Research.

It has always been very hard for me to talk about myself. As we know, writers of fiction do not necessarily invent but take the reality which they have lived or observed and imbue it with their subjectivity. Often their characters are disguised aspects of themselves, like the fragmented selves which confront and challenge each other in dreams. Even in a novel or a short story it is difficult to write in the first person because the choice of this narrative form (the only true one, according to certain writers and critics) requires a face-to-face meeting with the narrator, which inspires as much terror and bravado as a love-tryst, for it requires absolute honesty. And talking about oneself seems more arduous because one can't take refuge in the role of detached witness faithfully transcribing what an impartial observer might have remembered.

This kind of self-exposure frightens me and it extends beyond my writing to every kind of interview and questionnaire. I think that my reticence remains from an education that taught me that it was as rude to talk about oneself as to help oneself before others. Modesty and reserve were taught me, just as they were taught, more or less successfully, to all

French Canadian novelist, poet, and playwright.

Born: Québec City, Québec, October 5, 1939. Lived in the United States, 1963–74; now lives in Québec.

Education: Couvent Saint-Roch, Québec; Laval University (literature and philosophy), Québec.

Career: Clerical worker, 1956–57.

Recipient: L'Academie Francaise Prix de la Langue Francaise, 1961; Guggenheim fellowships, 1963, 1964; Le Prix France-Québec, 1966; Prix Medicis (Paris), 1966; Prix du Gouverneur General du Canada, 1969, 1979; York University (Toronto) honorary doctorate, 1975; Ordre du Canada, 1975; Prix Belgique, 1976; Calgary University honorary professor, 1978; Prix Athanase David, 1982; Prix de l'Academie Francaise, 1983; Nessim Habif prize (Belgium), 1991; honorary doctorate, Victoria University.

Agent: John C. Goodwin and Associates, 839 Sherbrooke Est, Suite 2, Montréal, Québec, Canada H2L 1K6.

Address: 448 Chemin Sims, Kingsbury, Québec, Canada J0B 1X0.

---

young girls of my age. The result is that when people talk endlessly about themselves I associate the habit with vanity or an absence of discretion. But there is also an element of vanity in the decision *not* to talk, though in my case it comes from my wish to remain a witness and to hear what other people have to say.

To talk about oneself is to bring to life times that lie deep in our subconscious memory. Remembering that somewhere in a dusty box were hidden photographs of my childhood, I found them and laid them out at random on a table. I looked at them curiously and saw familiar faces and objects that recalled, like a fragrance or a musical phrase, the faded memories of a past without precise boundaries. I saw again my mother's laced boots, a scarf she sometimes tied under her chin, my grandmother's muff, and then, huge and rounded, my father's first automobile. He is sitting very straight, proudly gripping the wheel, and I am kneeling on the backseat, smiling timidly, one of my hands bent against my chin in an almost worldly attitude, surprising for a five-year-old child. In fact, all the photographs of this period show a strangely serious little girl. In one, dressed in my Sunday-best, I am smiling, but my smile doesn't soften my severe look; in another, muffled in a snowsuit on a dismal winter day, I'm walking with a troubled gaze beside my grandmother, a woman with a strong, almost masculine bearing, straight and proud. In still another, my father and I are standing side by side in a shallow lake; my blond childish pigtails are in strange contrast to the grave, fixed expression in my eyes, a tranquil sadness. It wasn't caused just by the unpleasant sensation of cold water on my bare body, for I hated strenuous games and physical exercise when I was little. There was another cause; for as far back as I can remember, I was tormented by metaphysical anguish and by a morbid fear of death, so that I never shared the happy carelessness of other children. When I notice this same anguish in certain children, I wonder how it is that they have the power to imagine suffering so far beyond them and face it as they do in a state of complete moral solitude.

Our life was certainly not an easy one, and perhaps without knowing it my parents conveyed their own anxieties to me. I was born October 5, 1939, at the beginning of World War II, when the economy was struggling out of the Depression. My father, Fernando Blais, came from a family in Saint-Paul-de-Montmagny, a village close to the American frontier. The Blais family land descended, according to the custom in Quebec, from father to son, most often the eldest son. My father was one of seventeen children with many brothers ahead of him, so he had no hope of inheriting the family farm. Besides, like so many young people of his time he dreamed of living in a city, where, he said, "there was a future." He was bored by farming and the country. He decided to learn a trade with the hope of eventually running his own business. With this in mind, he studied refrigeration techniques at a school in Saint-Hyacinthe, then moved to Quebec City and found a job in a factory for the manufacture of dairy products; there, he was responsible for the maintenance and repair of the machinery. At that time, Quebec was in the midst of an economic slump, jobs were rare and salaries low. Many bosses took advantage of the situation by making their employees work long hours for inadequate pay and without overtime, and held the threat of dismissal over their heads. My father worked hard and earned very little, clinging to his dream of his own business and considering himself lucky to have a job at all. It was just at this time that he met my mother.

Véronique Nolin was the daughter of a Quebec City carpenter and had always lived in the city. "Your mother lived in the Upper City," said my father proudly. This was the more prosperous part of the city, as opposed to the Lower City. Véronique was a schoolteacher who dreamed of marrying and having children. She and Fernando met in church at Vespers, which isn't surprising to anyone who knows about the link between the history of Quebec and its powerful Roman Catholic Church. I remember that my mother often described the scene of their meeting with a mocking look in her lively, intelligent eyes and added, "Your father has always been faithful to the Church." As for her, she wasn't too fond of priests and pious people and had sworn to herself that her house would never be invaded by frocked clerics sermonizing over one of her good meals. Of course she was a believer—it was inconceivable not to be at that time—but less so than my father. His temperament combined with religion made him a fatalist who did not permit himself to be angry or rebellious. He was (and still is) tolerant and magnanimous and because

Fiction

La Belle Bête, 1959; translated by Merloyd Lawrence as *Mad Shadows*, 1960.

Tête blanche, 1960; translated by Charles Fullman, 1961.

Le Jour est noir, 1962; translated by Derek Coltman as *The Day Is Dark*, in *The Day Is Dark* [and] *Three Travelers*, 1967.

Une Saison dans la vie d'Emmanuel, 1965; translated by Derek Coltman as *A Season in the Life of Emmanuel*, introduction by Edmund Wilson, 1966.

Les Voyageurs sacrés, 1966; translated by Derek Coltman as *Three Travelers*, in *The Day Is Dark* [and] *Three Travelers*, 1967.

L'Insoumise, 1966; translated by David Lobdell as *The Fugitive*, 1978.

The Day Is Dark [and] *Three Travelers: Two Novellas*, translated by Michael Harris, 1967.

David Sterne, 1967; translated by David Lobdell, 1973.

Manuscrits de Pauline Archange (first book in series), 1968; with *Vivre! Vivre!: La Suite des manuscrits de Pauline Archange*, translated by Derek Coltman as *The Manuscripts of Pauline Archange*, 1970.

Vivre! Vivre!: La Suite des manuscrits de Pauline Archange (second book in series), 1969; with *Manuscrits de Pauline Archange*, translated by Derek Coltman as *The Manuscripts of Pauline Archage*, 1970.

Les Apparences (third book in series), 1970; translated by David Lobdell as *Dürer's Angel*, 1974.

Le Loup, 1972; translated by Sheila Fischman as *The Wolf*, 1974.

Un Joualonais, sa joualonie, 1973; as *A Coeur joual*, 1974; translated by Ralph Manheim as *St. Lawrence Blues*, 1974.

Une Liaison parisienne, 1975; translated by Sheila Fischman as *A Literary Affair*, 1979.

Les Nuits de l'underground, 1978; translated by Ray Ellenwood as *Nights in the Underground: An Exploration of Love*, 1979.

Le Sourd dans la ville, 1979; translated by Carol Dunlop as *Deaf to the City*, 1980.

Visions d'Anna, ou le vertige, 1982; translated by Sheila Fischman as *Anna's World*, 1985.

Pierre, la guerre du printemps 81, 1984; as *Pierre*, 1986.

L'Ange de la solitude, 1989.

Poetry

Pays voilés, 1963; as *Veiled Countries*, in *Veiled Countries* [and] *Lives*, 1984.

Existences, 1964; as *Lives*, in *Veiled Countries* [and] *Lives*, 1984.

Veiled Countries [and] *Lives*, translation by Michael Harris, 1984.

Plays

La Roulotte aux poupées (produced Montréal, 1962); translated as *The Puppet Caravan* (televised, 1967).

Eléonor (produced Québec, 1962).

L'Exécution (produced Montréal, 1967), published, 1968; translated by David Lobdell as *The Execution*, 1976.

Fièvre, et autres textes dramatiques: Théâtre radiophonique (includes *L'Envahisseur; Le Disparu; Deux Destins; Un Couple*), 1974.

La Nef des sorcières (Marcelle), with Nicole Brossard, Marthe Blackburn, Luce Guilbeault, France Théoret, Odette Gagnon, and Pol Pelletier, (produced Montréal, 1976), published, 1976; translated by Linda Gaboriau as *A Clash of Symbols*, 1979.

L'Océan; Murmures (broadcast, 1976), published, 1977; translation by Ray Chamberlain of *L'Ocean* published as *The Ocean*, 1977; translation by Margaret Rose of *Murmures* published in *Canadian Drama/L'Art Dramatique Canadien* (Ontario), fall 1979.

Sommeil d'Hiver, 1984.

Fière, 1985.

L'Ile (produced Montréal, 1991), published, 1988; translated by David Lobdell as *The Island*, 1991.

Un Jardin dans la tempête (broadcast, 1990); translated by David Lobdell as *A Garden in the Storm*.

Television Plays

L'Océan, 1976.

Journal en images froides, Scénario, 1978.

L'Exil, L'Escale, 1979.

Radio Plays

Le Disparu, Premières, 1971.

L'Envahisseur, Feuillaison, 1972.

Deux Destins, Premières, 1973.

Fièvre, Premières, 1973.

Une Autre Vie, Premières, 1974.

Un Couple, Premières, 1975.

Une Femme et les autres, Premières, 1976.

Murmures, Premières, 1976.

L'Enfant-vidéo, Scénario, 1977.

Le Fantôme d'une voix, Premieres, 1980.

Other

Author of introduction, *The Oxford Book of French-Canadian Short Stories*, edited by Richard Teleky, 1980.

"L'Exil," in *Liberté*, January–February 1981.

Contributor, *Contemporary Authors Autobiography Series*, Volume 4, 1986.

Voies de pères, voix de filles, 1988.

---

of this he endured resignedly an exhausting job that gave him hardly any free time. His boss required him to be on call day and night. My mother was outraged by this but swallowed her resentment, and it was only much later, when the workers formed a union and went on strike, that she enjoyed the sweet taste of revenge.

I was the eldest of five children: two brothers and three sisters. Since my father was always at work, my mother had the whole task of bringing us up. We didn't see Father much but we knew that his hard work kept the wolf from the door. He had to put aside his dream of being his own master because my mother thought it would be too risky and that he should wait for a more propitious time. It never came, either because my mother argued him out of it or because, tired of waiting, he gave up the whole idea.

When I emerged from my stubborn or melancholic silence I was a very talkative child, my mother tells me, and I loved having long conversations with the grocer, the telephone operator, and the plumber. Like all children, I loved to have an audience, to dazzle the grown-ups. When I was three or four years old and the adults were chatting in the living room, I used to bring in several volumes of the encyclopedia and pretend to read them with great interest. (I remember a similar scene in Sartre's *Les Mots*.) Enchanted by my precocity, the adults predicted a brilliant career for me.

I was sent to the parish elementary school and then to the Saint-Roch convent where, at my request, I was a boarder for a few months. I was delighted to be rid of household chores and the noisy, importunate presence of my little brothers and sisters, but also because I was surrounded by unfamiliar beings whose lives seemed more fascinating because they were so different from ours. But my exile as a boarder didn't last long for I fell sick and my mother decided that I should live at home, so I became a day-student.

In the course of those years at the convent I discovered literature and the world outside the convent gates and fell in love with books. By a combination of willpower and trickery we could secretly get hold of books we were forbidden to read: Baudelaire, Rimbaud, Verlaine, Flaubert, Balzac, Proust, and later, Zola, Gide, Lautréamont and the Surrealists. I wrote poems for the *Journal du Couvent*, and drafts of novels, and I began to dream about having a career as a writer. The same determined ruses that had enabled me to get books that I wanted was useful when I decided to broaden my culture by studying music. We didn't have a piano at home and my parents had no intention of buying one, so it seemed absurd to my mother that I kept insisting on having lessons. When I saw that she wouldn't give in I pleaded my cause with one of the nuns at the convent, who telephoned my mother to beg her to change her mind. She succeeded without difficulty (I was standing next to her, which infuriated my mother), not because my mother agreed with her argument but because she didn't want anyone to know that we couldn't afford it. I had counted on her pride for the success of my little strategy and my victory filled me with joy—and terror, since I knew what was in store for me at home. The piano was bought and took its place in the living room, and for a few months inspired my frenetic devotion. But I quickly got tired of finger exercises, just as my mother had anticipated, and the piano fell silent except when some visitor arrived who could play it. But this incident, which my mother still recalls with annoyance as one of the innumerable examples showing my stubborn and inflexible character, was a valuable lesson which convinced me that if only I were clever, strong-minded, and tenacious enough I could have anything I wanted.

But it was much less simple to persuade my parents that I needed a university education. They had four young children and they wouldn't hear of it. Moreover, they didn't take my passion for literature seriously and dreamed of my having a secure future, assured by my taking a secretarial course. So, much against my will, I had to learn how to type and take dictation. My years at the convent had given me a taste for study and discipline and I still kept my love for the pagan beauty of Roman Catholicism. Perhaps my admiration for Simone Weil, Georges Bernanos, Paul Claudel, and François Mauriac was born of the swarming aesthetic emotions which I think of as my religious feeling. But I hated the Catholic Church, its clergy, the nuns, and the ostracism of all those who were judged to be deviant. Much has been written about the crushing power and omnipresence of the Church in Quebec; the overthrow of the Church's power and the triumph of the laity is still recent enough, I think, to remember the courageous struggle which had its climax in the Quiet Revolution. But I am afraid that we are threatened all over again with a rebirth of a mediaeval kind of religion and that we will be victims again of the same intolerance and bigotry, which in the name of morality once forbade my books to be sold in bookstores. I still have a vivid recollection of the poverty of intellectual life in Quebec at the time when I came of age and I hope never again to see a time when the same kind of religious hysteria will trample on works of art.

Les Manuscrits de Pauline Archange, published in 1968, tells of the struggle of a young woman in this bigoted society to win her freedom as a writer; the three novels which compose it are the story of a painful search for knowledge in an ignorant world which violently rejects everything unfamiliar. I had seen how the efforts of a young immigrant doctor, who lived with his family in our parish, to set up a kind of literary meeting-place, were perceived as suspect and dangerous. He had probably been alarmed by the cultural void he saw around him and foresaw the sad fate that threatened the gifted young people who were being suffocated by a society which frowned on books and ideas. He wanted to make it possible for them to come together, exchange books, and read their work. I went enthusiastically to these meetings until, at the instigation of the parish priest, the well-meaning parents forbade their children to go.

And yet it was to a priest, Père Georges-Henri Lévesque, that I owe the publication of my first novel. Père Lévesque had founded the School of Social Sciences at the Laval University and was an admirably progressive man who had done much for the intellectual life of Quebec. With my usual determination, I began to pester him by sending him letters, poems, short stories, and novels, convinced that he would end by being moved, if not by my talent (of which I had no doubt) then by my persistence. At this time I was still living with my parents and had had various jobs: as a clerk in a biscuit factory, a cashier in a bank, a salesgirl in a department store—all with an absence of enthusiasm that exasperated my employers. Seeing that I was determined to write, my mother had fixed up a little worktable in her room where the sound of my typewriter was less likely to wake up the other children, but I always had to stop working when my father wanted to sleep. Since I worked in the daytime and wrote at night, the situation became impossible. I dreamed of an attic room like Balzac's and waited patiently for Père Lévesque to notice me.

Finally, thanks to Père Lévesque, I had the means to rent a room in Old Quebec; it was small and ugly, and freezing in winter, but it was "a room of one's own," and just what I needed. I was enchanted by my new domain and surprised by my parents' unhappy reaction, for they thought of it as futile misery that I imposed on myself in the name of a dream of glory, and that it could only lead to defeat and poverty. In vain, they tried everything to convince me—didn't I want a family, children, a decent life?—and then tried to make me more comfortable. On Sundays they came with the children, bringing blankets, clothes, and food so as to be sure that I stayed alive and well, and this with a touching solicitude which my brother Michel remembers to this day. And he remembers his big sister whom he hardly knew, who seemed unique and far away.

Blais publishes her first novel at age 19.

My first novel, *La Belle Bête*, was published in 1959 when I was nineteen. In general, the reviews were crushing. The book occasioned a dispute which pitted those who liked it against the others, the more numerous, who claimed to be horrified by it. But it didn't stop me from writing and when I had time I took courses in literature and philosophy at Laval University. But if the severe judgement of *La Belle Bête* didn't completely discourage me, it did frighten me a little and calmed the violence of the mental images I dreamed of using in my work. *Tête Blanche*, which was published a year later, shows this restraint. *La Belle Bête* was an adolescent nightmare brimming with passion and vitality about the erotic love of a mother for her handsome retarded son and the jealous hatred felt for him by his ugly sister. *Tête Blanche* was closer to the classic novel form; it was a study of a gifted young delinquent boy and of his surroundings, his school, and his family. After all the sound and fury of *La Belle Bête* this was a relatively calm book, a little the way *L'Insoumise* would be after the stir caused by *Une Saison dans la Vie d'Emmanuel.*

At the time *Tête Blanche* was published I was still living in Quebec. Exasperated by the narrow provincial life of the city I suddenly decided to leave, and for another reason—that I had fallen in love with a filmmaker who lived in Montreal. I told my parents that I had found a job there and they encouraged me to go, convinced this time that I'd made the right decision. I rented a room in a boardinghouse on Prince Arthur Street and perhaps for the first time in my life had the feeling that I was really free. I was twenty-two years old.

My life in Montreal was composed of writing, reading, music, and German language courses that I took at the Goethe Institute. Now and then I worked in the City Archives under the wing of Louise Myette, who was studying German with me and later became my literary agent. A grant from the Canada Arts Council then allowed me to go to France, and there I made enduring friendships. But the thing that really changed my life (and it was something many writers hoped for even if they didn't admit it) was praise and understanding from the great critic, Edmund Wilson.

A new life in Montreal.

One summer evening I got home to find a note for me saying that a Mr. Wilson had tried to reach me on the telephone. A few days before that Père Lévesque had told me that a great American critic was coming soon and that it was important for me to meet him. Ironically, I didn't know who Edmund Wilson was, so Père Lévesque hastened to tell me about his work and his great influence and suggested a few books for me to read before his arrival. At that time I was familiar with French literature but had read only a few American writers: some Henry James, Melville, Fitzgerald, Hemingway, Faulkner, and Steinbeck, but I had to read much more, I thought, to be worthy to meet Edmund Wilson. So I rushed to a bookstore to find books to fill the vacuum and began to read as anxiously as if I were preparing for an oral examination.

Edmund Wilson was at that time making a study of Canadian literature (*O Canada*, published in 1965) and he wished to meet some of the writers whose work he was studying. He arranged for us to meet at the

Ritz-Carlton where he was staying with his wife, Elena. I had never set a foot in the Ritz, had never even imagined crossing its dazzling threshold under the eyes of the man in uniform, as so many people did with complete indifference. But ever since that first time I've felt a superstitious attraction to the slightly faded charm of the Café de Paris. Its heavy dark blue velvet curtains seem even in the daytime to cast a warm shadow, lit softly by lights which suggest the whispering intimacy of a boudoir. But when I was getting ready to meet Edmund and Elena I was preoccupied by my clothes: a blouse and skirt and a long raincoat which was much too hot for that August afternoon; I felt awkward, ignorant, and timid and I was sure in advance that I was going to disappoint them, for they undoubtedly expected to meet a learned, brilliant, and graceful young woman.

I had counted on having a drink to get me over my shyness, but since the waiter thought I was a minor he refused to give me one. I had to dig into a worn little handbag I'd been trying to hide to find my card proving that indeed I had come of age. Edmund found this incident, which happened again several times, very amusing, and couldn't resist mentioning it in his book.

Edmund was very kind to me that day but it was Elena whose smiling gentleness put me at ease. Of my meeting with her that day I remember best the extraordinary brilliance of her blue eyes. Edmund expressed his admiration for my work and promised to recommend me for a grant from the Guggenheim Foundation, which would allow me to write full time. After we had shaken hands I went off in a state of ecstatic joy and hope, reeling with dreams of the future.

Two long months went by without news and I was sure Edmund and Elena had forgotten me completely. I was even more impatient then than I am now and the delay seemed intolerable. It was the terrible autumn of 1962, when for endless hours we faced the imminent possibility of nuclear war. I remember that people I saw in the street, far from being petrified by the thought that the Soviet Union might not withdraw its missiles from Cuba, went to work as though their changeless routine would prevent the catastrophe and ensure a connection between yesterday and tomorrow. "Worse than dogs, they didn't imagine their own death," wrote Céline about the young soldiers who were about to die on the front, torn to pieces by a shell, but in the meantime, ate, drank, and slept just as usual. Sometimes I think that the indifference and scepticism of many people in the face of the nuclear threat, as though they are hiding their heads in the sand or passively accepting the inevitable, comes from their inability to imagine the horror of it. My books are haunted by my own anguish; in my most recent novels— *Visions d'Anna, Pierre ou la*

THE GAY AND LESBIAN LITERARY COMPANION

Guerre du Printemps '81—I have written about the mutilated lives of characters whose *joie de vivre* has been shattered by the piercing light of their vision of disaster. They are enclosed in their state of painful lucidity, unable to feel pleasure which seems futile beside the death of our planet. The young people in these books are no longer fictional characters, but real human beings struggling to survive, broken by their own visions.

A few days after we heard that the Soviet Union had withdrawn its missiles from Cuba I got a friendly letter from Edmund saying that I would certainly get the Guggenheim grant. He also sent me the poems of A. E. Housman and Edna St. Vincent Millay. As he had foreseen, the grant came and in the month of July 1963, I moved to Cambridge, Massachusetts. I found a little apartment which I moved into without even taking the trouble to furnish it properly, for I was in a hurry to begin work on what was to become *Une Saison dans la vie d'Emmanuel*.

After *Tête Blanche* I had written two books: *Les Voyageurs Sacrés* and *Le Jour est Noir*, half novels, half poetry, which because of their lyrical quality seem to me to betray my immaturity then as a writer. But in spite of its weaknesses, *Les Voyageurs Sacrés* still touches me when I reread it because it is a daring attempt to combine music, poetry, and sculpture in a lucid, aesthetic unity, symbolised by the converging paths of the three lovers who meet and embrace each other in various European cities.

Edmund Wilson said that *Le Jour est Noir* reminded him of Walter de la Mare, whose work I had not yet read. With its publication, my reputation in Quebec as a "somber" writer was firmly fixed. From then on, it was customary to speak of me as a depressing writer who loved misery and felt at home in a morbid, ugly world—Ugliness with a capital U being the opposite of Beauty, like Good and Evil, in the minds of people who distinguished so easily between virtue and vice. Some of them even said that I used "blackness" as a device to help me write my novels. I was particularly exasperated by this view after the publication, in 1965, of *Une Saison dans la Vie d'Emmanuel*; its biting humor and uncompromising irony were completely ignored by a chorus of reviewers who angrily denounced its falseness and the depravity of the characters. It has often been said that the children in my books have revolting habits, and above all, that I talk too much about them. This way of stigmatizing a book makes me indignant both because it is unjust (I shall say more later about this) and because to me it is a form of literary terrorism which denies an artist the freedom to explore his chosen world. Nevertheless there were certain critics, like Jean Ethier-Blais, who wrote enthusiastically about my book, and I got a favorable reception in the United States and in France, where it won the Prix Médicis in 1966.

Guggenheim grant leads to a writing life in Cambridge.

Marie-Claire Blais around 1965, when *Une Saison dans la Vie d'Emmanuel* was published.

In Cambridge I worked on the first draft of my novel and in my free time I discovered the exciting life of an American university-town in the sixties. Edmund had said in one of his letters that he wanted to introduce me to some of his friends in Wellfleet and he brought one of them, Mary Meigs, to Cambridge where the three of us had lunch together. I felt intimidated and fascinated by this tall, thin woman with graying hair and bangs cut just above her blue eyes. I liked her immediately, and was drawn by her uncertain laugh and quick smile, by her grace, and by a sort of elegance in her conversation. Not long after our lunch together, I went to Wellfleet and saw the house where she lived with Barbara Deming, an old house on a hill, with locust trees surrounding it and the pine woods behind. The house and studio were full of books and of her paintings and drawings, and I discovered in her a very good painter who was to introduce me to a world of form and color which until then had been unknown to me. She invited me to work in her studio and to use her brushes and paints, and I discovered an inexhaustible world where I could take refuge and abandon myself as one would to a game without penalties and without any rules. I got into the habit of illustrating my notebooks and the margins of letters, and I quickly took over this new space, a place of repose where my anguish and agitation as a writer, the tangle of emotions that threatened to choke me, were soothed and dissipated.

When Mary invited me to live in her house, I left Cambridge for Wellfleet, a haven of peace, where I looked forward to being able to do some good work. Mary and Barbara led a healthy and disciplined life which by contrast to my own—disorderly and impulsive—seemed almost monastic. They lived a kind of golden mean, without any excesses, went to bed early and got up early in order to work. I did my best to imitate them, partly because I didn't want to disturb their working times, and also because I felt vaguely ashamed of my restlessness and imprecise schedule when I felt that I was under their ascetic gaze. I also felt that for the time being their rigor was good for me and would help me in my

THE GAY AND LESBIAN LITERARY COMPANION

work. It seemed to me that I was being shown the way of most writers, which was to shut oneself up in one's room and work for a certain number of hours every day. I worked "like an angel," Mary said in her book, *Lily Briscoe: A Self-Portrait*. And in fact, I did a tremendous amount of work during those years in Wellfleet, which I might not have done as well in other circumstances, particularly since I wasn't in good health. But now I don't practice that kind of discipline anymore. I need to be in perpetual motion, travelling, writing as I go, wherever my needs or my phantasy tells me to go. My writing has come to need this kind of movement; it has taken on its color and is reflected in long sentences like ocean waves with hardly any punctuation to slow their rhythm.

In Wellfleet, even if I was an exemplary disciple, I needed to get away from my too-calm life and dive into the delicious excitement of a city. I needed streets swarming with complicated lives, bars full of slightly crazy or melancholy people, the feeling of living dangerously. This need, which I have had since I was a small child, reminds me of one of Colette's heroines, Minne. Sometimes it would get me into situations that were really dangerous, but most of the time it helped to sharpen my imagination which proceeded almost without my knowing it to create a danger that wasn't really there. I laugh when I think about it now; nevertheless my ventures into unknown worlds gave me valuable impressions which I would use in the novels that were already beginning to take shape in my mind.

Our life in Wellfleet, in spite of its happy moments, was difficult for me because I had no place in that closed little society, and I spoke hardly any English. Our happiest times were spent together. I remember the hours we spent reading out loud and I can still hear Barbara's grave voice reading Ibsen's *The Wild Duck*, which, along with *The Doll's House*, is the Ibsen play I like best.

Barbara (who died in 1984) was an extraordinary being who was ready to give her life for the causes she believed in. Once she had committed herself she never wavered and she always remained loyal to her beliefs. She was active in the pacifist and civil rights movements which became more radical in response to the violence unleashed against the non-violent demonstrations of Martin Luther King, Jr. and his followers. If a political action ended in prison Barbara saw it out to the end. She was in prison many times and spent a month in the Albany, Georgia, jail, an experience which inspired her beautiful book *Prison Notes*.

The pacifist movement became more powerful with the increased involvement of the USA in Vietnam. Sometimes, members of the New England Committee for Non-Violent Action would gather in our house

Wellfleet: A haven of peace.

to discuss strategies, which included fasting and non-violent actions. Neither Mary nor I was capable of living with Barbara's fervor and we continued our work as artists, but with feelings of guilt. Almost every day I wrote down my reflections on the day's events, on the activists who came to the house, and I smile now at my scruples of conscience, exacerbated by the indomitable courage of Barbara. As I leafed through these notebooks full of watercolors and crayon drawings, I came on a newspaper clipping about an American Quaker who set himself on fire on the steps of the Pentagon as a protest against the war. The horror of this was quickly forgotten in the flood of atrocities committed in Vietnam, but it made a profound impression on me. François Reine, one of the characters in my novel *David Sterne*, kills himself in the same way, and his friend David is deeply troubled by François' intransigence, his insistence on a sacrifice that will do nothing to stop the war, on his own useless death. "Cursed be the martyrs, who are loved neither by God nor men!" says David Sterne. "Whether it be heaven or hell, whether the flame rises straight and pure into the sky or races across the dry plain, what difference does it make to us, François Reine? Aren't our bodies embers extinguished in the same way? Don't we always rediscover the same void, the same nothingness at the moment of death?"

During those troubled days I kept on working as hard as ever. *Une Saison dans la Vie d'Emmanuel* had won the Prix Médicis and my editor, Jacques Hébert, decided that Les Editions du Jour would do a deluxe edition with Mary's illustrations. I had been amazed by the richness of imagination of her drawings which were unlike anything else she had done and gave me the feeling that I was in real communication with another artist. When I wrote the book I intended it to be tender and humorous, casting an ironic eye on the tragedy and cruelty of humble lives. It is true that the setting is one of extreme hardship but the characters are full of life, of sensuality, and friendship. And it is in a comic spirit that Jean- Le-Maigre, le Septième, and even Héloïse, who leaves her convent to enter a brothel, try to survive and rebel against destiny. Far from being lugubrious, the book is brimming over with vitality and ferocious humor, and a rebellious dignity and grace are shown in Jean-Le-Maigre's refusal to give way to sadness and bitterness. Mary gave form to all my beloved characters.

After *Une Saison dans la Vie d'Emmanuel* I wrote *L'Insoumise*, an impressionistic book in softer colors, in which the characters are imprecise sketches of people which suggest how opaque and impenetrable human beings are to those who try to discover their mysteries or understand the fragile links which hold them together. They are unsuccessful and wander anxiously in uncertainty and doubt, holding tight to their own secrets and their own suffering. In *Visions d'Anna*, published in 1982, there is another kind of invading fog, induced by drugs; it has almost an autonomous existence which threatens Anna's life. She is helpless to get rid of it and sinks into a comatose state which affects everything she experiences. *Visions d'Anna* for me is about life as a dream shown in a succession of fugitive images bound by a steady rhythm, as regular as that of sleep.

At the time I was writing *L'Insoumise* I was also working on a play, *L'Exécution*, the hero of which, Louis Kent, was to find his full stature in my latest novel, *Pierre ou la Guerre du Printemps '81*. The play was produced in Montreal by the Théâtre du Rideau-Vert, directed by Yvette Brind'Amour. At about the same time, a film version of *Une Saison dans la Vie d'Emmanuel* which had been made in France by Claude Weiss, also was shown in Montreal. I came often to Quebec in connection with my work as a writer and spent a couple of summers in a somewhat flimsy prefabricated house Mary and I had had placed on a piece of land I bought near the beach in Grande-Vallée, in the Gaspé Peninsula. The house was battered by storms even in summer and was blown down by a particularly ferocious gale one winter. We had also acquired a big piece of land in Val-David and had had a sugaring-house rebuilt and insulated so that it served as a refuge, a place of silence and peace. It is still there among the old maples, and a jungle of young spruces and maples has grown up around it. I still have a dream of transforming the land into an artists' colony.

In 1970, Mary and I moved to France and lived for four years in an old house in Brittany—La Salle en Sulniac—and in a succession of apartments in Paris, where I went to see friends, to work, and to absorb the life of the city. It was both in Paris and in Montreal that I found material in the streets and in bars for my two books which study homosexual love: *Le Loup* and *Les Nuits de l'Underground*; Lali, in the latter, and Sébastien, in the former, live only for love and sex, drawn to the beings they meet "in the warm shadows of a bar." The characters in both books talk about homosexual love with complete naturalness and simplicity, without guilt-feelings, at times denouncing the hypocrisy of people who lead a double life which they think they are hiding when they noisily condemn what they are living in secret: "… as fathers they punish what they cherish as lovers." Lali and Sébastien celebrate their freedom to love while living lives that hold little promise of happiness.

Two other novels are the result of my shuttling between two continents and come out of the meeting of two worlds which are slowly coming together in Quebec and France. *Un Joualonais, sa Joualonie* reminds us by its title of the inebriating awakening in Quebec, when we glorified for

Marie-Claire Blais in Kingsbury, Eastern Townships, Quebec, in 1981.

a while our impoverished French, called *joual*, in a rebellious attempt to be different from the mother-country, or to have an identity of our own. *Une Saison Parisienne*, on the other hand, is about a naïf young poet who falls in love with a bourgeoise Frenchwoman and then lives her life of perverse refinement, scented with the perfume and culture of old France. This woman, Madame d'Argenti, has nothing in common with Florence, the heroine of *Le Sourd dans la Ville*, who breaks all her ties to her bourgeois milieu to engage in a solitary journey towards death. I wrote this book while I was alone in the Alps and in a little inn in Hudson, Quebec; this relentlessly lucid book which perhaps seems sharp and hard, is nevertheless my favorite. In the book, people, animals, even a chair which falls over in an empty room, are invested with radiant life and the most despairing characters know that nothing is more precious than the lives that they may lose.

After several years of exploring Mexico and the Caribbean Islands, where I met the young people I wrote about in *Visions d'Anna* and in *Pierre ou la Guerre du Printemps '81*, I decided to live for a few months of the year in Key West, at the end of the Florida Keys, a little town full of light, of sweet-smelling flowers and tropical plants; as a northerner deprived of sun and warmth in winter, I never cease to be delighted by it. I've become deeply attached to "my" island and to my friends there. I spend hours watching the ocean and the milky transparency of the water that slides up the beach. I think of Tennessee Williams who lived and worked there such a short time ago as I silently watch his cousin, Stella, reading my hand, her head bent over misfortunes she sees and would like to wish away. Barbara Deming, too, only two years ago as I write this was still working on her own nearby island, Sugarloaf Key, struggling bravely and unsuccessfully against cancer. I think of "Grass," the first poem in James Merrill's *Late Settings:*

The river irises
Draw themselves in.
Enough to have seen
Their day. The arras

Also of evening drawn,
We light up between
Earth and Venus

On the courthouse lawn,
Kept by this cheerful
Inch of green
And ten more years—fifteen?—
From disappearing.

Time goes so swiftly. We write to survive, to escape death—that was the aspiration of Pauline Archange, who had the pretentious naïveté of her years. At forty-six, having lost most of my illusions, wouldn't I say that one writes because life is unbearable without the solace of writing? I am sitting on the beach beside a child who is carefully torturing his soldier-toy without the least desire to hide his cruelty, and my mind is already busy with the task of describing the somewhat terrifying aspect of this little being lost in primitive fantasies. I try ceaselessly to plumb the depths of human nature, extract heavy ore which I have to turn into something light and fluid. I have a book about Virginia Woolf on my knees, and read what she repeated herself: "Sacrifice nothing to the clarity of my vision." I have the painful task of creating a limpid, transparent style which will carry the subjects which obsess me. I tirelessly pursue this fugitive idea, indefinable, which, like love, is like a mirage that draws me toward the horizon forever, in pursuit of something intangible. But isn't it this vision of the ideal, like the vision of the beloved, which spurs us on and sometimes even recalls us to life?

BLANCHE McCRARY BOYD

BLANCHE McCRARY BOYD'S writing career has spanned more than 20 years, at least two genres, and several artistic identifications. Her first novel, *Nerves*, was published in 1973 by Daughters, Inc., a collectively run publishing house—founded by writers June Arnold, Bertha Harris, Parke Bowman, and Charlotte Bunch—that was dedicated to bringing new feminist voices to print. (Their greatest success was Rita Mae Brown's first novel, *Rubyfruit Jungle*, also published in 1973, which has since become a lesbian classic.)

Essay by
MICHAEL BRONSKI

On the surface, *Nerves* was a domestic Southern gothic that chronicled and explored the troubled underpinning of the dysfunctional nuclear family from the point of view of 14-year-old Diane. But the trappings of the family gothic—a genre that has appealed to other Southern women writers, such as Flannery O'Connor and Carson McCullers, and gay male writers, like Tennessee Williams and Harlan Greene—are subverted by Boyd's conscious intervention of a feminist politic. The byzantine and often emotionally unhealthy family relationships (so often the trademark of the gothic) are viewed as the direct result of male power. The narrative tensions in *Nerves* come from the struggle of the female characters to create their own autonomy and overcome not only the power of their past family history, but the troubled history of the American South itself. This theme was repeated and expanded in Boyd's next two novels, *Mourning the Death of Magic* and *The Revolution of Little Girls*. The setting of each of the novels is Charleston, South Carolina, where Boyd was born and raised and returned to live several times as an adult.

Each of Blanche McCrary Boyd's novels creates an essentially female-centered universe in which the younger women—Diane in *Nerves*, Galley in *Mourning the Death of Magic*, and Ellen in *The Revolution of Little Girls*—constantly encounter emotional, psychic, and sometimes material obstacles to their gaining some autonomy over their lives and sexuality. Each of these characters becomes, at some point in their lives, a lesbian. But Boyd's novels never reduce complex emotional and political arrangements to a simple case of gender disenfranchisement,

The narrative tensions in many of Blanche McCrary Boyd's novels come from the struggle of the female characters to create their own autonomy and overcome not only the power of their past family history, but the troubled history of the American South itself.

and in each of the novels it is the younger women's mothers and aunts who are coagents of their disempowerment. In the context of Boyd's female-centered universe, this creates a situation in which the generations of women characters refract and reflect one another. Halfway through *The Revolution of Little Girls* (Boyd's most successful and critically acclaimed novel), Ellen is pursued by a small troop of phantom pre-pubescent girls who are at once a materialization of past and possible selves, as well as a sign that the need to break from the past is inevitable.

Many of these themes are also present in *The Redneck Way of Knowledge,* a collection of nonfiction pieces that originally appeared in the *Village Voice.* Many of the fictionalized events of the novels reappear as personal *reportage,* although Boyd's social concerns—especially about racial issues—are delved into more deeply. In "Growing Up Racist" she explores the complexities of being Southern and attempting to embrace an anti-racist politic. In "Ambush" she describes the complicated social relationships that led to a clash of violence and murder between the Ku Klux Klan and the Communist Worker's Party. Issues of race are also present in the novels— Lena, in *Nerves,* wonders "if it was nerves making her see, for the first time, how much of her life was built on the lives of black people…. [I]t was as if, when she walked on her carpets, she stepped on bodies"—and Boyd is particularly concerned with how white women, already socially constrained, deal with their own complicity in racial oppression.

Boyd writes from the perspective of a white Southern lesbian who understands the complexity of her position as an oppressed gender and sexual minority, as well as a member of a dominant racial class. Her writing continually attempts to mediate and understand the imbalance of power in her life and to establish her own autonomy and sense of self.

THE REVOLUTION OF LITTLE GIRLS

Excerpt reprinted from *The Revolution of Little Girls,* Vintage Contemporaries, copyright 1991 by Blanche McCrary Boyd.

When I was in the eleventh grade, my English teacher, Mr. Endicott, dropped his college ring down Reggie Lucas's shirt, then reached inside to retrieve it. Mr. Endicott had been to military college and perhaps thought such behavior could be passed off as horseplay.

American novelist and essayist.

Born: Charleston, South Carolina, 1945.

Career: Teaches writing at Connecticut College, New London, Connecticut.

Address: c/o Connecticut College, Box 1421, New London, Connecticut 06320, U.S.A.

He'd been reading *Our Town* to us out loud. Most students at Plaxton High majored in Home Economics or Agriculture, and Mr. Endicott had been teaching at Plaxton High for fifteen years. At some point in his career he had probably discussed literature and assigned papers, but by the time I was in his class, we diagrammed sentences on the blackboard or else he read to us. There was no point in giving us assignments, because we wouldn't do them.

In the first act of *Our Town*, a typical day in Grover's Corners, New Hampshire, is described. I was as bored by Mr. Endicott's droning as everyone else when Reggie Lucas raised his hand. "Bill," he said winningly, "are you sure you went to VMI? Do they even *have* English majors at VMI?" Reggie smiled, baring large white teeth. We were not allowed to call Mr. Endicott by his first name.

Reggie had a blond, waxed flattop and the most attractive collarbones I had ever seen. We'd ridden together in the back seat of a car the week before, all the way home from a basketball tournament. My friend Marla had arranged this. Reggie wasn't very interested in me sexually but found Marla's invitation worth exploring. In the car he kissed me several times, and I was so thrilled to have my fantasy fulfilled that I couldn't actually feel anything. "I just don't want to do this," Reggie said, nibbling wetly on my neck. "I've got to play again tomorrow night." I kissed him back woodenly, worried about what to do with my tongue. "Jesus," he groaned after a while, leaning back and pointing to the crotch of his warmup pants. "You've done it to me now. This is your fault."

"What?" I said, refusing to look down.

"I *knew* this would happen," he said. "*Look* at it."

I stared hard at the couple in the front seat, who were pretending to be deaf. "Reggie," I said, suddenly inspired, "what do you think of Mr. Endicott?"

"He's a queer," Reggie snarled at the fogged window beside him. "Everybody knows that."

"But what do you think of him?"

"I think he's a queer."

I decided to try a different approach. "If you could have anything in the world you wanted, what would it be?"

He looked darkly hopeful. "I'll show you," he said, grabbing my wrist.

I snatched my hand away. "Really, Reggie. What would you want?"

"A Corvette," he said and folded his arms across his chest. He shut his eyes and pretended to sleep.

Outside the other back window, which was unfogged by Reggie's distress, I watched the dark South Carolina landscape slide by, catching glimpses of Spanish moss in live oak trees, dense stands of pine, the shacks where black people lived. White people's houses were few. The rural Lowcountry was mostly black, and the schools had not yet been integrated. Our district was over thirty miles long. The trips to ball games were tedious. I felt disappointed and embarrassed about Reggie, so I composed a new note for Mr. Endicott:

> When you're driving your car
> and relief seems so far
> remember that suffering is always random
> but you are protected by your friend
> the Phantom.

I had begun these notes a few weeks before. The first one I left of the dashboard of his car. After that I scribbled them on his blackboard, before class. He seemed very happy about them. "I have an admirer," he'd say.

Mr. Endicott was a tall, masculine man, but his buttocks were a bit thick, probably from sitting down for fifteen years, and he had a generous mouth. "I know what he does with those rubber lips," I once heard Reggie's friend Cliff say.

In English class Reggie flirted contemptuously with Mr. Endicott, both to entertain the rest of us and to stall the readings. Mr. Endicott was intrigued by Reggie's insolence, and he usually stopped whatever he was doing to smile and chat.

"VMI was tougher than the army, Reggie," he said. "I promise you it was tougher than playing basketball."

"Why weren't *you* in the army?" Cliff asked. He was a burly boy with small, blinky eyes.

Mr. Endicott smiled. "Somebody had to bring y'all some culture."

Perhaps this is why I liked Mr. Endicott: he could be sarcastic and pleasant at the same time.

"Cliff," Mr. Endicott said, "you aren't by any chance the Phantom, are you?"

"Nah," Cliff said, "it's Reggie."

I was hurt by this exchange, because neither Cliff nor Reggie was smart enough to rhyme anything, even partially.

"Let me see your ring," Reggie said.

Mr. Endicott hesitated, then rose from his desk and walked toward him. Maybe he just wanted to stand next to him. I could understand that. He handed Reggie his ring.

Reggie examined it and threw it to Cliff, whose chair was next to mine.

Mr. Endicott didn't know what to do, so he just stood there awkwardly. After a few seconds, Cliff threw the ring back, and Mr. Endicott's hand snatched it out of the air right in front of Reggie's.

Reggie grabbed Mr. Endicott's wrist and they struggled.

"Here, if you want it so much," Mr. Endicott said, and he dropped the ring down the back of Reggie's shirt.

We were very quiet except for the sound of our breathing. It was English class and something wrong had happened. No one knew what to do.

"I'll get it," Mr. Endicott said, resuming his grown-up teacher's tone. He reached his hand matter-of-factly inside Reggie's shirt.

Reggie leaped from his seat, and I could see him trembling. He pulled out his shirttail and the ring hit the linoleum floor with a brief, muffled sound. It rolled toward me and stopped right by my penny loafer. I picked it up. It was a heavy gold school ring with a blue stone.

Mr. Endicott looked grateful as I handed it to him. He went back to his desk and took up reading *Our Town* again.

It's hard to explain what happened next. The class was so tense and unnerved that we began to listen desperately to the play. Dr. Gibbs was chastising his son George for not doing his chores and leaving his mother to chop wood. *Our Town* was set in 1900, but I didn't think that could account for all the differences from Plaxton that I was noticing. My father had died in an automobile accident; Reggie's father was a butcher at Mack's Meats; Cliff's father was our town doctor and, as everyone knew, he beat his son—that's where the scars on Cliff's back came from.

When Dr. Gibbs got disgruntled because Mrs. Gibbs was staying too long at choir practice, I began to giggle. The women on the way home from choir practice had stopped on the corner to gossip about the town drunk: "Really," one of them said, "it's the worst scandal that ever was in this town!"

I was trying to stop giggling when Mrs. Gibbs arrived home and Dr. Gibbs complained, "You're late enough," and Mrs. Gibbs replied, "Now, Frank, don't be grouchy. Come out and smell my heliotrope in the moonlight."

I started to laugh out loud. I didn't know what heliotrope was, and this remark struck me as hilariously off-color.

Mr. Endicott stopped reading. I put my head down on the desk but I knew he was looking at me. "Try to get hold of yourself, Ellen." The pleasant sarcasm was back in his voice.

But this laughter was like nothing that had ever happened to me. My face felt hot, and my new contact lenses were floating off my eyes. I gripped the edges of my desk as Mr. Endicott continued to read.

A few minutes later Mr. Webb, Dr. Gibbs's neighbor, went up to his daughter's room to see why she wasn't in bed. "I just can't sleep yet, Papa," she said. "The moonlight's so *won*-derful. And the smell of Mrs. Gibbs's heliotrope. Can you smell it?"

A howling noise escaped me. I began to pound helplessly on my desk.

"My dear," Mr. Endicott said, "heliotrope is a flower."

I stood up, squinting to hold my lenses in place. I could hardly breathe, much less speak. The laughter was brutalizing me with its terrible release, and I was no longer sure if I was laughing or crying.

Now Mr. Endicott sounded concerned. "Do you want to go home, my dear?"

I pulled my books against my chest, nodding.

"Go by the office."

I struggled down the hallway, still laughing, my face soaked with tears. In the principal's office I couldn't speak so I wrote a note to the secretary and pushed it across her desk: GOING HOME. CAN'T STOP LAUGHING.

* * *

Seven years passed.

Reggie married Marla's other friend, Janine. He inherited Mack's Meats, and he and Janine had two children. Soon after birth the girl died of spinal meningitis; the boy was slow and timid.

Right out of high school Cliff surprised everyone by marrying Marla. He surprised everyone again by becoming a successful antique dealer in Charleston, thirty miles away from Plaxton. Cliff soon learned to talk comfortably and grammatically about Edwardian, Victorian, or antebellum, but on Sundays he remained content to watch ballgames on TV with Reggie, while Marla and Janine made chili or fried chicken and pies with Cool Whip on top.

Mr. Endicott developed a hearing problem and had to give up teaching. He became a furniture restorer, a job he could do in his own garage. Sometimes he did freelance work for his former student, Cliff.

I moved to California and got enmeshed in a number of pursuits I considered radical and beautiful.

* * *

"It makes me want to throw up," my mother said, in reference to my newly declared homosexuality.

We were driving in her new Mercedes to the country club to have dinner and play bingo. My mother did not really like the new Mercedes, so she was letting me drive it. She'd bought it because she could afford it, but a Datsun, she'd informed me as she handed me the keys, was definitely a superior car.

"You don't like this car because you've gained too much weight to be comfortable under the steering wheel," I said as we pulled out of the driveway of her condominium, past the guard house.

"The steering wheel is too large and it is incorrectly placed."

"I think the steering wheel's just fine."

My mother was wearing a red jersey dress and lots of gold jewelry. She admitted that she would limp tomorrow from her high heels. I was wearing a black dress and high heels, to prove to her that I still liked being a woman. I would probably limp tomorrow too.

We pulled into the country club lot and parked under the moss-draped arms of a huge live oak tree. When I came around the car to open her door and help her out, I kissed her on the cheek. "Does that make you want to throw up?"

My mother was shorter and heavier than me. The woman I changed my life over was taller and thinner, and embracing her was nothing like kissing my mother on the cheek.

She hugged me miserably. "Honey, I'm afraid people will try to hurt you about this."

"Me too, Momma. I'm afraid too."

"Couldn't you change your mind?"

"I don't think so." Over her shoulder, beyond the smooth green fairway, I watched the Ashley River slide turbidly by.

* * *

Cliff and Reggie were watching a different river through the plate-glass window in Reggie's den. "I always wanted to live on this river," Reggie said. He would say this every Sunday, but today there was something vague in his voice, something about loss.

"You did it, Bo." That was what Cliff always said too. But yesterday Cliff closed a deal on an eighteenth-century house in the historic area of Charleston. His voice was as wistful as Reggie's.

Reggie did not want Cliff to move away from Plaxton. He said that it was one thing to work in Charleston, but moving there was another. "It's too far from my store out here, Bo," Cliff said. "Ain't nobody in Plaxton gonna buy anty-cues."

Reggie closed the curtains. He was thinking about butchers' wounds. Butchers always sliced toward their abdomens, and sometimes they got cut. His father had cut himself once in twenty years, perforating his intestine, but it was lung cancer that killed him. "My daddy always wanted to live on this river."

* * *

My mother was winning at bingo. She was playing so many cards she had to put some on an extra chair beside the table. She mumbled for the caller, an adenoidal, bored young woman, to slow down. "Honey, why don't you tell her to slow down." My mother was too polite, herself, to complain to anyone directly.

"I'm too well brought up to do any such thing," I said, but when I walked up front to collect one of her $25 prizes, I conveyed her request. The girl gave me a bovine look and nodded. I wasn't quite sure what the nod meant. Southerners are as polite as cattle, except when they're not. When they're not, they might shoot you or chase you around the yard with a hatchet.

"Thank you, honey," my mother whispered, when I reseated myself at the table.

Later, at home, she tied a pair of underpants around her head to protect her hairdo. "It just works better than anything else. I know it looks silly." In our pajamas we had a nightcap, bourbon for her, brandy for me, and kept the television running in the background. On the news was a picture of Bobby Seale tied to a chair with his mouth taped shut.

"My father's sister was …" my mother said. "Of course we didn't call it … we didn't call it anything."

"How did you know she was? You can call it gay."

"Well, she lived with another woman who was younger than she was, and she raised her child with her. Also, she was mannish."

"Do you think I'm mannish?"

"And Cousin Bryce, when he was going to marry that girl he brought home for Christmas? Then excused himself from dinner and went upstairs and shot himself with the shotgun? I think he was, too."

"Do you think I'm mannish?"

"I don't know what to think about you, Ellen. Gay seems like such an inappropriate word."

"Well, anyway, thank you for giving me the family history."

* * *

Reggie and Cliff were watching the same newscast: Bobby Seale's trial had been severed from that of the rest of the Chicago Eight, who were now the Chicago Seven. Popcorn was spilled across the coffee table. Marla and Janine were asleep on the sofa. Reggie and Cliff were drunk. "How'm I gonna get her into the car?" Cliff said.

"Look at that nigger," Reggie said, pointing at the television. "I tell you, I'm glad somebody burned the high school down. So much for having to go to school with them."

Cliff raised Marla's limp arm and dropped it. "I guess she's not driving."

"Remember those pig balls?" Reggie said. "Castrating pigs was about the only good thing we learned in Agriculture." He made a noise that was half-whispered but as high-pitched as a scream.

Janine stirred on the sofa without waking.

"If I close one eye I see fine," Cliff said. "Too bad I've got to drive with two."

"Remember how we left 'em on Endicott's doorstep? With a note from the Phantom? Old Endicott, old rubber lips. He probably thought it was a compliment. He probably thought that crazy girl did it. Ellen. The one who laughed."

Cliff was helping Marla to her feet. "Don't be so goddamn dumb, Reggie. Don't be such an asshole. Of course he knew we did it. Of course he knew that."

* * *

Three months after I returned to California, my lover left me and returned to her husband, a man who wore his shirts half buttoned, exposing a chestful of hair and gold chains. She grew her nails long again, and painted them red. "I just couldn't handle it," she said.

"It?" My lover had been a radical who said the word *lesbian* as easily as my mother said *segregation*. "What about being revolutionaries? What about custody of the cats?"

"My shrink says I was going through a phase. You can keep the cats."

We were standing close to each other, but I was looking at the poster of Emma Goldman on the wall behind her. "Don't you think you could've figured this out a bit sooner?"

For several months I stayed in bed listening to Linda Ronstadt records. Linda Ronstadt, I felt sure, understood suffering. I drank half gallons of wine, smoked marijuana, and inhaled hundreds of hits of laughing gas. Nitrous oxide is the propellant for whipped cream dispensers. Whippets, we called them. Dealers sold the cartridges with a small instrument that emptied them into balloons. I didn't laugh much, but my lungs developed enough to inhale an entire balloon in one breath.

* * *

Mr. Endicott liked the mall. It was a safe place to walk, and his doctors had told him to exercise. He couldn't go to bars anymore because the music hurt his ears, and going to the Battery to cruise wasn't safe at his age. But in the bright artificial light of the mall he could walk and look. The smooth, careless bodies of the young seemed a kind of museum, and he felt harmless enough, looking. When he was tired, he would sit in the center of the mall by the fountain. The noise of the water was soothing.

My mother and I found him there, eating a cup of frozen yogurt.

Mr. Endicott was wearing a plaid wool shirt, and his gray hair was combed neatly. His eyes had the dreamy quality that the hard of hearing sometimes develop.

"Look," my mother said, "isn't that your old high school English teacher?"

My mother had recently had her facelift, and it was too soon for her to be out in public. She still looked bruised and puffy and garish. "Like Frankenstein," she'd said, cheerfully putting on her sweatsuit that morning. She had twelve identical sweatsuits, each in a different color. Today she was wearing powder pink, topped with dark glasses.

Blanche McCrary Boyd in 1985.

I was holding my mother's elbow. "Yes. It is." When she'd asked me to take care of her during her recovery, I was both troubled and touched. I was taking my duties seriously.

"Hello there, stranger!" my mother said gaily, seizing Mr. Endicott's hand. "Look who's come home!"

Mr. Endicott seemed alarmed because he didn't recognize either of us at first. I'd been out of high school twenty-five years. I wasn't sure he'd ever met my mother; at any rate, she looked as if she'd been beaten up in a barroom fight.

"Ellen?" Mr. Endicott's eyes were watery and vulnerable. "Is that you?"

"One and the same," I said.

He fumbled with his yogurt cup. "My stars. I thought you would never come back to South Carolina. I thought you were too big for us."

"She is! She is!" my mother said. "She's written a bestseller cookbook and even a screenplay! She's come home to help me with my facelift! Don't I look like Frankenstein?"

"Do you remember my mother?" I said.

* * *

Late the next afternoon I drove out toward Plaxton in my mother's Mercedes. The car was seventeen years old, seasoned and comfortable, and, according to my mother, the best car she'd ever had. The offending steering wheel had been replaced by a mahogany Nardi she'd ordered from the Beverly Hills Motoring Accessories catalog.

The road across the marshes had become a divided highway. At the Plaxton River, I noticed that the huge oak that used to hang into the water was gone. The banks had been cleared, and where the tree once was a small ranch house now stood. The house had a picture window, but the curtains were closed.

Past Plaxton, the road became the familiar two-lane blacktop crowded by fecund brush. In clearings were the same old shacks or small brick houses. A black snake slithered across the pavement. In the distance the road looked wet and shiny. "It's a mirage," my father had told me when I was a little girl. "The heat causes it." I had loved the word *mirage* and would say it over and over, gazing at the end of the road.

In Plaxton, the Chevrolet dealership still looked as if it only stocked two or three cars. The drugstore was boarded up, but a combination convenience store and gas station was new. Mack's Meats had expanded from a small cinderblock building to a larger cinderblock building.

I pulled in beside the phone booth near the gas pumps at the convenience store and sat there for a few minutes. It was cool in the air-conditioned car, but I was sweating. Finally I got out and called my home in Vermont.

Meg's voice, husky and mocking, answered on the tape machine: "This is Tammy Faye Bakker. Jim and I can't come to the phone right now, because we're praying over my hairdo."

"Meg," I said after the beep, "I hate these damn phone jokes. Anyway, picture this. I'm standing in a parking lot across from Mack's Meats in Plaxton, South Carolina, and a boy I was ferociously attracted to in high school is probably over there working. It's damn hot. I'm going to dinner tonight at my high school English teacher's house. I'll call back tonight. I miss you."

The asphalt was sticky under my tennis shoes.

There were no customers in the store. "Is Reggie around?" I asked the girl behind the counter. Slight and bored, she looked familiar. One of the Glendennings, I decided. She directed me through a doorway to Reggie's cluttered office.

He was sitting behind a metal desk, punching figures into an adding machine. "Ellen! Is it really Ellen?"

We hugged hard. His hair had turned gray and his teeth were yellow, but he still looked fine. "You always had the best collarbones," I said into his neck. "How's Janine?"

"Fine, fine. Did you see my daughter out there? We finally had another daughter. She's on the junior varsity." When he smiled I saw that one of his darkening teeth had been capped and had a bluish cast.

We sat and passed the time for a few minutes. There was a map of a steer on the wall, each part labeled with the cuts of meat it provided. Reggie's daughter brought us coffee. I could see, now, how much she looked like Janine. The fact that there were no customers was misleading. Reggie said that he did mostly slaughtering, and business was good. "Janine's gotten fat as a house. You wouldn't believe it." He laughed appreciatively.

I was surprised to see that Reggie was no taller than I was. "Reggie, did you used to be taller, when you played basketball?"

He frowned. "I played guard."

"How's Cliff?"

"That shit. You can know somebody your whole life and not know anything about them."

* * *

Dinner at Bill Endicott's house began awkwardly. He was lonely, he said, and he'd burned the pork chops. Did I like opera?

His house, low-ceilinged and airless, was jumbled with broken antiques. "I don't know much about opera," I said, and he turned down the scratchy record he was playing. His stereo was of obviously poor quality, a weekend special from some discount house.

"Cliff loved it. He gave me this record. It's a rare recording. Very rare."

"Cliff from high school? That Cliff?"

He nodded, smiling. "Cliff died last year, you know."

"Cliff died?" I realized I was beginning to sound stupid. "I'm sorry. It's just that I saw Reggie today, and he didn't even tell me."

"Well, they grew apart."

Over his shoulder I saw a framed eight-by-ten photograph on an end table. Cliff's small, blinky eyes stared out of it. Mr. Endicott turned and picked it up and handed it to me.

I spoke carefully. "I didn't know."

"I worked for him some, Ellen, restoring furniture. Maria had a bad time, but I think she's all right now. She's a sweet girl."

"What did he die of?"

"Cancer."

We sat down at his kitchen dinette set. Its plastic wood contrasted with the faded antiques in the rest of the house. "Bill," I said, "did you know I'm gay too?"

He was pouring iced tea for us and hadn't heard.

"Bill," I said when he was looking at me, "I wanted you to know I'm gay."

Emotion rushed across his face. "Cliff told me."

"How …"

"He was an antique dealer, and he found out these things."

"Bill, did Cliff die of AIDS?"

"Of course not," he said too quickly, handing me the bowl of red rice. "Cliff was happily married. I worked for him. That was all."

I understood that he was lying to me. He'd probably made his decision to lie about Cliff long ago. I was sorry, because I would have liked for us to talk. "It's nice to see you again" was all I said.

He looked grateful, watching my lips. "It's nice to see you too, Ellen."

I tried to think of a question that wouldn't intrude. "How did you and Cliff get to know each other?"

He clutched his fork, and his faded eyes brightened. "In high school he used to write these notes on my blackboard. Do you remember the Phantom?"

I nodded and looked down, concentrating on cutting my pork chop.

"Well, he wrote me a very mean one and left something very mean on my doorstep. I won't say what. Then he came to my house to apologize, and we talked."

The pork chops really were burned. The red rice was flavorless, the broccoli frozen, served from a boiled plastic bag.

I smiled and looked Bill right in the eyes. "What a wonderful story," I said.

After dinner I lay sprawled on his sofa drinking cup after cup of instant coffee while he played me his scratchy opera records. He sat in a pink Victorian wing chair with his head tilted back, and once tears ran down his face. "Can you hear it?" he kept saying. "Can you hear it?"

"I hear it," I said.

MALCOLM BOYD

THE COMPLEX VARIETY of career paths taken by activist Malcolm Boyd are bound together by a common theme: expressing the truth of one's inner nature and spiritual needs with openness and honesty. Since his ordination as an Episcopal priest in 1955, Boyd has written on a broad field of subjects, from his 1965 collection of prayers for the contemporary world, *Are You Running with Me Jesus?*—which brought him national acclaim—to the meditation texts of *The Book of Days*, and articles in popular periodicals and newspapers, such as *Ms.*, *Parade*, the *New York Times* and the *Washington Post*. His contributions to the evolving body of American gay and lesbian journalism are similarly diverse, with features on such topics as the emerging gay community in the former Soviet Union and the struggle of homosexuals with organized religion for recognition and equality at the altar appearing frequently in the *Advocate*. Much of Boyd's gay-themed writing is autobiographical in nature, as he uses his own life as a forum for the explication of his views and insights on social reforms, spirituality, and political change. The three works for which he is most widely known, *Take Off the Masks*, *Look Back in Joy: Celebration of Gay Lovers*, and *Gay Priest: An Inner Journey*, reveal the development of Boyd's private journey and growth.

At the time of its initial publication in 1978, two years after John McNeill's groundbreaking study *The Church and the Homosexual*, *Take Off the Masks* was virtually unique as an autobiography of an openly gay member of the clergy, preceded only by Troy Perry's *The Lord Is My Shepherd and He Knows I'm Gay* in 1972. Despite the subsequent appearance of such works as Zalmon Sherwood's *Kairos: Confessions of a Gay Priest*, Johannes DiMaria-Kuiper's *Hot under the Collar*, and the anthology *Lesbian Nuns: Breaking Silence*, Boyd's volume retains its primacy as the opening dialogue against the subordination of human spiritual needs to the bureaucracy of faith, a condition that he termed "Churchianity." The demand that individuals be seen as precious, unique, and valuable, irrespective of race, beliefs, or sexual orientation, is an outgrowth of Boyd's own outreach ministry at Colorado State University in 1959, as well as his involvement in the civil rights movement. Through the story of the

Essay by
ROBERT B. MARKS
RIDINGER

author's life and passage into wholeness, *Take Off the Masks* inveighs against the separation of people by barriers of any kind. The idea that a prominent clergyman would not only admit to being homosexual but actually celebrate it as a spiritual gift contributed both to the growth of a separate gay and lesbian approach to religious matters and to the evolution of a more accepting theology.

The format of the brief essays that form the body of *Look Back in Joy: Celebration of Gay Lovers* recalls the pages of *Are You Running with Me, Jesus?* The collection frankly explores the gamut of emotions that comprise gay relationships of all types, from the most transient encounters to lifetime commitments. The final section presents vignettes from the construction of Boyd's own partnership. Taken as a whole, the work is a melding of the activist focus of much of the author's previous writing with the spiritual aspects emerging from the gay and lesbian movement of the 1980s. The growing spiritual aspect of the gay and lesbian movement is more fully developed and explored in such anthologies as *Gay Spirit: Myth and Meaning* and *Amazing Grace: Stories of Lesbian and Gay Faith*.

Gay Priest: An Inner Journey is in many ways a combination of the passion, anger, and purpose of *Take Off the Masks* and the poetic style of *Look Back in Joy*. It completes the inner picture of the writer by deepening his sense of life experience, a quality that was also achieved in Boyd's *Half Laughing/Half Crying: Songs for Myself*, published in 1986. The conflict between religion and society for possession of the souls of gays and lesbians has been played out in the words of dozens of books, essays, and poems since the Stonewall Riots of 1969. The writings of Malcolm Boyd offer a consistently humane perspective on this debate as seen from the battlefield of integrity, faith, and sexuality.

AUTOBIOGRAPHY

Reprinted from *Contemporary Authors Autobiography Series*, volume 11, copyright 1990 by Gale Research, updated in 1994.

Three parts of my life have defined me as far back as I can remember. I am a writer. I am religious. I am gay.

My childhood was very much out of the ordinary. Growing up in Manhattan as the only child of rich parents, I was terribly alone and lonely. Servants were the only people close to me. A chauffeur taught me how to tie shoelaces and read the face of a clock. Instead of playing with other children, I had a succession of governesses. One, English to the core, was tweedy, affectionate, but firm. My family resided near Central Park, and every day my governess and I made our way around the reservoir, she on foot, I riding my tricycle.

Inside Central Park was an old stone observatory which became a castle for me. My governess had given me a book about British kings, queens, princes, princesses, palaces, gardens, and wars. I lived inside my own fantasy world, and my fantasies came to life when I climbed around the observatory, its stairways and turrets. Of course, I knew the story of *The Prince and the Pauper*, and alternately played both roles in my daydreams.

Later, I had a German governess. Her name was Angela. She had an affair with the doorman of our apartment building. She knew that *I* knew, so discipline was out of the question. When I was supposed to be in bed and asleep, I insisted that she allow me to listen to "Chandu the Magician" on the radio. It was scary, all shadows and serpents, and I was blissfully terrified.

Malcolm Boyd outside Saint Augustine by-the-Sea Episcopal Church in Santa Monica, California, in 1987.

When my parents separated, I was nine years old. My mother was given custody of me. We left New York and visited my maternal grandmother in Oklahoma. Then we settled down to live in Colorado Springs, Colorado, and later, Denver. My father, Melville Boyd, a financier, remained in New York. I hated everything outside New York, and was an utter snob about it. The Sunday edition of the *New York Times* didn't reach Colorado Springs until the following Thursday (or Saturday, maybe even the next Monday in case of a blizzard). I devoured the "Arts and Leisure" section. Theatre, dance, opera, books: these were my real world.

I listened to opera broadcasts from the Met each Saturday. The first time I ever heard the "Liebestod" sung by Flagstad and Melchior was one of the most exciting moments of my early life. On Saturdays I also visited the public library. Always I returned a stack of eight or ten books, and brought home a new batch. I read avidly the most sophisticated novels and nonfiction.

These were odd years because I was, in the classic sense of the word, a sissy. I knew nothing of sports. My friends comprised one or two adult women. Lonely and isolated, I could not identify with anyone of my own age. The junior high school newspaper became a salvific force in my life when I began to write for it.

American theologian, novelist, playwright, and editor.

Born: New York City, June 8, 1923.

Education: University of Arizona, Tucson, B.A. 1944; Divinity School of the Pacific, B.D. 1954; Oxford University, Oxford, England, 1954–55; studied at an ecumenical institute in Geneva, Switzerland; Union Theological Seminary, New York City, S.T.M. 1956; participated in a work-study program at Taizé Community, France, 1957.

Partnerships: Companion of Mark Thompson.

Career: Copywriter, scriptwriter, and producer of radio programs, Foote, Cone & Belding (advertising agency), Hollywood, California, 1945–46; writer and producer, Republic Pictures and Samuel Goldwyn Productions, Hollywood, 1947–49; cofounder, vice president, and general manager, Pickford, Rogers, & Boyd, New York City, 1949–51; rector, St. George's Episcopal Church, Indianapolis, Indiana, 1957–59; Episcopal chaplain, Colorado State University, Ft. Collins, 1959–61; Protestant chaplain, Wayne State University, and assistant priest, Grace Episcopal Church, Detroit, 1961–64; assistant pastor, Church of the Atonement, Washington, D.C., 1964–65; national field representative to American universities and colleges, Episcopal Society for Cultural and Racial Unity, 1965–68; writer-

priest in residence, St. Augustine by-the-Sea Episcopal Church, Santa Monica, California, 1981–; director, Institute of Gay Spirituality and Theology, Los Angeles, 1987–. Lecturer, World Council of Churches, 1955 and 1964; columnist, *Pittsburgh Courier*, 1962–65; participated in voter registration drives in Alabama and Mississippi, 1963 and 1964; resident fellow of Calhoun College, Yale University, New Haven, Connecticut, 1968–71, associate fellow, 1971–75; resident guest, Mishkenot Sha'ananim, Jerusalem, Israel, 1974; host of television programs, including *Sex in the Seventies*, CBS-TV, 1975; president of Los Angeles chapter of PEN, 1984–87; chaplain, AIDS Commission of the Episcopal Diocese of Los Angeles, 1989–; contributing editor, *Renewal and Integrity Forum*; contributor of reviews and articles to newspapers and periodicals, including *Los Angeles Times Book Review*, *New York Times*, *Advocate*, *Ms.*, *Modern Maturity*, *Episcopalian*, *United Church Herald*, and *Christian Century*.

Memberships: Film Awards Committee, National Council of Churches, 1965; Los Angeles City/County AIDS Task Force, beginning 1985.

Recipient: Integrity International Award, 1978; Union of American Hebrew Congregations Award, 1980.

Address: c/o St. Augustine by-the-Sea Episcopal Church, 1227 Fourth Street, Santa Monica, California 90401, U.S.A.

In that pretelevision era, major artists braved snow and ice to appear in Colorado Springs. I saw Paderewski, Flagstad, Lotte Lehmann, Marion Anderson, John Charles Thomas, Lawrence Tibbett, Lily Pons, and many others. More to the point, I got in the habit of interviewing them whenever they were available. God knows why they spent their valuable time with a kid in short pants from the local junior high school paper.

When violinist Mischa Elman sat for my first interview, my questions were awful, stilted, unimaginative, and obvious. He said angrily that I needed to do more research. Lotte Lehmann was a lovely and gracious subject. And, she treated me as an adult. Could it be she was simply lonely out on the road in the hinterlands? Did she see me as a sophisticated and sensitive boy providing a pleasant interlude? Carl Van Doren, urbane and kind (he gave me three hours for our interview), was joined by Harold Laski, H. V. Kaltenborn, and a small legion of authors and social critics as my subjects. After Josephine Antoine, a Metropolitan Opera soprano, gave a concert in the Ute Theatre, I interviewed her. Learning from our conversation that I sang, too, she asked me to perform "O Sole Mio" for her onstage. My mother, arriving to drive me home, was startled to hear my voice thundering through the empty hall.

My mother had gone to work as a teacher, for my family's money was wiped out in the Depression. Beatrice, who is ninety-one as I write this, has always possessed strong inner resources. In her youth she taught and cared for Navajo children in the Arizona desert during an influenza epidemic. Then, after working for forty years, she retired at the age of seventy and commenced another twenty years of volunteer teaching at the Children's Hospital of Los Angeles.

After my mother and I moved to Denver, I continued interviewing celebrated men and women in the arts and letters. Wanda Landowska entered my life unforgettably when she insisted on my staying to lunch after our chat. She prepared a salad and served it with fresh bread and tea.

During this period I won first prize in the Sons of the American Revolution essay contest, received an honorable mention in a *Scholastic* magazine competition, placed third in my high school's poetry contest, wrote editorials for my school newspaper, the *Spotlight*, and was the *Denver Post* correspondent from my high school. Chosen by the National Honor Society in my junior year, I was studious and deeply concerned about world events and politics. A regular reader of the *Nation* and the *New Republic*, I became sharply aware of racism at home and the emerging Holocaust in Europe. I wrote long letters expressing my views about these matters to the *Rocky Mountain News* and the *Denver Post*.

I still remember my first opera, *Rigoletto*, performed by a traveling troupe, and Noel Coward's *Private Lives*. Despite such icing on the cake, this period of my life was utter hell. I felt an alien in a strange place. No one, I was sure, understood me at all. Any serious attempt to communicate with another human being seemed hopeless. I was "different." How could I cope with forever being The Outsider? I looked at easygoing, popular, handsome athletes and knew I was totally shut out of their world of acceptance, glamour, achievement (in my eyes), and fun. Girls either ignored me or found me a eunuchlike jester, someone to laugh with and confide in. I quickly learned how to provide laughs and counseling for such people. Although I was convinced no one gave a tinker's damn about what I wrote, I continued turning out page after page of poems, essays, and reviews for any publication willing to print it.

Religion was at the center of my life, although I was not conventionally "pious." There was a lot of rage inside me. God was not distant, I knew, but close by and caring. Although God siphoned off some of my rage, a lot of it remained. The church, I understood, was a vastly amusing, very political, highly eccentric organization close to God, but also capable of the devil's subversion. I saw strong, dynamic church leaders locked in conflict with one another over careerism, absurdly minute territorial rights, and foppish matters of protocol. Egos were dominant. While the sheer drama of the church was compelling, both in its liturgy and behind-the-scenes soap operas, instinctively I knew Jesus the Galilean stood in stark contrast to such polished posturing and burnished gold. I could scarcely, and seldom, find Jesus in the church that seemed to go out of its way to condemn the world in his name. I perceived that the church, at its worst, was an imperial and self-serving empire whose own machinery took precedence over human needs.

My paternal grandfather, who died before I was born, was an Episcopal priest in New York. I still have a photograph of him. Garbed in vestments, he appears a gentle and kind man with soft, compassionate eyes. While I was a youth living in Denver, Paul Roberts, an Episcopal priest, became a role model for me that cut sharply against my negative image of clergy. Dean of Saint John's Cathedral, he was gutsy, honest, plain, an eloquent preacher, and possessed a sturdy sense of humor as well as a keen social conscience. I stayed in touch with him through succeeding years. He was a marvelous man, an exemplary Christian. But even his positive presence in my life was not enough to make the church as an institution appealing to me.

When I went away to college, I dropped the church like a hot potato. It bored me, droning on endlessly with those whining, irrelevant prayers. Clergy seemed a breed apart, mostly cold, clammy men with whom one felt ill at ease. Did they *ever* take their clerical collars off? What did they do in *bed?* Were there *any* simply natural moments when they weren't "on"? I didn't want to hear any more about "sin"; I yearned to experience and enjoy life.

During my four years of college, I never found out who I was, and no one was able to help me. Still The Outsider, I learned how to play a splendid masquerade. I drank beer every night at the Speedway, the "in" bar for the college set at the University of Arizona. (My lungs were poor, and this was the reason I attended Arizona instead of Dartmouth; I remained the easterner in my allegiances.) My writing became perfunctory; there was no sense of intellectual challenge or creative growth, and my former idealism seemed to ebb. I wrote for the yearbook and newspaper, and published a gossip sheet called the *Bar Nuthin*.

While I dated girls, I longed for boys. Boys surrounded me in the highly erotic setting of my fraternity, the most macho on campus. I had to learn to wear a mask, hide my feelings, repress my strongest desires, and show a face that bore little resemblance to my real self.

After college I moved to Los Angeles in the mid-forties, studied how to write radio scripts, and was hired by the Hollywood office of one of the largest and most powerful American advertising agencies. Soon I produced a fifteen-minute soap opera five days a week at Foote, Cone and Belding, along with a Sunday evening news broadcast. And, I wrote a few scripts for dramatic programs.

Malcolm Boyd with Mary Pickford at the Hollywood Advertising Club in 1949.

Hollywood was in the last stages of its "golden age" when I left the agency to work for a movie studio. All doors were apparently open for me, a good-looking, well-educated, clean-cut, hard-working young guy starting out. Quite innocent, I met the stars, dined in legendary restaurants and clubs, spun dreams, and became a success.

Serious writing was out the window. So was religion. I didn't know what to do about being gay—it didn't seem *gay* at all, just an awful burden to be "a homosexual." So I put my pent-up sexual energy into my work, and soon had the workaholic force of a one-person Niagara Falls.

When I met Mary Pickford, I was in awe. She was the empress of the entertainment world, the first great woman star, the first modern media celebrity (with Charlie Chaplin), and a millionairess. We met when I worked on a movie she coproduced, *Sleep, My Love*, starring Claudette Colbert. Pickfair, Mary's home, was at that time nearly as well known as the White House. She entertained U.S. presidents, European royalty, and international stars. Mary opened Pickfair to me. I learned to swim in its pool and stayed in the guest house which had hosted the Mountbattens and Queen Marie of Romania. I quickly grew accustomed to Hollywood stars whose foibles were amusing but their egos tedious.

Mary and I formed PRB, Incorporated, a production company, and moved to New York. Shortly I was having brunch with Mrs. William Randolph Hearst, cocktails with Adele Astaire, and was being called the

"Golden Boy" by society columnist Cobina Wright. As a young gay man in search of his identity, I entered into a close friendship with Mary, who called herself my "spiritual mother."

Mary drank heavily in a sad *Long Day's Journey into Night* sort of way. This boozing was dead serious, self-destructive, obsessive, and rooted in extreme human anguish. Mary, "America's Sweetheart," was lost. I cared for her deeply, but was unable to help her.

I was lost, too. I had settled for glamour (which I found quite drab) instead of pursuing spiritual and intellectual truth. The parts of myself that responded to this, I repressed. I was locked in an "I-Thou" relationship with God that was intense, troubled, and unfulfilled. I needed desperately to enter into a human relationship that combined sexual and spiritual elements, but that possibility seemed remoter than going to the moon. I lacked the basic rudiments of self-definition, and also feared the sexual mystery of myself. I wasn't able to share it with anyone else, except in the most casual and shifting of brief encounters.

Glancing around me at the personages inhabiting Mary's heady milieu, I realized I didn't *want* this. I couldn't bear to look ahead to twenty or thirty years of such aggressive success-manufacturing and image-making, accompanied by spiritual despair. I yearned to open up windows in my claustrophobic life. Was there a vaster and infinitely more comprehensive life outside? Could I learn to exercise my intellect and provide oxygen for my soul? I wanted to try. I withdrew from Hollywood, went out to the desert, prayed and meditated. Gradually an inner life came into focus as a possibility for me. And, I knew a fire burned there. My life was undergoing a major turning point, an extraordinary change.

From "Golden Boy" to priest.

I decided I wished to be an Episcopal priest, and, after applying to the diocese of Los Angeles, was admitted as a postulant to holy orders. In 1951 I departed Hollywood for a seminary in Berkeley, California. My going-away lunch at Ciro's, when the entertainment industry formally told me good-by, was star-studded and tearful. Columnist Hedda Hopper reported that even the bartender bowed his head for the Lord's Prayer. My departure shared newspaper headlines with actor Robert Walker's youthful death and Mary Astor's suicide attempt.

The following three years at the Church Divinity School of the Pacific allowed little time or energy for either writing or pursuing my gay identity. I devoted all my time to the Bible, liturgics, homiletics, church history, Christian education, and ethics. The next year I went to England and studied at Oxford. Also, I closely observed such church experiments in evangelism as the "industrial mission" and "house-church." That winter was spent at the Ecumenical Institute of the World Council of

Churches at the Chateau de Bossey, near Geneva in Switzerland. Then I commenced two years of graduate theological studies at Union Theological Seminary in New York City.

Here, I wrote a graduate paper which became my first book. Carefully grounded in scholarship (my teachers included Reinhold Niebuhr and Hendrik Kraemer), it attempted to relate Christian theology to the mass media. In other words, I was constructing a bridge between two quite different worlds I'd inhabited. Doubleday published *Crisis in Communication* in 1957. When the book was completed, I had to be hospitalized briefly. I was as close to a nervous breakdown as I would ever be. The stress had been relentless.

During the next year at Union Theological Seminary I completed my second book, *Christ and Celebrity Gods* (Seabury Press). It should have been Part II of the first book, as it explored the same themes. Now I went to work in my first parish, a tiny church in an impoverished inner-city area of Indianapolis. The sophisticated young mandarin of academia was, at least on the surface, turning into a kind of worker-priest. The dean of the nearby cathedral was Paul Moore, Jr., who would later become bishop of New York and remain one of my close friends for a lifetime.

In 1959 I was asked to become the Episcopal chaplain at Colorado State University in Fort Collins, Colorado. In that small-town environment I staged a series of "Espresso Nights," with readings and dance, and directed a reader's theatre-style presentation of T. S. Eliot's *Cocktail Party*. The diocesan bishop strongly opposed such outreach and the implicit meaning of my work. I was forced to resign.

Four books emerged from this period, all published by Morehouse-Barlow of New York. They are *Focus: Rethinking the Meaning of Our Evangelism* (1960); *If I Go Down to Hell* (1962); *The Hunger, The Thirst* (1964); and *On the Battle Lines: A Manifesto for Our Times* (1964), which I edited. I had gone to France in 1957 to spend three months living and working in the Taizé Community, an ecumenical Christian brotherhood. It engaged in farming, medicine, and art, as well as theological work. Taizé combined the contemplative with the active life, believing each necessarily complements the other. My experience at Taizé, which deeply affected my life, I wrote about at length in *If I Go Down to Hell*. However, the book proved to be a disappointment because I was unsuccessful in communicating my ideas and feelings in a clear way that embodied their urgency, and in relating these to my own inner struggle and a more universal, existential one.

Compelled to leave my chaplain's post in Colorado, I was invited to become Episcopal chaplain at Wayne State University in Detroit, which occupies a sprawling, urban campus in the heart of the city. I lived in a ramshackle apartment house across from the university. At this time I became involved in the civil rights movement, participating in a 1961 "Prayer Pilgrimage" Freedom Ride and dozens of other demonstrations, frequently being arrested for my beliefs and actions to combat racism. Nothing else I ever did meant so much to me. I was ready to lay down my life for what I perceived as justice. I was with Martin Luther King, Jr., on numerous occasions and had great admiration for him. In Detroit, I held discussion meetings about civil rights in my apartment, which were often impassioned and attracted large and diverse groups of people, including the brother of Malcolm X and Viola Liuzzo, whose murder would shortly make her a nationally known activist martyr.

I wrote four dramatic sketches, all related to the civil rights struggle. *Boy* was about a middle-age African-American shoeshine man; *A Study in Color* featured a white man dressed in black, wearing a black mask, and a black man dressed in white, wearing a white mask. I appeared in both short plays when we presented them in Detroit coffeehouse theatres. Neither Detroit paper would review them, but the *New York Times* did. They were later performed nationally on college campuses, off-Broadway, in cathedrals, and on NBC-TV. The two other dramatic sketches were *They Aren't Real to Me*, a comedy about a reverse racial situation, and *The Job*, a humorous but bitterly ironic monologue.

During 1963 and 1964, I wrote *Are You Running with Me, Jesus?* At the outset I rented a small house in a Detroit suburb to provide a space where I could work completely alone without interruption. A friend, Richard A. English, who later became the dean of the School of Social Work at Howard University, drove me there, and planned to come back once a week during a two-month period to bring me a supply of food. I settled down to write.

However, the civil rights struggle would not conveniently leave me alone. These were the days when the youthful civil rights martyrs Goodman, Schwerner, and Chaney were missing in Mississippi. Every night I watched the Huntley-Brinkley news on TV for an update on the search for them until their bodies were found.

Not long before, I had visited Jackson, Mississippi, to attend the funeral of Medgar Evers, the black civil rights leader who was killed there. Going to the Evers home, I saw a field of tall grass nearby in which the killer had hid, holding his gun. Now, in my rented house in an all-white Detroit suburb, I noticed there was a vacant lot alongside it that was also filled with tall grass.

Soon telephone calls started. When I answered, I heard heavy breathing, but no word was ever uttered. The calls came intermittently throughout the day and night. I had given the number of the house to no one. I realized these calls must be placed by someone trying to terrify me. Then it dawned on me that they must be coming from someone *who could see me* from a nearby house. The caller had apparently watched Richard and me arrive. His black face in that determinedly all-white neighborhood had triggered fear and hatred.

Seated at my typewriter, with my back to a window that opened on the field of tall grass, I nervously waited for the phone to ring again, and again, bringing its message of hate. When I answered, I pleaded in vain for the caller to talk, or listen to me; to permit some kind of an honest, open dialogue between us. A sullen silence prevailed, which clearly carried a genuine threat to my safety. When Richard arrived the next time, bringing my food, I asked him to get me out of there as fast as he could.

During the coming months I worked on *Are You Running with Me, Jesus?* in my inner-city apartment overlooking the Wayne State University campus. As I structured these poems/prayers, I found my voice. I was able to communicate my thoughts and feelings effectively, it seemed, for the first time. I felt battered and tired; I had just been fired from the chaplaincy in Detroit because rich, powerful people in the church opposed what I was doing. Why was I so controversial? I didn't know where to go from here. I felt down, drained, unaccepted, and perhaps even unacceptable. It is no wonder that my prayers have been compared to psalms in their swings of up and down, their primitive cries from the heart and unvarnished look at life.

William Robert Miller became my editor when he accepted the book for Holt, Rinehart and Winston. Bill offered invaluable advice in helping me complete the book for publication. But he was shortly fired, gone in a bureaucratic shuffle. Joseph Cunneen replaced him as editor, leaving his own strong mark on the book. Holt expected *Are You Running with Me, Jesus?* to sell around four thousand copies, and ignored the book.

It changed my life when it became a sensation and a best seller. Arthur Cohen, editor in chief at Holt, suddenly took me seriously as a writer. So did other people. Sales mushroomed. Soon I read the prayers during a month's engagement at San Francisco's *hungry i* and on campuses in every part of the U.S. Visiting Newport, Rhode Island, to read them at the Jazz Festival, I was invited by Hugh D. Auchincloss, the financier, to use his family's cabana at Bailey's Beach. When Auchincloss unexpectedly showed up, he didn't greet me or shake hands, but blurted out, "Why don't you write any prayers for stockbrokers?" The book's title

Are You Running with Me, Jesus? becomes a best seller.

quickly became part of contemporary folklore, appearing on banners in parades and demonstrations, and seen as an integral part of pop culture.

Are You Running with Me, Jesus? had fourteen editions in hardcover, fourteen in paperback (Avon). The *New York Times* wrote, in a review published months after publication: "Terse, sometimes slangy, always eloquent prayers ... Their eloquence comes from the personal struggle they contain—a struggle to believe, to keep going, a spiritual contest that is agonized, courageous, and not always won ... A very moving book." The *San Francisco Chronicle* observed: "These prayers are vital, extremely contemporary, and have caught on in the ferment of the new cultural revolution." Senator Eugene J. McCarthy wrote a poem titled *Are You Running with Me, Jesus?* that was published in the *New Republic:*

> Are you running with me, Jesus
> asks the Reverend Malcolm Boyd
>
> May I ask the same?
>
> I'm an existential runner
> Indifferent to space.
> I'm running here in place.

I didn't wait long enough for my next book to appear. The pressure from Holt was unyielding. I was caught in a very heady experience of success. So I let *Free to Live, Free to Die* come out perhaps a year earlier than it should have. In retrospect, I wish that *Are You Running with Me, Jesus?* had been followed by *As I Live and Breathe: Stages of an Autobiography,* which I wrote a bit later. I find *Free to Live, Free to Die* an uneven work, containing both some of my best writing and some of my worst. The *Christian Century* wrote: "I give thanks for it. Boyd is a prophet for our times. His words speak with disturbing power to believer and unbeliever alike." The *Chicago Tribune* called it a "drama of redemption." The book's first printing was eighty thousand copies. It moved into two paperback editions (New American Library). The seemingly stark secularity of this book was a shock to many readers who expected a sequel to *Are You Running with Me, Jesus?* I believe these people had never understood how deeply radical that work is. Did its subject matter of "prayers" mask its offense? *Free to Live, Free to Die* possessed no such layer of protection. Yet it is a profoundly spiritual work, albeit without stereotyped trappings. To a number of people it appears even antireligious. It is largely misunderstood.

James Silberman was my editor for my next two books at Random House. The first was *Malcolm Boyd's Book of Days* (1968), with a subsequent paperback edition from Fawcett. A number of people fell in love with this book, but it was distinctly a minor work. I find it curiously detached from myself, having a format that is more packaged than personal. Bennett Cerf thought it should be titled *Half Laughing/Half Crying*, a title that I used nearly twenty years later for another book. *Book Week* wrote: "Malcolm Boyd wants to break down ghetto walls, tear off masks, remove barriers." *Look* exclaimed amusingly: "A smashing iconoclast!"

Within seven months I was arrested twice for participating in Peace Masses inside the Pentagon. It seemed the epitome of theatre of the absurd, enacted in real life. In one mass I delivered the sermon. A police officer with a bullhorn engaged in an unrehearsed dialogue with me. He tumbled out the words "You are under arrest." I responded antiphonally, "If the salt has lost its taste, how shall its saltness be restored?" My image at this time was defined by Robert Frank's photograph on the cover of *Are You Running with Me, Jesus?*: sophisticated but sincere, tense-eyed but with soul, a swinger but certainly on the saintly side.

When *As I Live and Breathe: Stages of an Autobiography* appeared, R. W. B. Lewis wrote in its foreword: "Malcolm Boyd's mission is altogether in the American grain. It harks back to the days of Emerson and Theodore Parker and Orestes Brownson, to those restive ministers who found their church had gone dry ... and who in their attempt to restore vitality to the religious life expanded their ministerial activities into the whole range of human experience.... Malcolm Boyd is the irregular man, the informal man, but (anything but an alienated man) he always prefers to do his work and have his say *within* the peripheries of whatever establishment he is inhabiting.... How Malcolm arrived at his so-to-say regularized irregularity is the subject of this book, and an utterly absorbing account it is."

I attempted to tell my story chronologically in the book, but spent almost no time on my youth, and an inordinate amount of it on civil rights. The *New York Times* called the book "a story of our times" and noted: "The vibrations of church and society and race and war are so tightly interwoven that you can never separate them." I felt this book was my proudest, most elegantly written, most beautifully produced book. The *New Yorker* wrote: "His experiences are moving and his concern is affecting." The only problem with *As I Live and Breathe*—and it's a major one—is that I remained closeted at the time. So did an indispensable part of my life in the book.

Washington, D.C., became my home for a couple of years after I left Detroit. I found it a cold and impersonal city. Also I had a back problem, felt terribly lonely in a harsh spotlight of celebrity, and withdrew into myself. My personal life was spartan and devoted to writing. I made

"Rebel Priest" leaves Detroit.

Malcolm Boyd speaks with Boston University students about religion, the draft, Vietnam, and morality, at one of many such college gatherings in the mid-1960s.

appearances on national television as "the rebel priest" and read my celebrated and now-familiar prayers and meditations. At this point I could not walk through an airport without causing at least a slight stir, being asked for autographs, or even running into a vociferous, demanding, youthful group of fans. All this only served to heighten my isolation.

From the church I heard conflicting messages. A fundamentalist minister in the Midwest, obviously critical of me, asked almost accusingly (as if expecting a negative response) if I had ever experienced an act of conversion. I told him offhandedly that I sometimes had three in a good day, but could go five weeks without one. The minister seemed an enemy. However, I perceived the essential church as passionately alive in the midst of sensitive, crazy, changing, and growing people. Here, I found a quiet celebration of Jesus, the antihero, who died on the cross in God's identification with human injustice, suffering, failure, and hope.

I went to Yale in 1968 in response to R. W. B. Lewis's invitation to reside in Calhoun College as a visiting fellow. (I returned there for a second year in the early seventies.) Now I was quite estranged from the institutional church. Indeed, I felt that it and I were in a *Who's Afraid of Virginia Woolf?* marriage. Love and hate ran deep. At Yale, William Sloane Coffin, Jr., who was the chaplain there, kindly asked me to preach. But aside from an occasional visit to the Yale chapel, I seldom attended a service.

Norman Mailer was also a fellow of Calhoun College. I remember when he visited the college and held court. Everybody sat on the floor around the chair where he sat. He pontificated, issuing opinions as from a throne. Norman apparently viewed himself as Hemingway's literary heir. He seemed to enjoy his role as an avant-garde filmmaker, drank a lot, and cultivated a persona of an aging social and political enfant terrible.

Years later, when I lived in Los Angeles and was president of PEN there, Norman visited from New York as president of PEN American Center in the East. We were at a literary cocktail party in Venice given by producer-restaurateur Tony Bill. The bartender was Mac McNeel, a young woman who worked at Bill's Venice restaurant, 72 Market Street, and was a faithful member of my parish church, Saint Augustine by-the-Sea. After handing Norman a fresh drink, she told him, "Mr. Mailer, it's a shame you missed Malcolm's sermon last Sunday. It was great. You would have loved it." Norman looked completely nonplused.

Twenty-five years earlier Norman had addressed a Vietnam Day protest in Berkeley when I preached at a jazz mass in San Francisco's Grace Cathedral. Columnist Ralph J. Gleason compared us under the heading "Two Moments in a Revolution" in the *San Francisco Chronicle*. He wrote: "Agnostic that I am, Rev. Boyd's sermon was the most impressive I have heard in years, and ... [Mailer's] was the most impressive political speech in a generation."

While I was at Yale, I lived in the Master's house of Calhoun College with R. W. B. Lewis and his wife Nancy. They became close friends. Nancy and I particularly enjoyed cooking together. It became a hobby, and, with the assistance of students, we prepared ambitious and mouth-watering dinners for various celebrated visitors. Nancy and Dick's own home in nearby Bethany, Connecticut, became a familiar and welcome haven. Here, I enjoyed meeting friends of theirs, John and Barbara Hersey, Bill and Rose Styron, and the Red Warrens.

I'll always remember fondly my first dinner invitation to their Bethany farmhouse. I came out from Calhoun College for the evening. It was snowing, but seemingly no more than usual for a winter's night. We dined informally at their kitchen table, with a Helen Frankenthaler painting looking down at us from a vantage place on the wall near the stove. When it came time for me to go, we opened the front door and an icy blast of air hit us in the face. We beheld a maelstrom of swirling snow. I stayed there three days and nights as a blizzard raged.

Neither milk nor the *New York Times* reached the door. Of course, we could not get out in the car to shop. So Nancy and I found a lamb bone, placed it in an iron pot, added vegetables, herbs and spices, and prepared a stew. With the passing of days, we added whatever ingredients we could lay our hands on. It became miraculously like the feeding of the five thousand with loaves and fishes. Inside the house we had fire, food and drink, intermittent conversation, stretches of silence for reading or writing, and the slow, easy formation of an emerging friendship. I hated it when the sun came up on the morning of the fourth day, the *Times* appeared at the door, and it was time for me to go. But Nancy invited me to dinner on Friday, two days away.

During this period of my life a publisher would inevitably expect me to go on a national book tour, visiting major cities for media appearances, when a new title of mine came out. A book tour is, I believe, as physically and emotionally demanding as Wimbledon or the U.S. Open. F. Scott Fitzgerald never rose at dawn for an author's appearance on "Good Morning America." Neither George Sand nor Elizabeth Barrett Browning ever raced in a cab on a rainy morning to be interviewed on "Today." One day in New York when I was on the move from dawn to 9:00 P.M., a Boston radio station asked me to do a telephone interview from my hotel room that night between 11:00 P.M. and midnight. I was exhausted, but my publisher asked me to accept the interview, saying it would be a snap. At ten o'clock I dozed off.

When the phone rang, I picked up the receiver and a voice asked, "Is Malcolm there?" I moved my head on the pillow. As I listened, the radio announcer told his audience that Pauline Kael would join us. Kael, the most articulate of film critics, was seated in the Boston studio. I pulled my body to a sitting position in the bed. I was plunged headlong into an erudite, sophisticated, fast-moving discussion, like a lobster pointed toward boiling water. I never caught up.

All interviews are arduous, but long ago I learned not to give a print interview over a meal. Without fail, a waiter barges in at a key moment of one's confession. My two best print interviews took place in taxis racing toward airports. One was for the *Toronto Globe and Mail*, the other for the *Chicago Tribune*: No frills, all existentialism.

My relationships with other writers have proved highly interesting. Naturally I have interacted with many of them as president of PEN. I have dined with Christopher Isherwood in Los Angeles, shared a microphone with Studs Terkel in Chicago, given a reading with Langston Hughes in Cleveland, and shared a speaker's platform with Ralph Ellison in New York. (Nancy Lewis shared with me his wife, Fanny's, recipe for a salad that's become a favorite of mine; its ingredients include marinated mushrooms, a sliced tart apple, a sweet onion, and watercress.)

One night in Madrid I missed going out on the town with James Baldwin because my back hurt, and I rested instead. I never met Graham Greene, but, in October 1954, Mrs. Greene asked me to dinner at her home near Oxford. She showed me her doll's house. It was immense, expensive, intricate; each little room was perfect with a carpet, chairs, tables, drapes, and she was inordinately proud of it.

I was visiting New York in 1989 when R. W. B. Lewis was asked to read from the work of Henry James at the Cathedral Church of Saint John the Divine. That night, James and Henry David Thoreau were formally inducted into the American Poets' Corner. Nancy and I sat together as James Merrill read two speeches from *The Ambassadors*. Then Dick read a Jamesian letter written in 1896 in Rome, the concluding pages of *The Wings of the Dove*, and a letter to H. G. Wells. He appeared remote and distant, robed in black, as he stood at the cathedral lectern. How different he looked in this public setting from the close friend with whom I have shared hour upon hour of conversation over food and drink. I felt such a somber, heavy image did not capture his great humor, vitality, irony, anger, and passion. Years before, his photograph in the *Times* accompanied the announcement that he had just been given the Pulitzer Prize for *Edith Wharton*. (Later, Dick and Nancy were co-editors of *The Letters of Edith Wharton*.) Following Dick's extremely formal and sedate appearance at Saint John the Divine, it was good to engage in the most ordinary of chats with him while holding a drink in Paul and Brenda Moore's home.

Authors and artists as celebrities are fascinating to me. In the mid-seventies when I lived in the creative center of Mishkenot Sha'ananim in Jerusalem, Friedrich Durrenmatt was there when I arrived. Virgil Thomson had just departed, and soon to arrive were Simone de Beauvoir, Lukas Foss, Stephen Spender, Alexander Calder, and Arthur Rubinstein. Interaction was quite natural and left to the individuals involved. I lived there when the thirty-ninth International Congress of PEN met in Jerusalem in 1974, and guests of honor included Saul Bellow, Heinrich Boll, Eugene Ionesco, V. S. Pritchett, and Yehuda Amichai.

The "celebrity factor" of becoming a well-known writer touched my own life during this period. I was written about and interviewed. I found myself in situations with other well-known people. For example, Teddy Kollek, the mayor of Jerusalem, and I became friends. At first we kept seeing each other in the streets. I walked two or three miles daily. Teddy was never a mayor to sit in his office. He was constantly out, on the go, moving rapidly, interacting with a wide variety of people. When I was a member of Teddy's invited party for a Christmas Eve midnight mass in Bethlehem, I found a pleasant companion in a middle-aged woman in the party who dressed plainly, wore flat shoes, and had an engaging sense of humor. Afterward we became separated from the others in a great crush. Seemingly we missed our ride. We started to walk on foot the highway leading from Bethlehem to Rachel's Tomb. The night was bitter cold.

"We haven't formally met, have we?" she asked. "No. I'm Malcolm Boyd," I replied. "I'm the Baroness de Rothschild," she said. Hiking beneath the stars, we engaged in an animated conversation. Shortly a car appeared to whisk us back to Jerusalem. A couple of days later the Baroness asked me to tea at her Jerusalem home. "But you don't really want *tea*, do you?" she asked. "Let's have scotch." And she invited me to join friends at her home for New Year's Eve. Stephen Spender was among the other guests. It was a low-key, quiet evening. In a few days the Baroness returned to her castle in France.

While living in Jerusalem I ate many meals at a popular "French kosher" restaurant that was a bit like a private club. The staff became familiar and, in fact, once catered a party in my honor in another part of the city. Often I would just sit at the bar in the restaurant, order a drink, and dine on a salade Nicoise or a light plate of veal piccata. One evening, the owner asked me to sign a leather-bound guest book which he placed in my hands. I thumbed through its pages. Henry and Nancy Kissinger were on one page, Elizabeth Taylor and Richard Burton on another. It seemed everyone, from Frank Sinatra to Zubin Mehta, had written a few words. What should I say? Sipping another drink, I drew a picture. Soon it covered two pages in the book. I had arrows pointing everywhere. A few days later the owner told me the president of Israel came in to dinner the next night. He had never signed the guest book and was asked to. But when he got to my mini-mural, he called the owner to his table. "What's *this?*" he asked. "Tell me, what's *this?*"

Blending private and public lives.

We authors have public lives and private ones. Some of us do not wish to have the former; or we try to place a fence around the latter. During the sixties my public life was under klieg lights, while my closeted sexuality kept my private life a hidden preserve. In 1968, when I edited *The Underground Church* (Sheed and Ward; Penguin paperback), I became publicly identified with the book almost as if I were "the bishop" of the underground church. *Time* said that I named it. The publisher's jacket copy, which I did not see until the book appeared, offered this commentary about me: "He is the unofficial national chaplain to the disaffected or alienated Christian of whatever age who has been 'turned off' by the official Church. At the same time, he serves the official Church as prophet-preacher, critic-gadfly, and quintessential priest."

My own picture of my life and role was not nearly so neat. I found myself plunged into seemingly endless controversy. I had a persona that aroused the strongest emotions, positive and negative. I hated that kind of polarization of attitudes. Was I a kind of battleground for other people's wars? People who didn't read me apparently had as many opinions about me as those who did.

I moved to fiction for *The Fantasy Worlds of Peter Stone and Other Fables.* The stories concerned (1) a Jewish candidate for the U.S. presidency, (2) a coffeehouse priest who comes close to secular canonization by the New Age, (3) a woman's visions that cause her to found a new worldwide religion, and (4) a young man selected by a celebrated Italian filmmaker to portray Jesus Christ in a spectacular biblical movie. I wrote an additional story about a cathedral that was bombed, but the piece never seemed to come together, and I dropped it. Harper and Row published the book; Avon did a paperback edition. *Publishers Weekly* wrote: "Boyd is lighter, brighter and fresher than he has ever appeared before in print. The fables are delightful and wise." It surprised me that the book was not a sales success, because a number of critics went out of their way to praise it. For example, the *New York Times* wrote: "Malcolm Boyd turns his considerable talents from off-beat apologetics to satire and shows himself to be provocative, witty, and highly entertaining." Too provocative? Too witty? Did "highly entertaining" cut against the image created by *Are You Running with Me, Jesus?* that called for a soberer, self-conscious moral tone?

I followed *Peter Stone* with an altogether different book. Looking at the traditional interview—and having been interviewed myself more than two thousand times in various media—I wished to open up the form, freshen it, try something new, find some offbeat life and energy. So when I decided to write a book of interviews, I set out to correlate my central subject with a group of related people surrounding him or her. I began with a Chicano leader in Colorado, and interviewed a dozen or so associates and followers. Next came members of a midwestern commune, intellectuals and idealists trying to forge a new life with a new set of rules or approaches. One chapter comprised a group of Vietnam veterans.

Malcolm Boyd engages in conversation in a downtown Dallas, Texas, bar in 1967. While in Dallas attending a session of the National Council of Churches, Boyd had spoken of an "underground church" whose members were concerned with such matters as poverty, war and peace, sex, and race.

Another I devoted to Hugh Hefner and his *Playboy* empire. He intrigued me as an American folk figure. I interviewed his mother, college room-mate, girlfriend, valet, and A. C. Spectorsky, author of *The Exurbanites*, who had become a *Playboy* editor. The book was published by Holt, Rinehart and Winston. The *Rocky Mountain News* observed: "His service here is that of a medium … [He] transmits, with honesty, straightforward-ness and no small measure of integrity, an inexorable heartbeat of America, in its steady pulse, in its worrisome murmur."

For several years I crisscrossed the United States, speaking on countless campuses. Airports and motels seemed to frame my life. When I read my prayers with guitarist Charlie Byrd, Columbia Records taped us and produced two albums of our work. In my personal life I felt lonely and driven. While I was a fellow at Yale, the *Yale Daily News* invited me to write a weekly column. On September 24, 1968, I said in my first col-umn: "As I feel strongly that we have come to a period of necessary and painful silences, I hope to share them in creative community instead of bearing them simply in isolation."

After *My Fellow Americans*, which was such a secular book, it seems strange that my next books narrowed to tighter religious themes. *Human Like Me, Jesus* was a new prayer book. I like parts of it very much. It epit-omizes my belief that prayer is light years away from talking to God in Old English and occurs in everyday life, mostly in our actions. Prayer is found in a supermarket and on a highway, in bed and the kitchen, beneath a tree and clouds, on a picket line; in anger, frustration, joy, betrayal, fulfillment, ordinariness, and ecstasy. I wrote prayers while visit-ing an old cemetery, and about a black-student center on a university campus, a rollicking party, people in love, and reading letters and scrap-books in an attic. Simon and Schuster published the book; Pyramid did the paperback. The *Boston Globe* wrote: "He has come of age. Concerned, caring people across the nation will be pleased with his latest book."

However, *Human Like Me, Jesus* clearly lacks the raw energy and spiritual power of *Are You Running with Me, Jesus?* By this time dozens of imitations of the latter book had appeared. A few were superb, others pedestrian and banal, imitating style while largely ignoring content. At this time I wrote my next three books for Word Books. *The Lover* is a tapestry interweaving stories that tell, again and again, of the immanence of God. Word Books was more a religious than a mainstream publisher; my readership had always been more mainstream than religious. Consequently, this book did not reach my readership. This frustrated me because critics loved it; it is a shame that a bridge between critics and readers could not be traveled. The *Atlanta Constitution* commented:

"Modern life seen with poetic vision. He is the secular saint." *Publishers Weekly* said: "Malcolm Boyd is fast becoming an American institution."

In *The Runner,* which followed—and was designed to complement *The Lover*—I attempted to portray Jesus Christ in a new, and different, light *in relation to* his followers. "It is a kind of Pilgrim's Progress a la Bunuel, Ionesco or Arrabel," said the *Christian Century. Publishers Weekly* offered this highly interesting observation: "He may stand the best chance among a small group of his writing contemporaries of revealing the common meeting ground where young and old alike might put down roots in a Christianity seen freshly without cant or cliché."

My next book was an attempt to do this. A rather obvious idea on the surface, it turned out to offer fresh and innovative insights. I keep running into people who say *The Alleluia Affair* remains a favorite book of theirs. A favorite of mine too, it's about a Christ nailed to a cross in an Indianapolis church who climbs down and starts walking the streets. Other Christs come down from crosses all over the world from Rio to Johannesburg, Beirut to Paris. These Christs go to work, talk to people, enroll in school, and live ordinary lives. Soon the crosses are empty. But they start filling up again. People begin to notice other men and women whom *they* place on the crosses. My favorite scene in the book takes place inside a lavish new cathedral by an ocean. Jesus is the central figure in an immense stained-glass window. He leaps from it, shattering the glass.

I paid my visit to Mishkenot Sha'ananim in Jerusalem before I wrote *Christian.* It is a collection of essays. These concern such diverse topics as Jewish-Christian relations, Israel, mass evangelism, Billy Graham, religious films including *Godspell* and *Jesus Christ Superstar,* and the future of faith in America. I wanted to call the book *Bread and Butter Issues of Faith.* I never managed to pull the various pieces together into a unified work. To my surprise, *Publishers Weekly* called it "His most mature and searching book." I wasn't terribly angry in the book (perhaps I needed to be), and took a somewhat lofty, objective view of things. But I had fun writing about a restaurant that had previously been a church building. The bar was allegedly where the choir loft had stood. I saw lots of irony and "post-Christianity" in the situation.

Am I Running with You, God? is something of a mystery to *me.* I wonder why I wrote it, but the answer seems to be that the material within its pages existed mainly in the form of various published magazine pieces, and the publisher wished to collect these in a book. The form is largely meditations. *Publishers Weekly* said that I mingled "intense prayer-poems with confessional meditations and personal responses to the world of social and spiritual struggle," and added: "His insights into what is spiritually 'phony' and 'true' go deeper than most of the self-help psychotherapy books that flood today's market."

Inevitably one might ask why I have written so many books. In one sense, they are my children. Quite a family. I have learned that they have lives altogether separate from mine. They grow up, leave home, and embark on the damndest adventures. I can't help them from getting burned, entering into relationships I question, or cultivating wrong company. I have my favorite books, but should keep this information from the others.

Writing is my passion. Some people breathe; I write. "Keep breathing" one might say to others. "Keep writing" is invaluable advice for me. I know that I am not a "great" writer. Fine. That is not the point at all. I strive to be professional, to dig ever deeper into my own truth, and to communicate. Communication is very important to me, though paradoxically, I am not a gregarious person, and its practical requirements do not come easily to me in ordinary, daily living. I am, in fact, a classic loner who needs to integrate one's own life with others, yet sets up barricades and spins spiderwebs.

I collaborated on my next book with Paul Conrad—and loved the experience. I want to collaborate more often with interested, skilled, creative coworkers. Paul, who draws editorial cartoons for the *Los Angeles Times* and its syndicate, joined me in a book entitled *When in the Course of Human Events*. Paul has won three Pulitzer Prizes for his work, and is an enormously gifted man with a strong social conscience. His editorial cartoons, at their best, deal with such subjects as racism, the homeless, political corruption, and world peace. He has both a sense of humor and a sense of outrage. I wrote short texts to complement his cartoons. The *Chicago Daily News* wryly commented: "Should be right next to every Gideon Bible in every hotel room in the land."

The mystery of being gay.

These days my life was changing. I slowed down, allowing myself much space and time for reflection and introspection. Based in Ann Arbor, Michigan, I spoke on a number of U.S. university campuses and wrote reviews and articles for magazines and newspapers. Gradually I was building up to the moment of coming out as a gay man. I found it an extraordinarily sensitive thing to do.

The mystery of being gay puzzles and astonishes me. What, if any, unique mission or vocation is involved in this? Gay used to stand for pretense and patterned choreography, playing prescribed roles and wearing masks. "Make it gay" was the watchword. It meant "put on the ritz," "keep the act going," "don't let down your guard," "keep on smiling"—

especially to conceal one's sadness. But there has been a change. Gay now means new honesty. Where it used to signify wearing a mask, now it is a call to take off the masks. Its definition has shifted from form to content, sheer style to reality.

So, gay has something (I believe) of universal meaning to say to everybody. Take off the masks of repressed anger, self-pity, sexual deceit, hypocrisy, social exploitation, and spiritual arrogance. Let communication be an event that involves people, not a charade of puppets. Be yourself. Relate to other selves without inhibition and pretense. Help others to be themselves too.

Taking the matter this seriously, it is only natural I should have needed time to burrow inside my consciousness and explore my faith. I have always done this when I approached great turning points of my life. Often I have stayed in monasteries. In 1957, for example, when I lived in the Taizé Community in France, during the days I worked hard in the fields. At morning worship I liked to watch the subtle reflection of stained-glass on the stones in a restored twelfth-century Romanesque chapel. Sunlight streamed through small windows behind the altar, creating a pool of color on the floor. At first I perceived simply pure blue or yellow. Then, red ran slowly along the sharp edge, making a design, a movement.

One of the artistic ministries of the Taizé Community was filled by a lay brother who created sculpture, mosaics, canvases, frescoes, stained-glass windows, and etchings. When he visited Algiers for the first time (he told me), he had contacts with the nationalistic movement, saw police brutality, and discovered the racial problem. Afterwards he made a stained-glass window for a church in Strasbourg showing a black man playing a saxophone. And, he painted "Vierge Noire," a black Virgin and child. She wore a yellow gown, white hennin, a blue ring on her finger, and a single gold bracelet, this against a vivid red background. I remember that he used dehumanization as his theme in a painting, *David and Goliath:* "transposé dans un univers modern la victoire de l'Esprit sur la matière." Young David stood naked and quietly confident, holding a flower, in front of monolithic structures of steel in which people were cruel to each other, and helpless, and there was a sense of demonic power.

Always I have observed a sense of strongly contrapuntal values within monastic communities. Not that they're perfect. But, at their best, they struggle for an ideal, and reject any too easy, glib solution for either social or personal problems. There is an authentic intellectual vitality within any spiritually alive community. Always I love being literally astounded by a new idea, challenged by a thought that never occurred to me.

One day in the madly energized sixties I found myself near the Trappist Abbey of Gethsemani in Kentucky. I decided to drop in on Thomas Merton, who lived there. He greeted me as a long-lost friend, showing remarkable high energy and humor. He had read and liked *Are You Running with Me, Jesus?* Inside his hermitage we talked, laughed, shared, gossiped, and discussed a world of ideas and topics within a span of a few hours. He provided Kentucky bourbon, which we sipped as a form of communion.

A turning point: coming out.

Now a major turning point in my life beckoned once again. In 1976, grappling with the idea of coming out as a gay man and immersing myself in reflection, I sought the meaning of Marianne Moore's words, "The cure for loneliness is solitude." I identified strongly with Sam Keen's description of his experience with solitude: "A drop of calm, a moment of silence, a thimbleful of the Void is enough to reverse the paranoid movement of the mind." I settled into the seasons, getting to know their moods and qualities. It required me to look into a mirror, see Malcolm Boyd without flinching, and decide that I must not run away any longer from God, other people, or my true self. As I wrote later in *Take Off the Masks*, I reduced the speedometer of my life toward zero. The arrival of the daily mail took on all the significance of a visit from a god. Wrapped in silences, I slowly became at ease with demons whom I had feared.

Vistas outside and inside myself merged in landscapes of stark whites, blacks, and browns. Sometimes flowers punctuated, or even splashed, these landscapes with marks of color. Snow on the ground provided the whiteness for nearly half the year. Trees were black sentinels then; later they became brown, surrounded by the greenness of their foliage. A few of the trees were among my beloved friends. I talked to them, touched them, more than once I placed my arms around a tree to hug it.

I fed, and watched, birds. For a time a lively cardinal visited me daily. I felt a closeness grow between us. Then on an ice-cold morning I found its small red body resting in death outside the door. What could I do as a final gesture of friendship? I carried it into a nearby area and buried its remains beneath frozen winter leaves.

After blocking earlier escape routes of my life, and working my way through a number of dilemmas and problems, the moment finally arrived for my coming out. Afterward, *People* magazine tried to describe how many people had apparently viewed me: "blunt, restless, eloquent and above all, open." Yet it noted the brooding presence of a mask in my public life: "He kept one aspect of his life deeply private: his homosexuality." In 1978 I wrote a book about my experience, *Take Off the Masks* (Doubleday). New Society Publishers published the paperback, still in print. I wrote in its introduction: "My life is in mid-course. I want to involve my life in the whole struggle for human liberation and understanding ... I do not *ask* for my right to life, liberty and the pursuit of happiness in what will inevitably be the final years of my life. This right belongs to me. I claim it. For anyone who knows what it is to wear a heavy, stultifying, and imprisoning mask in life, I write this book. I offer my witness. Let's take off the masks."

The book proved to be an event. The *Washington Post* called it "Boyd's honest, courageous account of his freedom march toward integrity and psychological health." *Library Journal* wrote: "A man reborn who learns to love himself, other people, and God, step by bloody step. He reveals the flesh and soul of a media-myth we thought we knew."

A few years later I wrote another book that is a recollection of my gay relationships over a life span, some lasting and significant, others fleeting and transitory, a few mixed with fantasy. *Look Back in Joy: Celebration of Gay Lovers* was published by Gay Sunshine Press in 1981. I consider it daring, original, and a work other people can identify with. A new edition was published by Alyson Publications of Boston in the fall of 1990, accompanied by photographs by Crawford Barton. Poet Will Inman said of the book: "He tries to lead us to see ourselves, not with guilt but compassion, with clear eyes and courage, reaching to the roots of the spirit within us toward healing. His book is one of the necessary ongoing gospels of our uncertain and struggling time." The *Los Angeles Times* said: "By sharing the unextraordinariness of love's long suffusion into his life, Malcolm Boyd has shared with us his neatest trick of all."

St. Martin's Press published *Half Laughing/Half Crying*, which is, in effect, a reader containing a goodly sampling of my written work. It may have been a bit premature; in any event, it moved out-of-print fairly briskly. *Publishers Weekly* commented: "Boyd has explored how people maintain their humanness in the face of forces that try to break them or reduce them to stereotypes ... [His] relentlessly honest self-portrait inspires the reader to examine his or her own preconceptions."

Gay Priest: An Inner Journey followed from St. Martin's, with a subsequent paperback in Stonewall Inn Editions. Michael Denneny of St. Martin's Press became a friend in the process of our getting out the book. He had emerged, along with Sasha Alyson, as one of the key figures and best editors in gay publishing. In order to understand this book, one must take note of the subtitle. It is, truly, an *inner* journey. The *New York Times*

Malcolm Boyd with life-partner Mark Thompson in 1988.

called it "Part memoir, part meditation, part manifesto."

After I came out, my first telephone call was from author Frank Deford, then a senior writer for *Sports Illustrated* and an old friend. He had read the story in a New York newspaper on a plane en route to Dallas. He said, "Gee, I don't know what to say. They don't make Hallmark cards for this." We laughed, but a human tidal wave of reaction struck me within a few hours. The story was carried on the wire services and featured in newspapers, TV flash announcements, and radio broadcasts throughout the country. I sensed instinctive human support rather than hostility or rejection, although I heard that someone burned all my books. Paul Moore, as bishop of New York, supported me courageously in the face of scattered demands that I be punished by the church. I had to adjust to a new life out of the closet. I found this moment a painful one because I felt stark naked in front of the world. Yet it brought me personal freedom and the most remarkable opportunity to start over with a new lease.

During the eighties I resumed an anchored place in the church as writer-priest-in-residence at Saint Augustine by-the-Sea Episcopal Church in Santa Monica, California. It meant that I returned to regular preaching in a church pulpit. I regard the sermon as an art form, albeit a neglected one, and love to preach. To my surprise and delight, I feel very relaxed and at home within the church as I prepare to celebrate my fortieth anniversary as an Episcopal priest. I am impressed by the depth of faith shown by congregations like St. Augustine's that engage in serious social activism and remain open to the world as well as to God. I find staggered levels of incredible meaning in the eucharist, the church's central act of worship, and rejoice in a liturgical role as its celebrant.

In the past few years I have served three terms as president of the Los Angeles Center of PEN (1984–1987), and have been a member of the Los Angeles City/County AIDS Task Force and chaplain of the AIDS Commission of the Episcopal Diocese of Los Angeles. My life has come together in ways I would not earlier have believed possible. My gay personhood is integrated with the rest of my life. I live in a fulfilling relationship with my life-partner, Mark Thompson. Also a writer, he has been senior editor of the *Advocate*, the national gay newsmagazine, for many years, and is author of *Gay Spirit: Myth and Meaning, Long Road to Freedom*, and *Gay Soul*. The twenty-fifth anniversary edition of *Are You Running with Me, Jesus?* was published by Beacon Press in the spring of 1990, and I later wrote *Rich with Years*, which was published by HarperCollins.

At seventy, I look forward with a certain childlike innocence to the year 2000. A reviewer for the *New York Times* once called me "a balding Holden Caulfield." Perhaps I am. I realize that I have always been more like *The Glass Menagerie*'s Tom, who was "pursued by something," than like a knight consciously searching for the Holy Grail.

TAKE OFF THE MASKS

Walking inside, I realized it was a gay bar. It was warm, smoky, and noisy, and I happily immersed myself in the pack of people. I nursed my beer and surveyed the mixed crowd. There was a short, cute blond over by the jukebox ... a romantic Byronic type with longish dark hair two place away from me at the bar ... and next to him a collegiate number with a pug nose.... Then I saw someone who took my breath away, a Moorish prince who had apparently just stepped out of one of those Turkish cigarette ads.

I got next to him and started up a conversation by talking about the sleet. His responses were brief, his look veiled, but I sensed in him the same desperate need, and the same anger, that I had encountered in Jonathan at that overlook in the Sierra.

He came home with me. I made love to him. He tried to respond, and at moments I felt a flooding outpouring of himself as he clutched me. But then he'd retreat into some bastion of hostility, looking at me with smoldering eyes.

I wanted to talk to him. To explain ... explain what? The only language I could trust was the language of my body, and I flung meanings at him that I barely understood myself. How could I make him understand?

He rose from the bed like a pillar of amber, like an avenging angel—and noticed my clerical collar on top of the bureau. He picked it up with great delicacy. As I stood beside him, he looked at me. "You a priest?"

Excerpts reprinted from *Take Off the Masks*, HarperCollins, copyright 1993 by Malcolm Boyd.

MALCOLM **BOYD**   95

Nonfiction

Crisis in Communication, 1957.
Christ and Celebrity Gods, 1958.
Focus: Rethinking the Meaning of Our
Evangelism, 1960.
If I Go Down to Hell, 1962.
The Hunger, the Thirst, 1964.
Are You Running with Me, Jesus? 1965;
revised, 1990.
Free to Live, Free to Die, 1967; revised
and abridged, 1970.
Malcolm Boyd's Book of Days, 1969.
As I Live and Breathe: Stages of an
Autobiography, 1969.
Human Like Me, Jesus, 1971.
When in the Course of Human Events,
with Paul Conrad, 1973.
Christian: Its Meanings in the Age of
Future Shock, 1975.
Am I Running with You, God? 1977.
Take Off the Masks, 1977; revised,
1984; revised, 1993.
Look Back in Joy: Celebration of Gay
Lovers, 1981; revised, with pho-
tographs by Crawford Barton, 1990.
Half Laughing/Half Crying: Songs for
Myself, 1986.

Gay Priest: An Inner Journey, 1987.
Edges, Boundaries, and Connections,
1992.
Rich with Years: Daily Meditations on
Growing Older, 1993.

Fiction

The Fantasy World of Peter Stone, and
Other Fables, 1969.
The Lover, 1972.
The Runner, 1974.
The Alleluia Affair, 1975.

Plays

They Aren't Real to Me, produced New
York, 1962.
The Job, produced New York, 1962.
Study in Color, produced New York,
1962.
Boy, produced New York, 1964.
The Community, produced New York,
1964.

Editor

On the Battle Lines, 1964.
The Underground Church, 1968.
Amazing Grace: Stories of Lesbian and

Gay Faith, with Nancy Wilson, 1991.

Contributor

Christianity and Contemporary Arts,
1962.
Witness to a Generation, by Edward
Fiske, 1967.
You Can't Kill the Dream, 1968.
Gay Spirit: Myth and Meaning, edited by
Mark Thompson, 1987.
Contemporary Authors Autobiography
Series (autobiographical sketch),
Volume 11, 1990.

Other

My Fellow Americans (interviews),
1970.
Are You Running with Me, Jesus?
(screenplay; based on author's book
of the same title), with Ervin Zavada.

Adaptations

All of Boyd's plays have appeared on
television.
The Job, Study in Color, and Boy were
produced as films by the Anti-
Defamation League of B'nai B'rith.

"Yes."

"Well, how about that!" His eyes suddenly burst into flame. "I don't want to make it with a priest."

"Why? What's the matter with being a priest?"

"I've got no time for the goddamn church. It hates gays. The church hates humanity. The church hates God because God made people. You're a fucking priest in the goddamn church."

I saw the fist coming toward me, felt a crash of pain....

When I regained consciousness, I raised my head and looked around the apartment. Nothing was disturbed, nothing taken. But the room was empty.

Then I saw it, crushed and twisted, lying on the floor—my clerical collar. I was drained.

All night I sat in a chair, gazing into the jet darkness inside the room. What sense was I supposed to make out of being a priest *and* a gay human being? What connection was there between these?

Somehow *I* provided a connection. Inside myself. In my tortured, seeking life. But how was it possible? How?

"Who am I, then?" I asked the darkness.

There was no response out of the heavy silence.

* * *

The mystery of being gay puzzles and astonishes me. Why are there gays? What does it mean to be the Jew, the black, the gay, someone who must suffer in a particular way within the "normal majority" culture? What, if any, unique mission or vocation is involved in this? One is compelled to ask such questions when one is different and belongs to such a sharply defined minority.

Gay used to stand for pretense and patterned choreography, playing prescribed roles and wearing masks. "Make it gay" was the watchword. It meant "put on the ritz," "keep the act going," "don't let down your guard," "keep on smiling"—especially to conceal your sadness.

But there has been a change. Gay now means a new honesty. Where it used to signify wearing a mask, now it is a call to take off the masks. Its definition has shifted from form to content, sheer style to reality.

So, gay has something of universal meaning to say to everybody. Take off the masks of repressed anger, self-pity, sexual deceit, hypocrisy, social exploitation, and spiritual arrogance. Let communication be an event that involves people, not a charade of puppets. Be yourself. Relate to other selves without inhibition and pretense. Help others to be themselves, too.

The journey toward self-honesty includes the study of one's myths. Everybody has them. So do you and I. Since we invariably create many of our personal myths, it should not be extraordinarily difficult for us to perceive them honestly.

Also, most of us have painstakingly constructed our own masks, the ones that we wear and change ritualistically as we move from one situation to another, from this relationship to that. To take off the masks is to stop the ritual for its own sake and let life replace it.

What happens to a person whose mask has been shed? Speaking for myself, I feel better than ever before. I am incredibly energized. I acknowledge the mystery of my creation and my own mission within it. The reality of myself, as a person created in God's image, is openly shared for the first time. I am grateful that I did not go to the grave without sharing it happily. My closet door is unhinged. Light and air are flooding into that claustrophobic dungeon cell in which I spent more than fifty years of my life.

Beyond all expectation, I have discovered release and freedom, joy and love. Isn't the purpose of our lives to develop and evolve with every breath we take, in every second we live? I have been able to risk everything, and this at an age when many people begin to settle in for their end.

With great zest I celebrate life. I have countless friends. I am filled with joy and gratitude. I love. I am evolving as a person. How could I possibly ask for anything more?

I have learned that a mask is a lie, that it obscures deep truths, that it gets in the way of life. The time has come to take of the masks.

MARION ZIMMER BRADLEY

ACCORDING TO SCIENCE FICTION and fantasy author Marion Zimmer Bradley in *Jamie, and Other Stories: The Best of Marion Zimmer Bradley*, women's liberation, not space exploration, is the great event of the twentieth century. Influenced by C. L. Moore and Leigh Brackett—female pioneers in the male-dominated field of science fiction of the 1930s and 1940s—Bradley is one of the first science fiction writers to feature independent female characters such as Cassiana in 1954's "Centaurus Changeling," Taniquel in 1964's *The Bloody Sun*, and Melitta of Storn, the hero of 1970's *The Winds of Darkover*. She is also one of the first continually to explore the universe of gender roles and human relationships.

Bradley denies that she is a feminist, and decries the use of literature as propaganda and polemic. A storyteller above all else, she emphasizes in her essay in *Women of Vision* that "it's okay for a woman in a story to have whatever love life suits her, but the real work of the world must come first." Nevertheless, her enthusiasm for women's rights and gay rights is apparent in her works.

A lifelong science fiction and fantasy fan turned prolific author, Bradley is best known for her science fiction novels about the world of Darkover and for her best-selling mainstream Arthurian fantasy novel *The Mists of Avalon*. Her works also include many non-Darkover science fiction novels and short stories, fantasies based on myth and legend, lesbian romances written under pseudonyms, Gothics, bibliographies of gay and lesbian fiction, and a mainstream gay novel set in the circus milieu of the forties, *The Catch Trap*. As the editor of *Marion Zimmer Bradley's Fantasy Magazine* and many Darkover and non-Darkover anthologies, Bradley has served as role model and mentor for the work of her numerous fans—some of whom, such as Mercedes Lackey, Jennifer Roberson, and Diana Paxson, have built successful professional writing careers of their own.

The artistry of Bradley's writing has progressed steadily throughout her career. Having learned her craft by writing potboilers—formula fic-

Essay by
JEANETTE SMITH

Marion Zimmer Bradley is one of the first science fiction writers to feature independent female characters and to explore continually the universe of gender roles and human relationships.

tion tied to strict deadlines and genre parameters—she was finally freed of length restrictions by publisher Don Wollheim of DAW Books. The resulting work, *The Heritage of Hastur* in 1975, marks the beginning of her mature Darkover novels in which adventure is combined with in-depth exploration of psychological, sexual, spiritual, and social issues. It was at this time that Bradley made the decision not to be locked into the concepts of the earlier novels. In 1979 an extensive rewrite of *The Bloody Sun* was published, and in 1981 a completely new novel, *Sharra's Exile*, based on the events in *The Sword of Aldones*, replaced that novel in the official Darkover chronology.

Bradley was able at last to take the time to realize her literary potential in two carefully researched and well-written mainstream fantasies based on myth and legend, *The Mists of Avalon* in 1982, and *The Firebrand* in 1987. *The Mists of Avalon* gained international recognition for Bradley's work beyond her cult Darkover fandom.

Bradley writes with awareness and sensitivity about differences in cultures and lifestyles. Many of her characters initially hide their true identities and struggle to adapt to alien ways. Attempting to hide her Terran background from her Darkovan Renunciate sisters, Magda Lorne remarks literally and figuratively in the novel *Thendara House*, "I never realized how Terran I was until I *had* to be Darkovan 28 hours a day, ten days a week."

Eventually most of Bradley's characters come to terms with who they are. This can be a complex multi-level process developed through several novels. For instance, in the Darkovan trilogy *The Shattered Chain*, *Thendara House*, and *City of Sorcery*, Magda learns to accept the activation of her "laran" psi powers, openly to express her awakened love for her freemate Jaelle n'ha Melora and for her lover Camilla n'ha Kyria, to understand and respect the female-centered orientation of the Free Amazons/Order of Renunciates, to develop a healthy pride without guilt in her professional accomplishments, and to reconcile many social and spiritual aspects of her Terran/Darkovan cultural heritage.

Many of Bradley's characters are developed according to a similar plot formula. As they come of age sexually or psychically or both, they progress from feeling alien and outcast to forming a bond with a group, family, or individual, while retaining responsible self-determination. For example, in the Darkover novel *The Heritage of Hastur*, young Lord Regis Hastur experiences the awakening of his psychic "laran," accepts his gay identity and his love for schoolmate and paxman Danilo Syrtis, and chooses to take control of his destiny as the heir to the Comyn telepathic dynasty rather than escape to Terra. Likewise, in the mainstream gay novel *The Catch Trap*, trapeze artist Tommy Zane sorts out his sexual identity while trying to fit into the family and circus culture of the Flying Santellis. For the love of Mario Santelli, Tommy chooses to forgo a promising career as a flyer to become Mario's catcher.

Not all of Bradley's plots, however, are developed according to a simple formula. In the science fiction novel *The Ruins of Isis*, Unity scholar Cendri Owain observes the subjugation of men by the Matriarchate of the planet Isis. While she makes friends with powerful woman leaders and participates in traditional Isis mating rituals, Cendri never completely loses her culture shock. In the end she and her husband accept each other as loving equals and work together to bring legal and educational equality to men and women on the planet. Similarly, the plots of Bradley's short stories about Lythande, the Adept of the Blue Star, depend on the premise that Lythande remain hidden and an outsider. As she travels disguised as a male minstrel (her lyrics consist of paraphrases of Sappho), her identity as a woman is divulged only at the risk of losing her magic powers. Bradley portrays Lythande as a woman cursed to conceal her true self forever.

Bradley peoples her worlds with characters representing many types of gender roles and relationships. According to researcher Marilyn Farwell, *The Mists of Avalon*, although predominantly heterosexual, contains a clear lesbian subtext. While the two loves of the priestess Morgaine's life are men, Lancelot and Accolon, the concept of sisterhood in the Goddess is pervasive throughout the novel and is intensified in several love scenes between Morgaine and another priestess, Raven.

Native Darkovan culture exhibits a vast variety of relationships, in contrast to Terrans who are depicted mostly as conservative heterosexuals. Two forms of Darkovan marriage are recognized, the permanent *di catenas*, using bracelets representing chains, and freemate marriage, a more temporary legal bond between a man and woman or between two women. *Nedestro* children born out of wedlock are accepted casually, as are gay relationships preceding heterosexual marriage. Female lovers of women, such as Camilla n'ha Kyria, and female lovers of men, such as Rafaella n'ha Doria, serve together in the Free Amazons/Order of Renunciates.

American novelist, genre writer, critic and musician. Has also written as Lee Chapman, John Dexter, Miriam Gardner, Morgan Ives, and Elfrida Rivers.

Born: Albany, New York, June 3, 1930.

Education: New York State College for Teachers (now State University of New York at Albany), 1946–48; Hardin-Simmons University, Abilene, Texas, B.A. 1964; graduate study at University of California, Berkeley.

Career: Editor of *Marion Zimmer Bradley's Fantasy Magazine.*

Recipient: Hugo Award nomination, 1963; Nebula Award nominations, 1964 and 1978; Invisible Little Man Award, 1977; Leigh Brackett Memorial Sense of Wonder Award, 1978; Locus Award for best fantasy novel, 1984.

Address: P.O. Box 72, Berkeley, California 94701, U.S.A.

Heterosexuals, gays, lesbians, and bisexuals on Darkover share the stage with virginal or celibate Keepers of the towers where psychic matrix technology is controlled, and with the rarely seen indigenous residents of Darkover, the androgynous *chieri*, who appear as their partners desire them to be. The Explorers in the non-Darkover novel *Endless Universe* are sterile (they steal or purchase children to replenish their numbers) and are quite lacking in sex-role differentiation. In Bradley's early short story "Centaurus Changeling," the natives of the planet Megaera practice polygamy.

Bradley also introduces characters who sexually exploit and enslave others, such as the men of the Darkovan Dry Towns who keep their women in chains, the women of Isis who brand their men with property tattoos and call them "it" rather than "he," and the gay character Dyan Ardais in *The Heritage of Hastur* who uses his "laran" power to humiliate and terrorize Danilo Syrtis both psychically and sexually. Ajax murders and then brutally rapes the corpse of the Amazon warrior Penthesilea in *The Firebrand,* and in *Rediscovery* Ryan Evans plots to use the Darkovan drug kireseth to increase the "useful life" of child prostitutes.

Bradley more than balances her portrayal of the dark side of human relationships, however, with positive influences such as the Free Amazons/Order of Renunciates, who renounce the marital enslavement of the Dry Towns, and the "laran" breeding program of the Comyn telepaths. In addition, there is a men's resistance movement on Isis, with its motto, "We were not born in chains." In the name of the Goddess, groups such as the Amazon tribes and Priestesses of the Serpent Mother in *The Firebrand*, the Wise Sisterhood in *City of Sorcery*, and the Priestesses of Avalon in *The Mists of Avalon* all provide similar counterweights to those who would dominate and enslave.

Inherent in Bradley's storytelling is a message of acceptance and respect for oneself and for others, an affirmation of human rights and human dignity. Her explanation of the matter in *Sword and Sorceress: An Anthology of Heroic Fantasy* is characteristically plain-spoken and modest: "There is only one purpose in fiction, and that is to entertain the reader, and to make her—or him—think."

SHARRA'S EXILE

I said, "They *can't* marry you off to Beltran, just like that! You are Head of a Domain and Keeper...."

"So I thought," she said dispassionately. "But if I were not Head of a Domain, he would not want me—I do not think it is me he wants. If he simply wanted to marry into the Comyn, there are other women as close to the center of power; Derik's sister in Alanna was widowed last year. As for my being the Keeper—I do not think the Council wants a Keeper in power there, either. And if I marry—" she shrugged. "There's the end of that."

I remembered the old stories that a Keeper maintains her power only through her chastity. It's drivel, of course, superstitious rubbish, but like all superstitions, it has a core of truth. *Laran*, in a Comyn telepath, is carried in the same channels as the sexual forces of the body. The main side effect, for men, is that prolonged or heavy work in the matrixes temporarily closes off the channels to sex, and the man undergoes a prolonged period of impotence. It's the first thing a man, working in the Towers, has to get used to, and some people never learn to handle it. I suppose for many people it would seem a high price to pay.

A woman has no such physical safeguard. While a woman is working at the center of a circle, holding the tremendous forces of the amplified linked matrixes, she must keep the physical channels clear for that work, or she can burn up like a torch. A three-second backflow, when I was seventeen years old, had burned a scar in my hand that had never really healed, the size of a silver coin. And the Keeper is at the very center of those flows. While she is working at the center of the screens, a Keeper remains chaste for excellent and practical reasons which have nothing to do with morality. It's a heavy burden; few women want to live with it, more than a year or two. In the old days, Keepers were vowed to hold their office lifelong, were revered and treated almost as Goddesses, living apart from anything human. In this day and age, a Keeper is simply required to retain her chastity while she is actively working as a Keeper, after which she may lay down her post, conduct her life as she pleases,

Excerpt reprinted from *Sharra's Exile*, DAW Books, copyright 1981 by Marion Zimmer Bradley.

Novels

The Catch Trap, 1979.

Romance Fiction

I Am a Lesbian (as Lee Chapman), 1962.
Spare Her Heaven (as Morgan Ives), 1963.
My Sister, My Love (as Miriam Gardner), 1963.
Twilight Lovers (as Miriam Gardner), 1964.
Knives of Desire (as Morgan Ives), 1966.
No Adam for Eve (as John Dexter), 1966.

Gothic Fiction

The Strange Women (as Miriam Gardner), 1962.
Castle Terror, 1965.
Souvenir of Monique, 1967.
Bluebeard's Daughter, 1968.
Dark Satanic, 1972.
Drums of Darkness: An Astrological Gothic Novel, 1976.
The Inheritor, 1984.
Witch Hill, 1990.

Fantasy Fiction

The House between the Worlds, 1980.
The Mists of Avalon, 1982.
Web of Darkness, edited by Hank Stine, illustrations by V. M. Wyman and C. Lee Healy, 1983.
Web of Light, edited by Hank Stine, illustrations by C. Lee Healy, 1983.
Night's Daughter, 1985.
Lythande (anthology), with Vonda McIntyre, 1986.
The Fall of Atlantis (includes *Web of Light* and *Web of Darkness*), 1987.
The Firebrand, 1987.
Black Trillium, with Julian May and Andre Norton, 1990.

Science Fiction

The Door Through Space (bound with *Rendezvous on Lost Planet* by A. Bertram Chandler), 1961.
Seven from the Stars (bound with *Worlds of the Imperium* by Keith Laumer), 1962.
The Colors of Space, 1963.
Falcons of Narabedla [and] *The Dark Intruder, and Other Stories*, 1964.
The Brass Dragon (bound with *Ipomoea* by John Rackham), 1969.
Hunters of the Red Moon, with Paul Edwin Zimmer, 1973.
Endless Voyage, 1975; expanded as *Endless Universe*, 1979.
The Ruins of Isis, edited and illustrated by Polly and Kelly Freas, 1978.
The Survivors. with Paul Edwin Zimmer, 1979.
Survey Ship, illustrations by Steve Fabian, 1980.
Warrior Woman, 1988.

"Darkover" Series

The Sword of Aldones [and] *The Planet Savers*, 1962; with introduction by Bradley, 1977; as *Planet Savers: The Sword of Aldones*, 1984.
The Bloody Sun, 1964.
Star of Danger, 1965.
The Winds of Darkover (bound with *The Anything Tree* by John Rackham), 1970.
The World Wreckers, 1971.
Darkover Landfall, 1972.
The Spell Sword, 1974.
The Heritage of Hastur, 1975.
The Shattered Chain, 1976.
The Forbidden Tower, 1977.
Stormqueen! 1978.
The Ballad of Hastur and Cassilda (poem), 1978.
The Bloody Sun [and] *To Keep the Oath*, 1979.
Contributor, *Legends of Hastur and Cassilda* (short stories), edited by Bradley, 1979.
Two to Conquer, 1980.
The Keeper's Price, and Other Stories (short stories), 1980.
Contributor, *Tales of the Free Amazons* (short stories), edited by Bradley, 1980.
Sharra's Exile, 1981.
Children of Hastur (contains *The Heritage of Hastur* and *Sharra's Exile*), 1981.
Hawkmistress! 1982.
Contributor, *Sword of Chaos, and Other Stories* (short stories), edited by Bradley, 1982.
Thendara House, 1983.
Oath of the Renunciates (contains *The Shattered Chain* and *Thendara House*), 1983.
City of Sorcery, 1983.
Contributor, *Free Amazons of Darkover: An Anthology* (short stories), edited by Bradley, 1985.
Red Sun of Darkover (short stories), with the Friends of Darkover, 1987.
The Other Side of the Mirror, 1987.
Contributor, *Four Moons of Darkover* (short stories), edited by Bradley, 1988.
The Heirs of Hammerfell, 1989.
Domains of Darkover (short stories), with the Friends of Darkover, 1990.
Leroni of Darkover (short stories), with the Friends of Darkover, 1991.
Renunciates of Darkover (short stories), with the Friends of Darkover, 1991.
Rediscovery: A Novel of Darkover, 1993.
Towers of Darkover, edited by Bradley, 1993.

Short Stories

"Centaurus Changeling," in *Magazine of Fantasy and Science Fiction*, April 1954.
The Parting of Arwen (as Elfrida Rivers), 1974.
The Jewel of Arwen, 1974.
Contributor, *Thieves' World*, edited by Robert Lynn Asprin, 1979.
The Best of Marion Zimmer Bradley, edited by Martin H. Greenberg, 1985.
Contributor, *Spell Singers*, edited by Alan Bard Newcomer, 1988.
Jamie, and Other Stories: The Best of Marion Zimmer Bradley, edited by Martin H. Greenberg, 1992.

Nonfiction

Checklist: A Complete, Cumulative Checklist of Lesbian, Variant, and Homosexual Fiction in English, with Gene Damon, 1960.

Men, Halflings, and Hero Worship (criticism), 1973.

The Necessity for Beauty: Robert W. Chambers and the Romantic Tradition, 1974.

Editor, A Gay Bibliography, 1975.

Experiment Perilous: Three Essays in Science Fiction, with Alfred Bester and Norman Spinrad, 1976.

"One Woman's Experience in Science Fiction," in Women of Vision, edited by Denise DuPont, 1988.

Other

Songs from Rivendell, 1959.

Translator, El Villano en su Rincon by Lope de Vega, 1971.

In the Steps of the Master (teleplay novelization), 1973.

Can Ellen Be Saved? (teleplay novelization), 1975.

Contributor, Essays Lovecraftian edited by Darrell Schweitzer, 1976.

The Darkover Cookbook, 1977.

The Maenads (poetry), 1978.

Author of introduction, The Breaking of the Seals by Francis Ashton, edited by Hank Stine, illustrations by Randy Bruce, 1982.

Editor and contributor, Greyhaven: An Anthology of Fantasy, 1983.

Editor, Sword and Sorceress: An Anthology of Heroic Fantasy (multiple volumes), 1984–.

Contributor, Contemporary Authors Autobiography Series (autobiographical sketch), Volume 10, 1989.

Editor, Spells of Wonder, 1989.

Author of foreword, Harper's Encyclopedia of Mystical and Paranormal Experiences, edited by Rosemary E. Guiley, 1991.

marry and have children if she wishes. I had always assumed that Callina would elect to do this; she was, after all, the female Head of the Domain, and her oldest daughter would hold the Domain of Aillard.

She followed my thoughts and shook her head. She said wryly, "I have never had any wish to marry, nor met any man who would tempt me to leave the Tower. Why should I bear a double burden? Janna of Arilinn—she was your Keeper, was she not?—left her post and bore two sons, then fostered them away, and came back to her work. But I have served my Domain well; I have sisters, Linnell will soon be married, even Merryl, I suppose, will some day find a woman who will have him. There is no need...." but she sighed, almost in despair. "I might marry if there was another who could take my place.... but not Beltran. Merciful Avarra, not Beltran!"

"He's not a monster, Callina," I said. "He's very like me, as a matter of fact."

She turned to me with wild anger, and her voice caught in her throat. "So you'd have me marry him too? A man who would bring an army against Thendara, and blackmail my kinsmen into giving him the most powerful woman in the Council for his own purposes? Damn you! Do you think I am a *thing*, a horse to be sold in the market, a shawl to be bartered for?" She stopped, bit her lip against a sob, and I stared at her; she had seemed so cold, remote, dispassionate, more like a mechanical doll than a woman; and now she was all afire with passion, like a struck harp still vibrating. For the first time I knew it; Callina was a woman, and she was beautiful. She had never seemed real to me, before this; she had only been a Keeper, distant, untouchable. Now I saw the woman trapped and frantic behind that barricade, reaching out—reaching out to me.

She dropped her face into her hands and wept. She said through her tears, "They have put it to me that if I do not marry Beltran it will plunge the Domains into war!"

I could not stop myself; I reached out, drew her into my arms.

"You shall *not* marry Beltran," I said, raging. "I will kill him first, kinswoman!" And then, as I held her against me I knew what had happened to both of us. It was not as kinswoman that I had vowed to shelter and protect her. It went deeper than that; it went back to the time when she had fought to save Marorie's life and had shared my agony and despair. She was Tower-trained, she was a memory of the one good time in my entire life, she was home and Arilinn and a time when I had been happy and real and felt my life worthy; a time when I had not been damned.

I held her, trembling with fright, against me; clumsily, I touched her wet eyes. There was something else, some deeper, more terrible fear behind her.

I murmured, "Can't Ashara protect you? She is Keeper of the Comyn. Surely she would not let you be taken from her like this."

We were deeply in rapport now; I felt her rage, her dread, her outraged pride. Now there was terror. She whispered, her voice only a thread, as if she feared that she would be heard, "Oh, Lew, you don't know—I am afraid of Ashara, so afraid.... I would rather marry Beltran, I would even marry him to be free of her...." and her voice broke and strangled. She clung to me in terror and despair, and I held her close.

"Don't be afraid," I whispered, and felt the shaking tenderness I had thought I would never know again. Burned and ravaged as I was, scarred, mutilated, too deeply haunted by despair to lift my one remaining hand to save myself—still, I felt I would fight to the death, fight like a trapped animal, to save Callina from that fate.

... still there was something between us. I dared not kiss her; was it only that she was still Keeper and the old taboo held me? But I held her head against my breast, stroking her dark hair, and I knew I was no longer rootless, alone, without kin or friends. Now there was some reason behind my desperate holding on. Now there was Callina, and I promised myself, with every scrap of will remaining to me, that for her sake I would fight to the end.

RITA MAE BROWN

RITA MAE BROWN is perhaps the widest read openly lesbian author publishing in the 1980s and 1990s. Like many other feminist and lesbian writers—Jewelle Gomez, Dorothy Allison, Robin Morgan, Sarah Schulman, and Barbara Smith—she got her start and found her inspiration in the energy of the early women's liberation movement. Although Brown is now read for her well-received and well-publicized mainstream novels (including a mystery series allegedly cowritten with her cat, Sneaky Pie Brown), many of her current readers know nothing of her more political past.

Born to an unwed couple ("Let's say I had illegitimate parents," she always quips), Brown was adopted by a working-class family while still a young child. She grew up in Florida and attended Howard Junior College as well as the University of Florida (from which she was expelled in 1963 for being a lesbian). After moving to Manhattan, Brown received her bachelor's degree from New York University and went on to the New York School of Visual Arts; she later received her doctorate from the Institute of Policy Studies in Washington, D.C. During this time, Brown became a very visible member of the newly emerging women's liberation movement and later the radical lesbians. She was also a member of the RAT collective, an underground newspaper that laid the groundwork for much early women's liberation theory. Later, Brown was a member of the "Furies" collective, which produced some of the movement's finest theoretical and positional works.

It was in this political environment that Brown began writing. Many of her early political essays are examples of precise, impassioned, and hard thinking. It was her political commitments that led Brown to write her first novel, *Rubyfruit Jungle*, published by the feminist, collectively run publisher Daughters, Inc. *Rubyfruit Jungle* (the title refers to female genitalia) was a runaway best seller, selling more than 35,000 copies in its first years. A cross between *The Adventures of Huckleberry Finn* (its heroine's name is Molly Bolt) and a lesbian *Tropic of Cancer* (Brown consciously served up her pungent social critiques with bawdy humor), *Rubyfruit Jungle*—even with its graphic lesbian sex and its heart-

Essay by
MICHAEL BRONSKI

107

Rita Mae Brown is probably the most popular openly lesbian author writing today.

on-its-sleeve progressive politic—managed to find a crossover audience.

Brown's identification with an overtly feminist press made the gender, sexual, and class politics in both *Rubyfruit Jungle* and the author's next novel, *In Her Day*, clearly apparent. *Six of One* drew upon these same themes but was positioned as more of a mainstream work, detailing the lives of the lovable eccentrics in Runnymead, a small town on the Pennsylvania-Maryland border (a setting to which Brown would later return in *Bingo*). Brown's concerns about the lives of working-class people, the social and psychological experiences of women, the reality of racism, and the oppression of lesbians are still present in this work but less explicitly articulated, woven into the subtext of the narrative.

In much of Brown's newer, mainstream work, there is a mixture of traditional plotting, raucous—sometimes bawdy—humor, and a keen sense of storytelling. *Southern Comfort* is a multi-generational family saga set in Montogmery, Alabama, that uses the same tone and character types as *Six of One* and *Bingo*. In *Sudden Death*, a *roman a clef* based on Brown's well-publicized affair with tennis champion Martina Navratilova, the author returns to some of the themes of her earlier feminist essays, examining the responsibilities and respect that women owe one another. In *High Hearts*, Brown again returns to the southern regionalism of her earlier novels, only this time with a Civil War setting and a heterosexual heroine who turns to transvestism in order to fight. When not writing fiction, Brown has also been very successful in writing for television, completing more then a dozen major projects and at least one produced screenplay.

VENUS ENVY

Excerpt from *Venus Envy*, Bantam Books, copyright 1993 by American Artists, Inc.

"Boss." Mandy walked in.

"Hey."

"You look good, girl," Mandy's smile was incandescent.

Odd. Frazier thought to herself that she and Mandy had worked cheek by jowl for three years, yet only now did she notice the high cast to her coffee-colored cheekbones.

American activist, novelist, poet, translator, essayist, and author of screenplays.

Born: Hanover, Pennsylvania, November 28, 1944.

Education: Broward Junior College, A.A. 1965; University of Florida; New York University, B.A. 1968; New York School of Visual Arts, Manhattan, cinematography certificate 1968; Institute for Policy Studies, Washington, D.C., Ph.D. 1976. With others, founded Student Homophile League at New York University, and opened the first women's center in New York City.

Career: Photo editor, Sterling Publishing, New York City, 1969–70; lecturer in sociology, Federal City College, Washington, D.C., 1970–71; visiting member of faculty in feminist studies, Goddard College, Plainfield, Vermont, 1973; writer-in-residence, Women's Writer's Center, Cazenovia College, New York, 1977–1978; president, American Artists, Inc., Charlottesville, Virginia, 1980–; visiting instructor, University of Virginia, Charlottesville, 1992.

Memberships: Former member of National Gay Task Force and National Women's Political Caucus; member of board of directors of Human Rights Campaign Fund (New York City), 1986; founding mother of Piedmont Women's Polo Club and Blue Ridge Polo Club; member of Farmington Hunt Club.

Recipient: Writers Guild of America award and Emmy award nomination for television special *I Love Liberty*, 1983; Emmy award nomination for miniseries *Long Hot Summer*, 1985; New York Public Library's Literary Lion award, 1986; named Charlottesville's favorite author, 1990.

Address: c/o American Artists, Inc., P.O. Box 4671, Charlottesville, Virginia 22905, U.S.A.

Agent: Julian Bach Literary Agency, Inc., 747 Third Avenue, New York, New York 10017, U.S.A.

"Did Mrs. Thornburg come to a decision about the Isidore Bonheur?"

"She's a whirlwind of indecision. However, the small hound picture sold today."

"Good."

Before Frazier could ask, Mandy added, "Darryl Orthwein from New York. I expect he'll roll it over in a year or two but that's okay."

"Shrewd collector, that one."

"I brought you something." Mandy reached into her voluminous bag and pulled out a box of fine French paper. "Here, write letters to Tomorrow."

Frazier opened the box and ran her forefinger over the smooth cotton finish. The pale-blue paper sported a tiny darker-blue freckling. "This is gorgeous. Mandy, where do you find these treasures?"

"Picked up the phone and called Paris. Fortunately, they believe in Federal Express. I love paper and I remembered the time when your father sent you reams of rice paper from Japan. The stuff was so beautiful it took you six months to work up to writing on it." Mandy laughed.

RITA MAE **BROWN**   109

"Had to learn to use a brush." Frazier held the paper on her lap. "This is very kind of you."

"I figure if you write a letter each evening for the next day, there will always be a next day." Mandy fought back the tears.

"Oh, Mandy …" Frazier choked up, then gained mastery of herself. "None of this makes any sense. I feel okay, sort of."

"What about the coughing?"

Frazier shrugged. "What bothers me is that every now and then I can't breathe, but I'm not in pain. That's what I hate about the morphine. I click this button here and presto, more drips into my veins. It feels great but how do I know how I really feel?" She turned her face to the window for a moment. "Well, maybe I never knew how I felt, period."

"I have this theory"—Mandy leaned forward, beginning her sentence with a favorite phrase—"that feelings are the essence of being human but it takes probably fifty years to trust them. Most of us are living from the neck up."

"Not Billy Cicero."

"His sex stuff is just another escape," Mandy stated flatly. "Anyway, I'm not sitting here in judgment of anyone in particular. I'm guilty too."

"You know, I was thinking when you walked in the door about how I spend more time with you than anyone but I don't know much about you, other than that you graduated from Smith, top of your class, did your graduate work at Yale, and worked in Rochester after that."

"You met my mother. To meet a woman's mother is to know what you need to know."

"Thanks, Mandy. Mine was in here yesterday sobbing because she wants me buried. My God, I can't even have control of my body when I'm dead. It's my body and I'll do with it what I want."

"Tell that to the anti-abortionists."

"You know what I mean." Frazier placed the stationery on the nightstand. "Is there any subject before the American public today more overworked than abortion?"

"Well, I don't know, but you scooted off the feelings discussion right fast."

"All right then, smartass, what are you feeling right this instant?" A flash animated Frazier's scratchy voice.

Mandy paused a long time, then spoke in a soft voice: "I don't want to lose you. And you look ravishing."

Frazier's chin wobbled. "I thought you tolerated me because I'm your boss. I mean, I'm white. Don't you hate me somewhere in your heart?"

"I'm not that petty, Frazier."

Tears splashed onto Frazier's ample bosom. "How am I to know? It's awkward. Maybe that's why I concentrated on work. I didn't grow up with black people as social equals. Or African-Americans or whatever the hell I'm supposed to call you all. You know what I mean."

"So we both lose." Mandy dropped her head and then lifted it again. "Sometimes I think we'll never stop paying. Not your people. Not my people. It will go on and on like some painful wave that never reaches shore. Since we're telling the truth, I'll tell you why I was reticent...."

"But fun, you were always fun." Frazier wiped her eyes.

"Thank you." Mandy pulled out Kleenex for herself and Frazier. "You might get angry."

"I don't care."

"Okay. I think you're gay. I think you've hidden from me and everyone. You go out nonstop, mostly with Billy, some other guys, too, but you know, I never feel any ... heat."

Frazier's shoulders tensed. "Maybe they're not the right guys. Or maybe I'm cold-blooded."

Mandy shook her head. "It's not the end of the world, boss."

"And when's the last time you saw anyone rewarded for being gay and telling the truth about it? It might not be the end of the world but it sure as hell isn't the road to success."

"I didn't take you for a coward." Mandy's voice dropped lower, then rose with renewed energy. "Then again, I understand no one has a right to know another person's business. But from my point of view, I'm left out. You never trusted me enough to include me in your life. Do you think I care for one minute about whether you're gay or straight? Don't you know me better than that?"

Frazier's chest tightened. She fought for every breath. No one had ever spoken to her like this before and she'd never told her secrets before, except to Billy, but that wasn't telling—that was sharing. "I trust you, Mandy, as much as I trust anyone." She inhaled and heard that nasty rattle. Mandy stood up and began lightly patting her on the back. That didn't work. Frazier pointed to the oxygen tank. Mandy quickly put the tube into Frazier's mouth and turned on the valve. Frazier took a few deep hits of pure O_2 and then removed the tube. "Sorry."

"I'm the one who's sorry. I should have kept my mouth shut."

Frazier breathed again from the tube. The little iridescent dots that had been dancing before her eyes disappeared. "I guess, I guess I thought no one would want to know the real me and now I'm leaving and no one will ever know me."

"I'd like to know you." Mandy smiled. "You're a genius at what you do. You're a good boss and I think you're a good person basically."

Frazier shook her head. She didn't know what to say.

Mandy spoke again. "Don't die a stranger. Tell the people you love who you are, or write them. Maybe they need you and you don't know it. Maybe you need them."

"I don't want to need anyone." Frazier's hands shook as she placed the oxygen tube back on the tank.

" 'No man is an island,' " Mandy recited from the poem.

"This woman has tried to be." She steadied herself and then told Mandy what she had never spoken to another person, other than Billy. "I am gay. Or maybe I'm not. Let's just say I'm operating sexually on all pistons, but emotionally I am much more attracted to women. I've tried to avoid it, you know. What this could cost me … My family, such as they are. Not my clients, thank God, but my social position. My reserve turned into a full-scale emotional retreat. So I avoid the issue by not falling in love, by keeping my distance, by … by working and working and working. It's just … too painful." Frazier fell back on her pillows. "People are cruel. *You* know that."

"I do, but I also know that plenty of them are wonderful and if you don't put yourself out there you'll never know. And you just put yourself out there and I …" Mandy swallowed her words, a hard knot of grief like a baseball in her throat.

"Mandy, I don't even know if I'll be here tomorrow. I have a surprise for you after I'm gone. It's the only way I can tell you how I feel. I'm not much good at this. Feelings exhaust me."

Mandy had much more to say but she could see the fatigue and she felt guilty for bringing it on. She kissed Frazier goodbye and left, wondering if she had been selfish in pushing her boss or if she had actually given Frazier a kind of gift.

* * *

Two hours later Frazier's phone rang. It was Mandy apologizing profusely. Frazier, just back from the X-ray lab, was happy to talk to anyone not involved in the medical profession.

"Stop worrying about it," Frazier commanded. "Just live for two when I'm gone—or name your firstborn after me."

"I'm not handling this very well." Mandy sobbed.

"You were the one who wanted to know!"

"No, not that. I'm not doing very well about your being sick. I'm sorry. I should be comforting you, not the reverse."

"Mandy, don't worry about it. Comfort my brother. On second thought, don't comfort my brother. He already has one mistress that I know of."

"Still?"

"Oh, yeah, the one with the cowboy boots and tits big as Texas. In fact, I think she is from Texas. Those girls down there are serious about hair too. I never saw so much hair on a woman's head. Of course, I've only seen her from a distance."

"What does Laura say about Miss Texas?"

"She thinks he's given her up."

"So how do you know he hasn't?" Mandy's natural curiosity was taking over.

"Because when he cried all over me—and I confess I cried back— he stank of Giorgio perfume. The stuff oozed right out of his pores. Laura wears Hermès, as you might suspect. Giorgio is much too loud for Laura. The Garden Club would turn up its collective nose, literally. Even the daffodils would shudder."

"Um, um," Mandy hummed.

"You got it, girl. My brother may be a failure in many respects but when it comes to women he's irresistible. It's hard for a sister to see a brother as sexy but ever since I can remember Carter has been a triumph of androgen, or whatever it is that attracts the girls like flies."

"My mother says women *are* like flies. They'll settle on shit or on sugar."

"Your mother doesn't like women much, does she?"

"Well, this statement was provoked by my sister's falling for a man Mother considered too dark for an Eisenhart. Mom's a horrible snob that way."

"Yeah, so's mine—about suitable matches. Before Charles married Diana I swear Libby would lie awake at night and plot how I might meet the Prince. 'If only he could see you, sweetie,' she'd say. 'They want you when they see you.'"

"True enough." Mandy paused a moment while her dog barked. "Enough, Duncan."

The Scottie barked harder.

"Duncan's true to form," Frazier remarked.

"Am I forgiven?"

"I said you were. Don't repeat yourself. You know how I hate to be bored."

"I know. Well, don't forget to write a letter to Tomorrow. Promise?"

"I will. Bye-bye."

"Bye, boss."

Frazier hung up the phone. Like the claws of physical desire, loneliness and longing seized her stomach. There was so much to live for. How could she have so squandered her time? She thought of the lips unkissed, the thighs uncaressed, the paintings she'd just missed purchasing. She thought of the music she adored and how she wished she had kicked off her shoes and danced in the dew on spring grass. Simple pleasures, animal delights, all were shoved aside in her ascent and in her fear that if she cavorted, frolicked, and played, she might betray herself. Spontaneity evaporated inside her.

Control. Control yourself. Control your destiny. Control your emotions. Well, she controlled all right. She controlled herself right out of any action that did not lead directly to her bank account.

She lay there and wondered why so many people who considered themselves aristocrats violently opposed displays of emotion, honest exchange. Not that the middle classes were much better. They preferred to talk about emotion rather than show it. The joke was that talking about emotion often vitiated the emotion. They wound up bloodless. Frazier's friends, the U.C.'s—the Upper Classes—preferred neither. A single poppy in a round crystal bowl sitting on a perfect terrace could elicit as much rapture from Billy Cicero's mother as an orgasm. Probably more. Small wonder that Billy, like the moon, never showed his mother his dark side.

Frazier kept returning to the lips unkissed. If only she had pressed her mouth between DeeDee Cheatam's shoulder blades in their Tri-Delta days. And Frances Peterson. She was so hot, with her long, long body and her ice-blue eyes. Who knew what might have happened if Frazier had just reached out once or twice or, well, more than that. Then she had spurned Victor Nederlander, which nearly killed her mother. What she remembered about Victor, her beau in her middle twenties, was the

WRITINGS

Novels

Rubyfruit Jungle, 1973.
In Her Day, 1976.
Six of One, 1978.
Southern Discomfort, 1982.
Sudden Death, 1983.
High Hearts, 1986.
Bingo, 1988.
Venus Envy, 1993.
Dolley, 1994.

Mystery Series with Sneaky Pie Brown

Wish You Were Here, 1990.
Rest in Pieces, 1992.

Poetry

The Hand that Cradles the Rock, 1971.
Songs to a Handsome Woman, 1973.
The Poems of Rita Mae Brown, 1987.

Screenplays

Slumber Party Massacre, 1982.
Rubyfruit Jungle.
Cahoots.

Television Series

I Love Liberty, 1982.
Long Hot Summer (remake of 1958 film based on *The Hamlet* by William Faulkner), 1985.
My Two Loves, 1986.
The Alice Marble Story, 1986.
Southern Exposure, 1990.

Television Films

The Girls of Summer, 1989.
Selma, Lord, Selma, 1989.
Rich Men, Single Women, 1989.
Sweet Surrender, 1989.
The Thirty-nine Year Itch, 1990.
Home, Sweet, Home, 1990.
The Mists of Table Dancing, 1987.

Essays

"Take a Lesbian to Lunch" and "Hanoi to Hoboken, a Round Trip Ticket," in *Out of the Closets: Voices of Gay Liberation*, edited by Karla Jay and Allen Young, 1972.
"The Last Straw," in *Class and Feminism: A Collection of Essays from the Furies*, edited by Charlotte Bunch and Nancy Myron, 1974.
"Living with Other Women" and "The Shape of Things to Come," in *Lesbianism and the Women's Movement*, edited by Nancy Myron and Charlotte Bunch, 1975.
A Plain Brown Wrapper, 1976.
"Queen for a Day: A Stranger in Paradise," in *Lavender Culture*, edited by Karla Jay and Allen Young, 1978.

Other

Translator, *Hrotsvitra: Six Medieval Latin Plays*, 1971.
Starting from Scratch: A Different Kind of Writer's Manual, 1988.

---

downy hair on his chest. She made him crawl over hot coals for sex and then she hurt him by not enjoying it. What would have happened if she'd let go? Every now and then she'd escape to Charlotte, North Carolina, to the Guest Quarters with someone, male or female, only to forget them after the weekend. As Frazier had good taste, they were nice people, people worth remembering.

Keep your distance. Don't get involved. Don't reveal too much. Keep it light. But people couldn't keep it light. They had emotions, even if Frazier didn't.

She was having them now. All the pain and even the pleasure she'd sidestepped in her thirty-five years had boomeranged into an anguish more profound than any physical pain. Again, Frazier gasped for breath. Her head pounded. She fumbled for the oxygen tube and managed to turn on the tank. The smooth, pure air clarified her mind as well as her lungs.

She had never truly loved anyone. Of course, she had never truly hated anyone either, but this lack of passion seemed a further incrimination of her refusal to become engaged, to connect. She sucked in another breath and with it her mind bent under the weight of her sorrows.

She grabbed for the *Common Service Book*, the gold letters *I.H.S.* beckoning in the lower right-hand corner. A frayed red silk page marker bore testimony to Libby's constant use. Frazier gulped in more air, then replaced the tube and turned off the oxygen. She composed herself as she opened the book to page 430, where her mother had placed the marker. It was the "Order for the Burial of the Dead" and Libby had underlined burial.

Furious, Frazier nearly tossed the book against the wall. The only thing restraining her from this small fit was the realization that the thud would disturb whoever was in the adjoining room, suffering with God knows what. She hoped they suffered merely the pains of their disease and not the pains inflicted by family.

She dropped the book back into her lap and the pages fluttered to 441. Her eyes fell on "Responsories."

V. *In pace in id ipsum dormiam:* I will lay me down in peace and sleep. None of us liveth to himself, and no man dieth to himself.

Verse: Whether we live therefore or die, we are the Lord's. None of us liveth to himself, and no man dieth to himself.

The shroud of mortality drew closer around Frazier's strong shoulders. A blue chill shot down her spine. She closed the book and fumbled in the nightstand for her solid gold Montblanc pen. Billy gave it to her on her last birthday, September 17. He laughed when she turned thirty-five and said that that was the age at which Dante wrote the *Inferno*, for thirty-five was believed to be the beginning of middle age in the Middle Ages. On her birthday card he wrote, "Welcome to the Middle Ages." The next day she called Fahrney's, a pen and stationery store in Washington, D.C., and discovered that the pen cost $8,500.

A phone book would serve as a desk. She yanked the Yellow Pages out of the drawer. When she took out one sheet of Mandy's paper the tube from the morphine drip swung in the way of her writing. Frazier tore it out of her vein.

"Goddammit, if I'm going to die I might as well feel it. I might as well feel something before I go!"

Then she began writing, writing, writing. Mandy suggested one letter per day to Tomorrow but Frazier wrote volumes. She wrote to Billy, to her mother and father, to Carter, to her Auntie Ruru, whom she adored, to Ann, to Kenny Singer, and lastly to Mandy. She was so tired by the time she got to Mandy that she wrote only, "Thank you."

By now, midnight beyond thought, she was withdrawing from the morphine. She felt sick to her bones. She put stamps on the envelopes and placed them on the nightstand by her bed.

She was going to die. She'd never felt so wretched. She shook. Nausea consumed her. She considered jamming the morphine needle back into her vein but she was determined to feel something, anything, this pain in her last moments. At least she would die knowing she had told the truth to the people she could have been close to—perhaps. Maybe her death or her truth could be a spur to them. Maybe they could change and find a few shards of happiness amidst the rubble of their psyches.

Frazier, trembling uncontrollably, clicked off the light. She remembered that it was Ash Wednesday. Why she would remember that she didn't know, but it stuck in her brain like a piece of cotton on the boll. She wondered if she should ring the nurse or call up her pastor for the Last Rites. No, she'd lived this life fundamentally alone. She might as well die alone. Frazier Armstrong fell into a boiling sleep from which she never expected to return.

The descent into Hell had begun.

QUENTIN CRISP

Essay by
ROBERT B. MARKS
RIDINGER

THE PHENOMENON KNOWN as Quentin Crisp was born Dennis Pratt in Sutton, Surrey, in 1908. Following a fairly conventional childhood and education at a public school, he embarked upon a life of being, as he frankly states in the opening pages of *The Naked Civil Servant*, "not merely a self-confessed homosexual but a self-evident one." This entailed a move to London in the late 1920s and a highly varied series of occupations, ranging from commercial artist to modeling and writing. Beginning with the 1938 work *Color in Display*, his literary creation has ranged from articles for the travel section of the *New York Times* to film commentary for *Christopher Street* and observations on society and manners for the *Advocate*. The three works for which he is best known as a gay writer are his two volumes of autobiography, *The Naked Civil Servant* and *How To Become a Virgin*, published in 1968 and 1981 respectively, and the 1989 compilation *Quentin Crisp's Book of Quotations*.

The Naked Civil Servant was, at the time of its initial publication in London, virtually the only such work by a homosexual who was open about his sexual identity. Covering the author's (often violent) experiences with the working-class population of London from 1926 until the late 1960s, the autobiography presents a virtually unparalleled account of the social atmosphere of Depression-era England, the Blitz and World War II years, and post-war recovery, from the perspective of a deliberately marginalized individual. Of particular interest to the student of gay and lesbian history are the descriptions of attitudes and fashions of speech and behavior among some homosexuals over the four decades. The title of *The Naked Civil Servant* is a reference to Crisp's periodic work as an artist's model. The work established the author's reputation as a wit and humorist with a clear sense of the absurd and a sharp eye for manners and aesthetics, and was adapted as a play for television in December of 1975. The book's 1981 sequel, *How to Become a Virgin*, covers the period in the author's life when his pen name was legally adopted and he immigrated to the United States. Crisp was, however, severely criticized by the London homosexual newspaper *Gay News* for representing an extremely effeminate and stereotyped image of gay men.

119

Following his relocation to New York City in 1977, Crisp developed his one-man show from the London pub theaters into the performance piece, *An Evening with Quentin Crisp*, which opened at Players Theatre in 1978. The piece is reminiscent of *Tru*, a work on the life of author Truman Capote, and the dramatization of Mark Twain's writings by actor Hal Holbrook; in this case, however, the author himself is on stage to play out the aesthetic quality initiated in *The Naked Civil Servant* and to answer questions.

Quentin Crisp's Book of Quotations: 1000 Observations on Life and Love by, for, and about Gay Men and Women presents selections from an assemblage of publications, ranging from the homoerotic poetry of the ancient world, to the more recent poems of Walt Whitman and Allen Ginsberg, to the California Penal Code. It traces the changing attitudes toward, and social acceptance of, homosexuality—among both heterosexuals and homosexuals—as reflected in print over the centuries. Offering his own view of the gay community's current relationship with mainstream society, Crisp notes in the preface, "If the gay community ever wished to enter the real world, it no longer does."

THE NAKED CIVIL SERVANT

Excerpt reprinted from *The Naked Civil Servant*, Cape, copyright 1968 by Quentin Crisp.

By this time my companion and I were living in King's Cross, a much more fertile region than the one we had just left. Baron's Court had been a no-man's-land in which the houses were blind with stained glass and, on the pavements, raw trees no thicker than your arm stood in straightjackets of chicken wire wincing at every breath of wind. Our new location was loud with the noise of steam trains and lousy with teashops that had a well-defined rush hour.

Things were better without, but they had grown worse within. We now shared a double room for which the rent was eleven shillings each and we were almost never apart. My roommate's idea of companionship included having me sit on the edge of the bath while he cleaned his teeth. My aversion caused me to live in a state of tension every moment that I was not alone, but the middle-class morality in which I had been so carefully reared prevailed. I hissed but I almost never shouted. I don't expect that this self-restraint would have lasted indefinitely but it didn't have to. After three months in King's Cross, news reached me from my mother which broke the siege.

My mother had a genius for making and keeping friends. This talent was instinctive and was exercised without a hope of profit. It was merely my good fortune that at least twice she was able to turn it to my account. The woman who many years before had introduced us to Mrs. Longhurst now, for my mother's sake, persuaded one of the directors of a vast firm of consulting electrical engineers to give me employment. I was absolutely amazed. He paid me two pounds ten shillings a week for eighteen months before coming to his senses. Until I had been in work long enough to become eligible for the dole (fifteen shillings threepence a week) I almost held my breath. After that point was passed, my relief became evident in my general demeanor and particularly in the returning length of my hair and my fingernails.

Quentin Crisp during a break from his one-man show in New York, January 1978.

Even greater than my joy at the prospect of one day being able to draw unemployment insurance was my ecstasy at moving into a room of my own. Once I had achieved this I was happy. All the reactions that other people have described to me when at last they found someone to live with—the heightened perception of the world around them, the inability to refrain from taking little skips as they walked—all these were mine on realizing that I might with luck never have to live with anyone again.

I was happy. The room I took (and even this I couldn't find without the help of the roommate I was so gladly leaving) was in darkest Pimlico. It had Nottingham lace curtains at the window, corned-beef linoleum on the floor, and a brass bedstead in one corner. Some of my friends said how lucky I was to have been let in, while others laughed the room to scorn and implored me to chi-chi it up. I didn't listen. I was happy.

At work I never once understood what I was doing. In theory I was employed as an engineer's tracer. This was one of the many kinds of work at which I could never hope to become proficient. Accuracy is alien to my nature. Many years later a woman asked me what a "point" was. When I told her it was a seventy-second part of an inch, she said, "But there isn't such a thing, really. Is there?" That is what I have always secretly thought. When I was given plans to trace, I copied the mistakes as well as the revisions and neither of them properly; when I was told to transfer the positions of electric pylons from one map to another I did so with such a jolly laugh that construction men telephoned from distant shires to ask what on earth was going on at head office. If any housewife has a pylon among her rose bushes, if any country clergyman has a pylon sticking up through his church roof, if any borough surveyor has a pylon

British actor, humorist, social critic, commercial artist, and memoirist.

Born: Dennis Pratt in Sutton, Surrey, December 25, 1908; immigrated to the United States in 1977.

Career: Actor in films, including *The Bride*, Columbia, 1985, and in stage productions, including *The Naked Civil Servant* and *The Importance of Being Earnest*.

Contributor to *New York* magazine and the *New York Times*.

Recipient: Special Drama Desk Award for unique theatrical experience, 1979.

Address: 46 East Third Street, New York, New York 10003, U.S.A.

blocking his main thoroughfare, may she or he read here that I apologize. May it comfort them to know that I was happy.

When I was not at work, I sat in my room and wrote plays, poems, libretti, stories, which were never to see the light of publication. The crippling weakness of all these works was that the ideas they sought to embody were far too highbrow for my sub-Tennysonian style. This is the main fault in all the writings that I have ever read in manuscript. The poverty from which I have suffered could be diagnosed as "Soho" poverty. It comes from having the airs and graces of a genius and no talent. But I was happy.

On evenings when I felt that I could write no more I went to visit friends, boys from cafés who had rooms in houses where no landladies fly, or girls with whom I had been at art school. The journey there and back I nearly always made on foot to show that I could. It was getting harder all the time.

Exhibitionism is like a drug. Hooked in adolescence, I was now taking doses so massive that they would have killed a novice. Blind with mascara and dumb with lipstick, I paraded the dim streets of Pimlico with my overcoat wrapped around me as though it were a tailless ermine cape. I had to walk like a mummy leaving its tomb. At every step one foot had to land directly in front of the other. My knees ground together. After about a mile of walking thus, my trousers began to wear out between the knees; after two miles I began to wear out. Sometimes I wore a fringe so deep that it completely obscured the way ahead. This hardly mattered. There were always others to look where I was going.

As my appearance progressed from the effeminate to the bizarre, the reaction of strangers passed from startled contempt to outraged hatred. They began to take action. If I was compelled to stand still in the street in order to wait for a bus or on the platform of an Underground railway station, people would turn without a word and slap my face; if I

Autobiographies

The Naked Civil Servant, 1968.
How to Become a Virgin, 1981.

Other

Color in Display, 1938.
How to Have a Lifestyle (social history), 1975.
Lettering for Brush and Pen, with A. F. Stuart, 1976.
Love Made Easy, 1977.
An Evening with Quentin Crisp (one-man show), produced New York, 1978.
Chog: A Gothic Tale, illustrations by Gahan Wilson, 1979.
Doing It with Style, with Donald Carroll, 1981.
Manners from Heaven: A Divine Guide to Good Behavior, with John Hofsess, 1984.
The Wit and Wisdom of Quentin Crisp, edited by Guy Kettelhack, 1984.
How to Go to the Movies (film criticism), 1988.
Quentin Crisp's Book of Quotations: 1000 Observations on Life and Love by, for, and about Gay Men and Women, edited by Amy Appleby, 1989.

Recordings

An Evening with Quentin Crisp, 1979.

Adaptations

The Naked Civil Servant was adapted as a television play, 1975.

was wearing sandals, passers-by took care to stamp on my toes; and once a crowd had started to follow me, it grew and grew until no traffic could pass down the road. If I didn't put a stop to this quickly, by getting on a bus or going into a shop, the police had to deal with it. Barging his way through the yelling crowd or coming at me from a side street, the constable would say, "You again. Move on." Then, turning on the rabble with raised arms, he would tell them that it was over—that there was nothing to see (both of which statements were untrue). In a weary voice, he would implore them to pass along the pavement. I was excited, exhausted, and worried by these crowds but, because I had never yet been savaged by them, I was not frightened. Because I still believed that I could educate them, I was happy.

MARY DALY

MARY DALY'S *The Church and the Second Sex*, published in 1968, placed her among the radical feminist theologians and resulted in her prompt dismissal from a teaching job at Boston College. Student demonstrations for "academic" freedom led to Daly's reinstatement, but the book, which discussed in bitter terms the submissive role of women in the Catholic Church, established Daly once and for all as an enemy of "the prevailing religion of the entire planet": patriarchy. Five years later, in *Beyond God the Father: Toward a Philosophy of Women's Liberation* she leapt into what Erica Smith called in *Herizons* "the post-Christian era"; Daly "began to understand more clearly the nature of the beast and the name of the demon: patriarchy, the interconnections among the structures of oppression in a patriarchal society and the destructive dynamics which these structures generate in their victims became more and more visible."

Essay by
DAYANA STETCO

In 1978's *Gyn/Ecology: The Metaethics of Radical Feminism*, Daly is concerned not only with those malfunctioning (she uses the term "male-functioning") mythologies of the Christian Church clearly hostile to women, but also with creating (discovering) the female cosmos, a space of self-representation and assertion where words lose their negative connotations. Hags, Crones, Harpies, Furies, and Spinsters are the true women who represent life. On the other side of the barricade, Daly places men, i.e., the enemy. But as Rita Mae Brown notices in her discussion of the book in *Washington Post Book World*, "Daly, in her righteous anger at the total rape of womankind, still does not address the question of why so many women comply in their own 'living-death'." However, *Gyn/Ecology* proposes solutions that will lead to the final triumph of women—and one of the main demands is the recognition of the power of language.

Pure Lust: Elemental Feminist Philosophy is an exploration of the depths of language and meaning. Considered by its author "a sisterwork to *Beyond God the Father* and *Gyn/Ecology*," *Pure Lust* moves through three realms: Archespheres (discerning our origins), Pyrospheres (reclaiming our passions and virtues), and Metomorphospheres (deep changes that occur when we break through the mazes of phallocratic

125

double-think.) *Pure Lust* is an existential journey, something that Daly names "the break through the foreground." It also plays on the double meaning of words and their interchangeability. Thus gynecide (the killing of women) is accompanied by the killing of words. Naturally, the author's task is to find the "right" words for the newly discovered female cosmos. *Webster's First Intergalactic Wickedary of the English Language*, "conjured by Mary Daly ... in Cahoots with Jane Caputi" in 1987, is considered by Julia Penelope in *Women's Review of Books* to be an "erratic, ecstatic, eccentric" piece of writing that deconstructs and reconstructs language in feminist terms. In a world where male language has "messed" with female minds, the acquisition of a new language is mandatory. Daly refuses again to be "at a loss for words"; if such a language does not exist, it is because the hidden layers of English have not been developed. The *Wickedary* offers women a language that can serve them. As Penelope puts it, "the Wickedary is a Sin-thesis." It is, in other words, Daly's theory of the original sin of language revisited.

TIDY REPORTS; UNTIDY RETORTS

Reprinted from *Pure Lust: Elemental Feminist Philosophy*, HarperSanFrancisco, copyright 1984 by Mary Daly.

In her book of Original Genius, *The Euguélionne*, the French Canadian feminist Louky Bersianik, writes Untidily of the curse of tidiness, as seen through the eyes of the Euguélionne, a visitor from another planet. A sample report:

FEATS BEHIND THE SCENES

—Achieve. Assist. Balance the budget. Balance the meals. Bandage cuts. Bawl in hiding. Blanche. Buy. Care for. Chill. Clear. Console. Cook. Cut out. Cut up. Darn. Do the dishes. Drive. Dry. Dry dishes. Economize. Educate. Empty the ashtrays. Empty the garbage cans. Encourage. Endure. Feed. Flatter. Fold. Forbid. Forgive. Freeze. Gather laundry. Gather up garbage. Give. Go shopping. Heat up. Help. Iron. Keep. Keep (yourself) young. Laugh. Love. Maintain. Make children. Make love. Make meals. Make peace. Make sure homework's done. Pare. Pay off bills. Peel. Play. Preserve. Punish. Rinse. Roast. Rub. Serve. Set table. Sew. Shout. Shut (yourself) up. Stop (yourself) shouting. Sweep. Tidy. Use up leftovers. Wash. Wax. *ETC.*[1]

On the most obvious level, tidiness suggests housework. According to recent studies the average working wife in 1982 spent 26 hours a week doing housework and the average husband spent 36 minutes.[2] Nags need to think not only of the physical exhaustion implied in this double-double work schedule of women, but also of the fragmentation of spirit and binding of creativity. Anyone who has produced a work of artistic, scholarly, or scientific achievement knows that one does not say: "Since I now have an hour to spare, I'll sit down and write for a while." Great works require time and space around them—which may appear to be "leisure" and which Virginia Woolf called "a room of one's own."

Even if she has "servants" to do the housework, a woman is supposed to be the "angel in the house," doing spiritual housework. Virginia Woolf made it clear that before women can write we must *kill* the "angel in the house," glorified by male authors.[3] The word *angel*, squeezed into this tidy context (derived from the tidy scribbler Coventry Patmore), is an example of the phenomenon of false faces imposed upon words under phallic rule. As we have seen, the word *angel* has breathtakingly biophilic meanings and suggests Elemental powers of be-ing. The petty perversity of Patmore's use of this word, his typically tidy twisting of this inherently

Mary Daly around 1978, when *Gyn/Ecology: The Metaethics of Radical Feminism* was published.

American teacher of theology and philosophy, feminist, and essayist.

Born: Schenectady, New York, October 16, 1928.

Education: College of St. Rose, B.A. 1950; Catholic University of America, M.A. 1952; St. Mary's College, Notre Dame, Indiana, Ph.D. 1954; University of Fribourg, Switzerland, S.T.D. 1963, Ph.D. 1965.

Career: Teacher of philosophy and theology, Cardinal Cushing College, Brookline, Massachusetts, 1954–59; assistant professor, 1966–69, and then associate profes-

sor of theology, 1969–, Boston College, Chestnut Hill, Massachusetts. Teacher of theology and philosophy, U.S. Junior Year Abroad programs, University of Fribourg, Switzerland, 1959–66.

Memberships: Member of American Academy of Religion, American Association of University Professors, National Organization for Women, Society for the Scientific Study of Religion.

Address: Department of Theology, Carney Hall, Boston College, Chestnut Hill, Massachusetts 02167, U.S.A.

Tidal Name, is comparable to snooldom's shrinking of the Goddess Isis to the dimensions of wimpy plastic madonnas.

An "Exotic" Example

The tidiness inflicted upon women, together with orders to impose this torture upon each other, combine to produce a climate of tidy torture. Within this prevailing climate, the everyday atrocities here "at home" go unrecognized and unreported, while "exotic" tidy practices in faraway lands become the objects of fascinated attention.

This phenomenon was blatantly exemplified in *National Geographic* in an article concerning the "beauty secret" of Padaung tribeswomen of Burma, often called "giraffe women." The article reports:

A relentless embrace of brass … armors the neck in a coil that weighs about 20 pounds, and measures a head-popping one foot high. The loops, draped with silver chains and coins and cushioned by a small pillow under the chin, signal elegance, wealth, and position.[4]

The author, a physician, does give some indication of the horror underlying this "elegance," including X-rays that reveal an unbelievable displacement of the clavicle and ribs by the loops, the first of which are twisted around a girl's neck when she is about five years old. The number of loops is augmented periodically. Moreover:

Rings worn on arms and legs may weigh a woman down with an additional thirty pounds of brass. Since leg coils hamper

WRITINGS

Nonfiction

Natural Knowledge of God in the Philosophy of Jacques Maritrain, 1966.

The Church and the Second Sex, 1968; revised with new "feminist postchristian" introduction by author, 1975; revised with new "archaic afterwords" by author, 1985.

Beyond God the Father: Toward a Philosophy of Women's Liberation, 1973.

Gyn/Ecology: The Metaethics of Radical Feminism, 1978; revised with new "intergalactic introduction" by author, 1990.

Pure Lust: Elemental Feminist Philosophy, 1984.

Webster's First New Intergalactic Wickedary of the English Language, with Jane Caputi, 1987.

Outercourse: The Be-Dazzling Voyage, 1993.

walking, the women waddle. Constrained from drinking in the usual head-back position, a ring wearer leans forward to sip through a straw.... And the voices of wearers, wrote British journalist J. G. Scott, sound "as if they were speaking up the shaft of a well."[5]

The readers of *National Geographic* were also informed that in the past the coils were removed as punishment for adultery. The head would then flop over and the woman would suffocate. Certain questions, significantly, are not raised in the article, for example: How could such a burdened, crippled woman possibly escape from a male who decided to force her into adultery? What comparable horror could have been inflicted upon him?

The attitude of the author (and most likely of the editors) is conveyed explicitly:

Legend claims that the brass rings protect the women from tiger bites, but actually the practice of wearing them helps maintain individual and tribal identity.[6]

As if to reinforce this message, the article is accompanied by colorful photographs of "giraffe women," most of whom are smiling, apparently in a state of full-fillment. Moreover, the reader is left with the depressing information that:

The custom, indelibly inscribed in Padaung culture, persists and, according to University of Illinois anthropologist F. K. Lehman, shows signs of a resurgence.[7]

While it may by true that the "custom" prevails only in a tribe of several thousand members, the article is of significance as an example of the media's mind-tidying tactics. For this kind of publication, by means of both overt and subliminal double-talk, functions to defeat rather than to liberate consciousness. This depressing effect is achieved in at least two ways.

First, the article manages on one level to minimize the horror of such mutilation. The fact that the "custom" affects relatively few women in a faraway land distances the female reader to some extent, so that the atrocity can be experienced superficially as unthreatening. Indeed, it sets up an unmentioned comparison/contrast in the reader's mind between the situation of the "giraffe women" and her own, even eliciting plastic feelings of gratitude for the benefits of modern civilization and its "liberation" of women. Since the "giraffe women" are smiling and since the loops are described as signifying elegance, wealth, and position and as helping the women maintain "individual identity," the reader may be seduced into thinking that the cultural difference between herself and these women is so vast that she is unable to give an "objective" estimation of their oppression. She is lured into non-identification with them as sister-women; and she is further mystified by her male acquaintances' disguised—or obvious—experience of the article as a piece of exotic, or even erotic, journalism. Moreover, in some circles (conservative, liberal, and "radical") any criticism could even bring down remonstrances for the critic's "sentimentality" or "cultural imperialism."

Second, on a deeper level, no matter how bamboozled a woman may be by such confusing media messages, the knowledge is absorbed that *women* are *mutilated* and vulnerable to the prevailing "customs." In the psyche of any woman reading such an article the connection is made between the "strange" condition of these "other" women and her own state. The fear-button that has been embedded deep in her soul is tidily tapped and the message recorded: "Stay in line, then you'll be fine."

Although the double-talk has conveyed, on the overt level, a sense of disconnection from the bizarre "giraffe women" and all of the horrors they are used to symbolize, the reader is allowed to make unspoken/unspeakable connections, privately. This terrifying private understanding is paralyzing so long as it remains private and to some extent subliminal. And there are, of course, reasons why a woman would keep it thus repressed, including fear of ridicule and of the common tidy labels. Yet only by making the connections explicit can she release her potted anger and fear, converting these into gynergizing Rage/Courage, burning the tidy bindings of her mind, Realizing her power.

Each time one woman encourages another to Realize such subliminal connections, severing the tidy ties, she is presentiating Presence. Each time she uses her Labrys to cut through the demonic double messages of tidydom she releases Tidings of Great Hope, for she is rendering the truth explicit and therefore accessible. Such Good Tidings free the flow of communications/connections. Potentially, this flow is Tidal, enabling those who are Touched by its healing waves to Race with the Race of Women.

MELVIN DIXON

Essay by
MICHAEL BRONSKI

AT THE TIME of his death due to complications from AIDS in 1992, Melvin Dixon was considered one of the most noted gay African American writers in the United States. In less than ten years he had produced two novels, a book of poems, two volumes of translations, and a work of literary and cultural criticism. All of the books met with positive critical press, and Dixon's literary scholarship was highly praised. While his scholarly work is respected—in particular his translations of Léopold Sédar Senghor's poetry and his critical volume *Ride Out the Wilderness: Geography and Identity in Afro-American Literature*—it is his fiction writing that is most innovative.

Most gay male literature since Stonewall has received scant attention from mainstream critics; gay writing by African American men has had to function under the double burden of being ignored by both the mainstream and a wide white gay readership. Although Dixon's *Vanishing Rooms* managed to gain some crossover critical reception and audience with white gay reviewers and readers, it did not receive the attention that other books of its stature have. This is due to Dixon's insistence on focusing on the primacy of African American themes and continually posing difficult questions about race, violence, and homophobia.

In *Trouble the Water*, Dixon takes two traditional genres: the return of a Northern African American to the South (a traditional black narrative theme that Dixon explored in depth in *Ride Out the Wilderness*) and the more extravagant Southern gothic. *Trouble the Water* tells the story of Jordan Henry, who was raised as a young boy by his strong-willed grandmother Mother Harriet in Pee Dee, North Carolina. Later in life, Jordan, now a Harvard graduate and professor, returns home with his wife only to be embroiled in a destructive struggle—orchestrated by his grandmother on her deathbed—that is centered around family history.

Trouble the Water draws on several African American literary traditions—the use of biblical imagery, the idea of home as being a haven of security, and the notion that education represents a form of economic and psychological progress—and then reverses them. The climb to the

American novelist, poet, translator, and educator.

Born: Stamford, Connecticut, May 29, 1950.

Education: Wesleyan University, Middletown, Connecticut, B.A. 1971; Brown University, Providence, Rhode Island, M.A. 1973, Ph.D. 1975.

Partnerships: Companion of Richard Horovitz (died).

Career: Assistant professor of English, Williams College, Williamstown, Massachusetts, 1976–80; member of the English department of Queens College of the City University of New York, Flushing, 1980–92. Contributing editor to *Callaloo.*

Recipient: National Endowment for the Arts poetry fellowship, 1984; New York Arts Foundation artist fellowship in fiction, 1988; Nilon Award, 1989.

Died: October 26, 1992, of complications from AIDS.

mountaintop, on which Pee Dee is situated, might have conjured up images of Moses, Noah, and the Transfiguration, but in Dixon's world there is no such enlightenment. Although Jordan returns to find his "roots" in Pee Dee, he discovers little emotional or historical comfort there, but rather a past that refuses to let go and move forward. While his advanced "Northern" education has situated him better in the world, it has not, as Booker T. Washington might imply in his writings, proved to be any emotional or physical panacea. History, Dixon seems to be saying, is always a trap unless we face it with unsentimental hearts and minds.

Dixon employs Southern Gothic themes—most notably those used by such white authors as William Faulkner, Flannery O'Connor, Lillian Hellman, and Tennessee Williams—in a more straightforward manner. Family secrets, festering hates, and deathbed manipulations are all consciously used by the author to explore the capability of the human heart for destruction. Mired in history and tradition, the residents of Pee Dee are trapped because they can see no other alternatives.

The characters in *Vanishing Rooms* are also trapped by history. The novel begin with Metro, the white lover of the African American Jesse, queer-bashed and murdered by a gang of white youths. From this beginning, Dixon has fashioned a series of three overlapping narratives: by Jesse, by Ruella, an African American woman who befriends him, and by Lonny, the troubled white boy who is part of the murderous gang. These interlocking chapters explicate the murder, detail Metro and Jesse's relationship, and describe Jesse's dealing with his grief at his lover's death.

If the plot structure of *Vanishing Rooms* turns on three narratives, its thematic structure revolves around three political ideas: the nature of homophobic violence, the social construct and parameters of male homosexuality, and the eroticization of race. Dixon approaches each of these contested topics and attempts to discover a "hidden" side to them that fuels his character's actions and ideas.

We see in the "Lonny" sections of *Vanishing Rooms* how the young man is both attracted to homosexuality and repulsed by his own feelings. When Metro is attacked and killed by the gang, Lonny undergoes a breakdown as well as a catharsis. Dixon seems to imply that the two prevailing thoughts about homophobia and homophobic violence—the first that it is simply a hatred of "difference," the second that it is a recognition and then an attraction—are both inadequate to describe the phenomenon. Lonny is neither *simply* a "homophobe" or *simply* a "closet case." Dixon's vision is too complex to allow either simplistic analysis to stand.

After Metro is murdered, Jesse finds comfort, as well as a sexual relationship, with Ruella. There is no doubt that Jesse remains homosexually identified throughout the novel and such interludes of heterosexual activity are quite rare in contemporary gay male fiction, even though it may occur in everyday life. Since the theoretical underpinnings of much gay fiction is to establish, in the face of overwhelming homophobia, the validity of homosexuality, non-homosexual behavior—and especially nurturing heterosexual behavior—is quite deviant. *Vanishing Rooms* attempts to broaden the boundaries of gay male fiction by insisting that we acknowledge, in our writings, the possibilities and realities of the actual world.

The relationship of Metro and Jesse forms the center of *Vanishing Rooms,* and although both of them attempt to be cognizant of what it means in a racist culture to be involved in an interracial homosexual relationship, at times they are unable to establish themselves as completely separate from their environment. The climax of the interpersonal problems comes when—in an attempt to be aggressively sexy and "low"—Metro calls Jesse a "nigger" during their lovemaking. Jesse is enraged and repeatedly hits Metro who responds by masturbating until he reaches orgasm. The interplay of racism and racist language, the pushing of the boundaries of eroticism, and the violence that ensues from reflexive, non-thinking action permeate the book. Although Dixon is clear about what constitutes racism, he is also insistent on examining the ways in which both Metro and Jesse contribute to their interpersonal violence.

In his fiction, Melvin Dixon attempted to push the boundaries of what is permissible in the traditions of African American and gay male fiction. By insisting that race and sexuality be dealt with in each genre, he enlarged the possibilities for all writers and readers.

RED LEAVES

"Red Leaves," copyright 1988 by Melvin Dixon, was reprinted from *Men on Men 2: Best New Gay Fiction*, Plume, copyright 1988 by George Stambolian.

You can't walk on 12th Street no more on account of the leaves covering the ground. Even in Abingdon Square just this side of Key Foods where only two or three maples give shade there are leaves everywhere, and when I walk outside I step on them. Some stick to my heels and scratch against the ground in a hurt voice. When it rains the leaves turn to mush and dirty my sneakers—not Adidas, but cheaper ones just as good. Even inside houses and buildings you got leaves brought in by all kinds of people. It's October, the season of yellow, copper, gray, and red, real red. The leaves are cut-off hands curling up like fists. If they grab for my sneakers, I just walk faster and harder to get them off. Like that faggot reaching for me out of the dirt and shedding red like some gray bone tree. You know the trees I'm talking about. You've seen them faggots. They all over this city like flies on shit. You hear the scratchy tumble of red leaves everywhere until someone rakes the place clean. Don't let nobody tell you that leaves don't talk. They pile up on you like something or someone is gonna burn.

The funny thing is whether it happened like you remember it happening or if your head changes it all, gets the people and action messed around. I'd talk to the other fellas, but they'd think I was trying to punk out, see, and make like it was more than it was. Simple. We was getting back at him for trying to come on to me. You know, like I was some goddamn bitch. He probably wanted all of us, not just me, although we got him really scared by then, turning pale and twitching his eyes like he couldn't believe it was really happening to him out there alone at 4:30 in the morning in October in 1975. Wasn't he smiling at us? I remember his lips curling up, then down, his mouth moving like he was eating up the beer stink and smoke until he gagged. He acted weak, hungry, drugged up worse than the rest of us, but almost like getting fucked in the ass was an end to it. The hunger, I mean. I could tell he was hungry. We all could.

That night wasn't the first time I seen him. In fact, I seen him several times and knew where he lived. Sometimes I seen him go toward the docks and meat-packing houses. Why? Drinks, maybe. There are a few bars around there, where I've never been. He could have been one of the guys, you know, going after a six-pack at the corner grocery. He wore track sneakers—real Adidas—and jeans and a plaid flannel shirt opened from the neck on down. That day you could feel the season change right in the air, so I thought it funny seeing the open V of his chest like that. The morning chill had cooled off what was left of Indian summer, but it was too early for leather jackets and thick collars. I thought he was one of the guys 'cause he didn't swish like them over at Sheridan Square that got makeup on or their hair too neatly trimmed around the neck. This guy walked like a regular fella. Someone you'd want to talk to, chase pussy with, or get shit-faced on Budweiser together like we do most nights. Yeah, I seen him. Lots of times. Sometimes he didn't know I was seeing him. Not until the day I was gonna meet Cuddles after his job when he actually come up close to me. It was near Cuddles' meat-packing house up by the docks and burned out piers where Little West 12th Street runs into traffic on the downtown detour from the closed up West Side Highway.

He was just walking and I was walking. I looked at him. He looked at me. I didn't mean nothing by looking at him close like that, face-to-face. He didn't *look* like no faggot. So I nodded "Hey, man," and kept on walking. I mean, I wanted to be civil and shit. He might be able to lay you on to some drugs. But I said what I said, and he nodded and both of us went our separate ways. Easy, see. But damn, man, no sooner do I reach the door to Cuddles' job where he's supposed to be waiting but ain't, than I turn around to see that guy looking at me. He was watching my ass. Checking me out like you check out a bitch. Like he wanted something from me. Needed it. Scheming how he was gonna get it. But he didn't make no moves. Cuddles finally came outside and slapped me on the shoulder. I turned around and the guy was gone. Good thing, too. With Cuddles I forgot about him 'cause we was gonna get Maxie and Lou and ride around. I didn't give a fuck about that guy looking at me. Before joining the others, Cuddles and me had a beer where they don't check IDs. A little pre-drink drink. Get ready for the night. We always had good times. We tight, Cuddles and me.

Cuddles' father makes him work after school. Trade school. My old man died too soon to make me do nothing. Half the time I live in the streets. I should quit school, get a full-time job. Get the cash Cuddles has most times—where I got to ask my Moms to spot me some coins, mostly for cigarettes. Don't need no subway fare. Just jump the turnstile soon as the train screeches in. I do the best I can. Cuddles is the one in the money. Ain't tight-assed about it either, which is why we hang together. I like him better than Maxie or Lou, but I can't tell them that, not even Cuddles 'cause he'll start calling me names and picking on me 'cause I'm only fifteen and he's older. Just a little older.

"Two drafts, what d'ya say?" I tell him.

"Just what I need. Throat's tight as a damn drum."

"Mine's like a hose, man. Only it's empty."

"What's eating you? I been working all day."

"Shit, man, this dude, you know, like the rest of them in the Village. Always coming on to you, checking you out like you some bitch."

"They think it's their turf, Lonny. We just tourists, you know."

"Yeah. Faggots is everywhere."

"You ain't got nothing to worry about, long as they keep a distance."

"But this dude act like he wanted it and could get it."

"He say anything to you, man."

"Naw, he just kept looking."

"He touch you, Lonny? He touch you?"

"Why you wanna know?" I say, but nothing else, just set my jaw tight so he'd know not to fuck with me. You can never tell about Cuddles. Always fucking with somebody.

"Drink up, Lonny. The guys gonna be mad cause we got a head-start." Cuddles slaps me on the shoulder and ruffles my stringy hair.

I'm grinning now, feeling stupid, too.

"I know what you need, man," he says. "Let's get the rest of the guys and blow outta here."

I don't say nothing more to Cuddles and just "Hey, man" to Maxie and Lou waiting for us at the cycle garage in Chelsea. Lou has his machine up on the racks and comes toward us wiping grease off his hands. Maxie sits on a locked bike and leans forward and back like he's speeding down I-95 and going into a long S-curve. He thinks he's in some kind of pro race, but ain't none of us old enough for the big time yet. Some places you got to be eighteen.

I'm just a year away from quitting school if I want. Maxie is out of school already, but he don't have a job. Maybe 'cause his round pink face is full of acne. Cuddles is blond and older than me by a couple of months. He's funny, and you never know if he's gonna turn on you, especially if he can act big around Lou and Maxie. Lou is eighteen and works at the cycle garage where we hang out. I usually get Cuddles after his job 'cause he's near where I live. We walk the rest of the way. Sometimes Cuddles has his moped and we ride over. Junior cycle, we call it. Wish I had one. Once I stole a ten-speed and spray-painted it over. I rode around, got Cuddles, and we rode double, Cuddles peddling and me on the seat, my hair blowing into spikes behind me and me holding Cuddles at the waist with my feet spread out from the double chain derailer. He told me not to hold on so tight. Lou laughed his nuts off at us riding up to the garage on a stupid bike like that. He called us silly shitheads. I didn't care since he's mostly friendly with Maxie and thinks we just punks anyway. That's when Cuddles tries to act tough. But when I told Lou how I stopped this kid in the park on the East Side, took the silver ten-speed right from under his ass, raced downtown and spray-painted it red, he looked at me weird like he didn't think I had the balls to do that on the East Side. "You a mean dude," he said. And I said, "Naw, just regular white trash." I grinned all over myself and slapped his palm. Slapped Cuddles on the palm too.

This time walking up on the guys already at the garage and with me feeling the slow buzz of brew on a warm day, I don't say much to Lou or to Maxie 'cause Cuddles is already talking big and laughing. Then I get the drift of some shit that really puts me out. "Man, what Lonny needs is some pussy," Cuddles is saying. "He ain't had none in so long he's watching the boys on Christopher Street." And Cuddles laughs, poking me in the side like I'm supposed to laugh too. But I'm hot in the face, red all over, itching to dance on somebody. But shit, Cuddles is my man, or supposed to be. He can turn on you and get Maxie and Lou on his side. Now they're all laughing.

"No shit. You mean Lonny's sneaking after some faggot pussy?" says Lou.

"Maybe Lonny just getting tired of the front door," says Maxie. "He wants to come round back."

"Can't get it open no more, huh, Lonny?" says Lou.

They make me feel like shit. I probably look like shit too. Damn Cuddles, I could kill him. Punch them all out. Why he had to goof on me like that when I was enjoying my buzz. When these guys start loudmouthing, no telling what they gonna do. "Naw, man," I tell them. "The only thing I do with a back door is shut it with my fist."

"You into fist-fucking!" Maxie screams. I don't even know what he's talking about. Then he balls up his greasy hands and starts waving all in my face like I'm gonna stand there and take it.

My hands get tight, maybe tighter than his. What I got to lose? "Yeah—and if you don't watch out, I'm gonna fist fuck yo face."

"Whoaaa," Maxie hollers, pretending to fall down, his mouth and eyes shoot open.

"Whoaa," says Cuddles, slippery as spit.

Then Lou goes, "Aw, man, we just messing with you. We know you cool."

"Yeah, he cool," says Maxie. "When you got a shitty dick, you gotta keep cool, and clean."

That's when I pull him off a that locked bike where he thinks he's king or something. Get him down tight between my legs, face red, and I'm about to beat his pink acne head to a pulp when Cuddles and Lou pull me back by my hair. I'd lose anyway. Maybe Cuddles and Lou know something I don't know.

"Cut the shit, man."

"Yeah, cut it."

I let him up. Maxie brushes himself off real calm like it was nothing but a punk getting out of hand. Being naughty. Shit. I push him away. "Next time you wanna give some lip," I'm saying. And I grab my cock in a mound, point it at him. "Wrap your lips around *this*."

"Whew," says Lou. "You don't need no taste that bad."

"Let's get the fuck out of this garage," says Cuddles. "Who's buying this time?"

We head for Key Foods and load up on two sixes. We get our regular bench in Abingdon Square which tries hard to be a park with a little grass and dirt, but it's mostly concrete benches and jungle gyms. We sit and sip and sit and sip. Can't wait for night to come, and I'm trying to be cool.

It ain't always bad, drinking with the guys. About what I dig most these days, biding time till I can quit school. Be out on my own. More time to hang out. We get so plastered sometimes that night comes up on us with a scare and you wonder where the day went. Night is all right by me in the summer, but in October, man, you see things start dying all over the place. Not just red leaves circling down from the trees, but the cold whooshing in, cleaning the air of summer dog shit and roach spray. I can tell it's gonna be an early winter. Long one too. Sooner than anyone expected, October came in like an old lady screaming burglary or rape.

On the concrete bench next to me Lou says beer and night get him horny. His eyes snap at any piece of ass walking by. "Not any piece," he says all loud and blustery. "Just the ass that squats to pee." He starts stroking himself and gets up, saying he got to have some woman, and beer sprays from his mouth. Maxie says he needs some woman too. They say "woman" cause they won't get anything calling it pussy. Cuddles stands next to Lou holding him up then pushing him aside. "Forget about the woman," Cuddles says. "I just want some snatch." He poses like a hero out of some spy flick or war movie. I listen to them laughing and cackling but I don't say nothing about women or anything else.

"Listen, if we all put our money together—"

"What money," I say. "I just blew what I had on beer."

"See, I told you he was small," says Maxie.

"Shit."

Cuddles says he got ten dollars left. "And I got ten," says Lou. "Twenty's enough."

"Ain't a bitch in town for that amount," I say. Nobody answers. Every time we start cutting up on beer or herb or cycling around, somebody gets horny and we end up talking about bitches and chasing leg.

"Drink up," Cuddles tells me.

"Let's blow back to the garage," says Lou. "Then the road to heaven."

We split up, riding double.

"Hey, Lonny," Maxie goes. "Don't hold so tight."

"Sorry."

I feel bad not having any money, but that's all right with the guys. We don't go to a house or a place with rooms. We ride uptown, along Broadway, near 79th Street where Cadillac headlights dim and slow to a cruising speed. Ten blocks further you see the bitches in miniskirts, all legs and face and not much chest, which is fine with me. Maxie pulls to a curb where Lou and Cuddles are leering at somebody. I stay at the bike while Maxie walks over to them. Suddenly she's laughing out loud like they was the funniest thing she ever seen. She waves her hand away and goes back to her pose in the door of a bakery closed for the night. Maxie goes ahead a half block further and approaches another and another one until he comes running back to me.

"Any go?" Lou asks for all of us. Me included.

"Yeah, some bitch around the corner at Ninety-first. You guys down?"

"Yeah," Cuddles says and looks at me. I say yeah too.

We go on up to 91st Street and turn in between Broadway and Amsterdam. We stop at the first abandoned building, which is really near Columbus. The woman—I'll say woman too this time—has dyed blond hair that looks like straw under the street lamp. She pulls at her skirt and pops gum in her mouth. "Hurry up now," she says. "I ain't got all night. For this little shit money, I'm doing you a favor. Be glad I got the real money early. Roscoe be on my ass if he finds out. Be on all your asses, too."

She enters the dim hallway and Maxie and Low follow her up to the first floor. I wait with Cuddles against the parked cycles. They are gone only about fifteen minutes when she comes out again. "Anybody got a jacket? It's damn cold up there."

Cuddles hands over his jacket. Up close now I see she's not much older than me, maybe younger. I wonder why she's doing this. I want to say something to her but I don't. Besides, what can I say? I'm here. Cuddles winks at me and points to her swaying ass as she goes back inside. We wait.

When our turn comes Maxie and Lou watch the bikes. Cuddles goes first. He doesn't take off his pants all the way, just unzips his fly and plows in. He's fast. Faster than I'll ever be. Maybe. It's already my turn. Her face turns up to me from the floor, her eyes tiny like they're holding something in. "What's the matter? You scared?"

I don't say anything. I make my eyes tiny, like hers.

"If you don't come on, you lose. Ain't no discounts, now." And she laughs. Cuddles laughs, too. I climb on top, my clothes tight at the waist.

I feel around her titties and she turns her tiny eyes away from me, arching her back. "Stop fumbling with my chest. Ain't nothing there." I want to say I like it like that, but I don't say nothing. This close I can see her teeth ain't clean.

Cuddles moves toward the door, keeping a lookout. I try to say something but she starts moving her hips around and my dick pops out of my pants. The tightness is gone, I'm all in her now and working, watching her face, her head shaded by the denim jacket and her tiny eyes doing nothing like she's the middle of a sunflower or a wheel of cloth spinning now until her eyes open up on me doing what I'm doing.

Cuddles comes over and just stands there like I'm taking too much time. Shit, he got his. I'm getting mine. He watches me. I try to say something, anything. His eyes hold me. Her eyes pinch tiny again and I feel the pull way down between my legs. I get it in my throat and say, "You see me, Cuddles." And he says, "Yeah, man." The girl breathes deeply, but she don't say nothing. It's just me and Cuddles. Me and him with words. "You see me getting this pussy?"

"Yeah, I see you, man."

"I'm getting it. I'm getting it, Cuddles." And my head goes light all of a sudden as if a weight was easing off me and going her way, maybe his. My hands grip the ends of the jacket like they're the spokes of a wheel turning me. My head circles faster than my body or her head below mine as I push my face against the cloth and away from her tiny eyes and straw hair. I feel Cuddles' eyes on me again, then her eyes on me. The smell of denim and armpits makes me tingle all over and tingle again until my whole body heaves and pulls. The jacket lets go the smell of grease and body all in my face and I can't do nothing but let go myself. The bitch had nothing to do with it. Riding on empty, I ease up. She smooths her shirt back into place. I don't say nothing and she don't say nothing. We walk outside.

Maxie hands her the twenty dollars. She looks like she could cast a spell. "You better be glad Roscoe ain't around. He'd be on all your asses for this lousy twenty bucks."

We rev up for the ride downtown. Cuddles brushes off his jacket and climbs behind Lou at the handlebars. "I was just shiting you, Lonny, about that faggot stuff. You cool, man. I seen you. You cool."

"I know," I tell him. "I know I'm cool." I slap him on the back. I climb up on Maxie's bike. I ain't grabbing tight this time. In a minute we're gone.

* * *

Like I keep telling you. October is a bitch, a mean red bitch. And you still don't believe me. Shit, you got the red leaves, you got early nightfall and twisted chilly mornings freezing you back into bed. You got people in scarves and caps tilted to the side like Hollywood detectives. You got October. What more do you want? You want red leaves clogging the sewers? You want legs and arms splayed out like tree limbs after a storm? You really don't believe in fall, huh, or how people can change too, just as fast. You want all this? Then you're no better than that faggot who wanted me.

He said his name was Metro. Just like that, he said it, out of the blue. So I said, "Yeah." Nothing more. The way he looked at me I could tell he was thinking he'd seen me around and knew I'd seen him around, too, and after saying hello just once he could come up to me a week later and tell me his funny name.

I was on my way to meet Cuddles who had the smoke this time. I had my mind on herb and didn't really see him until he was close enough to speak. "Metro," he said. I thought he was asking for directions. But he stuck out his hand cause it wasn't a place he was telling me, it was his name. I felt a load on me from the moment he spoke. All I said was "yeah." He didn't take the hint. He waited for more. Maybe he was thinking the cat got my tongue and he wanted it. I looked closer. He was about my height and build. Had wavy hair, not stringy like mine. He looked like any regular guy, except he spoke first in a drawl straight out of *Gone with the Wind*, then changed back to a normal voice. He said again his name was Metro. What could I do? He waited until I told him my name, but I never did. I finally said, "You know what you are?"

"Metro."

"Shit, man. You better get out of my face." And I left him standing there at the corner of West 12th and Bank looking like he just lost some money or came home to find his apartment broken into and his stereo and favorite records gone. With the wind. How do I know he even had a stereo? I don't know. He never invited me in to smoke dope or listen to records. Which is the only reason anyone would go with him. With a name like Metro what would you expect?

I didn't expect nothing at all. The third time I seen him walking into the corner building, I knew he lived there. I wasn't meeting Cuddles this time. I didn't know why I was even in the neighborhood. You get used to meeting friends in late afternoon and it gets to be routine. Metro was dressed in a suit, no jeans, no flannel plaid, no white undershirt poking from inside the open collar. He looked like one of those Wall Street businessmen, he looked so square, so regular. He might have been somebody's husband or somebody's father even though he wasn't *that* old. You should know about fathers. They're the most important people to a kid trying to be a man, when everyone is out to get you or fix you into a can or a crate going six feet down.

My father built things. He was a carpenter mainly. He'd build things, take things apart and build them again. But he was also an electrician, a house painter, a wallpaper hanger, a welder, a car mechanic, a plumber. All for money and for fixing up other people's houses. He could fix anything. A regular jack-of-all-trades, a handyman. I remember he used to make toys for us at Christmas because he couldn't buy any. We was living in the Bronx then and my father would load up his beat-up station wagon every morning and go off on the jobs people called him for.

He owned his business. He *was* his own business. That's what Moms said to write in the blank beside "father's occupation" on school registration forms every September, "self-employed." I didn't even know what it meant, because my father never talked to us. He didn't tell us about who we were. I mean, as a family. And since I didn't know who I was aside from nothing or no one, I thought I could be anybody I damn well pleased.

"You ain't never had a chance, did you?" Moms said once.

"What you talking about? I'm anybody I'm strong enough to be."

"And mean enough," she said, shaking her head like she did when my father died. He worked all the time and kept his feeling locked inside until his heart burst open. The fucking load he must have been carrying. Shit, I could have carried some of that load.

"You ain't never had a chance," Moms said again.

"I make my own chances. I'm self-employed."

* * *

Naw, Metro couldn't have been anybody's husband or father. You could tell by the way he walked and, if you listened close enough, by the way he talked. But he had what you call opportunities. Maybe if you don't ever have kids you can build things for yourself. Do things. He just made the mistake of wanting to do me.

"You can come up to visit sometime, you know. Now that you know where I live."

"You mean me?"

"Sure. What's your name?"

"Lonny."

"I'm Metro."

"You told me before. Remember?"

"Yes. I thought you didn't remember. You didn't say anything."

"I didn't know what to say. Besides, where'd you get a name like that?"

"You'll see."

"Listen, man, you trying to get wise or something?"

"Let's be friends, Lonny."

"I got to go now."

"Some other time, then?"

"Sure, man, sure."

"Call me Metro. I like that."

"Sure."

I got away and ran all the way to Cuddles' place. He wasn't even expecting me. But I was there just the same, leaning against the corner beam of the loading platform. It was about five feet off the ground so that the packing trucks could be loaded from the level of the storage and work areas. I could have been holding up the very corner of the building myself or at least the sign saying Holsworth Meat and Poultry Packing, where you could actually see the sides of beef, the blood and fat making the loading platform slippery and the whole place smell like rotten armpits.

Maybe it was the heat. Or just me, hot with my tangled nerves sizzling electric. All from talking with that guy Metro and running breakneck speed to Cuddles' job like it was the only safe place. I was hot standing there thinking about Metro and hating myself for letting him talk like that to me. Shit, he talked like he knew who I was or who I could be. Like he could actually see into my corduroy jacket, his eyes like fingers in my clothes and touching me. You ever get that feeling talking to someone? Shit. I hated him for thinking he knew who I was and could come on to me like I was some bitch. He didn't know who he was messing with. Sure, I told him my name. We was just talking. Wouldn't you talk before you realized his eyes were fingers crawling all over you? I know you would, mostly because you'd think a guy wouldn't do that to another guy. Later, you'd swear he touched you. Wouldn't you? You'd think that talking was all right. It was only some words between you, not hands. You'd think that as long as he didn't touch you it would be all right to speak. Long as neither of you was touching. It don't mean that you're one of them, just cause you say "Lonny," like I did. We was only talking, man. But when you realized his eyes were fingers taking hold, you'd hate him even more for pulling it off, undressing you right there with his eyes and laughing at your naked ass or shriveled-up cock. You'd be mad enough to kill him.

"You lying," Cuddles says when I tell him. "You lying, man."

"Naw, I ain't."

"Shit, man. Wait till I see Maxie and Lou."

"What for?"

"We oughta kick his ass."

"Look, Cuddles. Maybe we can just forget it, huh?"

"Naw, man, You one of us. What happens to you, happens to us. You forgetting the pledge."

"What pledge?" I ask after him, and he's dancing on the same short circuit I'm on.

When we catch up with Maxie and Lou it's Cuddles doing the talking. "Man, we should celebrate," he yells, looking me over.

"Celebrate what?" I ask.

"Losing your cherry to a faggot, what else?" he says.

My face burns. "He didn't touch me, man."

"Aw, Lonny, we know you got a little bit," says Maxie, grinning.

"Don't start no shit," says Lou.

"Maybe that's what I'm smelling," says Cuddles, moving up then back from me and flailing his arms like he's brushing me off.

"You mean the shit on *your* breath," I say, stepping up to him.

And Maxie jumps up, saying "Whoa," and Lou goes "Whoa," and I go "Whoa."

Cuddles backs off. "I'll fix your ass," he says. "Fix it real good."

"Aw, man, we been low too long now, let's ride high," says Maxie.

"Beer and smoke?" I ask.

"Yeah."

"Let's ride and fuck the night," adds Lou. He revs up the cycle with Cuddles holding tighter to him than I ever held. At the first red light Cuddles turns to me saying he'll fix me real good. I tell him where to put that shit.

Around midnight after five trips to Burger King for fries and hot apple pies to ease the munchies, we get back to the garage in Chelsea. I am high, yeah, I admit it. Feeling good. We stop cutting up with each other and just enjoy being so bloated we can barely move. We keep talking shit, though, like it is all we can say. But I still feel funny about Metro earlier in the afternoon. Then a numbing tingle comes through my face like I'm getting high all over again or just burning slowly inside.

Then I feel light again as if something is about to happen to ease the beer and marijuana out of me on a cool streak and I'd lift off the garage floor, lift up from the street and concrete and glide out to 12th Street and Bleecker again, then to West 4th where I'd be sure to see him and we'd talk. Just talk. Maybe this time I would get to hear his stereo. Maybe he likes the same music I do. Maybe he really is like me or Maxie or Cuddles or Lou, just a little haywire. But we leave the garage again and move in a group through the meat-packing section of lower West 12th and up toward Bleecker where men walk alone or in twos passing us. Lou scowls. Cuddles sets his shoulders broad. We're a solid block and tough.

Them faggots is just maggots on rotting meat. They move away from us and off the sidewalk quick. Lou and Cuddles laugh, and I hardly know their voices. When I laugh too, just to be laughing, the chuckle comes out of some gray pit inside me and the voice isn't mine, honest. The shit you can carry just waiting for a time like this to stink.

Some guy up ahead is selling loose joints for a dollar. "All our joints loose," says Maxie, laughing and trying to unzip his pants. When we come up to him Maxie asks, "Got fifteen?"

"We'll get blasted to hell," I say. But no one answers. They all look like they know something I don't.

Maxie asks for change for a twenty. I see Cuddles and Lou sneak in close, so I move in close. They guy fumbles around his pockets and gives me the joints to hold. As soon as he brings out a wad of bills it's a flurry of green and fists. Cuddles first, then Maxie, Lou and me pounding hard on the upbeat.

"That's all the money I got," the guy whines. Cuddles pushes him away from us. The flash of metal makes the kid back right into Lou who feels his ass. Cuddles gets a feel, too. His face goes red and his voice quivers, "Leave me alone. You got what you wanted."

"You oughta be glad we don't make you suck us off," Lou says, pushing him away. "Now get the fuck outta here."

The kid disappears down a side street. We count the new joints and money and move in close ranks like an army of our own, the baddest white boys out that night. Everyone else moves off the sidewalk as we approach, some we even push deliberately into the street just close enough to a car to scare them clean out of their designer jeans and alligator shirts. The funniest shit is that some of them have on combat jackets and here we are doing the combat. We blow some of the cash at the liquor store off Sheridan Square.

On a vacant stoop near West 4th Street, we finish off the beer and the joints and divide up the rest of the money. Everything is sweet now. Sure we have our fights and fun and great highs. So what if they don't last long.

Sure as shit and just as loud as the beer and smoke would let him, Cuddles goes, "Lonny, man, how's Beatrice these days?"

"Don't be bringing my Moms into your shit."

"Keep it clean, guys," says Maxie.

"I was trying to keep it clean," Cuddles starts. "But the bitch had her period right when I was fucking her."

In a second I'm on him with fists and feet. He deserves no better. "We dancing this one, asshole."

"Yo, man, cool it," say Lou. He and Maxie pull me off Cuddles, but not until I land some good ones. Cuddles is too high to fight good. I could be faster myself, but what the hell.

"Aw, man," Cuddles says, rolling to his side, sliding down the concrete stairs away from me. "I just wondered if she knew about your boyfriend. You know, the one you said lived around here."

"Whoaa," says Maxie. "Lonny getting faggot pussy again? Keeping it all to himself?"

"It ain't true, man," I say.

"What ain't true?"

"This guy just told me his name, that's all. I didn't say anything else. Nothing."

"Why he tell you his name then?"

"Cause he wanted to, that's why. You jealous Cuddles?"

"Shit, man."

"He wanted to do something, I guess," I say.

"Of course he wanted to," says Maxie.

"He was trying to rap to me," I say, but I'm talking too much and can't stop. "Like I was some bitch."

"He touch you, man? He touch you?" Maxie asks.

"Shit," says Cuddles. "Faggots everywhere."

"I ain't no faggot," I say.

"He touch you, man?" asks Maxie.

"Like you touched that reefer kid back up there?"

"That's different, Lonny. We was on top."

"Shit," says Cuddles. "Pass me another joint."

"Me, too."

"Pass Lonny another joint. He cool."

"Thanks."

Hours pass. Or minutes that seem like hours. The streets are suddenly quiet and so are we. But in the kind of quiet sneaking up and banging like a fist on your face that makes you think something's about to happen and no laughing or getting high can stop it. What you do won't be all that strange, either, more like something you always thought about doing but never did. I hate that feeling. It makes me think that something's burning in me that I don't know about. And I've got to let it out or choke on the fumes.

Cuddles is the first to see him strolling down the street. He nudges me and Maxie. Maxie nudges Lou, who's half asleep and stroking himself hard again.

"Aw shit." My voice gives it away.

"That's him, ain't it?" asks Cuddles. "That's Lonny's faggot, ain't it?"

"I didn't say that," I say, but it's too late.

"He the one touch you?" ask Maxie.

"That's the one," says Cuddles.

"How do you know?"

"*You* told me," Cuddles says, but his voice also tells me something I can't get a hold of. They ease into the street and wait. I join just to be joining them. Metro approaches dizzily, either drunk or high or plain out of it, but not as bad as the rest of us. Cuddles speaks up like he has it all worked out in his head.

"Hey, baby," he goes, in a slippery, chilly voice.

"Huh?" says Metro.

"Hey subway, baby," Cuddles goes again.

"The A train, right? I just took the A train," says Metro.

"We got another train for you, baby. A nice, easy ride."

I can't believe what Cuddles is saying. I try to hide my surprise by not looking at Metro, but they both scare me like I've never been scared before. It's something I can't get hold of, or stop.

"Metro. Why do they call me Metro?" he goes, talking to himself all out of his head now. Does he even see these guys, hear them?

"Hey, baby," says Lou, getting close to him.

I stay where I am near the concrete steps.

"Ooh, baby," says Maxie, joining in.

"They call me the underground man," says Metro, his words slurring. "You wanna know why? I'll tell you why." His eyes dart to all of us, locking us in a space he carries inside for someone to fill. Then he sees me for the first time. He stops, jaws open, eyes wide. "Is that you, Lonny?"

I say nothing. The guys are quiet too.

"You wanna know why, Lonny? Cause I get down under. Underground. Metro. Get it?" Then he laughs a high, faggoty laugh. And

I don't know him anymore. He suddenly stops. No one else is laughing. He feels something's wrong. He looks straight at me, then at the others now tight around him.

"Lonny, what's going on? Who are these guys?"

Cuddles touches him, his hand gliding down Metro's open shirt. Metro's eyes get round.

"Lonny, I don't know these guys."

"That's right," says Maxie. "We're Lonny's friends. Ain't that right, Lonny?"

I say nothing. Lou kicks me square in the shins. "Yeah," I say. "Yeah." But nothing more.

"And when Lonny tells us you go under, man, you give it up nice and easy, don't you?" says Cuddles.

Metro reaches into his pockets and pulls out a raggedy leather wallet. "I don't have much money." He shows the wallet around so we see the single ten spot inside. "That's all there is. You want it? It's all I have."

"No, baby," says Cuddles. "Keep your money. Right, fellas?"

"Right."

Metro looks worried. "My watch? I don't have anything else. Nothing, honest. You can check if you want."

"We don't want your watch," says Lou. His hand falls to Metro's ass, feeling it. Then to the front, gathering Metro's balls into a hump, and slowly, ever so slowly releasing them.

"Lonny says you been after him."

"After him? I don't understand. What are they saying, Lonny?"

I don't say nothing, but I want to say something. When I step closer, I feel metal pointing in my side, a blade tearing my shirt. Cold on my skin.

"Yeah," I say. "You been after me."

Cuddles steps up. "You want to such his cock? Take it up the ass?"

"Hold it, Cuddles," I say.

"Naw, you hold it," says Maxie. "You could be like that too, for all we know. Ain't that right fellas?"

"Shit, man. You tell him, Cuddles. Tell him he's crazy to think that. You seen me with that girl."

"Naw, man. *You* show us," Cuddles says.

They hustle me and Metro into an alley near an abandoned building. Maxie and Lou hold Metro by the armpits. Cuddles twists my arm behind my back and from his open breath I know he's grinning ear to ear. "Aw, man," he whispers to me. "We just having fun. Gonna shake him up a little."

"What about me?"

Cuddles says nothing more. He looks at the others.

Maxie pushes Metro to the ground. The alley carries his voice. "You wanted to suck him, huh? Well, suck him."

Cuddles unzips my pants.

"I didn't touch you, Lonny. I never touched you."

"You lying, subway man," says Cuddles.

"Ask him," Metro says. "Did I touch you, Lonny? Ever? You can tell them. Please, Lonny. I never touched you."

All eyes are on me now, and even in the dark I can see the glimmer of Metro's eyes looking up from the ground. From the sound of his voice I can tell he's about to cry. Suddenly, the click of knives: Lou's and Maxie's. Metro faces away from them and can't see. I see them, but I say nothing. Cuddles twists my arm further. The pain grabs my voice. His blade against my skin. "I told you I'd get back at you, shithead."

Pain all in me. Metro jerks forward. "Ouch," he feels the blade, too. Then Metro's mouth in my pants. Lips cold on my cock. Then warmer. Smoother. Teeth, saliva, gums. I can't say anything, even if I want to.

It don't take me long. I open my eyes. Metro's head is still pumping at my limp cock, but his pants are down in back and Lou is fucking him. Lou gets up quickly, zips up his pants. Maxie moves to take his place. I move out of Metro's mouth, open in a frown this time or a soundless cry. Maxie wets his cock and sticks it in. Cuddles pumps Metro's face where I was. Metro gags. Cuddles slaps his head back to his cock and I hear another slap. This one against Metro's ass and Lou and Maxie slap his ass while Maxie fucks him. Lou has the knife at Metro's back and hips. He traces the shape of his body with the blade. Metro winces. "Keep still, you bastard. Keep still," Lou says.

I try to make it to the street, but Cuddles yanks me back. He hands me a knife and I hold it, looking meaner than I am. "You ain't ever had a chance," I'm thinking and realizing it's for Metro, not for me. Cuddles finishes and pulls out of Metro's dripping mouth. His fist lands against Metro's jaw, slamming it shut. I hear the crack of bone and a weak cry. The next thing I know Maxie, still pumping Metro's ass and slapping his cheeks with the blade broadside, draws blood, and once he finishes he shoots the blade in, gets up quickly, pulling the knife after him. Lou's hand follows. Then a flash of metal and fists.

"Shit, man. Hold it," I yell. "I thought we was only gonna fuck him. What the hell you guys doing?"

"Fucking him good," says Lou.

"Stop. For God's sake, stop."

But they don't stop.

"Oh my God. Oh my fucking God." It's all I can say, damn it. And I hear my name.

"Lonny?"

"Oh my God."

"Lonny?" Metro's voice is weak, his words slurring on wet red leaves. "Help me."

Lou and Maxie jump together. "Let's get the fuck outta here."

"Yeah," says Cuddles. He kicks Metro back to the ground where his arms and legs spread like the gray limbs of a tree.

"Oh my fucking God." I keep saying it, crying it. But it's too late. The guys scatter into the street like roaches surprised by a light. Running. They're running. I look back at Metro and he rolls toward me. His still eyes cut me like a blade. "Never touched you," the eyes say. "Never touched you."

I hold my breath until my ears start to pound. I hold my head. I run, stop, run again. The knife drops somewhere. I run again. Don't know where the fuck I'm going, just getting the hell out of there. Don't see anybody on the street and not for the rest of the night. Not Lou, not Cuddles. Not anybody else at all.

* * *

October is red, man. Mean and red. Nobody came back there but me, see. And Metro was gone by then. Somebody had raked the leaves into a clean pile. I ran through it and scattered the leaves again. Once you get leaves and shit sticking on you, you can never get them off. And when you start hearing the scratchy hurt voices coming from them, the red leaves I mean, not patches of skin or a body cut with knives, or a palm of broken fingers, you'll start talking back, like I do. You stop hanging out at the meat-packing warehouses on lower West 12th or walk the loading platforms mushy with animal fat and slime where your sneaks slip—not Adidas, but cheaper ones just as good.

When I found Cuddles and told him about the talking red leaves, he said to get the fuck away from him, stop coming around if I was gonna talk crazy and dance out of fear like a punk. But I wasn't dancing. My feet was trying to hold steady on the loading platform but my sneaks wouldn't let me. You ever hear the scratchy voices of leaves? You ever try to hold steady on slippery ground?

Like I was telling you and telling Cuddles, after Maxie and Lou cut us loose and before Cuddles cut me loose. Mine wasn't the only hand on his ass or on his face that night. Metro tried to make me. He wanted it that way. They all do. Man, October is a mean, red bitch. I know. But what if it ain't the only bitch? What if you could answer the leaves and tell them to stop falling 'cause winter is here now. It's cold, getting colder. Aw shit, man, trees don't talk.

They had the body marked out in chalk on the ground behind some blue sawhorses saying, "Police Line Do Not Cross." It was right where we left him. I saw it glowing. "Here's Metro," I told myself. Here's anybody, even me. A chalk outline and nothing inside. A fat white line of head, arms, body, and legs. A body curled into a heap to hold itself. Like the shape of a fallen leaf or a dead bird, something dropped out of the sky or from a man's stretched out hand. It was amazing. But it was also the figure of somebody. A man. Any man. So I walked around the outline, seeing it from different angles. How funny to see something that fixed, protected from people or from falling leaves or from the slimy drippings from sides of beef. The outline wasn't Metro. It was somebody like me.

Once I saw the chalk figure I couldn't get enough of it. I kept coming back and walking slower and slower around it, measuring how far it was from the police barricade and from where I stood looking down at it, sprawled where we left him. But I figured out a way to keep looking at it and not step in the garbage scattered nearby. You know, leaves, rags, torn newspapers, bits of dog hair, blood maybe, and lots more leaves. I went three steps this way and three steps that way, keeping the chalk outline in sight and missing the garbage and dog shit. One two three, one two three. Up two three, down two three. Then I saw one of the neighbors watching from a window and I cut out of there. But I knew by then how to keep the chalk outline of a man and not fall like a leaf.

That night I came back. The chalk shape was glowing brighter under the street lights like crushed jewels. I took off my shirt and pants and didn't even feel cold. I crossed the barricade and sat inside the chalk. The glow was on me now. It was me. I lay down in the shape of the dead man, fitting my head, arms, and legs in place. I was warm all over.

The police came and got me up. Their voices were soft and mine was soft. They pulled a white jacket over me like some old lady's shawl. I shrugged a little to get it off, but my arms wouldn't move. When I looked for my hands, I couldn't find them. The police didn't ask many questions, and I didn't say nothing the whole time. Besides, there was no red leaves inside the chalk, not a single one. At the precinct a doctor talked to me real quiet like and said the leaves would go away forever if I told him everything that happened to the dead man and to me. But they didn't call him Metro, they called him some other name with an accent in it. A name I didn't even know. I asked the doctor again about the leaves. He promised they would go away. "What about the blood?" I asked. "Will I step in the blood?"

"Not if you come clean," he said.

"What about my sneaks?" I asked him. "Will they get dirty?"

ANDREA DWORKIN

ONE OF THE MOST vital and, until recently, least examined aspects of the literature of the gay and lesbian liberation movements that emerged during the 1970s is its interaction with, and treatment of, themes of importance to the women's movement. The demands of openly lesbian feminists created a crisis of conscience within the Women's Liberation movement; no less a figure than Betty Friedan referred to them as the "lavender menace." A stream of writing of diverse viewpoints—which arose out of the fierce debates aimed at assisting newly awakened women with the complex task of understanding and defining their multiple oppressions—sought to explore the roots of then-current political and social limits and the ways in which these might be challenged. A particularly influential group of militant authors gradually coalesced in the San Francisco Bay Area, represented by such women as poets Pat Parker and Judy Grahn, and the philosopher Susan Griffin. While each would come to find her own voice with which to call for change, few were as insistently controversial as their counterpart in the New York City area, Andrea Dworkin.

Born in Camden, New Jersey, in 1946, and raised on the street where poet Walt Whitman's house stood, Dworkin began writing in elementary school and debated whether to become a writer or pursue a career in law. One of her goals was to alter society; she based her final decision—as she later stated in an interview—on her belief that "the change that happens from writing is very deep." Involving herself in demonstrations against the Vietnam War—and the entire counterculture movement—while a student at Bennington College, Dworkin's first direct experience of the costs of promoting alternative political positions came when she was arrested during a demonstration and held for four days in the New York City Women's House of Detention. Upon her release, she immediately went public with graphic descriptions of the ways in which she had been brutalized by both prison employees and inmates. No woman, Dworkin protested, whatever her status, should be subjected to such indignities.

Essay by
ROBERT B. MARKS
RIDINGER

157

Andrea Dworkin became a writer because of her belief that "the change that happens from writing is very deep."

The anger and outrage generated by this event fueled her initial determination to explore and challenge what she saw as a male-dominated system of power allocation in contemporary society. In 1974, following a period of travel and residence in Crete and the Netherlands, the first of her books appeared. The result of three years of thought, it bore a simple blunt title. *Woman Hating: A Radical Look at Sexuality* conveyed both Dworkin's subject and manifesto.

In the opening paragraphs of the book's introduction, Dworkin outlines her basic agenda for promoting change. "This book is an action, a political action where revolution is the goal. It has no other purpose," she writes. "The commitment to ending male dominance as the fundamental psychological, political and cultural reality of earth-lived life is the fundamental revolutionary commitment, ... a commitment to transformation of the self and transformation of ... reality on every level, ... an analysis of sexism, ... what it is, how it operates on us and in us."

Such rhetoric represents a logical extension of one of feminism's basic tenets into a complete framework for cultural dissection. But, while many feminists and lesbian separatists would have otherwise agreed with some of her premises, Dworkin's radical, vigorous attacks on any institution or practice that she viewed as oppressive to women—in any form—swiftly marked her as independent and distinctive. Between 1974 and 1976, riding the wave of publicity generated by her first work, Dworkin became a familiar figure on the lecture circuit, speaking at Smith College, at a conference held at Boston College entitled "Alternatives to the Military-Corporate System," at a host of major universities in and around New York City, as well as to the National Organization for Women. The complete texts of nine of these speeches were published in 1976 as *Our Blood*. Of particular value to the history of homosexual literature is the address she delivered on June 28, 1975, at a rally for Lesbian Pride Week held in Central Park. Published as "Lesbian Pride," it sets out clearly the author's vision of what it means to be a lesbian in all its manifestations and provides a standard for the evaluation of her subsequent writing from this perspective.

The majority of works published after *Our Blood* continued the analysis of feminist issues Dworkin began in *Woman Hating*. The issue of pornography was most notable among them. With the formation of the San Francisco–based Women Against Violence in Pornography and the

American feminist, novelist, and essayist.

Born: Camden, New Jersey, September 26, 1946.

Education: Bennington College, B.A. 1968.

Career: Has worked as a waitress, receptionist, secretary, typist, salesperson, factory worker, paid political organizer, and teacher. Regular contributor to periodicals, including *America Report*, *Christopher Street*, *Gay Community News*, *Ms.*, *Social Policy*, and *Village Voice*.

Memberships: Member of PEN, Women's Institute for Freedom of the Press, Authors League of America.

Agent: Elaine Markson, 44 Greenwich Avenue, New York, New York 10011, U.S.A.

Media in 1976, the topic swiftly occasioned considerable debate within all sections of the women's community. Dworkin's view of pornography as a genre that both justifies and celebrates male power over women—thus supporting the basic tenets of the American ideal of masculinity—should be seen in the context of both lesbian feminist philosophy and the women's liberation movement's anger at the reduction of women to the status of objects. Realizing her early dreams of effecting change in society through legal channels, Dworkin and lawyer Catherine MacKinnon drafted an ordinance that defined pornography as a type of sex discrimination; moreover, the ordinance allowed that those hurt by pornography have been deprived of their civil rights. The ordinance was passed into law in Indianapolis, Indiana, and Minneapolis, Minnesota. It was in the process of being introduced in Los Angeles and Cambridge, Massachusetts, when it was declared unconstitutional in 1986. Some of the ordinance's most vocal opponents were feminists who believed that its passage would place limits on the rights of women to explore all types of sexuality. Dworkin published a collection of writings tracing her involvement with this subject in 1989, under the title *Letters from a War Zone*.

Most of Dworkin's literary work dates from after 1980. Highly varied in form, her pieces range from contributions to *Ms.* and the *Village Voice* to works published in *Gay Community News* and *Christopher Street*. Her only collection of short stories, *The New Woman's Broken Heart*, was followed by two autobiographical novels: *Ice and Fire* and the more lengthy *Mercy*, notable for its author's simultaneous praise and condemnation of Walt Whitman for his unrealistic dreams of true democracy in America. Through her professional affiliations with the Authors League of America, the Women's Institute for Freedom of the Press, and PEN, Dworkin continues a tradition of radical lesbianism—born of Stonewall—into the future.

BIOLOGICAL SUPERIORITY: THE WORLD'S MOST DANGEROUS AND DEADLY IDEA

1

"Biological Superiority" was first published in 1977; here it is reprinted from *Letters from a War Zone*, Dutton and Lawrence Hill Books, copyright 1993 by Andrea Dworkin.

All who are not of good race in this world are chaff. (Hitler, *Mein Kampf*)[1]

It would be lunacy to try to estimate the value of man according to his race, thus declaring war on the Marxist idea that men are equal, unless we are determined to draw the ultimate consequences. And the ultimate consequence of recognizing the importance of blood—that is, of the racial foundation in general—is the transference of this estimation to the individual person. (Hitler, *Mein Kampf*)[2]

Hisses. Women shouting at me: slut, bisexual, she fucks men. And before I had spoken, I had been trembling, more afraid to speak than I had ever been. And, in a room of 200 sister lesbians, as angry as I have ever been. "Are you a bisexual?" some women screamed over the pandemonium, the hisses and shouts merging into a raging noise. "I'm a Jew," I answered; then, a pause, "and a lesbian, and a woman." And a coward. Jew was enough. In that room, Jew was what mattered. In that room, to answer the question "Do you still fuck men?" with a No, as I did, was to betray my deepest convictions. All of my life, I have hated the proscribers, those who enforce sexual conformity. In answering, I had given in to the inquisitors, and I felt ashamed. It humiliated me to see myself then: one who resists the enforcers out there with militancy, but gives in without resistance to the enforcers among us.

The event was a panel on "Lesbianism as a Personal Politic" that took place in New York City, Lesbian Pride Week 1977. A self-proclaimed lesbian separatist had spoken. Amidst the generally accurate description of male crimes against women came this ideological rot, articulated of late with increasing frequency in feminist circles: women and men are distinct species or races (the words are used interchangeably); men are biologically inferior to women; male violence is a biological inevitability; to eliminate it, one must eliminate the species/race itself (means stated on this particular evening: developing parthenogenesis as a viable reproductive reality); in eliminating the biologically inferior species/race Man, the new *Ubermensch* Woman (prophetically foreshadowed by the lesbian separatist[3] herself) will have the earthly dominion that is her true biological destiny. We are left to infer that the society of her creation will be good because she is good, biologically good. In the interim, incipient SuperWomon will not do anything to "encourage" women to "collaborate" with men—no abortion clinics or battered woman sanctuaries will come from her. After all, she has to conserve her "energy" which must not be dissipated keeping "weaker" women alive through reform measures.

The audience applauded the passages on female superiority/male inferiority enthusiastically. This doctrine seemed to be music to their ears. Was there dissent, silent, buried in the applause? Was some of the response the spontaneous pleasure that we all know when, at last, the tables are turned, even for a minute, even in imagination? Or has powerlessness driven us mad, so that we dream secret dreams of a final solution perfect in its simplicity, absolute in its efficacy? And will a leader someday strike that secret chord, harness those dreams, our own nightmare turned upside down? Is there no haunting, restraining memory of the blood spilled, the bodies burned, the ovens filled, the peoples enslaved, by those who have assented throughout history to the very same demagogic logic?

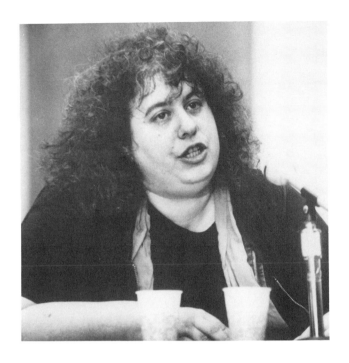

Andrea Dworkin speaks to a federal commission on pornography in New York, January 1986. Two years later Dworkin, along with Catharine A. MacKinnon, outlined her philosophy on the issue in *Pornography and Civil Rights: A New Day for Women's Equality.*

In the audience, I saw women I like or love, women not strangers to me, women who are good not because of biology but because they care about being good, swept along in a sea of affirmation. I spoke out because those women had applauded. I spoke out too because I am a Jew who has studied Nazi Germany, and I know that many Germans who followed Hitler also cared about being good, but found it easier to be good by biological definition than by act. Those people, wretched in what they experienced as their own unbearable powerlessness, became convinced that they were so good biologically that nothing they did could be bad. As Himmler said in 1943:

> We have exterminated a bacterium [Jews] because we did not want in the end to be infected by the bacterium and die of it. I will not see so much as a small area of sepsis appear here or gain a hold. Wherever it may form, we will cauterize it. All in all, we can say that we have fulfilled this most difficult duty

for the love of our people. And our spirit, our soul, our character has not suffered injury from it.[4]

So I spoke, afraid. I said that I would not be associated with a movement that advocated the most pernicious ideology on the face of the earth. It was this very ideology of biological determinism that had licensed the slaughter and/or enslavement of virtually any group one could name, including women by men. ("Use their own poison against them," one woman screamed.) Anywhere one looked, it was this philosophy that justified atrocity. This was one faith that destroyed life with a momentum of its own.

Insults continued with unabated intensity as I spoke, but gradually those women I liked or loved, and others I did not know, began to question openly the philosophy they had been applauding and also their own acquiescence. Embraced by many women on my way out, I left still sickened, humiliated by the insults, emotionally devastated by the abuse. Time passes, but the violence done is not undone. It never is.

2

I am told that I am a sexist. I *do* believe that the difference between the sexes are our most precious heritage, even though they make women superior in the ways that matter most. (George Gilder, *Sexual Suicide*)[5]

Perhaps this female wisdom comes from resignation to the reality of male aggression; more likely it is a harmonic of the woman's knowledge that ultimately she is the one who matters. As a result, while there are more brilliant men than brilliant women, there are more good women than good men. (Steven Goldberg, *The Inevitability of Patriarchy*)[6]

As a class (not necessarily as individuals), we can bear children. From this, according to male-supremacist ideology, all our other attributes and potentialities are derived. On the pedestal, immobile like waxen statues, or in the gutter, failed icons mired in shit, we are exalted or degraded because our biological traits are what they are. Citing genes, genitals, DNA, pattern-releasing smells, biograms, hormones, or whatever is in vogue, male supremacists make their case which is, in essence, that we are biologically too good, too bad, or too different to do anything other than reproduce and serve men sexually and domestically.

The newest variations on this distressingly ancient theme center on hormones and DNA: men are biologically aggressive; their fetal brains

THE GAY AND LESBIAN LITERARY COMPANION

were awash in androgen; their DNA, in order to perpetuate itself, hurls them into murder and rape; in women, pacifism is hormonal and addiction to birth is molecular. Since in Darwinian terms (interpreted to conform to the narrow social self-interest of men), survival of the fittest means the triumph of the most aggressive human beings, men are and always will be superior to women in terms of their ability to protect and extend their own authority. Therefore women, being "weaker" (less aggressive), will always be at the mercy of men. That this theory of the social ascendancy of the fittest consigns us to eternal indignity and, applied to race, conjures up Hitler's identical view of evolutionary struggle must not unduly trouble us. "By current theory," writes Edward O. Wilson reassuringly in *Sociobiology: The New Synthesis*, a bible of genetic justification for slaughter, "genocide or genosorption strongly favoring the aggressor need take place only once every few generations to direct evolution."[7]

3

> I have told you the very low opinion in which you [women] were held by Mr Oscar Browning. I have indicated what Napoleon once thought of you and what Mussolini thinks now. Then, in case any of you aspire to fiction, I have copied out for your benefit the advice of the critic about courageously acknowledging the limitations of your sex. I have referred to Professor X and given prominence to his statement that women are intellectually, morally and physically inferior to men ... and here is a final warning ... Mr John Langdon Davies warns women "that when children cease to be altogether desirable, women cease to be altogether necessary." I hope you will make note of it. (Virginia Woolf, *A Room of One's Own*)[8]

In considering male intellectual and scientific argumentation in conjunction with male history, one is forced to conclude that men as a class are moral cretins. The vital question is: are we to accept *their* world view of a moral polarity that is biologically fixed, genetically or hormonally or genitally (or whatever organ or secretion or molecular particle they scapegoat next) absolute; or does our own historical experience of social deprivation and injustice teach us that to be free in a just world we will have to destroy the power, the dignity, the efficacy of this one idea above all others?

Recently, more and more feminists have been advocating social, spiritual, and mythological models that are female-supremacist and/or matriarchal. To me, this advocacy signifies a basic conformity to the tenets of biological determinism that underpin the male social system. Pulled toward an ideology based on the moral and social significance of a distinct female biology because of its emotional and philosophical familiarity, drawn to the spiritual dignity inherent in a "female principle" (essentially as defined by men), of course unable to abandon by will or impulse a lifelong and centuries-old commitment to childbearing as *the* female creative act, women have increasingly tried to transform the very ideology that has enslaved us into a dynamic, religious, psychologically compelling celebration of female biological potential. This attempted transformation may have survival value—that is, the worship of our pro-creative capacity as *power* may temporarily stay the male-supremacist hand that cradles the test tube. But the price we pay is that we become carriers of the disease we must cure. It is no accident that in the ancient matriarchies men were castrated, sacrificially slaughtered, and excluded from public forms of power; nor is it an accident that some female supremacists now believe men to be a distinct and inferior species or race. Wherever power is accessible or bodily integrity honored on the basis of biological attribute, systematized cruelty permeates the society and murder and mutilation contaminate it. We will not be different.

It is shamefully easy for us to enjoy our own fantasies of biological omnipotence while despising men for enjoying the reality of theirs. And it is dangerous—because genocide begins, however improbably, in the conviction that classes of biological distinction indisputably sanction social and political discrimination. We, who have been devastated by the concrete consequences of this idea, still want to put our faith in it. Nothing offers more proof—sad, irrefutable proof—that we are more like men than either they or we care to believe.

DAVID B. FEINBERG

Essay by

MICHAEL BRONSKI

THE ADVENT OF AIDS, first reported in the *New York Times* in July of 1981, completely changed the tone and terrain of gay male fiction writing. While most post-Stonewall gay male fiction dealt with either coming out as a gay man, coming to terms with being a gay man, or discovering a place in the gay community, the reality of AIDS essentially fractured the limited scope of such inquiries. To a large degree, pre-AIDS gay male literature was a literature of discovery; post-AIDS, it is now a literature of immediate crisis. The tensions and quandaries of individuals, as well as a community, who are living with the continual onslaught of serious illness were bound to affect both the style and the narrative content of gay male writing in the 1980s and 1990s. The novels of David Feinberg are good examples of one kind of narrative strategy for dealing with the AIDS crisis. Immediate in tone and subject, Feinberg captures the social and psychological hysteria surrounding AIDS, containing it in a loosely knit, highly effective genre of first-person, confessional narrative.

David Feinberg was born in 1956 in Lynn, Massachusetts. He attended the Massachusetts Institute of Technology and later received an M.A. from New York University. While living for a time in Los Angeles, he came out in 1977 after attending the Gay Pride March. Feinberg began writing fiction in Los Angeles, and his first novel, *Calculus*, remains unpublished. After moving to New York City, he joined a gay male writing group and finally found a narrative voice with which he was comfortable. This voice—decidedly Jewish, definitely New York, and emotionally volatile—became the inspiration for B. J. Rosenthal, the narrator of his two novels *Eighty-Sixed* and *Spontaneous Combustion*. During this time the gay community began to organize against the AIDS epidemic and Feinberg joined AIDS Coalition to Unleash Power (ACT UP), an AIDS activist group that focused upon direct-action politics. Feinberg's involvement with ACT UP focused his political energy and greatly influenced both the tone and the content of his two novels.

In its first half, entitled "1980: Ancient History," *Eighty-Sixed* is a cross between the non-linear structure of a Jack Kerouac novel and the

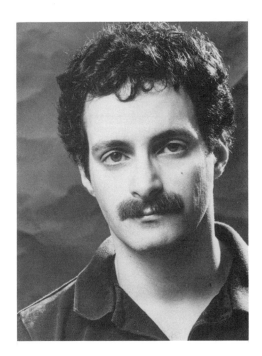

David Feinberg captures the social and psychological hysteria surrounding AIDS in his novels *Eighty-Sixed* and *Spontaneous Combustion*.

intense self-revelation/self-analysis of the work of Philip Roth. B. J. Rosenthal's voice is so strong and consistent that it allows Feinberg to deliver a tirade of description, opinion, and digression. He spins a circuitous plot involving his character's experiences with work, the search for sex, and the attempts to enjoy the delights of Manhattan while overcoming a sense of guilt whenever he has fun. In the book's second half, "1986: Learning How to Cry," AIDS begins to infiltrate Rosenthal's world when many of his friends and sex partners begin getting sick. It is then that Feinberg's (and Rosenthal's) compulsive narration begins to build to a strong emotional climax. And although there are no enormous plot developments—issues of work, sex, and guilt are joined by the need to take care of a sick friend—Feinberg effectively describes the enclosing terror and fear of living in a world dominated by AIDS.

Spontaneous Combustion takes up where *Eighty-Sixed* leaves off. B. J. Rosenthal discovers that he is HIV-positive, falls in love with his (heterosexual) doctor, looks for a lover, and joins ACT UP before ultimately getting used to the fact that he may, at some point in the future, become symptomatic with AIDS. Like *Eighty-Sixed,* the structure of *Spontaneous Combustion* is essentially a long jazz riff on the nature of life, sex, and death. Feinberg's most salient narrative coup is his ability to capture the frenetic quality of New York gay life without sacrificing either the mordant wit that acts as a defense against AIDS or the ever-present emotional terror of the disease.

As a stylist, Feinberg uses prose that recalls, curiously, the "then I did this, and then I did that" conversational poetry of gay poet Frank O'Hara. Neither *Eighty-Sixed* nor *Spontaneous Combustion* has a traditional narrative structure; rather, they move along, incident by incident, in an artful approximation of everyday life. The use of such a style attempts to convey the more open structure of urban gay life. Feinberg's use of camp, trenchant wit, and epigrammatic speech recalls the writings of Oscar Wilde as well as such gay stylists as Alfred Chester and Neil Bartlett.

In his tone, Feinberg clearly recalls the novels of Philip Roth by incorporating the compulsive self-analysis and the heightened awareness of being an "outsider." Roth's identity is that of a Jew who feels he lives outside the Jewish community. Likewise, Feinberg's is that of a gay Jew whose sexuality places him outside the Jewish community. Moreover, Feinberg's Jewishness marks him as an outsider to the gay community, and his health status as HIV-positive places him (irrevocably) outside the realm of the healthy. This sense of being the "outsider" allows Feinberg to establish his credentials as a social critic who is passionately concerned with questions of personal and social morality. For Feinberg, the moral questions of how casual sexual partners treat one another is as important as how ACT UP is attempting to force the United States government to act honorably and ethically about AIDS.

BREAKING UP WITH ROGER

How We Broke Up I

We broke up over omelets in a rather inexpensive restaurant in the East Village. I was dipping his French fries in ketchup. "Smoking is very glamorous," I said, putting two French fries in my nose à la Brooke Shields, pretending they were cigarettes.

"Breaking Up with Roger," June 1989, reprinted from *Spontaneous Combustion*, Viking Penguin, copyright 1991 by David B. Feinberg.

"Maybe you should stop that?" Roger Taylor suggested softly. Still, his voice was twelve octaves beneath my own harridan's shriek.

I had ordered an exotic omelet, which arrived with a mound of creamy green pesto that resembled avian cloaca from a rare and possibly extinct specimen. "Should I be eating garlic? Are we going to be kissing later tonight?" I asked, smearing my Italian bread with gobs and gobs of sauce.

"I don't think so," said Roger.

He cleared his throat.

"You'll probably hate me after I tell you what's on my mind."

"Oh, are you going to drop me?" I inquired, disingenuously. "Don't bother me with last week's news. I was *just* about to drop you. *Thanks for saving me the trouble.*"

"Shouldn't *I* be telling *you* this?" he asked, moderately relieved.

"Or do you mean that maybe we should sort of cool down for a while—you know, try to be apart and think about things and maybe dump one another in few weeks or so? Is that what you're trying to say?" I questioned.

"Something along those lines," he admitted. "I guess you're not as upset as I'd imagined."

"Why should I be upset, you cad, you hypocrite, you imbecile, you hateful scourge of society, you insect, you Precambrian layer of igneous material, you spineless creature, you jerk, you simpleton, you heartbreaker, you infidel, you bore, you know-nothing, you atheist, you Pet Shop Boys fanatic?" I said, as I tossed a glass of Mondavi Cabernet Sauvignon 1987 (a fruity, subtle, full-bodied varietal) at Roger, who was wearing a lesbian-identified lumberjack shirt.

He ducked. The slim and elegant waitperson ("Hi, my name is Gregory, and I'll be your server this evening"), who wore enough mousse in his neatly coifed hair to style seventeen Farrah Fawcetts, managed to catch the entire volume of liquid in a flask that he carried for such occasions.

Why Did We Break Up?

1. We had absolutely nothing in common, aside from HIV-antibody status.

2. Roger was deeply committed to a long-term till-death-do-us-part-or-at-least-till-I-run-out-of-conditioner relationship, and I, a novice at deep, meaningful, fulfilling relationships, had read only fifty pages of *The Male Couple's Guide to Living Together* in preparation.

3. I was a closet radical who went to demonstrations and shouted in protest and even once got arrested in the hopes of being strip-searched by the policeman of my dreams; Roger was so apolitical he didn't even *vote* in the last election (and if he *had* voted, he would have voted for *Bush,* but only because the name Dukakis didn't sound "presidential").

4. I was a proabortion atheistic knee-jerk pinko faggot; Roger was a Catholic who had spent several years unsuccessfully trying to cure himself of homosexuality because of the obvious religious conflict. Moreover, Roger was deeply offended by Madonna's video "Like a Prayer," whereas I worshiped her and secretly yearned to lick her stigmata.

5. Roger liked to have fun, and I preferred to suffer. Roger liked going out to bars and dancing on tabletops and smoking unfiltered cigarettes and eating brunch with other homosexuals of his ilk, whereas I preferred to stay home in my wreck of an apartment to the point of agoraphobia, reading the works of Schopenhauer, drinking bitters. Roger was extremely loyal to a highly selective group of friends numbering three, whereas in all of my relationships I was fundamentally promiscuous, and my acquaintances numbered in the hundreds. I'm sure he eventually smelled the rancid stench of my constant infidelity, which I was able to conceal so ingeniously that even I wasn't aware of it.

6. Roger was a virgin, and I was a whore. I would rush away a moment after ejaculation to wash off the *deadly* spermatozoa, and Roger would happily lie in puddles of spuck for days. I masturbated constantly—I'm masturbating this very second!—and Roger would rarely, if ever, perform an act of self-pollution, possibly because subconsciously the voice of God was telling him that it was a sin and he would go straight to hell if he did it, but more likely because he found it boring.

7. I was a pseudointellectual and a poseur and snob, and Roger was not particularly interested in printed matter when it didn't concern the internal mechanisms of automobiles: Whereas I read Kafka, Roger read car manuals.

8. I had complained that I didn't have enough time for a job, gym, reading, movies, plays, therapy, doctor's appointments, the beach, running, AIDS activism, museums, galleries, endless phone calls, visiting friends in the hospital, cleaning the apartment, doing the dishes, the laundry, ironing shirts, making dinner, eight hours of sleep each night, and a relationship; Roger responded sympathetically by casually eliminating the final item of my list.

9. Roger fell instantly, profoundly, completely, and eternally in love with me the moment we met: He told me he was experiencing deeper feelings for me than he had experienced for anyone else in the past eight years since his first cocaine-addicted lover named Larry, the first of three cocaine-addicted lovers named Larry (funny how we all have a "type"). And of course, two months later, after I returned from a ten-day separate vacation, he fell instantly, profoundly, completely, and eternally out of love with me. That was, of course, the point when I was gradually realizing that my feelings for him were growing to the point that separation would be unthinkable and I was actually considering releasing the floodgates of my frozen and stultifying emotions for a moment and admitting that maybe, just maybe, I might be in love with Roger; although, as one would expect, I only really fell in love with Roger two weeks after our tragic breakup.

How We Broke Up II

We broke up over dinner at the Heartbreak Restaurant, down in Soho.

The walls of the Heartbreak Restaurant were covered with repulsive art that changed every month: One month photorealistic canvases of grossly enlarged contorted faces blanketed the scene; this month, nonrepresentational splotches of violent shades of red. Our table, raised and centrally located, had two spotlights focused on it. The sound system

American novelist and essayist.

Born: Lynn, Massachusetts, November 25, 1956.

Education: Massachusetts Institute of Technology, S.B. 1977; New York University, M.A. 1981.

Career: Manager of MLACC for Modern Language Association of America since 1981. Regular contributor of stories and reviews to *Tribe, Outweek, Advocate, Gay Community News, Mandate, James White Review,* and *QW.*

Memberships: Active member of AIDS Coalition to Unleash Power (ACT UP).

Recipient: Lambda Literary Award for Gay Men's Fiction; American Library Association Gay/Lesbian Book Award for Fiction; New York Public Library Books to Remember Committee.

Address: c/o Modern Language Association of America, 10 Astor Place, New York, New York 10003, U.S.A.

---

played dramatic music from some unspecified *film noir* of the forties. On a videoscreen above the bar I could see Barbara Stanwyck with tears running down her black-and-white profile.

Roger was prompt and sweating slightly. I staggered to our table, having subsisted on vodka and cranberry juice during the past few weeks. The waiter left us separated checks when we ordered and informed us that tips were requested in advance of service, since very few meals were completed at the Heartbreak Restaurant.

"I have something to tell you," Roger began gently.

"Oh, are you going to drop me?" I inquired, disingenuously. "Don't bother me with last week's news. I was *just* about to drop you. *Thanks for saving me the trouble.*"

"There's no need to be nasty," he chided.

"What can I say? We laughed, we cried, we had good times, we had bad times. If you don't get on that plane, you'll regret it: maybe not today, maybe not tomorrow, but some day. Laszlo needs you more than I do. When you remember me," I said, arm poised with a glass of pink champagne, "and you will, you will, think of me kindly," I continued, tossing the contents at my white alligator shirt and stalking angrily out of the restaurant, to thunderous applause.

How Did We Meet?

We met in typical approaching-the-fin-de-siècle manner: at a People With AIDS Coalition Singles Tea. We had both come with friends who didn't want to go alone, hardly expecting to meet anyone ourselves, merely as support. My friend Jim said I would be Rhoda to his

Mary. Our friends had both developed full-blown AIDS; at the time Roger and I were asymptomatic antibody-positive.

The official *yenta*, a nice Jewish boy with aspirations in the profession of musical theater, asked exceedingly embarrassing questions of the gathered group to help narrow down our choices. Audience members raised their hands, indicating answers in the affirmative. "Who has more than twenty-seven T-cells? Who has less than fifteen hundred T-cells? Who is currently in a relationship with a member of the clergy and willing to have six to ten additional relationships on the side? Who has never had a relationship that lasted longer than the Broadway run of *Moose Murders*? Who owns an apartment in Zechendorf Towers? Who lives in a Salvation Army shelter? Who bites their nails? Who has a two-thousand-watt blow-dryer? Who has a penis that is ten inches or larger? (Please see me later in the back.) Who will have oral sex with a condom? Who will have oral sex with a condom only if the condom has a penis inside? Who is on aerosol pentamidine? Who owns their own nebulizer? Who rents? Who won more than ten thousand dollars in the New York lottery? Who goes to the gym more than five times a week? Who goes to twelve-step meetings more than twice a day? Who uses deodorant on a regular basis? Who shaves more than his facial hair? Who shaves more than his facial hair daily in the Chelsea Gym shower? Who has been in therapy for longer than ten years? Who hasn't been north of Fourteenth Street in ten years? Who has appeared as a model in *Mandate* magazine? Who used to hustle? Who is allergic to pubic hair? Who has slept with more than one thousand men in the past ten years? In the past five years? In the past ten weeks? Who has been disowned by his family? Who has disowned his family? Who likes to wear lace occasionally? Who is currently wearing frilly underwear? Who wouldn't mind displaying them to the group?" And so on.

By the time all of questions were asked, the only remaining question would be "Your place or mine?"

How We Broke Up III

One day it just happened. It was over. It ended. After a while I lost interest. We just let it fade away and die. I went home quietly and took an overdose of sleeping pills and turned on *Carson*. I went home quietly and called up the phone-sex line and had a lovely time. I went home quietly and baked a dozen hash brownies and sat there, eating them, watching a rerun of the final episode of *Berlin Alexanderplatz* on Arts and Entertainment. I went home quietly and rented a masseur and had a lovely time; he stole my stereo, my CD player, my VCR, and my personal computer, along with most of my software. I didn't care. Life was meaningless. I made a conscious effort to at least appear upset to the outer world. I failed. It was over. I didn't even notice his absence. I looked in my little black book and easily found a substitute. It ended quietly. There were no harsh words. We both agreed that we had relatively little in common, and although we did have a pleasurable experience, it was best to part. It was enough to just go home and cry into my Laura Ashley designer pillows and play Billie Holiday CDs and drink absinthe and smoke opium from a hookah and try to forget.

My old flame. I can't even remember his name.

What Did Roger Look Like?

Roger had deep, bright, sensitive brown eyes; thick, full, sensuous lips; a short, neatly cropped brown beard; and well-groomed brown hair thinning along the temples, indicating a high production of testosterone. He was extremely tall, at least for me: six foot one or two. He looked to be in his mid-to-late thirties. He was bundled in a plaid overshirt and jacket, possibly concealing several defects, for we met in the dead of winter. His clothing was rather unremarkable, leading me to the mistaken impression that he wasn't overly interested in fashion. His voice was deep and satisfying.

Later I would discover he had a not inconsiderable member, henceforth to be referred to in voice several octaves lower than my normal range as his "tool."

How We Broke Up IV

We broke up in a civilized manner. Afterward we returned to our respective apartments and shot ourselves with a single silver bullet in the head, between the eyes. Moments before, we had neatly laid newspaper around to catch spills and notified our menservants. We left our wills in plain sight. Unfortunately, we had named one another as executors and had, in fact, left the bulk of our estates to one another. The wills were in probate for years.

Why Did I Approach Roger?

I kept my eye on Roger throughout the question-and-answer period. He'd occasionally look in my direction. Jim and I came to the singles tea expecting the usual emergency-room overflow crowd, the kind of congregation one might find at Lourdes or at one of Louise Hays's evangelical lectures, ready to throw away their crutches and dance onstage with tambourines and ethyl rags. It wasn't quite that awful; still, it was like a bad night at the Barbary Coast: The pickings were pretty slim. Early on during the mass interrogation Jim and I decided that Roger was the only appealing prospect. Jim threw in the towel early, complaining that Roger hadn't noticed him. I then announced my intention to secure him.

So afterward I walked up, introducing myself. "Even though we're completely incompatible, since you are homeless and I am a complete slob, I would like to give you my phone number."

"I'm not homeless," said Roger, in a deep baritone that reverberated at the based of my spine.

"You didn't raise your hand at any of the questions regarding place of residence," I pointed out.

"I live on Long Island. It wasn't on the list."

In former years this would have been an automatic cause of disqualification—the red light, the buzzer, the seat-eject, the trapdoor, the shepherd's hook, you name it. However, in the approaching-the-fin-de-siècle manner, one uses a less exacting set of criteria in selecting possible dates. In other words, we've lowered our standards. There was a time when I didn't date men who smoked cigarettes, were in any of the design professions, wore leather pants, had tit rings, appreciated the opera, drank to excess, danced in the gym, or had been in therapy for more than ten years. Now, however, I'm just looking for a warm body to cuddle, hopefully with a life expectancy longer than that of my five-day deodorant. The rest is immaterial.

How We Broke Up V

Roger and I broke up every week, on Friday. After considerable experimentation we had decided that Friday would be optimal, giving us the rest of the weekend for a Harlequin "second chance at romance." We were doomed to repeat our breakup scenes endlessly, with only minor variations, in our version of Boyfriend Hell. One week I would break up with Roger; the following week, he would break up with me. One week I would toss a glass of chablis at Roger; the following week, he would retaliate with a glass of Mogen David wine, kosher for Passover. Yet, inextricably linked, powerless to resist, we remained faithful to our Friday-night assignations.

How Did Our First Date End in a Rather Typical Manner?

We promised not to start too fast and ended up having sex on the first date anyway.

"You seduced me!" he accused. "It was that look you gave me, with those big brown eyes of yours."

"They're hazel. If only you were paying attention."

"Whatever. It must have been what you whispered in my ear."

At every step Roger hesitated, from the door to the chair to the couch to the bed. Ever the disinterested participant, I was willing to offer no advice, either pro or con. I neither encouraged nor discouraged his advances; of this, I am certain he will dispute me. "I would rather get to know you better," he said on the couch, enveloping me in his brawny arms and kissing me on the cheek, "before we continue."

I offered the suggestion that we contain ourselves to necking and petting above the waist, with at least one foot on the floor at all times. Roger consented. All too soon, we went the way of all flesh. "Would you hate me if I stopped here?" asked Roger.

"Of course not," I murmured, circling his sensitive nipples with my tongue.

Perhaps we were both too passive to stop.

Was it my fault? I mentioned the possibility of a change of venue to the bed, in the interest of basic human comfort. Roger *was* six foot two, and my farcical couch was tiny, a suburban sleeper suitable for Japanese apartments and preadolescents. I had bought this midget divan for the express purpose of avoiding sleeping with a siren from the Midwest who had visited me roughly nine years earlier intent on converting me to the wonderful world of bisexuality—she who, like Marilyn Chambers, was "insatiable."

Of necessity, shoes were removed. At that point it only made sense to continue disrobing. Socks, pants, and expandable watch-bands were sporadically tossed in the direction of the couch. I hid under the sheets, burrowing deep down under like a gopher, curling up into a fetal position. Roger soon followed.

We were down to our underwear. "Would you feel foolish if we stopped here?" asked Roger.

Answering neither yes nor no, I went to the kitchen for twin glasses of water. When I returned, Roger lay flat on the bed, arms outstretched, legs spread, a pillow replacing his white Jockey shorts. His eyes were closed. Following the most primitive of all categorical imperatives, I doffed my shorts and dove in.

Was it a momentary lapse of reason, a convenient case of temporary amnesia, or merely situational ethics of the most abhorrent and venal kind? For some reason, in the heat of passion I invariably forget the logic behind not sleeping with someone on the first date. I vowed to spray-paint the elusive reasons in day-glo block letters on the ceiling for precisely these occasions.

We all have our own personal scales of intimacy. Perhaps mine was skewed? It ranged from such relatively impersonal contact like shaking someone's hands, greeting them on the street, having violent and profound sex with them, exchanging first names, sharing recreational drugs with them, pointing out unseemly semen stains in public to avoid undue embarrassment, to exchanging last names, adding phone numbers to the quick-dial feature of auto-memory, naming one another as correspondents in divorce cases, exchanging house keys, and so on.

Sleeping with someone was rather low on my scale of familiarity. "Don't take it personally," I rushed to reassure Roger, who feared we had gone too far and was consequently banging his head against the plaster. "What happened to you could have happened to anyone."

How We Broke Up VI

I was coming home from work late one evening. I decide to take the shortcut through Great Jones Alley. I patted my wallet self-consciously. I heard footsteps behind me. I started to pick up my pace. Soon, we were both running. I made a quick left into a blind alley. I was stuck. There was no way out.

He had a flashlight shining on me. I couldn't see his face. And then he spoke, that deep familiar voice of gravel. "This is for the emotional scars you've given me these past six months."

"But, Roger," I began, "I didn't mean to hurt you—" That was when I felt something harsh splashing on my eyes. I screamed. Battery acid. I was blinded for life.

Why Doesn't Anyone Go Slow Anymore?

Because there just isn't enough time.

How We Broke Up VII

Once we broke up, we severed all contact. I believe Roger moved to Baltimore the following autumn, with an insurance broker. I remained firmly ensconced in my venomous flat in Hell's Kitchenette. Christmas cards were not exchanged. Birthdays were forgotten. A few years later, it was as if I had never known Roger at all.

How Long Were Our First Three Dates?

Roger wanted to stay over. I acceded to his wishes, although my omnipresent infinite list of things to do weighed heavily on my mind.

It was a very long first date.

A few weeks later, I realized that each of our first three dates extended longer than twelve hours. Perhaps we were getting serious? I consulted my horoscope for clues. The enigmatic forecast was immediately covered with the wet quicksand of my failing memory.

When Did Roger Learn My Phone Number?

Roger learned my phone number by heart after our first date; I always referred to the yellow stickum on the bulletin board, next to the laundry ticket and the film-festival schedule. I ultimately didn't memorize his number until about two weeks *after* we broke up.

How Did Roger Kiss?

Every kiss was an event. Roger's kisses were gentle morning dew on my cheeks, teasing passes of a butterfly's wings at my lips, mad B-52 bombing runs on my mouth, kamikaze attacks on my throat, atomic-bomb explosions on my nipples, urgent stingray bites on my pelvis, laconic feathers slowly wafting their way earthbound on my stomach.

"Look!" he would say, pointing his finger toward the ceiling.

"What is it?"

"No, the other way," he'd continue, veiling his approach with subterfuge, throwing me off the track with false promises of Halley's comet. I would turn my head, following the imaginary trajectory of his fingertip to the sky.

He would bring his finger to my lips. "Shhh."

If I turned to look at him, he would warn, "Don't watch."

Shy and secretive, he would make his gentle approach, with all of the stealth of an invisible jet-bomber. "Don't move!"

I pretended I was in Bermuda, merely hallucinating Roger. I felt Roger wanted to protect me, rejuvenate me to the point of being too young to realize I was naked. "You don't want to spoil it, do you?" said Roger with his eyes.

Every kiss was magic. I can only fail in my attempts to describe the unbearable lightness of Roger's lips. Thus inclined, he would make his gradual approach. "Excuse me, what's that?" he would say. A piece of lint? A freckle? An invisible spot?

I would feel gentle, sweet soft contact on the cheek as Roger kissed the locus of our deception. "Got it!" he'd announce successfully. "It's gone now."

Who wouldn't swoon?

What Were We Afraid Of?

I was afraid of dying.

Roger was afraid of getting sick.

He said he didn't mind dying; it was just the getting sick that he hated.

I said, "Are you crazy? Nobody wants to die."

How Did We Get Along with One Another's Friends?

I hated all his friends, and he couldn't stand any of mine; every chance meeting was fraught with peril. It was safest when we stuck to our apartments and ordered out Chinese, rented old horror flicks, and had copious amounts of sexual intercourse.

The snideness of his friends' responses was unparalleled in the history of queendom. Roger's friends discussed accessories constantly, along with fashion utensils, sexual appliances, household demographics, make-up secrets, interior deconstructionism, and skin-care secrets. They all worked in the madcap world of design: remixing music videos, deranging window displays, bending hair, slinging hash, filing teeth, and so on.

My friend Cameron didn't fare any better with Roger. The three of us met in a Mexican restaurant. Cameron chose that moment to inform Roger that Madonna's latest blasphemous video had changed his life. Cameron then made us move to another table because the lighting was rather unflattering. For some reason that escapes me, Cameron grated on Roger's nerves, although Roger was kind enough not to bring it to my immediate attention.

Did Roger Sleep Naked at Night?

Of course he did.

What Kind of Underwear Did Roger Wear?

Roger wore plain full-cut white underwear, and I wore gray Calvin Kleins because I took vitamin B, and pee stains were rather unattractive.

How Does Roger Drop Men?

"I try to drop men as soon as I know that it won't work out," explained Roger to me on one of our twenty-three-minute post-breakup phone calls. "I don't believe in dragging out an affair. I try to be as gentle as possible in my approach. I usually hint around. I never break up over the telephone. It's always in person—usually over a chef salad."

"All I wanted was to better my personal record of three months for a relationship," I whined in reply. "I was hoping to break one hundred days. Maybe *Time* magazine would do an article on our relationship, like a recently inaugurated president. 'Roger and Me: The First Hundred Days.'"

"Everything was wrong from the start with us. The first time I saw you, sort of goofy looking, slouched down in that chair, an admitted slob, hair all over the place, painter's overalls with one suspender—not the height of fashion in my book, if you ask me."

"I don't recall posing the question," I replied, stung. "At least I've never been involved with cocaine addicts."

"Maybe it was a blind spot on my part."

"It's not as if I had any fantasies of sex with a grease monkey either."

"You were weird from the beginning. I should never have even dated you. Yet for some reason I was drawn to you. I don't know why."

What Did I Always Want to Do with Roger?

I always wanted to go for a drive on his motorcycle, with my long blond hair blowing in the wind, hugging him tight around the waist of his leather jacket, holding on for dear life as he sped around a curve. Unfortunately, at the time I was a brunette with a crew cut. And when I finally found the appropriate wig, Roger had already sold his Harley Davidson.

Roger had wanted a motorcycle for years, but when he finally got one, he was too nervous to drive it with any regularity.

Who Called the Other First after Our Tragic Breakup?

I suppose it was me.

Does Size Matter?

"And suppose I had a two-inch penis," asked Roger during one of our twenty-three-minute post-breakup phone calls. "If after you looked into my big brown eyes and boyishly sat next to me on the couch and then seduced me with your lips and took me over to the bed, leading me like the blind leading the blind, and then as we tussled on the bed and you caressed my legs, my thighs, my loins, feeling around, very casually, for some hardened *tool,* and then licking my bountiful chest, suppose after you had finally undressed me, taken off my shirt, my pants, then my underwear, you found that I had a two-inch penis. Would you have still loved me the same?"

"I probably would have pressed the bed-eject mechanism and sent you out flying through the window onto the hard sidewalk."

"You wouldn't have loved me for my charm, my wit, my sweet, loving kindness?"

"Of course not."

"I can't believe how shallow you are. You never loved me for what I am, just for a *thing.*"

"What about me? What about if I had a two-inch penis?"

"That's beside the point," responded Roger, in the sullen voice of a child refused. He paused for dramatic effect, long enough to let the dark and heavy cloud of guilt envelop me. "I was just playing with you," said Roger. "I was just teasing. You can tell, can't you?"

"How long is it, anyway?" I asked, wanting to quantify my lust once and for all.

"I never actually measured it. I think maybe eight and a half or nine inches. The last time I measured was when I was twelve. I don't know. It may have grown since then."

How Did I Fall in Love with Roger?

I fell in love with Roger over the phone approximately two weeks after our tragic breakup. Let me describe the progress of love: It is a slow

Novels

Eighty-Sixed, 1989.
Spontaneous Combustion, 1991.

Short Stories

"The Age of Anxiety," in *Men on Men 2*, edited by George Stambolian, 1988.

"If a Man Answers," in *Men on Men 4*, edited by George Stambolian, 1992.

Essays

"Queer and Loathing at the FDA: Revolt of the Perverts," in *Tribe*, (Baltimore), winter 1989.
"Notes From the Front Line," in *NYQ* (New York), 8 December 1992.
"Memorial Services From Hell," in *Gay Community News* (New York), April 1993 (special March on Washington promotional issue).

and fitful process, fraught with complications; it follows a narrow and tortuous path; it is accomplished through a series of almost imperceptible gradual shifts and the accretion of idiosyncracies and minute details of personality. My love, the love of a callous and jaded cynic from the island of Manhattan, was like a snowball in hell surreptitiously gathering frost from the freezer of a poorly maintained Kelvinator in the devil's locker room. And as I gradually fell in love with Roger, he became more and more remote from me: He was firmly resolved to uproot our geminate lust and render asunder the tendrils of our mutual affection. He became impermeable to my entreaties. My methods were inappropriate, my directives invalid, my tactics incoherent, as he remained inaccessible.

Love is Lucy van Pelt, Charlie Brown, and that goddamned football. Every autumn, Lucy convinces Charlie Brown that she won't pull it away at the last minute. Stupidly, he makes his approach, gathers speed, focuses all of his kinetic energy onto his right foot, lifts, and Lucy removes the ball as he is almost upon it; he kicks the air and falls flat on his back. Charlie Brown is in traction for months; he is psychologically paralyzed for life. Yet he persists in learning nothing from the experience, repeating it the following fall.

What Do I Plan on Doing?

I plan on seducing Roger back, so *I* can drop *him* properly.

Why Wouldn't It Have Lasted Anyway?

"Guess what I have?" asked Roger one day during one of our twenty-three-minute phone calls, about two months after our tragic breakup.

"Thrush."

"How'd you know?"

"I assumed it was something bad," I answered. "I assumed it wasn't something *that* bad, or you would have been more alarmed. Thrush is the least serious thing that you could have. Don't worry; it goes away. It's no big deal."

"I guess I should expect something like thrush with my T-cells."

"How low are they?"

"I dunno. They were around one hundred sixty in January," he replied.

"One hundred sixty! Why didn't you tell me? If I had known your count was that low, I wouldn't have even bothered attempting a relationship with you," I lied. "I was looking for a long-term relationship. Two, three, maybe even four weeks! And you obviously couldn't sustain that. You might as well have worn an egg-timer in place of your heart."

Why Didn't I Just Let Go Once and for All like Every Other Eligible Homosexual in Manhattan and Quite a Few Ineligible Ones and Go to the Spike on Saturday Night at One A.M.?

Because I didn't want to meet all of my six thousand ex-boyfriends at once. Every Saturday night there's a meeting of the Benjamin Rosenthal Ex-Fan Club. They convene at the Spike at midnight, at the wall by the pool table, to dish me.

Why???

Roger, sweet Roger. When I found out about the lymphoma, I wanted it to be anyone but you. I was already stuck with survivor's guilt, and neither of us was dead. Yet. But what do you expect from someone who wrote the book on the power of negative thinking (*How to Lose Friends and Irritate People*)? I always wanted to know why tumors were constantly compared to fruits, generally of the citrus variety. Roger had a tumor the size of a navel orange in his liver. As the famous Chinese philosopher Laotzu once said, "This sucks the big one."

Why did it have to be you, Roger? Why not me? This was the tragic knife in the side, the dagger at one's heart. I'm the personification of evil, whereas you were never anything but good, except, of course, when you callously dropped me, three cocaine addicts, and countless others.

So our eventual reconciliation, the first time we actually saw one another since our tragic breakup, which I have magnified into legend, into history, into melodrama, into an archetypal primal scene, took place at a Jewish hospital on the East Side. Were there strains of music in the hallways as I entered, men in somber rented tuxedos playing violins in the airshaft that his room looked out on? No, only silence, soundless television in the background. All three of Roger's hideous friends were there, in solidarity against me. And inevitably, I found myself falling in love with Roger for one last time.

We made out on the hospital bed after his friends left. Roger threatened to hang me from the ceiling, using the curtain tracks, and then to grease up his arm. He was just kidding, which was a good sign. In a few days he'd start chemo. "I guess my hair will fall out," he said, sorrowfully.

"It was bound to happen sooner or later."

"But I'm only twenty-six," he said.

"I know. I know."

I don't know why, but I almost cried when he told me over the phone, and I stopped myself. Does this make any sense? Does anything make any sense anymore? My friend Seymour Goldfarb died during the weekend we waited for Roger's liver biopsy. I went out to the hospital on Long Island to say good-bye to him on Saturday. He was breathing roughly, eyes closed. By Sunday he was gone.

What Does Roger Dream Of?

Roger dreams of a lover to take care of him the way he took care of his best friend, Bill, a few years ago. He still keeps Bill's photo in his wallet. Bill was one of the first to come down with AIDS, back in the early eighties.

Now Bill's mother comes to visit Roger at his home. A nervous nicotine addict with a three-pack-a-day habit, she invariably blows smoke into his face. Although she annoys him, he is too polite to tell her. Even when Roger chain-smoked around me, he was always careful to notice in which direction the wind blew. Since Roger got sick, he lost the taste for cigarettes.

The Future of Our Relationship

We talk on the phone every other day. Sometimes he calls me, but usually I call him.

I tell Roger that he's my pal. He likes the sound of the word "pal." I tell Roger that we'll be pals forever.

KATHERINE V. FORREST

ALTHOUGH SHE HAS written a number of novels featuring complex themes and plots, Katherine Virginia Forrest is perhaps best known for her series of police procedurals featuring lesbian detective Kate Delafield. The popularity of the Delafield books is due in large part to both their tight construction and empathetic heroine. "My objective in the series is to present entertaining fiction and also lesbian life in process," the author once noted: "a woman in a high visibility job who must deal with her sexual identity in a totally homophobic atmosphere."

Essay by
JANE JURGENS

Forrest introduced readers to her fictional sleuth in *Amateur City*. In this work—as well as the other books in the mystery series—Forrest presents Delafield as strong, self assured, and independent, but not above engaging in a romantic interlude while investigating a case. Delafield is, however, a "closeted" figure who goes to great lengths to separate her personal and professional life. On the job, she is diligent, correct, and patient, with a meticulous eye for detail. Mindful of the human element in her work, she has compassion for both the victim and the victim's family.

In *The Beverly Malibu*, Delafield, together with her partner Ed Taylor, investigates the especially gruesome murder of Owen Sinclair, a Hollywood director living in a Los Angeles apartment complex called the Beverly Malibu. During the course of the investigation, Forrest introduces a cast of bizarre characters and individual side plots that keep the reader guessing at the outcome. To further complicate matters, Delafield becomes involved emotionally and sexually with two of the prime suspects.

Delafield is pressured to take on a case involving the murder of Teddie Crawford, a young gay man, in *Murder By Tradition*. As her investigation proceeds, the LAPD detective is drawn so deeply into the case that it imperils both her career and her personal life. For the first time, despite her careful attempts to keep her sexual orientation separate from her professional life, Delafield is ultimately threatened with exposure.

Katherine V. Forrest is perhaps best known for her series of police procedurals featuring lesbian detective Kate Delafield.

Apart from her "Delafield" work, Forrest has also written a number of thematically complex novels. Her first work, *Curious Wine*, is a sustained romantic fantasy about love, exploration, discovery, and intense passion involving two women, Diana Holland and Lane Christianson. In *Daughters of a Coral Dawn*, the author introduces readers to Megan, Laurel, and the other women of Cybele who have fled their homeland—Earth—in search of a world of their own without men. *An Emergence of Green* explores themes of jealousy, indecision, loyalty, and doubt, as well as the emergence of lesbian identity in all its complexity. Forrest has also collaborated with Barbara Grier in a compilation of lesbian erotica entitled *The Erotic Naiad: Love Stories by Naiad Press Authors.*

***Katherine Forrest told the* Companion:**

"From the beginning, lesbian and gay lives were my writing focus because of my own membership in a community starved for accurate images of itself in print. My work is intended as a reflection of our lives, and of a cultural identity that incorporates all races, all colors, all creeds. Gay and lesbian literature, in my opinion, has become the most dynamic literature in America because of the sheer diversity of lesbian and gay lives. As a people, we have literally had to invent our lives, and, as lesbian editor Carol DeSanti of Dutton has remarked, ours remain 'the only untold stories'."

DAUGHTERS OF A CORAL DAWN

Excerpt reprinted from *Daughters of a Coral Dawn*, Naiad Press, copyright 1984 by Katherine V. Forrest.

Once we completed our home-based education and ventured out into the world we thought it would be more difficult to hide our gifts, especially when we all performed spectacularly well scholastically, and later, professionally. But we had one overwhelming advantage: We were women. Scant significance was attached to any of our accomplishments.

It was Diana, now a geneticist, and Demeter, a meditech, who made the first great contribution to our future. They discovered through experimentation that most Vernan genes are dominant and consequently mutation-resistant.

Canadian novelist and author of short fiction.

Born: Windsor, Ontario, April 20, 1939.

Education: Wayne State University, Detroit, Michigan, and University of California, Los Angeles.

Career: Fiction editor, Naiad Press, Tallahassee, Florida.

Memberships: Member of International PEN.

Recipient: Lambda Literary Award for *The Beverly Malibu* and *Murder By Tradition*.

Address: P.O. Box 31613, San Francisco, California 94131, U.S.A.

"It's why you had girls," Diana explained to Mother. "You couldn't have had a male no matter what."

Venus, our biologist, joined in further research. Additional experiments showed that our life expectancy was thirty years longer than an Earth male's; that unlike Mother who was pure Vernan, we were more likely to bear only two or three babies at most at one time, all girls; and that they would inherit the intellectual capacity of their mothers.

Selene the poet and Olympia the philosopher made the final valuable contributions, documenting and forecasting the continuing irrationality of Earth beliefs, customs, and mores, and clearly demonstrating the need for concern—and change.

* * *

We have just completed a week-long meeting of extraordinary scope, and have made our plans.

We will marry. We will all have as many births as our individual situations allow. And pass the word on to our daughters.

Isis has shown that if we have multiple births, and succeeding generations continue at that rate, exponentially there will soon be a female population explosion.

And we are perfectly concealed. Men will continue to notice us only for their sexual and nesting needs—which is what we want them to do. And by the time they observe that there has been an astonishing number of births of baby girls, it will be much too late.

I am Minerva the historian, and this is the first chapter of our saga ...

KATHERINE V. **FORREST** 185

WRITINGS

Novels

Curious Wine, 1983.
Daughters of a Coral Dawn, 1984.
An Emergence of Green, 1986.
Flashpoint, 1994.

"Kate Delafield" Novels

Amateur City, 1984.
Murder at the Nightwood Bar, 1987.

The Beverly Malibu, 1991.
Murder By Tradition, 1991.

Short Stories

Dreams and Swords, 1987.

Editor

The Erotic Naiad, with Barbara Grier, 1992.

The Romantic Naiad, with Barbara Grier, 1993.

ELSA GIDLOW

ELSA GIDLOW, a pioneer Bay Area lesbian poet, was the first American female poet of the early twentieth century to write almost exclusively and explicitly from an openly lesbian viewpoint. She was born in Yorkshire, England, in 1898, and her freethinking English parents moved when she was six to primitive quarters in the tiny schoolless French Canadian village of Tetreauville, Québec. Between early fear of her hard-drinking, ambitious father (who often declaimed popular poems), household chores, and helping her overburdened but always singing mother with younger children, Gidlow soon found her own secret place, a large rock between giant tree roots at the edge of a stream, where she developed a poetic fantasy life, an abiding dislike for snow, a longing for knowledge, and a hope for a salubrious climate.

Essay by
JIM KEPNER

Her "practical" father—who took correspondence courses, taught first-aid to railroad workers, and traveled comfortably on the job while keeping his wife tight-budgeted and pregnant, hoping for another son— thought Elsa's interest in poetry impractical. After a year traveling across Canada on the railroad as his secretary, Gidlow moved with her family to Montréal when she was 16. There she took a typing job, joined a library, experienced her first passionate friendship (the woman she loved got married), brought together a bohemian literary group, published a "little magazine" with much gay material, and took courses at McGill College (now University). At school she and her friends discovered the works of Havelock Ellis, Edward Carpenter, Baudelaire, Rimbaud, Verlaine, and other writers who seemed liberating at the time. Finding the classic literature of India also deeply influenced her.

Gidlow was inspired during her adolescence by reading press accounts of the feminist protests of the Pankhursts and their compatriots in London. Having seen her father's appalling treatment of her mother, the many infant deaths in the poor village, and having been accosted by men who exhibited themselves, she resolved very early never to marry. In "Footprints on the Sands of Time" she wrote, "When I filled out forms, I used to wonder if I really existed. For example: grammar school (none); high school (none); college (none); degrees (none); post graduate record

British, Canadian, and American poet and philosopher.

Born: Hull, Yorkshire, 1898; grew up in Montréal; came to the United States in the early 1920s.

Partnerships: Companion of 1) Violet Henry-Anderson (deceased); 2) Isabel Quallo.

Education: McGill College (now University).

Career: Journalist and editor of in-house industry periodicals, 1918–21; English secretary, Consulate of Serbians, Croatians and Slovenians, Montréal, 1922; poetry editor, then associate editor, *Pearson's*, New York City, 1921–26; editor, *Pacific Coast Journal of Nursing*, San Francisco, 1926–28; free-lance writer, 1940–68. Contributor to periodicals, including *Canadian Bookman, Feminist Studies, Forum, Pacific Weekly*, and *San Francisco Review*. Cofounder and owner of publishing house Druid Heights Books.

Memberships: Cofounder, 1962, treasurer, and member of the board, Society for Comparative Philosophy.

Recipient: Southern California Women for Understanding Lesbian Rights Award, 1981.

Died: Marin County, California, June 8, 1986, of a heart attack.

(none); honors and awards (none); marriages (none); children (none); religious affiliation (none). I do have a birth certificate."

Gidlow called poetry "a poet's way into the world, a path to connection … a key to unlocking her deepest self, discovering where that self joins with all that appears to be outside of it, ultimately to realize inseparability from the 'self' of every other being, human and non-human. If that suggests religion I cannot deny the resemblance … it comes to me forcibly that I am in the realm of the sacred … in its gut level place in human life, most particularly in the life of woman … our awe in the face of the whole mystery of our being, of Being itself, not any institutionalized doctrine or belief."

She published her first collection of poetry, *On a Grey Thread,* a book of explicit and passionate lesbian love verses, in 1923, when she "was too ignorant and too courageous to know better." Unmolded by the literary lions of the early twentieth century, her verse always lacked the defensiveness of so many gay and lesbian writers. She trusted her love and gloried in it—no lurking in the dark, no fear of discovery, no sense of guilt, no wallowing in willful degradation.

In *Ask No Man Pardon: The Philosophical Significance of Being Lesbian,* a 1975 pamphlet, she notes the continued fear and ignorance regarding Sapphic love; she also notes the contrast between the social imperatives, "Male and female created he them" and "go forth and multiply," and Nature's apparent love of diversity and spontaneity. "It appears to be natural to delight in union," she says, regardless of whether procreation is intended. If the way of the woman who takes delight in other

WRITINGS

Poetry

On a Grey Thread, 1923.
California Valley with Girls, 1932.
From Alba Hill, 1933.
Wild Swan Swinging, 1954.
Letters from Limbo, 1956.
Moods of Eros, Mill Valley, California, 1970.
Makings for Meditation: A Collection of Parapoems, Reverent and Irreverent, illustrations by Dearie Swick, 1973.

Sapphic Songs: Seventeen to Seventy, 1976; revised as *Sapphic Songs: Eighteen to Eighty, the Love Poetry of Elsa Gidlow*, 1982.

Other

Wise Man's Gold (drama in verse), 1972.
Ask No Man Pardon: The Philosophical Significance of Being Lesbian (essay), photographs by Ruth Mountaingrove, 1975.

Elsa, I Come With My Songs: The Autobiography of Elsa Gidlow, 1986.
Contributor, *A Lesbian Love Advisor* by Celeste West, illustrations by Nicole Ferentz, 1989.
Shattering the Mirror.

Adaptations

Selections from *Sapphic Songs* were set to music by K. Gardner as *Two Sapphic Songs*, 1982.

---

women "was unnatural, as claimed, why was so much pressure, so much conditioning, required to mold ... her to the socially prescribed role? ... Who instructs the dolfin, or the pine ... how to grow and function? How should they need instruction, being cells of the being of the Universal Mother, carrying within themselves her design?" She notes that botanists regard each new variation with interest and excitement, never asking if the fritillary butterfly is abnormal for not conforming to the pattern of the monarch. While not demeaning the contribution of mothers, she discusses the signal contributions that women-loving women have made and can make to society if they are not forced into roles contrary to their own natures.

In 1981 the Southern California Women for Understanding and the International Gay and Lesbian Archives held a reception for Gidlow in the Hollywood Hills after presenting SCWU's 1981 Lesbian Rights Award to her. Her last remaining copy of *On a Grey Thread*—possibly the first book of open lesbian verse published in America—as well as a lock of the long hair she had cut in 1923 (swearing never again to wear it long), and other historically important personal mementos, were displayed under glass on the patio—and stolen. Miraculously, they were returned to the Archives weeks later by a chagrined woman who said, "My lover is a klepto," and left.

Gidlow left behind a frank, sensitive, and challenging autobiography in *Elsa, I Come with My Songs*, and was a contributor to Celeste West's *A Lesbian Love Advisor*. In her graceful and moving appearance in the film *The Word Is Out*, asked when she became a lesbian, Gidlow replied, "I never know what that means! I feel I was born this way!"

FOR THE GODDESS TOO WELL KNOWN

Poem first published in
Sapphic Songs, Druid
Heights Books.

I have robbed the garrulous streets,
Thieved a fair girl from their blight,
I have stolen her for a sacrifice
That I shall make to this night.

I have brought her, laughing,
To my quietly dreaming garden.
For what will be done there
I ask no man pardon.

I brush the rouge from her cheeks,
Clean the black kohl from the rims
Of her eyes; loose her hair;
Uncover the glimmering, shy limbs.

I break wild roses, scatter them over her.
The thorns between us sting like love's pain.
Her flesh, bitter and salt to my tongue,
I taste with endless kisses and taste again.

At dawn I leave her
Asleep in my wakening garden.
(For what was done there
I ask no man pardon.)

ALLEN GINSBERG

ALLEN GINSBERG grew up in Paterson, New Jersey, in a house full of politics and poetry. His father, Louis, was a teacher and a published poet known in literary circles in New York. His mother, Naomi, plagued with bouts of paranoia and delusion over her political causes, nonetheless was active in communist groups throughout her years before incarceration in various asylums. The young Ginsberg grew up under the conventionality of his father's poetry and the duress of a sick mother whom he was often called upon to care for. He eventually rebelled against both parents out of shame and anger and then strove to merge their different worlds into his own writing.

Essay by
PAUL CHRISTENSEN

From early adolescence on, Ginsberg was aware of homosexual stir-rings, and for the need to conceal them. After being drawn to Columbia in pursuit of a man he was attracted to in high school, Ginsberg seeming-ly led a double life as a student and tormented closet lover. He wrote much bad verse in those years, then in 1945 befriended the novelist Jack Kerouac, who had dropped out from Columbia several years earlier. Ginsberg was expelled for sheltering Kerouac in his dorm room and for having scrawled an obscenity on his dorm window. He moved into a communal apartment nearby and fell in with the demimonde society of William Burroughs and his cronies in the drug and skin trades. He flung himself into the fleshpots of 42nd Street, and took his "real" education in the underground classics of the era from Burroughs, who tutored Kerouac; Lucien Carr, a classmate; and Neal Cassady, an idol of the Beats to come.

Ginsberg drifted briefly, but his bad-boy persona was only skin deep. He returned to Columbia to study until 1948, when he became entangled in the fencing of stolen property then being stored in his apartment by Herbert Huncke. Huncke was reputedly the coiner of the word "Beat," a word that referred to the tired, down-and-out, and jazz-crazed postwar generation coming of age in America. Ginsberg copped a plea of insanity and rusticated in Columbia's own psychiatric ward, where he met Carl Solomon, his second tutor in underground culture. Ginsberg's 1955 mas-terpiece "Howl" is dedicated to this well-read, savvy bohemian.

Allen Ginsberg at the Beat Hotel on Rue Gît-le-Coeur, Paris, in 1956, a year after the publication of "Howl."

After writing orderly and rhyming verses, which William Carlos Williams, a willing mentor and member of the original Modernist generation, dismissed as amateurish, Ginsberg tossed aside his literary ambitions, taking odd jobs in New York. He was stymied by a conventional education and the misadventures of his love life.

When Neal Cassady came into New York City from Denver in 1946, leaving behind a father who was a notorious derelict of that city's Skid Row, he took command of the Burroughs group with legendary spiels on any subject. Ginsberg and Kerouac both listened, spellbound by a spontaneous street-honed eloquence not heard since pioneer days. They took notes, labored over his style, and—with the aid of mind-altering drugs—began to incorporate that lush cascade of words into their own writing. Kerouac was the more adept at it, and was soon advocating a new mode of prose that strung together vast outpourings of mind from chemically induced states. The outcome was his ground-breaking 1957 novel, *On the Road.*

Ginsberg's progress was slower, with more to give up from his father's example. Cassady had liberated him, and Kerouac and Burroughs provided alternative art forms. Not until he left New York in December of 1953, bound for Mexico and California—where his sometime lover, Cassady, now resided—did he make the plunge to open forms and write his classic, "Siesta in Xbalba," which predates "Howl."

Ginsberg's homosexuality was a link to his mother's underground life as a communist; both went against the American grain. It was not until his romance with Cassady that he came out to friends. Now, with Burroughs's world opened to him and art as its expression, he devised a method of splicing and rapid-fire phrasing that gave him a voice. Minted with that voice was his vision of a natural world of harmonious dynamics. Ginsberg abandoned conventional philosophy (and literature) to cultivate a view of nature as the sum of erotic forces willingly merging to create life, a view he derived in part from study of the Modernist poet Ezra Pound.

Homosexuality was at the base of his esthetic; a code of permissive sexuality eliminated the resistance and seduction of orthodox love. Cleared of these antithetical principles, Ginsberg's poetry could apply the dynamics of homosexuality to the rest of experience, and begin to merge

THE GAY AND LESBIAN LITERARY COMPANION

the otherwise irresolvable and antagonistic elements of life into a cosmic hymn. Out of such musing (and close study of the elliptical joinery of the Japanese haiku) came a spontaneous poetry, made famous by his phrase "hydrogen jukebox" in "Howl," where fragments and categorical opposites form polysemous wholes. Ginsberg has said his youthful studies of Cezanne's painting, with their cubist angles joined together to form human figures and landscapes, was another breakthrough to his method.

Ginsberg lecturing at Washington's Evergreen State College in 1980.

Ginsberg's language took a path around the more aggressive forms of conventional grammar, where a subject is made to strike or transform an object through the verb. In Ginsberg's poetry, images cohere loosely through enjambments and strings of hyphenated clauses, fusing together the desiderata of daily life into "reality sandwiches," as he later called them. His world is slightly skewed through drugs or an aroused surrealistic humor. A parade of low-lifers, tramps, ragamuffins, drag queens, addicts, and criminals—the marginal life Whitman had blessed in his 1855 "Song of Myself"—convenes in the poetry of *Howl, and Other Poems* in 1956, *Kaddish* in 1961, and *Reality Sandwiches* in 1963.

"Howl" champions the downtrodden while castigating the "system" in America. The nemesis of the young and free-spirited is a puritanical government living by the old oppositional philosophy. Ginsberg deconstructs some of that authority in "Howl" and in his 1958 "Kaddish," an elegy to his dead mother in which he employs elements of repressive Christianity, militarism, and corporate oligarchy in defining a version of "Moloch," the god who devours children. Early on, Ginsberg was against war; he had declared himself a homosexual in World War II and received a psychological discharge. Thereafter he opposed war as commercial venturing that squandered innocent life. He was active against the Vietnam War as well.

"Howl" attacked the power elite, but a poetry of encompassing reality in all its forms was the weapon he aimed at smug propriety and repression. Where others hid their sexual preferences under masks of conven-

ALLEN **GINSBERG**   193

American poet.

Born: Newark, New Jersey, June 3, 1926.

Education: Columbia University, A.B. 1948.

Career: Served in the U.S. military during World War II; discharged. Worked variously as a spot welder in the Brooklyn Naval Yard, 1945, as a dishwasher, 1945, and on various cargo ships, 1945–56; worked as a literary agent, a reporter for a New Jersey union newspaper, and as a copy boy for *New York World Telegram*, all 1946; night porter for the May Co. in Denver, Colorado, 1946; book reviewer for *Newsweek* in New York City, 1950; market research consultant in New York City and San Francisco, 1951–53; instructor at the University of British Columbia, Vancouver, Canada, 1963; founder and treasurer of the Committee on Poetry Foundation, 1966–; organizer of the Gathering of the Tribes for a Human Be-In, San Francisco, 1967; cofounder, codirector, and teacher, Jack Kerouac School of Disembodied Poetics at the Naropa Institute (the first Buddhist-inspired accredited college in the western hemisphere), Boulder, Colorado, 1974–. Has given poetry readings and has exhibited his photographs around the world in such countries as Austria, England, France, Germany, India, Japan, Peru, Poland, and Russia. Participant and speaker at numerous conferences, including the Gay and Lesbian Writers Conference in San Francisco, 1990. Has appeared in numerous films, including Robert Frank's *Pull My Daisy*, 1960, *Wholly Communion*, 1965, *Don't Look Back*, 1967, and *Renaldo and Clara*, 1978.

Memberships: Member of the National Institute of Arts and Letters, PEN, and the New York Eternal Committee for Conservation of Freedom in the Arts.

Recipient: Woodbury Poetry Prize; Guggenheim fellowship, 1963–64; National Endowment for the Arts grant, 1966; National Institute of Arts and Letters award, 1969; National Book Award for Poetry for *The Fall of America*, 1974; National Arts Club Medal of Honor for Literature, 1979; National Endowment for the Arts fellowship, 1986.

Address: P.O. Box 582, Stuyvesant Station, New York, New York, U.S.A.

---

tion, Ginsberg drew his sexual life directly into poetry, graphically describing his amours and orgasms in vivid, sometimes lurid detail. "Sweet Boy, Gimme Yr Ass" and "Come All Ye Brave Boys" from *Mind Breaths* in 1978 are representative of the genre: dense, erotic, and funny, motivated partly by a desire to shock the heterosexual reader. Even with sex on dining tables and floors, in backseats and bedrooms, there is no power play by the lover; in many of these erotic episodes Ginsberg plays the submissive partner, the clown, the meek hedonist taking pleasure from willing participants. He says in "Love Returned" of a young lover, "I don't have to beg ... he's willing & trembles."

Ginsberg met his lifelong companion Peter Orlovsky at a Christmas party in San Francisco in 1954; Ginsberg has celebrated this relationship as the mainspring of harmony in his life. The troubled affair with Cassady, who had married in his absence, and misadventures with females before and after, added a plaintive note to his earlier, self-absorbed lyrics; with Orlovsky the poems shift to boisterous eroticism and excess. Against such freedom lay the establishment with its war economy and waste, its repression and relentless exploitation of "consumers." Here

Ginsberg's writing celebrates sexual freedom and its ideological corollaries, civil rights, ecology, and pacifism.

WRITINGS

Poetry

Howl, and Other Poems, introduction by
William Carlos Williams. 1956; as
Howl Annotated, with facsimile man-
uscript, 1986.
Siesta in Xbalba and Return to the States,
1956.
Kaddish, and Other Poems, 1958–1960,
1961.
Empty Mirror: Early Poems, 1961.
The Change, 1963.
Kral Majales ["King of May"], 1965.
Wichita Vortex Sutra, 1966.
TV Baby Poems, 1967.
*Airplane Dreams: Compositions from
Journals*, 1968.
Ankor Wat, with Alexandra Lawrence,
1968.
Scrap Leaves, Tasty Scribbles, 1968.
Wales—A Visitation, July 29, 1967,
1968.
The Heart Is a Clock, 1968.
Message II, 1968.
Planet News: 1961-1967, 1968.
For the Soul of the Planet Is Wakening…,
1970.
The Moments Return, 1970.
Ginsberg's Improvised Poetics, edited by
Mark Robison, 1971.
New Year Blues, 1972.
Open Head, 1972.
Bixby Canyon Ocean Path Word Breeze,
1972.
Iron Horse, 1972.
*The Fall of America: Poems of These
States, 1965–1971*, 1972.
*The Gates of Wrath: Rhymed Poems,
1948–1952*, 1972.
*Sad Dust Glories: Poems during Work
Summers in Woods, 1974*, 1975.
*First Blues: Rags, Ballads, and
Harmonium Songs, 1971–1974*, 1975.
Mind Breaths: Poems 1971–1976, 1978.
*Poems All Over the Place: Mostly
Seventies*, 1978.
Mostly Sitting Haiku, 1978; revised and
expanded, 1979.
Careless Love: Two Rhymes, 1978.
*Straight Hearts' Delight: Love Poems and

Selected Letters, with Peter Orlovsky,
1980.
*Plutonian Ode, and Other Poems,
1977–1980*, 1982.
Collected Poems, 1947–1980, 1984.
White Shroud Poems: 1980–1985, 1986.

Prose

Prose Contribution to Cuban Revolution,
1966.
*Allen Verbatim: Lectures on Poetry,
Politics, Consciousness*, edited by
Gordon Ball, 1975.
Your Reason and Blake's System, 1988.

Letters

The Yage Letters, with William S.
Burroughs, 1963.
The Visions of the Great Rememberer,
1974.
To Eberhart from Ginsberg, 1976.
*As Ever: Collected Correspondence of
Allen Ginsberg and Neal Cassady*,
with Neal Cassady, 1977.

Journals

*Indian Journals: March 1962–May 1963;
Notebooks, Diary, Blank Pages,
Writings*, 1970.
*Notes after an Evening with William
Carlos Williams*, 1970.
Journals: Early Fifties, Early Sixties, edit-
ed by Gordon Ball, 1977.
Japan and India Journals, 1960–64, by
Joanne Kyger, with photographs by
Ginsberg and others, 1981.

Contributor

The Marijuana Papers (essays), edited by
David Solomon, 1966.
*Background Papers in Student Drug
Abuse*, edited by Charles Hollander,
1967.
*Pardon Me Sir, but Is My Eye Hurting
Your Elbow?* (plays), edited by Bob
Booker and George Foster, 1968.
Contributor of commentary, *May Day
Speech*, by Jean Genet, 1970.

Poetics of the New American Poetry
(essays), edited by Donald M. Allen
and Warren Tallman, 1973.
Philip Glass: The Hydrogen Jukebox,
1992.

Photograph Books

Reality Sandwiches, 1963.
Allen Ginsberg and Robert Frank, 1985.
Allen Ginsberg Fotografier 1947–1987,
1987.
Allen Ginsberg: Photographs, introduc-
tion by Robert Frank, with pho-
tographs by Ginsberg, 1991.
Snapshot Poetics, 1993.

Other

Translator with others, *Poems and
Antipoems* by Nicanor Parra, 1967.
Compiler, *Documents on Police
Bureaucracy's Conspiracy against
Human Rights of Opiate Addicts and
Constitutional Rights of Medical
Profession Causing Mass Breakdown of
Urban Law and Order*, 1970.
The Fall of America Wins a Prize (speech
text), 1974.
Chicago Trial Testimony, 1975.
*Madiera and Toasts for Basil Bunting's
Seventy-fifth Birthday*, with others,
edited by Jonathan Williams, 1977.
The Cantos (125–143) Ezra Pound, with
Robert Creeley, edited by Michael
Andre, 1986.
Nuke Chronicles, with others, 1980.

Recordings

*Songs of Innocence and of Experience by
William Blake Tuned by Allen
Ginsberg*, 1970.
Birdbrain, 1981.
First Blues: Songs, 1982.
The Lion for Real, 1989.

Adaptations

Kaddish (play; produced Brooklyn
Academy of Music, Brooklyn, New
York, 1972).

was the only enemy to pagan joy, and like his mother Naomi before him, he railed against these powers at poetry readings, sit-ins, and meditations with peaceniks and anti-nuke groups.

Ginsberg's writing is a coherent celebration of sexual freedom and its ideological corollaries, civil rights, ecology, and pacifism. He drew ideas from a wide variety of sources to write his poetry and was attracted to Hinduism and Buddhism because of their theology of harmonious relations between spirit and flesh, gods and mortals, death and life. These too play a prominent role in his poems as forms of human integration.

Like Robert Duncan, his counterpart on the West Coast, Ginsberg believed in a mode of spontaneous composition in which to capture the mind at play. Man corrupts only when he imposes a stifling logic to his thoughts; the raw energies of nature are inherently virtuous and coherent, but human eyes are often blind to the original beauty of creation. The sexual urge in all its forms is part of that original energy; like Whitman, Ginsberg celebrates love between men as another of its forms and a binding power of otherwise formless masses of humanity.

TO AUNT ROSE

Aunt Rose—now—might I see you
with your thin face and buck tooth smile and pain
        of rheumatism—and a long black heavy shoe
          for your bony left leg
limping down the long hall in Newark on the running carpet
       past the black grand piano
        in the day room
           where the parties were
   and I sang Spanish loyalist songs
     in a high squeaky voice
       (hysterical) the committee listening
    while you limped around the room
     collected the money—
Aunt Honey, Uncle Sam, a stranger with a cloth arm
    in his pocket
      and huge young bald head
        of Abraham Lincoln Brigade

Reprinted from *The Norton Anthology of Poetry*, 3rd edition, 1983.

ALLEN **GINSBERG**

—your long sad face
　　　　　your tears of sexual frustration
　　　　　　　　(what smothered sobs and bony hips
　　　　　　　　　　　under the pillows of Osborne Terrace)
—the time I stood on the toilet seat naked
　　　　　and you powdered my thighs with Calomine
　　　　　　　against the poison ivy—my tender
　　　　　　　　　　and shamed first black curled hairs
what were you thinking in secret heart then
　　　　　　　knowing me a man already—
and I an ignorant girl of family silence on the thin pedestal
　　　　　　　of my legs in the bathroom—Museum of Newark.
　　　　　　　　　　Aunt Rose
　　　　　Hitler is dead, Hitler is in Eternity; Hitler is with
　　　　　　　Tamburlane and Emily Brontë

Though I see you walking still, a ghost on Osborne Terrace
　　　　　　　down the long dark hall to the front door
　　　　　　　limping a little with a pinched smile
　　　　　　　　in what must have been a silken
　　　　　　　　　　flower dress
　　welcoming my father, the Poet, on his visit to Newark
　　　　　　　—see you arriving in the living room
　　　　　　　　　dancing on your crippled leg
　　　　　　　and clapping hands his book
　　　　　　　　　had been accepted by Liveright

Hitler is dead and Liveright's gone out of business
The Attic of the Past and *Everlasting Minute* are out of print
　　　　　　　Uncle Harry sold his last silk stocking
　　　　　　Claire quit interpretive dance school
　　　　　　　　Buba sits a wrinkled monument in Old
　　　　　　　　　Ladies Home blinking at new babies

last time I saw you was the hospital
　　　　　　　pale skull protruding under ashen skin
　　　　　　　blue veined unconscious girl

in an oxygen tent
the war in Spain has ended long ago
Aunt Rose

JEWELLE
GOMEZ

THE FICTION AND POETRY of Jewelle L. Gomez is a hybrid of politics and imagination. Although Gomez is a noted writer with a novel, two books of poetry, and a collection of essays to her name, she is also known as an astute political organizer and activist.

Essay by

MICHAEL BRONSKI

Born in Boston in 1948, Gomez graduated from Northeastern University in 1971 and Columbia School of Journalism in 1973. Her earliest work was in public television and between 1968 and 1971 she worked on the Boston-based series *Say Brother*, one of the first weekly Black television programs. In the mid-1970s she helped produce the Children's Television Workshop in New York. After years of teaching creative writing and Women's Studies, she became, in 1989, the director of the Literature Program of the New York State Council on the Arts, where she remained until 1993.

During this time Gomez was also involved as a social activist with a special interest in issues of lesbian and gay representation. She was a founding board member of Gay and Lesbian Alliance Against Defamation (GLAAD), an organization that agitated against homophobic depictions in the print and electronic media, as well as a member of the Feminist Anti-Censorship Taskforce, a group founded to supply a feminist, sex-positive analysis of anti-pornography campaigns.

While much of Gomez's two books of poetry—*The Lipstick Papers* in 1980, and *Flamingoes and Bears* in 1986—celebrates lesbian life and sexuality, much of her other writing consists of more detailed analyses of how lesbian and gay male culture can understand and articulate erotic and political differences. In a keynote address presented at the 1991 Creating Change Conference in Arlington, Virginia, Gomez spoke about the need for the lesbian and gay community to analyze how it uses and misuses power: "We have power. White men have power they use over each other and over women. They use it to the benefit of each other and the few lesbians they find acceptable. Lesbians use their power of acceptance in their various social circles for each other and against others they don't think are cool enough or well-dressed enough ... [b]lack gays use our

Jewelle Gomez is both a noted writer—with a novel, two books of poetry, and a collection of essays to her name—and an astute political organizer and activist.

power to 'dis' to keep ourselves isolated from the movement … [s]ome lesbians curse the power of sexual imagery without ever examining what that power means to lesbians."

Part of Gomez's analysis of power is manifest in how the lesbian and gay community, as well as the mainstream media, construct images of homosexuals. On a 1990 panel celebrating butch/femme identity, held at the Gay and Lesbian Community Center in Manhattan, Gomez noted: "As a writer who's also black, who's also a lesbian, a good part of my early life was spent examining mythology and stereotypes that were damaging to me. In order for me to write characters and create situations that I thought were true to the spirit of people I wanted to represent, I had to confront many stereotypes." Gomez's warning against stereotypes is moderated, however, by an injunction against looking for easy acceptability. At the Creating Change Conference she noted that "desire for acceptance is the antithesis to the desire for change. I fight every day not to return to that desire to be accepted into the familiar order of things."

Gomez's novel, *The Gilda Stories*, is an eloquent explication of her political theories. Spanning 200 years—from 1850 to 2050—*The Gilda Stories* tells the story of an African American lesbian vampire making her way through history and across cultures in a continual attempt to make sense of her life. By reclaiming several genres—the horror story, the picaresque, and the social history novel—and reimagining them from a lesbian-feminist point of view, Gomez inserted her sensibility and politics and managed to interrupt and change a traditionally male narrative. The effect of *The Gilda Stories* is not only to present us with positive images of lesbians but also to allow us to see how a whole range of traditional writing, by excluding women, gay people, or people of color, is limited by its own exclusive point of view. As such it is as much a work of literary criticism as it is a novel in its own right.

American novelist, social activist, and teacher of creative writing.

Born: Boston, Massachusetts, September 11, 1948.

Partnerships: Companion of Diane Sabin, beginning 1992.

Education: Northeastern University, B.A. 1971; Columbia University School of Journalism, M.S. 1973.

Career: Worked in production, WGBH-TV, Boston, for *Say Brother*, 1968–71; WNET-NY, New York City, 1971–73; and for the Children's Television Workshop, New York City, 1970s; worked in various capacities, including stage manager, at Off-Broadway theatres, 1975–80; lecturer in women's studies and English, Hunter College, 1989–90; director of Literature Program, New York State Council on the Arts, 1989–93.

Memberships: Founding board member, Gay and Lesbian Alliance Against Defamation (GLAAD); member of Feminist Anti-Censorship Taskforce (FACT); member of board of advisors, Cornell University Human Sexuality Archives, National Center for Lesbian Rights, and *Multi-Cultural Review* magazine.

Recipient: Ford Foundation fellowship, 1973; Beards Fund award for fiction, 1985; Barbara Deming/Money for Women Award for fiction, 1990; Lambda Literary awards for fiction and science fiction for *The Gilda Stories*, 1991.

Agent: Frances Goldin, 305 East 11th Street, New York, New York 10003, U.S.A.

JEWELLE GOMEZ TOLD THE COMPANION:

"The strategic efforts of the dominant culture to make invisible or belittle the contributions and influence of people of color, women, and lesbians in the United States make my writing a survival technique for myself and the millions of others like me. I write out of a deep sense of history that was instilled by living with my great-grandmother until I was 22 years old. She looked at history with an unflinching eye, but still felt hopeful about the world. That is the perspective I try to take in my fiction and essays. I want to write about larger-than-life characters who still reflect the struggles that each of us must face every day. That is why writing fantasy fiction appeals to me. I enjoy creating in a form that is considered lightweight because so many 'heavy' ideas can be slipped in. The principals of feminism and all the social changes they imply can be made to represent the value system of benign vampires without feeling didactic.

"Another important element which I became aware of because of my great-grandmother, and which I bring to my work, is the importance of acknowledging and using our full selves as we go about our work. My great-grandmother was African American, but she was also Native American. She was born on a reservation in Iowa and lived to see the first man walk on the moon. She carried with her many contradictions, as we all do. In order to be fully myself, and to write as fully as I want, I keep all the elements of my life under consideration: Black, lesbian, feminist, former Catholic, part of the Black Nationalist movement of the 1960s and the anti-war movement of the 1970s. All these elements of who I am are important and none should be sacrificed. I think I write for all of the people who were important to me in each of the phases of my life, whether it's my best friend from high school, my regular customers when I used to wait tables in a bar, the women who worked with me at Gimbels department store or the students who take my courses, or other writers I admire, living or dead."

DON'T EXPLAIN

Boston 1959

Reprinted from *Love, Struggle & Change*, edited by Irene Zahava, copyright 1988 by The Crossing Press. Lyrics to "Don't Explain" are by B. Holiday and A. Herzog, Jr., Northern Music Co. (ASCAP).

Letty deposited the hot platters on the table, effortlessly. She slid one deep-fried chicken, a club-steak with boiled potatoes and a fried porgie platter down her thick arm as if removing beaded bracelets. Each platter landed with a solid clink on the shiny formica, in its appropriate place. The last barely settled before Letty turned back to the kitchen to get Bo John his lemonade and extra biscuits and then to put her feet up. Out of the corner of her eye she saw Tip coming in the lounge. His huge shoulders, draped in sharkskin, barely clearing the narrow door frame.

"Damn! He's early tonight!" she thought but kept going. Tip was known for his generosity, that's how he'd gotten his nick-name. He always sat at Letty's station because they were both from Virginia, although neither had been back in years. Letty had come up to Boston in 1946 and been waiting tables in the 411 Lounge since '52. She liked the people: the pimps were limited but flashy; the musicians who hung around were unpredictable in their pursuit of a good time and the "business" girls were generous and always willing to embroider a wild story. After Letty's mother died there'd been no reason to go back to Burkeville.

Letty took her newspaper from the locker behind the kitchen and filled a large glass with the tart grapejuice punch for which the cook, Mabel, was famous.

"I'm going on break, Mabel. Delia's takin' my station."

She sat in the back booth nearest the kitchen beneath the large blackboard which displayed the menu. When Delia came out of the bathroom Letty hissed to get her attention. The reddish-brown skin of Delia's face was shiny with a country freshness that always made Letty feel a little warm.

"What's up, Miss Letty?" Her voice was soft and saucy.

"Take my tables for twenty minutes. Tip just came in."

The girl's already bright smile widened, as she started to thank Letty.

"Go 'head, go 'head. He don't like to wait. You can thank me if he don't run you back and forth fifty times."

Delia hurried away as Letty sank into the coolness of the over-stuffed booth and removed her shoes. After a few sips of her punch she rested her head on the back of the seat with her eyes closed. The sounds around her were as familiar as her own breathing; squeaking Red Cross shoes as Delia and Vinnie passed, the click of high heels around the bar, the clatter of dishes in the kitchen and ice clinking in glasses. The din of conversation rose, levelled and rose again over the juke box. Letty had not played her record in days but the words spun around in her head as if they were on the turntable:

"… right or wrong don't matter
when you're with me sweet
Hush now, don't explain
You're my joy and pain."

Letty sipped her cool drink; sweat ran down her spine soaking into the nylon uniform. July weather promised to give no breaks and the fans were working over-time like everybody else.

She saw Delia cross to Tip's table again. In spite of the dyed red hair, no matter how you looked at her Delia was still a country girl: long and self-conscious, shy and bold because she didn't know any better. She'd moved up from Anniston with her cousin a year before and landed the job at the 411 immediately. She worked hard and sometimes Letty and she shared a cab going uptown after work, when Delia's cousin didn't pick them up in her green Pontiac.

Letty caught Tip eyeing Delia as she strode on long, tight-muscled legs back to the kitchen. "That lounge lizard!" Letty thought to herself. Letty had trained Delia: how to balance plates, how to make tips and how to keep the customer's hands on the table. She was certain Delia would have no problem putting Tip in his place. In the year she'd been working Delia hadn't gone out with any of the bar flies, though plenty had asked. Letty figured that Delia and her cousin must run with a different crowd. They talked to each other sporadically in the kitchen or during their break but Letty never felt that wire across her chest like Delia was going to ask her something she couldn't answer.

She closed her eyes again for the few remaining minutes. The song was back in her head and Letty had to squeeze her lips together to keep from humming aloud. She pushed her thoughts onto something else. But when she did she always stumbled upon Maxine. Letty opened her eyes. When she'd quit working at Salmagundi's and come to the 411 she'd promised herself never to think about any woman like that again. She didn't know why missing Billie so much brought it all back to her. She'd not thought of that time or those feelings for a while.

She heard Abe shout a greeting at Duke behind the bar as he surveyed his domain. That was Letty's signal. No matter whether it was her break or not she knew white people didn't like to see their employees sitting down, especially with their shoes off. By the time Abe was settled on his stool near the door, Letty was up, her glass in hand and on her way through the kitchen's squeaky swinging door.

"You finished your break already?" Delia asked.

"Abe just come in."

"Uh oh, let me git this steak out there to that man. Boy he sure is nosey!"

"Who, Tip?"

"Yeah, he ask me where I live, who I live with, where I come from like he supposed to know me!"

"Well just don't take nothing he say to heart and you'll be fine. And don't take no rides from him!"

"Yeah, he asked if he could take me home after I get off. I told him me and you had something to do."

Letty was silent as she sliced the fresh bread and stacked it on plates for the next orders.

"My cousin's coming by, so it ain't a lie, really. She can ride us."

"Yeah," Letty said as Delia giggled and turned away with her platter.

Vinnie burst through the door like she always did, looking breathless and bossy. "Abe up there, girl. You better get back on station. You got a customer."

Letty drained her glass with deliberation, wiped her hands on her thickly starched white apron and walked casually past Vinnie as if she'd never spoken. She heard Mabel's soft chuckle float behind her. She went over to Tip who was digging into the steak like his life depended on devouring it before the plate got dirty.

"Everything alright tonight?" Letty asked, her ample brown body towering over the table.

"Yeah, baby, everything alright. You ain't workin' this side no more?"

"I was on break. My feet can't wait for your stomach, you know."

Tip laughed. "Break! What you need a break for, big and healthy as you is!"

"We all gets old, Tip. But the feet get old first, let me tell you that!"

"Not in my business, baby. Why you don't come on and work for me and you ain't got to worry 'bout your feet."

Letty sucked her teeth loudly, the exaggeration a part of the game they played over the years. "Man, I'm too old for that mess!"

"You ain't too old for me."

"Ain't nobody too old for you! Or too young neither, looks like."

"Where you and that gal goin' tonight?"

"To a funeral," Letty responded dryly.

"Aw woman get on away from my food!" The gold cap on his front tooth gleamed from behind his greasy lips when he laughed. Letty was pleased. Besides giving away money Tip like to hurt people. It was better when he laughed.

The kitchen closed at 11:00 p.m. Delia and Letty slipped out of their uniforms in the tiny bathroom and were on their way out the door by 11:15. Delia looked even younger in her knife-pleated skirt and white cotton blouse. Letty did feel old tonight in her slacks and long-sleeved shirt. The movement of car headlights played across her face, which was set in exhaustion. The dark green car pulled up and they slipped in quietly, both anticipating tomorrow, Sunday, the last night of their work week.

Delia's cousin was a stocky woman who looked forty, Letty's age. She never spoke much. Not that she wasn't friendly. She always greeted Letty with a smile and laughed at Delia's stories about the customers. "Just close to the chest like me, that's all," Letty often thought. As they pulled up to the corner of Columbus Avenue and Cunard Street Letty opened the rear door. Delia turned to her and said, "I'm sorry you don't play your record on your break no more, Miss Letty. I know you don't want to, but I'm sorry just the same."

Delia's cousin looked back at them with a puzzled expression but said nothing. Letty slammed the car door shut and turned to climb the short flight of stairs to her apartment. Cunard Street was quiet outside her window and the guy upstairs wasn't blasting his record player for once. Still, Letty lie awake and restless in her single bed. The fan was pointed at the ceiling, bouncing warm air over her, rustling her sheer nightgown.

Inevitably the strains of Billie Holiday's songs brushed against her, much like the breeze that fanned around her. She felt silly when she thought about it, but the melodies gripped her like a solid presence. It was more than the music. Billie had been her hero. Letty saw Billie as big, like herself, with big hungers, and some secret that she couldn't tell anyone. Two weeks ago, when Letty heard that the Lady had died, sorrow enveloped her. A refuge had been closed that she could not consciously identify to herself or to anyone. It embarrassed her to think about. Like it did when she remembered Maxine.

When Letty first started working at the 411 she met Billie when she'd come into the club with several musicians on her way back from the Jazz Festival. There the audience, curious to see what a real, live junkie looked like, had sat back waiting for Billie to fall on her face. Instead she'd killed them dead with her liquid voice and rough urgency. Still, the young, thin horn player kept having to reassure her: "Billie you were the show, the whole show!"

Once convinced, Billie became the show again, loud and commanding. She demanded her food be served at the bar and sent Mabel, who insisted on waiting on her personally, back to the kitchen fifteen times. Billie laughed at jokes that Letty could barely hear as she bustled back and forth between the abandoned kitchen and her own tables. The sound of that laugh from the bar penetrated her bones. She'd watched and listened, certain she saw something no one else did. When Billie had finished eating and gathered her entourage to get back on the road she left a tip, not just for Mabel but for each of the waitresses and the bartender. "Generous just like the 'business' girls," Letty was happy to note. She still had the two one dollar bills in an envelope at the back of her lingerie drawer.

After that, Letty felt even closer to Billie. She played one of the few Lady Day records on the juke box every night, during her break. Everyone at the 411 had learned not to bother her when her song came on. Letty realized, as she lay waiting for sleep, that she'd always felt that if she'd been able to say or do something that night to make friends with Billie, it might all have been different. In half sleep the faces of Billie, Maxine and Delia blended in her mind. Letty slid her hand along the soft nylon of her gown to rest it between her full thighs. She pressed firmly, as if holding desire inside herself. Letty could have loved her enough to make it better. That was Letty's final thought as she dropped off to sleep.

THE GAY AND LESBIAN LITERARY COMPANION

Sunday nights at the 411 were generally mellow. Even the pimps and prostitutes used it as a day of rest. Letty came in early and had a drink at the bar and talked with the bartender before going to the back to change into her uniform. She saw Delia through the window as she stepped out of the green Pontiac, looking as if she'd just come from Concord Baptist Church. "Satin Doll!" was on the juke box, wrapping the bar in cool nostalgia.

Abe let Mabel close the kitchen early on Sunday and Letty looked forward to getting done by 10:00 or 10:30, and maybe enjoying some of the evening. When her break time came Letty started for the juke box automatically. She hadn't played anything by Billie in two weeks; now, looking down at the inviting glare, she knew she still couldn't do it. She punched the buttons that would bring up Jackie Wilson's "Lonely Teardrops" and went to the back booth.

She'd almost dropped off to sleep when she heard Delia whisper her name. She opened her eyes and looked up into the girl's smiling face. Her head was haloed in tight, shiny curls.

"Miss Letty, won't you come home with me tonight?"

"What?"

"I'm sorry to bother you, but your break time almost up. I wanted to ask if you'd come over to the house tonight … after work. My cousin'll bring you back home after."

Letty didn't speak. Her puzzled look prompted Delia to start again.

"Sometime on Sunday my cousin's friends from work come over to play cards, listen to music, you know. Nothin' special, just some of the girls from the office building down on Winter Street where she work, cleaning. She, I mean we, thought you might want to come over tonight. Have a drink, play some cards…."

"I don't play cards much."

"Well not everybody play cards … just talk … sitting around talking. My cousin said you might like to for a change."

Letty wasn't sure she liked the last part: "for a change," as if they had to entertain an old aunt.

"I really want you to come, Letty. They always her friends but none of them is my own friends. They alright, I don't mean nothin' against them, but it would be fun to have my own personal friend there, you know?"

Delia was a good girl. Those were the perfect words to describe her, Letty thought smiling. "Sure honey, I'd just as soon spend my time with you as lose my money with some fools."

They got off at 10:15 and Delia apologized that they had to take a cab uptown. Her cousin and her friends didn't work on Sunday so they were already at home. Afraid that the snag would give Letty and opportunity to back out Delia hadn't mentioned it until they were out of their uniforms and on the sidewalk. Letty almost declined, tempted to go home to the safe silence of her room. But she didn't. She stepped into the street and waved down a Red and White cab. All the way uptown Delia apologized that the evening wasn't a big deal and cautioned Letty not to expect much. "Just a few friends, hanging around, drinking and talking." She was jumpy and Letty tried to put her at ease. She had not expected her first visit would make Delia so anxious.

The apartment was located halfway up Blue Hill Avenue in an area where a few blacks had recently been permitted to rent. They entered a long, carpeted hallway and heard the sounds of laughter and music ringing from the rooms at the far end.

Once inside, with the door closed, Delia's personality took on another dimension. This was clearly her home and Letty could not believe she ever really needed an ally to back her up. Delia stepped out of her shoes at the door and walked to the back with her same, long-legged gait. They passed a closed door, which Letty assumed to be one of the bedrooms, then came to the kitchen ablaze with light. Food and bottles were strewn across the pink and gray formica-top table. A counter opened from the kitchen into the dining room, which was the center of activity. Around a large mahogany table sat five women in smoke-filled concentration, playing poker.

Delia's cousin looked up from her cards with the same slight smile as usual. Here it seemed welcoming, not guarded as it did in those brief moments in her car. She wore brown slacks and a matching sweater. The pink, starched points of her shirt collar peeked out at the neck.

Delia crossed to her and kissed her cheek lightly. Letty looked around the table to see if she recognized anyone. The women all seemed familiar in the way that city neighbors can, but Letty was sure she hadn't met any of them before. Delia introduced her to each one: Karen, a short, round woman with West Indian bangles up to her pudgy elbow; Betty, who stared intently at the cards though thick eyeglasses encased in blue cat-eye frames; Irene, a big, dark woman with long black hair and a gold tooth in front. Beside her sat Myrtle who was wearing army fatigues and a gold Masonic ring on her pinky finger. She said hello in the softest voice Letty had ever heard. Hovering over her was Clara, a large red woman whose hair was bound tightly in a bun at the nape of her neck. She spoke

Poetry

The Lipstick Papers (poetry), 1980.
Flamingoes and Bears (poetry), 1986.

Fiction

"Don't Explain," in *Love, Struggle &*

Change: Stories by Women, edited by
Irene Zahava, 1988.
The Gilda Stories (novel), 1991.

Essays

"A Celebration of Butch-Femme

Identities in the Lesbian
Community," in *The Persistent Desire:
A Butch-Femme Reader*, edited by
Joan Nestle, 1992.
Forty-three Septembers, 1993.

with a delectable southern accent that drawled her "How're you doin'" into a full paragraph that was draped around an inquisitive smile.

Delia became ill-at-ease as she pulled Letty by the arm toward the French doors behind the players. There was a small den with a desk, some books and a television set. Through the next set of glass doors was a livingroom. At the record player was an extremely tall, brown-skinned woman. She bent over the wooden cabinet searching for the next selection, oblivious to the rest of the gathering. Two women sat on the divan in deep conversation, which they punctuated with constrained giggles.

"Maryalice, Shelia, Dolores … this is Letty."

They looked up at her quickly, smiled, then went back to their preoccupations: two to their gossip, the other returned to the record collection. Delia directed Letty back toward the foyer and the kitchen.

"Come on, let me get you a drink. You know, I don't even know what you drink!"

"Delia?" Her cousin's voice reached them over the counter, just as they stepped back into the kitchen. "Bring a couple beers back when you come, OK?"

"Sure, babe." Delia went to the refrigerator and pulled out two bottles. "Let me just take these in. I'll be right back."

"Go 'head, I can take care of myself in this department, girl." Letty surveyed the array of bottles on the table. Delia went to the dining room and Letty mixed a Scotch and soda. She poured slowly as the reality settled on her. These women were friends, perhaps lovers, like she and Maxine had been. The name she'd heard for women like these burst inside her head: bulldagger. Letty flinched, angry she had let it in, angry that it frightened her. "Ptuh!" Letty blew air through the teeth as if spitting the word back at the air.

She did know these women, Letty thought, as she stood at the counter smiling out at the poker game. They were oblivious to her, except for Terry. Letty remembered that was Delia's cousin's name. As

Letty took her first sip, Terry called over to her. "We gonna be finished with this game in a minute Letty, then we can talk."

"Take your time," Letty said, then went out through the foyer door and around to the livingroom. She walked slowly on the carpet and adjusted her eyes to the light, which was a bit softer. The tall woman, Maryalice, had just put a record on the turntable and sat down on a love seat across from the other two women. Letty stood in the doorway a moment before the tune began:

"Hush now, don't explain
Just say you'll remain
I'm glad you're back
Don't explain ..."

Letty was stunned, but the song sounded different here, among these women. Billie sang just to them, here. The isolation and sadness seemed less inevitable with these women listening. Letty watched Maryalice sitting with her long legs stretched out tensely in front of her. She was wrapped in her own thoughts, her eyes closed. She appeared curiously disconnected, after what had clearly been a long search for this record. Letty watched her face as she swallowed several times. Then Letty moved to sit on the seat beside her. They listened to the music while the other two women spoke in low voices.

When the song was over Maryalice didn't move. Letty rose from the sofa and went to the record player. Delia stood tentatively in the doorway of the livingroom. Letty picked up the arm of the phonograph and replaced it at the beginning of the record. When she sat again beside Maryalice she noticed the drops of moisture on the other woman's lashes. Maryalice relaxed as Letty settled onto the seat beside her. They both listened to Billie together, for the first time.

JUDY GRAHN

SINCE BEING DISCHARGED from the armed forces for lesbianism in 1961, Judy Grahn has worked consistently in her writing to redefine gay and lesbian existence in positive and powerful terms. As Grahn relates in the preface to *Another Mother Tongue: Gay Words, Gay Worlds*, the less-than-honorable discharge, rejection by several family members and friends for her sexuality, and several other incidents including being beaten in public "for looking like a dike" made her "angry and determined enough to use my life to reverse a perilous situation." Grahn further states in the preface that if she had been born into the earlier tribal culture of her European ancestors, she would have been one of the European equivalents of a shaman, such as a hag or wise-woman. Born into twentieth-century America, she says she instead became "a very purposeful Lesbian poet."

Essay by
JAYNE RELAFORD
BROWN

Grahn's purpose has been in public evidence since her first book of poems. She explains in *Another Mother Tongue* that she titled the first collection *Edward the Dyke* "to begin to defuse the terror people have of the word" and "to tie it to me, so I could never deny it." *Edward the Dyke* was published by the Woman's Press Collective, which Grahn, Wendy Cadden, and other women began in 1970. Even before 1970, however, Grahn had been active on behalf of homosexual rights. In 1963 she joined the Mattachine Society in front of the White House for an early gay rights protest; in 1964 she wrote a pro-homosexual article for *Sexology* magazine, using the name "Carol Silver" as a pseudonym. Under her own name, she first published several poems from *Edward the Dyke* in the *Ladder*, an underground lesbian magazine.

Since 1970, Grahn has been drawn to increasingly ambitious projects. *The Common Woman Poems* is a cycle of verse that both depicts and valorizes the lives of "ordinary" women. Her long poem "A Woman Is Talking to Death," weaves together the description of a fatal motorcycle accident with a meditation on racism, lesbian existence, betrayal, and love as redemption. Mary J. Carruthers's *Hudson Review* essay, "The Re-Vision of the Muse," notes that these elements are combined to portray "the futility of trying to work within a society fascinated by destruction."

American poet, playwright, novelist, and writer of nonfiction.

Born: Judith Rae Grahn in Chicago, Illinois, July 28, 1940.

Education: San Francisco State University, B.A. 1984; and at various other institutions.

Career: Served in the U.S. armed forces; discharged in 1961. Has held a variety of jobs, including waitress, short-order cook, clerk, barmaid, artist's model, typesetter, photographer's assistant, and nurse's aide, all prior to 1969; cofounder, publisher, editor, and printer, Women's Press Collective, Oakland, California, 1969–78; instructor of literature and lesbian cultural classes at New College of California, San Francisco, beginning in 1984; instructor of a course on Gertrude Stein at Stanford University, 1988; teacher in women's writing programs in Cazenovia, New York, Ithaca, New York, Berkeley, California, and San Francisco; gives lectures and poetry readings; conducts workshops.

Recipient: American Poetry Review Poem of the Year Award, 1979; National Endowment for the Arts grant, 1980; Before Columbus Foundation American Book Award, 1983; American Library Association Gay Book of the Year Award, 1985; with Alice Walker, Tillie Olsen, Janice Mirikitani, and Alice Adams, Women's Foundation (San Francisco) Women of Words Award, 1985; Lambda Book Award for Nonfiction, 1988; Outlook Foundation Pioneer Gay Writer Award, 1989.

With *The Queen of Wands*, Grahn has commenced a four-volume cycle of poems based on the four suits of the Tarot deck. She has moved into prose with *Another Mother Tongue*, a ten-year research and writing project that both traces and creates a history of gay culture. *The Highest Apple*, originally intended to be a chapter of *Another Mother Tongue*, links Sappho with eight other lesbian poets from the nineteenth and twentieth centuries, including Grahn herself, to create a theory of lesbian poetics. Grahn has gone on to expand her prose efforts with *Mundane's World*, her first novel, and *Really Reading Gertrude Stein*, a series of poetic critical essays introducing selected writings by Stein.

Grahn's writings draw generously from myth, tribal cultures, history, and personal experience to create a new mythology of gayness as a way of being. *The Queen of Swords*, a poetic play, equates a modern woman's coming out process with the story of the mythological figures of Inanna and Persephone, who journey to the underworld then return to the land of the living. In *Another Mother Tongue*, Grahn traces the roots of words, symbols, and attributes associated with gayness in order to establish the idea of a gay culture and spiritual function that transcends temporal and national boundaries. For example, she traces the word "dyke," or "dike," back to the goddess Dike, whose name means "balance" or "the path," and relates this balancing attribute to gay identity and purpose. "One of the major homosexual/shamanic functions in any society," states Grahn in *Another Mother Tongue*, "is to *cross over* between these two essentially different worlds [of male and female] and reveal them to each other."

Grahn brings this same valorization of what it means to be gay to her poetry, as is evidenced in the title poem from *She Who:* "I am the wall at the lip of the water / I am the rock that refused to be battered / I am the dike in the matter, the other / I am the wall with the womanly swagger / I am the dragon, the dangerous dagger / I am the bulldyke, the bulldagger." Continuing the work she began with her first book, Judy Grahn continues to use her office as poet and writer to transform and create positive meanings for being lesbian and gay.

Judy Grahn told the Companion:

"I think it is important for people to know that an open, working-class lesbian poet who surfaced in 1970 with the word 'dyke' in the title of her first book is now considered literary canon. I've seen my work taught in conjunction with Plath, Rich, Plato, and Milton, and best of all, used by common people to transform their lives. Now I feel capable of becoming a world class philosopher, using the best gifts of my communities and my spirits to help reshape the world."

HELA (DEATH)

Reprinted from *The Queen of Wands*, The Crossing Press, 1982.

In the South and in the West
the sun is a monster
eating your water, eating
the juice right out of your bones,
and blinding your eyes,
your brain.
The sun takes photographs
they say, burning a record
of the day's events
into the filmy leaves of tress—
those wise old women-sticks.
The middle of the sun is dark, an eye.
At Hiroshima, they say
the radiation was a white
storm, the center of a flash.
Some people who vanished
in it left their shadows
on the wall, a still life
photograph.
I am Hela. I am used for all

purposes. I do not care.
I clean down to the bone earth.
I sear. I flare.
I take photographs
of what is no longer there.

THE MOST BLONDE WOMAN IN THE WORLD

Reprinted from *The Queen of Wands*, The Crossing Press, 1982.

The most blonde woman in the world
one day threw off her skin
her hair, threw off her hair, declaring
"Whosoever chooses to love me
chooses to love a bald woman
with bleeding pores."
Those who came then as her lovers
were small hard-bodied spiders
with dark eyes and an excellent
knowledge of weaving.
They spun her blood into long strands,
and altogether wove millions of red
webs, webs red in the afternoon sun.
"Now," she said, "Now I am expertly loved,
and now I am beautiful."

1974, WE WERE FIVE DYKES

Reprinted from *Another Mother Tongue: Gay Words, Gay Worlds*, Beacon Press, copyright 1984 by Judith Grahn.

The year was 1974. We were five dykes, living in an all-women's household. We were highly visible and vocal Lesbian feminist organizers, a little grungy and eccentric in jackets and baggy pants, for we did not have a stake in what we looked like. We had started the first women's bookstore, the first women's collective press for publishing books, and a newspaper. Occupationally we were a carpenter-mechanic-accountant, a copy editor, a printer-poet, an electronics assembler, and a print-artist. One day a woman came into the bookstore begging us for help. Her boyfriend, she said, was trying to kill her because she did not want to see him anymore. She was afraid to tell her friends because he would tell them she was a whore. So he had beaten her up. He called her on the phone day and night to threaten and terrify her; he banged on her door in the middle of the night, and only that morning in broad daylight he had thrown a crowbar through her front door, which happened to be made of glass. And he had sworn he was coming in to get her. She spent

Poetry

The Common Woman Poems, 1969.

Edward the Dyke, and Other Poems, 1971.

Elephant Poem Coloring Book, 1972.

Contributor, *No More Masks!: An Anthology of Poems by Women,* 1973.

A Woman Is Talking to Death, 1974.

She Who: A Graphic Book of Poems with Fifty-four Images of Women, 1978.

The Work of a Common Woman: The Collected Poetry of Judy Grahn, 1964–1977, introduction by Adrienne Rich, 1978.

The Queen of Wands, 1982.

Spider Webster's Declaration: He Is Singing the End of the World Again, 1983.

Contributor, *The Penguin Book of Homosexual Verse,* edited by Stephen Coote, 1983.

Descent to the Roses of the Family (chapbook), 1986.

The Queen of Swords, 1987.

Contributor, *Gay and Lesbian Poetry in Our Time,* edited by Carl Morse and Joan Larkin, 1988.

Contributor, *The American Reader,* edited by Diane Perita, 1991.

Contributor, *Before Columbus Foundation Poetry Anthology,* 1991.

Contributor, *An Intimate Wilderness,* edited by Judith Barrington, 1991.

Contributor, *Lesbian Culture,* edited by Julia Penelope and Susan Wolfe, 1993.

Plays

The Cell, produced Yellow Springs, Ohio, 1968.

She Who, produced San Francisco, 1973.

The Queen of Wands, produced Ithaca, New York, 1985.

The Queen of Swords, produced Oakland, California, 1989.

Novels

Mundane's World, 1988.

Nonfiction

"Menstruation: From the Sacred to the Curse and Beyond," in *The Politics of Women's Spirituality,* edited by Charlene Spretnak, 1982.

Another Mother Tongue: Gay Words, Gay Worlds, 1984; updated and expanded, 1990.

"Flaming without Burning: The Role of Gay People in Society," in *Advocate,* March 1985.

The Highest Apple: Sappho and the Lesbian Poetic Tradition, 1985.

"Vessels of Life and Death: Gay Spirituality in 1986," in *Advocate,* December 1986.

Really Reading Gertrude Stein: A Selected Anthology, 1989.

Contributor, *Classical and Medieval Literature Criticism,* 1989.

"Drawing in Nets," in *Conversant Essays: Contemporary Poets on Poetry,* edited by James McCorkle, 1990.

"The Common Woman, A Map of Seven Poems," in *Inversions: Writing by Dykes, Queers, and Lesbians,* edited by Betsy Warland, 1991.

"Healing from Incest through Art," in *She Who Was Lost Is Remembered,* edited by Louise Wisechild, 1991.

Blood, Bread and Roses: How Menstruation Created the World, 1993.

Editor

Lesbians Speak Out, 1974.

And author of introduction, *True to Life Adventure Stories,* Volume 1, 1978; Volume 2, 1989.

Other

Author of article, in *Sexology* (as Carol Silver), c. 1964.

Movement in Black, foreword by Audre Lorde, 1978.

Author of introduction, *The Shameless Hussy: Selected Poetry and Prose,* 1980.

"Boys at the Rodeo" (short story), in *True to Life Adventure Stories,* Volume 2, edited by Grahn, 1989.

Recordings

Where Would I Be without You: The Poetry of Pat Parker and Judy Grahn, 1975.

Lesbian Concentrate, 1978.

March to Mother Sea: Healing Poems for Baby Girls Raped at Home, 1990.

A Woman Is Talking to Death, 1991.

Adaptations

The Common Woman Poems (one-woman stage play), performed in Australia.

Edward the Dyke (stage play), performed off-Broadway.

A Woman Is Talking to Death (interpretive dance), performed in Seattle.

"Contemplating Chrystos" (interpretive dance), performed in San Francisco.

"Funeral Plainsong" (musical presentation), performed in New York.

hours cowering on the floor at the back of her apartment. The police had told her they couldn't—or wouldn't—do anything. They advised her to move.

"I don't want to move," she raged. "I love my apartment. Why should I move? He's the one who's in the wrong. Besides, he could just follow me home from work and start it all over again." We agreed. And we agreed to help. But, we told her, "You will have to help too."

That evening we went to her house, which had many windows and was as filled with lively plants as a hothouse garden. "We are starting a vigil here," we told her. "One or two of us will stay with you until the problem is solved."

She smiled gratefully. We did not smile in return.

"What are you doing to defend yourself?" we asked. She did not know.

"What do you want us to do to stop him?" we asked.

"Kill him," she said.

"No, no," we replied. "But you must protect yourself from direct physical attack and learn to feel safe in your house." We located hammers, umbrellas, heavy dictionaries, flowerpots, bricks, sticks, and the like and arranged them strategically around the house, showing her what to do with them. We talked a lot to each other about guns, knives, karate. We got her to agree to tell some of her friends about what was happening and to keep their numbers near her phone for emergencies.

Then we talked among ourselves about what plan of action to take, loud enough so she could hear there were a thousand alternatives to the drastic, essentially passive reaction "kill him." She went into the kitchen, returning with cookies and brownies. "I baked these for you," she said, smiling at us as though we were football heros. We ignored her cookies.

"Why do you wear such helpless clothes?" we asked. "How can you run or kick in those shoes, that tight skirt?" She didn't know. "The police aren't going to help you," we said. "And for the most part neither are your friends. And you can't expect us to stay with you forever. We're not your personal bodyguards. You have to learn to defend yourself." She changed her clothes and began to pay attention to our plans. We asked questions about her boyfriend's habits. What does he value, we asked, his car, his motorcycle? Where does he work, where does his wife work, where do they live? Are his parents in town? Where do you think he is most vulnerable? We made a plan, one, two, three, four. First we would talk to him; if that didn't work then we would contact his wife, go see her if necessary, then his boss; if none of those tactics worked, we would go wreck his car.

She listened in amazement. She had believed the only way to stop him was to murder him. The two oldest among us—women in their forties—got on the telephone to him and took turns talking.

"Hello there," they said. They used his full name, they mentioned his address. "We're from the Women's Defense League of Oakland. We're a special protection group for women, and we've gotten a very serious complaint about you." They described his actions to him in detail. They mentioned his wife's name and where they both worked. "We've been checking up on you and we know quite a lot. If you don't agree—right now—to leave this woman completely alone, we're going to institute action." They left the nature of the action to his imagination. He began to stutter, then bluster, and finally to crack and beg them not to tell his wife.

He did not go near the woman again. Within two days she had changed her attitude toward her life, becoming much more assertive, especially with the several boyfriends she had. She came into the bookstore a month later to report to us and to thank us woman to woman. "This guy got drunk at my house last night and I ordered a cab, trundled him into it, and got rid of him," she crowed in triumph. She again owned her own space and peace of mind. And now that she was no longer using them to pay us for "protecting" her while she continued being Miss Helpless, we ate her cookies.

RADCLYFFE HALL

RADCLYFFE HALL, the famous English author of *The Well of Loneliness*, was born near Surrey Lawn, West Cliff, near the town of Bournemouth. As the child of a wealthy and privileged, albeit troubled, family, she received a university education at King's College in London with a brief post-college year in Dresden, Germany. Although she was given the name of Marguerite Radclyffe-Hall, she was raised as a boy and wrote under the name of Radclyffe Hall. To her friends and acquaintances she was known as John.

Essay by
JANE JURGENS

Between 1906 and 1915, Hall composed five volumes of poetry; in all but one of these, she is explicit in her expression of same-sex love. *A Sheaf of Verses* and *Poems of the Past and Present*, written soon after she had met Mabel Veronica Ballen ("Ladye"), her literary patron and her first long-standing friend and lover, are filled with passionate declarations expressing confidence and power. In *Songs of Three Counties, and Other Poems* and *The Forgotten Island*, Hall continues her lyrical declarations of earthly love to a woman but introduces a religious note in an expression of love and devotion to God.

Between 1924 and 1936, Hall published seven novels and a collection of short stories. Only two of Hall's novels deal directly with lesbian themes: *The Unlit Lamp* and *The Well of Loneliness*. In both of these works, Hall pleads for the individual's freedom to pursue happiness and fulfillment and for public sympathy and compassion for the homosexual. *The Unlit Lamp*, a precursor to *The Well*, explores the role of parental manipulation and control in a growing lesbian relationship. In this story about the Ogden family, Hall focuses on the relationship between Mrs. Odgen and her daughter Julia, and Julia's relationship with Elizabeth Rodney. Julia is torn between her growing love and devotion toward Elizabeth and her mother's jealousy and disapproval.

The Well of Loneliness undoubtedly represents Hall's bravest and best-known work. Published in England in 1928, the book was initially well received by critics. Famous English critics of the Bloomsbury Circle, such as Desmond MacCarthy and Rebecca West, praised the novel more

Oil-on-canvas portrait of Radclyffe Hall painted by Charles Buchel in 1918.

for its positive social statement on lesbianism, less for its artistic skill. Despite the added support of the general public, the novel was banned in England in the year of its publication under the Obscene Libel Act. In the book, Stephen Gordon, the female protagonist, is a lesbian in search of an identity. Isolated from herself in body and mind, Stephen is the "sexual invert," the outcast of society who must yield to the power that drives her. She often envies women who are able to accept their own bodies and their femininity.

Both *The Unlit Lamp* and *The Well* seem to support the theory that homosexuality is biologically determined, inherited from the parents, and is, therefore, unavoidable and irreversible; however, Hall does not rule out the possibility that upbringing and general environment are factors in the development of the homosexual identity. Despite *The Well's* somber mood, moralistic tone, and dated content—at least by contemporary standards—the novel has endured and has enjoyed immense popularity.

Lady Una Troubridge, Hall's companion and lover for almost 30 years, recorded their life together in a work entitled *The Life and Death of Radclyffe Hall*. Published soon after Hall's death in 1943, Troubridge's book provides many insights into their long life together which was, by and large, happy and fulfilling but not without conflicts. If Troubridge's account can be taken as true, it suggests that Hall's portrayals of lesbians, especially that of Stephen Gordon in *The Well*, were not autobiographical, though many readers have interpreted them in this manner. Hall, according to Troubridge, seems to have fully and enthusiastically accepted herself as a lesbian and a woman and, because of this, enjoyed a more serene existence than her lesbian characters did. Despite this variance between her real and literary worlds, Hall's fiction and poetry represent a prominent and pioneering effort in support of lesbianism.

Radclyffe Hall's poetry and fiction, notably her celebrated (and initially banned) novel *The Well of Loneliness*, represent a prominent and pioneering effort in support of lesbianism.

English novelist, poet, and author of short stories.

Born: Bournemouth, Hampshire, c. 1886.

Education: In Germany and at King's College, London.

Partnerships: Companion of Ladye Mabel Batten, 1908–16; companion of Lady Una Troubridge.

Recipient: James Tait Black Memorial Book Prize, c. 1926; Femina-Vie Heureuse Prize, c. 1926; Eichelbergher Humane Award gold medal, c. 1926.

Died: London, October 7, 1943.

THE WELL OF LONELINESS

Came the thought of that unforgettable scene with her mother. "I would rather see you dead at my feet." Oh, yes—very easy to talk about death, but not so easy to manage the dying. "We two cannot live together at Morton.... One of us must go, which of us shall it be?" The subtlety, the craftiness of that question which in common decency could have but one answer! Oh, well, she had gone and would go even farther. Raftery was dead, there was nothing to hold her, she was free—what a terrible thing could be freedom. Trees were free when they were uprooted by the wind; ships were free when they were torn from their moorings; men were free when they were cast out of their homes—free to starve, free to perish of cold and hunger.

At Morton there lived an ageing woman with sorrowful eyes now a little dim from gazing for so long into the distance. Only once, since her gaze had been fixed on the dead, had this woman turned it full on her daughter; and then her eyes had been changed into something accusing, ruthless, abominably cruel. Through looking upon what had seemed abominable to them, they themselves had become an abomination. Horrible! And yet how dared they accuse? What right had a mother to abominate the child that had sprung from her own secret moments of passion? She the honoured, the fulfilled, the fruitful, the loving and loved, had despised the fruit of her love. Its fruit? No, rather its victim.

She thought of her mother's protected life that had never had to face this terrible freedom. Like a vine that clings to a warm southern wall it had clung to her father—it still clung to Morton. In the spring had come gentle and nurturing rains, in the summer the strong and health-giving sunshine, in the winter a deep, soft covering of snow—cold yet protecting the delicate tendrils. All, all, she had had. She had never gone empty of love in the days of her youthful ardour; had never known longing, shame, degradation, but rather great joy and pride in her loving. Her love had been pure in the eyes of the world, for she had been able to indulge it with honour. Still with honour, she had borne a child to her mate—but a child who, unlike her, must go unfulfilled all her days, or else live in abject dishonour. Oh, but a hard and pitiless woman this mother must be for all her soft beauty; shamelessly finding shame in her offspring. "I would rather see you dead at my feet...." "Too late, too late, your love gave me life. Here am I the creature you made through your loving; by your passion you created the thing I am. Who are you to deny me the right to love? But for you I need never have known existence."

And now there crept into Stephen's brain the worst torment of all, a doubt of her father. He had known and knowing he had not told her; he had pitied and pitying had not protected; he had feared and fearing had saved only himself. Had she had a coward for a father? She sprang up and began to pace the room. Not this—she could not face this new torment. She had stained her love, the love of the lover—she dared not stain this one thing that

remained, the love of the child for the father. If this light went out the engulfing darkness would consume her, destroying her entirely. Man could not live by darkness alone, one point of light he must have for salvation—one point of light. The most perfect Being of all had cried out for light in His darkness—even He, the most perfect Being of all. And then as though in answer to prayer, to some prayer that her trembling lips had not uttered, came the memory of a patient, protective back, bowed as though bearing another's burden. Came the memory of horrible, soul-sickening pain: "No—not that—something urgent—I want—to say. No drugs—I know I'm—dying—Evans." And again an heroic and tortured effort: "Anna—it's Stephen—listen." Stephen suddenly held out her arms to this man who, though dead, was still her father.

But even in this blessed moment of easement her heart hardened again at the thought of her mother. A fresh wave of bitterness flooded her soul so that the light seemed all but extinguished; very faintly it gleamed like the little lantern on a buoy that is tossed by tempest. Sitting down at her desk she found pen and paper.

She wrote: "Mother, I am going abroad quite soon, but I shall not see you to say good-bye, because I don't want to come back to Morton. These visits of mine have always been painful, and now my work is beginning to suffer—that I can not allow; I live only for my work and so I

Poetry

'Twixt Earth and Stars: Poems, 1906.
A Sheaf of Verses: Poems, 1908.
Poems of the Past and Present, 1910.
Songs of Three Counties, and Other Poems, 1913.

The Forgotten Island, 1915.

Novels

The Forge, 1924.
The Unlit Lamp, 1924.
A Saturday Life, 1925.
Adam's Breed, 1926.

The Well of Loneliness, 1928.
The Master of the House, 1932.
The Sixth Beatitude, 1936.

Other

Miss Ogilvy Finds Herself (short stories), London, 1934.

---

intend to guard it in future. There can now be no question of gossip or scandal, for everyone knows that I am a writer and as such may have occasion to travel. But in any case I care very little these days for the gossip of neighbors. For nearly three years I have borne your yoke—I have tried to be patient and understanding. I have tried to think that your yoke was a just one, a just punishment, perhaps, for my being what I am, the creature whom you and my father created; but now I am going to bear it no longer. If my father had lived he would have shown pity, whereas you showed me none, and yet you were my mother. In my hour of great need you utterly failed me; you turned me away like some unclean thing that was unfit to live any longer at Morton. You insulted what to me seemed both natural and sacred. I went, but now I shall not come back any more to you or to Morton. Puddle will be with me because she loves me; if I'm saved at all it is she who has saved me, and so for as long as she wishes to throw in her lot with mine I shall let her. Only one thing more; she will send you our address from time to time, but don't write to me, Mother, I am going away in order to forget, and your letters would only remind me of Morton."

She read over what she had written, three times, finding nothing at all that she wished to add, no word of tenderness, or of regret. She felt numb and then unbelievably lonely, but she wrote the address in her firm handwriting: "The Lady Anna Gordon," she wrote, "Morton Hall. Near Upton-on-Severn." When she wept, as she presently must do, covering her face with her large, brown hands, her spirit felt unrefreshed by this weeping, for the hot, angry tears seemed to scorch her spirit. Thus was Anna Gordon baptized through her child as by fire, unto the loss of their mutual salvation.

JOSEPH HANSEN

Essay by
JIM KEPNER

JOSEPH HANSEN, a novelist, artist, and poet who also writes under the pseudonyms James Colton and Rose Brock, was born on July 19, 1923, in the railroad town of Aberdeen, South Dakota. Taught to read with "progressive" flash cards and forced by a strep throat infection at age seven into an eight-month isolation, Hansen developed his imagination through reading such works as Carl Sandburg's *Abraham Lincoln: The Prairie Years* at an early age. When he returned to school, he proved himself a bright student, and he made friends easily. In 1933, as the Great Depression ravaged much of America, Hansen's father lost his shoe store and the family moved to Minneapolis, Minnesota. It was there that Hansen learned to ice skate; he read books such as Jack London's *White Fang* and Mark Twain's *Huckleberry Finn*, and he wrote "Philosophy from a Boy to Older Folks," a treatise on solving national problems.

A few years later, the family joined the migration to California, driving an old Marmon with cartons and suitcases tied on, and sharing cramped quarters with in-laws on ten Altadena acres of citrus and beehives. Hansen began writing sonnets and putting the psalms of David into contemporary English, being guided briefly by Episcopal choirmaster-organist Raymond Hill through art books and classical recordings. As his love of music and literature grew, he tried writing a comic opera, edited the John Marshall Junior High School paper, acted in school plays, and immersed himself in evangelical church activities. For a time he entertained the notion of becoming a minister. It was his love of the written word, however, that eventually drew him in the direction of his life's work in writing.

Despite Hansen's respect for a religious and pure way of life, he admits to one theft: stealing, from the school library in 1938, William Rose Benet's *Fifty Poets*, an anthology in which each poet is represented by their best poem. The book was, and remains, precious to him, demonstrating that he was not alone in his hunger to write verse. "My family then were not my father, mother, sister, brother," Hansen stated in *Poetry News, Calendar & Reviews of Southern California Readings and Publications*. "My family were these: Edgar Lee Masters, Edward Arlington Robinson,

Anna Hampstead Branch, Robinson Jeffers ... and so many others. And once I had found them, I tried my faltering best to be worthy of them. I hope that somewhere, in some school library, at this moment, some 15-year-old misfit like my long-lost self has chanced to come upon a book of poems that will mean as much to him as that one meant to me."

Entering Pasadena City College in 1939, Hansen eased up on religion and found exciting new friends and activities. He worked as a page at the public library and discovered, in writers such as Walt Whitman, Henry David Thoreau, and Ralph Waldo Emerson, help for his self-doubts. His lover, Bobker Ben Ali of the Pasadena Playhouse, helped even more, introducing Hansen to the works of Homer, Socrates, Charles-Pierre Baudelaire, James Joyce, Jean Cocteau, Arthur Rimbaud, and composers Erik Satie and Igor Stravinsky—as well as a rich diet of theater. He spent many hours, still underage, at Hollywood's intimate jazz clubs, hearing great jazz for the price of a beer. In August 1943 he married an aircraft plant worker named Jane Bancroft, who had come into his place of work. They have one daughter, Barbara, and a West Los Angeles houseful of other kids, dogs, cats, and more exotic pets (Hansen's books *Strange Marriage* and *A Smile in His Lifetime* partly address their life together).

As Hansen finished school and began married life, he turned to his writing skills to earn a living. From 1962 to 1965 he was an editor of *ONE* magazine (the first openly sold "avowed" American publication for homosexuals). After an angry schism, he helped launch an aesthetically superior periodical, also titled *ONE*. He was later forced, for legal reasons, to rename the magazine *Tangents*. His work on *Tangents* included writing editorials, stories, reviews, and a news column. Jane contributed artwork, layouts, reviews, and an advice column. Aside from work with *Tangents* (also known as the Homosexual Information Center), Hansen and his wife participated in inter-group homophile movement activities during the late 1960s. *Todd*, a novel he later wrote under the pseudonym James Colton, was inspired by Los Angeles's Gay Liberation Front, organized at *Tangents*'s garage-office. The magazine folded in 1970, at a time when Hansen's fiction work was just becoming widely known. He felt that the periodical had said what it had to say to the homosexual audience. At this stage in his career, Hansen felt that he could reach a wider audience, one that included heterosexual readers, with novels.

It took years for Hansen to get published and, until 1970, his writing on homosexual themes appeared under the Colton pseudonym (*ONE* magazine editor Don Slater insisted he use a pen name). Starting with *Lost on Twilight Road* and concluding with *Todd* in 1971, the novels serve as some of the better gay erotica available, even if some were written

THE GAY AND LESBIAN LITERARY COMPANION

speedily. It is his fine mystery novels about masculine homosexual insurance adjuster David Brandstetter, however, that have solidified Hansen's popularity with readers both gay and non-gay. From *Fadeout* in 1970 (the first novel he sold to a major publisher), the series (which he had not intended to be ongoing) has been well received by both readers and critics, although his American reception was perfunctory until after he had received high praise and popularity in England; the *London Times* called him the best writer of his kind since Dashiell Hammett, who wrote such mysteries *The Maltese Falcon* and *The Thin Man*. Popularity for novels such as *Skinflick* and *Nightwork* followed in France, Holland, and Japan. *Early Graves*, published in 1987, was Hansen's first novel to deal with the issue of AIDS—a subject he took up with trepidation but handled masterfully. In the novel, Brandstetter investigates the murders of young men infected with the HIV virus. *Obedience*, written the following year, explores the Vietnamese community in Southern California.

Novelist, short story writer, and poet Joseph Hansen.

Because protagonists of his favorite mystery writer, Ross MacDonald, did not age or develop, Hansen decided to trace real growth and change in his own lead character, as well as the changes in the Southern California landscape that Brandstetter inhabited. The investigator and his male lovers aged through the series and gay life underwent many transformations—though Hansen spurns the term gay and any concept of gay community or uniqueness.

Hansen kept busy with other writings as well. *Backtrack,* published in 1982, covers a non-exploitive man-boy relationship and attacks a common stereotype of homosexual relationships. While gay characters predominate, the writing is non-exploitive—a change from the Colton novels, whose publishers wanted detailed and steady sex scenes. Hansen also wrote the non-mysteries *A Smile in His Lifetime*, dedicated to his wife, and *Job's Year*. In the 1950s, he worked on scripts for the TV series *Lassie;* in 1969 and 1974, he published the gothic novels *Tarn House* and *Longleaf* under the pseudonym Rose Brock (his mother's maiden name was Rosebrock); he also published a booklet of exquisite verse, *One Foot in the Boat*, in 1977, and produced many fine short stories.

Hansen insists he is a homosexual—not a gay—writer, as if that would make him a lesser writer. Still, his early Brandstetter novels have an elegance and an eye for interior decoration that set off his otherwise

American novelist, short story writer, poet, and educator. Also writes as Rose Brock and James Colton.

Born: Aberdeen, South Dakota, July 19, 1923.

Education: Public schools in Aberdeen, South Dakota; Minneapolis, Minnesota; and Pasadena, California, 1929–42.

Partnerships: Married Jane Bancroft in 1943; one daughter.

Career: Member of editorial staff of *One*, beginning 1962; cofounder and staff member, *Tangents*, 1965–70. Producer of radio show *Homosexuality Today*, KPFK-FM, Los Angeles, 1969. Creative writing teacher, Beyond Baroque Foundation, Venice, California, 1975–76; University of California, Los Angeles, beginning 1977. Contributor of verse to periodicals, including *Atlantic*, *Harper's*, *New Yorker*, and *Saturday Review*; contributor of short fiction to *Bachy*, *South Dakota Review*, *Tangents*, and *Transatlantic Review*; contributor of articles to *Armchair Detective*, *New Review*, and *Writer*.

Recipient: National Endowment for the Arts grant, 1974; British Arts Council lecture tour grant, 1975.

Agent: Stuart Krichevsky, Sterling Lord Literistic Inc., 1 Madison Avenue, New York, New York 10010, U.S.A.

spare, "hardboiled" style descended from authors like Hammett and Raymond Chandler. He created Brandstetter to confound the stereotypes with which homosexuals were too often portrayed, to illustrate that there are just as many "macho" homosexuals as there are effeminate ones—that homosexuals come in the same variety of personalities as heterosexuals. Asked if he is the model for Brandstetter, Hansen admitted some resemblance but, unlike his fictional creation, he admits to being a sensitive and emotional person. Asked if he saw a Brandstetter film in the future, he said in 1981 that offers had come and gone, but most studios were fearful of presenting a real gay character, one that strayed from the popular Hollywood image of a gallivanting, flamboyant queen. Perhaps today, Hansen's concept of homosexuals on film is more likely.

Not all gay critics approve of Hansen's work. James Levin argues in *The Gay Novel in America* that while the author's 1975 novel *Troublemaker* provides a full portrayal of the gay subculture rather than simply individual homosexual characters, Hansen begins to show contempt for gay liberation. Levin points in particular to the novel's expectation that gay relationships should abandon gender roles, and he also argues that Hansen's antagonism toward gay activism and goals increases in each successive novel. This argument is a bit one-sided; some of the gay activists that Hansen presents as caricatures are, in fact, caricatures in real life. Hansen's talent is his eye for what is contemptible and silly— as well as admirable—in gay life.

Hansen also involved himself in activities outside of writing. When police beat his daughter at a Century City, California, anti-war protest, his poster of police beating a demonstrator became a hit among many counter-culture groups. At the urging of a local businessperson, Hansen also started a series of poetry workshops. This eventually led to teaching creative writing at the Beyond Baroque Foundation, at the University of California at Irvine, and at the University of California's Los Angeles extension. A leading member of the Venice Poet's Circle, his verse has appeared in the *Atlantic*, *Harper's*, *New Yorker*, and *Saturday Review*.

AUTOBIOGRAPHY, 1992

Aberdeen is a railroad town in the flat northeast corner of South Dakota, and I was born there on a hot July afternoon in 1923, in a spindly frame house on Fourth Street, across from a livery stable. My pretty sister, Louise, eighteen, a reader of novels and a writer of moody verses, hated the stink of that livery stable. I suspect my brother, Bob, age nine, had too much else on his mind—every kind of sport in its season, a sandlot baseball game on the day I came squalling into the world—to fret much over horse smells.

My father, Henry, born forty-one years before in Des Moines of Norwegian immigrant parents, was short, bald, devoted to awful cigars, and ran a shoe store on Main Street. He had a sweet tenor voice, and often sang solos at the First Methodist Church. He could play any musical instrument he picked up. He made up funny rhymes on the spur of the moment, was clever at drawing, and was a marvelous mimic, especially hilarious with foreign accents, which were then fair game for comedy. He also built elegant kites and taught me to fly them. There was always plenty of wind in South Dakota.

My mother, Alma, aged thirty-nine when I arrived, was a small, dark woman with soulful brown eyes and a pensive mouth. She sang alto, played the piano, and taught all of us children to sing—church music but also tearful Irish tunes like "Mother Machree" and "Bendameer Stream," such Carrie Jacobs-Bond hits as "Just a-Wearying for You," and parlor favorites like "Somewhere a Voice Is Calling," whose writers' names I now forget. The attic of my memory echoes with dozens of treacly songs from those far-off days.

In 1927, we moved to a newly built house on the south edge of town—this time across from an apple orchard. Painted slate blue, with dark woodwork inside, it seemed cozy to me then. Old photographs I have looked at since show a gaunt barn of a place. Soon, I started school.

Reprinted from *Contemporary Authors Autobiography Series*, volume 17, copyright 1993 by Gale Research.

Somewhere I have a photograph of that foursquare brown brick building, taken on a winter day, and it looks bleak. But I liked it, earned good grades, appeared in patriotic playlets and tangle-footed Maypole dances, and made friends.

I learned to read with great suddenness. I have never understood why. South Dakota was among the first states in the nation to embrace Progressive Education, a product of the solemnly lunatic mind of John Dewey. We were taught to read not with phonics but with flash cards. As we sat in a circle on little red chairs, a teacher would hold up a card with a picture of a horse on it, then turn over the card where the word HORSE was printed.

This was no way to teach reading, almost everyone had an awful time learning from it, and some did not learn at all. But it was fine for me. I saw some method in the madness which I could not then, nor can I now, explain. In *Colloquium on Crime*, edited by Robin Winks (Scribners, 1986), I've told how at age seven I was sick for many months, and how, alone for long hours every day, I chanced to read my first adult book, *Abraham Lincoln: The Prairie Years*, by Carl Sandburg. Not a bad writer for a youngster to start off with, who would in time become a writer himself. I would follow Sandburg with Jack London and Mark Twain, but not until a few years later.

In 1932, the Great Depression and the dustbowl winds swept away the shoe store, the house, the car, and scattered our family. My sister, a graduate of Northern State Teachers College, who had for a time worked there as secretary to the president, went to try her luck in California. My father headed for Minneapolis to look for work. My brother thumbed his way from small college to small college, sleeping the nights in barns and haystacks. He had won medals in regional contests for his singing, and he hoped for a music scholarship, but his high school grades weren't good enough—he'd spent too much time on sports, playacting, and music.

My mother and I hung on in Aberdeen, moving from one dismal spare room to another—no doubt because my father couldn't send money for the rent. At one of these stops, seated by a window outside which bees tumbled in the blossoms of a lilac bush, I did my first writing. In an old stenographer's notebook of my sister's. It was plain to me that something had gone wrong with the country and, in a series of essays, I offered my ideas on how to put it right again. I titled this sage work "Philosophy from a Boy to Older Folks," and illustrated it with drawings in colored crayon.

In the summer of 1933 I got the surprise of my life when I stepped into the tiny grocery store near where we lived, to pick up a bottle of milk and a loaf of bread. "Charge it, please," I said. I always said that. The grocer, a skinny bespectacled man in a white apron, grabbed me by my shirt front, lifted me right off my feet, and told me he'd heard we were leaving town, and if my mother didn't pay him what she owed, he'd set the police on her. I was scared. And maybe my mother was scared too, but I doubt the grocer got his money. Where would it have come from?

Still, he was right—we did leave town. To me it was a fairy-tale flight. A beautiful, modishly dressed young lady drove us to Minneapolis in a new cabriolet with red leather seats and red wire wheels. Who was she? A stranger, at least to me. But with a kind heart. Glinda the Good? Why not? Minneapolis, however, was scarcely the Emerald City. We dwelt in dreary apartments and ate oatmeal. My father heaved coal into the vast basement furnace of some towering downtown church. With frostbitten fingers, my brother clambered around the outside of Sears Roebuck's upper stories, stringing festive SALE banners in the snow.

Minneapolis had many lakes that of course froze in winter when, to the delight of my father and Bob, who had feared I was hopeless at sports, I learned to skate. I was good at it, and spent every free hour I could on the ice. To my joy, I found that a couple of bullies who'd been making my life hell in the halls at school had weak ankles and could only flop around on the ice, helpless and red faced, shaking futile fists at me while I breezed circles around them, grinning. I could easily have knocked them down, and they knew it. They stopped calling me sissy after that.

Yet sometimes the snow piled up to the windowsills, and it was impossible to get to even the nearest lake—Powderhorn, it was called—and this was when I happened upon *White Fang* in our modest bookcase, and read it over and over again. Its only characters were dogs, which somehow comforted me. It wasn't dogs that had wrecked my world.

Still, after I'd pondered it doubtfully many times, the front illustration in a book of my brother's at last lured me away from *White Fang*. The drawing showed a fierce-looking bearded man in ragged clothes climbing in the window of a bedroom where a frightened boy cowered in a corner. I had to learn what that was all about. And thus began my reading and rereading of *Huckleberry Finn*, surely the best of all American novels.

It's not a book for boys, but Twain's disgust at the casual viciousness of white people toward blacks was clear to me from my first trip on that raft with Huck and Jim down the Mississippi. *Huckleberry Finn* is not only a stunning piece of writing, but a good book by a good man about a world that needed then as it still needs all the goodness it can get. I expect I took in this lesson unawares, but when I began to write novels myself I found I expected this stress on goodness from them too. I hope it sometimes shows.

After three hardbitten winters in Minneapolis, my mother and father decided between themselves to sell whatever they still had, including my mother's beloved piano. With the money, they bought a stately if mortally wounded old Marmon automobile. The plan was to go to California, where if we continued to starve, at least we wouldn't freeze. Instead of alerting me to this plan, they shipped me off to stay with cousins in Duluth. Bob was kept in the dark as well. He was on the road with a down-at-heel theatrical company that mostly performed in barns, and rarely got paid.

When the wife of the company's owner began to breathe passionately in his ear, Bob fled. He arrived home in Minneapolis to find no one there. The folks had written him a letter, but too late. He didn't know where they'd gone. They had gone to Owatonna, a German-speaking southern Minnesota town, my mother's birthplace, where her older sister Edith still lived, with a gawky son, my cousin Galen, half-blind, but a whiz at things electric and mechanical. (I loved their house, and moved it to California in my novel *Job's Year*, where it becomes Oliver Jewett's boyhood home.)

Because Tony Erchul, my Duluth cousin, worked for the county, when the folks sent for me he arranged for me to get halfway to Owatonna in a limousine filled with crippled charity children on their way to therapy in Minneapolis. I sat in front with the chauffeur, who scared me with how fast he drove. He was a great kidder, and when he put me on the bus, knowing how nervous I was about traveling alone for the first time in my life, gravely charged the driver not to forget that I was to be dropped in—Mankato.

The driver, of course, dropped me in Owatonna, where I belonged. Bob at last arrived there too, and as soon as Galen was able to get the Marmon into running condition, we tied cartons and suitcases all over her and set off in the furnace heat of July 1936, for California. We had enough money for gasoline and food but little to spare for overnight stops, and we slept in ancient, gone-to-seed hotels, or shacky tourist cabins, four to a room. In one such place, the only water came from a leaky tap outside the cabin door.

As the majestic old Marmon rolled westward along the scorching highways, my mother slumped in the backseat, sweating and moaning. I was afraid the heat was going to kill her. But I was the one who passed out, to be shocked awake by water from a garden hose splashing over me.

I lay on my back on a small patch of grass, and a sunburned farmwife in a J.C. Penney housedress stood over me, laughing easily, hosing me down, and saying, "Come on, now, sonny. Wake up, boy. You're all right." Where was that? Nevada? Possibly. If so, our nightmare in the sun was almost over.

My beautiful sister, Louise, who was a typist for a bank, lived with her foundry-worker husband, Joe Hubbard, among ten acres of grapefruit, lemons, limes, in Altadena. Joe kept bees that produced magnificent honey, dark and heady with sage. But however charitably and cheerfully the scheme began, moving three more adults (Bob was by now twenty-two) and a child into a one-room cabin led to friction. I was enchanted by the place, where deer sometimes peered in at us through the windows at night. I spent hours outdoors shooting at tin cans with the BB gun Joe Hubbard had given me, reading, daydreaming, playing with a trap-door spider I located under a hulking old pepper tree. In Minneapolis, I had written stories. Here I wrote poems.

But Bob, though he'd been working at some pretty dreadful jobs, was appalled when Joe Hubbard demanded he hire on among the hellish fires of the foundry, and moved out. When winter came, with its rainy nights, and the porch proved unsleepable, my father and mother and I left too—for spare rooms in the wisteria-covered cottage of one Miss Criss (she looked exactly like her name) in Pasadena. Here I labored earnestly at putting the Psalms of David into modern English. I don't know why. Perhaps as a form of prayer. God seemed to be ignoring us.

My father found occasional work as a shoe clerk, but the pay was poor, and the jobs chancy, so we were soon again, and often afterwards, on the move, in search of cheaper rent. This meant making shift in the cheerless brown rooms of other people's houses, but it was surely harder on my parents than on me. Humiliating, hopeless. I was a child. I got used to it. It was simply how things were.

I joined a boy choir at an Episcopal church, where I learned plain-song and the glorious English of the Book of Common Prayer. The choir-master-organist was Raymond Hill, charming, humorous, gifted, who took special interest in me. I was often at his house, where he saw to it that I heard a wide range of good music. His collection of records was fabulous—almost every week new shipments arrived from England, Germany, Italy. Browsing his shelves of art books, I began to learn something about painting, sculpture, architecture. He wangled me into a private school for brilliant boys where, with my stunted background, I was instantly lost, and survived only one wretched term.

Raymond sailed off to Rome to study Gregorian chant, and I returned to public school, where I soon became a chorister again—this time with a boy choir drawn from schools all over town, and shepherded by John Henry Lyons, a gigantic man who never wore any color but green. Even his shoes were green. The choir had three hundred members, but a core of thirty boys sometimes used to travel to nearby towns for recitals, usually at Christmastime. We were forbidden to sing on our way to these events, but on the way home in the bus, we sang our hearts out. The exuberance of those nighttime shouts of song echo among my happiest memories.

When we staged an all-boy version of "Pinafore," I was inspired to try my hand at writing a comic opera just like it, words and music—but my invention flagged after a lively opening chorus about sailing on the Tappan Zee. Soon I was eagerly typing out reportage with two fingers for the John Marshall Junior High School paper. Later, I was proud to be named its editor. I appeared in school plays, and won a gold medal for dramatic recitation and a silver one for public speaking—or was it the other way around?

The reason fundamentalist Christian characters sometimes figure in my novels and stories is that for a couple of years in my teens I fell among these people, at one point stooping so low as to become president of my Christian Endeavor group, a Sunday school teacher, and the lead singer in a gospel quartet. I attended vast evangelical youth conventions, and went to summer camps in the mountains where these sanctimonious children gathered in God's Great Outdoors not simply to hike, swim, ride horses, but to pray, sing, study the Bible, and be preached at without ceasing.

To try to snap me out of this unattractive phase, Raymond Hill—back from Rome with Doctor tacked to the front of his name—gave me *Elmer Gantry* to read. It didn't turn the trick. But when I reached such a peak of hysteria that I announced to my parents I had been called by God to become a minister, they did something they'd never done to me before, no matter what wild career— artist, actor, singer, symphony conductor—I'd proposed for myself. They laughed. And that brought me to my senses. They were good Christians both, but they saw that I'd gotten in too deep and that the time had come to drag me ashore.

Someone long ago posited a connection between religious mania and sex. And at this point, sex was plaguing me. My suddenly lanky, six-foot-tall body was giving me surprises I didn't know what to make of. To that point, I must have been the most completely asexual child who ever lived. Now, suddenly, here came rushing at me a whole new set of impulses I didn't want and couldn't handle. This was almost certainly why I fled to the arms of Jee-zuss. Other boys at that church, I now realize, were also scrambling to escape their homosexuality, though I didn't know it then.

In the midst of this confusion, in 1939, I started at a new school, Pasadena Junior College, which offered the last two years of high school and the first two of college. I met a set of shiny new friends, some of them two or three years older than I. With my smalltown, Midwest origins, I was not sophisticated. These youngsters dazzled me with what I took to be their maturity and worldliness. To my delight, they accepted me in spite of my rusticity, and I hurried to adopt their attitudes. Luckily I had a talent for mimicry.

I reported for the school newspaper and acted in stage and radio plays. For one of these, Dickens's *A Christmas Carol*, I wrote the script, with George Hodgkin, the most dazzling of my new chums. I hung out with them in cafes near the campus, talking, smoking Domino cigarettes, drinking coffee, listening to the jukebox. On sunny afternoons when we ought to have been in classrooms, we might pile into cars and head for the beach, or up into the rugged canyons above town, to read poetry, or hold grave adolescent discussions about the meaning of life. I worked after school as a page in the public library, so sometimes I had enough money to join them at movies in the evenings, and afterwards for hamburgers at drive-ins.

By now, my father had found a steady job selling shoes in a department store, and we were living in a small house by ourselves, on a rundown little street shaded by old pepper trees. For that house, that street, forty years later, I wrote an elegy in *A Smile in His Lifetime*. I had my own room, at last, but I'd seen the large, handsome houses of my new friends, and met their prosperous parents, and I was ashamed for them to see how shabbily I lived with parents who were old and poor. This was not only mean-spirited toward my parents, but shows how little I knew the good hearts of my friends. I had a lot of growing up to do.

As best I could with the small money that came my way, I began to fill my room (and my head) with books—Shakespeare's plays, Poe's tales, Walt Whitman's *Leaves of Grass*, Thoreau's *Walden* and Emerson's *Essays*. Whitman startled me by writing of feelings I had supposed doomed me. I had dreaded being classed with the mincing men my cruder schoolmates jeered at on the streets, or with a willowy distant uncle of mine, who in simpering middle age wore rouge and lipstick at his job behind the counter where customers paid their bills at the Pasadena gas company. Whitman's manly ease with his sexuality eased my worries, and Emerson's

"Self Reliance" urged me to be myself, no matter what the world might think.

But books, however wise, weren't enough. And for all the friends I had, I still felt lonely. Robert Ben Ali took care of this. Portly, and as Arabic in looks as his name suggested, he was a local *wunderkind*, whose play *Manya*, written at age seventeen, had been staged to nationwide publicity: one of its student actors, Bill Beedle, was given a movie contract that launched his career as William Holden.

Ben Ali's play was about Marie Curie, and for a while he and his mother clung to the hope that the studios would buy it to turn into a picture. Marie Curie's story did reach the screen, but not in Ben Ali's version. As to Holden, after his early success in *Golden Boy,* Ben Ali, with a car full of other youngsters who'd been in school plays with him, drove over to his Beverly Hills mansion to congratulate him. Holden refused to see them. Ben Ali was philosophical about it: "I suppose he was afraid we'd come to ask favors." But I could see that he was hurt.

He was more than lover, he was mentor, counselor, comforter, a spellbinding talker who flung open doors for me into the worlds of Homer and Socrates, of James Joyce and Jean Cocteau, of Rimbaud and Baudelaire, the music of Eric Satie and Igor Stravinsky, and Lord knows what and who else. I've been lucky all my life in my friends. They have been my university—the only one I was to have or to want.

Ben Ali lived with his mother in a tiny book-filled house on Allen Avenue, and was finishing up his studies at PJC. He continued to write plays and to direct plays at school and at the Pasadena Playhouse, where he saw to it that I got an education in theatre—there was a summer festival of all the Shakespeare comedies, another of famous American stage hits of the past—*Clarence, The College Widow, The Baby Cyclone.* All lavishly mounted, with first-rate professional casts. There were Ibsen and Strindberg and Chekhov. There was Onslow Stevens as a hulking Richard III, and a rumbling-voiced, gold-helmeted Odysseus in a play by Emil Ludwig. There were Restoration comedies dressed in velvets, lace ruffles, and silver shoebuckles. There were funny, sentimental Saroyan plays—*Jim Dandy* and *My Heart's in the Highlands.*

Lucille Ben Ali, a short, fat woman with a splendid nose, worked as a performer with delightful marionettes that she made herself. Her parks and recreation department paychecks kept food on the table, but it was not until Ben Ali took a night job at Lockheed Aircraft that they could afford a car, a wooden-sided station wagon. America was in the war by then, my brother, Bob, was in hazard day and night on a Navy minesweeper, my shining friends had scattered, to the army, navy, air force, coast guard. I dealt with the draft as did Oliver Jewett in *Job's Year*, and I won't repeat the story here.

I drifted restlessly from job to job—midnight want-ad tallyman for the *Los Angeles Times*, announcer for a tiny Pasadena radio station, page at the Henry E. Huntington Library and Art Gallery in San Marino, and in Hollywood at the Pacific Aeronautical Library. Still living with my parents, I wrote poems and plays. My heart lifted when a friend promised to get a play of mine produced at Christmastime on the new LA television station. Titled "I Have Been Here Before," it was about Jesus returning as a man to Bethlehem, and to the stable behind the inn, where he'd been born. That there were as yet few if any television sets in the city for anyone to see my play on didn't worry me. And it needn't have—the play was never produced.

In February 1943 I got a job clerking, for eighteen dollars a week, at the Pickwick Bookshop on Hollywood Boulevard. The bus ride from Pasadena took an hour, so with my typewriter, books, and clothes, I left my parents' roof in favor of a rented room on Yucca Street, a block from the store. I was thrilled to be living on my own at last, and immediately began to write a novel. Hell, wasn't it about time? I was nineteen. I had a lot to say, didn't I?

The cavernous bookstore and my dusty work there I have described in *Living Upstairs*. I've put into that novel also the wonderful jazz clubs that flourished along the shadowy night boulevard in those times, and the immortal performers—Jack Teagarden, Erroll Garner, Jimmy Noone, and others—I got to hear when for the price of a watery highball I could buy an enchanted hour on a wobbly stool at the bar. I was too young to drink legally, but so were most of the servicemen on leave who crowded these places, kids from the sticks, most of them, wide-eyed at being in fabulous Hollywood.

Now and then some non-hick would sit next to me and try to coax me to take him to my room for sex, but I was leery of strangers. For sex I wanted a friend, and I already had one. Ben Ali and I saw each other every weekend, driving in his trusty bangwagon to restaurants, galleries, concerts, ballets, the beach if there were gasoline coupons. But our time together—three years of it—was running out.

One Saturday morning, a young woman called Jane Bancroft came into the shop, saw me carrying an armload of books up an aisle, and for reasons still mysterious to me decided I was the boy for her. At that time, Jane was operating a router, a messy and dangerous job, at the Vega aircraft plant, and in her off-hours at home was designing glorious patterns

JOSEPH **HANSEN**   239

for textiles. Slender, narrow-hipped, tall for a girl, she wore bell-bottom jeans and cut her hair short like a boy's. I found her a treat to look at.

A Boston Brahmin, descended from the Massachusetts Bay Colony's first governor John Winthrop, she'd passed much of her childhood with her mother's family in Texas, where they also were old blood. Her self-assurance bespoke aristocratic heritage, all right, but her arresting vocabulary suggested the stables of Fort Bliss, the Army cavalry post at El Paso, where she'd spent a girlhood among horses, and the stockyards, where she'd worked cattle from horseback.

My single experience on horseback had resulted in a misunderstanding between me and my glum old mount, and I'd lost interest in riding then and there—so that side of Jane's experience didn't draw me, but she had a lively mind, had read widely, retained what she read, and could talk about it glowingly. Here was a bright new friend to learn from. Her interests ranged from the war news on the radio (and the political motives behind it) to the ancient Chinese poetry of Tu Fu and Li Po, from T. S. Eliot's theology to that of Boethius—she was reading *The Consolation of Philosophy* when we met—from Leonardo's drawings to those of Paul Cadmus, from Wanda Landowska's Bach recordings to the conductor Frank Black's current broadcast series of Mahler symphonies. If Ben Ali had read to me with vivid excitement all the Socratic dialogs, Jane had in her memory every myth in Ovid's *Metamorphosis*. My head grew dizzy, and my heart soon followed. We were married on August 4, 1943, at Los Angeles County courthouse, ate lunch in Chinatown, and rode home by streetcar. I had been given a whole day off for my honeymoon.

Our odd apartment I've described in *Living Upstairs*. We were lucky to get it—housing was hard to find during the war. And at first, fate smiled on us there. My account of the courageous struggle of Esther Takei, a Japanese-American girl, to return from internment camp to go on with her schooling in bigoted Pasadena, was published in a national magazine, *Common Sense*. Houghton Mifflin optioned a new novel I'd begun, after I'd scrapped the first one on Jane's advice. And in July of 1944, our daughter, Barbara, was born, one week short of my twenty-first birthday.

Then, as surprisingly as it had struck, luck deserted me, at least so far as writing went. Houghton Mifflin didn't want the novel once it was finished. And though I kept writing, nobody would buy a line I wrote, not articles, not short stories, not poems, not plays, and not novels. The publisher's enormous $500 advance was long gone, and I was back working.

Sometimes, to give me more time to write, Jane would take jobs at the Pickwick and other bookstores along the boulevard, while I kept one eye on the typewriter and the other on the baby. Except for our love for each other, these were years when it seemed always to be raining. It grew hard to keep believing in myself. I took to starting new novels, plays, stories, and not finishing them. What was the use? They all came limping back.

I missed singing, making music, and scraped together enough pennies to buy an autoharp. In the late 1940s, Burl Ives, Richard Dyer-Bennett, and Susan Reed had begun to sing folk songs, and I was fetched by their recordings and worked up a batch of songs on my own. Not that I craved a career in music. Writing was still my aim. But my generous friend from high school, George Hodgkin, now working at a big LA radio station, heard me sing and decided I ought to have a program on the air. He named it "The Stranger from the Sea," wrote the introductory copy, and produced and directed it.

It aired every week from December 1951 to December 1953. A small record company, Tempo, issued a couple of albums that sold well in and around LA. But they and all the broadcasts put together had earned me very little money for all my time and effort. And so I was relieved when George left radio for television, and "The Stranger from the Sea" was canceled. All my spare hours had gone into researching songs, arranging and memorizing them, and writing copy about them for the broadcasts, so for two years, I'd had no time for writing—or trying to write. I was glad to have that time restored.

Back in 1951, Jane's mother had made us the gift of a small house in the Hollywood hills—it figures in *A Smile in His Lifetime*. We had good times there. We added some interesting new members to our cat population, and Jane, in return for looking after a neighbor's horse, got to ride him whenever she wished. There was enough wilderness around us in those days to make riding a pleasure. Little Barbara had taken a liking to reptiles, and had as pets a handsome brown-and-yellow-banded king snake and a dignified desert tortoise who enjoyed Mozart. Then came a young horned owl with a broken wing whom we all took turns looking after until he mended. Cuthbert matured into a magnificent specimen, and after he soared off to live on his own in our wooded canyons, I wrote an article about him for *All-Pets* magazine.

But it grew clear to Jane and me that if we three were going to eat and have clothes to wear, one of us had better find steady work. I had been trying to sell encyclopedias door to door, but my heart wasn't in it. A friend of ours at the Technicolor plant in Hollywood got me a job there as a clerk-typist in the shipping department. It was dreary, but it meant a paycheck every week, so at the same desk, in the same windowless cinder-block room, I kept at that job for ten long years, writing when I could, but with dimming hopes.

In 1954, at my sister's house in Pasadena, my father died of pancreatic cancer, aged seventy-one. He was a sunny man and always good to me. I still dream of him. And only the other evening, when I stepped into the kitchen for something, I smelled smoke from his cigar. It was as if he'd left the room only a moment before.

Tom Lengyel, a young Hungarian with illustrious screenwriter relatives but whose own luck at the studios had been spotty, asked me for help in 1955. He had an in with the story editor of the television series "Lassie." If he could come up with scripts, he was sure she would buy them. The hitch was, he knew nothing about American farm life. This was where I came in. Jane furnished the story ideas, and between us— Tom standing at my shoulder teaching me scriptwriting as we went along—he and I turned out two episodes, "The Greyhound" and "The Hungry Deer," that were, for a fact, accepted, filmed, and broadcast. But I hated the writing process—everybody interfered, producer, advertising agency, sponsor, even Lassie's trainer—and I swore I would never again write for television. I was happy for Tom to have the screen credit—and most of the money, since he needed it worse than we did. After all, I was working.

Then, in 1956, I had some real luck with my writing. John Ciardi bought a poem of mine for the *Saturday Review* about a childhood episode in South Dakota. I wrote another with the same setting right away and the *New Yorker* bought it. And another, and another. The small checks didn't mean I could quit my job, but they were useful. For a year earlier, we'd taken in to live with us a recently divorced and penniless young woman friend and her three little kids.

This required more room than the small house in the hills afforded, and in 1957 the crowd of us moved into the low-roofed, green-sided, French-windowed house in southwest Los Angeles where Jane and I still live. By 1961, Jane was teaching steadily, and our friend Froncie, whose kids were now in school, also had found a job, so I was able to quit Technicolor and take a four-hour night job at a bookstore. This gave me more time to write, but still it was 1964 before I managed to sell a novel, and that to probably the least-distinguished publisher in the United States—or the world, for that matter. But before we get to that, let me outline what led up to the novel.

A year or two earlier, Wayne Placek, a friend and lover, alas now dead of AIDS, had introduced me to Don Slater, a feisty little Navy veteran, a gay activist long before the term was coined. He edited a small magazine for homosexuals called *ONE*, and soon he began publishing my short stories. Though by today's standards as chaste as a Sunday school paper, yet simply because of its subject matter, *ONE* sometimes ran into trouble with authorities, postal and other. So the paper's policy was that all its writers use pen names, to protect them from arrest and prosecution, possibly even jail. I protested, but Don was adamant, so I became James Colton.

And when, after publishing a handful of stories, I decided to try a novel along the same lines, figuring I might have a fan or two, I stuck with James Colton. Now, there was no graphic sex in "Valley Boy," but it shunned the tacitly agreed-upon formula of earlier homosexual novels—sin, suffering, and suicide—so no one in New York would touch it, not even the reputedly fearless Harlan Ellison, then head of a paperback imprint called Lion Books.

Finally, in desperation, I sent the tattered manuscript to Les Aday, who issued pulp-paper pornography from, of all unlikely places, Fresno, California. He gave it a soppy title, *Lost on Twilight Road*, and chose cover art featuring, unaccountably, a naked woman, but he did have the guts to print the book, and so, however humbly, I was a published novelist at last.

If this account of a *New Yorker* poet unable to find a decent publisher for his novel seems unlikely to you, you came into the world too late to know the fear and loathing a writer faced who, thirty years ago, treated homosexuality as simply another element of everyday life.

In 1965, Don Slater made me an editor of *ONE* magazine, and I soon saw that it urgently needed to change. The homosexuals who were our readers already knew what we were telling them. The straight world did not. If things were ever to improve for us, it was the straight world we must educate. This caused a rift at the magazine, with the result that one midnight, Don Slater, aided by a tough, wiry friend who owned a furniture van, stealthily whisked *ONE*, lock, stock, and barrel, out of its old headquarters to a place miles away, in Cahuenga Pass.

Threatened with lawsuits, we changed the magazine's name to *Tangents*. With no money, but with a smart, new design, sometimes even a dash of color, and with a lot of hard work, we kept it going for five years. I wrote editorials, articles, stories, book reviews, and a monthly column based on news clippings sent in by readers from around the country. Jane designed striking covers, drew graphics for the inside of the book, wrote reviews and an advice column. But by 1970, large circulation magazines like *Cosmopolitan* and *Playboy* had begun treating homosexuality candidly and sometimes even with goodwill and common sense. We had become redundant. Subscriptions dried up. We couldn't pay our printer. And we folded.

In the midst of all this, I kept writing novels, not ambitious in scope, but aimed at telling the truth. I was exploring what I had begun slowly to realize was my subject. *Strange Marriage* appeared in 1965 from the mail-order wing of Sherbourne Press, a new Los Angeles publisher. A collection of the stories I'd published in *ONE* and *Tangents* followed from Evergreen Classics, a busy San Diego publisher of gay pornography.

Then in 1966, I wrote a novel that I sensed was better than the first two by quite a stretch. But again, New York wanted nothing to do with it, nor did a swishy but firmly closeted editor at Sherbourne Press. And the novel ended up two long years later as a paperback from Brandon House in North Hollywood, whose editors insisted I add graphic sex scenes, and called it *Known Homosexual*. It is in the shops these days as *Pretty Boy Dead*—without the sex scenes.

Also in 1966, Jane, working at a newsstand, came upon a magazine called *South Dakota Review* and brought a copy home to me. Some years before, I'd written a story called "Mourner." Like several of my poems, it was based on a Dakota childhood memory, but though I'd sent it around, no editor had wanted it. John R. Milton at *SDR* liked it, and soon printed it. I've recounted the thrill of that in *SDR's* twenty-fifth anniversary issue (winter 1988), where the story makes a reappearance. John Milton not only founded and edited a first-rate literary magazine in an unlikely place, he kept it going through thick and thin, gave a lot of writers breaks, and I'm proud to call him my friend.

In *Pretty Boy Dead* I'd tried on for the first time the murder mystery form, and I felt I'd been less than successful with it. So I tried again. My aim was to write a book about a homosexual that heterosexuals would want to read, and there's no form that keeps readers turning pages like a mystery. But it must hew to the expected lines. I worked hard at this, and the result was *Fadeout*, featuring an insurance death-claims investigator, Dave Brandstetter, whom the *New Yorker* would later call "thoroughly and contentedly homosexual." I knew it was the best book I'd yet written, but again no establishment publisher would accept it. The year was 1967.

The two novels that followed I wrote hastily. I had lost my bookshop job, and I felt, having wasted months on a novel no one would buy, that it was past time I brought some money into the household. Jane and

Froncie were both working. So was Barbara by now, at a nearby electronics plant. I owed it to them to do my part. So I'm afraid there's not a lot of literary quality to *Cocksure* and *Hang-Up*. While they have some serious things to say, both are melodramas overloaded with pornography. But they did find publishers, of a sort, and the money did help.

I had begun writing another such novel, *Gard*, when life took a surprising new turn. Without warning me, a young New York writer, Leo Skir, who had sent me outstanding stuff when I was editing *ONE* and *Tangents*, showed my books to his agent, Oscar Collier, who then wrote offering to represent me. He sold *Tarn House* right away, a little Gothic novel I'd written in 1967, when such stuff was crowding the supermarket racks. I'd submitted it to eight or ten publishers, but hadn't been able to sell it on my own. On the strength of some chapters and an outline, Oscar sold *Gard* as well, to Michael de Forrest, at Award Books. As to *Fadeout*, he asked me to have patience. I knew what that meant, but wondered bleakly if he did.

Michael de Forrest, himself a novelist, advised me to scrap the melodrama and murder I'd had in mind for *Gard*, and simply write the story of the two main characters, a thirty-something writer of children's books, and a supposedly retarded seventeen-year-old neighbor boy, as their relationship develops through a seaside summer of loving and learning. I saw this as a chance to challenge the straight world's notion that homosexual men only exploit and abuse youngsters. Often they do, which is criminal. But sometimes they understand where others cannot or will not, and give unselfish help—emotional, educational, material.

But writing this nearly plotless kind of novel marked a change for me, it was difficult, and took time. When I had finished, I was pleased and moved by what I'd done. But by then, de Forrest had been fired and replaced by an editor who, without consulting me, gutted the novel, so I scarcely recognized it when the printed book arrived. I was outraged, but I had no money for lawyers, and no time for lawsuits.

It stuns me to realize now how I crowded my time in the 1960s, and how much energy I had. Not only was I working at the bookshop (until March 1966), editing *Tangents*, writing novels, playing the guitar, composing songs, singing on Saturday nights at a little restaurant, and painting pictures (a couple of which actually sold), but in October 1967 I began conducting weekly poetry workshops at the Bridge, a hippy bookshop in East Hollywood. I've described the place, its flower-child denizens, and their dreamy, drugged-out life-style in *A Smile in His Lifetime*.

The Bridge's life was brief, and in February 1969 a poet friend, John Harris, discovered George Drury Smith's Beyond Baroque gallery and printshop in Venice Beach, and we moved the poetry workshop there. I left in 1974, but the workshop persisted for at least a decade more, always open to all comers, always free of charge, sometimes argumentative, even explosive, but often good-humored and funny, and sometimes genuinely productive. Some good poets—James Krusoe, Lee Hickman, Kate Braverman, many others—took part, all of us teaching each other, learning from each other.

Toward the end of 1969, Oscar Collier telephoned me from New York—Joan Kahn, the Great Lady mystery editor at Harper & Row, had accepted *Fadeout*. Jane was teaching in her classroom in Santa Monica, Froncie was typing in an office near the airport, Barbara was assembling electronics at the Avnet plant, the youngsters were in school. I told our dog, Bantu, who lifted her head, wagged her tail once, lowered her chin between her paws, and went back to sleep. I told such of our snoozing cats as I could locate. Then I began ringing up anyone I figured there was a chance of reaching. This was the biggest and best news I would ever get in my life, and I simply had to tell someone, anyone. No one answered.

Alma Rosebrock Hansen died in February 1970 in the intensive care unit of a San Diego hospital, after a massive heart attack. She was eighty-six years old, and had outlived my father by sixteen years. These years she had spent with my sister, Louise, also a widow now, in a city whose glorious climate gave her back her health. Later, after an engineering career with various aircraft companies that took him from LA to Tucson to Pascagoula, Bob also settled with his wife, Hannah, and their children in San Diego, so though I never visited my mother there—we didn't get along—she had a loving family around her. I flew to San Diego to be with her at the end, but her mind was jumbled, and she didn't know me.

My reaction to having, after years of struggle, at last gained a first-rate book publisher was in some ways sensible—I hung up my guitar, I put away my paints and brushes, I was about to have a career. But then how can I explain to you or to myself plunging ahead in a kind of panic to write, this time for Olympia Press, two more sexually graphic James Colton novels? Part of the answer must be that deep down I didn't trust my good luck. I feared the Harper & Row connection was a fluke, and would never repeat itself.

The Outward Side was written in fifteen days, and shows it. Its subject—a young, married minister in a small town, trying to cope with his homosexuality—deserved better treatment. In *Todd* I tried to make up to Frances Green, my very nice editor, for such a rackety first book with a better one. The concept for *Todd* came in a rush late one night, when the house was asleep. I sat alone leafing over a favorite anthology, and chanced to read again John Crowe Ransom's moving lines, "A cry of absence, absence in the heart / And in the wood, the furious winter blowing," and saw a whole novel in those lines. I could hardly wait till morning to begin to write it.

Todd gives glimpses from inside of the boisterous gay liberation movement in the LA of the 1960s, but more interestingly to me, in the character of Todd, when he flees in fear from the chance to have a career as a concert pianist, and settles for playing "Stardust" in gay bars, I realize now I was depicting my own failure of nerve about tackling another book for Harper & Row. I had panicked. I couldn't remember how I'd fitted together the mystery plot of *Fadeout*. I was sure I couldn't manage it again. I used still another dodge. I took to broadcasting on the local Pacifica radio station a program called "Homosexuality Today" that popped the eyes and strained the tolerance of some of the left-liberal old guard at the station.

Then came *Fadeout*'s publication day, and good reviews, and I felt better. *Death Claims* was slow going, but in the end it proved to me I needn't worry about plotting. I had the knack. What I didn't have a knack for was making money. However good the press they received, the Brandstetter novels sold poorly. And paperback publishers had at that time stopped issuing reprints of any mysteries not by Agatha Christie. So when Oscar Collier telephoned one day to say he could get me three thousand dollars fast from some paperback outfit if I'd send him the outline of another Gothic novel, I did as he asked. And started writing the book.

But Oscar decided on his own that my proposal was too good for paperback, and showed it to Joan Kahn, who bought it at once. Now, my reading had equipped me with enough period detail to have written a paperback set in the South in 1880 without taking time out for research. But for a hardcover novel? From a major publisher? Jane brought me stacks of books from the library. I groaned, but to my surprise, I enjoyed the research. Harper & Row packaged the book handsomely, it sold well, and brought me letters from New Orleans readers praising how well I'd pictured a place I'd never seen.

By this time, the autumn of 1974, I was living in London on a grant from the National Endowment for the Arts. I'd completed the third Dave Brandstetter adventure, *Troublemaker*, just before I got the astonishing news about the grant. I'd scoffed at the idea that a mystery writer stood a chance, but I'd applied at the repeated prompting of Alexandra Garrett, of Beyond Baroque. Sadly, Sandy is no longer living. But I will always be grateful for her cheerful nagging. I had a big novel to write. This grant would buy me the time.

London was terrifically romantic to me, crowded with associations from a lifetime of reading. It seemed as if around every corner I ran into some name or sight that evoked a literary past I could link up with in my memory. The present was exciting too. I made friendships I still cherish—with the delightful novelist Beryl Bainbridge; with Ronald Harwood, the playwright who would later triumph with *The Dresser*; with Charles Osborne, biographer of Verdi and Schumann and Wagner, and a witty and erudite companion.

Ken Thomson, my lighthearted editor, whirled me around London in his red mini, visiting all the sights, and into the countryside as well to lunch in thatched villages, stroll through historic churches, climb the towering ruins of castles. With a neighbor, the stately, white-haired, drolly humorous Eric Walter White, retired head of the literary division of the British Arts Council, I saw operas and ballets at Covent Garden, and an awful *Yeoman of the Guard* at Saddlers Wells.

I saw at the Old Vic—of which my Cypriot taxi driver had never heard—Dame Peggy Ashcroft in Samuel Beckett's *Happy Days*, the best of his plays. I tramped through an endless Turner exhibition at the Royal Academy, and a rowdy Augustus John show at the National Gallery, got up by another friend, the biographer Michael Holroyd. With Michael, Beryl Bainbridge, Ron Harwood, and the gifted and personable poet David Harsent, I traveled to England's bleakly beautiful northeast, to make appearances in schools and pubs, reading our stuff and answering questions. On that trip we visited Hadrian's Wall, got a glimpse of Sir Walter Scott's fabled Cheviot Hills, low-lying, hazily blue, and climbed among the rocky ruins of Lindisfarne, the green and windblown Holy Isle.

But alone in my basement flat through the long nights of a London winter, and the brief, gray, rainy days, I wrestled with that wretched novel and got nowhere. I had a stupid love affair, drank too much, got into absurd scrapes, and wanted to go home. Back in Los Angeles, I put away the novel with a shudder, and got cracking on a new Brandstetter mystery. This was *The Man Everybody Was Afraid Of*, and to my stupefaction, Joan Kahn rejected it, claiming the plot was "put together with paperclips and bandaids." Before my luck changed, fourteen more publishers would vote with her. Those were scary months.

WRITINGS

Novels

Fadeout, 1970.
Death Claims, 1973.
Troublemaker, 1975.
The Man Everybody Was Afraid Of, 1978.
Skinflick, 1979.
A Smile in His Lifetime, 1981.
Gravedigger, 1982.
Backtrack, 1982.
Job's Year, 1983.
Nightwork, 1984.
Steps Going Down, 1984.
The Little Dog Laughed, 1986.
Early Graves, 1987.
Obedience, 1988.
The Boy Who Was Buried This Morning, 1990.
A Country of Old Men: The Last Dave Brandstetter Mystery, 1991.
Living Upstairs, 1993.

Short Stories

"Murder on the Surf," in *Mystery Monthly* (New York), December 1976.
The Dog, and Other Stories, 1979.
Brandstetter and Others: Five Fictions, 1984.

"The Olcott Nostrum," in *Alfred Hitchcock's Mystery Magazine* (New York), December 1987.
"The Owl in the Oak," in *Alfred Hitchcock's Mystery Magazine* (New York), March 1988.
Bohannon's Book: Five Mysteries, 1988.
"Molly's Aim," in *Ellery Queen's Mystery Magazine* (New York), June 1989.
Bohannon's Country, 1993.

Novels as Rose Brock

Tarn House, 1971.
Longleaf, 1974.

Novels and Short Stories as James Colton

Lost on Twilight Road, 1964.
Strange Marriage, 1965.
The Corrupter, and Other Stories (short stories), 1968.
Known Homosexual, 1968; revised edition published under name Joseph Hansen as *Stranger to Himself*, 1977; as *Pretty Boy Dead*, 1984.
Gard, 1969.
Cocksure, 1969.
Hang-Up, 1969.
The Outward Side, 1971.
Todd, 1971.

Contributor

The New Yorker Book of Poems, 1974.
Killers of the Mind, 1974.
Different, 1974.
Literature of South Dakota, 1976.
Years Best Mystery and Suspense Stories, 1984, 1985.
Murder, California Style, 1987.
Mammoth Book of Private Eye Stories, 1988.
City Sleuths and Tough Guys, 1989.
Under the Gun, 1990.

Other

One Foot in the Boat (poetry), 1977.
Contributor, *Colloquium on Crime: Eleven Renowned Mystery Writers Discuss Their Work*, edited by Robin W. Winks, 1986.
Rotten Rejections: A Literary Companion, 1990.

Adaptations

Four of Hansen's poems have been adapted into lyrics by composer Richard Rodney Bennett as *Vocalese*, produced London in 1983, and later broadcast by the British Broadcasting Corporation (BBC).

Meantime I began teaching weekly night classes in writing, first at Beyond Baroque, then at the Irvine campus of the University of California, and finally at UCLA. I loved teaching, and would go on with it for ten more years, winding up with four summers at Wesleyan University's writers conference in Connecticut. New England was another land rich with literary associations for me. And again I made new friends, among them the amiable conference director Jack Paton and his dear wife Sybil, the talented poets Dana Gioia and Henry Taylor, and the genial novelist George Garrett.

Henry Holt bought *The Man Everybody Was Afraid Of* in 1977, and began in 1980 to issue the earlier Brandstetter books in paperback, giving them new life. About this time, I chanced to tell a young writer friend, William Harry Harding, about my abandoned big novel. On a trip to New York, he mentioned it to Natalie Chapman, my Holt editor, Holt offered me a contract, and at last *A Smile in His Lifetime* got written. Five years had distanced me from the pain of the events I wanted to recount. I had thought through the point of the story, and how the book should be laid out. Bill Harding helped me generously with money to stretch the Holt advance, I wrote the novel with a high heart, and there were good, if sometimes shocked, reviews.

In 1970, I had written a little novel, *Backtrack*, that had never yet reached print. Sometimes this was because it was rejected, sometimes because managements changed and/or companies collapsed. In any case, twelve years later, it was still on my hands when, out of the blue, Lou Kannenstine of Countryman Press in Vermont wrote asking if I had anything he and his partner Peter Jennison might print. The moral is that a writer must never give up hope. So far as I know, *Backtrack* is still in print in Penguin paperback.

In New York in 1982, I met the handsome and likable Eleanor Sullivan, editor of *Ellery Queen's Mystery Magazine*, with the result that for the first time since *Tangents* folded I began to write short stories again. I've detailed this meeting in the introduction to *Bohannon's Country*. It would later, after years of maneuvering on my part, bring an end to *Ellery Queen's* ban on stories involving homosexuality. That introduction also tells how and why Hack Bohannon came to be, about whom I've now written some ten stories—which suggests that the six-year-old cowboy in that 1929 photo still lurks inside the graybeard he has become.

I met with some bruising reversals in the early 1980s, and my anger resulted in *Job's Year*, the story of an actor who, after a lifetime at his craft, decides he has misspent his life. Still, its first sentence begins with "He hopes..." and so does its last, and I think it is perhaps my best novel. For *Nightwork*, as often for the Dave Brandstetter mysteries, I chose a headline subject, the illegal dumping of toxic wastes in wilderness places. One reviewer noted that I had in this book come up with a new motive for murder—an uncommon event, if true. I dedicated *Nightwork* to Bob Ben Ali, and I'm glad I did. Grown frail from diabetes, and walking with a cane, he had only a year to live.

Steps Going Down I tackled as an exercise in writing a kind of crime novel different for me—with the killer instead of the detective as the central character. I had thought it would be easy—no complex plotting needed. It was not easy. I struggled with that book and its unsavory cast for fifteen wretched months. Because of the sheer awfulness of the story and everybody in it, it's the one book of mine that always makes me laugh aloud. With *Steps*, and with *The Little Dog Laughed*, I was temporizing. I'd been asked often when I was going to write about AIDS. And I shrank from the task.

But I owed it to my readers and finally steeled myself to read every scrap of paper I could find with words on it about AIDS. Once past the initial revulsion, I was so deeply moved, so emotionally involved, and found so much drama in this grisly situation that when I at last sat down at the typewriter, *Early Graves* wrote itself in five short months. It was a book I felt mattered. My publisher didn't give a damn.

In January 1986 Louise Hansen Hubbard died in San Diego of emphysema. She was eighty years old, and had been in failing health for some time, though her mind remained sharp to the end. I have a fuzzy color snapshot of her in her last months that moves me, because in it she sits surrounded by copies of my books, clutching *Job's Year* to her breast. Until I saw that picture, after her funeral, I had no idea my work meant anything to her.

All his life, Bob Hansen was active in little theatres, playing parts in comedies, musicals, dramas wherever he lived. He enjoyed it immensely, and with his talent gave pleasure to a lot of people. Recently, he lost his wife, Hannah, and he lives alone now, in San Diego. His daughter and her husband and kids live nearby, and see him often. Sometimes, even at age seventy-eight, he hops into his Volvo and travels to visit old friends around the state. Now and then, he talks of going to see Aberdeen again, but I don't think he will—the high school burned down, so did the First Methodist Church, and all his friends left long ago.

While I was writing *Obedience*, about the Vietnamese community in Los Angeles, an odd thing happened. People and events from my teen years began invading my mind, clamoring for attention. They wouldn't go away. And once I'd finished *Obedience*, I gave them their head and wrote a sprawling novel called "The Kids at Moon's." The cold reception it got from publishers I've recounted in *A Country of Old Men*, through the character of Jack Helmers, a grouchy old mystery writer.

I later rewrote and shortened "Kids" and, while it went the rounds in New York, I wrote a sequel, *Living Upstairs*, about my early days in Hollywood. It wasn't exactly snapped up, but thanks to thoughtful networking on the part of a caring friend, mystery novelist Michael Nava, it eventually reached the right editor.

Starting with "Kids" and *Upstairs*, I'd planned to write twelve novels about Nathan Reed, from age seventeen to seventy. Unrealistic for a writer crowding seventy himself? I didn't think so. One of my reasons for ending the Dave Brandstetter series was to clear the time. I was going to be writing, anyway, for as long as I could sit up and think, and I wanted to give some shape to my own life and times.

But for now, while I wait to see what happens to "The Kids at Moon's," I've put the third Nathan Reed novel aside, and am having fun writing short stories, trying angles new to me, as in "Molly's Aim" and "McIntyre's Donald." Those appear in *Bohannon's Country*, but I've written two more since, and a third is underway. I mean to have finished off five before 1992 runs out.

For 1993, I have only one plan. On the fourth of August, Jane and I will open a bottle of champagne. It will be our fiftieth wedding anniversary. Will we eat Chinese food? Why not? Hell—if we can find one, we may even ride a streetcar.

PATRICIA HIGHSMITH

IN HER ESSAY "Detective Fiction: The Modern Myth of Violence?" Brigid Brophy postulates that the popularity of the detective and crime novel is predicated not upon readers receiving a vicarious thrill in partaking in imaginary crime but in their relief that a perpetrator is always uncovered (and usually punished) at the end of the book. The emotional payoff of the crime novel isn't "who done it?" but the secure knowledge that the reader is (at least metaphorically) innocent. For Brophy, guilt is so integral to the contemporary human condition that readers need constant reassurance of their own innocence. The novels and stories of Patricia Highsmith posit an idiosyncratic response to Brophy's theorem because, in them, guilt and innocence are inextricably intertwined; often perpetrators go unpunished, while those who are technically innocent are punished. In Highsmith's world, "guilt" and "innocence" are relative, situational terms that depend more upon psychological states of mind than actual crimes or events.

Essay by
MICHAEL BRONSKI

Highsmith's output over four decades has been prodigious, including 20 crime novels, six collections of short crime fiction, and a how-to book for suspense writing as one of the earliest positive depictions of lesbian life. It has been her crime fiction, however, that has garnered the most acclaim. Her first novel, *Strangers on a Train*, was made into a classic film by Alfred Hitchcock, and several of her other novels also made the transition to the screen. Most notable of these are *The Talented Mr. Ripley*, which was made into *Purple Noon* by Louis Malle, and *Ripley's Game*, which was filmed as *The American Friend* by Wim Wenders. Highsmith's work has also been used as the basis for television scripts, particularly for the "Alfred Hitchcock Presents" series in the 1960s.

Much of Highsmith's fiction begins with ingenious, if contrived, plot devices—the traded murders of *Strangers on a Train*, the complicated foreign intrigue in *The Two Faces of January*, the elaborate forgery in *Ripley Under Ground*—but it is a finely honed psychological insight and delicate ironic sensibility that gives Highsmith's work its depth and resonance. It is the author's understanding of the intricacies of human nature that allows her to place her unpleasant characters in such unsavory situa-

tions and never let us lose sympathy for them. In Highsmith's work, the conscious act and the unconscious wish are never far apart; it is not uncommon in her books that a character wished dead by an enemy suddenly turns up dead or at least missing. Her genius is in allowing the reader to partake in crossing this thin line between desire and action, guilt and innocence.

Although most of Highsmith's male characters are ostensibly heterosexual, a strong theme of male homoeroticism runs through her work. In *Strangers on a Train*, the psychopathic Charles Bruno is characterized by such traditional homosexual male signifiers as a doting mother and a meticulous personal appearance. In the five books that chart the criminal career of Tom Ripley, Highsmith carefully hints at a homoerotic context in all of his male relationships even though Ripley enters into a heterosexual marriage and would never consider himself a homosexual. This homoeroticism is particularly strong in *The Talented Mr. Ripley*, the first of the series, as well as in *The Boy Who Followed Ripley*. This latter novel featured scenes in several gay bars, Ripley disguising himself by showing up in full drag, and a 16-year-old patricidal boy who falls in love with the protagonist. There are also strong hints of homoeroticism in such novels

American novelist. Has also written as Claire Morgan.

Born: Mary Patricia Plangman in Fort Worth, Texas, January 19, 1921; took stepfather's name. Has spent much of her time living in Switzerland.

Education: Barnard College in Manhattan, B.A. 1942.

Memberships: Member of the Detection Club.

Recipient: Mystery Writers of American Scroll and Grand Prix de Litterature Policiere, both 1957, for *The Talented Mr. Ripley;* Crime Writers Association of England Silver Dagger Award for best foreign crime novel of the year, 1964, for *The Two Faces of January;* Le Prix Litteraire, 1987.

Agent: Aarianne Ligginstorfer, Diogenes Verlag, Sprechstrasse 8, 8032 Zurich, Switzerland.

---

as *A Game For the Living* (1958), *The Two Faces of January*, *A Dog's Ransom*, and *People Who Knock on the Door.*

The persistence of male homoeroticism in Highsmith's work is indicative of, and consistent with, her interest in guilt and the unconscious. While none of Highsmith's characters who exhibit homoerotic feelings are particularly positive—everyone in Highsmith's world is, to some degree, guilty—they are not judged or condemned for their sexual desires. Male homoeroticism, for Highsmith, seems to signify for the writer an almost platonic state of natural desire and social transgression, of sexual innocence and societal guilt.

Interestingly, Highsmith's one overtly lesbian novel, *The Price of Salt,* is a fairly realistic look at lesbian lives in the 1950s. Although Highsmith is fully aware of the pressures of homophobia, the book is distinguished by a happy ending. This stands in sharp contrast not only to the bulk of writings about homosexuals of the period but also to the rest of Highsmith's work, which dwells, sometimes unremittingly, on the precariousness and instability of human emotions and relationships. Because *The Price of Salt* is an isolated work—there is nothing else like it in Highsmith's *oeuvre*—it is unclear if she intends it to be a psychological statement about lesbian sexuality. Because it was written and published at a time when most depictions of lesbianism or male homosexuality required some form of punishment, it was, and remains, a political statement. First published in 1952 under the pseudonym Claire Morgan, the book was reprinted by Naiad Press in 1984 with a new afterword by Highsmith under her own name.

Although Highsmith has a reputation as a crime novelist, it is a category that is far too narrow to suit the breadth and range of her psychological perceptions and her talents as a writer. Patricia Highsmith's work is essentially a meditation on what it means to be human—and therefore, in her terms, guilty—in the twentieth century.

THE PRICE OF SALT

Excerpt reprinted from *The Price of Salt*, Naiad Press, copyright 1991 by Patricia Highsmith.

Sometime that evening, Therese fell asleep in the car and woke up with the lights of a city on her face. Carol was resting both arms tiredly on the top of the wheel. They had stopped for a red light.

"Here's where we stay the night," Carol said.

Therese's sleep still clung to her as she walked across the hotel lobby. She rode up in an elevator and she was acutely conscious of Carol beside her, as if she dreamed a dream in which Carol was the subject and the only figure. In the room, she lifted her suitcase from the floor to a chair, unlatched it and left it, and stood by the writing table, watching Carol. As if her emotions had been in abeyance all the past hours, or days, they flooded her now as she watched Carol opening her suitcase, taking out, as she always did first, the leather kit that contained her toilet articles, dropping it onto the bed. She looked at Carol's hands, at the lock of hair that fell over the scarf tied around her head, at the scratch she had gotten days ago across the toe of her moccasin.

"What're you standing there for?" Carol asked. "Get to bed, sleepy-head."

"Carol, I love you."

Carol straightened up. Therese stared at her with intense, sleepy eyes. Then Carol finished taking her pajamas from the suitcase and pulled the lid down. She came to Therese and put her hands on her shoulders. She squeezed her shoulders hard, as if she were exacting a promise from her, or perhaps searching her to see if what she had said were real. Then she kissed Therese on the lips, as if they had kissed a thousand times before.

"Don't you know I love you?" Carol said.

Carol took her pajamas into the bathroom, and stood for a moment, looking down at the basin.

"I'm going out," Carol said. "But I'll be back right away."

Therese waited by the table while Carol was gone, while time passed indefinitely or maybe not at all, until the door opened and Carol came in again. She set a paper bag on the table, and Therese knew she had only gone to get a container of milk, as Carol or she herself did very often at night.

"Can I sleep with you?" Therese asked.

"Did you see the bed?"

It was a double bed. They sat up in their pajamas, drinking milk and sharing an orange that Carol was too sleepy to finish. Then Therese set the container of milk on the floor and looked at Carol who was sleeping already, on her stomach, with one arm flung up as she always went to sleep. Therese pulled out the light. Then Carol slipped her arm under her neck, and all the length of their bodies touched, fitting as if something had prearranged it. Happiness was like a green vine spreading through her, stretching fine tendrils, bearing flowers through her flesh. She had a vision of a pale-white flower, shimmering as if seen in darkness, or through water. Why did people talk of heaven, she wondered.

"Go to sleep," Carol said.

Therese hoped she would not. But when she felt Carol's hand move on her shoulder, she knew she had been asleep. It was dawn now. Carol's finger tightened in her hair, Carol kissed her on the lips, and pleasure leaped in Therese again as if it were only a continuation of the moment when Carol had slipped her arm under her neck last night. I love you, Therese wanted to say again, and then the words were erased by the tingling and terrifying pleasure that spread in waves from Carol's lips over her neck, her shoulders, that rushed suddenly the length of her body. Her arms were tight around Carol, and she was conscious of Carol and nothing else, of Carol's hand that slid along her ribs, Carol's hair that brushed her bare breasts, and then her body too seemed to vanish in widening circles that leaped further and further, beyond where thought could follow. While a thousand memories and moments, words, the first darling, the second time Carol had met her at the store, a thousand memories of Carol's face, her voice, moments of anger and laughter flashed like the tail of a comet across her brain. And now it was pale-blue distance and space, an expanding space in which she took flight suddenly like a long arrow. The arrow seemed to cross an impossibly wide abyss with ease, seemed to arc on and on in space, and not quite to stop. Then she realized that she still clung to Carol, that she trembled violently, and the arrow was herself. She saw Carol's pale hair across her eyes, and now Carol's head was close against hers. And she did not have to ask if this were right, no one had to tell her, because this could not have been more right or perfect. She held

Patricia Highsmith at age 27, shortly after her first novel, *Strangers on a Train*, was optioned as an Alfred Hitchcock film.

Novels

Strangers on a Train, 1950.
The Price of Salt (as Claire Morgan),
    1952; reprinted with new afterword
    by the author, 1984.
The Blunderer, 1954; as *Lament for a*
    Lover, 1956.
The Talented Mr. Ripley, 1955.
Deep Water, 1957.
A Game for the Living, 1958.
This Sweet Sickness, 1960.
The Cry of the Owl, 1962.
The Two Faces of January, 1964.
The Glass Cell, 1964.
The Storyteller, 1965.
Those Who Walk Away, 1967.
Ripley Under Ground, 1970.
A Dog's Ransom, 1972.
Ripley's Game, 1974.

Edith's Diary, 1977.
The Boy Who Followed Ripley, 1980.
People Who Knock on the Door, 1983.
The Mysterious Mr. Ripley (contains *The*
    Talented Mr. Ripley, *Ripley Under*
    Ground, and *Ripley's Game*), 1985.
Found in the Street, 1987.
Ripley Under Water, 1991.

Short Stories

The Snail Watchers and Other Stories,
    1970.
Little Tales of Misogyny (in German),
    1974; English edition, 1977.
The Animal Lover's Book of Beastly
    Murder, 1975.
Slowly, Slowly in the Wind, 1979.
The Black House, 1979.
Mermaids on the Golf Course, and Other

Stories, 1985.
Tales of Natural and Unnatural
    Catastrophes, 1987.

Other

Plotting and Writing Suspense Fiction,
    1966.

Adaptations

Strangers on a Train was adapted for a
    film directed by Alfred Hitchcock.
The Talented Mr. Ripley was filmed as
    Purple Noon by Louis Malle.
Ripley's Game was filmed as *The*
    American Friend by Wim Wenders.
Highsmith's work has also been used as
    the basis for television scripts, partic-
    ularly for the "Alfred Hitchcock
    Presents" series in the 1960s.

Carol tighter against her, and felt Carol's mouth on her own smiling mouth. Therese lay still, looking at her, at Carol's face only inches away from her, the grey eyes calm as she had never seen them, as if they retained some of the space she had just emerged from. And it seemed strange that it was still Carol's face, with the freckles, the bending blond eyebrow that she knew, the mouth now as calm as her eyes, as Therese had seen it many times before.

"My angel," Carol said. "Flung out of space."

Therese looked up at the corners of the room that were much brighter now, at the bureau with the bulging front and the shield-shaped drawer pulls, at the frameless mirror with the beveled edge, at the green patterned curtains that hung straight at the windows, and the two gray tips of buildings that showed just above the sill. She would remember every detail of this room forever.

"What town is this?" she asked.

Carol laughed. "This? It's Waterloo." She reached for a cigarette. "Isn't that awful?"

Smiling, Therese raised up on her elbow. Carol put a cigarette between her lips. "There's a couple of Waterloos in every state," Therese said.

ANDREW
HOLLERAN

WHEN ANDREW HOLLERAN'S *Dancer from the Dance* was published in 1978 it was an immediate popular and critical success. This was probably the first time a post-Stonewall gay novel captured the attention of mainstream reviewers. (Although such varied books as Gore Vidal's 1948 *The City and the Pillar*, James Baldwin's 1956 *Giovanni's Room*, and John Rechy's 1963 *City of Night* had attracted critical attention from the national press, they were not identified as belonging to the distinct genre of "gay fiction.") The positive reception of *Dancer from the Dance* set a standard for acceptance that much gay male and lesbian literature has attempted to live up to ever since. And although *Dancer from the Dance* seemed to appear out of nowhere—at least for mainstream critics, who had not been paying attention to the burgeoning field of gay writing that began around 1969—the novel and its author had secure roots in a contemporary and historical gay male sensibility.

Essay by
MICHAEL BRONSKI

The birth of the gay liberation movement in 1969 brought about an explosion of new venues for cultural and artistic expression as well as opening up new venues for gay work. Along with the founding of openly gay and overtly political newspapers, journals, and magazines such as *Come Out* (Manhattan), *Gay Sunshine* (San Francisco), and *Fag Rag* (Boston), gay men in many cities also formed writers groups in which they discussed ideas and politics, shared their work, and supported one another. In Manhattan, The Violet Quill Club—with members Felice Picano, Edmund White, Michael Grumley, Robert Ferro, George Whitmore, Christopher Cox, and Andrew Holleran—met irregularly to discuss the potential as well as the problems of autobiographical fiction. *Dancer from the Dance* was one of the first works of gay fiction to be published by a Violet Quill member. (Edmund White's *Nocturnes for the King of Naples* also came out in 1970.)

Although the subject matter of *Dancer from the Dance* was drawn from the glittering disco world of Manhattan's gay male nightlife, the book's tone was meditative, almost melancholic. Its main character, a beautiful young man named Malone, traverses the gay social world looking for salvation in the form of emotional or erotic transcendence. By re-creating, in hallucinatory imagery, New York City's sexual underground and by idealizing Malone as a beautiful lost soul, Holleran managed to invent—and join together—two complimentary mythologies: the jaded, sexual, material world juxtaposed with the reactions and experience of the young, unspoiled innocent. This first world was described earlier by such writers as John Rechy (in *City of Night* and *Numbers*) and served as the background for many of the pulp novels with gay male themes that were popular in the 1950s and 1960s.

The idea of the uncorrupted, homoerotic innocent originated in the poetry of the Uranian writers of the Victorian era and has continued to appear in gay writing ever since. By updating these themes to the very contemporary worlds of disco and Fire Island, Holleran created a new version of old gay myths that resonated with contemporary, post-Stonewall readers. While much gay male literature of the period was intent on vocalizing the idea that "gay is good" as a much needed remedy to accepted social, moral, and legal homophobia, Holleran's gay world had a dark side as well.

Holleran published his much-awaited second novel in 1983. *Nights in Aruba* also told the story of an innocent who is torn between the personal, social, and political freedom of gay life and his duties as a son to his aging parents. This theme of split desire echoed *Dancer from the Dance*, and while the first book posited the dichotomy as innocence and experience, the second manifested it as the difference between a closeted, ostensibly heterosexual life and an open gay one. Although *Nights in Aruba* was well received by gay and straight critics it did not have the social impact of *Dancer from the Dance*. This was possibly because AIDS was beginning to emerge as *the* most important issue in the gay male community and most other discussions about coming out, dealing with family, and inventing a new social and physical world that accommodated homosexuality seemed less pressing. It was at this time that Andrew Holleran moved from New York City, where he had spent the better part of a decade, to a small town near Gainsville, Florida.

Andrew Holleran began writing essays about AIDS—mostly for *Christopher Street*—in the mid-1980s. These were collected in *Ground Zero* and in a surprising way they are a continuation and an obverse reflection of the world of *Dancer from the Dance*. The sense of doom and a tragic underside to gay sexuality that permeates Holleran's writing in *Dancer*, and to a lesser degree *Nights in Aruba*, has completely manifested itself in *Ground Zero*. But Holleran is careful never to make easy analogies that imply that AIDS is somehow a natural result of gay male sexual activity, as others have done. The sense of doom and despair in *Dancer* is a metaphysical condition of being human. In all of his essays on AIDS

Holleran takes a forthrightly, materialistic position: AIDS is a physical condition that is caused by a virus; it has no other meanings.

Holleran is even suspicious about his own inclination and ability to write about AIDS. In an essay published in *Tribe*, Holleran writes: "I'm horrified to say this, but in a real sense AIDS is incredible material. It's not material in the sense that it's an aesthetic object, because it's happening and it's too real. At the time AIDS began not only did I not want to write about it, I also felt deeply worthless writing about it. I felt that of all the things you can do about AIDS, writing about it is one of the most pointless."

Much of *Ground Zero* has to do with Holleran's attempt to find a comfortable way to write about AIDS. If art

Andrew Holleran with writer Felice Picano in 1980.

and literature is an act of transformation, how is it possible to transform this basic terrible, and terrifying, fact of the human condition? In *Ground Zero* Holleran writes about friends who have died, memories from pre-AIDS years, the limitations of art, and the inescapable state of mourning in which he and many of his friends live. In an attempt to describe AIDS—not the disease, but the state of a culture living with the disease—Holleran spends most of his time writing around it, discussing the reflections, circumstances, and parameters of what he calls "the plague" rather than the illness itself. What is most evident in Holleran's writings on AIDS is how the idea of family—once posited in *Nights in Aruba* as antithetical to the social and sexual camaraderie of gay life—now takes on new meanings. While *Dancer from the Dance* offers a look at gay social relationships, they are not as resonant as the nuclear family ties of *Nights in Aruba*. Throughout *Ground Zero* Holleran describes the love and caretaking exhibited by a gay male community in the same terms he had earlier ascribed to biological families.

AIDS, in *Ground Zero*, is too huge, too indefinite, and too complex an experience to capture in the act of writing. The essays in *Ground Zero* are some of the best writing that has been done about AIDS precisely because Holleran realizes, and admits, not only the limits of art, but the limits of human understanding as well.

FRIENDS AT EVENING

I saw Mister Lark at the Stanford Hotel last night—which, at Seventh Avenue and Twenty-second Street, is not a place history has noticed any more than the people who walk by. One block north is the Chelsea Hotel, whose rooms have housed, and still do, writers and musicians, poets and designers. But the Stanford Hotel has none of the reflected glory of the arts, or even of its seemingly English, substantial, semiaristorcratic name—whatever it once was, it is now, to be perfectly frank, a welfare hotel. And like those big old establishments in Atlantic City whose names conjured up the great country houses of England—the Marlborough-Blenheim, for instance—but whose windows looked down on a wooden boardwalk, brown beach and umber surf, the Stanford Hotel surveys a very un-English scene: black and Hispanic women on the stoop watching their children skip rope, play hopscotch, do back flips, as if in the dirt road of a small Southern town or a village in the mountains above San Juan. In summer the entire hotel seems to be on the sidewalk, but even in winter, no matter what the weather, there are always a few people out—certainly children, doing flips and skipping rope while waiting for their parents to come out of the bar on the corner called Soul Heaven. The music at Soul Heaven is on tape, and the tapes are so good that when I walk past the bar I stop—no matter what the weather; and even in a blizzard you can hear the music—to listen to a few songs.

Last night on my way to meet Mister Lark for Louis's funeral, it happened that Gladys Knight was singing the theme from "Claudine" ("Make Yours a Happy Home") and I had to ask myself where else on earth but this bar would I have been able to hear this song; one of my favorites a decade ago, one Louis and I used to dance to. A very light snowfall was trying to begin, but it was so feeble it resembled chips of paint falling from an apartment ceiling, and the children were skipping rope as if it were an August night. The song has just that unpretentious mix of happiness and sadness that one listens for in vain in so much contemporary music, and I was feeling very sentimental when who should come up with a little grocery bag in hand, the kind they give you for one small item, but Mister Lark.

"Mother of God, you're on time," he said in a murmur which melded his words together in one continuous stream—a sound that baffled me for years till I realized it was the sound the priest makes giving you absolution on the other side of the grille. "How few people one can even count on for that fundamental courtesy!" he said. "So small, yet so enormous! A real index of character! I do not want to be late for the service. He Who Gets Slapped expects us to pick him up on Madison Avenue.

He'll pay for the cab downtown." He grabbed my arm. "Do you remember this song?" I said.

"Remember it?" he said. "It is the story of my life!" And we stood there listening for a moment; until, just as Gladys Knight was starting the final chorus, the pay phone on the corner rang. Mister Lark reached right out and picked it up, as if it were his own. (Perhaps it *was*. I was so accustomed to Mister Lark's phoning me from subway stations and street corners, I assumed he had no phone of his own.) He listened for a moment and then said, "No I am *not* horny. I am, in fact, on my way to a funeral … I know *perfectly well* which window you're in, and I have no intention of looking up … I find penis size irrelevant, I do not talk dirty on the phone. I think that is for people who have never *quite* grown up!" he said, and put the receiver down with a clatter.

A small group of children gathered round and were staring up at Mister Lark. "Hello Charles, hello Antoinette, hello Delores, hello Paul," he said. "How are you this evening? Aren't you supposed to be doing your homework?" He set his paper bag on the metal platform beside the telephone, reached into the pocket of his coat, pulled out a little book whose cover had been ripped off, and began to leaf through it. "Louis's phone book," he murmured. "His brother and I ripped it in half, to divide the job of notifying people about the funeral tonight. I have a few more people to get a hold of," he murmured, and then, after putting a coin in, dialed a number he read in the book. He turned and smiled at the children, who continued to stare. It was just as well—"Make Yours a Happy Home" was succeeded by David Ruffin singing "Love Is What You Need," another song I hadn't heard in a long time. Mister Lark, however, began to frown, deeper and deeper, and finally he looked at me and said, "Do you suppose there is some equivalent of methadone for people who *cannot* stay off the phone? Could we set up toy telephone clinics for such people who cannot bring themselves to hang up? There is, after all, such a thing as consideration for others. The telephone does not exist to be abused," he said. (I waited to see what he would do: Mister Lark was the only person I knew who told the operator it was an emergency if someone's line was busy. Then, after the operator had broken in to say, "I'm sorry, I've an emergency," and the person interrupted felt his heart go into his throat at the imminence of bad news, he would hear the murmurous incantation of "My dear boy I'm so sorry, but I had to tell you *not* to meet me at eight o'clock *at the fountain*, but *inside* Alice Tully Hall. All right?") He sighed as he leafed through the little book, the phone cradled between his chin and shoulder, and finally stamped his foot. "That's it!" he said. "I've done my best!" And he threw the telephone down onto the metal prongs. I waited for him to dial the operator and declare an emergency, but instead he sighed, put the book back in his pocket, and picked up the paper bag. "*Avanti*," he said, and held out a hand with his pinky extended, a little hook I was to grasp, and be pulled along in the wake of his big black overcoat, past the children with wide eyes and pigtails and, around the corner, the middle-aged women in dresses the color of Kool-Aid and nylon bomber jackets, and their male companions in straw hats and old pea coats, who, with their bottles of beer in hand, gave the whole block a theatrical, artificial air; as if it were merely a theater set for *Porgy and Bess*. Mister Lark turned to me in the garish fluorescent light of the small tiled lobby and said: "Forgive me if I make you walk. But I would no more go in that elevator than I would go to a party given by Bobby Durwood." On the last few words his voice got louder, his enunciation sharper, in the tone of abused tenants everywhere, and the bare beginnings of the half-snicker, half-snort Mister Lark used in place of a laugh were aborted in the face of the immediate task: ascending the narrow stairs on which people sat rolling joints and listening to portable radios in little clouds of bright fluorescent light on each tiled landing, till we arrived at the top, dim floor and Mister Lark, panting, filmed with sweat, unlocked the gray metal door to his apartment. There was someone inside already: a man whose face was vaguely familiar. "Do you know Ned Stouffer?" said Mister Lark as the man smiled and held out his hand; he'd been standing at the window with his hands on the windowsill looking out when the door swung open.

"I think we have met," said Ned, "at Curtis's New Year's Eve party. How are you," he said, and shook my hand.

"Ned is just back in town for Louis's funeral," said Mister Lark. "I'm sorry he had to come back for such an awful reason," he said, his voice low, murmurous, gloomy. Then he grasped his friend's hands. "But I'm so glad to see him again!" He reached down and picked up a magazine on the table and held it out to us. It was called *Black Woman, White Stud*. "Have you seen this?" he said. "The 'portfolio' of the woman who lived here before me with her eight-year-old son. I can't bring myself to throw it away. Oh God. Look at him now," he said. We turned and saw across the amber radiance of the streetlight outside the window a naked white man standing in his window masturbating. "Can you imagine?" said Mister Lark. "And I'm over here, reading Montaigne! Of course," he said as the man turned around and put his buttocks to the glass, "it might make a difference if he were twenty-nine, good-looking, and Brazilian. But with *that* ass! Wouldn't you *hide it from everyone*? Tell me, what would you like to drink?" He held out an arm to the refrigerator. "I've got apple juice, tap water, and puree of beets. Unless you'd like tea," he said. Ned took apple juice and I took tea, and we sat down on the Styrofoam cush-

American novelist and nonfiction writer.

Born: c. 1943.

Education: Harvard University; University of Iowa.

Career: Served with U.S. Army in West Germany (now Germany).

ion which occupied what might be called a windowseat overlooking the skip-rope and games of the children on Twenty-second Street.

"*Mi casa es su casa,*" said Mister Lark, his voice swelling with the pride of a host whose friends are finally under his roof. "In the words of the Supremes—someday we'll be together! At the Stanford Hotel. I'd like to say Eugene O'Neill wrote *Mourning Becomes Electra* here, but I'd be lying if I did. In fact, though every street in Manhattan but this was *once* the playground of the Astors, nothing ever happened here. I'm in famous company—just around the corner from the Chelsea, which I'm told is so social these days poor Chris Potter takes a room at the Y," he snicker-snorted, "when he wants to get some writing done. Otherwise it's up and down the halls in a frenzy of gossip. Only the other day my friend Nicky Nolledo was in the lobby when one of the guests who'd just died was carried past on a stretcher, and the man at the desk looked up and said: 'Checking out?'"

He snicker-snorted and said: "I just thought I'd share that with you, since I have no cakes and cookies to serve, not even an Entenmann's!" (The paper bag he'd brought back from the store contained, I saw now, a product whose blue-and-white box promised the *safe home removal of ear wax*.) He raised his teacup and said to us: "I am reminded of a line from the perhaps overrated, but occasionally divine, Walt Whitman, which I shall use to toast you. 'It is enough to be with friends at evening,'" he said. We smiled. "Although," he added, putting his cup down, "the occasion that brings us here tonight, that is, the one we are going to, is not one Whitman would have imagined. Poor Louis! Lying in what I'm sure will be a closed coffin, considering how he looked the last time I went to the hospital."

"How did he die?" said Ned, frowning. "I mean, what was the final thing that did it?"

"The final thing, indeed," said Mister Lark. "I'm not sure, exactly. An intestinal infection, I believe. There was also blindness and herpes of the brain. Ron Pratt died of a tuberculosis formerly found in *birds*. Peter Ord of CMV running riot in his veins. As to what in Louis's case—the heart just stopped beating. What made the heart stop beating I can't say.

ANDREW **HOLLERAN** 265

I saw on television last night a gazelle brought down by lions on the Serengeti—the claws, the teeth, the *weight* of two lions, and still the gazelle almost escaped! That's what it's like to kill a man. The virus has to work itself into a perfect rage, a swarm, an irresistible tide that pours through the broken gates before anything so big, so vital, so complex as a *man* can be killed. And then," he laughed, "what does the virus do? Dies, because the thing it's been feeding on is dead. Foolish, isn't it? A parasite is more sensible—it knows when to stop. It even establishes a relationship. But I find it hard to find a place in God's plan for the virus."

"I still can't believe it," said Ned, looking down at the floor. "I feel so bad I didn't visit him more."

"But you had to leave town!" said Mister Lark. "How is your father? Hmmmm?"

"Well," he said, "a stroke takes a long time to recover from. And of course you never know if there won't be another stroke. But we send him to physical therapy and—just live from day to day, I guess. Were you with Louis at the end?"

"I was just going up to the hospital," said Mister Lark. "It was last Saturday morning. I had a few errands to run uptown—I planned to be there at ten. But I called first from the bookstore. A nurse answered the phone, said he'd died. And would I come up and please collect his things? They don't wait, you know, they get the room ready for the next patient! The private duty nurse on the night shift called Louis's brother at three in the morning to say Louis was dead, and she could not find her check! Can you imagine? *Moving right along!* The heartlessness of people is incredible! When I got there, everything he owned was in a plastic bag. His room was like the church door Luther nailed his theses to. Plastered with big crosses, skull and bones. *Poison. Stay Out. Do not enter without gloves and mask.* You'd have thought someone was making plutonium inside. But no," he said, "it was just darling Louis, looking more and more each day like the world's oldest man."

"Was he *very* skinny?" said Ned.

"Yes. One day he asked me to hand him the towel at the foot of his bed. And he lay it across his forehead. And I thought: What is he doing that for? And he said: 'Don't you think I look like Mother Theresa?'"

"Making a joke about it!" said Ned.

"Yes," said Mister Lark.

"And did he?" said Ned.

"Look like Mother Theresa?" said Mister Lark. "Exactly." A cockroach scuttled out onto the rug between us. Ned reached out with his foot and stepped on it. "We are to the gods as flies to wanton boys," Mister Lark intoned. "God just reached out with His foot and stepped on Louis. Only he didn't die *right away*."

"Is there family here?"

"Yes," said Mister Lark. "They flew up from Georgia. His brother lived with him the last three months, you know. An angel. Odd, isn't it, how at the end, the family takes you back? How many men have gone back home when they got sick?"

"And how many men have been cared for by their friends," said Ned. "Like you. I'm sure there'll be a terrific turnout tonight."

"Well, he knew so many people," said Mister Lark, "from so many milieus! He was always at the newest nightclub, in the newest pants, doing the newest dance! Sometimes I think he died just because he did everything *first*—"

"That's a funny way to look at it," said Ned.

"Funny ha-ha, or funny peculiar?" said Mr. Lark, as he opened a jar, scooped some cream out, and began to apply it to his face in small, ever-widening circles.

"Somewhere in between," said Ned.

"I suppose it is. But when I am lying awake at night, I think of it that way, sometimes. I think of it so many ways. My mind *swarms* with metaphor." His hands made tiny circles till his face was entirely green. He plucked a tissue from a box of Kleenex and began to remove it all in short, deft strokes.

"Do you think it's going to stop?" said Ned.

"No," said Mister Lark. "I think we are all going to die."

There was a silence; we could hear the throb of the bass of whatever song was playing in the bar below beating against the night. A few snowflakes began to meander down past the streetlight when I turned to look behind us; the man across the street was now lying before his window with his legs thrown up into the air, and an index finger circling his asshole.

"Do you really," said Ned in a soft voice.

"Yes," said Mister Lark. "Think of how many people we know who are already dead. Don't you make lists? Lists of people dead, lists of people living you worry about, lists of people you don't worry about, lists of people who would tell you if they got it, lists of people who wouldn't," he said as he wiped his face with a tissue. "Lists of people *you'd* tell if *you* got it, lists of people you wouldn't. Lists of people you'd care for if they got sick, lists of people you *think* would care for you, lists of places you'd like to be when you get it, lists of methods of suicide in case you do."

He sighed. "Dreadful lists!"

"But what about this list," said Ned. "Of people whose lovers have died of it, but who are perfectly all right themselves!"

"That list we recite several times each day," said Mister Lark. "That list is our only hope. Five men in New York who are perfectly intact, even though their entire household has died. Who will always wonder, like the survivors of any catastrophe, why was I spared?"

"So you think nothing will ever, ever be the same," said Ned.

"Nothing," said Mister Lark, screwing the cap on his jar of face cream. "We're all going, in sequence, at different times. And will the last person please turn out the lights?"

"I agree," said Ned.

"And that's why," said Mister Lark as he stood up, "each moment is so precious! Each friend who's still alive! Let us go then, you and I, when the evening is spread out against the sky, like a patient etherized upon the table."

He bent down and picked up the dead roach with a napkin.

"I feel bad killing that cockroach," said Ned. "It's the same thing."

"I know," said Mister Lark.

Louis's phone book fell out of his pocket with a thud; he picked it up in his other hand, and straightened up. "Did I tell you who's in Louis's phone book," he said, tossing the napkin and the roach into a wastebasket. "His brother and I ripped it in half to call people about the funeral." He opened the book up and began to read: "Mary Tyler Moore."

"Mary Tyler Moore!"

"Walter Cronkite."

"Walter Cronkite!"

"Lena Horne."

Ned smiled.

"Halston," Mister Lark said. "Dan Rather. Lauren Bacall. Jeff Aquilon. Roy Cohn. Liz Smith." He looked up. "He used them when he was arranging the fashion show for muscular dystrophy. But he put them in his book. Do you see? *He wanted Mary Tyler Moore in his phone book.*"

"That's *so* Louis," said Ned as he shook his head. "And what are the rest?"

"A lot of Spanish names," said Mister Lark, "of no particular importance."

"Not in official circles," said Ned.

"Shall we go?" said Mister Lark. "It's almost six o'clock." He looked at us. "We must make a stop uptown first. You know, He Who Gets Slapped is waiting."

"I'm so excited," Ned smiled as he stood up.

"No more than He Who Gets Slapped," said Mister Lark. "When I told him you were back, he began to sing on the telephone." We took our cups to the heaped sink—miraculous flies, even in the dead of winter, droned over the sticky patina on the dishes—put on our coats, and went out into the hall.

Mister Lark wrapped a long scarf around his neck so that it hung down his overcoat on either side, like the stole a priest wears to hear confession. "You never really know in the Stanford Hotel," he said as he went down the narrow, vomit-colored hall whose fluttering fluorescent light gave the place a nervous aspect, "if anything will be left when you get back. Imagine a methadone addict operating a hot plate! I *always* expect to see the towering inferno when I come up out of the IRT. So I follow the advice given in the *Times* to people traveling to countries on the verge of revolution," he said. "I take my valuables with me." And he pulled out of his pocket his wallet, first edition of Hart Crane, and Louis's phone book.

"How are you, good evening, *bon soir, buenas noches, auf wiedersehen*." Mister Lark smiled and nodded to the people sitting on the stairs as we descended the five flights to the lobby, which was now filled with excited men shouting Spanish. Mister Lark kissed the tips of his fingers and fluttered them in the direction of the crowd. "Don't wait up!" Ned said, stepped down the three cement stairs onto the sidewalk, turned and waited for us. Even though it was snowing on this late March night, the stoop and walls of the hotel were lined with its tenants taking the air. "Hello Lulu," Mister Lark said with a smile, as one of the women in a pea coat waved at him. "Hello Stan, hello Bertha Mae." He turned and said in a lower voice as we walked to the corner: "Don't you think these people look *exactly* like the inhabitants of a small town in the Mississippi delta?"

"I'm sure they are," said Ned. "And they just got on the bus one day."

"Well," said Mister Lark, "they may be destitute, but they've got the two things that count—rhythm and a complete immune system! Taxi?" he said, turning when we reached the corner. "Or the IRT?"

ANDREW **HOLLERAN**   269

"Taxi," said Ned. "My treat."

"You are," said Mister Lark, "a breath of fresh air."

Ned raised his arm and turned south, as Mister Lark cried "Get a Checker, get a Checker!" Minutes later we got into one, in a faint cloud of snowflakes, and began driving uptown. The streets were still so warm the snow was melting the moment it touched the asphalt. "Do you miss the city?" I said to Ned. "God! Yes," he said. "Terribly. Right now, it's just one big cemetery, but it still gets me so excited. When the plane started to descend, my stomach tightened and I began to shake."

"No!"

"And when I got *off*, I wanted to kneel down and kiss the tarmac, like the Pope. I didn't know *how* I was going to get into town from Newark. I was so impatient!"

"Next time," said Mister Lark, "you should have a helicopter lower you onto your apartment building. I never leave," he said.

"I used to walk this street every night on my way to the gym," Ned said.

"The McBurney Y?" said Mister Lark.

"Yes," said Ned. "It started to get yuppie by the time I left New York, it was filled with women in leotards doing yoga, and men taking karate, but when I first joined, it was a backwater. Dim and dingy, Puerto Rican boxers, sex in the air! You know?"

"I do indeed," Mister Lark murmured as we sped uptown; he was so frugal with what little money he had, taxis were one of the things he seldom allowed himself, no matter how sorely tempted; even though, he said, the IRT was something no man over thirty should go into unless in search of sex; and that was now out of the question. A taxi so enchanted him we might as well have been going uptown in the sleigh Ludwig of Bavaria used on snowy nights when he was bored and depressed, two things Mister Lark never was. He turned to us with a starstruck expression on his face, dazzled by the lights, the rushing, cold damp wind beside the window he'd left open at the top. "Boxers often do, you know," said Mister Lark. "Boxers *never* do," said Ned, "and never *are*. Just as homosexuals *never* wore rubber thongs into the shower, never boxed, and never played basketball."

"I knew one," said Mister Lark, "who did all three! Then he had his teeth filed down, and tipped with silver, and moved to Vermont to paint."

"Rick Satterwaite!" said Ned.

"Yes," said Mister Lark.

"He was divine," said Ned.

"But spaced out," said Mister Lark. "Though moving to Vermont when he did seems in retrospect, *very* sensible. *His* blood, no doubt, is pure as cows' milk!" He looked at Ned. "I used to see you at McBurney very late, on Saturday."

"That was my favorite time!" said Ned. "The last half hour in the locker room on a Saturday—there was something poetic about it."

"Now it's quite bustling, and busy, and renovated," said Mister Lark, "and some new director has increased the membership, and refurbished the weight and locker rooms, and it's full of copy editors learning self-defense. I don't know where I'll go when my membership runs out. Do you think there are still *seedy* gyms in Brooklyn? With old-fashioned swimming pools? The McBurney pool is—"

"A footbath," said Ned. "I used to wait an hour to get a lane. But the things I saw in it! I've showered beside creatures who could have—" He struggled for words.

"Persuaded the gods to come down from Olympus for an afternoon," said Mister Lark.

"Exactly!"

"But now the gods no longer seem interested in us as lovers," said Mister Lark. "Driver! Driver!" he said through the opening in the scratched plastic screen between the front and backseats. "Let us out on the next corner! There's been a change of plans!" The driver came to an abrupt halt, Mister Lark said to Ned, "I'll explain in a moment," and got out, while Ned paid the fare.

In a moment we were all on the cold, wet, and windy sidewalk across from the Fashion Institute of Technology. "Why did you do that?" asked Ned.

"There are two reasons to change taxis," said Mister Lark, his fine hair blowing about his head in the wind. "The first one I learned when I was taking drugs in the East Village—the feeling someone is following you. Now I think that's *why* people take drugs! To feel someone *is* following them. In my case, someone was. Because I wrote a somewhat nasty review of a novel by a man whose name I won't mention here. I knew I had crossed off our relationship with the article—I was young and drunk on language—even though it was the truth. But he actually began to follow me everywhere. You remember Warhol was shot by that crazy woman around that time? I had a job with *Saturday Review*, I was taking cabs then. I used to change taxis five times in twenty blocks. Which introduced me to the second reason for changing cabs," he said as Ned held up his arm and shouted "Taxi!" at the one approaching. "And that," he said as it stopped before us, "is the driver." We piled into the beackseat; this time there was no plastic panel between is and the front seat; the driver turned and smiled at us with big dark eyes, strong white teeth, in a pale olive face. "Julio," said Mister Lark, glancing at the information on the visor, "how do you do? And where are you from originally?"

"Ecuador," said the driver with a smile.

"Ah," said Mister Lark, "the kingdom of the Incas! Would you take us, proud descendant of Atahualpa, to the southeast corner of Madison Avenue and Seventy-fifth Street? Go through the park, please." He turned to us, and murmured: "The park is so lovely at night in this kind of weather. Gusty emotions on wet roads on autumn nights!" He put his hand between his teeth and bit it to repress the urge to shriek. "Now you were saying, dear boy, about the McBurney Y. Hmmmmm?"

Ned smiled and put his head back.

"The shower shoes? Hmmmm?" said Mister Lark.

"Just that after the gym," said Ned as we rattled north, "I'd go to the baths! I'd walk home from McBurney after being surrounded by these Puerto Ricans, down Sixth Avenue, and then veer over to Man's Country on Fifteenth Street to see who was standing in line," he said. "Or I'd go in and stand there till the urge went away. But the urge seldom went away," he said in a quiet voice. "I was in love with the two Cubans who worked the window. It was so cheap in those days, you could go in for three dollars. Three dollars! Movies cost five. And a night at Man's Country was infinitely more thrilling than any movie could possibly be. I think Man's Country killed Louis."

"What?" said Mister Lark as we stopped at a light on Thirty- fourth Street.

"He had a pass," said Ned. "He was a friend of the owner, and Louis could go there any hour of the day or night—it was only a block from his apartment—and check in. And get a room, unless they were sold out. They were never sold out. For some reason Man's Country never caught on—which is why I liked it. The Fire Island crowd, the circuit queens all went to the St. Marks. Man's Country was utterly off the beaten path. *No one I knew went there. Except Louis.* We loved it! I used to see him there, standing naked in the doorway of his room. When he saw me coming, he'd put one arm up and another on his hip, and kind of *lounge* in the doorway—like Elizabeth Taylor in *Cat on a Hot Tin Roof.*" He laughed. "One night Spruill saw him like that, and said: 'You'd better put that thing away, or people are going to throw peanuts at it.'"

"Put what away?" said Mister Lark.

"His dick," said Ned. "He had a gargantuan penis! *That's* what killed Louis—he came into his penis."

"Came into his penis!" said Mister Lark as we drove though Herald Square.

"You know the French saying," said Ned. "A woman comes into her beauty. Well, Louis came into his penis."

"But," Mister Lark spluttered, "he always had his penis! He didn't inherit it in midlife!"

"But he did," said Ned in a calm, reasonable voice. "I mean, of course his penis was always there between his legs, but it might just as well have not been. When we met him in the Pines in 1971, he was always in drag—of one kind or another. I remember one night Louis was coming up the stairs of the Sandpiper in one of his bizarre getups—torn fatigues, lamé tank top, and a towel, I think—and the man next to me said, 'Who is that?' And the person next to him replied: 'Some Jewish queen from outer space.' Remember? Louis used to stand outside the Sandpiper in a big red ball gown with black beads, black fan and fake camellia in his snood, and curtsy to boys he adored. He was like a child. And he had, at that time, not the slightest inkling that he had a penis! I mean it was there, but he never used it. And then, toward the end of the seventies—he realized the ... value of what he had."

"What value? said Mister Lark.

"Why, everything," Ned said, "in the little world we were living in. That penal colony! The whole point, as it were. The central symbol. The Eucharist. What everyone, on some level, was looking for, what everyone would not pause in their search until they found."

"You mean the great, the distinguished thing," said Mister Lark.

"Yes," said Ned.

"Surely you exaggerate."

"I don't," said Ned. "A homosexual *is* his penis. A homosexual cemetery should have just three things on the gravestone: name, date, and dimensions of dick."

"You've grown bitter in Ohio!" said Mister Lark.

"There's nothing else to do," he smiled.

"And you've forgotten about the meeting of two minds and souls, the escape from loneliness, or what it really is. What Plato called it—the desire to be born in beauty."

"Oh, Richard," said Ned. "How many homosexuals even get to, much less operate on that level? Most of them are looking for a good firm cantaloupe. They find a dick they like, pitch their tents, and unharness the camels."

"Oh!" said Mister Lark. "And you're the great romantic!"

"You can be romantic, and still face facts," said Ned.

"I thought you couldn't," said Mister Lark.

"And the facts are these," said Ned. "Louis came into his penis. And when he did, he began having sex—because now all those famous models he used to faint over were now lying in the bathtub in the Strap waiting to be pissed on! If the penis was right! And his was. So in the middle of the night, if he couldn't sleep, or in the middle of the afternoon, if he had an hour between appointments, he would drop into Man's Country. It was like a harem he could drop in on. A harem. That's what it was. A family. A home. A men's club. A place of refuge. And *what* a place of refuge! Two things in life are as exciting to me now as the first time I experienced them—"

"The ocean, and autumn nights," said Mister Lark.

"Taking off in an airplane, and hearing the door of a bathhouse close behind me," said Ned.

"Oh dear," said Mister Lark.

"And Louis felt the same," said Ned, "though he didn't carry the guilt I did. He had that wonderful gift—the ability to enjoy life. Which is why he had so many friends."

We came to a stop in dense traffic south of Columbus Circle. Ned looked out the window. "Do you think there's a car show at the Coliseum?" he said. "Or a health food fair? Or a convention of mind-control seminars? Should we just take the first right, and forget about going through the park?" But we could not even have done that at the moment: fenders, taillights, grilles enclosed us on all sides—we were trapped. "Something's going on," said Ned. Mister Lark leaned forward. "*Que está el problema?*" Mister Lark said to Julio.

"*Qué es el problema,*" said Ned. Mister Lark turned and looked at him. "Spanish has two verbs for being," Ned said. "*Está* is impermanent, *es* is permanent."

"Ah," said Mister Lark.

"*Qué es el problema,*" Julio said with a smile, and a nod, as he glanced at us in the rearview mirror, his large dark eyes glowing in the radiance of the reflected headlights bouncing off the taxi in front of us.

"*Como está Usted? Qué es el problema?*" murmured Ned.

"*Como está Usted? Qué es el problema?*" said Mister Lark. He covered his eyes with his hands. "Stuck in traffic?" he said. "Do facial isometrics, plan a party menu, learn to use Spanish verbs *es* and *está*. Not a moment wasted in the life of a modern American maintaining a balance among all the elements of his split identity. Oh, darlings! When did the world become a microwave oven?" He uncovered his face, rolled down the window, and yelled: "Precious! Excuse me, sir? Hello! Darling! Cupcake! Pudding face! Yes, I just want to know—has the water main burst up there? Is Mrs. Onassis going to the Opera?" Mister Lark held his head out the window to hear what a man on the sidewalk was saying to him. "There's been an accident," he said, coming back inside, "on the night of Louis's funeral."

"Let's get out," Ned said. "And get another cab on Fifth."

"*No!*" Mister Lark leaned toward us. "You'll never find another one like this, believe me! His voice is like a waterfall in a rain forest. He's got a *soul*."

"Richard, they all have souls," said Ned, still hanging on to the strap. "The question is, do they have immune systems?"

Mister Lark spluttered.

"The question is do we," said Ned. "And the answer is no."

"Do you think *you're* infected?" said Mister Lark.

"I'm sure of it," said Ned.

"But you haven't taken the test!"

"I don't have to," said Ned. "If I'm not infected, no one is. I was living at the baths."

"But you just looked," said Mister Lark.

"*Sometimes* I looked," said Ned. "Sometimes I touched."

"But—"

"You were at the theater," said Ned. "The opera, the reading. The rest of us were much lower on the ladder of love."

"You're turning bitter, aren't you," said Mister Lark. "You've been watching television, and shopping in supermarkets, and they've taken their toll. You're going to repent, like Saint Augustine, and turn against the past!"

"*You're* safe," said Ned. "Because I think of you as not having sex."

"This is hardly the time, or place, for *exposés*," said Mister Lark.

"I'm serious," said Ned. "You have the most precious gift of all! Your health. Your peace of mind. Your body, uninvaded. You are Sicily before the Normans. America before the white man. Mexico before the Spanish. Hawaii before the missionaries. You're intact. You're virgin. You're on fire." The taxi lurched. "You're even moving," he said as Julio, speaking rapidly in Spanish and honking the horn, suddenly floored the accelerator, sped round a car he saw, in passing, was broken down, flew past the police barricades, and on up Central Park West. "Thank God I'm not in labor," said Ned, lighting a cigarette. Mister Lark leaned forward to speak to Julio, then stopped, sat back and turned to us. "Would you say Louis *es* or *está* dead?"

"*Está*," said Ned. "*Está muerto.*"

"But why?" said Mister Lark. "Surely his deadness is not an impermanent condition. He is dead forever."

"Not if you believe in the psychic in the Beresford I used to see," said Ned, as the doormen and canopies and lighted facades of apartment buildings went by, "who told me I'm going to be a pediatrician in Bombay in my next life."

"You don't believe such nonsense," said Mister Lark.

"No, I don't," said Ned. "I believe Louis is dead, and we'll never see him again."

"So do I," said Mister Lark with a sigh, as he looked over at the buildings going by. "And at the same time I can't believe your theory about his getting sick. In fact, I find it hard to believe anything about this nightmare except one fact—"

"What's that?" said Ned.

"*The wrong people are dying,*" he said, turning to us as he veered into the park.

"The wrong people?"

"You know how Louis always used to say the wrong people are having babies? Well, now the wrong people are dying. The germophobes, the anal-retentive, the small and mean and cold and ungenerous are going to survive. The ones like Louis, who loved life, will not. Because life's chief pleasure ... is sex. And sex is what killed him."

"Africa is what killed them," said Ned. "Africa killed Louis. We are infected with a disease that got started in the garbage dump of a slum in Zaire."

He looked out the window at the skyline of Central Park South blazing though the dark trees. "And that's why it seems so awful," said Ned, "so out of proportion to what we were doing."

"And what was that?" said Mister Lark.

"Enjoying life," said Ned, "liberty, and the pursuit of happiness."

"Which you found twice!" said Mister Lark.

"Yes," said Ned. "Snookums, and Shithead." We went beneath a bridge and saw, when we emerged, the new wing of the Metropolitan Museum and the Temple of Dendur glowing pale cinnamon in its bath of golden light. "It looks just like an airplane hangar!" said Mister Lark. "I always expect to see the Spirit of St. Louis hanging there. *Eyes left!*" he said as we turned south on Fifth Avenue and the lighted facade of another apartment building loomed in the darkness. "*Mrs. Onassis!*"

"Have you ever seen her?" said Ned.

"Once, at the opera," said Mister Lark. "Her head is enormous. It just floated down the aisle in the glare of flashbulbs, like a spaceship." The taxi turned left off Fifth Avenue. "I have terrible news for you, Ned, about He Who Gets Slapped."

"What?" Ned said in an alarmed voice.

"Oh no, not that," said Mister Lark. He crossed himself. "You know how many happy days and nights we have spent in his flat, you know what teen tramps we have been there, what conversations, what pasta, what journeys downtown have all begun under his roof, when downtown was divine decadence and not dreadful death," he said.

"Yes," said Ned.

"Are you wearing a disposable incontinent brief?"

"Of course."

"The Whitney Museum purchased Curtis' building, and is *evicting* the tenants! They are going to tear it down to build an extension, an addition by Michael Graves that gives new meaning to the word 'silly,'" he said as the cab pulled up to the corner of Seventy-fifth Street and Madison Avenue. The driver turned to us with a smile. "Bravo, Julio!" said Mister Lark. "I would follow you across the Andes! In fact, if some evening you get off work and do not feel quite like going home, stop by. I have so many questions about Ecuador." He took a card from his wallet and handed it to Julio. Ned leaned forward to read the meter, paid Julio, and got out after me; Mister Lark stayed in the taxi to talk with Julio, as we waited beneath the portal of the Whitney Museum, which was still lighted within. Across the street, a showroom with mannequins in the windows was a brilliant cube of light.

"Have you ever *seen* a woman in a Givenchy?" said Ned.

Our host rounded the corner in a black chesterfield with the collar turned up, a paper bag in his arms, fluttered his hand in the air, and said: "Hi, where's Richard?"

"Still in the cab," I said.

"And here's my baby!" he said, embracing Ned.

"Happy to be back?" said Curtis.

"Very!" said Ned. "And to see *you!*"

Curtis went to the door of his building—a glass pane in the door already shattered, graffiti on the wall beneath the mailbox—looked back and said: "Don't wait for La Gioconda! Come in and have a drink!"

"I can't believe they're going to tear this down!" Ned said as we went up the worn, shabby, carpeted stairs to the third floor. "It's ten years of our lives!"

"Twenty of mine," said Curtis.

"And what about the bookstore next door?"

"It's all going," said Curtis as he unlocked the door. "The Huns! Evicting us all," he said, "and everybody sick, or sick with fear. God, these are hideous times!" he said, hanging up his coat in the hall as we went past him into a white room with vases of irises and votive candles. "These be real bad times," he said. Ned turned around and took it in: the books that covered one wall from floor to ceiling, the clay horses on the mantlepiece, the long tiled table at which he'd sat so many evenings, the tall bookcase whose titles my eyes had played over often without being able to determine a theme among them, save the eclectic chaos of twentieth-century.

"The thing now is to gain weight," said Curtis, pointing to a platter of bread, cheese and roast beef on the table. "You're supposed to look healthy, and healthy is fat. I was with Louis and Spruill one day in an elevator in the D&D Building, when Louis was looking very gaunt. And a friend we all knew got on, saw Louis, and said, 'How are you?' And Louis said: 'I have cancer.' Which really shut the friend up—he got off at the next floor just to recover from the shock. When he left, Spruill turned to Louis and said: 'Don't tell them you have cancer. Tell them you've been swimming laps!'" Ned and Curtis laughed. "Can you imagine?" Curtis smiled. "So how does the city look?"

"Gorgeous," said Ned. "Driving across the park tonight was as thrilling as the first time I did it."

"With Louis throwing up out the window," said Curtis. "Wasn't that it? The night we met you at Marty Rowan's party?"

"How's Spruill?"

"Livid."

"He's been evicted too?"

"The whole building. The whole past is going up in smoke!"

"And Spruill?"

"He's going to the south of France with Martion Lafarge. To sulk."

Ned smiled. "Actually it's because he's even more terrified than we are," said Curtis. "He won't go to the funeral of his friends because he's afraid the germs are floating in the air." Ned sighed. He looked around the room as if he could not believe he was there. "I miss you all so much," he said. "My most important relationship now is with my Chevrolet."

"A Chevrolet can't give you AIDS," said Curtis.

"No," said Ned, "and it can't talk to you when you're driving home alone from the bars. Actually, my most important relationship is with the car radio," he said.

"How's your father?"

"Okay," he said.

There was a silence. Curtis lighted a cigarette. I went into the front room to see it again. It looked as if it had not been used in some time. On the mantlepiece were photographs, one of Louis in a ship captain's uniform, another of him in a pale blue gown on the boardwalk on Fire Island. The windows were open an inch or two, and the room was chilly; a cold film of air stole over the sills. It was March—that strange, dead time in the city, when the season is not one thing or the other—when the nights lack the clarity of deepest winter, when cabs are warm and doorways magical. The apple trees in the park were not yet in bloom, or bodies shorn of their layers of clothes, or the buses running to Jones Beach. It was just March: when people were tired of winter, and everything they'd been doing; when life stands empty, like the squash courts at the gym, a month ago impossible to get on, and now brightly lighted, doors ajar. That odd time of desuetude and mud, bad complexions and soot, trash and litter blowing in the wind, and the whole town—as at the end of August—not quite functioning, for the same reason one cannot pedal a bike between gears. It was, in all its exhaustion and bleak mood and griminess a perfect time to consign Louis to the shades. "Would you tell me if *you* had it?" Curtis was saying when I returned to the other room.

"I—don't know," said Ned.

"You don't, do you?"

"Not at the moment," said Ned. "But I'm sure it's in me, along with the one thousand other things swimming in my blood. My sister says I was naive. Not to be more careful, suspicious, mistrustful."

"Of what?" said Curtis.

"Other people's hygiene."

"We didn't have any reason to worry about other people's hygiene! We had penicillin."

"But we didn't stop, even when we knew," said Ned.

"Knew but didn't believe," said Curtis. "For a while, there was a gap, you know. On Friday we were rational, celibate. On Saturday night we were terrified, and in bed with someone. We didn't know Third World diseases. Doctors at the Ford Foundation knew about those. We didn't know some Australian flight attendant was going to sleep with someone in Africa on Monday, and then with David on Fifty-first Street on Tuesday. Would you have believed me if I had taken you aside on one of these night you loved, with Mario and Raul and Umberto in the front room with the candles lighted and their beards and mustaches black as coal, and said to you: 'Ned, don't fall in love with them, they're carrying a virus from Kinshasa that can shrivel you up to ninety pounds, give you cancer and kill you in two weeks!' You'd have looked at me and said: What science fiction movie did you see on Times Square this afternoon, dear?" He put down his cigarette and said: "We knew, but we didn't believe!"

"But why was I in love with Umberto and Mario anyway?" said Ned, standing up and turning around in a circle with his hands in his pockets.

"And Raul!"

"And Raul," Ned said.

"Because they were good-looking, nice guys!"

"But why was I *sleeping* with them?"

"Because you wanted to merge your unity with their oneness," said Mister Lark as he came into the room. "There are thirty-seven dialects in the Andes of Ecuador," he said as he bent down to smell the irises, "and the word in one of them for potato is *yoringo*." He straightened up and turned to us. "Curtis, Ned is turning bitter. Like Saint Augustine in middle age, he has decided to renounce his past, his sensual youth. A typical reaction to middle age. Tell him the virus is merely a tragic accident that has nothing to do with either Africa, or our sex lives. Tell him it does not invalidate the thing which still persists in the midst of all this horror—I mean," he murmured, "the incalculable, the divine, the overwhelming godlike beauty of the … male body. And then ask him about his bizarre explanation for Louis' death—not to mention all of homosexual life. He thinks, silly boy, it is all centered on the penis!" he said, and, looking

Novels

Dancer from the Dance, 1978.
Nights in Aruba, 1983.

Short Stories

"Nipples," in *Aphrodisiac: Fiction from Christopher Street,* 1980.
"Ties," in *First Love/Last Love: New Fiction from Christopher Street,* edited by Michael Denneny, Charles Ortleb, and Thomas Steele, 1985.
"Friends at Evening," in *Men on Men,* edited by George Stambolian, 1986.
"Lights in the Valley," in *Men on Men* 3, edited by George Stambolian, 1990.
"Sunday Morning: Key West," in *The Faber Book of Gay Short Fiction,* edited by Edmund White, 1991.

Essays

"Four by Andrew Holleran: Nostalgia for the Mud; Fast-Food Sex; Dark Disco; Male Nudes and Nude Males," in *The Christopher Street Reader,* edited by Michael Denneny, Chuck Ortleb, and Thomas Steele, 1983.
"The Fear," in *Personal Dispatches: Writers Confront AIDS,* edited by John Preston, 1988.
Ground Zero, 1988.
"An Essay," in *Tribe* (Baltimore), spring 1990.
"My Uncle Sitting Beneath the Tree," in *A Member of the Family,* edited by John Preston, 1992.

Other

Author of introduction, *The Normal Heart* by Larry Kramer, 1985.
Author of afterword, *Men on Men 4,* edited by George Stambolian, 1992.

---

back over his shoulder, disappeared through the kitchen doorway, to use (I felt sure) the telephone.

"Leave me some message units!" Curtis shouted after him. But all he heard in response was the noise of dialing.

Curtis turned to Ned. "He's right, you know," said Curtis. "You can't revise the past. There's no point in introducing a fact which was not a fact at the time."

"But we should have foreseen it," said Ned.

"Oh," said Curtis, tapping his cigarette against the ashtray and looking down at it, "there are lots of things we should have foreseen. But what did the man say? Life is understood backwards, but lived forwards. That's the problem, dear."

"You're *so* rational," sighed Ned.

"That's what I told myself when I fell down on the boardwalk one summer night this summer on Fire Island and started screaming: We're all going to die. We're all going to die!"

"Did you do that?" said Ned.

"Ask Richard," said Curtis. "He had to pick me up and calm me down."

"Richard," Ned said, glancing at the kitchen, "I don't worry about at all."

"Because he never has sex," said Curtis. "He just talks to them. Sex for Richard is having dinner with the driver of the cab you just got out of. Sex for Richard is learning the word for potato in Inca."

"There is no law in physics more implacable than the one in New York which says the moment someone exits a room, he will be discussed," said Mister Lark, coming back into the room, with the scarf still around his shoulders, carrying Louis's phone book in his hands as if it were a breviary. Curtis and Ned smiled.

"It's only because you fascinate us," said Curtis. "It's only because we know nothing of your private life."

"That is because I have no private life," said Mister Lark. "I am entirely public. I spend my life in shower rooms and theater lobbies. Which is how I met Louis—sneaking into a matinee of *My Fair Lady* after the intermission. How many years ago." He sighed. "The last person I was to call does not answer," he said, sitting down in one of the cane-back chairs. "Have I ever told you how much I admire you all for not having answering machines?" he said.

"Why?" said Curtis.

"Because," said Mister Lark, "you maintain, by not having one, 'the pathos of distance.' Nietzsche." He sighed as he leafed through the little book whose binding was ripped and whose cover was gone—a book torn in half—and said: "Even Louis, toward the end, succumbed. Even Louis had an answering machine installed—"

"Because he was becoming very social," said Ned.

"Very," said Mister Lark.

"Curtis thinks Africa killed Louis, too."

"Unless tomorrow a scientist announces it was all caused by chicken salad in a restaurant on Forty-first Street," said Curtis. "Or fake fog in discotheques. Or the newsprint that comes off on your hands from the Sunday *Times*. The point is we don't know," he said. "The point is, we might as well be living in Beirut. Shall we go?" he said, standing up. "It's almost eight o'clock."

He and Ned went around the room blowing out the votive candles—as if extinguishing the decade—and Mister Lark turned off the Brazilian music. We paused at the edge of the room to put on our coats. "Take one last look," said Curtis at the door. "In another year it'll be a big white room filled with television sets showing videos from Milan to L.A."

"God!" said Ned. "No wonder everyone who works at the Whitney is always at the Mineshaft."

And with a flick of his hand, Curtis plunged the room behind us into darkness, as if it too were just a theater set. We went down the worn stairs and emerged onto Madison Avenue, which looked exactly like what Mister Lark said it was after seven o'clock: The Gobi Desert.

Nothingness stretched dreamily in both directions. Mister Lark led Curtis south into the darkness in search of taxis, and Ned, hands in his overcoat, his hair shining copper-bright in the light of the bookstore, surveyed the new titles in the window and then turned.

"This reminds me of old times," he said, "except, of course, we're going to Louis's funeral. But all our evenings began just like this."

"Were you all very close?" I said.

"Close?" he said. He looked at me. "We were the Four Supremes! And now Louis is the Dead Supreme. I still can't understand it."

"It must've been wonderful," I said. "You must miss it a great deal."

"Between you and me?" he said. "Not to leave this bus stop? I was very discouraged *before* all this began. I stayed in New York five years too many."

"Why?"

"Because the first five years were magic," he said, "and I kept hoping the second five would be too. But then you reach middle age, you'd rather have birds and trees and the sound of rain on the roof. That's all. Curtis and Richard belong here. Some part of them never ages. Richard is like the cockroach—he'll survive everything. When Curtis and I are gone, Richard'll still be going to the Opera, looking for Jackie O. But I was ready to leave before I did. I was listening to the radio one night in Ohio, some woman with a great voice began singing 'More Than You Know.' Have you ever heard the lyrics to 'More Than You Know'?"

"Yes," I said. "Something about man of my dreams."

"'Oh how I'd die,'" he said, "'oh, how I'd cry, if you got tired and said good-bye.' Well, when I was in New York those first five years, I used to hear that song and turn to mush. When I heard it last fall in Ohio one night in my car, I thought: 'This is the clinical description of a masochist.'" He smiled. "For the *first* five years, it was fun being a masochist."

"And then?" I said.

"Everything, including masochism," he said, "becomes a habit after a while. And once it does, you should go. No one should live in this city unless he's in a state of extreme romantic excitement. I'm no longer in a state of romantic excitement," he said.

There was a silence. "Why not?" I said.

"I can't romanticize this," Ned said, nodding south. "I can't romanticize taxicabs, or men with Spanish names. I … can't romanticize *me*."

"What can you romanticize?" I said.

"Budapest," he said, "in a light snow. Having wine in a cafe, with a pale, handsome waiter with very bony hands."

"So you *still* think you'll fall in love, somewhere else …"

"Though the settings get more and more exotic," he said. "In fact I'm happy just waking up in the morning. Louis, just before he died, was planning to go around the world."

There were shouts, a flurry of raised arms; we looked south and saw a cab, captured, and our friends getting in. My heart was pounding when I reached them, either from the run or that never-failing feeling of excitement that accompanies the entrance of any cab in New York City; as if one renews one's life each time a meter switches on. "Ah, Octavio," Mister Lark was saying in that priestly voice as we got in. "And what part of Buenos Aires?"

CHRISTOPHER ISHERWOOD

WHEN CHRISTOPHER ISHERWOOD died on January 4, 1986, he was widely mourned as a deeply revered icon of contemporary Anglo-American gay culture, a courageous teacher who had wrestled with themes that haunt the twentieth-century psyche—alienation and isolation, sexuality and spirituality—and who had voiced the fears and aspirations of gay men in difficult and dangerous times. His fascinating life's journey from an angry young man of the 1920s and 1930s to the ironic moralist and gay liberation activist of the 1970s and 1980s was itself the source of his art. Isherwood found in his mirror the personal reflection of universal predicaments, yet his work was never self-indulgent. Indeed, his greatest contribution to gay literature was to depict the homosexual as a faithful mirror of the human condition.

Essay by
CLAUDE J. SUMMERS

He was born Christopher William Bradshaw Isherwood on August 26, 1904, into an old and distinguished family, the principal landowners in Cheshire, England. In May of 1915, while a student at St. Edmund's preparatory school in Surrey, he learned of the death of his father in World War I, a loss that would haunt his early writings. He was educated at Repton School and Corpus Christi College, Cambridge, but was sent down from the university without a degree in 1925 for answering examination questions facetiously. Shortly thereafter he renewed his friendship with W. H. Auden, his former classmate at St. Edmund's, with whom he was to share a sporadic and unromantic sexual relationship for over ten years. Auden, who quickly emerged as his generation's greatest poet, cast Isherwood in the role of literary mentor and soon introduced him to a fellow Oxford undergraduate, Stephen Spender. The trio formed the nucleus of the "Auden Gang," the young poets and novelists who dominated the English literary scene of the 1930s.

From 1930 to 1933, Isherwood lived in Berlin, where the city's political excitement and sexual freedom became the stuff of his art. He immersed himself in the world of male prostitutes, living almost anonymously in shabbily genteel and working class areas of the city and translating his experience of the demimonde into what would eventually become the definitive portrait of pre-Hitler Germany, the "Berlin

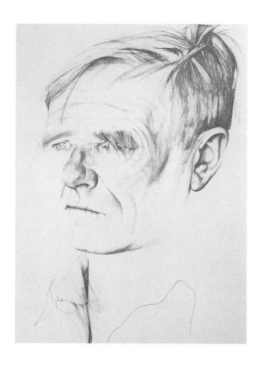

Portrait of Christopher Isherwood by friend and lover Don Bachardy, whom Isherwood described as "the ideal companion to whom you can reveal yourself totally and yet be loved for what you are, not what you pretend to be."

Stories." During his stay in Berlin, Isherwood fell in love with a working-class youth, Heinz, with whom he later wandered restlessly from one European country to another in search of a place where the two could settle together.

The odyssey finally ended when Heinz had to return to Germany, where he was arrested and sentenced to prison for homosexual activities, then to service in the German army. Isherwood's knowledge of Heinz's conscription in the German army contributed to his pacifism on the eve of the outbreak of World War II.

Having collaborated with Auden on three avant-garde plays and having supported various leftist causes, Isherwood gained a reputation for ideological commitment in the 1930s. But partly because of his growing self-consciousness as a homosexual, he deeply distrusted communism and became increasingly uncomfortable with the vacuity of political rhetoric of all stripes. In 1939, Isherwood and Auden emigrated to the United States, settling at first in New York City. But whereas Auden found the city exhilarating, Isherwood was soon deeply depressed. He decided to settle in Los Angeles, where he soon found a job in the motion picture industry. In 1940, under the influence of a Hindu monk and surrogate father, he converted to vedantism, a philosophy that influenced all his later work.

Isherwood was a conscientious objector during World War II and became a United States citizen in 1946. In 1953, he fell in love with an 18-year-old college student, Don Bachardy, who later achieved independent success as a portrait artist. The relationship lasted the rest of Isherwood's life. At the conclusion of his 1980 autobiography, *Christopher and His Kind*, he described Bachardy as "the ideal companion to whom you can reveal yourself totally and yet be loved for what you are, not what you pretend to be." During the 1970s and 1980s Isherwood and Bachardy were active participants in the burgeoning American gay liberation movement, a movement that Isherwood's work of the 1950s and 1960s had anticipated and inspired.

The impact of Isherwood's homosexuality on his writing is pervasive and incalculable, experienced both directly and indirectly. His interest in certain psychological predicaments and in recurring character types and themes, as well as his fascination with the anti-heroic hero, his rebellion against bourgeois respectability, his empathy with "The Lost" (his

British-born American novelist, playwright, editor, and translator.

Born: High Lane, Cheshire, August 26, 1904; immigrated to the United States, 1939; naturalized citizen, 1946.

Partnerships: Companion of artist Don Bachardy.

Education: Repton School, 1919–22; Corpus Christi College, Cambridge, 1924–25; medical student at King's College, London, 1928–29.

Career: Secretary to French violinist Andre Mangeot and his Music Society String Quartet, London, 1926–27; private tutor, London, 1926–27; English teacher, Berlin, Germany, 1930–33; film scriptwriter, Gaumont Films, England; dialogue writer, Metro-Goldwyn-Mayer, Hollywood, California, 1940; worked in hostel for Central European refugees, American Friends Service Committee, Haverford, Pennsylvania, 1941–42; coeditor, with Swami Prabhavananda, *Vedanta and the West*, Vedanta Society of Southern California, 1943–45. Guest professor, Los Angeles State College (now California State University, Los Angeles) and University of California, Santa Barbara, 1959–62; Regents Professor, University of California, Los Angeles, 1965, and University of California, Riverside, 1966.

Recipient: Brandeis University Creative Arts Award, 1974–75; PEN award for body of work, 1983; Common Wealth Award for distinguished service in literature, 1984.

Died: January 4, 1986, in Santa Monica, California, of cancer.

---

code name for the alienated and the excluded), and his ironic perspective, are all related to his awareness of himself as a homosexual. Even when suppressed or disguised for legal or artistic reasons, homosexuality is a felt presence in Isherwood's novels. It is a crucial component of the myth of the outsider that he developed so painstakingly, and a symbol not merely of alienation and isolation, but also of individuality and of the variousness of fully human possibilities.

In his early works, Isherwood presents homosexuality unapologetically and naturally. He domesticates aspects of gay life that lesser writers sensationalized, and he reveals considerable insight into the dynamics of gay relationships. His first novel, *All the Conspirators*, published in 1928, indicts the repression of homosexual feelings, a motif that recurs throughout his canon; while his second novel, 1932's *The Memorial*, brilliantly portrays a homosexual's grief at the loss of his best friend in World War I. *The Berlin Stories* (consisting of the novels *The Last of Mr. Norris*, 1935, *Sally Bowles*, 1937, and *Goodbye to Berlin*, 1939), which brought him international fame, depicts a wide range of homosexual characters, from Baron Kuno von Pregnitz, whose secret fantasies revolve around English schoolboy adventure stories, to Peter Wilkinson and Otto Nowak, who share a spoiled homosexual idyll on Reugen Island. In *The Berlin Stories*, the unhappiness that plagues the gay characters is attributed not to their homosexuality but to their infection with the soul sick-

Christopher Isherwood (left) and longtime friend and fellow writer W. H. Auden leaving London, England in 1938 for a journey to China.

ness that denies life and distorts reality, an infection that they share with everyone else in the doomed city. In the early works, the gay characters are juxtaposed with the heterosexual ones to reveal beneath their apparent polarities a shared reality of the deadened spirit.

Isherwood's American novels, beginning with *The World in the Evening,* published in 1954, focus more directly on the social plight of the homosexual in a homophobic society. In these novels, Isherwood anticipates the concerns of the nascent gay liberation movement, as he presents homosexuals as a legitimate minority among the sea of minorities that constitute Western democracies. By conceiving of homosexuals as an aggrieved minority, Isherwood both softens the stigma linked to homosexuality and encourages solidarity among gay people, while also implying the possibility of a political redress to injustice by forming alliances with other disadvantaged minorities. The dilemma faced by the gay characters of Isherwood's later novels is crystallized in their apparently irreconcilable needs to assert their individuality and to feel a sense of community.

In Bob Wood, the Quaker artist of *The World in the Evening,* Isherwood offers one of the earliest sympathetic portraits of a gay activist in Anglo-American literature. Wood bitterly criticizes the heterosexual majority for its failure to accept the gay minority. Sick of futile discussions of the etiology of homosexuality, he would like to "march down the street with a banner saying, 'We're queer because we're queer because we're queer.'" But even this protest, wildly unlikely in the 1940s, when the action of the novel takes place, is impossible: his lover, Charles, a Jew who has changed his name, "is sick of belonging to these whining, militant minorities." After much soul searching, Wood finally enlists in the Navy, despite the ban against homosexuals in the United States military. His motives are defiant rather than patriotic: "what they're claiming is that us queers are unfit for their beautiful pure Army and Navy—when they ought to be glad to have us." Wood's militancy and his solidarity with other homosexuals are extremely rare in the literature of the 1950s.

Novels

All the Conspirators, 1928.

The Memorial: Portrait of a Family, 1932.

The Last of Mr. Norris, 1935; as *Mr. Norris Changes Trains*, 1935; in *The Berlin Stories*, 1946.

Sally Bowles, 1937; in *The Berlin Stories*, 1946.

Goodbye to Berlin, 1939; in *The Berlin Stories*, 1946.

Prater Violet, 1945.

The Berlin Stories (contains *Mr. Norris Changes Trains*, *Sally Bowles*, and *Goodbye to Berlin*), 1946; as *The Berlin of Sally Bowles*, 1975.

The World in Evening, 1954.

Down There on a Visit, 1964.

A Single Man, 1964.

A Meeting by the River, 1967.

Plays

With W. H. Auden, *The Dog beneath the Skin; or, Where Is Francis?* (produced in London, 1936), 1935.

With W. H. Auden, *The Ascent of F6* (produced in London, 1937), 1937.

With W. H. Auden, *A Melodrama in Three Acts: On the Frontier* (produced in Cambridge, England, 1938), 1938; as *On the Frontier: A Melodrama in Three Acts*, 1939.

The Adventures of the Black Girl in Her Search for God (based on a novella by George Bernard Shaw; produced in Los Angeles, 1969).

With Don Bachardy, *A Meeting by the River* (based on novel by Isherwood; produced in Los Angeles, 1972; on Broadway, 1979).

With W. H. Auden, *Plays, and Other Dramatic Writings: W. H. Auden and Christopher Isherwood, 1928–1938*, edited by Edward Mendelson, 1988.

Screenplays

With others, *Little Friend*, 1934.

With others, *A Woman's Face*, 1941.

With Robert Thoeren, *Rage in Heaven* (based on novel by James Hilton), 1941.

With others, *Forever and a Day*, 1943.

With Ladislas Fodor, *The Great Sinner*, 1949.

Diane, 1955.

With Terry Southern, *The Loved One* (based on novel by Evelyn Waugh), 1965.

With Don Magner and Tony Richardson, *The Sailor from Gibraltar* (based on novel by Marguerite Duras), 1967.

With Don Bachardy, *Frankenstein: The True Story* (based on novel by Mary Shelley; produced, 1972), 1973.

Autobiographies

Lions and Shadows, 1938.

Kathleen and Frank, 1971.

Christopher and His Kind, 1980.

October, illustrations by Don Bachardy, 1983.

Editor

Vedanta for the Western World, 1945; as *Vedanta and the West*, 1951.

Vedanta for Modern Man, 1951.

Great English Short Stories, 1957.

Translator

Penny for the Poor by Bertolt Brecht, 1937; as *Threepenny Novel*, 1956.

With Swami Prabhavananda, *Bhagavad-Gita: The Song of God*, 1944; as *The Song of God: Bhagavad-Gita*, 1951.

And editor, with Swami Prabhavananda, *Crest-Jewel of Discrimination* by Swami Shankara, 1947.

Intimate Journals by Charles Baudelaire, 1947.

And editor, with Swami Prabhavananda, *How to Know God: The Yoga Aphorisms of Patanjali*, 1953.

Other

With W. H. Auden, *Journey to War*, 1939.

The Condor and the Cows: A South American Travel Diary, 1949.

An Approach to Vedanta, 1963.

Ramakrishna and His Disciples (biography), 1965.

Exhumations: Stories, Articles, Verses, 1966.

The Legend of Silent Night (television special; adaptation of a story by Paul Gallico), 1969.

Essentials of Vedanta, 1969.

My Guru and His Disciple, 1980.

With Sylvain Mangeot, *People One Ought to Know* (poems), 1982.

The Wishing Tree: Christopher Isherwood on Mystical Religion, edited by Robert Adjemian, 1987.

"Mr. Lancaster," in *The Faber Book of Gay Short Fiction*, edited by Edmund White, 1991.

"Hollywood Homophobia Doesn't Stop Everyone," in *Advocate*, 14 January 1992, 76.

Adaptations

I Am a Camera (stage adaptation by John Van Druten of *The Berlin Stories*) was produced in 1951.

Cabaret (a stage musical adaptation by Joe Masteroff, John Kander, and Fred Ebb of *I Am a Camera* and *The Berlin Stories*) was produced on Broadway in 1966.

Cabaret (screen adaptation by Jay Preston Allen of the stage musical) was filmed in 1972.

Isherwood's sensitivity to the injustices felt by homosexuals is also apparent in 1964's *Down There on a Visit*. Ambrose, an expatriate Englishman who has created an anarchic community on a Greek island, fantasizes a homosexual kingdom in which heterosexuality is illegal:

"meanwhile it'll be winked at, of course, as long as it's practiced in decent privacy. I think we shall even allow a few bars to be opened for people with those unfortunate tendencies, in certain quarters of the larger cities." This comic riff parodies the unjust reality in which homosexuals are excluded from the larger community, even as it also betrays Ambrose's secret desire for involvement in the world.

In Isherwood's 1964 masterpiece *A Single Man*, the need for community is also an issue. Focusing on George, a late-middle-aged and lonely expatriate Briton grieving at the death of his lover of many years, the novel more fully develops the context of gay oppression than do the earlier works and places it within a still larger context of spiritual transcendence. *A Single Man* regards the assertions of individual uniqueness and minority consciousness as necessary worldly and political goals, but it finally subsumes them in the vedantic idea of the universal consciousness. In making concrete this resolution, the novel presents a moving portrait of male homosexual love, and George emerges as an "Everyman" figure whose homosexuality is a simple given. Presaging the gay liberation movement, *A Single Man* presents homosexuality as a human variation that should be accorded respect and depicts homosexuals as a minority whose grievances need to be addressed.

Isherwood's final novel, *A Meeting by the River*, pivots on the unsuccessful attempt of a bisexual movie producer to dissuade his younger brother from taking final vows as a Hindu monk. The producer, Patrick, finally retreats to a cowardly conformity, but his Whitmanesque vision of a homosexual union "in which two men learn to trust each other so completely that there's no fear left and they experience and share everything together in the flesh and in the spirit" complements his brother's search for spiritual brotherhood in a monastery. This vedantic novel discovers in the concept of brotherhood a means of escaping the imprisoning ego.

Described by Gore Vidal as "the best prose writer in English," Isherwood was a masterful stylist, a subtle ironist, a witty and compassionate moralist, and an insightful observer of the human condition. He was, in fact, one of the best writers of his generation. Central to his achievement was his depiction of homosexuality in casual, occasionally elevated, and always human terms. Incorporating gay liberation perspectives into his novels, especially the need for solidarity among homosexuals and the recognition of homosexuals as a legitimate minority, Isherwood created characters whose homosexuality is an integral part of their personality and an emblem of their common humanity.

ON HIS QUEERNESS

When I was young and wanted to see the sights,
They told me: 'Cast an eye over the Roman Camp
If you care to.
But plan to spend most of your day at the Aquarium—
Because, after all, the Aquarium—
Well, I mean to say, the Aquarium—
Till you've seen the Aquarium you ain't seen nothing.'

So I cast an eye over
The Roman Camp—
And that old Roman Camp,
And that old, old Roman Camp
Got me
Interested.

So that now, near closing-time,
I find that I still know nothing—
And am not even sorry that I know nothing—
About fish.

First published in
Exhumations, Simon &
Schuster, Methuen,
copyright 1966 by
Christopher Isherwood.

CHRISTOPHER **ISHERWOOD**

LARRY KRAMER

"KRAMER EQUALS CONTROVERSY," wrote Paula Span in the *Washington Post*. From the time he burst on the gay literary scene with his novel *Faggots*, Larry Kramer has waged a war within and against a community built on sexual freedom. At first and for many years a seeming lone voice in the wilderness, Kramer has slowly won gay men from many circles over to his call for a more responsible gay male community, one that would think less about sex and more about compassion. Along the way, he has openly attacked high-profile figures both inside and outside the gay community, the former breaking a tacit rule against criticizing one's own. As well, few have done more to advance the cause of people infected with HIV, from his participation in the founding of both the Gay Men's Health Crisis and the AIDS Coalition to Unleash Power (ACT UP), to his prolific writings of both fiction and nonfiction concerning the AIDS crisis.

Essay by
BRADLEY BONEY

Kramer's writing career began in 1969 after almost a decade working in London for Columbia Pictures and United Artists, with the screen adaptation of D. H. Lawrence's novel *Women in Love*. Although the film reproduces the affectionate relationship between Rupert and Gerald (as well as the homoerotic nude wrestling match) from the novel, its primary focus remains on the two heterosexual relationships. Kramer himself was still a closeted gay man during this time, taking female dates to parties and having short-term affairs with several of them. Despite an Academy Award nomination for his *Women in Love* screenplay, Kramer was fired from his next film project and, in 1971, moved to New York City where he began writing plays.

Kramer's first attempts in the theater are all but forgotten. His first play, *Four Friends*, opened and closed on the same night in 1973. His second, *Sissies' Scrapbook*, opened a year later to mixed reviews and only a slightly longer run at Playwrights Horizons. Frustrated by his own inability to sustain a lasting personal relationship (either gay or straight), Kramer began writing a novel about one gay man's search for love in a world concerned primarily with sex. "There wasn't a relationship in the

293

Larry Kramer, founder of the AIDS Coalition to Unleash Power (ACT UP), at his
Greenwich Village home in 1989.

American playwright, novelist, and activist.

Born: Bridgeport, Connecticut, June 25, 1935; grew up in a suburb of Washington, D.C.

Education: Yale University, New Haven, Connecticut, B.A. 1957.

Career: Served in the U.S. Army, 1957. Messenger, William Morris Agency, New York City, 1958; telex operator, Columbia Pictures, New York City, 1958–59; assistant story editor, Columbia Pictures, New York City, 1961; production executive, Columbia Pictures, London, 1961–65; assistant to the president, United Artists, 1965; associate producer, *Here We Go Round the Mulberry Bush* (film), United Artists, 1967; producer, *Women in Love* (film), United Artists, 1969; writer and activist, New York City, 1971–. Frequent contributor to periodicals, including *Advocate, New York Native, New York Times,* and *Village Voice.*

Memberships: Cofounder of Gay Men's Health Crisis, New York City, 1981; founder of AIDS Coalition to Unleash Power (ACT UP), 1987.

Recipient: Academy of Motion Picture Arts and Sciences nomination, for best screenplay adaptation, and British Film Academy nomination, for best screenplay, 1970, both for *Women in Love;* Foundation of the Dramatists Guild Marton Award, 1986; City Lights Award, for best play, 1986; Sarah Siddons Award, for best play, 1986; Olivier Award nomination, for best play, 1986; Human Rights Campaign Fund's Arts and Communication Award, 1987; Obie Award, Lucille Lortel Award, and the Dramatists Guild Hull-Warriner Award, 1993, all for *Destiny of Me.*

Address: c/o Arthur B. Kramer, Esquire, 919 Third Avenue, New York, New York 10022, U.S.A.

world that could sustain the promiscuity we were asking these relationships to sustain," he told Dinitia Smith in *New York.*

Although his novel, *Faggots,* appeared in 1978 to caustic reviews from the gay press (for example, the *Gay Community News* called it "appalling" and "offensive" because of its satirical critique of promiscuity, then widely regarded as a fundamental plank of the gay liberation platform), it also generated a positive response. Having sold more than 400,000 copies over the years, it is now considered a cornerstone of the gay literary canon. At the time, however, Kramer became the villain of the gay press, while authors like Ethan Mordden and Andrew Holleran, whose *Dancer from the Dance* provides an admiring and sympathetic portrait of the gay 1970s in counterpoint to Kramer's novel, became the darlings.

In 1980, the sight of a young man carrying his dying lover on New York's Fire Island awakened the true activist in Kramer. A year later, with the AIDS crisis still in its early stages and a gay community largely in denial, Kramer called 80 of his friends to his apartment, where, that evening, they founded the Gay Men's Health Crisis, an AIDS services organization. Kramer was in almost constant disagreement with the rest of the group over political strategy and safe-sex recommendations, and he was eventually ousted from the organization in 1983. Still a writer, but now an AIDS activist as well, Kramer combined his two careers in his 1985 play *The Normal Heart*. What Mark Caldwell in *Dissent* called "covert psychoautobiography," *The Normal Heart* is the angry story of Ned Weeks, a Kramer-based character who founds an AIDS organization, fights with the other members, eventually gets kicked out, and loses his lover to the disease before the final curtain. The play continues Kramer's attack on promiscuity ("All we've created is generations of guys who can't deal with each other as anything but erections"), attacks Ronald Reagan and the *New York Times*, and "outs" then–New York City mayor Ed Koch, years before Michelangelo Signorile popularized this practice in *OutWeek*. Ironically, it is Kramer himself who creates the line that best sums up all the attacks he has received within the gay community, when a character says to Ned, "After years of liberation, you have helped make sex dirty again for us—terrible and forbidden."

Kramer produced a phenomenal success with *The Normal Heart*. The play holds the record for the longest run at the New York Shakespeare Festival's Public Theatre and has received over six hundred world-wide productions. Although many reviewers agreed with Paul Berman in the *Nation* when he called the script "amateurish," *The Normal Heart* was almost universally praised for its frank and overt handling of such an urgent social crisis. Years later, Jack Kroll in *Newsweek* called it "the breakthrough play on [AIDS]."

Kramer did not sit still. In 1987, through a rallying call-to-arms at New York's Lesbian and Gay Community Services Center, he founded the AIDS Coalition to Unleash Power (ACT UP), a direct-action group committed to ending the AIDS crisis. In 1988, Kramer himself tested positive for HIV. He wrote numerous essays and op-ed pieces in both the gay and straight press, many of which were collected and published as *Reports from the holocaust: The making of an AIDS activist*. The book, which concludes with a lengthy essay written specifically for the collection, provides an excellent history of the AIDS movement, albeit from one point of view. In the final essay, Kramer continues his attack on serial sex: "There's no question that the promiscuity of some gay men was unwittingly responsible for AIDS killing so many of us." He also found himself, once again, under attack as well. Gregory Kolovakos in the *Nation* called Kramer a "hate-monger," his politics "meanspirited and exclusionary," and his point "the old wages-of-sin argument."

In the same year that *Reports from the holocaust* was published, New York's WPA Theatre produced Kramer's new play, *Just Say No*. A farce of sexual hypocrisy, the play was ill-received in its scheduled limited run. It would seem at this point that Kramer was becoming, as John M. Clum states in *Acting Gay*, "better known as AIDS polemicist and activist than as playwright." Kramer, however, produced another major success in 1992 with *The Destiny of Me*, which opened to favorable reviews at New York's Lucille Lortel Theatre, and played runner-up to Tony Kushner's "Gay Fantasia," *Angels in America* for the 1993 Pulitzer Prize. Continuing the story of *The Normal Heart*'s Ned Weeks, now HIV–positive and undergoing experimental treatment, the play weaves in flashbacks from Ned's childhood as he struggles with his emerging homosexuality. William A. Henry III said in *Time*: "More than a play about AIDS and death, *The Destiny of Me* is a play about homosexuality and life. It is irate, not about dying but about having been unable to live and love."

Kramer is currently at work on his second novel, titled *The American People*. Though still an activist, he now commits more time to writing. As he told Victor Zonana in the *Advocate*, "I would like to say emphatically that I am not burned-out or tired. There just comes a time when you have to decide how your resources can be better spent." Always controversial, Kramer has nonetheless garnered respect from most in the gay community and press (even those he vehemently attacks), and is now a regular columnist for the *Advocate*. In an essay for the *New York Times*, Kramer clarifies the importance of his homosexuality in his journey to acceptance: "This journey, from discovery through guilt to momentary joy and toward AIDS, has been my longest, most important journey, as important—no, more important—than my life with my parents, than my life as a writer, than my life as an activist. Indeed, my homosexuality, as unsatisfying as much of it was for so long, has been the single most important defining characteristic of my life."

THE NORMAL HEART

Scene 3

The law office of BEN WEEKS, NED's older brother. BEN always dresses in a suit and tie, which NED never does. The brothers love each other a great deal; BEN's approval is essential to NED. BEN is busy with some papers as NED, sitting on the opposite side of the desk, waits for him.

BEN: Isn't it a bit early to get so worked up?

NED: Don't you be like that, too?

BEN: What have I done now?

NED: My friend Bruce and I went out to Fire Island and over the whole Labor Day weekend we collected a grand sum of $124.

Writer and AIDS activist Larry Kramer combined his two careers in his 1985 play *The Normal Heart*, which one reviewer dubbed a "covert psychoautobiography" about a Kramer-like character, Ned Weeks, who founds an AIDS organization.

BEN: You can read that as either an indication that it's a beginning and will improve, or as a portent that heads will stay in the sand. My advice is heads are going to stay in the sand.

NED: Because so many gay people are still in the closet?

BEN: Because people don't like to be frightened. When they get scared they don't behave well. It's called denial. (*Giving NED some papers to sign.*)

NED: (*Signs them automatically.*) What are these for?

BEN: Your account needs some more money. You never seem to do anything twice. One movie, one novel, one play … You know you are now living on your capital. I miss your being in the movie business. I like movies. (*Unrolls some blueprints.*)

NED: What are those?

BEN: I've decided to build a house.

NED: But the one you're in is terrific.

BEN: I just want to build me a dream house, so now I'm going to.

NED: It looks like a fortress. Does it have a moat? How much is it going to cost?

THE GAY AND LESBIAN LITERARY COMPANION

Plays

Four Friends (produced New York, 1973).

Sissies' Scrapbook (produced New York, 1974).

The Normal Heart (produced New York, 1985), introduction by Andrew Holleran, 1985.

Just Say No (produced New York, 1988), 1989.

The Destiny of Me (produced New York, 1992), 1993.

Other

Women in Love (screenplay; adaptation of the novel by D. H. Lawrence), 1969.

Faggots (novel), 1978.

Reports from the holocaust: The making of an AIDS activist (nonfiction), 1989.

"129,001 and Counting" (speech), in *Village Voice*, 10 December 1991, 18.

"A Man's Life, and the Path to Acceptance" (essay), in *New York Times*, 4 October 1992, B-1.

Adaptations

Indecent Materials (theater piece; produced New York Shakespeare Festival, 1990).

BEN: I suspect it'll wind up over a million bucks. But you're not to tell that to anyone. Not even Sarah. I've found some land in Greenwich, by a little river, completely protected by trees. Ned, it's going to be beautiful.

NED: Doesn't spending a million dollars on a house frighten you? It would scare the shit out of me. Even if I had it.

BEN: You can have a house anytime you want one. You haven't done badly.

NED: Do I detect a tinge of approval—from the big brother who always called me lemon?

BEN: Well, you were a lemon.

NED: I don't want a house.

BEN: Then why have you been searching for one in the country for so many years?

NED: It's no fun living in one alone.

BEN: There's certainly no law requiring you to do that. Is this ... Bruce someone you're seeing?

NED: Why thank you for asking. Don't I wish. I see him. He just doesn't see me. Everyone's afraid of me anyway. I frighten them away. It's called the lemon complex.

BEN: I think you're the one who's scared.

NED: You've never said that before.

BEN: Yes, I have. You just didn't hear me. What's the worst thing that could happen to you.

NED: I'd spend a million bucks on a house. Look, Ben—please! (*He takes the blueprints from him.*) I've—we've started an organization to raise money and spread information and fight any way we can.

LARRY **KRAMER**

BEN: Fight who and what?

NED: I told you. There's this strange new disease …

BEN: You're not going to do that full-time?

NED: I just want to help it get started and I'll worry about how much time later on.

BEN: It sounds to me like another excuse to keep from writing.

NED: I knew you would say that. I was wondering … could your law firm incorporate us and get us tax-exempt status and take us on for free, what's it called, *pro bono*?

BEN: *Pro bono* for what? What are you going to do?

NED: I just told you—raise money and fight.

BEN: You have to be more specific than that. You have to have a plan.

NED: How about if we say we're going to become a cross between the League of Women Voters and the United States Marines? Is that a good-enough plan?

BEN: Well, we have a committee that decides this sort of thing. I'll have to put it to the committee.

NED: Why can't you just say yes?

BEN: Because we have a committee.

NED: But you're the senior partner and I'm your brother.

BEN: I fail to see what bearing that has on the matter. You're asking me to ask my partners to give up income that would ordinarily come into their pocket.

NED: I thought every law firm did a certain amount of this sort of thing—charity, worthy causes.

BEN: It's not up to me, however, to select just what these worthy causes might be.

NED: Well, that's a pity. What did you start the firm for?

BEN: That's one of the rules. It's a democratic firm.

NED: I think I like elitism better. When will you know?

BEN: Know what?

NED: Whether or not your committee wants to help dying faggots?

BEN: I'll put it to them at the next meeting.

NED: When is that?

BEN: When it is!

NED: When is it? Because if you're not going to help, I have to find somebody else.

BEN: You're more than free to do that.

NED: I don't want to do that! I want my big brother's fancy famous big-deal straight law firm to be the first major New York law firm to do *pro bono* work for a gay cause. That would give me a great deal of pride. I'm sorry you can't see that. I'm sorry I'm putting you in a position where you're ashamed of me. I thought we'd worked all that out years ago.

BEN: I am not ashamed of you! I told you I'm simply not free to take this on without asking my partners' approval at the next meeting.

NED: Why don't I believe that. When is the next meeting?

BEN: Next Monday. Can you wait until next Monday?

NED: Who else is on the committee?

BEN: What difference does that make?

NED: I'll lobby them. You don't seem like a very sure vote. Is Nelson on the committee? Norman Ivey? Harvey?

BEN: Norman and Harvey are.

NED: Good.

BEN: Okay? Lemon, where do you want to have lunch today? It's your turn to pay.

NED: It is not. I paid last week.

BEN: That's simply not true.

NED: Last week was … French. You're right. Do you know you're the only person in the world I can't get mad at and stay mad at. I think my world would come to an end without you. And then who would Ben talk to? (*He embraces BEN.*)

BEN: (*Embracing back, a bit.*) That's true.

NED: You're getting better at it.

TONY KUSHNER

AT AGE 36, playwright Tony Kushner did not have a long list of productions to his credit, but he did have a Pulitzer Prize for a play that
Newsweek called "the biggest event involving the gay movement in the
history of American popular culture." That play was *Angels in America*,
which opened to rave reviews at the Royal National Theatre in London
in 1992, and found an equally enthusiastic reception among critics and
audiences alike on Broadway the following year. Subtitled "A Gay
Fantasia on National Themes," *Angels in America* actually comprises two
companion plays, *Millennium Approaches* and *Perestroika*, each of which
runs for three and one-half hours. Epic in scope as well as in design,
Angels in America goes further than any other contemporary gay literary
work in its use of gay characters and traditionally gay themes to examine
a complex political, cultural, and historical reality that transcends gay
ghettos and embraces all of American society.

Viewing the 1980s through the intersecting lenses of Reaganite politics, the burgeoning gay community, and the emerging AIDS epidemic,
Angels in America explores such themes as denial, hypocrisy, repression,
self-loathing, self-acceptance, and self-love. Kushner's truly inspired master stroke was the decision to include among his cast of characters an historical figure, the highly controversial attorney Roy Cohn, who gained
notoriety in the 1950s as the chief counsel to Senator Joseph McCarthy.
As McCarthy's trusted assistant, Cohn zealously pursued an anti-
Communist crusade that destroyed the lives of countless Americans and
culminated in the executions of Julius and Ethel Rosenberg for treason.
What makes Cohn such a sublime focal point for Kushner's epic drama is
the fact that this unscrupulous lawyer (who flouted the Constitution in
his efforts to prosecute its perceived offenders) vehemently asserted his
hatred of homosexuals while denying his own homosexuality. Moreover,
he vigorously asserted that he was suffering from liver cancer right up to
his death in 1986, when it was patently clear that he was dying of AIDS-
related causes.

In addition to Roy Cohn, *Angels in America* focuses on Cohn's fictional protegé Joe Pitt, a Mormon from Salt Lake City, Utah, who must

Essay by
MICHAEL BRODER

Tony Kushner won the Pulitzer Prize for his Broadway play *Angels in America*, which has been called "the biggest event involving the gay movement in the history of American popular culture."

confront the fact that he is a homosexual; Joe's wife, Harper, whose psychotic hallucinations contain some of the play's profoundest truths; Prior Walter, whose battle with AIDS transforms him into a prophetic recipient of angelic revelation; and Prior's lover Louis Ironson, who finds that despite his sweeping human-istic rhetoric, he does not have the courage to stand by Prior when the latter becomes ill. Joining these central figures is a wide range of peripheral charac-ters, straight and gay, living and dead, human and divine, in a sweeping panorama that encompasses the most elemental realities of mortal life and the most sublime fantasies of divine imagination. "Part One of the play is about despair," Tony Kushner told *Vogue*. "Part Two therefore must be about hope, but … our hope may simply be, as Prior says, an addiction to being alive."

Angels in America came to Broadway at a piv-otal moment in gay America's struggle to join the mainstream, just one month after a massive march on Washington for the rights of sexual minorities that itself drew momentum from highly publicized ballot initiatives to limit gay rights in Oregon and Colorado, and an intense public debate on the armed forces' ban on military service by homosexuals. Kushner's work also followed closely on a number of other plays dealing with AIDS, the gay community, and gay-straight interaction, including Larry Kramer's *The Destiny of Me*, Paul Rudnick's *Jeffrey*, and William Finn's Broadway musical, *Falsettos*. But Kushner's play enjoyed far greater critical and pop-ular acclaim than any previous drama about gay life in the age of AIDS, and—despite the fact that his first commercial productions went virtually unnoticed—left the author widely acknowledged as one of the best and most important young playwrights of his generation.

American playwright.

Born: New York City, c. 1956; raised in Lake Charles, Louisiana; lives in Brooklyn, New York.

Education: Columbia University, 1978, and the New York University graduate theater program.

Career: Worked as a switchboard operator at the United Nations Plaza Hotel, 1979–85; assistant director at the St. Louis Repertory Theatre, 1985–86; artistic director, New York Theatre Workshop, 1987–88.

Memberships: Member, AIDS Coalition to Unleash Power (ACT UP), a direct action political advocacy group.

Recipient: National Endowment for the Arts fellowship, 1985, 1988; London *Evening Standard* Award for drama; Los Angeles Drama Critics Circle award; Pulitzer Prize in drama for *Millennium Approaches*, 1993.

MILLENIUM APPROACHES

Scene 8

Late that night. Joe at a payphone phoning Hannah at home in Salt Lake City.

JOE: Mom?

HANNAH: Joe?

JOE: Hi.

HANNAH: You're calling from the street. It's … it must be four in the morning. What's happened?

JOE: Nothing, nothing, I …

HANNAH: It's Harper. Is Harper … Joe? Joe?

JOE: Yeah, hi. No, Harper's fine. Well, no, she's … not fine. How are you mom?

HANNAH: What's happened?

JOE: I just wanted to talk to you. I, uh, wanted to try something out on you.

HANNAH: Joe, you haven't … have you been drinking, Joe?

JOE: Yes ma'am. I'm drunk.

HANNAH: That isn't like you.

JOE: No. I mean, who's to say?

HANNAH: Why are you out on the street at four a.m.? In that crazy city. It's dangerous.

JOE: Actually, Mom, I'm not on the street. I'm near the boathouse in the park.

Reprinted from *Angels in America: A Gay Fantasia on National Themes,* Theatre Communications Group, copyright 1993 by Tony Kushner.

TONY **KUSHNER**   305

Tony Kushner's *Angels in America* has been optioned for film by Robert Altman.

HANNAH: What park?

JOE: Central Park.

HANNAH: CENTRAL PARK! Oh my Lord. What on earth are you doing in Central Park at this time of night? Are you …

Joe, I think you ought to go home right now. Call me from home.

(Little pause)

Joe?

JOE: I come here to watch, Mom. Sometimes. Just to watch.

HANNAH: Watch what? What's there to watch at four in the …

JOE: Mom, did Dad love me?

HANNAH: What?

JOE: Did he?

HANNAH: You ought to go home and call from there.

JOE: Answer.

HANNAH: Oh now really. This is maudlin. I don't like this conversation.

JOE: Yeah, well, it gets worse from here on.

(Pause.)

HANNAH: Joe?

JOE: Mom. Momma. I'm a homosexual, Momma.
Boy, did that come out awkward.

(Pause)

Hello? Hello?
I'm a homosexual.

(Pause)

Please, Momma. Say something.

Plays

La Fin de la Baleine: An Opera for the Apocalypse (produced New York, 1982).

Yes Yes No No: The Solace-of-Solstice, Apogee/Perigee, Bestial/Celestial Holiday Show (produced St. Louis, 1985; directed by Kushner).

The Heavenly Theatre (produced New York, c. 1986).

In Great Eliza's Golden Time (produced St. Louis, 1986).

The Illusion (adaptation of a play by Pierre Corneille; produced New York, 1988).

A Bright Room Called Day (produced London and New York, 1990).

Angels in America: A Gay Fantasia on National Themes, Part 1: *Millennium Approaches* (in West End, and Los Angeles, 1992; on Broadway, 1993), 1993; Part 2: *Perestroika* (produced on Broadway, 1993), 1993.

Adaptations

Robert Altman has acquired the film rights to *Angels in America*.

HANNAH: You're old enough to understand that your father didn't love you without being ridiculous about it.

JOE: What?

HANNAH: You're ridiculous. You're being ridiculous.

JOE: I'm ...

What?

HANNAH: You really ought to go home now to your wife. I need to go to bed. This phone call.... We will just forget this phone call.

JOE: Mom.

HANNAH: No more talk. Tonight. This ...

(*Suddenly very angry*) Drinking is a sin! A sin! I raised you better than that. (*She hangs up*)

DAVID
LEAVITT

DAVID LEAVITT'S work exhibits not only "a genius for empathy," as Wendy Lesser noted, reviewing *Family Dancing* in the *New York Times Book Review*, but also a canniness, an instinct for the ordinariness of life. In his stories and novels, it is what people hold in common, including those things that divide them, that provide him with his subject. It is not surprising, then, to find that families play so prominent a part.

Essay by
KEVIN RAY

In his debut collection of stories, *Family Dancing*, published in 1985, Leavitt introduced elements that would carry through his next three books: homosexuality, family, illness, and the ways in which individual lives strain the bonds of affection. His characters—educated, articulate, middle-class—love one another and fail to love. Jonathan Keates, writing in London's *Times Literary Supplement*, has said that "the kind of people David Leavitt writes about are exceedingly hard to dislike. Their waking thoughts, and occasionally their dreams as well, are furrowed with mutual solicitude, their arms sinewy from the exercise of reaching out, their consciences pitted with minor and tolerable quilts." In "Territory," a young gay man returning home to visit his mother, bringing with him the lover she has known of but never met, discovers that love is not immediately or infinitely elastic. "I'm very tolerant, very understanding," his mother tells him. "But I can only take so much." Borders are overstepped, and revealed by the transgression. Similarly, Rose, the wife and mother in Leavitt's first novel, *The Lost Language of Cranes*, pushes beyond what she is willing to accept by the admission that not only her son but her husband too is gay, and is lost or abandoned, as much by her own choice as by the choices others make.

Where in the work of many gay writers, women are omitted or somehow erased, in Leavitt's fiction women are central and essential. They appear, however, as either facilitators, bringing men together, or as aggravated and aggrieved judges. Many critics have pointed out that his female characters are commonly the most strongly drawn in his work, yet their position is agonistic, unresolved.

In David Leavitt's fiction, it is what people hold in common that assumes primary importance.

Excerpt reprinted from *Equal Affections*, Harper & Row, copyright 1989 by David Leavitt.

Women retain the center in Leavitt's later work. His second novel, *Equal Affections*, offers another analogue of the reluctant mother. Indeed, one can see in *Equal Affections* a drawing-together of the individual notes he has sounded from the start. In his circling back to common themes and familiar characters, Leavitt appears to be tapping the sides of a very particular box, testing it, not so much finding weaknesses in it as trying, as if for the first time, to see exactly what is there. His is an art of limited but precise dimensions. "I've never thought of myself as naive," he commented in an essay he wrote for *Esquire* in 1985. "I've never imagined that I might lead a sheltered life. I am, after all, 'sophisticated,' have been to Europe, understand dirty jokes and the intricacies of sexually transmitted diseases. This is my milieu, the world I live in, and I have almost never stepped beyond its comfortable borders. A safety net surrounds my sophisticated life, and the question is, of course, how did it get there? Did I build it myself? Was it left for me?"

EQUAL AFFECTIONS

Inside Walter's computer, meanwhile, the erotic masque continued unabated. So many newcomers were logging on that the channel was often packed, particularly on Friday nights. You could try to get through for hours and receive nothing but a busy signal, a situation that enraged the old-timers; Bulstrode was constantly collecting signatures on electronic petitions, or sending angry e-mail to the administrative offices of the service, which were located in Duluth. Other than that, things went on as usual; every time he logged on, Walter was happy to see a few familiar names embedded in the pornographic cast list. Lies continued to be told and tolerated. What did it matter? It was not as if any of them would ever actually meet. Two of the regulars, Mastermind and PandaBear, had met, and it had been a disaster; they had arranged a secret rendezvous in a Washington, D.C., hotel, yet when the momentous weekend finally arrived, no sooner were they checked into their room than they had logged back onto the computer, under the joint handle "Master/Panda." All Friday evening they were there, and Saturday as well. What had gone wrong? Walter wondered. Had the sight of the oth-

American novelist and author of short stories.

Born: Pittsburgh, Pennsylvania, June 23, 1961; grew up in Palo Alto, California.

Partnerships: Companion of author and teacher Gary Glickman.

Education: Yale University, New Haven, Connecticut, B.A. (Phi Beta Kappa) 1983.

Career: Reader and educational assistant, Viking-Penguin, Inc., New York City, 1983–84. Contributor of essays and stories to periodicals. Member of PEN.

Recipient: Yale University Willets Prize for fiction, 1982; O. Henry Award, 1984; PEN/Faulkner Award nomination, and National Book Critics Circle Award nomination, both for *Family Dancing*, 1984; Guggenheim fellowship, 1989.

Agent: Andrew Wylie, 48 West 75th Street, New York, New York 10023, U.S.A.

er's physical body been more than each of them could bear? Or had each merely been so disappointed at the unmasked reality of the other that in order to salvage what they could of their fantasies, they had elected to return to the electronic medium where their courtship had begun? The problem with real intimacy, Walter had long ago learned, is that you cannot just shut it off. Real people have a way of banging against the doors you've closed; they know your name, your phone number. They live with you. And that, he decided, was not altogether bad. What the computer had offered was the safety of isolation, the safety of control. Voices, words, telephone numbers came through the circuits, but you could always hang up, you could always log off. There was nothing to risk, nothing to lose, even with Bulstrode. And even so, from those heights of safety, those heights of self-protection and anonymity, Walter longed for nothing more than the rich landscape of the dangerous human earth. It was funny—for most of his life he had kept his eyes focused straight ahead, on the law, or else on some fantasy of escape, to Europe, to Asia; he had assumed that by looking only forward, he could eventually lose the sadness and dissatisfactions of his childhood. But the further he went, the more Walter realized that, like it or not, he was inextricably bound with the people who had mattered to him and who mattered to him now, the people whose loves defined him, whose deaths would devastate him. He would never, could never be Bulstrode, self-invented, untouchable, a journeyer among the keys. And for this he was glad.

When they were at the hospital, when Louise was dying, Walter had stood for hours just outside the glass partitions of her room. Inside, beyond the glass, Danny and April and Nat wept and raged and struggled through Louise's death, Louise struggled through Louise's death. All that separated him from the spectacle of them was a piece of glass. It could have been a television, or a window, or a mirror, but in fact it was a door,

Stories

Family Dancing, 1984.
A Place I've Never Been, 1990.

Novels

The Lost Language of Cranes, 1986.
Equal Affections, 1989.

Other

"The New Lost Generation," in *Esquire*, May 1985.

"New Voices and Old Values," in *New York Times Book Review*, 12 May 1985.

Author of introduction, *These Young People Today: Writers under 35* (special issue of *Mississippi Review*), spring/summer 1986.

"Italy's Secret Gardens," in *Vogue*, June 1988.

"The Way I Live Now," in *New York Times Magazine*, 9 July 1989.

"Almodovar on the Verge," in *New York Times Magazine*, 22 April 1990.

"Mad about Milan," in *Vogue*, March 1990.

"When You Grow to Adultery," in *The Faber Book of Gay Short Fiction*, edited by Edmund White, 1991.

Adaptations

The Lost Language of Cranes (teleplay; British production appeared as part of "Great Performances" series), PBS, 1992.

and every hour or so someone came out, usually crying. What right did he have to complain? He was just there for Danny; it wasn't his mother. Yet there was the door. And someday probably not too long from now, he was going to have to walk through that door; he was going to have to confront himself what was waiting for him on the other side of that door.

The computer was not a door.

He shut off his computer. Somewhere across the house was Danny. What to do? What to say to him? He started walking, then, for a moment, hesitated. Don't be an idiot, he chided himself. Go to him.

Danny was sitting at the kitchen table, reading the newspaper. Approaching him from behind, Walter was suddenly flushed with affection for his clean-shaven neck, his comfortable, round head. "Danny—" he said.

"Yes?"

"Danny, I—" He faltered. Danny put down the paper, swiveled the chair around to face him.

"What is it, Walt?"

"I missed you," Walter said.

Danny looked up at him. Walter had his arms folded behind his back and his head bent forward, like that of a penitent child.

"But I haven't gone anywhere," Danny said quietly.

"I have."

Danny reached up a hand, lightly brushed it over Walter's cheek.

"And are you back?" he said.

"I'm back," Walter said. "I'm back."

AUDRE LORDE

ONE OF THE MOST extraordinary facets of the explosion of gay and lesbian literature since the Stonewall Riots in 1969 is the multitude of ways in which the common experiences of the community have been drawn, sung, and celebrated in poetry and prose. Of less prominence, until recently, has been that body of writing addressing the needs, dreams, and hopes of gay men and lesbians outside mainstream homosexual culture. While some of this exclusion has been the result of a conscious choice on the part of group members—such as adherents of the Radical Faerie philosophy—often this marginalization is due to the reflection, within the homosexual world, of attitudes and trends prevalent in society at large. The most powerful of these have been racism and discrimination against women—as challengers of social limits and often on the basis of their status and sexual orientation. While writings by openly gay black men have only recently become a recognized part of the literature (with such anthologies as Joseph Beam's *In the Life*, for example), black women have possessed a visible and active presence in the creation of the current homosexual world almost from its birth through both their willingness to challenge accepted liberationist philosophies and the power of their individual and collective voices. One of the first and most influential of these voices was that of Audre Lorde.

Audre Geraldine Lorde was born in New York City in 1934; she was raised to fit the mold of many young women maturing in that metropolitan area. She enrolled at the National University of Mexico in 1954 and continued her postsecondary education at Hunter College and Columbia University, where she received her bachelor's degree and her professional certification in the field of librarianship in 1961. Lorde joined the staff of the Mount Vernon Public Library, the first in a series of positions which, over the next three decades, would expose her to the disparate influences of Saint Clare's School of Nursing, Lehman College, City College of the City University of New York, and the John Jay College of Criminal Justice. Her marriage to Edwin A. Rollins in 1962 completed the matrix out of which her public sharing of private insights, griefs, and fierce joys would soon begin to arise in her first book of verse.

Essay by
ROBERT B. MARKS
RIDINGER

313

Audre Lorde explained and celebrated her life as black, female, and lesbian through her poetry, fiction, essays, and journals.

The diversity of her creative gifts would prove to be well matched to the breadth of issues facing the communities of lesbians, women, and African Americans she would address in her personal essays and journals—and especially in her vital and intense poetry.

To understand a written work, the reader must have a clear picture of its author's vision—of the private road he or she has followed in developing both as an artist and a human being. Lorde presents a particularly complex picture due to the wide variety of causes and environments she has experienced. Nowhere in her work is this more openly presented than in her 1982 volume *Zami: A New Spelling of My Name; A Biomythography*. In an interview with Mari Evans for the 1984 publication *Black Women Writers: A Critical Evaluation*, she noted that she began to write because there was no visible source saying what she needed and wanted to hear to serve as a channel for the pain of her gradual comprehension of the world. *Zami* is perhaps the most coherent expression of this, telling, as it does, a dual story of her life from childhood in Harlem before World War II to her completion of higher education in 1962 and the coalescence of her identities as both lesbian and aware black woman in America. Lorde's characterization of the text as a new species of writing, a "biomythography," is in keeping with her adoption of—and search for—traditional ancestral beliefs and symbols from prior generations of women.

This search had a particularly personal aspect for her, a granddaughter of the Caribbean island of Grenada, as she recalled the tales her mother told her of the ways of the offshore island of Carriacou where she had been raised prior to immigrating to New York City. In some ways, the key to Lorde's entire career as a writer and activist lies in a description of her mother's island home on the opening page of *Zami*. "This is the country of my foremothers, my fore-bearing mothers, those Black island women who defined themselves by what they did." Self-definition through chosen actions and open admittance of the joys and sorrows of making those choices are threads common to much of her work throughout her life. Even the title reflects her choice to claim her heritage: Zami is "a Carriacou name for women who work together as friends and lovers," a beautifully apt term for the fusion and fashioning of diverse cultures evident in all her works. The book is also representative of a more limited group of lesbian autobiographies, foreshadowing later works such as Holly Near's 1990 work *Fire In the Rain, Singer in the Storm* and *Long Time Passing: Lives of Older Lesbians*, a collection published in 1986.

The two volumes of essays and speeches compiled from those delivered by Lorde at various institutions of higher learning and political conferences in the gay and lesbian community during the 1980s provide the reader with both a window into the continuing growth of her consciousness as lesbian and activist and as a bridge into the deepening power of her poetic voice. The first, 1984's *Sister Outsider*, contains 15 selections written or delivered between 1976 and 1983, including an extended interview and self-analysis conducted with fellow lesbian poet Adrienne Rich. Of the essays, the text of a paper given at the Modern Language Association's December, 1977, meeting in Chicago as part of the "Lesbian and Literature" panel is a particularly valuable sample of Lorde's deeply personal visions. Other papers touch upon the creative uses to which anger can be put as a generator of change, explore the concept of "the personal as political," or discuss eroticism as a source of power for women.

Sister Outsider's 1988 successor, *A Burst of Light*, presents five shorter essays dealing with Lorde's first three years of living with cancer, her views on the then-ongoing discussion of sadomasochism within the lesbian community (represented by such writers as Pat Califia), frank and moving opinions on being a lesbian mother, and the comparative situation of African Americans and the blacks of South Africa under apartheid. Readers of black lesbian and gay writings of any political slant will find the third essay, "I Am Your Sister: Black Women Organizing Across Sexualities," valuable for the links it establishes with other major writers such as Langston Hughes, Alice Dunbar-Nelson, and Angelina Weld Grimke, and the perspective it provides on the emergence of contemporary male poets such as Essex Hemphill and Assoto Saint.

Lorde's encounters with the pain of cancer and mastectomy may also be traced through the pages of the 1980 prose collection *The Cancer Journals*, which she termed "a piece of meaning words on cancer as it affects my life and my consciousness as a woman, a black lesbian feminist mother." Recognition of the place of such a testament in lesbian literature came with the designation of *The Cancer Journals* as the American Library Association's Gay Task Force Book of the Year for 1981.

The truest voice of Lorde will, however, be found in her poetry, for as she stated in the opening line of her 1977 essay *The Transformation of Silence into Language and Action:* "I have come to believe over and over again that what is most important to me must be spoken, made verbal and shared, even at the risk of having it bruised or misunderstood."

American librarian, educator, poet, essayist, and author of short stories. Also wrote as Rey Domini.

Born: New York City, February 18, 1934.

Education: National University of Mexico, 1954; Hunter College (now Hunter College of the City University of New York), B.A. 1960; Columbia University, New York City, M.L.S. 1962.

Partnerships: Married Edwin Ashley Rollins in 1962 (divorced 1972); one son, one daughter.

Career: Librarian, Mount Vernon Public Library, Mount Vernon, New York, 1961–63; head librarian, Town School Library, New York City, 1966–68; lecturer in creative writing, City College, New York City, 1968; lecturer in education department, Herbert H. Lehman College, Bronx, New York, 1969–70; associate professor of English, John Jay College of Criminal Justice, New York City, beginning 1970; professor of English, Hunter College, New York City, 1981–87; Thomas Hunter professor, 1987–92. Visiting professor, Tougaloo University, Tougaloo, Mississippi, and Atlanta University, Atlanta, Georgia, both 1968. Visiting lecturer throughout the United States, Europe, Africa, and Australia. Founder, Kitchen Table: Women of Color Press and Sisterhood in Support of Sisters in South Africa. Poetry editor, *Chrysalis* and *Amazon Quarterly*. Contributor of short stories to *Venture* magazine as Rey Domini.

Recipient: National Endowment for the Arts grants, 1968, 1981; Creative Artists Public Service grant, 1972, 1976; National Book Award nominee, 1974; American Library Association Gay Task Force Book Award, 1981, for *The Cancer Journals*; Borough of Manhattan President's Award, 1987, for literary excellence; Before Columbus Foundation's American Book Award, 1989; Triangle Publications Group's Bill Whitehead Award for lifetime contribution to literature, 1990; Sappho Award for contribution to literature on multicultural lesbian identity, 1990; Fund for Free Expression Award, 1991; named New York State Poet Laureate, 1992; honorary doctorates: Oberlin College, Haverford College, State University of New York at Binghampton.

Died: St. Croix, Virgin Islands, November 20, 1992, of liver cancer.

Beginning with her earliest book, 1968's *The First Cities*—written while she was the recipient of a grant from the National Endowment for the Arts—she focused a spare, sharp eye of language on life and love, including her lesbian relationships. Three of her collections, *Cables to Rage*, *From a Land Where Other People Live*, and *New York Head Shop and Museum* were published in the 1970s by Detroit's Broadside Press, one of the centers of publication for new African American poets such as Nikki Giovanni. It would be these editions of Lorde's work that would begin to bring her influence to the wider audience of black lesbian writers, as exemplified by the early writings of California lesbian poet Pat Parker. The imagery in *The First Cities* and *Cables to Rage* is a blend of uniquely spicy twists of language, the topics central to life as a black person in America at that time. These works came to be recognized as some of the most vital contributions to the Black Arts Movement. The poems of these first volumes were later collected and published under the title *Coal* in 1976. Perhaps most significant for the history of modern black gay and lesbian poetry is "Martha," which one critic noted as "the first poetic expression of Lorde's homosexuality."

A Creative Artists Public Service grant in 1972 provided the basis for generating her third book of poetry, *From a Land Where Other People Live*, published in 1973. Its lines express a maturation of the anger over injustices that had been present in *Cables To Rage*, as well as addressing more fully the author's identity as an African American woman and that role's differing dimensions as mother, sister, and teacher. Her nomination for the National Book Award for poetry for the year also served to further widen public awareness of Lorde as a leading feminist voice. Her fourth book, the 1974 *New York Head Shop and Museum*, is perhaps the most overtly political, using her visions of New York City as a matrix to explore her radical political views and foretelling the depth and power of such successor volumes as 1978's *The Black Unicorn*. Through the founding of Kitchen Table: Women of Color Press and her work as poetry editor of *Chrysalis* and *Amazon Quarterly*, Lorde attempted to provide the rising generations of women writers who would follow her with the venue she had not been able to find for the literary reflection of her inner selves.

Indefatigable in both claiming her life and cherishing her many-faceted insights, Lorde's honors included being named poet laureate of New York State in 1991. She died at her home on St. Croix in the Virgin Islands in late November of 1992, a victim of the liver cancer she had lived with for over a decade.

POETRY IS NOT A LUXURY

The quality of light by which we scrutinize our lives has direct bearing upon the product which we live, and upon the changes which we hope to bring about through those lives. It is within this light that we form those ideas by which we pursue our magic and make it realized. This is poetry as illumination, for it is through poetry that we give name to those ideas which are—until the poem—nameless and formless, about to be birthed, but already felt. That distillation of experience from which true poetry springs births thought as dream births concept, as feeling births ideas, as knowledge births (precedes) understanding.

As we learn to bear the intimacy of scrutiny and to flourish within it, as we learn to use the products of that scrutiny for power within our living, those fears which rule our lives and form our silences begin to lose their control over us.

Reprinted from *Sister Outsider*, The Crossing Press, copyright 1984 by Audre Lorde.

For each of us as women, there is a dark place within, where hidden and growing our true spirit rises, "beautiful/and tough as chestnut/stanchions against (y)our nightmare of weakness/" and of impotence [as written in "Black Mother Woman," first published in *From a Land Where Other People Live*, Broadside, 1973, and collected in *Chosen Poems: Old and New*, Norton, 1982].

These places of possibility within ourselves are dark because they are ancient and hidden; they have survived and grown strong through that darkness. Within these deep places, each one of us holds an incredible reserve of creativity and power, of unexamined and unrecorded emotion and feeling. The woman's place of power within each of us is neither white nor surface; it is dark, it is ancient, and it is deep.

When we view living in the european mode only as a problem to be solved, we rely solely upon our ideas to make us free, for these were what the white fathers told us were precious.

But as we come more into touch with our own ancient, noneuropean consciousness of living as a situation to be experienced and interacted with, we learn more and more to cherish our feelings, and to respect those hidden sources of our power from where true knowledge and, therefore, lasting action comes.

At this point in time, I believe that women carry within ourselves the possibility for fusion of these two approaches so necessary for survival, and we come closest to this combination in our poetry. I speak here of poetry as a revelatory distillation of experience, not the sterile word play that, too often, the white fathers distorted the word *poetry* to mean—in order to cover a desperate wish for imagination without insight.

For women, then, poetry is not a luxury. It is a vital necessity of our experience. It forms the quality of the light within which we predicate our hopes and dreams toward survival and change, first made into language, then into idea, then into more tangible action. Poetry is the way we help give name to the nameless so it can be thought. The farthest horizons of our hopes and fears are cobbled by our poems, carved from the rock experiences of our daily lives.

As they become known to and accepted by us, our feelings and the honest exploration of them become sanctuaries and spawning grounds for the most radical and daring of ideas. They become a safe-house for that difference so necessary to change and the conceptualization of any meaningful action. Right now, I could name at least ten ideas I would have found intolerable or incomprehensible and frightening, except as they came after dreams and poems. This is not idle fantasy, but a disciplined attention to the true meaning of "it feels right to me." We can train ourselves to respect our feelings and to transpose them into a language so they can be shared. And where that language does not yet exist, it is our poetry which helps to fashion it. Poetry is not only dream and vision; it is the skeleton architecture of our lives. It lays the foundations for a future of change, a bridge across our fears of what has never been before.

Possibility is neither forever nor instant. It is not easy to sustain belief in its efficacy. We can sometimes work long and hard to establish one beachhead of real resistance to the deaths we are expected to live, only to have that beachhead assaulted or threatened by those canards we have been socialized to fear, or by the withdrawal of those approvals that we have been warned to seek for safety. Women see ourselves diminished or softened by the falsely benign accusations of childishness, of nonuniversality, of changeability, of sensuality. And who asks the question: Am I altering your aura, your ideas, your dreams, or am I merely moving you to temporary and reactive action? And even though the latter is no mean task, it is one that must be seen within the context of a need for true alteration of the very foundations of our lives.

The white fathers told us: I think, therefore I am. The Black mother within each of us—the poet—whispers in our dreams: I feel, therefore I can be free. Poetry coins the language to express and charter this revolutionary demand, the implementation of that freedom.

However, experience has taught us that action in the now is also necessary, always. Our children cannot dream unless they live, they cannot live unless they are nourished, and who else will feed them the real food without which their dreams will be no different from ours? "If you want us to change the world someday, we at least have to live long enough to grow up!" shouts the child.

Sometimes we drug ourselves with dreams of new ideas. The head will save us. The brain alone will set us free. But there are no new ideas still waiting in the wings to save us as women, as human. There are only old and forgotten ones, new combinations, extrapolations and recognitions from within ourselves—along with the renewed courage to try them out. And we must constantly encourage ourselves and each other to attempt the heretical actions that our dreams imply, and so many of our old ideas disparage. In the forefront of our move toward change, there is only poetry to hint at possibility made real. Our poems formulate the implications of ourselves, what we feel within and dare make real (or bring action into accordance with), our fears, our hopes, our most cherished terrors.

For within living structures defined by profit, by linear power, by institutional dehumanization, our feelings were not meant to survive.

Kept around as unavoidable adjuncts or pleasant pastimes, feelings were expected to kneel to men. But women have survived. As poets. And there are no new pains. We have felt them all already. We have hidden that fact in the same place where we have hidden our power. They surface in our dreams that point the way to freedom. Those dreams are made realizable through our poems that give us the strength and courage to see, to feel, to speak, and to dare.

If what we need to dream, to move our spirits most deeply and directly toward and through promise, is discounted as a luxury, then we give up the core—the foundation—of our power, our womanness; we give up the future of our worlds.

For there are no new ideas. There are only new ways of making them felt—of examining what those ideas feel like being lived on Sunday morning at 7 a.m., after brunch, during wild love, making war, giving birth, mourning our dead—while we suffer the old longings, battle the old warnings and fears of being silent and impotent and alone, while we taste new possibilities and strengths.

ZAMI: A NEW SPELLING OF MY NAME

Excerpt reprinted from *Zami: A New Spelling of My Name,* The Crossing Press, copyright 1982.

Gerri was young and Black and lived in Queens and had a powder-blue Ford that she nicknamed Bluefish. With her carefully waved hair and button-down shirts and gray-flannel slacks, she looked just this side of square, without being square at all, once you got to know her.

By Gerri's invitation and frequently by her wheels, Muriel and I had gone to parties on weekends in Brooklyn and Queens at different women's houses.

One of the women I had met at one of these parties was Kitty.

When I saw Kitty again one night years later in the Swing Rendezvous or the Pony Stable or the Page Three—that tour of second-string gay bars that I had taken to making alone that sad lonely spring of 1957—it was easy to recall the St. Alban's smell of green Queens summer-night and plastic couch covers and liquor and hair oil and women's bodies at the party where we had first met.

In that brick-faced frame house in Queens, the downstairs pine-paneled recreation room was alive and pulsing with loud music, good food, and beautiful Black women in all different combinations of dress.

There were whipcord summer suits with starch-shiny shirt collars open at the neck as a concession to the high summer heat, and white gabardine slacks with pleated fronts or slim ivy-league styling for the very

Poetry

The First Cities, 1968.
Cables to Rage, 1970.
From a Land Where Other People Live, 1973.
The New York Head Shop and Museum, 1974.
Coal, 1976.
Between Our Selves, 1976.
The Black Unicorn, 1978.
Chosen Poems, Old and New, 1982; revised as *Undersong: Chosen Poems Old and New*, 1992.
Our Dead Behind Us, 1986.
The Marvelous Arithmetics of Distance: Poems 1987–1992, 1994.

Contributor

Beyond the Blues: New Poems by American Negroes, edited by Rosey Poole, 1963.

Sixes and Sevens, edited by Paul Bremen, 1963.
New Negro Poets, U.S.A., edited by Langston Hughes, 1964.
The New Black Poetry, edited by Clarence Major, 1969.
Natural Process: An Anthology of New Black Poetry, edited by Ted Wilentz and Tom Weatherly, 1970.
Afro-American Poetry, edited by Bernard Bell, 1972.
Black Sister: Poetry by Black American Women, 1746–1980, edited by Erlene Stetson, 1981.
Confirmation: An Anthology of African-American Women, edited by Amina and Amiri Baraka, 1983.

Essays

Sister Outsider: Essays and Speeches, 1984.
A Burst of Light: Essays, 1988.

Other

"Poems Are Not Luxuries," in *Chrysalis*, Number 3, 1977.
Uses of the Erotic: The Erotic as Power, 1978.
"Scratching the Surface: Some Notes on Barriers to Women and Loving," in *Black Scholar*, April 1978.
"Man Child: A Black Lesbian-Feminist's Response," in *Conditions: Four*, winter 1979.
"An Open Letter to Mary Daly," in *Top Ranking: A Collection of Articles on Racism and Classism in the Lesbian Community*, edited by Joan Gibbs and Sara Bennett, 1980.
The Cancer Journals (personal diary), 1980.
Zami: A New Spelling of My Name; A Biomythography, 1982.

---

slender. There were wheat-colored Cowden jeans, the fashion favorite that summer, with knife-edged creases, and even then, one or two back-buckled gray pants over well-chalked buckskin shoes. There were garrison belts galore, broad black leather belts with shiny thin buckles that originated in army-navy surplus stores, and oxford-styled shirts of the new, iron-free Dacron, with its stiff, see-through crispness. These shirts, short-sleeved and man-tailored, were tucked neatly into belted pants or tight, skinny straight skirts. Only the one or two jersey knit shirts were allowed to fall freely outside.

Bermuda shorts, and their shorter cousins, jamaicas, were already making their appearance on the dyke-chic scene, the rules of which were every bit as cutthroat as the tyrannies of Seventh Avenue or Paris. These shorts were worn by butch and femme alike, and for this reason were slow to be incorporated into many fashionable gay-girl wardrobes, to keep the signals clear. Clothes were often the most important way of broadcasting one's chosen sexual role.

Here and there throughout the room the flash of brightly colored below-the-knee full shirts over low-necked tight bodices could be seen, along with tight sheath dresses and the shine of high thin heels next to bucks and sneakers and loafers.

Femmes wore their hair in tightly curled pageboy bobs, or piled high on their heads in sculptured bunches of curls, or in feather cuts framing their faces. That sweetly clean fragrance of beauty-parlor that hung over all Black women's gatherings in the fifties was present here also, adding its identifiable smell of hot comb and hair pomade to the other aromas in the room.

Butches wore their hair cut shorter, in a D.A. shaped to a point in the back, or a short pageboy, or sometimes in a tightly curled poodle that predated the natural afro. But this was a rarity, and I can only remember one other Black woman at that party besides me whose hair was not straight-ended, and she was an acquaintance of ours from the Lower East Side named Ida.

On a table behind the built-in bar stood opened bottles of gin, bourbon, Scotch, soda, and other various mixers. The bar itself was covered with little delicacies of all descriptions; chips and dips and little crackers and squares of bread laced with the usual dabs of egg-salad and sardine paste. There was also a platter of delicious fried chicken wings, and a pan of potato-and-egg salad dressed with vinegar. Bowls of olives and pickles surrounded the main dishes, with trays of red crab apples and little sweet onions on toothpicks.

But the centerpiece of the whole table was a huge platter of succulent and thinly sliced roast beef, set into an underpan of cracked ice. Upon the beige platter, each slice of rare meat had been lovingly laid out and individually folded up into a vulval pattern, with a tiny dab of mayonnaise at the crucial apex. The pink-brown folded meat around the pale cream-yellow dot formed suggestive sculptures that made a great hit with all the women present, and Pet, at whose house the party was being given and whose idea the meat sculptures were, smilingly acknowledged the many compliments on her platter with a long-necked graceful nod of her elegant dancer's head.

The room's particular mix of heat-smells and music gives way in my mind to the high-cheeked, dark young woman with the silky voice and appraising eyes (something about her mouth reminded me of Ann, the nurse I'd worked with when I'd first left home).

Perching on the edge of the low bench where I was sitting, Kitty absently wiped specks of lipstick from each corner of her mouth with the downward flick of a delicate forefinger.

"Audre ... that's a nice name. What's it short for?"

My damp are hairs bristled in the Ruth Brown music, and the heat. I could not stand anybody messing around with my name, not even with nicknames.

"Nothing. It's just Audre. What's Kitty short for?"

"Afrekete," she said, snapping her fingers in time to the rhythm of it and giving a long laugh. "That's me. The Black pussycat." She laughed again. "I like your hairdo. Are you a singer?"

"No." She continued to stare at me with her large direct eyes.

I was suddenly too embarrassed at not knowing what else to say to meet her calmly erotic gaze, so I stood up abruptly and said, in my best Laurel's-terse tone, "Let's dance."

Her face was broad and smooth under too-light makeup, but as we danced a foxtrot she started to sweat, and her skin took on a deep shiny richness. Kitty closed her eyes part way when she danced, and her one gold-rimmed front tooth flashed as she smiled and occasionally caught her lower lip in time to the music.

Her yellow poplin shirt, cut in the style of an Eisenhower jacket, had a zipper that was half open in the summer heat, showing collarbones that stood out like brown wings from her long neck. Garments with zippers were highly prized among the more liberal set of gay-girls, because these could be worn by butch or femme alike on certain occasions, without causing any adverse or troublesome comments. Kitty's narrow, well-pressed khaki skirt was topped by a black belt that matched my own except in its newness, and her natty trimness made me feel almost shabby in my well-worn riding pants.

I thought she was very pretty, and I wished I could dance with as much ease as she did, and as effortlessly. Her hair had been straightened into short feathery curls, and in that room of well- set marcels and D.A.'s and pageboys, it was the closest cut to my own.

Kitty smelled of soap and Jean Naté, and I kept thinking she was bigger than she actually was, because there was a comfortable smell about her that I always associated with large women. I caught another spicy, herblike odor, that I later identified as a combination of coconut oil and Yardley's lavender hair pomade. Her mouth was full, and her lipstick was dark and shiny, a new Max Factor shade called "Warpaint."

The next dance was a slow fish that suited me fine. I never knew whether to lead or to follow in most other dances, and even the efforts to decide which was which was as difficult for me as having to decide all the time the difference between right and left. Somehow that simple distinction had never become automatic for me, and all that deciding usually left me very little energy with which to enjoy the movement and the music.

But "fishing" was different. A forerunner of the later one-step, it was, in reality, your basic slow bump and grind. The low red lamp and the crowded St. Alban's parlor floor left us just enough room to hold each other frankly, arms around neck and waist, and the slow intimate music moved our bodies much more than our feet.

That had been in St. Alban's, Queens, nearly two years before, when Muriel had seemed to be the certainty in my life. Now in the spring of this new year I had my own apartment all to myself again, but I was mourning. I avoided visiting pairs of friends, or inviting even numbers of people over to my house, because the happiness of couples, or their mere togetherness, hurt me too much in its absence from my own life, whose blankest hole was named Muriel. I had not been back to Queens, nor to any party, since Muriel and I had broken up, and the only people I saw outside of work and school were those friends who lived in the Village and who sought me out or whom I ran into at the bars. Most of them were white.

"Hey, girl, long time no see." Kitty spotted me first. We shook hands. The bar was not crowded, which meant it probably was the Page Three, which didn't fill up until after midnight. "Where's your girl-friend?"

I told her that Muriel and I weren't together any more. "Yeah? That's too bad. You-all were kinda cute together. But that's the way it goes. How long you been in the 'life'?"

I stared at Kitty without answering, trying to think of how to explain to her, that for me there was only one life—my own— however I chose to live it. But she seemed to take the words right out of my mouth.

"Not that it matters," she said speculatively, finishing the beer she carried over to the end of the bar where I was sitting. "We don't have but one, anyway. At least this time around." She took my arm. "Come on, let's dance."

Kitty was still trim and fast-lined, but with an easier looseness about her smile and a lot less makeup. Without its camouflage, her chocolate skin and deep, sculptured mouth reminded me of a Benin bronze. Her hair was still straight-ended, but shorter, and her black Bermuda shorts and knee socks matched her astonishingly shiny black loafers. A black turtleneck pullover completed her sleek costume. Somehow, this time, my jeans did not feel shabby beside hers, only a variation upon some similar dress. Maybe it was because our belts still matched—broad, black, and brass-buckled.

We moved to the back room and danced to Frankie Lymon's "Goody, Goody," and then to a Belafonte calypso. Dancing with her this time, I felt who I was and where my body was going, and that feeling was more important to me than any lead or follow.

The room felt very warm even though it was only just spring, and Kitty and I smiled at each other as the number ended. We stood waiting for the next record to drop and the next dance to begin. It was a slow Sinatra. Our belt buckles kept getting in the way as we moved in close to the oiled music, and we slid them around to the side of our waists when no one was looking.

For the last few months since Muriel had moved out, my skin had felt cold and hard and essential, like thin frozen leather that was keeping the shape expected. That night on the dance floor of the Page Three as Kitty and I touched our bodies together in dancing, I could feel my carapace soften slowly and then finally melt, until I felt myself covered in a warm, almost forgotten, slip of anticipation, that ebbed and flowed at each contact of our moving bodies.

I could feel something slowly shift in her also, as if a taut string was becoming undone, and finally we didn't start back to the bar at all between dances, but just stood on the floor waiting for the next record, dancing only with each other. A little after midnight, in a silent and mutual decision, we split the Page together, walking blocks through West Village to Hudson Street where her car was parked. She had invited me up to her house for a drink.

The sweat beneath my breasts from our dancing was turning cold in the sharpness of the night air as we crossed Sheridan Square. I paused to wave to the steadies through the plate-glass windows of Jim Atkin's on the corner of Christopher Street.

In her car, I tried not to think about what I was doing as we rode uptown almost in silence. There was an ache in the well beneath my stomach, spreading out and down between my legs like mercury. The smell of her warm body, mixed with the smell of feathery cologne and lavender pomade, anointed the car. My eyes rested on the sight of her coconut-spicy hands on the steering wheel, and the curve of her lashes as she attended the roadway. They made it easy for me to coast beneath her sporadic bursts of conversation with only an occasional friendly grunt.

"I haven't been downtown to the bars in a while, you know? It's funny. I don't know why I don't go downtown more often. But every once in a while, something tells me go and I go. I guess it must be different when you live around there all the time." She turned her gold-flecked smile upon me.

Crossing 59th Street, I had an acute moment of panic. Who was this woman? Suppose she really intended only to give me a drink that she had offered me as we left the Page? Suppose I had totally misunderstood the impact of her invitation, and would soon find myself stranded uptown at 3 a.m. on a Sunday morning, and did I even have enough change left in my jeans for carfare home? Had I put out enough food for the kittens? Was Flee coming over with her camera tomorrow morning, and would she feed the cats if I wasn't there? If I wasn't there.

If I wasn't there. The implication of that thought was so shaking it almost threw me out of the car.

I had had only enough money for one beer that night, so I knew I wasn't high, and reefer was only for special occasions. Part of me felt like a raging lioness, inflamed in desire. Even the words in my head seemed borrowed from a dime-store novel. But that part of me was drunk in the thighed nearness of this exciting unknown dark woman, who calmly moved us through upper Manhattan, with her patent-leather loafers and her camel's-hair swing coat and her easy talk, from time to time her gloved hand touching my denimed leg for emphasis.

Another piece of me felt bumbling, inept, and about four years old. I was the idiot playing at being a lover, who was going to be found out shortly and laughed at for my pretensions as well as rejected out of hand.

Would it be possible—was it ever possible—for two women to share the fire we felt that night without entrapping or smothering each other? I longed for that as I longed for her body, doubting both, eager for both.

And how was it possible, that I should be dreaming the roll of this woman's sea into and around mine, when only a few short hours ago, and for so many months before, I had been mourning the loss of Muriel, so sure that I would continue being broken-hearted forever? And what then, if I had been mistaken?

If the knot in my groin would have gone away, I'd have jumped out of the car door at the very next traffic light. Or so I thought to myself.

We came out of the Park Drive at Seventh Avenue and 110th Street, and as quickly as the light changed on the now deserted avenue, Afrekete turned her broad-lipped, beautiful face to me, with no smile at all. Her great lidded, luminescent eyes looked directly and startlingly into mine. It was as if she had suddenly become another person, as if the wall of glass formed by my spectacles, and behind which I had become so used to hiding, had suddenly dissolved.

In an uninflected, almost formal voice that perfectly matched and thereby obliterated all my question marks, she asked, "Can you spend the night?"

And then it occurred to me that perhaps she might have been having the same questions about me that I had been having about her. I was left almost without breath by the combination of her delicacy and her directness—a combination that is still rare and precious.

For beyond the assurance that her question offered me—a declaration that this singing of my flesh, this attraction, was not all within my own head—beyond that assurance was a batch of delicate assumptions built into that simple phrase that reverberated in my poet's brain. It offered us both an out if necessary. If the answer to the question night, by any chance, have been no, then its very syntax allowed for a reason of impossibility, rather than of choice—"I can't," rather than "I won't." The demands of another commitment, an early job, a sick cat, etc., could be lived with more easily than an out-and-out rejection.

Even the phrase "spending the night" was less a euphemism for making love than it was an allowable space provided, in which one could move back or forth. If, perhaps, I were to change my mind before the traffic light and decide that no, I wasn't gay, after all, then a simpler companionship was still available.

I steadied myself enough to say, in my very best Lower East Side Casual voice, "I'd really like to," cursing myself for the banal words, and wondering if she could smell my nervousness and my desperate desire to be suave and debonair, drowning in sheer desire.

We parked half-in and half-out of a bus stop on Manhattan Avenue and 113th Street, in Gennie's old neighborhood.

Something about Kitty made me feel like a roller coaster, rocketing from idiot to goddess. By the time we had collected her mail from her broken mailbox and then climbed six flights of stairs up to her front door, I felt that there had never been anything else my body had intended to do more, than to reach inside of her coat and take Afrekete into my arms, fitting her body into the curves of mine tightly, her beige camel's-hair billowing around us both, and her gloved hand still holding the door key.

In the faint light of the hallway, her lips moved like a surf upon the water's edge.

It was a one-and-a-half-room kitchenette apartment with tall narrow windows in the narrow, high-ceilinged front room. Across each window, there were built-in shelves at different levels. From these shelves tossed and frothed, hung and leaned and stood, pot after clay pot of green and tousled large and small-leaved plants of all shapes and conditions.

Later, I came to love the way in which the plants filtered the southern-exposure sun through the room. Light hit the opposite wall at a point about six inches above the thirty-gallon fish tank that murmured softly, like a quiet jewel, standing on its wrought-iron legs, glowing and mysterious.

Leisurely and swiftly, translucent rainbowed fish darted back and forth through the lit water, perusing the glass sides of the tank for morsels of food, and swimming in and out of the marvelous world created by colored gravels and stone tunnels and bridges that lined the floor of the tank. Astride one of the bridges, her bent head observing the little fish that swam in and out between her legs, stood a little jointed brown doll, her smooth and naked body washed by the bubbles rising up from the air unit located behind her.

Between the green plants and the glowing magical tank of exotic fish, lay a room the contents of which I can no longer separate in my mind. Except for the plaid-covered couch that opened up into a double bed that we set rocking as we loved that night into a bright Sunday morning, dappled with green sunlight from the plants in Afrekete's high windows.

I woke to her house suffused in that light, the sky half seen through the windows of the top-floor kitchenette apartment, and Afrekete, known, asleep against my side.

Little hairs under her navel lay down before my advancing tongue like beckoned pages of a well-touched book.

How many times into summer had I turned into that block from Eighth Avenue, the saloon on the corner spilling a smell of sawdust and liquor onto the street, a shifting, indeterminate number of young and old Black men taking turns sitting on two upturned milk crates, playing checkers? I would turn the corner onto 113th Street toward the park, my steps quickening and my fingertips tingling to play in her earth.

And I remember Afrekete, who came out of a dream to me always being hard and real as if the fine hairs along the underedge of my navel. She brought me live things from the brush, and from her farm set out in cocoyams and cassava—those magical fruit that Kitty bought in the West Indian markets along Lenox Avenue in the 140s or in the Puerto Rican *bodegas* within the bustling market over on Park Avenue and 116th Street under the Central Railroad structures.

"I got this under the bridge" was a saying from time immemorial, giving an adequate explanation that whatever it was had come from as far back and as close to home—that is to say, was as authentic—as was possible.

We bought red delicious pippins, the size of French cashew apples. There were green plantains, which we half-peeled and then planted, fruit-deep, in each other's bodies until the petals of skin lay like tendrils of broad green fire upon the curly darkness between our upspread thighs. *There were ripe red finger bananas, stubby and sweet, with which I parted your lips gently, to insert the peeled fruit into your grape-purple flower.*

I held you, lay between your brown legs, slowly playing my tongue through your familiar forests, slowly licking and swallowing as the deep undulations and tidal motions of your strong body slowly mashed ripe banana into a beige cream that mixed with the juices of your electric flesh. Our bodies met again, each surface touched with each other's flame, from the tips of our curled toes to our tongues, and locked into our own wild rhythms, we rode each other across the thundering space, dripping like light from the peak of each other's tongue.

We were each of us both together. Then we were apart, and sweat sheened our bodies like sweet oil.

Sometimes Afrekete sang in a small club farther uptown on Sugar Hill. Sometimes she clerked in the Gristede's Market on 97th Street and Amsterdam, and sometimes with no warning at all she appeared at the Pony Stable or Page Three on Saturday night. Once, I came home to 7th Street late one night to find her sitting on my stoop at 3 a.m., with a bottle of beer in her hand and a piece of bright African cloth wrapped around her head, and we sped uptown through the dawn-empty city with a summer thunder squall crackling about us, and the wet city streets singing beneath the wheels of her little Nash Rambler.

There are certain verities that are always with us, which we come to depend upon. That the sun moves north in the summer, that melted ice contracts, that the curved banana is sweeter. Afrekete taught me roots, new definitions of our women's bodies— definitions for which I had only been in training to learn before.

By the beginning of summer the walls of Afrekete's apartment were always warm to the touch from the heat beating down on the roof, and chance breezes through her windows rustled her plants in the window and brushed over our seat-smoothed bodies, at rest after loving.

We talked sometimes about what it meant to love women, and what a relief it was in the eye of the storm, no matter how often we had to bite our tongues and stay silent. Afrekete had a seven-year-old daughter whom she had left with her mama down in Georgia, and we shared a lot of our dreams.

"She's going to be able to love anybody she wants to love," Afrekete said, fiercely, lighting a Lucky Strike. "Same way she's going to be able to work any place she damn well pleases. Her mama's going to see to that."

Once we talked about how Black women had been committed without choice to waging our campaigns in the enemies' strongholds, too much and too often, and how our psychic landscapes had been plundered and wearied by those repeated battles and campaigns.

"And don't I have the scars to prove it," she sighed. "Makes you tough though, babe, if you don't go under. And that's what I like about you; you're like me. We're both going to make it because we're both too tough and crazy not to!" And we held each other and laughed and cried about what we had paid for that toughness, and how hard it was to explain to anyone who didn't already know it that soft and tough had to be one and the same for either to work at all, like our joy and the tears mingling on the pillow beneath our heads.

And the sun filtered down upon us through the dusty windows, thought the mass of green plants that Afrekete tended religiously.

I took a ripe avocado and rolled it between my hands until the skin became a green case for the soft mashed fruit inside, hard pit at the core. *I rose from a kiss in your mouth to nibble a hole in the fruit skin near the navel stalk, squeezed the pale yellow-green fruit juice in thin ritual lines back and forth over and around your coconut-brown belly.*

The oil and sweat from our bodies kept the fruit liquid, and I massaged it over your thighs and between your breasts until your brownness shone like a light through a veil of the palest green avocado, a mantle of goddess pear that I slowly licked from your skin.

Then we would have to get up to gather the pits and fruit skins and bag them to put out later for the garbagemen, because if we left them near the bed for any length of time, the would call out the hordes of cockroaches that always waited on the sidelines within the walls of Harlem tenements, particularly in the smaller, older ones under the hill of Morningside Heights.

Afrekete lived not far from Genevieve's grandmother's house.

Sometimes she reminded me of Ella, Gennie's grandmother, who shuffled about with an apron on and a broom outside the room where Gennie and I lay on the couch. She would be singing her nonstop tuneless little song over and over and over:

Momma kilt me

Poppa et me

Po' lil' brudder

suck ma bones ...

And one day Gennie turned her head on my lap to say uneasily, "You know, sometimes I don't know whether Ella's crazy, or stupid, or divine."

And now I think the goddess was speaking though Ella also, but Ella was too beaten down and anesthetized by Phillip's brutality for her to believe in her own mouth, and we, Gennie and I, were too arrogant and childish—not without right or reason, for we were scarcely more than children—to see that our survival might very well lay in listening to the sweeping woman's tuneless song.

I lost my sister, Gennie, to my silence and her pain and despair, to both our angers and to a world's cruelty that destroys its own young in passing—not even as rebel gesture or sacrifice or hope for anything living of the spirit, but out of not noticing or caring about the destruction. I have never been able to blind myself to that cruelty, which, according to one popular definition of mental health, makes me mentally unhealthy.

Afrekete's house was the tallest one near the corner, before the high rocks of Morningside Park began on the other side of the avenue, and one night on the Midsummer Eve's Moon we took a blanket up to the roof. She lived on the top floor, and in an unspoken agreement, the roof belonged mostly to those who had to live under its heat. The roof was the chief resort of tenement-dwellers, and was known as Tar Beach.

We jammed the roof door shut with our sneakers, and spread our blanket in the lee of the chimney, between its warm brick wall and the high parapet of the building's face. This was before the blaze of sulfur lamps had stripped the streets of New York of trees and shadow, and the incandescence from the lights below faded this far up. From behind the parapet wall we could see the dark shapes of the basalt and granite out-croppings looming over us from the park across the street, outlined, curiously close and suggestive.

We slipped off the cotton shifts we had worn and moved against each other's damp breasts in the shadow of the roof's chimney, making moon, honor, love, while the ghostly vague light drifting upward from the street competed with the silver hard sweetness of the full moon, reflected in the shiny mirrors of our sweat-slippery dark bodies, sacred as the ocean at high tide.

I remember the moon rising against the tilted planes of her upthrust thighs, and my tongue caught the streak of silver reflected in the curly bush of her dappled-darkly maiden hair. *I remember the full moon like white pupils in the center of your wide irises.*

The moons went out, and your eyes grew dark as you rolled over me, and I felt the moon's silver light mix with the wet of your tongue on my eyelids.

Afrekete Afrekete ride me to the crossroads where we shall sleep, coating in the woman's power. The sound of our bodies meeting is the prayer of all strangers and sisters, that the discarded evils, abandoned at all crossroads, will not follow us upon our journeys.

When we came down from the roof later, it was into the sweltering midnight of a west Harlem summer, with canned music in the streets and the disagreeable whines of overtired and overheated children. Nearby, mothers and fathers sat on stoops or milk crates and striped camp chairs, fanning themselves absently and talking or thinking about work as usual tomorrow and not enough sleep.

It was not onto the pale sands of Whydah, nor the beaches of Winneba or Annamabu, with cocopalms softly applauding and crickets keeping time with the pounding of a tar-laden, treacherous, beautiful sea. It was onto 113th Street that we descended after our meeting under Midsummer Eve's Moon, but the mothers and fathers smiled at us in greeting as we strolled down Eighth Avenue, hand in hand.

I had not seen Afrekete for a few weeks in July, so I went uptown to her house one evening since she didn't have a phone. The door was locked, and there was no one on the roof when I called up the stairwell.

Another week later, Midge, the bartender at the Pony Stable, gave me a note from Afrekete, saying that she had gotten a gig in Atlanta for September, and was splitting to visit her mama and daughter for a while.

We had come together like elements erupting into an electric storm, exchanging energy, sharing charge, brief and drenching. Then we parted, passed, reformed, reshaping ourselves the better for the exchange.

I never saw Afrekete again, but her print remains upon my life with the resonance and power of an emotional tattoo.

PAULA MARTINAC

IN BOTH HER NOVELS and short fiction, Paula Martinac is largely concerned with highlighting the experiences of women. Though the characters she chooses to feature are often homosexual, the focus on lesbians is by no means a given, and she is often able to target the many common denominators among women of differing sexual orientations. Her stories in *Voyages Out 1: Lesbian Short Fiction*, a collection that features Martinac's stories along with those of Carla Tomaso, tend to focus on lesbian issues. These include transitions in relationships and the challenge of "coming out." Ray Olson, writing in *Booklist*, also noted that these stories feature "the subtler, emotional politics between family members, friends, and lovers." The topic in *The One You Call Sister: New Women's Fiction*, of which Martinac is both editor and contributor, is the special relationship between sisters, some lesbians and some not. "Nonsisters may find a new world in the casual clutter of these images of family life," Sally S. Eckhoff remarked in *Village Voice*. "Sisters trying to solve the mysteries of their attachments will also gain some insight," Eckhoff continued, "but may feel in the end that they're looking at an unfinished picture." *Belles Lettres* reviewer Lynne M. Constantine predicted that readers will need to stop to digest each story, because they "so powerfully evoke memory, sensation, regret, longing, and hope that each one will stall any reader who lets it in to the place where fiction touches us most intimately."

Martinac's first novel, *Out of Time*, draws readers into the mystery of an old photo album and the woman who finds it. Susan uncharacteristically steals the book from an antiques shop, and finds herself wondering about the four women in its pictures. Her curiosity turns to obsession when the women begin to talk to Susan, eventually seducing her and luring her into their 1920s world. Through her exploration of the women's lives, Susan learns about her own history as a lesbian. "Martinac's talent for mood, mystery, and literary seduction shine in this unusually impressive debut," a *Kirkus Reviews* contributor commented.

Essay by
DEBORAH A. STANLEY

PAULA MARTINAC TOLD THE COMPANION:

"My longer fiction has mostly to do with history and time. I am interested in continuity over time—how different periods in history relate to the present and what lesbians and gay men in particular can learn from them. I am intrigued by photographs and movies and often blend descriptions of them into my narrative; it is their ability to catch specific lost moments in time that fascinates me. Much of my short fiction has been concerned with either family issues or the everyday lives of gay people. Whenever possible, I reach for humor in my fiction, which is almost always set in New York City."

One reviewer praised the way Paula Martinac's stories "so powerfully evoke memory, sensation, regret, longing, and hope."

Excerpt reprinted from *Out of Time*, Seal Press, copyright 1990 by Paula Martinac.

OUT OF TIME

I began to go to them in daydreams. I went to them with questions on my lips.

What was it like for you then?

Where was your work? What did you eat? What books did you cry over? What was a kiss like in 1962? How did women find each other?

How did I find you?

"Silly girl," said Harriet, with a smile that melted butter, "we found *you*."

* * *

"What's this?" Catherine asked, from the living room. I was chopping vegetables at the kitchen counter, watching her anxiously as she made her way to the coffee table and touched the leather scrapbook with one soft hand. "Susan," she said, "what's this?"

"Open it up," I said, trying to be casual but nearly chopping my finger into the eggplant.

American novelist and author of short stories.

Born: Pittsburgh, Pennsylvania, July 30, 1954.

Education: Chatham College, Pittsburgh, B.A. 1976; College of William and Mary, Williamsburg, Virginia, M.A. 1979.

Career: Editor of *Conditions* magazine, 1988–90.

Memberships: Cochair, Board of Directors, New York City Lesbian and Gay Community Services Center; member of International Women's Writing Guild.

Recipient: Lambda Literary Award for lesbian fiction, 1990; Puffin Foundation grant for teaching of lesbian writing, 1990.

Address: c/o Seal Press, 3131 Western Avenue, Suite 410, Seattle, Washington 98121, U.S.A.

I thought she gave a little gasp as she opened it, but it was probably me. She had only turned two or three pages when she said, "Where did you find this?"

"At an antiques store downtown," I answered, giving up the chopping to stand beside her as she lingered over the pages. "It was raining."

She nodded as if to say she understood. "Who are they?"

I recited their names in a litany.

"Oh," she said. Then, "1920. 1926."

"Yes," I said, aware all along that she would know the dates exactly, without having to look at the backs of the photos.

She closed the cover gently. "I can't remember," she said, "when I've heard of something this extraordinary. Finding a lesbian scrapbook in an antiques shop."

I smiled.

"They're just beautiful," Catherine said, opening the cover again.

"Catherine," said Harriet and Lucy in unison. "Catherine Synge."

* * *

I kept the scrapbook on the shelf with the other lesbian books I had collected. The vitality of Lucy, Harriet and The Gang seemed to give new life to them. Sometimes, when I was in the bedroom, I heard some unexplained racket in the living room and became convinced that it was The Gang, having a little get-together on the bookshelf.

The women didn't live for Catherine the way they did for me, but I shared the book with her anyway. She was, after all, a historian of women, rational but sensitive all at the same time. But I was hesitant to tell her the experience I was having with The Gang. Catherine had related many stories about growing up in her traditional Irish family, in which

PAULA **MARTINAC** 335

her immigrant grandmother talked a lot about spirits and saints and other seemingly fantastic things. She had rebelled against it at a young age; and even though she felt she had a deeper appreciation of her culture now, she still drew the line at all things magical. Partly because of that, she'd gone into history, the discipline that depends on facts.

We spent many evenings those first few weeks at my apartment pouring over the scrapbook. It was now my favorite thing to do. I refused to travel with the book, I was afraid of loose photographs falling out all over Manhattan. I couldn't bear the thought of losing even one mounting corner....

* * *

"Do you believe in time travel?" I asked Margielove one day as I was sprawled out in the shop, organizing the postcards into neat categories. "How about voices from the past?"

She looked at me cautiously from behind pink, heart-shaped sunglasses. I thought her the perfect person to ask, because she was frozen in the sixties.

She was, I'm sure, about to say "Yes." She was about to tell me all the voices she had heard, Jimi Hendrix and Janis and Malcolm X. But just as she was opening her mouth, just as the words were forming, I picked out of the shoebox an old postcard from Montauk and flipped it over. In a familiar hand, I read, "Dearest S., Had to get away from the city. The weather's beautiful, the beach a dream. Hope you're getting on without us. Kisses, L. and H."

I must have gasped or cried out, because Margielove was suddenly beside me, towering over me in her fluorescent pink caftan. "What is it?" she said. "You turned completely white." I handed her the postcard, which she read without surprise. "Someone you know?" she asked.

When I looked at it again, I realized I was going crazy. The handwriting was totally foreign, the card addressed to "Miss Gertrude Blain" in Hicksville, N.Y. "Dear Friend," it said, "Did you have a good time last night? Best wishes, N.S." I stared up at Margielove in disbelief.

"Kind of funny," she said, reading it once again.

"I have to go home now," I said, and she agreed without asking questions.

As I was barreling out of the door, with Margielove saying, "Take care, Susan," from behind me, I plowed right into Catherine, who was on her way to my apartment. It was our night to go to the Lesbian Archives.

"Susan," she said, taking me by both arms. I was shaking under her touch. "You look like you've seen a ghost. What is it?"

WRITINGS

Novels

Out of Time, 1990.
Home Movies, 1993.

Short Stories

"The Good Daughter," in *Focus: A Journal for Lesbians,* May/June 1983.
"Like Mother, Like…," in *We Are Everywhere: Writings by and about Lesbian Parents,* 1988.
"The Tenants," in *Conditions* (Brooklyn, New York), Number 15, 1988.
"Little Flower: A Love Story," in *Binnewater Tides,* summer 1989.
"Mineola, Mineola," in *Sinister Wisdom* (Berkeley, California), summer/fall 1989.
Editor and contributor, *The One You Call Sister: New Women's Fiction,* 1989.
Voyages Out 1: Lesbian Short Fiction, with Carla Tomaso, Seattle, 1989.
"Heroines," in *Conditions* (Brooklyn, New York), Number 17, 1990.
"Pitching Woo," in *Queer City,* 1991.
"Unusual People, Extraordinary Times," in *Art & Understanding,* January–February 1993.

"Catherine," I said softly, feeling like I was melting into the sidewalk, "take me home."

* * *

Later, after I'd taken a nap, I stood staring at Catherine in a confused way from the doorway of the bedroom. I felt a little like an amnesia victim who is just regaining memory.

"What happened back there?" she asked. I remained in the doorway, bracing myself on the door frame with both hands.

"I was hallucinating," I said.

"About what? And what were you doing in that shop? Don't you have to teach class today?"

I sat down next to her on the couch, and she offered me the box of saltines she'd been nibbling from. I took one and bit it in half.

"Things are becoming too real," I said.

"What things?" she persisted, but I didn't answer. Instead I picked up the scrapbook from its place on the coffee table. "Susan," said Catherine, sternly, "do you have to do that now?" I flipped through to the photos of The Gang at Montauk. They stood in a tight line, their arms entwined, perched on a precipice overlooking the sea at Montauk Point. If they had been fragile women, they would have blown away.

But they stood their ground, a firm and impenetrable chain. Elinor, the tallest and sturdiest, held onto her hat. Sarah, beside her, let her hair blow wildly across her face. Harriet, next, pushed her hair aside so everyone could see her clearly. Lucy, at the other end, the second tallest, looked longingly sideways at Harriet.

Did I really, I wondered, take the picture?

"I'm sorry," I said to Catherine, "what did you say?"

"I said, were you hallucinating about these women? Susan, can you hear me?" Her voice was getting louder and louder, as if she believed hallucinations could destroy your hearing. Or maybe because she could see I was somewhere else.

And then, as if by the power of suggestion, I was. I was lowering the camera to my side.

"Thank you," I smiled, "for the lovely postcard. I was worried about you."

"Everyone needs some time away," Harriet said.

"We should be getting back soon," Elinor pointed out, smoothing her skirt and stepping away from the cliff. "Sarah has a meeting to attend."

"You shouldn't worry," Lucy said, maybe to me, maybe to Elinor.

"I'm worried about you," someone was saying, and I could tell by the long, cool fingers pressing into my arm that it was Catherine.

"You shouldn't worry." I smiled. I looked down at my watch. "We have an appointment, don't we? At the Archives?"

"Oh, shit," she said. "I totally forgot to cancel."

I closed the scrapbook and replaced it on the table. "So let's keep it," I said.

ARMISTEAD MAUPIN

ARMISTEAD MAUPIN'S popular *Tales of the City* novels have appealed to a wide audience, overcoming the gays-only stigma attached to many openly homosexual authors who feature homosexual characters in their work. Although Maupin's work presents issues important to the gay community to a wide audience (a role that he has relished, especially since the epidemic of AIDS), there are elements, which are largely responsible for his popularity, that threaten to undermine the literary viability of his work. The episodic, soap opera–style format of the novels, nearly all of which were first published serially in San Francisco papers, has been criticized as contrived melodrama. Maupin's burlesque of contemporary society has also been read in different ways by different readers, with the line between satire and cliché sometimes becoming difficult to distinguish.

Despite such criticisms, the long history of the continuing series—six novels over an 11-year span—provides a poignant social history of the gay community, contrasting the hedonistic late 1970s with the tragedy that has pervaded the AIDS era. The books follow a recurring cast of characters, who originally shared a San Francisco boarding house, and each installment is rife with historical artifacts, including everything from cocaine and bath houses to AZT and the Persian Gulf War. Maupin's books are more than documents of popular culture, however, and it is his mix of literature and politics that has invited comparisons to earlier socially conscious authors. Several critics have placed Maupin in the same tradition as nineteenth-century British novelist Charles Dickens, citing Maupin's dramatization of social issues and his affection for the serial format. While the comparison is somewhat apt, Maupin illustrates his contemporary allegiances by replacing Dickens's sentimentality with satire. This combination has obvious popular appeal, and it has allowed Maupin to outline his position on several gay-related issues.

Maupin's homosexual characters are diverse, as capable of both good and bad as their heterosexual counterparts. Maupin also portrays these two groups, gay and straight, as being involved in the same behavior en route to the same conclusions. Gay characters, such as Michael "Mouse" Tolliver, become involved in numerous sexual relationships in

Essay by
JEFF HILL

339

Armistead Maupin's episodic, soap opera–style "Tales of the City" novels, most of which were first published serially in San Francisco papers, have been both criticized as contrived melodrama and considered Dickensian in their social commentary.

the earlier installments of the series; heterosexuals like Mary Ann Singleton go through a similar stage of experimentation. In Maupin's later novels, these escapades yield to longer-term relationships that demand greater commitment and offer greater satisfaction. In this manner, Maupin indicates that sexual orientation has no discernible effect on other aspects of an individual's behavior and that, in many respects, the two groups share similar ideals. This point is carried further by the relationships that develop between homosexuals and heterosexuals in Maupin's work. In daring to put gays and straights together, Maupin breaks down the sexual identity segregation that exists in many works of gay literature. This process emphasizes similarities as much as differences, and demonstrates that strong bonds can develop between homosexuals and heterosexuals.

Coexistent with this intermingling of people with different sexual orientations is an honesty about sexual identity. Maupin's gay characters are generally open about their sexuality, and the heterosexuals are aware and accepting of same-sex relationships. This arrangement provides an implicit message that became more explicit in the course of the *Tales* series: that gays should openly admit their sexual orientation. Maupin's most strident advocacy of coming out occurs in *Sure of You*, the final novel in the series, when Tolliver castigates a fashion designer who hides his homosexuality behind a conventional marriage. Maupin has further promoted a message of sexual openness in his frequent public appearances, and he sees a direct correlation between his roles as activist and writer. "It was no accident that my literary drive emerged as soon as I stopped hiding my sexuality," he related in a *Contemporary Authors* interview. "There was this irresistible urge to tell everything I knew, to explain myself, to demystify a subject that had scared me silly for years."

Since closing the *Tales* series, Maupin has explored new literary interests. His 1992 novel, *Maybe the Moon*, is narrated by a 31-inch-tall Hollywood actress who struggles to revive her failing career. By concentrating on such a unique character, Maupin is able to cultivate his pen-

American novelist, journalist, and public speaker.

Born: Washington, D.C., May 13, 1944; grew up in Raleigh, North Carolina.

Education: University of North Carolina at Chapel Hill, B.A. 1966.

Partnerships: Companion of Terry Anderson.

Career: Served with the U.S. Navy in Vietnam, 1967–70; Lieutenant Reporter, Charleston *News and Courier,* Charleston, South Carolina, 1970–71; reporter, Associated Press, San Francisco, California, 1971–72; account executive, Lowry, Russom, & Leeper Public Relations, San Francisco, 1973; columnist, *Pacific Sun,* San Francisco, 1974; publicist, San Francisco Opera, 1975; author of serial column "Tales of the City," for *San Francisco Chronicle,* 1976–77, 1981, and 1983; commentator, KRON-TV, San Francisco, 1979. Author of serial column for San Francisco *Examiner,* 1986. Author of dialogue, *La Perichole,* by Jacques Offenbach, produced by the San Francisco Opera Company. Public speaker on gay issues.

Recipient: Freedoms Foundation Freedom Leadership Award, 1972; Los Angeles Metropolitan Elections Commission Communications Award, 1989; American Library Association's Gay/Lesbian Book Award, 1990, for exceptional achievement.

Agent: Amanda Urbin, International Creative Management, 40 West 57th Street, New York, New

chant for social outcasts while at the same time broadening his literary repertoire. After spending an extended period with the cast of the *Tales* novels, it may take several other variations like *Maybe the Moon* before he earns a critical response that is equal to his popular success. Regardless of Maupin's fate in this regard, he has done much to familiarize the general public with homosexual lifestyles and issues and has rendered compelling, comforting, and entertaining portraits of his gay and lesbian characters.

THINKING OUT LOUD

In less than twenty-four hours Michael's paralysis was complete. He could blink his eyes and move his lips, but the rest of him was horribly still. He looked at his visitor using a mirror angled over his bed.

"Hi, lover," he said.

"Hi."

"Shouldn't you be at the office?"

"It's O.K. Slow day."

Michael grinned. "Me too."

"I talked to Mary Ann. She and Burke are coming over later."

Excerpts reprinted from *More Tales of the City,* HarperPerennial, copyright 1979 by The Chronicle Publishing Company.

ARMISTEAD **MAUPIN**   341

"God, I'm popular today! Miss Congeniality. Brian and the Three Graces just left."

"Who?"

"That's what I call 'em now. Mona and Mrs. Madrigal and Mother Mucca."

Jon laughed. "They're quite a trio."

"Yeah. And it's good for Mona, too. I'm glad."

"Are you ... doin' O.K., Michael?"

"Well ... I remembered something funny today."

"Yeah?"

"When I was a kid, fourteen or so, I used to worry about what would happen when I didn't get married. My father was married when he was twenty-three, so I figured I had nine or ten years before people would figure out that I was gay. After that ... well, there weren't a whole lot of good excuses. So you know what I used to hope for?"

Jon shook his head.

"That I'd be paralyzed."

"Michael, for Christ's sake!"

"Not like this. Just from the waist down. That way, I could be in a wheelchair, and people would like me, and I wouldn't have to worry about what they'd say when I didn't get married. It seemed like a pretty good solution at the time. I was a *dumb* little kid."

"You're also a maudlin grownup. You can't dwell on this stuff, Michael. It's not healthy for you to ... Hey, I almost forgot. *Chorus Line* is coming back. I sent for our tickets today."

"Nice fake."

"Goddammit, Michael! Will you stop being so ... melodramatic! I hate to disappoint you, but you're not gonna ..."

"The word is die, Babycakes."

"You're not, Michael. I'm a doctor. I know."

"You're a gynecologist, turkey."

"You *like* playing this scene, don't you? You're getting off on this whole goddamn Camille—"

"Hey, hey," Michael's voice was gentle, consoling. The flippancy was gone. "Don't take me seriously, Jon. I've just gotta talk, that's all. Don't listen to what I'm saying. O.K.?"

"You got a deal."

"You know what? They've got me on The Pill. I mean, they call it steroids or something, but it's still The Pill. I've been tripping on that all morning. I'm on The Pill, and my gynecologist spends more time with me than my doctor does. Isn't that a hoot?"

Jon smiled. "That's pretty good, all right."

"Maybe there's a lot to be said for all this. I mean, for one thing, I can go for hours at a time without looking nellie. If they could prop me up or something, I'd be *dynamite* in a dark corner at The Bolt!"

* * *

Mary Ann arrived half an hour later. Michael winked at her in the mirror.

"Hi, gorgeous. Where'd ya get that Acapulco tan?"

"Hi, Mouse. Burke's here too."

"I see. Hello, Hunky."

"Hi, Michael."

"The coast is clear, kiddo. Not a rose in sight."

The couple laughed nervously. "Mouse," said Mary Ann, "I picked up your mail for you. Do you ... want me to read it to you?"

"What is it? A pink slip from the Clap Clinic?"

Mary Ann giggled. "I think it's from your parents."

Michael said nothing. Jon cast a warning glance at Mary Ann, who instantly tried to backtrack. "I can leave it, Mouse ... and maybe later Jon can—"

"No. Go ahead."

Mary Ann looked at Jon, then back to Michael. "Are you sure?"

"What the hell."

So she opened the letter.

SAVING THE CHILDREN

Mary Ann began to read:

Dear Mikey,

How are you? I guess you're back from Mexico by now. Please write us. Your Papa and I are real anxious to hear all about it. Also, how is Mary Ann and when will we get a chance to meet her?

Everything is fine in Orlando. It looks like we'll do fine with this year's crop, even with the frost and all. The homosexual boycott may make orange juice sales drops off a little, but Papa says it won't make any difference in the long run, and besides it won't …

Mary Ann looked up. "Mouse … I think we should save this for some other time."

"No. It's O.K. Go on."

Mary Ann looked at Jon, who shrugged.

"I've handled it for half my life," said Michael. "Another day won't make a difference."

So Mary Ann continued:

… besides it won't do anything but show Jesus whose side we're on.

You remember in my last letter I said we didn't say anything in our resolution about renting to homosexuals, because Lucy McNeil rents her garage to that sissy man who sells carpets at Dixie Dell Mall? I thought that was O.K., because Lucy is a quiet sort who has stomach trouble, and I didn't think it would be Christian to upset her unduly.

I guess the man was right when he said the road to Hell is paved with good intentions, because Lucy has all of sudden become real militant about the homosexuals. She said she wouldn't sign our Save Our Children resolution, and she called us all heathens and hypocrites and said that Jesus wouldn't even let us kiss His feet if He came back to earth today. Can you imagine such a thing?

I was real upset about it after the meeting until your Papa cleared it up for me. You know, I never thought about it much, but Lucy never did marry, and she was really pretty when her and me used to go to Orlando High. She could of gotten a real good husband, if she had set her mind to it. Anyway, your Papa pointed out that Lucy takes modern art classes at the YWCA now and wears Indian blouses and hippie clothes, so I guess it's possible that the lesbians have recruited her. It's mighty hard to believe, though. She was always so pretty.

Etta Norris had a Save Our Children get-together at her house last Saturday night. It was real nice. Lolly Newton even brought a Red Devil's Food Cake she made using Mrs. Oral Roberts' recipe from Anita Bryant's cookbook. That gave us the idea of making lots of food from the cookbook and selling it at the VFW bazaar to raise money for Save Our Children.

We are all praying that the referendum in Miami will pass. If the homosexuals are allowed to teach in Miami, then it might happen in Orlando. Reverend Harker says that things have gotten so bad in Miami that the homosexuals are kissing each other in public. Your Papa doesn't believe that, but I say that the devil is a lot more powerful than we think he is.

Mikey, we had to put Blackie to sleep. I hate to tell you that, but he was mighty old. I know the Lord will look after him, like he does with all His creatures.

Bubba says hi.

Love,
Mama

Mary Ann moved to Michael's bedside, addressing him directly without using the mirror. "Mouse ... I'm really sorry."

"Forget it. I think it's a riot."

"No. It's awful. She doesn't know what she's saying, Mouse."

Michael smiled. "Yes she does. She's a capital-C Christian. They *always* know what they're saying."

"But she wouldn't say that, Mouse. Not if she knew. Not her own son."

"She'd say it about somebody else's son. What the hell's the difference?"

Mary Ann looked back at Jon and Burke, tears streaming down her face. Then she reached out and touched the immobile figure in the bed.

"Mouse ... if I could change your life for you, so help me I'd— "

"You can, Babycakes."

"What? How?"

"Got your Bic handy?"

"Sure."

"Then take a letter, Miss Singleton."

Tales of the City Series

Tales of the City (originally serialized in *San Francisco Chronicle*), 1978.

More Tales of the City (originally serialized in *San Francisco Chronicle*), 1980.

Further Tales of the City (originally serialized in *San Francisco Chronicle*), 1982.

Babycakes (originally serialized in *San Francisco Chronicle*), 1984.

Significant Others (originally serialized in *San Francisco Examiner*), 1987.

Sure of You, 1989.

28 Barbary Lane: A Tale of the City (contains *Tales of the City*, *More Tales of the City*, and *Further Tales of the City*), 1990.

The Complete Tales of the City, 1991.

Back to Barbary Lane: The Final Tales of the City, 1991.

Other

Author of introduction, *Mrs. Miniver* by Jan Struther, 1985.

Author of introduction, *Drawings of the Male Nude*, illustrations by Don Bachardy, 1985.

Heart's Wheel (musical), with others, music by Glen Roven, 1990.

"Suddenly Home," in *The Faber Book of Gay Short Fiction*, edited by Edmund White, 1991.

Maybe the Moon (novel), 1992.

Beach Blanket Babylon (dialogue for a stage show).

Adaptations

A television screenplay adaptation by Richard Kramer of *Tales of the City* ran as a limited series on Channel Four, England, in 1993.

LETTER TO MAMA

Dear Mama,

I'm sorry it's taken me so long to write. Every time I try to write to you and Papa I realize I'm not saying the things that are in my heart. That would be O.K., if I loved you any less than I do, but you are still my parents and I am still your child.

I have friends who think I'm foolish to write this letter. I hope they're wrong. I hope their doubts are based on parents who loved and trusted them less than mine do. I hope especially that you'll see this as an act of love on my part, a sign of my continuing need to share my life with you.

I wouldn't have written, I guess, if you hadn't told me about your involvement in the Save Our Children campaign. That, more than anything, made it clear that my responsibility was to tell you the truth, that your own child is homosexual, and that I never needed saving from anything except the cruel and ignorant piety of people like Anita Bryant.

I'm sorry Mama. Not for what I am, but for how you must feel at this moment. I know what that feeling is, for I felt it for most of my life. Revulsion, shame, disbelief—rejection through fear of something I knew, even as a child, was as basic to my nature as the color of my eyes.

No, Mama, I wasn't "recruited." No seasoned homosexual ever served as my mentor. But you know what? I wish someone had. I wish someone older than me and wiser than the people in Orlando had taken me aside and said, "You're all right, kid. You can grow up to be a doctor or a teacher just like anyone else. You're not crazy or sick or evil. You can succeed and be happy and find peace with friends—all kinds of friends—

who don't give a damn *who* you go to bed with. Most of all, though, you can love and be loved, without hating yourself for it."

But no one ever said that to me, Mama. I had to find it out on my own, with the help of the city that has become my home. I know this may be hard for you to believe, but San Francisco is full of men and women, both straight and gay, who don't consider sexuality in measuring the worth of another human being.

These aren't radicals or weirdos, Mama. They are shop clerks and bankers and little old ladies and people who nod and smile to you when you meet them on the bus. Their attitude is neither patronizing nor pitying. And their message is so simple: yes, you are a person. Yes, I like you. Yes, it's all right for you to like me too.

I know what you must be thinking now. You're asking yourself: What did we do wrong? How did we let this happen? Which one of us made him that way?

I can't answer that, Mama. In the long run, I guess I really don't care. All I know is this: If you and Papa are responsible for the way I am, then I thank you with all my heart, for it's the light and the joy of my life.

I know I can't tell you what it is to be gay. But I can tell you what it's not.

It's not hiding behind words, Mama. Like family and decency and Christianity. It's not fearing your body, or the pleasures that God made for it. It's not judging your neighbor, except when he's crass or unkind.

Being gay has taught me tolerance, compassion and humility. It has shown me the limitless possibilities of living. It has given me people whose passion and kindness and sensitivity have provided a constant source of strength.

It has brought me into the family of man, Mama, and I like it here. I *like* it.

There's not much else I can say, except that I'm the same Michael you've always known. You just know me better now. I have never consciously done anything to hurt you. I never will.

Please don't feel you have to answer this right away. It's enough for me to know that I no longer have to lie to the people who taught me to value the truth.

Mary Ann sends her love.

Everything is fine at 28 Barbary Lane.

Your loving son,

Michael

KATE
MILLETT

SINCE THE PUBLICATION of *Sexual Politics* in 1970, Kate Millett has been in the public eye. This has not always been to her benefit, as she is quick to point out in her several autobiographical memoirs. But it is this conflict between the public and the private—juxtaposed with her deeply held belief that the personal is the political—that is at the basis for all of Millett's thinking and writing. In all of her work Kate Millett has attempted to pose and explore difficult social, political, and philosophical questions. She has often drawn upon her own life and experiences to elucidate and exemplify these questions and just as often has been attacked not only for her inquiry but for personalizing her investigation.

Kate Millett was born to a middle-class, but impoverished, family in St. Paul, Minnesota, in 1934. She was an excellent student and graduated with a B.A. with highest honors from the University of Minneapolis in 1956, and an M.A. from Oxford University in 1958. She started a career as a sculptor, painter, and photographer in 1959 and moved to Tokyo where she taught English, studied sculpting, and married Fumio Yoshimura, a noted Japanese sculptor. After moving back to the United States in 1963 she taught at Barnard College for several years and entered a Ph.D. program at Columbia University, from which she received her degree in 1970. Her doctoral thesis, titled *Sexual Politics*, which combined literary analysis, sociology, and anthropology, was published that year and became an instant best-seller with over 80,000 copies sold the first year.

Sexual Politics was perhaps the first major theoretical work of the second wave of feminism, and as such it defined the ideas, strategies, and goals of the woman's movement. It also catapulted Millett into the limelight as a major spokeswoman for the movement. In the midst of this media blitz Millett came out as a lesbian—she was asked at a lecture about her sexual identity and answered, as she always did, honestly—a disclosure that was quickly reported in the mainstream press and caused great discussion within the women's movement itself.

Essay by
MICHAEL BRONSKI

349

Kate Millett in 1971, a year after the publication of her best-selling first book,
Sexual Politics, which combined literary analysis, sociology, and anthropology.

American feminist, sculptor, photographer, painter, educator, and nonfiction writer.

Born: Katherine Murray Millett, St. Paul, Minnesota, September 14, 1934.

Education: University of Minnesota, Minneapolis, B.A. 1956 (Phi Beta Kappa); St. Hilda's College, Oxford University, Oxford, England, M.A. 1958; Columbia University, New York, Ph.D. 1970.

Partnerships: Married Fumio Yoshimura in 1965 (divorced in 1985).

Career: Artwork has appeared in numerous exhibits, including Minami Gallery, Tokyo, Japan, 1963; Judson Gallery, Greenwich Village, New York, 1967; Los Angeles Woman's Building, Los Angeles, California, 1977. Professor of English at University of North Carolina at Greensboro, 1958; kindergarten teacher in Harlem, New York, 1960–61; English teacher at Waseda University, Tokyo, 1961–62; professor of English and philosophy at Barnard College, New York, 1964–69; professor of sociology, Bryn Mawr College, Bryn Mawr, Pennsylvania, 1971; distinguished visiting professor at State College of Sacramento, California, 1971–. Contributor of numerous essays to newspapers and periodicals including *Ms.*, *Semiotext(e)*, *New York Times*, and *Nation*.

Memberships: Member of National Organization of Women; Congress of Racial Equality.

Agent: Georges Borchardt, 136 East 57th Street, New York, New York 10022, U.S.A.

While most of the reviews of *Sexual Politics* praised its intelligence, erudition and political acumen, it was also met with some resistance. The woman's movement was still regarded as a threat and it was not uncommon to find critical pieces that referred to "woman's libbers" and "screeching feminists." Even some favorable reviews took exception to Millett's using the blatantly homosexual works of Jean Genet as a blueprint for reviewing gender and sexual roles. Millett's public lesbianism made her an easy target for those who wanted to dismiss her work, her life, and the women's movement itself.

As the pressure of the public life increased and Millett was forced into a celebrity status she never sought, her own life began to spin out of control. This period is documented in *Flying*, in 1974, an autobiographical work that details the emotional and psychological dislocations she experienced after the publication of *Sexual Politics*. Not only did she receive public censure for her opinions and her open lesbianism, but her family, particularly her mother, was very upset with her. Millett, however, was determined to be as honest as possible and *Flying*—which she dedicated to her mother—was an attempt to explore exactly what feminists meant when they claimed that the personal was the political.

The revelations of *Flying* were mild compared with those of *Sita*, in 1977. Based on entries from her 1975 journal, *Sita* described and analyzed a destructive sexual and emotional relationship she had with an older woman while living in Berkeley, California, after the publication of *Flying*. While many in the women's movement and the gay and lesbian liberation movement wanted to believe that a relationship between two women would avoid the power struggles and emotional inequities they associated with heterosexuality and heterosexism, Millett's brilliant dissection of human sexual and emotional obsession and destruction within a lesbian relationship was a political breakthrough. The possibility that women might act destructively and hurtfully to one another was an unpopular political and emotional truth that those within the movement did not want to hear. Because Millett used her own life to illustrate her ideas of the complexities of women's experience of sexuality, desire, and power, many wrote off *Flying* and *Sita* as overly self-absorbed and egotistical.

Millett followed *Sita* with *The Basement: Meditations on a Human Sacrifice*, in 1980. Based on a true incident in which a young woman was systematically abused, tortured, and finally murdered by a group of teenage boys and girls led by an older woman in whose care she had been placed, *The Basement* is one of Millett's bravest works, for in it she poses the questions of why and how women are capable of the same destructive behaviors usually associated with men. Millett was not interested in the simplistic, easy analysis of male power and privilege and was attempting to explore the intricacies of human, and female, behavior. As usual, Millett was a character in *The Basement*—this time serving as reporter and interrogator as well as subject—and included herself and her own life in her investigation of how powerlessness, as well as power, can corrupt.

Going to Iran, published in 1982, documents Millett's trip to Iran after the fall of the Shah and before the rise of the Ayatollah Khomeini. After the collapse of the Shah's regime, a strong feminist movement was fermenting in Iran as part of a broader movement for freedom and social justice. Millett and photographer Sophie Keir documented this movement, as well as the state's opposition to it. In the end Millett and Keir were arrested and expelled by the new government. *Going to Iran* is not only the story of a specific time and place but an examination of how revolutions fail and how political oppression functions on an everyday, personal level.

The publication of *The Loony-Bin Trip* in 1990 brought Millett back into the public eye. In 1973—during the time described in *Flying*—Millett had been briefly committed to a mental hospital by her family. After this she was medicated on lithium to control her mood swings. In 1980, after deciding that the drug was destructive to her creativity as well as her daily life, she made the decision to stop taking it. As her behavior changed, her family and friends reacted and Millett was forced to endure several institutionalizations. In *The Loony-Bin Trip*, Millett argues that "insanity" and "mental illness" are socially constructed labels used against anyone who deviates from the accepted norm. Once again Millett has used her own private life to explore public issues. *The Loony-Bin Trip* was a popular and critical success and engendered heated discussion over a variety of issues, from the uses of psychotropic drugs to the role of the artist in society. The power of the book comes from Millett's willingness to break through—as she always has—the artificially constructed categories of "private" and "public" and to make those vital connections between the personal and the political.

SITA

Am I crazy? Buying a present. Passing a store and feeling the impulse. This morning I would have throttled her, struck, even struck her dear tender face. And now, buying a present. Just lost my last argument with her and I want to buy her a present. Sitting across from her at the teashop today, I knew for sure she would never live as I am living, in someone else's town, someone else's house, with the pretext of a silly marginal course paying only a token salary while I wheeled and dealed in my world, slept with other people while she waited up nights. Unthinkable. It is this that humbles me, this knowledge that she would not endure my circumstances one single week. And perceiving this, I worried most that she would despise me, because I gave in, took every insult. I cannot ask for gratitude, yet I so fear her contempt.

And having passed the afternoon with "other people," the other people she advises me to cultivate, having sat through coffee and a young filmmaker's epic about trains—miles of footage lavished on the Metroliner because the young woman who did it declares it's actually the "feminine spirit," the passion of her life, and so forth—I am hanging about in front of a record store hankering to go in and buy a present. The audience was so savage during the question period that I came to the filmmaker's defense, complimented the photography, the technique, the ghostlike effect in the old photographs she used. "There are always ghosts in a love affair, other people on stage," Susan Griffin whispered to me while we waited for the film to begin. "And ghosts of all the old moments of the love itself, the lovers as they were a month, a year ago, the love of then. Which is not the love of now," I said. Susan's a playwright, we were being literary. When they invited me for dinner after the film, I begged off, half regretting it later. For it had felt good being with other people, almost like New York. A life of appointments and friends and conversation. Not to be buried in that house. Morose, solitary, lugubrious place with night coming on. And yet I wanted to be alone again. To expect her

Excerpt reprinted from *Sita,* Simon & Schuster, copyright 1977 by Kate Millett.

Kate Millett stands beside one of her drawings at a New York exhibit of her work, called "Nudes," that coincides with the publication of *Sita* in 1977.

again. To go home and wait. Knowing she'll be late. And passing a store, wanted to go in and buy her a present. Noticing the records, feeling the impulse.

Lovers and presents. How we used to buy them, hardly a day without them. Mostly hers. Flowers, records, a book or something to eat, trivia even. Flowers, heaps of them. Spending way beyond her means. The whole kitchen of plants she gave me when I moved in at Sacramento. Begonias, the two moccasin plants I used to literally run to water after our weekends in San Francisco. Furious they would be at me, crying out over neglect at the end of two days. Sita courting me those days. Something I hardly understood then. I had never known gifts in such profusion.

Now it's I who buy the presents. Passing the record store and then going back. Not knowing what to buy till I remember the Alice Stuart that Sherman has. Alice Stuart, recalling the name just when I need it, tossing it to the clerk. "Central aisle." Steward, no, Stuart, no, next to it, finding it just when I'd given up. The one with the motorcycle on the cover. And another one too that I haven't heard yet. Clerk wrinkles her nose at the other. Maybe she does me a favor. "It's early and not very good." "All right, just this one then."

Waiting for her downstairs, the record on the couch where I will not forget it. The rain in torrents. Will she stay at school? Put up with a friend? Go to Neal's? The time passes. Nine-thirty, when I expected her. Then ten. And past ten. And still the rain. Huge impersonal flood. How will she ever survive it? Then a taillight reflected through the glass of the front door. Seeing it like some sort of miracle, unforeseen, beyond desert. I call to her from the open door. Her voice answering me, her brown coat around my arms.

Settled on the sofa, we sit where she sat that night with Pia, comforting her after the quarrel with Valerie, and I hovered in the kitchen, cooking a chicken to comfort them. But tonight I sat where Pia sat, tonight it is I, the center of her attention, her delight. She crows over the record and plays it, listening in my arms. For the first time in weeks I feel she is actually present when she is with me. Her body speaks to me. "Makes you want to dance," she whispers. I remember dancing as from some former life. "Friday let's go dancing at Peg's," she says, bouncing

THE GAY AND LESBIAN LITERARY COMPANION

nearly, having thought of it. Excited by her nearness, her kisses, the pressure returned against my body. But afraid to press further.

In bed she seems ready for me. Permitting me brief access, one bittersweet opportunity to enter and be her lover. Does she remember him and compare, measure me against him, Neal of only last night. If I went down on her, would I find him there, his odor still about her after a shower? Forget it, take what you have, what is given in her sweetness, her willingness. The aftereffect of the other perhaps, the rebate, but still mine. Yet so short this turn of mine before she finishes, expels me, ceases to respond. My own inability or her lack of interest?

Then leaning over me, taking me, always what she prefers. Her face looking down on the joy given, registered unashamedly, uncontrollably. Her satisfaction. Her godlike powers. In and out of me each time stronger more certain more inevitable until she has found a new touch, slowly ever so slowly, touching the whole outer flesh, each stroke separate resonant astounding. I dare not speak, even encourage her with words as I love to do, sly lechery of language to excite us both, forgone now, I can only cry out softly with each stroke as she guides, controls, masters, nurtures, and completes. I the creature given over, straining, accepting, accepting all I am given. Stroke after stroke, curious the high of it, the cool of it, and the plateau of it surprising and a little frightening. Wave after wave of heat. Stillness and motion, then the sudden shuddering. Have you ever done this to me before, I ask, bewildered, ever quite like this? That miracle, the finding, the discovery of new sensation where all was familiar, all had been known.

I am lifted, I am hidden, I am in danger and suspended in air and fall and rise again and dizzy, then battered, then exalted. I am her cunt and against my will I tell her so, slavish, owned, devoted, open, a thing to be used. At the mercy of her force and her strength and her fingers, her caprice or her tenderness or her majesty over me. Her eyes open to me, giving pleasure, knowing her certainty to make me rich or afraid or victorious with each caress. Giving because it pleases her to give now, this moment. As it pleased her to give another last night. And I can only admire, prisoner of the touch of her hand on the quick of me, the slow mysterious move of her fingertips around the lips of my mouth gaping to be filled with her, pleading for her fullness and her force in me, the blow of her arrival at the cervix, itself another mouth, another door opening to her touch. Have me, have me, I'm yours, altogether yours, my mind saying what I refuse to say aloud or say only to repent it, the complete abnegation submission surrender, the long fingers of her assaulting me breathless or sly shove high and now and now this instant. Crying out in the lit-

Kate Millett speaks at a poets conference.

tle cries she gives me, crooning to me as I come to her, my creator, comforter. A coming strange and strangely disappointing....

* * *

Thinking that I have now, my stated interval, my term of time. Thinking it as I watch her at breakfast. My stretch of days, my allotment of proximity, days, weeks, months. Then nothing. Go back to New York and it will be over. But for now there is this, guaranteed. Thinking it as I watch her over breakfast. Warm, secure in her presence, momentarily secure, watching her eat. Her poise, her assurance, her movement taking a piece of toast and buttering it, both dainty and bold somehow, and curiously admirable to me, smooth and fluid like the smoothness of her skin. Admiring the shape of her breasts in their green sweater, her long legs as she stands and goes into the kitchen, Her movements as she cleaned the ice box last night, the stride, the efficiency. Even her confidence before a mess of spoiled vegetables, some recalcitrant stain. I would have made a project of this, dreaded it all day, stretched it to hours if I'd gotten to it at all. She does it in four whirling minutes. Even the arcane fitting of the plastic shelves, those troublesome boxes at the bottom, all deceitfully easy under her command, trays sliding neatly back into place.

THE GAY AND LESBIAN LITERARY COMPANION

Then her committee arrived for a meeting she'd assured me would last only three minutes. I went upstairs to read and be out of the way. Discovered I had left the glass of wine I was drinking downstairs. Too late. The book I'm reading inescapably dull, the print too fine, my neck begins to ache from reading prone on the bed. Try again, sitting up. Worse still. They have been down there an hour already. I begin to hate and resent them. It's dinnertime, why don't they go home? Percy, his boasting noise coming up through the floor. Then a white man's voice, nasal, irritating, going on about his asinine "five-point scale" for making decisions. "We must ask ourselves, will this experience benefit my intellectual and emotional growth?" I close my eyes, this sort of language always gives me the creeps. California hokum, therapeutic weekends, how can she bear these people? But this project, this "dialogue between male and female: toward a new communion and understanding," is at the moment the darling of her heart. It has already consumed two of our evenings and will devour a three-day weekend in February. It is about to overcook tonight's own chicken as well. The male voice goes on: "Does it take me to restful places likely to nourish and stimulate that growth?" Charming, well-modulated moron. Go home, the chicken will be overdone. This is my dinner you are drying out. I have a headache from hunger, from being cooped in a room like a domestic animal.

And when they finally left two hours later, she rescued me. Hearing her step on the stairs, I had already forgiven everything. The dear soft voice of her apology. How charming the Italian in its accent, which fluctuates according to the occasion but is always stronger when she is confused or sorry or ill at ease. Or perhaps it is the Portuguese, for it is the Indian in her that apologizes or waits, once waited two whole days for me when I missed a plane. Light-years ago. Never mind, she is laughing, hugging me, laughing at them, laughing with delight that they are finally gone, laughing at the chicken. And I am laughing too, warm in her embrace, the scent of her lovely sweater, the silk around her neck, the fine gold of the bracelet at her wrist. I forget everything in her presence: the absurdity of my position here, the unfairness. They are dismissed in an instant by her complicity, her romantic transformation of all life into an assignation. She'd once spoken, smiling, of "the proper conduct of a love affair." I had never realized that love affairs were conducted, I thought they merely happened. I had much to learn....

* * *

Her face in light of two candles. I've done a London broil, striving for variety as meat chef. This one from a real butcher, not the usual Safeway thing. It's too rare for her, she says, "but it has a lovely taste." More wine and we edge toward what is usually a quarrel, but tonight we stay precariously balanced in a serious discussion. And then lapse into sentiment. She draws her chair closer. "And what am I to do when you leave? Does that ever enter your mind?" It had come up in the kitchen while we were cooking. "When do you take that trip to Puerto Rico?" I ask. "April twenty-sixth." "Then I guess I won't see you again; I have to speak in San Diego the twenty-fifth." And I'd been planning to go home to New York at the beginning of May. New York again without even saying goodbye? Suddenly the wall in front of me, the end. I look up at the cupboards, off to the stove. Her back is to me, preparing the salad. "How long will you be gone?" "Just four days." "Then maybe I could wait till you get back before I fly East." "You could spend the weekend in San Diego, it's beautiful down there. You might even want to go down a few days ahead." She goes on in her California tour-guide manner. I listen, incredulous. Can those last days together be so unimportant to her that she can cheerfully pack me off to look at scenery instead? As always it is so hard to understand the brisk managing side of her, the capriciousness.

Is it caprice now, her hand on my shoulder, asking about the future? "We have a lot to discuss here. Your belongings. The house. If you're coming back. All of it." One candle gutters. Her eyes by the light of the single candle, so very beautiful, so full of feeling, tenderness. Compelling. "Maybe if I had a connection that could keep on supplying me with underground classes at substandard wages?" I tease her, opening the way. Wondering, as I do it, if I want to come back, so unsure myself. Yet part of me assumes it now; I will come back, I will always come back. It will go on, it will always go on. "You don't seem eager," I say, nudging her, sorry the very instant I do it, not having meant to, wanted to. "I don't want to push you. Not until we both know what we want." "And the fact is, we don't," I conclude. We smile. A wan, hopeless smile.

"Now when I think of leaving, it makes me very sad. It hadn't been this way when I first came. Things were so hard then that leaving was rescue. Now that we've come closer together I dread the time I go back." "It will be very lonely here without you." Her eyes telling me this, canceling the others, the friends and lovers and diversions. "It's very lonely in New York too, damn bleak in that loft a lot of the time." "Maud used to tease me, that when I came back from Europe last fall I almost systematically started surrounding myself with things and people and activities." Her hands move, describing the things and people and activities, moving them around the polished surface of the dining-room table like small wooden counters. "Maud used to tease me that under it all I knew just as well as she does that there's the house wine and there's champagne. It's that simple. You're my champagne." Laughing. "And you know my extravagant tastes." Her eyes, mischievous and full of light, snapping in the warm glow around her face. "I'd be able to forget for days in a row, and then when I'd be dressing or walking to lunch, I'd suddenly remember. I have felt the greatest tenderness for you, more than I've ever felt in my life for anyone." She puts her lovely head on her arms, her white sweater gleaming around her shoulders in the candlelight. Utterly beautiful to me. I sit drinking wine, loving her, admiring, telling her my admiration, adoring her in words, words I am normally too shy to say. Emboldened a little by the wine, by our closeness tonight, our final ability to talk. Even to talk without argument or bitterness. We are lost in our situation, hopeless as the distance between our worlds, a whole continent, three thousand miles, two radically different ways of life.

There is the art world and my need of it, which she saw when she came to explore it at Christmas; a small foreign child she was while I dragged her through slums, through the Village and SoHo, exclaiming softly, "Now I see, now I finally see where you live." We talked of it again, the sense she has of being excluded there, her hatred of New York, her love of California. "But if I went to New York, if I arrived at your door, the door of your loft, you couldn't stand it." "I think it would be super," I say. "No, you don't. Four days maybe, but not much beyond that." Wondering if she's right, if I want New York to be alone in, free, my own place.

But wanting while she goes off to telephone Maud, wanting simply to admit how empty and alone New York really is. Wanting to say that Dobie, for example, is just a nice guy to build bookcases or go dancing with, but that's all. That only twice was I drunk or dumb enough to sleep with him and it wasn't any good. That even Dobie prefers platonic friendship out of some dingbat romantic notions of his own. Wanting for some crazy reason to tell her all, to show her the utter barrenness of my days there, admit even that I'd been sleeping with Ruth and that it is nothing but guilt and disaster and that when I go back I won't do it again, that the whole thing with Ruth is a species of crime because she loves me and I do not, cannot love her, maybe—the terrible thought again—as I am Sita's crime because she cannot love me. The old analogy;

KATE **MILLETT**   359

as Ruth is to me, so am I to Sita. Wanting to tell her New York is solitude, that there is no one and nothing there for me. And yet not saying it. Shyness? Self-protection?

She comes back to the table to talk again and drink wine. It could work, she says, hard as it is to live our lives together only half the time. It could work. She wants me to come back next winter. We talk late and until we are very tired. As she was undressing in Paul's room, where she keeps her clothes, I found her and my arms brought her to bed with me.

During the night she escaped, but I did not mind, waking to a bit of a hangover to see that it's barely dawn. Coming back from the toilet, I walk softly, crossing the treacherous floorboards before her open door.

"Come here." I stop like a thief in a pantomime. And then dive into the warmth next to her. "Snuggling"—surely the most pleasant thing in the world. Scrunching further and further into the mattress as we struggle closer and closer warmer and warmer nearer and nearer, our bodies like a letter fitting into an envelope, my legs over her legs, our hips sliding against each other, her arm tighter and tighter around my shoulders, my face nestled more and more firmly into her collarbone. It is bliss. The simplest and most primitive bliss. A childlike, sexual, friendly, animal bliss.

PAUL MONETTE

UPON RECEIVING THE 1992 National Book Award for *Becoming a Man: Half a Life Story*, Paul Monette was catapulted into global recognition as one of the most famous gay writers in the world. At the same time, he was living with AIDS and, in a race against time with the perils of the disease, attempting to complete a book of essays entitled *Last Watch of the Night*.

Essay by
MALCOLM BOYD

On a balmy April afternoon in 1993 I chatted with Monette in his warm, cozy, art-filled home in the Hollywood hills above Los Angeles's fabled Sunset Strip. Although he had just returned from a radiation treatment for AIDS, he was alert and energized as ever. I asked him to describe his greatest strength and primary weakness as a writer. "My chief weakness was the closet," he said. "It made virtually everything I wrote until I came out a kind of ventriloquism. Now it turns out I find my greatest strength in exploring myself and my own psyche, testing myself against a rigorous standard of honesty."

Monette explained that he has been influenced as a writer by the essays of Joan Didion and the fiction of Flannery O'Connor. "There's a kind of willingness there to probe a harrowed world. They taught me honesty about writing. But I think the larger influence on the course of my work was the gay generation after the liberation of Stonewall. What I had written earlier was about nothing. When I finally found I could write about being gay, I knew everything was possible. Now I do not write or think in isolation from my tribe. I go with its vicissitudes and triumphs and its constant changing. The hatred of my enemies has spurred me forward."

He finds enormous significance in the emergence of gay and lesbian writing as a powerful force in literature. "It's immensely affirming and exciting that we have produced this documentation of our lives. We are a literature and a psychology that has bloomed with astonishing rapidity. In my lifetime the most powerful literature has come from communities in crisis. Most American writing, however, has become pallid, self-conscious university stuff with precious little to say. In fact, I left poetry

361

Paul Monette with Mary Oliver, winners of the National Book Awards in 1992. Monette won the non-fiction category for *Becoming a Man: Half a Life Story*.

American poet, novelist, and memoirist.

Born: Lawrence, Massachusetts, in 1945.

Education: Phillips Academy, Andover, Massachusetts; Yale University, New Haven, Connecticut, B.A. 1967.

Partnerships: Companion of Roger Horwitz (died, 1986); companion of Stephen Kolzak (died, 1990); companion of Winston Wilde since 1990.

Career: Taught at Milton Academy and Pine Manor College.

Memberships: Active supporter of ACT UP (AIDS Coalition to Unleash Power) and advocate for gay and lesbian rights.

Recipient: National Book Critics Circle Award nomination, 1988; National Book Award for *Becoming a Man: Half a Life Story*, 1992; honorary degrees from State University of New York College at Oswego, 1992, and Wesleyan University, 1993.

---

behind (with the exception of *Love Alone: Eighteen Elegies for Rog*) because too much of it was writing about nothing, written to a small group of colleagues to get their approval and grants."

I asked Monette to offer an overview of the gay/lesbian content of his past work. He said that his novel *Taking Care of Mrs. Carroll* afforded him a breakthrough moment: "I was proud to have that Dietrich figure at the center, a lesbian from another generation. And all the camp and romanticism of the gay scene in the '60s and early '70s found expression." He discussed his two novels *The Gold Diggers* and *The Long Shot* as a single entity: "I was trying to explore the relationship between gay men and straight women. I did not feel ready to talk about lesbians. Both novels are about friendship and making a family that is not a blood family, but a chosen one. These are gay people and how they live their lives."

Monette feels that his novel *Lightfall* was an anomaly in his work because he was under pressure from his publishers when he wrote it to stop dealing with gay themes. "It is prophetic in that it's about a crazed fundamentalist. It wasn't an easy time for me because I really doubted myself." His next novel, *Afterlife*, provides a broad spectrum of a number of people confronting AIDS. "Everything changed for me after Roger [Horwitz, Monette's lover] was diagnosed with AIDS in 1985. This book records some of the rage of people I admire like Larry Kramer and organizations like ACT UP."

His novel *Halfway Home* is, for Monette, his "lucky star." He said: "I really did get to write the gay love story I always wanted to do. It feels like my best book. I was not afraid to have lesbian characters. I exulted in them. The chosen family wins hands-down. I was able to generate a story that, even in the midst of death, could make the connection of intima-

PAUL **MONETTE**   363

Paul Monette is perhaps best known for his memoirs, *Borrowed Time: An AIDS Memoir* and *Becoming a Man: Half a Life Story*.

cy." *Borrowed Time: An AIDS Memoir* is about his lover Roger's diagnosis and dying. "It struck chords deeper than itself," Monette told me. "I wish I was as wise as the narrator. It lifted me out of myself and enabled me to speak of matters that touched all my people."

His autobiographical work *Becoming a Man: Half a Life Story* brought Monette the maximum of fame and literary acceptance. "I never expected to write nonfiction prose at all. I never thought of myself as a journalist or an essayist. It was totally unknown territory. Although I had all of my education and discipline to help me, it was new. Yet art is inevitably political if one grows up in calamitous times." How, I wondered, does Monette place himself within a larger literary or historical sphere? "This is what is causing so much trouble for the white straight men who wield the power and teach the courses. I am part of the turmoil in which we're trying to add new voices and give a feel of a multicultural world. But I don't feel separatist. One person's truth if told well does not leave anybody out."

Referring to AIDS, which has consumed so much of his health and energy, Monette explains that he has continued to write as a way of continuing to breathe. "I've been pleasantly surprised by how [much] I am giving back to my community. There's so much alienation from ourselves as gays and lesbians—the conquest of our own self-hatred—I'm glad to be a figure that gives hope." His life's focus has shifted because of the battleground of his illness. "My life has narrowed to my house and my life with Winston and my two dogs. I'm trying to go over the pieces of my life and see what I cherish and what I believe. This is what I am doing in *Last Watch of the Night*. Simplify—simplify—simplify. I'm not sure what my final words will be."

Paul Monette has confronted being gay in America and AIDS in his work in a deeply involving, confrontational way. Hans Castorp, in Thomas Mann's classic novel *The Magic Mountain*, regretted that he did not live in demanding times. A writer like Monette living today is challenged by a plethora of human and moral crises. The "imprisoned writer" and the "censored artist" are commonplace in our world. A writer provokes controversy, and often wrath, when he or she refuses to bow to conventional demands to remove art's sting and trivialize on demand creative work.

Monette is a symbol of freedom of expression at a moment when serious attempts are being made to suppress such expression, reduce it to a low common denominator, or harness it to serve merely utilitarian purposes. Yet a creative writer cannot thrive in deadening isolation, cut off from the demanding issues and personalities of his or her time. Brutality, prejudice, discrimination, and all forms of dehumanization demand a response as a part of a writer's pact with conscience. A writer cannot remain detached from the shadowy figures—evocative of sculptor Alberto Giacometti's art—who inhabit our city streets in the guise of homeless people; or racism, sexism, and homophobia; or the pandemic of AIDS. Paul Monette's best work in *Borrowed Time* and *Becoming a Man* penetrates the dark night of our collective soul. At precisely this point, he melds his work with his life.

BORROWED TIME

How do I speak of the person who was my life's best reason? The most completely unpretentious man I ever met, modest and decent to such a degree that he seemed to release what was most real in everyone he knew. It was always a relief to be with Roger, not to have to play any games at all. By a safe mile he was the least flashy of all our bright circle of friends, but he spoke about books and the wide world he had journeyed with huge conviction and a hunger to know everything.

He had a contagious, impish sense of humor, especially about the folly of things, especially self-importance. Yet he was blissfully unfrivolous, without a clue as to what was "in." He had thought life through somehow and come out the other side with a proper respect for small pleasures. "*Quelle bonne soirée,*" as Madeleine once exclaimed after dinner one night with us in Les Halles, a bistro called Pig's Foot. Wonderful evenings were second nature to us by then, with long walks at the end, especially when we traveled. Days we spent cavorting through museums, drunk on old things, like ten-year-olds loose in a castle. Roger loved nothing better than a one-on-one talk with a friend, and he had never lost track of a single one, all the way back to high school. The luck of the draw was mine, for I was the best and the most.

We met on the eve of Labor Day in 1974, at a dinner party at a mutual friend's apartment on Beacon Hill, just two days before Roger was to start work as an attorney at a stately firm in Boston. He was thirty-two; I was twenty-eight. Summer has always been good to me, even the bittersweet end, with the slant of yellow light, and I for one was in love before the night was done. I suppose we'd been waiting for each other all our

Excerpt reprinted from *Borrowed Time*, Harcourt Brace Jovanovich, copyright 1988 by Paul Monette.

PAUL **MONETTE** 365

lives. The business of coming out had been difficult for both of us, partly because of the closet nature of all relations in a Puritan town like Boston, partly because we were both so sure of what we wanted and it kept not coming to life.

"Spain!" Roger writes in his diaries in 1959, after three days' hitch-hike from Paris to Madrid. "If only I had a friend!"

For if there was no man out there who was equal and simpatico, then what was the point of being gay? The baggage and the shit you had to take were bad enough. But it all jogged into place when we met, everything I'd brooded over from the ancient Greeks to Whitman. It all ceased to be literary. My life was a sort of amnesia till then, longing for something that couldn't be true until I'd found the rest of me. Is that feeling so different in straight people? Or is it that gay people have to keep it secret and so grow divided, with a bachelor's face to the world and a pang like dying inside?

The reason he got such a late start as a lawyer was that Roger lived a whole other life first. During his freshman year at Harvard Law he was simultaneously writing his dissertation for a Ph.D. in Comparative Literature. That work grew out of a decade of Europe and books, the bohemian ramble, complete with beret in one black-and-white of the period. A month before he was diagnosed, we saw a production of Philip Barry's *Holiday*, and Roger laughed on the way out, saying he'd done exactly what Barry's hero longed to do—retire at the age of twenty.

He left Brandeis after his freshman year and went straight to Paris, where he worked as a waiter and flirted with being a poet. The *patronne* of Restaurant Papille was Madeleine Follain, a painter by vocation, the daughter of Maurice Denis and wife of the poet Jean Follain. Roger reveled in all that passionate life of art, and the journal of his nineteenth year, two hundred close-typed pages, burns with the search for the perfect feeling and the words to speak it. When he finally graduated from Brandeis, he returned to Paris for two more years, working at Larousse and Gallimard. Then he took a long sojourn in the Middle East, where his aunt was married to an Israeli diplomat. Once he wandered for weeks through Ethiopia, eating goat around village fires, walking up-country to monastic caves at Lalibala, till even the guide lagged back for fear of bandits.

Then in 1965 he packed in at Harvard's Widener Library, reading French, reading everything really, till he finally concentrated on the novels of Henri Thomas. He was senior tutor in Dudley House and took his meals at a co-op on Sacramento Street, a chaotic Queen Anne tenement bursting with Harvard and Radcliffe students, all at full throttle. Roger

WRITINGS

Poetry

The Carpenter at the Asylum, 1975.
No Witnesses, drawings by David Schorr, 1981.
Love Alone: Eighteen Elegies for Rog, 1988.
West of Yesterday, East of Summer, 1994.

Novels

Taking Care of Mrs. Carroll, 1978.
The Gold Diggers, 1979.
The Long Shot, 1981.
Lightfall, 1982.
Afterlife, 1990.
Halfway Home, 1991.

Memoirs

Borrowed Time: An AIDS Memoir, 1988.
Becoming a Man: Half a Life Story, 1992.

Other

Nosferatu: The Vampire (adaptation of screenplay by Werner Herzog), 1979.
Scarface (adaptation of screenplay by Oliver Stone), 1983.
Predator, 1986.
Havana, 1991.
Midnight Run, 1990.
(Author of foreword) *A Rock and a Hard Place* by Anthony Godby Johnson, 1993.

---

used to look back on those years at graduate school with a sort of amazement: to think that life could clear you a space just to sit and read! How he savored Harvard, the elm alleys and the musty bookstores, this place that had turned him down at seventeen and left him crying on the stoop of his parents' three-decker in Chicago.

Whereas I had fumbled my way through Andover on a scholarship, too dazed to do much thinking in the thick of an atmosphere that felt as exotic to me as Brideshead. Yet I breezed into Harvard and Yale on half of Roger's intellect, with whole hockey squads of my privileged classmates. Four years later I had neither the analytic cast of mind nor the stamina for graduate work. I made a half-wit decision to be a poet—that was the good half—without preparing any sort of career cushion. I ended up teaching at a prep school out of Boston, with the sinking feeling that I had *become* one of the privileges of the upper class.

But I wrote poems and papered the East with them. My particular Left Bank was Cambridge in the early seventies, where poets passed through in caravan, some in sedan chairs, some like an underground railway. Parties in Cambridge had totems in every corner—Lowell, Miss Bishop, I. A. Richards ("Is *he* still alive?"), visiting constellations rare as Borges.

In 1974 I was waiting for my first book of poems to come out and generally going about feeling heavily crowned with laurel. Yet the poems seethe with loneliness, the love that dared not speak its name like a stranglehold on the heart. Roger had just completed a year working in public television for a show called *The Advocates*, where bloody Sunday issues were debated hotly by brainy types. The show Roger was proudest of was about gay marriages. He'd been instrumental in pulling the brains together and airing a wildly controversial notion—single all the while, of course.

We weren't kids anymore. We'd been hurting dull as a toothache for years. When we came together as lovers we knew precisely how happy we were. I only realized then that I'd never had someone to play with before. *There* was a lost time that wanted making up in spades. Six weeks before Roger died, he looked over at me astonished one day in the hospital, eyes dim with the gathering blindness. "But we're the same person," he said in a sort of bewildered delight. "When did that happen?"

LESLEA
NEWMAN

UNDER THE ASSUMPTION that humans cannot live without nourishment—spiritual, emotional, and actual—and under the assumption that writers and readers meet best on planes that offer these essentials among sensual details, one finds in Lesléa Newman's writing food for the goddess, food for thought, food for a large populace.

Essay by
CARMEN EMBRY

Her work, whether directed to children or an adult readership, continually explores issues of lesbian identity and Jewish identity, as well as the political relationships between women and food. Saturated in Yiddish, these predicaments of struggle, discovery, and acceptance are so steeped in unique details that they rise above the formulaic, illustrating that Newman heeds her own advice. In "Writing as Self-Discovery" she encourages beginning writers to fill the pages with "sensory detail," noting that "the more specific images you have, the more alive your writing will be." From detailing a gray hospital setting in "Sunday Afternoon" to etching holy domesticity in "One Shabbos Evening," Newman abides by this literary philosophy.

To such vivid settings, she adds solid characterization. In *A Letter to Harvey Milk*, a 1988 collection of short stories, Newman compacts a virtual universe of characters. Rachel, in "The Gift," grows from five years old to adulthood in video-like glimpses, rejecting, accepting, and finally celebrating her Judaic background. Like a *tallis*, her faith and beliefs finally rest easily on her shoulders. Other characters confront issues such as AIDS, relationship struggles, incest— less than desirable situations, but somehow comfortably universal—as they do in another sound collection, *Secrets*.

Her work also highlights eating disorders. *Good Enough To Eat* chronicles the daily struggles of a young woman suffering from bulimia. Throughout most of the novel, the reader finds her possessed and obsessed with food. Sharing an apartment with a whimsical gay man and a vague straight woman, the character continually checks her designated refrigerator shelf, weighing its contents and her self-worth simultaneously. After dipping into her roommate's cache, she chastises herself: "Here

Lesléa Newman's writings find an audience with children, young adults, and adults.

you are popping out of your clothes and still you go on eating and eating like there's nothing wrong with you." Later she adds, "It was only a bit of cottage cheese."

These food dilemmas show up elsewhere in Newman's writing. From her poetry, where in "Hunger" she notes that her "thighs grow fat and get in each other's way," to *Somebody to Love: A Guide to Loving the Body You Have*, where she offers candid advice and writing suggestions designed to empower women through their body images, Newman burns the torch for self-acceptance.

She offers the same realistic exposure for children in *Belinda's Bouquet*, the story of a young girl who arrives at self acceptance. Belinda moves from being a tormented child, teased on the bus for being fat, to a reflective individual after hearing a tale about a gardener who attempts to put all of her marigolds on a diet to make them "thin like the irises," at which point they naturally whither and droop.

Newman manages to step clear of the didactic and continues instead the same Aesopian insight she offered in the groundbreaking book *Heather Has Two Mommies*. In this book, Heather, raised by two lesbians, is confronted in school with a concept of a father, and the child is reduced to tears because she doesn't have the "typical" nuclear family. She learns that many children, not just those with lesbian parents, often have no such family structure. One classmate has a single mother; another has two fathers; still another is part of an adoptive family.

Newman continues her pioneering work in *Gloria Goes to Gay Pride*, in which she offers a variety of characters who pivot around Gloria as she participates in the parade. Gays, lesbians, straights, all colorfully portrayed, call for understanding. However, because of content deemed sensitive by several libraries across the nation, Newman's books for children have caused considerable controversy over the issue of lesbian/gay censorship.

American educator, poet, novelist, and author of short stories and children's fiction.

Born: Brooklyn, New York, November 5, 1955.

Education: University of Vermont, B.S. 1977; Naropa Institute, certificate in poetics 1980.

Career: Manuscript reader, *Mademoiselle* and *Redbook*, New York City, 1982; book reviewer and writer, *Valley Advocate*, Hatfield, Massachusetts, 1983–87; teacher, University of Massachusetts continuing education, Amherst, 1983–85; director and teacher of creative writing summer program for high school women, Mount Holyoke College, South Hadley, Massachusetts, 1986–88; founder and director, Write from the Heart: Writing Workshops for Women, Northampton, Massachusetts, 1987–. Lecturer and conductor of writing workshops at educational institutions, including Yale University and Amherst, Smith, Swarthmore, and Trinity colleges. Regular contributor to *Conditions*, *Heresies*, *Common Lives*, *Sinister Wisdom*, and *Sojourner*.

Memberships: Member of Society of Children's Book Writers, Authors League of America, Poets and Writers, Feminist Writers Guild, Publishing Triangle, and Academy of American Poets.

Recipient: Massachusetts Artists Foundation fellowship in poetry, 1989; Lambda Literary Award for *Gloria Goes to Gay Pride*, 1992; *Highlights for Children* fiction writing award for "Remember That," 1992.

Agent: Charlotte Raymond, 32 Bradlee Road, Marblehead, Massachusetts 01945, U.S.A.

Address: Write from the Heart, P.O. Box 815, Northampton, Massachusetts 01061, U.S.A.

Newman's three collections of poetry, *Love Me Like You Mean It*, *Just Looking for My Shoes*, and *Sweet Dark Places*, reflect yet another outlet for her creativity. Again the human predicament is scoped, illuminated, and celebrated. Her lines reflect real-life situations—sometimes painful, sometimes playful, always candid—as she continues to explore her lesbianism and Jewish identity.

This quest cumulates and unfolds in her 1992 novel *In Every Laugh a Tear* where Newman writes about a mid-life Jewish lesbian caught in the midst of outrage over her grandmother's induction into a nursing home. As Shayna immerses herself into Bubbe's life, sharing the frustrations and fears of aging, Newman consistently stays the great observer, pulling back from any *schmaltz* and offering instead a grandmother who opens a dresser drawer to offer "two American cheese sandwiches." Yet the old woman's wisdom is not lost. Watching the multitudes pass through the home, she notes: "*Nu*, welcome to God's waiting room." And when the matriarch finally passes, a much stronger Shayna exchanges keepsakes with her mother and promises of commitment with her lover.

In all genres Newman's literary style offers a succession of surprises as she swings from first to third person effortlessly. From hard cadence to a lazy stream of consciousness, the works reveal a woman unafraid of risks. Newman, in an interview for the *Springfield Sunday Republican*, stated that writing is "like being an explorer—when you get scared, you should keep going."

Newman's work, certainly a tribute to her culture and sexual orientation, manages to offer a bridge for those who cannot claim such background elements, offering education, enlightenment, and entertainment. One comes away decidedly hungry for more as she assumes her rightful place in the literary canon.

Lesléa Newman told the Companion:

"Ever since I was a child I have written poems and stories in order to try and understand the world around me, the world inside me, and the relationship between the two. Issues of identity and belonging have always been important to me; the position of being an outsider gives one a unique perspective. I write about being a woman, being a Jew, and being a lesbian, living in a difficult world in difficult times. Humor runs rampant throughout my work; I use it to remind myself that even in the most trying of times, there is much to be joyful about."

ONE SPRING

Reprinted from *Eating Our Hearts Out: Personal Accounts of Women's Relationship to Food*, The Crossing Press, copyright 1993 by Lesléa Newman.

The air was thick with promise
of lilacs and rain that evening
and the clouds hovered about my shoulders
like the mink stole in my mother's closet
I tried on from time to time.
I was sixteen and I knew it.
I tossed my head like a proud pony
my hair rippling down my back in one black wave
as I walked down the sultry street
my bare feet barely touched the ground
past sounds of a television
a dog barking
a mother calling her child
my body slicing through the heavy air
like a sailboat gliding on lazy water.

When the blue car slowed alongside me
I took no notice
until two faces leaned out the open window.
"Nice tits you got there, honey."
"Hey sweetheart, shine those headlights over here."

"Wanna go for a ride?"
I stopped,
dazed as a fish thrust out of water
into sunlight so bright it burns my eyes.
I turn and walk away fast
head down, arms folded,
feet slapping the ground.
I hear, "Nice ass, too,"
then laughter
the screech of tires
silence.

All at once I am ashamed of my new breasts
round as May apples,
I want to slice them off with a knife
sharp as a guillotine.
All at once I am mortified by my widening hips,
I want to pare them down with a vegetable peeler
until they are slim and boyish.
All at once I want to yank out my hair by the roots
like persistent weeds that must not grow wild.
But I am a sensible girl.
I do none of these things.

Instead I go home, watch TV with my parents,
brush my teeth and braid my hair for the night.
And the next day I skip breakfast,
eat only an apple for lunch
and buy a calorie counter,
vowing to get thinner and thinner
until I am so slim I can slip
through the cracks in the sidewalk
and disappear. And I do.

RED, WHITE AND NO LONGER BLUE

You want to know why I'm eating blue spaghetti with tomato sauce and tofu all by myself on the fourth of July? There's a simple, logical, one word explanation: Margaret.

She left me. I was looking forward to spending a whole day with her smack dab in the middle of the week. You know, we'd get up late, make love, hang out, drink coffee, go back to bed, have a picnic, watch the fireworks. Well, that was the plan, but it seems my Margaret was off

Reprinted from *Eating Our Hearts Out: Personal Accounts of Women's Relationship to Food*, The Crossing Press, copyright 1993 by Lesléa Newman.

LESLEA **NEWMAN**   373

Novels

Good Enough to Eat, 1986.
In Every Laugh a Tear, 1992.

Short Stories

A Letter to Harvey Milk, 1988.
Secrets, 1990.

Young Adult Fiction

Fat Chance! 1993.

Children's Fiction

Heather Has Two Mommies, illustrations
 by Diana Souza, 1989.
Gloria Goes to Gay Pride, illustrations
 by Russell Crockfer, 1991.
Belinda's Bouquet, illustrations by
 Michael Willhoite, 1991.
Saturday Is Pattyday, 1993.

Remember That, forthcoming.
*Too Far Away to Touch, Close Enough to
 See,* forthcoming.

Poetry

Just Looking for My Shoes, 1980.
Love Me Like You Mean It, 1987.
Sweet Dark Places, 1991.

Plays

After All We've Been Through, produced
 Durham, North Carolina, 1989.
Rage, produced New York, 1991.

Nonfiction

"Writing as Self-Discovery," in *Writer,*
 January 1988.
*Somebody to Love: A Guide to Loving the
 Body You Have,* 1991.

*Writing from the Heart: Inspiration and
 Exercises for Women Who Want to
 Write,* 1993.

Other

Editor and author of introduction,
 *Bubbe Meisehs by Shayneh Maidelehs:
 Poetry by Jewish Granddaughters about
 Our Grandmothers,* 1989.
Editor, *Eating Our Hearts Out: Personal
 Accounts of Women's Relationship to
 Food,* 1993.
Editor, *Bearing the Unbearable: Stories of
 Losing Loved Ones to AIDS,* forth-
 coming.

Adaptations

A Letter to Harvey Milk was produced by
 Yariv Kohn, York University,
 Canada, 1990.

---

somewhere making fireworks of her own. With someone else. And like a poorly written soap opera, I was the last to know.

So, while the rest of Boston was celebrating the birth of our nation (or protesting it, whatever turns you on), I was alone. All by myself with no picnic ingredients, no party to go to, no one to *ooh* and *aah* with down at the Esplanade when it got dark and they shot those babies up in the air.

I moped around most of the day, and then around five o'clock I snapped out of it. I had no right to feel sorry for myself. I was young, healthy, employed and reasonably good looking, with a roof over my head and food on the table. That's when I decided, what the heck, I'd make myself a festive meal and have a private celebration. Hell, I'm a woman of the nineties. I don't need anyone, right? I can take care of myself.

So, due to the day being what it was, and me being the cornball that I am, the meal had to be red, white and blue. I opened the refrigerator and immediately saw red, a jar of Paul Newman's tomato sauce. Perfect. Red was for blood, anger, revenge; how dare that bitch leave me for somebody else? I'm the best thing that ever happened to her. And she knew it, too. Or used to know it.

Now I was feeling blue. Blue food was trickier. I didn't have any blueberries in the fridge. On to the pantry. Would navy beans count?

Hardly. How about a can of green beans? Almost, but not quite. Although some people have trouble telling the difference between blue and green and some people don't even think there is a difference. I found that out a few years ago when I was waiting for the T at Harvard Square. A music student from Japan struck up a conversation with me, pointing at my sweater with her flute case. "That's a nice green sweater," she said, though my sweater happened to be blue. When I told her that, she smiled and said there was only one word for blue and green in Japanese, which sounded quite lovely and meant the color of the water. I started wishing that train would never come, but of course it did and off I went, only to meet Margaret three days later as a matter of fact. But I refuse to think about that now. Anyway, the point is, if I was Japanese the green beans would do just fine, but then again if I was Japanese, I'm sure I wouldn't give a flying fuck about the fourth of July.

Back to the pantry. That's when I spotted those little bottles full of food coloring: red, green, yellow and blue. I'd gotten them last year for St. Patrick's Day, to make bona fide green mashed potatoes for Margaret. The blue bottle was still full. What could I dye with it?

Why, spaghetti of course. We used to color spaghetti when I taught day care. We'd save this special activity for a freezing Friday in February when the kids were off the wall from being cooped up all week, and the teachers were going bananas from five days of dealing with seventeen pairs of mittens, boots, snowsuits, scarves, sweaters, hats and jackets. To while away the afternoon, we'd cook up a huge vat of spaghetti, dye it different colors and throw it against the wall, where it would stick, making a mural I'm sure Picasso himself would have been proud of.

I put up a pot of water, contemplating blue: sadness, an ocean of tears, Lady Day singing the blues, red roses for a blue lady, that was me all right. Sigh.

Two down, one to go. White. Like every good dyke, I didn't have any white bread, white flour, white sugar or white rice in my cupboard, but I did have that handy dandy item that no lesbian household is complete without: a virgin block of tofu sitting on the top shelf of the fridge in a bowl of water. I chopped it up, thinking about the white: a blank page, empty space, tabula rasa, clean sheets, starting over, yeah.

So I set the table and sat down with my very own red, white and blue meal, feeling angry, empty and sad. To tell you the truth, the plate in front of me wasn't very appealing. I took a bite anyway and smiled. Not too bad, actually. A little chewy maybe, but other than that, okay. After I forced four bites down past the lump in my throat, it hit me: it wasn't just the fourth of July I was celebrating; it was Independence Day. I was celebrating my independence by eating a completely ridiculous meal and the best part about it was I didn't have to explain it or justify it or defend it or hide it or even share it with anyone. I tell you, the fifth bite was delicious and after that the food just started tasting better and better. As a matter of fact, I don't remember spaghetti ever tasting so good. I had seconds and then thirds. I ate it with my fingers, I let the sauce drip down my chin, I picked up the plate, and licked it clean. Yum, yum, yum. My country 'tis of me.

FELICE PICANO

FELICE PICANO is a leader in the modern gay literary movement. Among his works are many novels—both gay and straight—several books of poetry, plays, short stories, a guide to gay sex, and service as a contributor and editor of numerous books. His active involvement in the development of gay presses and a gay literary movement is widely acknowledged. Throughout his life Picano has shaken the status quo. He states in his fictionalized memoirs *Ambidextrous: The Secret Lives of Children:* "I'd already been a fornicator and petty criminal at eleven years old, a drug addict and homosexual at twelve, a seducer, a sexual exhibitionist and successful purveyor of pornography at 13." It seemed only logical he would help create the gay literary genre.

Essay by
MICHAEL A. LUTES

Following two years of service as a social worker in East Harlem, New York, Picano left for Europe "to break all ties and become a homosexual," he perfunctorily states in *Men Who Loved Me.* After his return from Europe he filled managerial positions in several New York bookstores and performed free-lance writing on the side. While working at Rizzoli's Bookstore, he signed on with literary agent Jane Rotrosen. Through her efforts, Picano's first novel, *Smart as the Devil,* was published in 1975. *Smart as the Devil,* an Ernest Hemingway Award finalist, was followed by two other "straight" novels, *Eyes* in 1976, and *The Mesmerist* in 1977. All three were commercial successes. It was not until 1979, however, that Picano "came out" in his first openly gay thriller, *The Lure.* From that point onward, his literary work was dedicated to the advancement of gay literature.

In 1977 Picano founded the first gay publishing house in New York City, SeaHorse Press. He designed the business as a complete gay endeavor. It would publish solely gay literature and would employ only gay bookbinders, typesetters, artists, and distributors. Some of the most prominent gay literary works of the last two decades can be attributed to SeaHorse. Works by Martin Duberman, Dennis Cooper, Gavin Dillard, Brad Gooch, Doric Wilson, and others fill their catalogues. Several years later Picano collaborated with two other small gay presses to form the Gay Presses of New York (GPNY). By the mid-1980s the alliance held

more than 70 gay and lesbian titles in print. One of its most notable books was Harvey Fierstein's *Torch Song Trilogy*. GPNY also published Picano's *Slashed to Ribbons in Defense of Love, and Other Stories* and *Ambidextrous*.

Through his work with SeaHorse and GPNY, Picano was influential in gay literary circles. He met frequently with Edmund White, Robert Ferro, Andrew Holleran, George Whitmore, Michael Grumley, and Christopher Cox. This literary circle became known as the Violet or Lavender Quill Club, the first openly gay author group. The group publicized their books and toured the country promoting them, and its members soon became some of the prominent gay literary figures of the 1980s. From the Violet Quill Club sprang such works as Picano's *Late in the Season* and *An Asian Minor: The True Story of Ganymede*, Ferro's *Family of Max Desir* and *The Blue Star Conspiracy*, Holleran's *Nights in Aruba*, Whitmore's *Confessions of Danny Slocum*, and White's *Boy's Own Story*— as well as numerous others.

The Lure, Picano's quintessential "coming out" novel, succinctly connected his first three straight books, written with a more commercial approach, and his openly gay style that emerged through his affiliation with the Violet Quill Club and SeaHorse. *The Lure* is a fine example of a gay thriller set in Manhattan. The protagonist of the book, Noel Cummings, agrees to act as bait to trap the perpetrator of a series of gay murders. Along the way Cummings discovers his own gay identity. The controversial gay lifestyle of late 1970s New York is openly and unapologetically presented in *The Lure*. As James Levin states in *The Gay Novel in America*, "The theme of coming out was done many times before, but seldom so well as here.... Picano has integrated the homosexual subculture into the traditional thriller." Will Meyerhofer, writing in *Contemporary Gay American Novelists*, finds it to be "the finest example of the gay thriller, a classic."

Picano followed in 1980 with his second gay book, *An Asian Minor*. This was a lighthearted, campy takeoff on a Greek myth. The short novella, with erotic drawings by David Martin, expands the tale from Ovid adding a gay liberation slant. Meyerhofer points out in *Contemporary Gay American Novelists* that this was the first time a Greek myth had been updated with gay sensibility and a high degree of homoeroticism.

Two of the books that Picano is most proud of are his fictionalized memoirs *Ambidextrous: The Secret Lives of Children* in 1985, and *Men Who Loved Me* in 1989. *Ambidextrous* covers his school years from ages 10 to 14, while *Men Who Loved Me* is the author's viewpoint from his early 20s. The books are structured in the style of musical sonatas, complete with variations and fugues. Picano commented in *Contemporary Authors Autobiography Series* that "the books contain all I've learned so far of style, form, and technique in rendering the funny, tragic, sad, frustrating, incomprehensible and ambiguous quotidian of our lives."

Picano's books of poetry, *The Deformity Lover, and Other Poems* and *Window Elegies*, along with other select pieces, express a sense of coming to terms with human nature or contemporary urban living. Many contain autobiographical snippets, often experimental in form, including self interviews, imaginary dialogues, and letters to unknown individuals.

Felice Picano's contribution to contemporary gay literature has been immense. His founding of one of the first gay publishing firms, SeaHorse Press, and his involvement in establishing GPNY have fostered a profound growth in the gay literary genre. Over the course of the last several decades, Picano, along with members of the Violet Quill, has been responsible for some of the most heralded gay literature of the 1980s and 1990s. Picano claimed in *Contemporary Gay American Novelists* that perhaps "the reason I lived through these times, knew these people, suffered these losses, became a writer, is so I might bear witness to that era (of AIDS), these people, and these great losses, and make it literature."

Born: New York City, February 22, 1944.

Education: Queens College of the City University of New York, B.A. 1964.

Career: Social worker, New York City Department of Welfare, New York City, 1964–66; assistant editor, *Art Direction*, New York City, 1966–68; assistant manager, Doubleday Bookstore, New York City, 1969–70; free-lance writer, 1970–72; Rizzoli's Bookstore, New York City, assistant manager and buyer, 1972–74; free-lance writer, 1974–; book editor, *New York Native*, 1980–83.

Founder and publisher of SeaHorse Press Ltd., 1977–; cofounder and copublisher of the Gay Presses of New York, 1980–. Instructor of fiction writing classes, YMCA West Side Y Writers Voice Workshop, 1982–84.

Recipient: Ernest Hemingway Award finalist, c. 1975.

Agents: Jane Berkey (for works published prior to 1992), Jane Rotrosen Agency, 226 East 32nd Street, New York, New York 10016, U.S.A; Malaga Baldi, P.O. Box 591, Radio City Station, New York, New York 10101, U.S.A.

Felice Picano told the *Companion:*

"Gay and lesbian culture has grown so quickly, flourished so, and become so pervasive (and sometimes so important) in our lives that it is very difficult for younger people to realize that it wasn't always there. It wasn't. For those of us who helped to build it, brick by brick, those early, merciless attacks against us and our work in the media (often by closeted gays), the lifelong enmities created, and the continuing closed doors against us in the highest artistic circles are constant reminders of the price we paid for being pioneers. Even worse are those younger lesbians and gays now in power who ignore and overlook us and our work—which is often at its most mature—and who only present their generation. Those who ignore history are doomed to repeat its mistakes."

AUTOBIOGRAPHY, 1991

Reprinted from *Contemporary Authors Autobiography Series*, volume 13, copyright 1991 by Gale Research.

My mother used to tell us stories. Growing up in eastern Queens during the fifties in the midst of a middle-class, television-age, melting-pot neighborhood, my mother used to tell us stories of growing up a generation before in New England.

Her storytelling was immediate and fully recalled—"That reminds me of the time I was working on Westminster Street when the hurricane hit," she'd begin, just like that. It was limpidly related, unbound by extraneous facts or irrelevant information, rising to a climax—"We had to stay in the building all night, without electricity, watching the Providence River rise above the tops of cars. We laughed and lit candles and sang.

But were we scared!" Sometimes she ended with a moral, not always, but you always knew the end—"You can still see the high-water mark from the '38 hurricane on some downtown buildings!"

I knew some characters in her stories: my mother's mother was alive until 1955 and Grandpa outlived her by twenty years. My uncles Billy and George and Rudy visited with their wives and children, as did my mother's nephew Henry, oddly enough her age, who'd been her escort in adolescence. But they had minor roles: my mother's stories were about her boyfriend Bill, whom she always called "Sourpuss," and Clemmy, short from Clementine. My mother had a nickname too—"Anna Banana"—because of the long, drooping curls she'd worn as a girl. And since her stories ranged willy-nilly, day to day, from her earliest years to just before she and my father married, we were sometimes confronted by confusions, mysteries.

How did our parents know each other? Visiting our grandparents in Thornton, Rhode Island, we could see from the second-floor bedrooms our other grandma—Soscia's—chicken coops, vegetable garden, and, hidden in peach trees, her house. My mother sent us to our grandma Soscia's house, though she never went herself. We'd walk down State Street to Fletcher Avenue around the hill. Coming back we'd cut through the connecting gardens and climb the tall, grassy hill, under which lay an old Indian graveyard, where we'd hunt shards and shreds of anything in the least bit old.

We knew our grandparents—adjoining neighbors—weren't friendly. Knew that our parents' marriage was one (but not the only or the earliest) reason why not. That was one mystery.

We knew why Grandma's name was Soscia and not Picano: she'd remarried after her husband died of the Spanish flu in 1918, remarried and had three more children, Betty, Mike, and Little Tony—to distinguish him from Anthony Picano, known as Big Tony. But there was more mystery. My father's stories weren't about growing up in Rhode Island, but in New York: Ozone Park, though his siblings had grown up in Thornton and he'd once been my mother's classmate in an early grade. Why? My father's face would darken when he spoke of his stepfather, a man he hated with an intensity undiminished to this day. So my father's evil stepfather became another character in my mother's stories, with clever, gloomy, fortunate Sourpuss, and humorous, daring, social Clemmy.

When the Second World War was over and gasoline no longer rationed, we'd drive up to Thornton in a new, wooden-backed station wagon, along new highways spun like black ribbons through

Connecticut's green hills, and we'd see and confirm places from my mother's stories—the trolley along Plainfield Street to funny-sounding Onleyville, Farmer Smith's fields stretching for miles, the orchards on the cliff above Atwood Avenue; in Providence itself, we'd play in Roger Williams Park, walk along Broadway, where a great-aunt lived in a huge Victorian house, or ascend Benefit Street on College Hill, where another aunt lived near Brown University, not far from where Poe and H. P. Lovecraft had resided. We'd drive to Barrington, where cousins lived on the waterside, or down to Bristol and Newport, or directly south to Rocky Point Amusement Park and Scarborough Beach, or further to Point Judith and Galilee. We'd even spend a July in a cottage in Petasquammscut, until it seemed we'd reclaimed all our mother's past and then some.

The more we reclaimed, the more the mysteries grew. Who was the boy in that old photo and why would no one speak of him? Who was that Air Force captain in that other photo? Why had we never heard of him? How come, if our mother was engaged to Sourpuss for so many years, she'd ended up marrying our father? Why was it some relatives hadn't spoken to each other in decades? Why was it our father had as a boy gone to live with Aunt Carrie and Uncle Recco? Why did we live not in Rhode Island, but in Queens? Not near my father's uncles and cousins, but an hour away, away from all relatives, at the city line?

I and my older brother and sister and cousins would pool rumors and data and try to figure it out, pushing into that treacherous, ultimately unknowable area of "what grown-ups do"—and why. We seldom came up with the answers.

Now, decades later, I've realized how those daily examples of my mother's storytelling and her sense of the importance of those stories have influenced me, perhaps decided me, to become a writer. Equally, unconsciously, influential for me in terms of *what* I'd write were my attempts to solve those mysteries in and between our parents' families—and our physical distance, even exile, from the rest of them.

I was born in New York City at midnight between the 22nd and 23rd of February in 1944, the third child of Phillip and Anne Picano. I have three birth certificates for two days giving three times. My mother was awake at my birth and said it was just before midnight, and I was the easiest birth of her children despite my size—ten and a half pounds. With my father home asleep, she named me—after my paternal grandfather.

My father had also been Felice, son of Felice, son of Felice, etc., all the way back to mid-nineteenth-century Itria, a mountain town known for olive oil in the province of Roma. In Italy, Felice is a common male name, as I discovered when I lived there; one with literary connotations: poet Felice Romani wrote libretti to operas by Verdi, Bellini, and Donizetti that every Italian knows. My father didn't grow up in Italy, but here, and he'd often fought over his name—in effect over being Italian. He'd legally changed his name. He didn't want any child of his to suffer from the same prejudice.

For my mother, with her New England sense of tradition, a family name, no matter how odd or difficult to bear, must be passed to the next generation. She had a point: after my books were published in England, Argentina, and France, I received letters from Picanos there tracing their lines back to one or another Felice Picano from Itria. And an archeologist placed my family name with geographical exactitude. She'd come across it in a story in an Italian grade-school reader. More recently, in *Smithsonian Magazine*, I found a forebear—Giuseppe Picano. In an essay on Neapolitan wood sculpture in the eighteenth century, art critic Hilton Kramer wrote that Giuseppe had moved from Itria to Naples and for several decades dominated his field with crucifixions, *pietàs*, and carved *baldachins*, some still extant in local churches.

I've never fought over my name: people have been befuddled by it, misspelled and mispronounced it (Fuh-leese is right); people have asked if I'm Spanish or Greek or if it's a *nom de plume*. Due to my name, I've been instantly unique from early on in life. Later I realized being special for a name wasn't enough: spoiled by the attention, I sought a way to solidly earn it.

For my generation, being Italian was limited to a name and a few guarded family recipes my grandma Soscia gave my mother, herself a fine cook with an international cuisine. Being Italian was reduced to biannual visits to my father's relatives in Ozone Park, where Italian was spoken by adults when they didn't want us to know something, and where Uncle Recco read Italian-language newspapers while the tantalizing odors of lemon and anise and hazelnut arose in the kitchen, preceding delicious confections served with tiny cups of *espresso*, candy-covered almonds, and doll-sized glasses of sherry. Catholic icons, calendars, and a cousin who became a nun completed the exoticism of these visits, and we never tired of correcting adults who referred to someone nonItalian as "American," saying, "We're American too. All of us!"

Until I was three years old, we lived in Richmond Hill, Queens, in an apartment above a supermarket my father and my uncle Tony owned and which flourished during the war, even when Tony went off to become a much-decorated hero in the Pacific theater, and despite the fact that (as my parents insisted) they thought black-market sales unpa-

Felice Picano (right) with siblings Carol, Bob, and Jerry, around 1950.

triotic. When the city took over the block to build the Van Wyck Expressway, my father bought land for a store off one new service road, and a house further away, in eastern Queens.

My brother Bob and sister, Carol, two and three years older than me, recall the apartment and store and our neighbors on Liberty Avenue. They recall trolley cars on the street and weekly serial shows on the radio. I don't. My awareness begins later, on long blocks of single and attached houses with front and backyards, grass, bushes, trees, a neighborhood rife with kids on skates and bikes, playing in the street at all seasons of the year, or in furnished basements watching TV. This defines me as Post War, in the van of the largest baby boom in history that would change our country, and eventually the world.

I led a cushioned life until the fourth grade. There, one day, quite by accident, I had my first encounter with unreasoning prejudice, and met my first life enemy.

In the book titled *Ambidextrous: The Secret Lives of Children*, published in 1985, I wrote of this encounter in detail. It centered on my ambidexterity. I'd learned to read and write on my own, using my older siblings' schoolbooks and notebooks. I watched them write and taught myself that, too. My mother—pregnant with my younger brother, Jerry—would correct me. By the age of four I read at first-grade level; when I entered kindergarten, I was reading third-grade books. One reason for my early success in any subject I was interested in was that I'd learned alone, forging my own methods. I used both hands to write and was very fluid in printing and script. I'd begin a sentence with my left hand and continue it with my right hand. In drawing, I'd shade and color-in using two crayons simultaneously.

My fourth-grade teacher, a middle-aged man, opposed my ambidexterity, my creativity, anything in fact but using my right hand. He went further, he used me as an example of everything wrong with a child. The more intolerant he became, the more I resisted. My parents didn't believe me when I told them of his irrational behavior. His persecution worsened. I was appalled by the injustice of my situation, trapped, on my own for the first time in my life. No one, not even my God, seemed able to help me. I began to rebel, in school and out. An explosion between my teacher and I was inevitable and it occurred. I was ten years old. I'd been a perfectly behaved child at home and at school—but when our little war was over, I'd become a monster of egotism and suspicion, filled with hatred.

And I was forever left-handed.

I settled more warily into a new class with a new teacher and got through the next two years easily. Following some quite high IQ tests, I was offered a chance to enter a special program in junior-high school: doubled science, music, art, social studies, two foreign languages, and tons of extracurricular activities. In recompense, we'd be socially and intellectually at the top of the school—and we'd skip the eighth grade!

I found I could learn at this advanced, subject-crammed, condensed level with only a bit more effort, since it depended so much upon autodidacticism, at which I was already a past master.

In *Ambidextrous*, I also wrote about my coming to sexuality, which happened between the ages of ten and thirteen, and involved several neighborhood girls and one boy. My third affair at the age of thirteen, recounted in the book, had more importance in that it led to my first piece of recognized writing, and my first artistic crisis.

The situation, briefly put, was that I realized one day that the surprising sexual relationship I'd been having with our ninth-grade class's "Ice Princess" had been completely set up and was being directed and watched by her father, an optics expert confined at home to a wheelchair by wounds suffered in the war. I ended the relationship.

Shortly later, when our English teacher had us write stories for a city-wide fiction contest, I wrote up what had happened with the girl and her father, greatly toning down the content, but not the situation nor its denouement. My story was much admired and picked to represent our grade in the contest. To my amazement, the story was sent back. The contest committee deemed it disrespectful of adults, in bad taste, overly mature, and even thought it was plagiarized. My teachers and even our dean weren't able to help me.

As a result, I became cynical and hard. It would be another decade and a half before I wrote fiction or showed it to anyone.

I had no special teacher in high school or college who intuited I had what it took to be a good writer and encouraged me.

Dr. Beringause conveyed his love for poetry: his clear, vivid analyses opened up the inner workings of poetry. Dr. Day's course in eighteenth-century British literature was sheer delight due to his legerdemain in making long-dead authors and their writings live again. James Wilhelm's seminar on Dante's work, life, and times was memorably comprehensive.

Though I was an art major—painting, sculpting, making collage—by my junior year I began to minor in cross-departmental literature using my alleged command of foreign tongues. I read six books a week, trying to keep plots and characters of Leskov and Genet apart from those in Henry James, William Faulkner, and Tolstoy.

Three students in most of my lit. courses were Steve, Barry, and Alan, who I joined during breaks between classes talking— arguing—in the "Little Caf," a small, older dining area favored by the bohemian elements on campus at Queens College, among which I suddenly found myself. But no matter how much Pinter or Proust that Alan or Barry or Steven read, they lived for, all but breathed, film. Not "movies," but film—experimental American film and any foreign-language one they could find. For them the novel was dead; literature completely moribund: film was the art form of the future. A few years younger and more restrained, I was less sure.

I had loved movies since I was two years old and awakened in a movie theater, stood on my mother's seat, being bottle-fed and watching Marlene Dietrich as a gypsy wrestle another actress for Gary Cooper in *Golden Earrings*. Now, living in lower Manhattan, I was closest to the cinemas that showed Resnais, Bergman, Fellini, and Mizoguchi: my apartment became a meeting place for the group—one teacher called us the "Hell Fire Club"—and my roommate Michael was also swept up in our cinema-madness.

Graduation neared and I still had no idea what I wanted to do with my life. I'd passed tests for the Peace Corps, but I wavered. The dean of the English department recommended me for a Woodrow Wilson Fellowship. That would mean more school: a masters and Ph.D. degree, then becoming a professor. I didn't think I wanted that. I'd written amusing and original term papers, so I'd been recommended for the Writing Workshop at the University of Iowa, and had been accepted. But Iowa looked so flat, so treeless, and I was so tired of going to school!

That spring, 1964, I'd accompanied my friend Ruth Reisiger when she'd applied for a job with the New York City Department of Social Services. I'd taken the tests and interviews too. Ruth had trained to be a social worker, but I was less altruistic. Even so, when I discovered I'd be able to fulfill my military duty working for the Vista program—an American inner-cities version of the Peace Corps—I took the job.

At twenty, I was by no means a saint, but I'd been touched by several incidents bringing home our nation's social injustice. In 1962, the Black Muslim leader Malcolm X was to speak at Queens College. I knew he'd been a pimp and thief who'd become an eloquent speaker for Negro

Rights (as it was called). One day before his appearance, the college administration cancelled it, calling Malcolm X "detrimental."

The uproar among students was immediate. The school had barred us from our First Amendment rights, although it insisted it was acting "in loco parentis"—in the place of a parent—protecting us.

In the sixties, Queens had as intellectual and liberal a faculty as any college in the country. They agreed it was a free-speech issue and joined our protest. When the administration failed to restore Malcolm X's speaking date, we organized a boycott of classes, marching around the campus's main quad with signs, chanting slogans, filling up the dean's office. The boycott spread to the rest of the City University system. We were assailed on all sides—our education was paid for by city taxes!—but we held firm, and the administration was embarrassed into letting Malcolm X speak. To my knowledge this was the first such student action in the country.

One result was that the implicit racism of the school, the city government, much of the public and the press was made explicit. The college's Student National Coordinating Committee chapter grew in size and activism. We organized sit-ins at lunch counters in the tri-state area where we heard of de facto segregation. I joined, was arrested, and experienced firsthand the oiled heat of bigotry. That summer and the next, SNCC sent students down South to enroll Black voters. I had to earn my living and didn't go. One pal and classmate, Andrew Goodman, did go—and paid with his life.

Despite this background, by the time my two year "hitch" as social worker was over, I'd become disillusioned: I could only see the program's lacks and failures. Oddly, others thought I did a great job: they wanted to promote me, to pay my tuition to get a graduate degree in social work.

This was also a time of personal crises—among them my need to investigate my sexuality more fully, which I knew would be difficult to do in the sexually repressive U.S. I quit work and went to Europe.

In the second volume of my memoirs, I've written in detail about this period and of my return. I merely note here that I returned to a new apartment in Greenwich Village, a new group of friends, mostly involved in the arts, and mostly homosexual. Nineteen sixty-six to 1971 were to be my years of experimentation: with different groups of people, lifestyles, sexual and other relationships—and with psychedelic drugs.

Several people I met in this time influenced me greatly: among them the painter Jay Weiss, the writer Joseph Mathewson, the actor George Sampson, and Arnie Deerson. We—and others—were drawn by the charisma and generosity of Jan Rosenberry and formed a sort of group in 1968 and 1969. Jan was an advertising executive who tried to close the gap between the corporate world and rock music by befriending musicians and inviting them into TV commercials. Jan also opened his Manhattan flat to many people. It became a second home for some, an urban commune. His generosity toward me lay in his encouragement and his intelligent enthusiasm over any piece of writing—no matter how small or shallow—I showed him.

I'd written one story since the ill-fated one in junior high. In the "catalogue of my works," begun in 1974, it's listed as "Untitled: approx. 2,000 words, set in Cape Cod," with "artist from New York, and pre-teen local child" as characters. The subject is "betrayal." The entry reads: "August, 1966—MS missing. No typed copy." I.e. lost. I haven't a clue what it could be about.

As a social worker I'd written case histories, one of them complex enough to end up in the teaching manual. My next job was as a junior editor at a graphic-arts magazine. But there my writing was ephemeral, even the feature articles not worth saving. My next job was at a bookstore. As was the next. At the latter store I wrote an introduction to an exhibit of Jiri Mucha's works—and an interview with the Czech artist's son translated from the French, the only language we more or less shared.

My little catalogue shows other works I'd deemed important: one-act comedies written in the summer of 1968, with titles like "The Persistence of Mal-Entendu," and that fall, an unfinished novella that would become the seed upon which I built a career.

I was overqualified and overcompetent for any job I might land. It never failed—within months I'd be told I was the best employee, pushed into promotion, into pension plans and stock-sharing, my future in the company all laid out.

No way! I saw this period differently: as a time of testing and tasting and trying out. I would work as long as needed to save enough money to cover six to nine months of bills. Then I'd quit, giving as much advance warning as possible.

If asked, I'd say I was becoming a writer and needed time. And it's true that during these hiatuses from employment I taught myself the rudiments of poetry. I'd analyze, say, metaphor, then write a poem stressing metaphor—any topic would do—metaphor was what counted. Or I'd study form, say Spenserian Rhyme Royal, and use it to write a poem about my coffee cup or the first telephone call of the day—anything! Ditto with drama or comedy: I'd take any situation and turn it into a fifteen-page play. I'd even use authors I was reading, turn them into characters—with appalling results!

What I mostly did between stints of work was read, listen to music, go to movies and concerts, hang around with friends—anything but write. When a friend said it was an excuse for not working, for not tying myself to the "establishment," I couldn't deny it.

In the late winter of 1971, I was twenty-seven years old. I'd travelled, I'd had adventures, I'd lived in a variety of places among an assortment of people. A few months earlier I'd left the first bookstore I'd worked at, not only earlier than intended, but somewhat under a cloud, and with less savings than I would have liked. At the same time, a complicated and emotionally wrought romance with the late painter Ed Armour had begun to distort into something even more incomprehensible and unsatisfactory: I saw no way out but to end the relationship.

It was in this state of virtually total life crisis that I decided to become a writer. I dared myself: I staked everything on it.

I looked through notebooks and diaries, read scraps of plays and stories and finally lit on the 1968 novel fragment. After some scrutiny it seemed to hold up. A bit of thought and I began to outline it more fully. Amazement! I found I had characters, a plot, scenes, everything! As pieces of the novel began to fall into place in my outline I became excited. Certain scenes played themselves out in my mind—I could hear what my characters were saying to each other, could feel as they did, could see, smell, taste, know what it was like to *be* them.

Halfway through the outline, I threw it away and bought a hardcover notebook. I recopied the opening pages of the fragment from years before, crossed it out and began again. It took ten tries but I finally found the first line I wanted, then the first paragraph, the first page, the first chapter.

I wrote continuously after that, daily, whenever I could, whenever I wanted to. Late into the night sometimes, playing Bach's *Well-Tempered Clavier* on the stereo, letting his sense of structure and rhythm and Wanda Landowska's style subconsciously influence my own. When Bach became too rigid or monochrome, I'd switch to Solomon playing Beethoven's piano sonatas, or to Cortot's Chopin mazurkas.

Keyboard music—because the protagonist of my novel was a pianist. He'd been a child prodigy before the turn of the century, the toast of Europe in short pants, playing for Paderewski, Brahms, Sauer, Liszt. Now, in his mid-twenties, living in New York, he'd returned to playing. A college acquaintance came to a recital and asked him to record for his new cylinder company. At the same time my protagonist had met a young European couple: a beautiful, charming, brilliant duo filled with extraordinary ideas, capable of anything!

My novel was unusual in other ways. It was set in New York of 1913, on the eve of the First World War. All that I'd read of that period's avant-garde convinced me that it was not too different than the late sixties I'd just gone through: bohemian life-styles, controversial art movements, experimentation with life-styles, sex, drugs. The young Hesse, Gide, and Ezra Pound seemed more my contemporaries than my grandparents—the half-century between their blossoming and my life a stupid waste filled with world wars.

It's not difficult to recall what writing that first novel was like for me: the same excitement, the same depth of concentration, the same trancelike, out-of-time sense that I'm on another plane of existence happens whenever I'm truly involved in writing. In an interview I once said that writing was one of the three physical/mental/emotional highs of my life—along with sexual climax and using LSD-25—and the only sustainable one.

One thrill in writing this first book was being in such full command of a fictional world that when I needed a minor character, one simply appeared at the tip of my pen, with her own personal quirks and demeanor, dress and history. I wondered how long this unexpectedly Olympian power could last.

Working at top speed to avoid its collapse, I completed a first draft in two months: a record I would never surpass, especially given that the ms. was 150,000 words long. I read it over, made notes for emendations, then typed a second draft over the next six weeks. On May 20 of 1971, I had two copies of a readable ms. in hand. I'd titled it *Narrative and Curse*, after the scene in Wagner's opera *Tristan and Isolde*, performed during the novel's climax.

I'd not told anyone what I was doing. Jan, Arnie, most of my friends from the Twelfth Street commune, had moved to California. I knew only one person with enough experience, savvy, and connections to help me if what I'd written was at all good. I'd met Jon Peterson a few years before through Jay Weiss. He was intelligent, clever, and sophisticated: he'd produced plays off-Broadway, and introduced the actor Al Pacino. I phoned Jon and said I'd written a novel and needed an agent.

Jon was cautious. He would read the ms. first. He warned me not to be surprised if the agent turned it down. He was right in trying to calm me. But Jon read the novel quickly—and he loved it! He immediately got it to an agent friend, along with all of his enthusiasm. The agent read it and decided to represent my work.

In four months, I'd changed my life. Or so I thought.

By the time my savings ran out, my book still hadn't sold. I took part-time work and tightened my belt. As editor after editor turned it down, I saw I'd have to find a job. Through Dennis Sanders's recommendation I began work that fall at Rizzoli Bookstore.

Unlike the other bookstore I'd worked at, Rizzoli was unique. Truly international, its employees had to speak one or more foreign languages fluently. As a result our staff was unusual, many foreign-born, or Americans brought up abroad: many younger ones were biding their time while awaiting a break in their true careers as writers, painters, musicians—our manager had trained as a concert pianist. After I'd been there some months they seemed like a family—caring and close, but also emotional and irrational. Working at Rizzoli could be like a party where business also happened; at other times it was like being caught in the final act of some demented nineteenth-century opera.

After a year, my agent returned my ms. to me, unable to sell it. I was disappointed, but continued to work at the bookstore, and write.

Writing this novel had been creatively explosive: as though I'd been chock-filled with poems, stories, essays, plays, films, entire novels trying to get out. Among them would be my first published story, poem, and novel. But I'm getting ahead of myself.

For the next two and a half years I continued at Rizzoli, moving steadily upward in its hierarchy—my usual course—and becoming steadily discouraged about finding a new agent or selling my novel. One poem I wrote in this time is titled "The Waiting Room," which pretty much sums up how I felt—on the brink of, but held back.

Our children's book manager, Alex Mehdevi, had written and published *Tales from Majorca,* folk stories from his homeland. When I told Alex of my frustration at being unpublished he was kind enough to have his own literary agent read my novel.

Jane Rotrosen phoned me before she'd even finished reading my ms. The title should be changed, she said, and she had other minor suggestions but she agreed to represent the book—even with its previous history! She spoke fast and made an appointment for us to meet.

The Kurt Hellmer Literary Agency office on Vanderbilt Avenue was a warren of small, dark rooms filled with manuscripts and shelvesful of books. Jane and I went to the Pan Am Building, where we sat thirty floors above Park Avenue and she talked about my novel with all the detail, expertise, immediacy, and enthusiasm I could hope for. As soon as I made those minor changes, she would send out the book. We sealed the deal with a handshake—and Jane has been my literary agent ever since.

Months went by, yet no editors seemed willing to take the ms. Jane couldn't get a fix on why not. Was it too new? Its combination of fictional world, characters, and style *too* different?

In February of 1974, Jane took me to dinner for my thirtieth birthday. My novel remained unsold. Meanwhile at Rizzoli, I'd been promoted to store manager and my boss had just explained the company's expansion plans, and my role in them. I'd said what I'd told each employer—I was a writer: the first book contract I got, I would leave. He and I knew the chances of this happening diminished daily. His offer included salaries and positions beyond my expectations. I told Jane this and of the decision I faced: I wanted to be a professional writer!

We returned to my apartment and Jane asked what was in the notebooks atop my nonworking fireplace. Unfinished works. She went through them, and stopped at the outline and opening chapters of a novel I'd titled *Who Is Christopher Darling?*

I'd begun it in the summer of 1972, basing it on the Greek myth of Phaeton—son of Apollo who'd driven his father's chariot across the heavens far too close to the sun, and who had to be destroyed. My updating retained the allegory with a sharp twist, and it was told as a psychological thriller. Its ideas reflected my interest in child prodigies and savants, and in the language and mores of Elizabethan and Jacobean England.

Jane thought it publishable. If I wrote up a fuller outline detailing characters and scenes, she'd get it to editors already intrigued with my work.

In a few weeks Don Fine, publisher of Arbor House, signed me to finish the novel. It was to be retitled *Smart as the Devil*, a more commercial title, he and Jane thought (I didn't). I'd receive an advance against royalties large enough to pay my bills while I left my job and wrote the book. My boss was surprised when I told him all this but the money involved was so small he gave me leave and agreed to keep all our future plans open.

From March through early October of 1974, I worked on the novel, moving out to Fire Island Pines that summer into a cottage I shared with Jon Peterson and two new friends, lovers named Nick Rock and Enno Poersch. As they all worked part- or full-time, I had the place to myself and was able to make real progress. I wrote two drafts, revised a bit after Jane had read it, and again after Don Fine read it.

Smart as the Devil was published by Arbor House on February 28, 1975, my mother's birthday. It wasn't given a large printing, and was not well advertised or promoted. It was excellently if not extensively reviewed, picked by the Mystery Guild book club, and paperback rights were sold to Dell, giving me somewhat more income. The book became one of five finalists for the Ernest Hemingway Award—for the best first novel of the year—partly due to the uniqueness of entire sections having been written in seventeenth-century English. It didn't get the award, but the nomination gave my reputation a boost.

I returned to Rizzoli after finishing the novel, but I had a new book I was eager to write, based on a personal experience. When I'd returned from Europe I'd moved into a studio apartment in the "Village," its two windows facing the street. One night, I got a phone call from a young woman. After a variety of questions and answers, it turned out I didn't know her.

She knew me, plenty about me, virtually everything about me! It took a while to figure it out; then I realized, she had binoculars—I was being watched! Whenever she phoned after that, I tried to elicit information from her—I'd lived in London too! I found out little. One night a young woman slept over with me. The next day my voyeur phoned: her words and tone of voice angry and bitter. I found that odd, given how flip she'd been about the many more young men who'd slept over. When I pointed this out, she said it was because she didn't take the men seriously as rivals.

Clearly this went beyond sport: she'd developed a fantasy life about me. I was flattered—and freaked! As a social worker I sought help for her. She refused and threatened blackmail. I said I didn't care who knew what I did in my own home. I warned her not to call anymore—it was harassment, a Federal offense. From then until I moved, I would flinch every time my phone rang—was it her?—even though I'd changed my phone number and it wasn't listed. I kept my window shades down, but I felt aware at all times that I was being watched—that I might be in danger.

But I wondered what would have happened if I'd been different: if I'd been a young man as needy of a relationship as she seemed to be. What if the relationship had bloomed, became complicated by hidden neuroses, even psychoses in her and by his growing determination to know who she was and to find her?

That was the basis of *Eyes*, which Jane, Don Fine, and Linda Grey, the editor at Dell who'd bought *Smart as the Devil*, all liked. I sold it on several chapters and an outline and wrote it during the summer and fall of 1975.

Eyes was published in 1976, following a falling out with my publisher. Editing my ms., he'd excised a short chapter describing a crucial secondary character. I deemed it necessary to give weight and color to this character, whose role was almost that of a fairy-tale witch in what was an otherwise minutely realistic narrative. When the book was published, I found out he'd not put back the chapter and I broke off relations. My editor at Dell agreed to replace the chapter and it first appeared in the paperback edition.

This second published novel was well received, sold better than my first, got more attention—reviews from several women's magazines—and earned higher book club, paperback, and foreign advances. As the book became read by more people, I realized that in attempting to investigate an incident in my own past, I'd come to symbolize in my female voyeur the questions so many young women were facing themselves—how they could be equal to men yet still feminine; how be sexual and emotional yet intelligent; how be themselves yet appropriate companions.

When the paperback was published in 1977, Peter Caras's artwork—a woman's hands in close-up, holding binoculars through which a half-naked man can be seen looking back—was stunning and appropriate. It helped the book become a best-seller, though word-of-mouth played an even larger role.

Eyes sold well here and in England until quite recently. It was translated into French, German, Spanish, Portuguese, and Japanese. Several television and filmmakers were interested in it, and it was under option for over a decade. Even so, the "unhappy" ending—the only realistic one for the story—kept it from being produced. That and the fact that a woman's p.o.v. is required to make it work. I'd suffered over that while writing the book: had to, in effect, become a mentally disturbed woman to have it come out without compromise or faked emotion.

Even before *Eyes* was published I'd begun another novel. Some years before, a friend, Nunzio D'Anarumo, avid collector of Cupids and haunter of antique stores, sent me a copy of a New York *Telegraph* from St. Patrick's Day, 1900. The paper was yellowing and cracked but one front page article couldn't fail to catch my attention, accompanied as it was by a dramatic drawing of a man shooting a pistol in a crowded court building.

"Prosecutor Shoots Defendant!" The headline was datelined the previous day from a large city in Nebraska. I read it with interest and found it strange yet very much of its time and place. I put the aged newspaper away and thought I'd forget it.

The story continued to haunt me. Partly because it was bizarre and sensational: it wasn't every day a noted lawyer attacked the man he was prosecuting for conspiracy and murder. Partly because of the characters: the defendant was shady. He'd once used hypnotism for "painless dentistry" in the poorer section of town but had become influential through his connection with a woman—beautiful, wealthy, and recently widowed under odd circumstances. As intriguing were minor characters: the dead husband; his housekeeper; the handsome con man's old assistant. I found it easy to assess the social and business classes of a Midwest boomtown; its mores and its amusements.

I mentioned it to my agent, who thought it had possibilities. I began to research the story and discovered it had been written up in many national papers of its day and in even greater detail in Midwestern ones. The more I read, the more bizarre the story, its major and minor characters and their relationships became. I was certain I had a classic American tale: one never told before. My plan was to go to Nebraska and research the book where it happened then write it up as a nonfiction novel, the form popularized by Truman Capote.

Almost immediately, I hit snags. The town hall with the trial records had burned down in 1910. No local and no state library had existed to keep copies. Only one newspaper of the time was still in business and its archives didn't go back that far. The state's Historical Society forwarded data to me—it was jejune: I wanted those aspects of character and motive I thought essential for a book. I tried contacting survivors of the families involved but they wrote back saying either they wouldn't help or knew nothing.

After a time, I was able to put together my own idea of what had happened in that Nebraska town three quarters of a century before; not only during the course of the trial, but in the years before—and after.

I knew it contained mystery and color and humanity—enough for a good novel! That's what I'd write. I pored over letters and diaries of the year for the spoken tongue, then medical journals for what was known about psychology and how it was discussed by those who practiced it—*crucial* to my story. I even consulted a specialist in Territorial and Early State Law at the A.L.A. to get the correct trial law.

I wrote the novel throughout 1976. *The Mesmerist* was published by Delacorte in September of 1977, with excellent cover art—again by Peter Caras—which also appeared on the paperback. My original title was "The Mesmerist and Mrs. Lane," which I still think superior. *The Mesmerist* was chosen as an Alternate Selection by the Literary Guild. It was better promoted and advertised than my previous books, more widely and better reviewed. It sold triple the earlier books in hardback but eventually less in paperback—*Eyes* was such a runaway seller. *The Mesmerist* was translated into six languages and published widely abroad. The biggest immediate change for me was that I'd sold hardcover and paper-

Felice Picano at a publicity tour in Los Angeles, 1979.

back rights to Delacorte/Dell and in England and come up with a big enough sum for me to quit work at Rizzoli, move into a larger flat, keep a summer place myself, travel, even invest.

By mid-1978, I was launched as a writer. Bookstores held fifty-unit displays of my recent books. Even so, my first novel languished in a drawer, unpublished, unread, and I couldn't understand why.

I was leading a double life—at least in publication.

Since my return from Europe in the late sixties I'd been living in Greenwich Village: my associations predominantly gay men. After the Stonewall Riot of 1969, the Village became a mecca for lesbians and gays. Stonewall had begun as another police raid upon another Village gay bar. For many gays, fed up with outmoded laws and constant harassment, it was the last straw. Once word spread, the raid became a pitched battle on the streets in which police were outnumbered, overwhelmed, and humiliated. Riot squads were required to keep the peace in the area the entire following week. The true importance of the event became clear the day after the raid when a thousand gays—myself and my friends among them—gathered at Sheridan Square to protest the harassment. Protests continued, a political-action group formed—the Gay Liberation Front—and eventually splintered to include the more radical Gay

Activists Alliance. Within weeks, a political agenda was devised. The GAA began to meet, ironically, in a former firehouse on Greene Street: a minority had begun to empower itself.

And to celebrate itself. If Black was Beautiful! as the slogan had it, then Gay was Proud! Weekly meetings at the Firehouse were attended by larger groups and ended in a dance, helping to attract, centralize, and allow people to celebrate themselves. Out of the Firehouse rose other, less political gay and lesbian clubs. The first totally gay dance club was the Tenth Floor, a "private party" stressing Black and Latin Rock and Soul music in Manhattan's West Twenties, which attracted a crowd involved in music, design, and fashion. This same group had begun to transform Fire Island Pines into a stylish, unambiguously gay resort.

By 1975, a new gay social set had emerged, quite different from "Activists" with their academic and political background. Defined by membership in the arts, the media, recording and design professions, it was known as the "Pines-Flamingo Nexus," after the resort and the new discotheque with its five hundred members that had become its Manhattan center. This small, homogenous, sophisticated, self-conscious group began many trends in the next decade in fashion, music, and social behavior. Their imprint on gay life was instant, long-lasting, and ultimately international.

Some feared such "ghetto-ization," ergo the proliferation of more heterogenous clubs—among them Le Jardin, Twelve West, the Paradise Garage, Les Mouches, and Studio 54. The latter, Steve Rubell and Ian Schrager's glitzy club, caught the public's imagination, and soon designers, movie stars, and Social Register hopefuls were joining gays on its dance floor and in its lounges—and in summer, crowding the Botel and Sandpiper at Fire Island Pines. This same mixture of gays, jet-setters, entertainers, personalities, and talent formed a highly creative social and artistic community that gave the seventies a distinctive high-gloss style, culminating in the "Beach" party of 1979, a charity drive at the Pines that commanded a full page of the "Society" section of the *New York Times* the following day.

I'd become a part of this group almost from its inception: in Manhattan as a member of the dance clubs, in the Pines as a full-time summer resident from 1975 on. Since others were offering their photography, music, sculpture, illustration, and design, I decided to offer my poetry and fiction.

Magazines of gay writing had begun: Andrew Bifrost's *Mouth of the Dragon* in New York, and Winston Leyland's *Gay Sunshine Press* in San Francisco. Even Manhattan's *Gaysweek* began a bi-monthly "Arts and

Letters" section. Most of my earliest published poems and short stories appeared in these journals. Other gay magazines were *Fag Rag* and *Gay Community News* in Boston, *Body Politic* in Toronto, *New York City News, Christopher Street,* the *Native, Mandate, Stallion, Blueboy* et al. in New York, the *Advocate* and *Drummer* in California. I wrote for them all—reviews, poems, stories, essays.

I—and other writers—began to give readings of poetry and fiction at the newly started lesbian/gay groups mushrooming on campuses at Hunter College, Columbia, Princeton, and Stanford universities.

A question now arose: I had a book of poetry, another volume of short stories, all written out of and addressing my experiences as a gay man: how could I get these books out where they could be read?

The answer, according to my agent Jane, my editor Linda, and my friend Susan Moldow, who also worked in book publishing, was that I couldn't! Few gay-themed books were published—and they had always been special: Vidal's novel, Rechy's *City of Night,* Isherwood's *Single Man,* Baldwin's *Giovanni's Room.* No one could live off writing them, and no publisher would put out books by unknown gay writers, dramatists, or—heaven forbid!—poets. I was told to forget it, told to do what gay writers had done for years: keep them to myself, and continue writing nongay novels.

That struck me as unfair; worse, as usufructage; even a species of slavery. I'd begin my *own* publishing house and publish *nothing* but the work of gays. I'd hire, utilize, and work only with gays—artists, typesetters, printers, binders, distributors. I'd stock my books in lesbian/gay-owned bookstores. The company would be called the SeaHorse Press—named after the marine species in which the male bears and gives birth—and I felt it would work.

SeaHorse Press's first title was my *Deformity Lover and Other Poems*—chosen because the author didn't have to be paid. George Stavrinos's cover illustration and the high quality of all aspects of the book got it noticed. In the gay media, reviews were lengthy and laudatory—from its first line, the book *assumed* the reader and writer shared the gay experience and went on from there to detail and particularize that world. Critics also appreciated the book's range of styles and forms: lyric, epistle, ode, sonnet, dramatic monologue were all represented.

When the book was reviewed by nongay media, the reaction was far more mixed—some tried to but were unable to hide their prejudice. For others it was simply too different, too alien. One bright woman poet couldn't grasp why I would opt for rhythms that sounded to her like "popular music: phonograph songs!"—which was *exactly* what I wanted.

The poet/translator Richard Howard encouraged me, and the late Howard Moss, poetry editor of the *New Yorker,* thought the work strong and asked to see new poems; but he could never bring himself to publish any of my gay work. Others invited me to send work to those many small poetry quarterlies that seem to define American verse today.

I continued to write poetry and many newer poems were published in magazines and anthologies—a high-school textbook published one I thought fairly gay, "Gym Shorts," to illustrate "image."

Gym Shorts

You really look good in those gym shorts
now that they're worn
and you're filled out to fit them
so manly.
You used to look good way back then, too.
Was it ten years ago?
That long?

Yes. I saw the games. I was watching.
Watching those gym shorts
grip muscled sides
as you dribbled and sped
playing king of the court.
Watched how the gold stripe you alone wore
marked you apart from the bodies rising
when you netted the ball
as if picking a rose.
How your shorts sort of fluttered
against trembling thighs
when you sprang to the floor
and ceiling spotlights stroked you.

You were sweat and smiles and modest lies
leaning on the railing
at halftime.
You shivered. So I loaned you my coat.
You thanked me.
Those gym shorts were new then,
shining blue
like children's Christmas wishes.

FELICE **PICANO**   399

Three poems appeared in *The Oxford Book of Homosexual Verse*. I've only had one more book of poems published, a chapbook, *Window Elegies*, by the Close Grip Press at the University of Alabama in 1986, but I was pleased and honored to read it at the Poetry Society of America, a usually less adventuresome organization.

SeaHorse Press, however, was launched. Especially as my book went through four printings. The second title was *Two Plays by Doric Wilson*, the third, *Idols*, poems by the talented Dennis Cooper, then Kevin Esser's man-boy love novel *Streetboy Dreams*. Clark Henely's hilarious *Butch Manual* became a best-seller, and in 1980 I edited an anthology of poetry, drama, and fiction by lesbians and gay men, *A True Likeness*.

As the press continued to grow, so did its list—Alan Bowne's play *Forty-Deuce*, a collection of stories by Brad Gooch, *Jailbait* (cover photo by Robert Mapplethorpe), poetry by Robert Peters, Rudy Kikel, Gavin Dillard, and Mark Ameen, George Stambolian's interviews, *Male Fantasies Gay Realities*, and a translation from the French of gay novelist Guy Hocquenghem's novel *Love in Relief*. Later on, I'd use the prestigious SeaHorse imprint on titles I would edit for Gay Presses of New York—our reprint of the 1933 Charles Henri Ford/Parker Tyler novel *The Young and Evil* and Martin Duberman's *About Time: Exploring the Gay Past*.

The SeaHorse Press turned out to be a great deal of work, fun, and a way to meet lesbian and gay authors all over. But it didn't solve the problem of writing gay material and getting it to a wide readership.

While writing *The Mesmerist*, I was approached by a film producer at Universal Studios who wanted me to write a gay-themed movie. His idea was for me to explore the darker side of gay life in Manhattan. He offered a single image which, while striking, ended up remaining unused. There was a basis to his idea. Arthur Bell, openly gay columnist for the *Village Voice*, had been writing a series on several bizarre and grisly murders of gay entrepreneurs. Bell was chasing leads and tying together clues when his life was threatened; he stopped the series.

Through my own contacts, I could go further: sex partners, acquaintances, and a close friend worked in the hierarchy of discos, bars, bathhouses, and private sex clubs which had sprung up in Chelsea. I began to ask questions and what I discovered began to intrigue me.

A former lover, the playwright Bob Herron, was a community leader in the Village through the Jane Street Block Association. He told me of an undercover unit of the New York City Police Department formed to investigate the seemingly related murders Bell had reported. I met a member of this unit who answered some of my questions. Shortly after, the unit was disbanded. It was supposed to be investigated itself, but that never happened.

I had more than enough material and some of it was very hot. But I knew that presenting as factual what I'd found out would lead to death threats or worse: I'd fictionalize it. I put together an outline and got it to the film producer.

He was horrified. It was so gay, so raw, so disturbing and violent he could barely read my outline. No doubt, he was being realistic about its chances of being filmed in a homophobic industry. Upon my return from California I mentioned the outline to my editor, Linda Grey, who read it and, bless her, said, "It'll be a terrific book!" I wrote a single, gripping, opening chapter and Delacorte bought it.

The Lure was my fourth published novel, my most controversial, and until recently the best known. Someone recently called it "pulp." Someone else "a cult classic," which seems pretentious yet in terms of sales and influence isn't inaccurate. The hardcover was well packaged, promoted, and advertised and it was the first gay-themed book sold by the Literary Guild: an Alternate Selection. It sold very well in hardcover and paperback and was translated into many languages. Its greatest foreign success was in Germany, where it sold steadily for a decade under the title *Gefangen in Babel*. "Warning: Explicit Sex and Violence," the ad read for the book club advertising *The Lure*: and it's true, I've never written anything quite like it again and have resisted all requests and demands for a sequel or to have it made into a film.

I wrote it in Manhattan and at Fire Island Pines throughout 1978. A long time, given how tightly plotted the book is and how fast it reads: many people told me they were up all night reading it. Author Edmund White called it "hallucinatory—as though one were drugged."

Some gays hated *The Lure*—and me—for its uncompromising portrait of the sleazier scenes that had arisen out of Gay Liberation, of which few political activists were proud. To them, I was washing dirty laundry in public. Worse, I was providing damaging confirmation to those opposing gay rights. At the least I was betraying the movement.

My intentions were different: I'd wanted the reader—gay or not, male or female, young or old—to share what it was like being gay in Manhattan: experiencing fear, doubt, the constant questioning of one's own and everyone else's motives, yet joy and camaraderie and love too; and always, motiveless bigotry and hatred.

Most nongay reviews (*The Lure* was reviewed widely) and the mail I received confirmed that I'd succeeded in that task. No matter how badly I portrayed some gays or some aspects of gay life in the novel, no matter how thin a slice of gay life I'd concentrated on, I'd drawn it richly, in the round, sympathetically, and without the usual knee-jerk judgementalism. And I'd portrayed those arrayed against gays worse: irrational, ruthless, often deadly. Years later when *The Lure* was being used in college courses about minorities or about psychology or even about urban life, I knew my critics had been wrong: I felt justified.

I'd also achieved something else. With *The Lure's* success I'd tied together that work I'd been publishing—classed as "commercial fiction" despite that Hemingway Award nomination—with my own private life and interests. It was the first time these two disparate, even opposing, forces would come together for me—and to date, the last!

I'd met Edmund White socially in 1976. He'd just published *The Joy of Gay Sex* with Charles Silverstein, but I admired more White's stories and his earlier novel, *Forgetting Elena*. I'd also met George Whitmore around this time, and we became friends. George told me of a remarkable novel he'd read in galleys. Titled *Dancer from the Dance*, the new book was about the Pines-Flamingo crowd by an unknown author—Andrew Holleran. I read it and confirmed for myself his talent and the book's truth, humor, and brilliance. A few weeks later, at a party at the Pines, I was introduced to Holleran: we've been good friends ever since.

Dancer was published in the autumn of 1978. My *Deformity Lover* had come out earlier that year, as had a fascinating nonfiction book, *After Midnight*, by Michael Grumley, author of *Hard Corps*, a study of the S/M leather scene. Michael's lover, Robert Ferro, had published a short enigmatic novel, *The Others*, in 1977. George Whitmore was writing poetry and articles. Edmund's lover, Chris Cox, was compiling an oral history of Key West. In the spring of 1979, White's *Nocturnes for the King of Naples* was published; that autumn my novel *The Lure*.

In the following months, we seven were constantly thrown together within the gay cultural scene and found out we shared many interests. I don't recall who suggested we meet on a regular basis to read and discuss our work. I know the first meeting was held at George's apartment on Washington Square. Casually, later on, we came up with a name—the Violet Quill Club—sometimes called the Lavender Quill Club.

No matter how light-hearted we were in talking about it, once together we were in earnest. We'd seen what happened to gay writers before us who'd not been able to write about the gay experience, forced to tailor their talent to the heterosexual majority—William Inge, Thornton Wilder, Tennessee Williams, Truman Capote, Edward Albee. Few of those who had succeeded in what Roger Austen called "Playing the Game" for the sake of their careers had escaped personal damage:

alcoholism, psychosis, self-destruction, suicide. We refused to take that route, even though (especially for Edmund White and myself) a public coming out might well mean the destruction of our careers.

We knew not to expect our work to be critiqued fairly, even competently. The literarily powerful *New York Times* was virulently homophobic and reviews of gay-themed books were openly hostile, often written by "closeted" gay writers. But our books were sympathetically reviewed elsewhere, and other writers worked quietly in our cause.

Yet with public criticism on such a simplistic level, we lacked that dialogue we needed to grow in our work. The Violet Quill Club would provide it, as well as occasional technical aid in the niceties of prose fiction. We discovered we were all writing some sort of autobiography, but besides individual tales of growing up and "coming out" we hoped our gay-themed work could be enlarged to treat the "big" themes that have always attracted writers—love, death, how to live one's life.

Through appearances in *Christopher Street* and the *New York Native*, we became known as a group to other gay writers. As a group, we strengthened each other individually and began to wield influence. Those who admired our writing or our uncompromising stance called us the New York School. Those who felt excluded or threatened called us the Gay Literary Mafia. Many younger writers have told me that our work and our publicity lessened their own fear of ostracism and helped them define themselves as gay writers.

Our meetings were neither regular nor often: in all, no more than eight times over a year and a half. Like all groups with strong egos, the VQ Club eventually ended. With one exception, we all remained friends. In some cases even closer friends. In the years since, we would often meet together for "tea" or spend weekends at the Ferro family summer place on the Jersey shore, which we jokingly renamed "Gaywyck."

As of this writing—summer 1990—only three of us are still alive, and one of those three is infected: AIDS has taken and continues to take its toll. But the group's importance should continue to live on. The curators of the American Literature Collection at the Beinecke Library at Yale University believe the VQ Club to have been the key group in producing, popularizing, and legitimizing gay fiction in America: they are collecting our manuscripts and papers.

The VQ Club was responsible for an efflorescence of new books by its members, among them White's *Boy's Own Story* and *The Beautiful Room is Empty*, Ferro's *Family of Max Desir* and *The Blue Star*, Cox's *Key West*, Holleran's *Nights in Aruba*, Grumley's *Life-Drawing*, and Whitmore's *Confessions of Danny Slocum* and *Nebraska*. I'd completed my novel *Late in the Season* (1981) when we began to meet, but my novella *An Asian Minor: The True Story of Ganymede* (1981), and several short stories which I eventually collected, were written or rewritten for VQ Club meetings. Our discussions gave me enough confidence to later write more autobiographical works.

Late in the Season was published by Delacorte, although with a tenth of the attention given *The Lure*—because it was a "smaller" book. It was in fact something new: an "idyll," a love story about two attractive, successful middle-class gay men during one late summer month as their "marriage" is tested by, among other things, one of them having an affair with a young woman.

I'd written the book from a double p.o.v. as I had in *Eyes,* and in a way, it's a companion piece to that book. Except that it's a series of prose poems: aquarelles, even. It opens like this:

> It was a perfect day for composing. The morning mist had finally burned off the ocean, unfurling the blue sky like a huge banner of victory. Kites were fluttering at various levels of the warm, balmy air. From down the beach came the sweet-voiced distortions of childrens' cries in play—the last children of the season—adding extra vibrancy to their sounds, piercing the scrim of post-Labor-Day-weekend silence that had softly dropped a week ago. Already the first dying leaves of an autumn that came early to the seashore and would blaze madly for a mere month of picture-book beauty had flung themselves at the glass doors this morning. They had saddened Jonathan then, perched over his large mug of coffee, feeling the hot sun on his closed eyelids. But now the morning felt so clear and sunny, so absolutely cloudless, he felt he might strike it with the little glass pestle in the dining room bowl, and the day would ring back, echoing crystal, like a gamelan orchestra.

The novel's poetry has made it a lasting favorite among my readers. While it was sold to British and German publishers, *Late in the Season* attained a smaller, if more discriminating, readership than my earlier novels. It fell out of print at Dell and was reprinted in a trade paper edition by Gay Presses of New York, where it's been a steady seller.

As has been my gay short-story collection, *Slashed to Ribbons in Defense of Love,* published by GPNY in 1983, now in its third printing. I'd gathered all my stories from gay magazines, added the novella "And Baby Makes Three," and a final, autobiographical tale, "A Stroke." The

WRITINGS

Novels

Smart as the Devil, 1975.
Eyes, 1976.
The Mesmerist, 1977.
The Lure, 1979.
An Asian Minor: The True Story of Ganymede (novella), illustrations by David Martin, 1980.
Late in the Season, 1981.
House of Cards, 1984.
Ambidextrous: The Secret Lives of Children, Volume 1, 1985.
To the Seventh Power, 1989.
Men Who Loved Me: A Memoir in the Form of a Novel, 1989.

Poetry

The Deformity Lover, and Other Poems, 1978.
Window Elegies, 1986.

Contributor

Orgasms of Light, edited by Winston Leland, 1979.
Aphrodisiac: Fiction from Christopher Street, edited by Michael Denneny, 1980.
New Terrors Two, edited by Ramsey Campbell, 1980.
Modern Masters of Horror, edited by Frank Coffey, 1981.
On the Line, edited by Ian Young, 1982.
Getting from Here to There: Writing and Reading Poetry, edited by Florence Grossman, 1982.
The Christopher Street Reader, edited by Charles Ortleb and Michael Denneny, 1983.
The Penguin Book of Homosexual Verse, edited by Stephen Coote, 1983.
The Male Muse, Number Two, edited by Ian Young, 1983.
Not Love Alone, edited by Martin Humphries, 1985.
Men on Men, edited by George Stambolian, 1986.
Scare Care, edited by Graham Masterson, 1989.
Men on Men, Volume 3, edited by George Stambolian, 1990.
The Gay Nineties, edited by Phil Wilkie and Greg Baysans, 1991.

Other

Editor, *A True Likeness: An Anthology of Lesbian and Gay Writing Today*, 1980.
Slashed to Ribbons in Defense of Love, and Other Stories, 1983.
One O'Clock Jump (one-act play), produced off-off Broadway, 1986.
New Joy of Gay Sex, with Charles Silverstein, 1992.

Adaptations

Immortal! (play with music; based on *An Asian Minor: The True Story of Ganymede*), produced off-off-Broadway, 1986.
Eyes (screenplay; based on novel of same title), 1986.

---

book was published at a time when the short story was making one of its periodic comebacks. Besides fine reviews in the gay media, it was well received in general. *Writer's Digest* listed it along with collections by Barthelme, Carver, and Beattie as the best of the year.

Gay Presses of New York was put together in 1980 by myself, Larry Mitchell, who'd begun Calamus Press, and Terry Helbing, who'd begun the JH Press. Our idea was to combine administrative and overhead costs and to publish one new title per year. Our first book was a play in three parts the author wanted printed as one and produced in a single evening. Harvey Fierstein's *Torch Song Trilogy* still hadn't been produced as a trilogy when GPNY bought publication rights. The book came out in 1981, the play opened off-Broadway in 1982, where its successful run led it to Broadway, and it received the Tony Award in 1983.

The great success of *Torch Song Trilogy* allowed GPNY to flourish. We spread our net wide, pulling in lesbian authors, gay dramatists, non-fiction writers, novelists, etc. The 1985 catalogue showed 75 titles in print. I knew GPNY was secure when my partners bid for *my* new works along with commercial publishers. We continued to encounter bigotry:

book clubs wouldn't purchase rights directly from us, a large distributor wouldn't do business with us. Prejudice dies hard.

Throughout, GPNY has been hard work with little or no profit, done as a challenge and as a service to the readers and writers of the lesbian/gay community. When *Newsweek* ran a cover story on gay writing coming into the mainstream in 1989, it completely ignored GPNY and SeaHorse and Calamus, as well as other important lesbian/gay presses—Daughters Ink, Gay Sunshine Press—who were fully responsible for the inception and continued existence of a lesbian/gay literature.

I was happy enough for GPNY to publish my first book of memoirs. *Ambidextrous: The Secret Lives of Children* (1985) is a true story in the form of three novellas covering three years in my life, from the ages of eleven to thirteen. I began the first, "Basement Games," in the summer of 1983, driven by a need to deal with the most difficult problem I'd ever faced and the people involved. When I'd written it, I realized it was only one of three formative crises that had determined who I would become as a person and writer. I wrote "A Valentine" in the next few months, and spent the first third of 1984 writing the third and most complex section, "The Effect of 'Mirrors'."

The reception of *Ambidextrous* was strong enough for me to consider writing another volume. While I planned to be chronological, I didn't want a full sequential account. Like most lives, mine had gone through long fallow periods followed by sudden times of action: only those "highlights" would be my material.

I was impelled by more than memory and self-healing. I'd begun to feel increasingly limited and caged inside the novels I'd been writing. The tight, suspenseful plots and fully rendered p.o.v.s of characters required to drive my *House of Cards* (1984) and especially *To the Seventh Power* (1989) were making writing less "fun," more work. I tried other areas of writing: in 1985 and 1986 I worked on a screenplay of *Eyes* with director Frank Perry. I adapted my novella *An Asian Minor* at the request of director Jerry Campbell and it had a good off-Broadway run in 1986 as the play *Immortal!* That same summer my one-act play "One O'Clock Jump" was also produced off-Broadway.

Despite these distractions, I still wanted to use the individual "voice" I'd found in my poetry and short fiction and develop it into a more supple, varied, sophisticated prose. I was searching for new structures too, capable of the closest detail, yet open enough for sudden wide shifts in time, place, and character.

A short version of "The Most Golden Bulgari," the first part of the second book of my memoirs, appeared in George Stambolian's excellent anthology *Men on Men* in 1986. "A Most Imperfect Landing," the second part, was written in May 1987 and first published in a gay literary magazine, the *James White Review*, in 1989. I wrote the final part, "The Jane Street Girls," in the spring of 1988.

Gary Luke, editor of the Plume line at NAL, bought paper rights to *Ambidextrous* and hard/soft rights to *Men Who Loved Me*—as I'd cheekily titled the sequel. They were published together in the fall of 1989 and are the books I'm most proud of: they contain all I've learned so far of style, form, and technique in rendering the funny, tragic, sad, frustrating, incomprehensible, and ambiguous quotidian of our lives.

Not all reviewers grasped my purpose. While some found the books "distinguished" or "brilliant," others called them "bad jokes," "put on tell-alls." Unsurprisingly, complaints have been leveled at my prose for daring to mix "high" and "low" styles; also at the contents of the books for mixing the "popular" and "literary." Some British critics called the books flat-out lies, assuring their readers and me that children never have sex. But I'll continue to experiment with and develop this new style. At this time I'm utilizing it in a novel about the complex love-hate relationship of two gay friends over a busy, incident-filled, thirty-five-year period.

Looking over these pages, I see many deal not with myself, my life, my family, my friends, my work, but with larger issues: social and political forces—the Civil Rights and Student movements in the sixties, Gay Liberation and the world created by gays in the seventies. In a review of both memoirs in a Boston newspaper, Allan Smalling wrote: "Picano bids us to see his experiences as exemplary…Whether good or bad, his life experiences virtually define what it meant to come of age in America in the 'Fifties and 'Sixties."

The seventies and eighties too—once I feel I'm able to write about those decades—not an easy or happy task and not one I look forward to or think myself equal to. As one example of the problem I face, think on this: two of my Fire Island Pines housemates and friends were among the first known American men to have been stricken with and died of AIDS. This past decade has been one in which I've watched my entire community, an era, an entire way of life—as rich and full as any I've known—swept away by disease as utterly as the Holocaust swept away European Jewry, and with about as little response from the rest of the world.

As those few friends left to me continue to sicken and suffer and die, I often wonder if that's the reason I lived through those times, knew those people, suffered those losses, became a writer, learned the value of storytelling from my mother—so that eventually I might bear witness to that era, those people, this great loss, and make it literature.

MANUEL PUIG

MANUEL PUIG'S work was acclaimed in Latin America from the time his first novel *La traición de Rita Hayworth* (*Betrayed by Rita Hayworth*) was published in Argentina. At the time of his sudden death in 1990, he was arguably one of the best known Latin American authors of the last several decades. Puig is situated among the renowned group of writers, including Julio Cortázar, José Donoso, Carlos Fuentes, Gabriel García Márquez, and Mario Vargas Llosa, whose works began to draw attention to Latin American literature during the 1960s, the period of the so-called "Boom." Puig's work is unique among this literary group in that he combines an interest in popular culture with techniques of experimental fiction, while also turning a critical eye and ear on modern society and culture.

When Puig died, his work had reached many different audiences of readers around the world. Theater-goers and movie fans also became familiar with his name through the successful 1985 film based on his novel *El beso de la mujer araña* (*Kiss of the Spider Woman*), which he adapted for the stage as well. This novel, which is his fourth (he wrote eight in all), seems to have had the greatest impact on the general public, partly because it deals explicitly, and rather inventively, with the question of homosexuality. This question becomes a topic of discussion and debate for the novel's two protagonists, a homosexual and a heterosexual. These two characters are thrown together for several months in 1975 as cellmates in an Argentine prison. Valentín, the heterosexual, has been convicted of revolutionary activities, and his is the voice of political activism, of leftist—Marxist, to be precise—theory and practice; Molina, the homosexual, has been convicted of the "corruption of minors," and his is the voice of sentimental and romantic stories, of film fantasies and popular culture. In the juxtaposition of these characters, the novel stages an encounter between incompatible political values and views of homosexuality. What appears at the beginning as a difficult encounter of opposing characters and questions, however, becomes at the end an embrace that resolves apparently irreconcilable differences of political ideology and sexual preference.

Essay by
LUCILLE KERR

409

At the time of his sudden death in 1990, Manuel Puig was arguably one of the best known Latin American authors of the last several decades.

Readers familiar with other Puig novels may see in Molina something familiar to an adult version of the protagonist of *Betrayed by Rita Hayworth*, whose name is Toto. *Betrayed by Rita Hayworth* virtually tells the story of Toto's formation, and that formation, it is suggested, is both as an artist (perhaps a writer—Puig states in a number of interviews that the novel was autobiographical) and as a homosexual. In that first novel, however, the protagonist's possible sexual orientation is not a matter to which direct and sustained attention is paid, although the question of his sexual identification and preference does get raised here and there in a number of observations made by other characters. The novel seems to hint at but not state what otherwise remains as a constant, if not also critical, subtext to the story being told about its protagonist. It is a text that suggests but does not declare what the outcome will be for Toto, whose obsession with Hollywood movies and devotion to his mother are implicitly bound to one another. It could be argued, then, that this novel of formation is precisely that, a story about how sexual identity and artistic potential are simultaneously shaped through familial attachments and cultural interests.

With *Betrayed by Rita Hayworth* Puig provides a kind of case study not only of an individual but also of a family and a town in Argentina in the 1930s and 1940s. This novel is the first chapter, so to speak, in the overall story that is told in Puig's works. The story begins in that place and time with *Betrayed by Rita Hayworth*'s tale about childhood and ends in Brazil (where Puig lived for some years in the 1980s) with *Cae la noche tropical* (*Tropical Night Falling*) and its sketch of old age. In between, Puig fashions his own brand of serial and detective fiction in *Boquitas pintadas: Folletín* (*Heartbreak Tango: A Serial*) and *The Buenos Aires Affair: Novela policial* (*The Buenos Aires Affair: A Detective Novel*); an adventurous combination of Hollywood romance and science fiction in *Pubis angelical*; a story of political exile and personal entanglement in *Maldición eterna a quien lea estas páginas* (*Eternal Curse on the Reader of These Pages*); and a confusing confessional soap-opera story of young passion in *Sangre de amor correspondido* (*Blood of Requited Love*).

The path to *Kiss of the Spider Woman* and its explicit engagement with theories of homosexuality as well as its overt presentation of a homosexual character is not a thematically direct one. Indeed, in both his second and third novels, published between *Betrayed by Rita Hayworth*

Argentinean novelist and playwright.

Born: General Villegas, December 28, 1932.

Education: University of Buenos Aires beginning 1950; Centro Sperimentale di Cinematografia beginning 1955; studied language and literature at private institutions.

Career: Served as a translator, Argentina Air Force, 1953. Translator and instructor in Spanish and Italian, London and Rome, Italy, 1956–57; assistant film-director, Rome and Paris, France, 1957–58; worked as a dish-washer, Stockholm, Sweden, 1958–59; assistant film director, Buenos Aires, 1960; film subtitle translator, Rome, 1961–62; clerk, Air France, New York City, 1963–67. Contributor to *Omni.*

Recipient: *Le Monde* best foreign novel designation, 1968; San Sebastian Festival best script award, 1974, and jury prize, 1978; American Library Association Notable Book award, 1979; *Plays & Players* award, for most promising playwright, 1985.

Died: Cuernavaca, Mexico, July 22, 1990.

and *Kiss of the Spider Woman*, Puig focuses on the sentimental and sexual affairs of heterosexual characters. He also continues to rework, if not also revive, forms of popular or "low" art and culture, as the subtitles of *Heartbreak Tango* ("A Serial") and *The Buenos Aires Affair* ("A Detective Novel") clearly suggest. In the novels that follow *Kiss of the Spider Woman*, popular culture remains a thematic concern and popular narrative models inform both the stories Puig tells and the methods he deploys to tell them.

In *Kiss of the Spider Woman*, Molina, the homosexual character, tells the plots of Hollywood movies to his cellmate Valentín as a kind of nighttime entertainment. Molina is presented as a homosexual whose interests and identity are also bound up with popular culture. Molina's interest in sentimental and romantic forms of popular culture would seem to fit the "feminine" role he desires to play as a homosexual. The novel also focuses directly on the question of homosexuality in a series of footnotes that summarize scientific discourse and sociological studies about the origins and nature of homosexuality. In addition, the two characters talk about homosexual and heterosexual relations; and, based on their own rather different ideas and experiences, they even debate what the differences and similarities between those apparently disparate types of relationships ought to be.

The importance of Puig's writing with regard to the topic of homosexuality may, however, resides less in such explicit discussions about sexual orientation or in the direct representation of a homosexual character than in the way his works erode the hierarchies supporting traditional social orders and cultural codes. Furthermore, his work is significant for gay and gender studies not so much because one or two novels present homosexual themes or figures, but rather because such works both reconsider cultural forms and redefine social values. Puig's writing overall, as well as the novels that take up the question of homosexuality, upsets the privilege of traditionally authorized figures, such as being male and heterosexual, and forms of culture, such as "high" art and "canonical" literature. In his work, female and homosexual figures acquire new value, just as previously undervalued or "low" forms of culture are resituated in positions of importance and interest. Thus, if *Kiss of the Spider Woman* remains as Puig's best known work, it should be seen as representing not a narrow focus on one issue but a radical interrogation of contemporary culture and society.

KISS OF THE SPIDER WOMAN

Excerpt reprinted from *Kiss of the Spider Woman*, Knopf, copyright 1979 by Manuel Puig.

—How did it all begin?

—One day I went to a restaurant and saw him there. I was crazy about him right off. But it's a long story, I'll tell you some other time, or maybe, no I won't, I'm not saying anything to you anymore, who knows what you'll come out with.

—Just a minute, Molina, you're really wrong. If I ask about him it's because I feel somehow ... how can I explain it?

—Curiosity, that's all you feel.

—That's not true. I think I have to know more about you, that's what, in order to understand you better. If we're going to be in this cell together like this, we ought to understand one another better, and I know very little about people with your type of inclination.

—I'll tell you how it happened then, quickly though, so as not to bore you.

—What's his name?

—No, his name no, that's for me. No one else.

—Whatever you like.

—That's the only thing of his that I have all to myself, inside me, it's in my throat, and I keep it down there just for me. I'll never let it out ...

—Have you known him a long time?

—Three years today, the twelfth of September, the first day I went to the restaurant. But I feel so funny talking about this.

—Never mind. If you want to talk about it sometime, talk. If not, don't.

—Somehow I feel embarrassed.

—That's … that's how it is when it comes to really deep feelings, at least I think so.

—I was just with some friends of mine. Well, actually a couple of harlots, unbearable, the two of them. But cute, and sharp too.

—Two girls?

—No, dummy, when I say harlots I mean queens. And so one of them was rather bitchy to the waiter, which was him. I saw from the beginning how handsome he was, but nothing more. Then when my friend got really snotty with him, the guy, without losing his self-control at all, he put her right in her place. I was surprised. Because waiters, poor guys, they always have this complex about being servants, which makes it difficult for them to answer any rudeness, without coming across like the injured servant bit, you get what I mean? Anyway, this guy, nothing doing, he explains to my slutty friend just why the food isn't up to what it ought to be, but with such finesse, she winds up looking like a complete dope. But don't get the idea he acted very haughty—not at all, perfectly detached, handled the whole situation. So immediately my nose tells me there's something unusual, a real man. So the next week this woman heads straight to the same restaurant, but this time alone.

—What woman?

—Listen, I'm sorry, but when it comes to him I can't talk about myself like a man, because I don't feel like one.

—Go on.

—The second time I saw him he looked even cuter, in a white uniform with a Mao collar, it fitted him divinely. Like some movie star or something. Everything about him was perfect, the way he walked, the husky voice, but sometimes a slight lilt to it, kind of tender, I don't know how to put it. And the way he served! I'm telling you, it was poetry, one time I saw him do a salad, I couldn't believe! First he sat the customer at a table, because it was a woman, a real dog, and he sets up a little side table next to hers, to put the salad tray down right there, then he asks her, some oil? some vinegar? some of this? some of that? until finally he picks up the wooden fork and spoon and gets right down to mixing the salad, but I don't know how to explain it, like he caressed the lettuce leaves, and the tomatoes, but nothing softy about it—how can I put it? They were such powerful movements, and so elegant, and soft, and masculine at the same time.

—And what's masculine in your terms?

—It's lots of things, but for me ... well, the nicest thing about a man is just that, to be marvelous-looking, and strong, but without making any fuss about it, and also walking very tall. Walking absolutely straight, like my waiter, who's not afraid to say anything. And it's knowing what you want, where you're going.

—That's pure fantasy, that type doesn't exist.

—Yes it does so exist, and it's him.

—Okay, so he gives you that impression, but inside, at least as far as this culture goes, without power behind you no one walks tall, not the way you say.

—Don't be so jealous, there's just no talking to a guy about some other guy without getting into a fuss, you're all like women that way.

—Don't be stupid.

—See how you react, even insulting me. You men are just as competitive as women.

—Please, let's stick to a certain level, or let's not talk at all.

—What's with this level bit ...

—With you there's simply no talking, unless it's when you're spouting off about some film.

—No talking to me? I'd like to know why.

—Because you can't carry on a discussion, there's no line of thought to it, you come out with any nonsense at all.

—That isn't true, Valentin.

—Whatever you say.

—You're so damn pedantic.

—If you think so.

—Show me. I'd like to see how I don't come up to your level.

—I didn't say you don't come up to my level; I just meant you don't stick to the point when we carry on a discussion.

—You'll see. I do so.

—Why go on talking, Molina?

—Just go on talking and I'll show you.

—What do we talk about?

—Well ... Why don't you tell me what it means to you, being a man?

—You got me, that time.

—Let's hear then ... Give me your answer, what makes a man in your terms?

—Mmm ... his not taking any crap ... from anyone, not even the powers that be ... But no, it's more than that. Not taking any crap is one thing, but not the most important. What really makes a man is a lot more, it has to do with not humiliating someone else with an order, or a tip. Even more, it's ... not letting the person next to you feel degraded, feel bad.

—That sounds like a saint.

—No, it's not as impossible as you think.

—I still don't get you ... explain a little more.

—I don't know, I don't quite know myself, right this minute. You've caught me off guard. I can't seem to find the right words. Some other time, when my ideas are a little clearer on the subject, we can go back to it. Tell me more about your waiter at that restaurant.

—Where were we?

—The business of the salad.

—Who knows what he's doing now ... Makes me sad. Poor baby, there in that place ...

—This place is a lot worse, Molina.

—But we won't be in here forever, right? But him, that's it, he doesn't have any future. He's condemned. And I told you already what a strong character he's got, he isn't afraid of anything; but you can't imagine, sometimes, the sadness you see in him.

—How can you tell?

—It's in his eyes. Because he's got those fair eyes, greenish, somewhere between brown and green, incredibly big, swallowing up his face it seems like, and it's that look in his eyes that gives him away. That look that makes you see sometimes how bad he feels, how sad. And it's what attracted me, and made me feel more and more like talking to him. Especially when things in the restaurant got a little slow and I'd notice that melancholy look on him, he'd go to the back of the dining room, where they kept a table so the waiters could sit sometimes, and he'd stay quiet there, lighting up a cigarette, and his eyes would slowly get strange, sort of misty. I started going there more and more often, but in the beginning he barely said anything unless it was absolutely necessary. And I always ordered the cold meat salad, the soup, the main course, dessert and coffee, so he'd come back and forth to my table a whole lot of times, and little by little we began to have a bit of conversation. Obviously, he had me pegged right off, because with me it's easy to tell.

—To tell what?

—That my real name is Carmen, like the one in Bizet.

—And because of that he started talking more to you.

—Christ! you don't know very much, do you? It was because I'm gay that he didn't want to let me come near him. Because he's an absolutely straight guy. But little by little, dropping a few words here, a few there, I made him see I respected him, and he started telling me little things about his life.

—All this was while he waited on you?

—For the first few weeks, yes, until one day I managed to have a cup of coffee with him, one time when he was on day shift, which he hated the most.

—What were his regular hours?

—Well, either he came in at seven in the morning and left about four in the afternoon, or he'd show up about six in the evening, and stay until roughly three in the morning. And then one day he told me he liked the night shift best. So that aroused my curiosity, because he'd already said he was married, although he didn't wear any ring, also fishy. And his wife worked a normal nine-to-five job in some office, so what was going on with the wife? You have no idea how much trouble I went through to convince him to come have coffee with me, he always had excuses about things he had to do, first the brother-in-law, then the car. Until finally he gave in and went with me.

—And what had to happen finally happened?

—Are you out of your mind? Don't you understand anything at all? To begin with, I already told you he's straight. Nothing at all happened. Ever!

—What did you talk about, in the cafe?

—Well, I don't remember anymore, because afterwards we met lots of times. But first thing I wanted to ask him was why anybody as intelligent as he was had to do that kind of work. And now you can begin to see what a terrible story it was. Like, well, the story of so many kids from poor families who don't have the cash to study, or maybe don't have the incentive.

—If people want to study, some way they find the means. Listen … in Argentina an education's not the most difficult thing in the world, you know, the university's free.

—Yes, but …

—Lack of incentive, now that's something else, there I agree with you, yes, it's the inferior-class complex, the brainwashing society subjects everyone to.

—Wait, let me tell you about it, and you'll understand what class of person he is, the best! He admits himself how, for a moment in life, he gave in, but he's been paying for it too ever since. He says he was around seventeen, anyway I forgot to tell you, he had to work from the time he was a kid, even in elementary school, like all those poor families from certain neighborhoods in Buenos Aires, and after elementary school he started working in a mechanics shop, and he learned the trade, and like I said, at about seventeen, more or less, already in the flower of his youth, he started in with the chicks, making it like crazy, and then yes, even worse: soccer. From when he was a kid he could play really well, and at eighteen, more or less, he started in as a professional. And now comes the key to it all: why he didn't make himself a career out of professional soccer. The way he tells me, he was only at it a short time when he saw all that crap that goes on, the sport is riddled with favoritism, injustice of every kind, and here comes the key, the key to the key, about what happens with him: he can never keep his mouth shut; whenever he smells a rat, the guy yells. He's not two-faced, and doesn't know when to keep his mouth shut. Because the guy's straight that way, too. And that's what my nose told me from the very beginning, see?

—But he never got involved in politics?

—No, he's got strange ideas about that, very off-the-wall, don't even mention the union to him.

—Go on.

—And after a few years, two or three, he quit soccer.

—And the chicks?

—Sometimes I think you're psychic.

—Why?

—Because he also quit soccer on account of the chicks. Lots of them, because he was in training, but the chicks grabbed him more than the training.

—He wasn't very disciplined after all, it seems.

—Sure, but there's also something I didn't tell you yet: his fiancée, the one he was serious with, and got married to eventually, she didn't want him to keep on with the soccer. So he took a job in a factory, as a mechanic, but the work was fairly soft, because his fiancée arranged it for him. And then they got married, and there he was at the factory, almost immediately he'd become a foreman, or chief of some division. And he had two kids. And he was nuts about his baby girl, the oldest of two, and at six she ups and dies. And at the same time he was having a row at the factory, because they started laying off people, favoring those who had connections.

—Like him.

—Yes, he did start off on the wrong foot there, I admit it. But now comes the part that's so great about him, to me, and makes me forgive anything, listen. He took sides with some poor old guys at the factory who'd been working part-time but non-union, so the boss gave him the choice of getting tossed out on his ass or toeing the line … and so *he quits*. And you know how it is when you quit on your own—you don't get a red cent in severance pay, not a fucking thing, and he wound up out on the street, more than ten years he'd put in at that factory.

—By then he must have been over thirty.

—Obviously, thirty plus. So he began, imagine, at that age, looking for work. In the beginning he was able to manage without just taking anything, but eventually he got offered that job as waiter and had to take it, naturally.

—He was the one who told you all that?

—Mmm-hmm, basically, little by little. I think it was a relief for him, to be able to tell somebody everything, and get it off his chest. That's why he started to open up to me.

—And you?

—I adored him all the more, but he wouldn't let me do anything for him.

—And what were you going to do for him?

—I wanted to convince him there was still a chance for him to go back to school and get a degree or something. Because there's another thing I forgot to tell you: the wife made more than he did. She was a secretary in some company and slowly got to be sort of an executive, and he didn't go for that too much.

—Did you ever meet his wife?

—No, he wanted to introduce me, but deep down I hated everything about her. Just the thought of him sleeping beside her every night made me die of jealousy.

—And now?

—It's strange, but now it doesn't matter.

—Really?

WRITINGS

Novels

La traición de Rita Hayworth, 1968; translated by Suzanne Jill Levine as *Betrayed by Rita Hayworth*, 1971.

Boquitas pintadas: Folletín, 1969; translated by Suzanne Jill Levine as *Heartbreak Tango: A Serial*, 1973.

The Buenos Aires Affair: Novela policial, 1973; translated by Suzanne Jill Levine as *The Buenos Aires Affair: A Detective Novel*, 1976.

El beso de la mujer araña, Barcelona, Spain, 1976; translated by Thomas Colchie as *The Kiss of the Spider Woman*, 1979; translated by Allan Baker, 1987.

Publis angelical, 1979; translated by Elena Brunet, 1986.

Eternal Curse on the Reader of These Pages, translated by Puig from English into Spanish as *Maldicion eterna a quien lea estas páginas*, 1980; in English, 1982.

Sangre de amor correspondido, 1982; translated by Jan L. Grayson as *Blood of Requited Love*, 1984.

La cara del villano; Recuerdo de Tijuana, 1985.

Cae la noche tropical, 1988; translated by Suzanne Jill Levine as *Tropical Night Falling*, 1991.

Plays

El beso de la mujer araña (produced Spain, 1981); translated by Allan Baker as *Kiss of the Spider Woman* (produced London, 1985; Los Angeles, 1987); published with *Bajo un manto de estrellas: Pieza en dos actos*, 1983.

Bajo un manto de estrellas: Pieza en dos actos (produced Spain); published with *El beso de la mujer araña: Adaptación escénica realizada por el autor*, 1983; translated by Ronald Christ as *Under a Mantle of Stars: A Play in Two Acts*, 1985.

Misterio del ramo de rosas (produced Spain; as *Mystery of the Rose Bouquet*, London, 1987), translation by Allan Baker, 1988.

Screenplays

Boquitas Pintadas, 1974.

El lugar sin límites (adaptation of a novel by Jose Donoso), 1978.

Pubis angelical.

Other

"Growing Up at the Movies: A Chronology" (autobiography), in *Review*, Numbers 4–5, 1971–72.

Contributor, *Le texte familial; textes hispaniques* (colloquium), edited by Georges Martin and N. Castellaro, 1984.

Contributor, *Drama Contemporary: Latin America*, edited by Marion P. Holt and G. W. Woodward, 1986.

Adaptations

The Kiss of the Spider Woman (motion picture), Island Alive, 1985.

The Kiss of the Spider Woman (screenplay) by Leonard Schrader with an introduction by David Weisman, 1987.

The Kiss of the Spider Woman (musical), produced London West End, 1992; on Broadway, 1993.

—Mmm-hmm. Look, I don't know ... Now I'm glad she's with him, so he's not all alone, since I can't pal around with him any longer, those times at the restaurant when not too much is going on and he gets bored, and smokes so much.

—And does he know how you feel about him?

—Obviously he does, I told him everything, when I still had some hope of convincing him that, with us two ... something might really ... happen ... But nothing, nothing ever happened, no convincing him on that score. I said to him, even just one time in his whole life ... but he never wanted to. And after a while I was too embarrassed to insist on anything, and satisfied myself with friendship.

—But according to what you said, he wasn't doing so well with his wife.

—There was a period, it's true, when they were fighting, but deep down he always loved her, and what's worse, he admired her for making more than he did. And one day he told me something that I nearly strangled him for. Father's Day was coming up, and I wanted to give him something, because he's so much of a father to that kid of his, and it seemed like a marvelous excuse to get him a present, and I asked him if he'd like a pair of pajamas, and then, complete disaster ...

—Don't leave me hanging.

—He said he didn't wear pajamas, he always slept in the raw. And he and his wife had a double bed. It killed me. But for a while, it did seem like they were on the verge of splitting up, and that's how I kidded myself, such illusions I had. You have no idea.

—What kind of illusions?

—That he might come to live with me, with my mom and me. And I'd help him, and make him study. And not bother about anything but him, the whole blessed day, getting everything all set for him, his clothes, buying his books, registering him for courses, and little by little I'd convince him that what he had to do was just one thing: never work again. And I'd pass along whatever small amount of money was needed to give the wife for child support, and make him not worry about anything at all, nothing except himself, until he got what he wanted and lost all that sadness of his for good, wouldn't that be marvelous?

—Yes, but unreal. Look, there is one thing, you know, he could also go right on being a waiter but not feel humiliated about it, or anything like that. Because however humble his work is, there's always the option: joining the union movement.

—You think so?

—Of course! There's no doubt about it ...

—But he doesn't understand any of that.

—He doesn't have any ideas about politics?

—No, he's rather ignorant. And he even says some foul things about his union, and probably he's right.

—Right? If the union's no good he should fight to change it, so it gets better.

—You know, I'm a little tired, how about you?

—No, not me. Aren't you going to tell me a little more of the film?

—We'll see ... But you don't know, it all seemed so nice, to think I could do something good to help him. You understand, being a window-dresser all day, enjoyable as it is, when the day's finished, sometimes you begin to ask yourself what's it all about, and you feel kind of empty inside. Whereas if I could do something for him it'd be so marvelous ... Give him a little bit of happiness, you see what I mean? What do you think?

—I don't know, I'll have to analyze it some more; right now I couldn't really say. What don't you tell me a little more of the film now and tomorrow I'll talk about your waiter.

—Okay …

—They shut the lights off in here so early, and those candles give off such a foul smell, and they ruin your eyes too.

—And they burn up the oxygen, Valentin.

—And I can't sleep when I don't read something.

—If you want I'll tell you a little bit more. But the stupid thing is that I'm the one who'll be up later on then.

—Just a little more, Molina.

—Ohh-h … kay. Where were we?

—Don't start yawning at me, sleepyhead.

—What can I do? I'm sleepy.

—… Now you've got … me … doing it.

—So you're sleepy too, eh?

—Maybe I could get … some sleep.

—Mm-hmm, and if you wake up, think about this Gabriel business.

—Gabriel, who's Gabriel?

—My waiter. It slipped out.

—Okay, in the morning then.

—Mmm, see you in the morning.

—See how life is, Molina, here I am staying up at night, thinking about your boyfriend …

—Tomorrow you can tell me about it.

—Good night.

—Good night.

ADRIENNE RICH

DURING THE MORE than 40 years of her literary career, Adrienne Rich has evolved from a dutiful poet following the masculine poetic tradition of Robert Frost, W. H. Auden, and William Butler Yeats to a radical, lesbian feminist with a commitment to a global perspective. She began this evolution in 1951 with her first volume of poetry, published in the same year that she graduated from Radcliffe. This volume, entitled *A Change of World*, won the Yale Younger Poets Prize and contains a foreword by Auden in which he suggested that the new generation of poets, including Rich, would follow the tradition established by the "modern" generation of poets (T. S. Eliot, Frost, Yeats) because there had been no societal revolutions that would enable a poetic revolution. Auden, writing in 1951, had no way of foreseeing the impact of the anti-war, civil rights, and feminist movements on poetry in the coming decades. Those movements, as well as the writings of James Baldwin and Simone de Beauvoir, created dramatic changes in Rich's world view and resulted in revolutions in her poetry. Particularly, Rich's developing feminist consciousness, which can be seen as early as 1963 in such poems as "Planetarium," led to an increased awareness of her lesbianism. These alterations in Rich's view of the world and herself created the contradictions of her life that appear in her art. She demands that she be accountable for every part of her identity. In "Split at the Root," a 1982 essay published in *Blood, Bread and Poetry* which begins to examine the contradictions of her life, Rich lists her various identities: "The middle-class white girl taught to trade obedience for privilege. The Jewish lesbian raised to be a heterosexual gentile. The woman who first heard oppression named and analyzed in the Black Civil Rights struggle. The woman with three sons, the feminist who hates male violence.... The poet who knows that beautiful language can lie, that the oppressor's language sometimes sounds beautiful." Rich claims that each of these selves must be investigated in her work and in her life. Rich's unrelenting self-analysis in her prose and in her poetry has not always been well received by critics. Nonetheless, Rich demands an honesty of self and a continual critical examination of self.

Essay by
ANDREA R.
CUMPSTON

423

Adrienne Rich's first volume of poetry, *A Change of World,* won the Yale Younger Poets Prize in 1951. During the more than 40 years following, the writer has evolved into a radical, lesbian feminist with a commitment to a global perspective.

Part of Rich's continual evolution as a writer includes her struggle to critique and define women's voices, particularly lesbian voices, in her writing as well as in that of others. She has worked to create a poetry and prose that investigates the hidden, the silence, that surrounds what we say about ourselves as lesbians, as women, and as women of color. More particularly, Rich questions what lesbians and women in general purposely do not say or reveal about themselves and why. Although she understands the real problems of unemployment and economic survival, she questions the lesbian who creates art in an environment of self-imposed censorship. In "Conditions for Work: The Common World of Women," an essay originally written as the foreword to the anthology *Working It Out: 23 Women Artists, Scholars and Scientists Talk about Their Lives and Work,* Rich points out that the "whole question of what it means or might mean to work as a lesbian might have occupied an entire essay in this book." Subtly, Rich indicates that the failing of the lesbian artists in this volume occurs on the level of awareness of self and commitment to self-exposure. These women artists, scholars, and scientists might have written an essay on what it means to work as a lesbian, but no such essay appears. Awareness of self and of the history of one's community (whether that community is lesbian, gay, women's, African American, Hispanic, etc.) is critical for Rich. For the lesbian to find her history she must interpret "the silence and denial that has enveloped lesbianism" and "the social taboos [women in the past] lived among."

As part of a larger awareness of self and in an effort to create community among women, Rich has been working at least since 1976 to persuade all women to see the "lesbian in us." This figure of woman, the lesbian, causes much tension in the women's community. It is precisely for this reason that Rich critiqued the tension produced by heterosexism that inhibits women's communion with one another in "It Is the Lesbian in Us …" and in her landmark essay, "Compulsory Heterosexuality and Lesbian Existence." In these essays, Rich proposes that women, both lesbian and heterosexual, critically examine heterosexism as an institution

American poet, translator, and author of nonfiction.

Born: Baltimore, Maryland, May 16, 1929.

Education: Radcliffe College, A.B. (cum laude), 1951.

Partnerships: Married Alfred Haskell Conrad in 1953 (died, 1970); three children; since 1976, has lived with novelist and essayist Michelle Cliff.

Career: Conductor of workshops, YM-YWHA Poetry Center, New York City, 1966–67; visiting lecturer, Swarthmore College, Swarthmore, Pennsylvania, 1967–69; adjunct professor in writing division of Graduate School of the Arts, Columbia University, New York City, 1967–69; lecturer in SEEK English program, 1968–70, instructor in creative writing program, 1970–71, then assistant professor of English, 1971–72 and 1974–75, City College of the City University of New York; Fannie Hurst visiting professor of creative literature, Brandeis University, Waltham, Massachusetts, 1972–73; Lucy Martin Donelly fellow, Bryn Mawr College, Bryn Mawr, Pennsylvania, 1975; professor of English, Douglass College, Rutgers University, New Brunswick, New Jersey, 1976–78; A. D. White Professor-at-Large, Cornell University, 1981–86; Clark Lecturer and distinguished visiting professor, Scripps College, Claremont, California, 1983; Burgess Lecturer, Pacific Oaks College, Pasadena, California, 1986; professor of English and feminist studies, Stanford University, Stanford, California.

Memberships: Member of advisory boards, *Bridges: A Journal for Jewish Feminists and Their Friends*, 1986–93, Boston Women's Fund, and Sisterhood in Support of Sisters in South Africa. Member of Modern Language Association, National Writers' Union, American Academy of Arts and Letters, and American Academy of Arts and Sciences.

Recipient: Yale Series of Younger Poets prize, 1951; Guggenheim fellowships,1952 and 1961; Poetry Society of America's Ridgely Torrence Memorial Award, 1955; Friends of Literature (Chicago) Thayer Bradley Award, 1956; Phi Beta Kappa Poet, College of William and Mary, 1960, Swarthmore College, 1965, and Harvard University, 1966; National Institute of Arts and Letters award for poetry, 1961; Amy Lowell travelling fellowship, 1962; Bollingen Foundation translation grant, 1962; *Poetry* magazine's Bess Hokin Prize, 1963; Bautibak Translation Center grant, 1968; *Poetry* magazine's Eunice Tietjens Memorial Prize, 1968; National Endowment for the Arts grant, 1970; Poetry Society of America's Shelley Memorial Award, 1971; Ingram Merrill Foundation grant, 1973–74; National Book Award, 1974; National Gay Task Force Fund for Human Dignity Award, 1981; Modern Poetry Association/American Council for the Arts Ruth Lilly Poetry Prize, 1986; Brandeis University Creative Arts medal for poetry, 1987; National Poetry Association award, 1987; New York University's Holmes Bobst award for arts and letters, 1989; Lambda Literary Award for lesbian poetry, 1992; Publishing Triangle's Bill Whitehead award for lifetime achievement in lesbian and gay literature, 1992; Lenore Marshall/Nation Award, 1992; Poets' Prize, 1993; Harriet Monroe Award, 1994; MacArthur Fellow, 1994–99.

Address: c/o W. W. Norton Co., 500 Fifth Avenue, New York, New York 10110, U.S.A.

---

that oppresses all women. This critique can range from redefining the words that have been used to oppress lesbians ("dyke," "butch," "bulldagger") to coining the phrases "lesbian continuum" and "lesbian existence" as ways of re-visioning women's relationships with each other outside of the heterosexist framework. The terms "lesbian continuum" and "lesbian existence" have been misunderstood and misapplied by many Rich readers. Rich is concerned that the phrase "lesbian continuum" has been used "by women who have not yet begun to examine the privileges and solipsisms of heterosexuality, as a safe way to describe their felt connections with women, without having to share in the risks and threats of lesbian existence.... *Lesbian continuum*—the phrase—came from a desire to allow for the greatest possible variation of female-identified experience, while paying a different kind of respect to *lesbian existence*—the traces and knowledge of women who have made their primary erotic and emotional choices for women."

Rich has been working to create connections and to foster community among women in her poetry as well as in her prose. *Twenty-One Love Poems* is a series of sonnets concerning the problematics of lesbian love in a society that insists on the invisibility of lesbians. Rather than dwell on the problem of lesbian invisibility, Rich finds strong images of women in the landscapes that surround her. These images of power involve figurative and literal representations of women's bodies. In poem XI, "Every peak is a crater. This is the law of volcanoes, / making them eternally and visibly female. / No height without depth, without a burning core, / though our straw soles shred on the hardened lava." Rich creates a powerful image of a woman's body and sexuality in a landscape which has been raped and wasted because it has been depicted as female in a patriarchal society. This creation of new images of the female body and sexuality stems from Rich's stated desire in "Diving into the Wreck." She desires "the wreck and not the story of the wreck / the thing itself and not the myth."

Because Rich finds that language cannot express the whole of experience and its shifts, she dates her poems; she believes that each poem expresses the feelings and thoughts of the poet at that moment. She does not pretend to write universal, transcendent truths. Rather, her poems are a way of understanding experience. In such volumes as *Your Native Land, Your Life, Time's Power*, and *An Atlas of the Difficult World*, Rich explores the responsibility of a poet to her words and images. In these volumes, lesbianism becomes less a subject in itself than a fact of the poet's world, intrinsic to her experience. Lesbianism does not disappear, but becomes a part of a matrix of issues that Rich brings to her poetry, including an awareness of political movements and global feminisms. This matrix attests to Rich's commitment to making minority voices heard, to making the invisible visible. Rich insists on the complexity of our lives and carefully, with a keen sense of language, records that complexity in her poetry and prose.

In a letter written in November of 1990 to David Montenegro and published in *Points of Departure*, Rich discusses forms of censorship and the costs of artistically trivializing minority voices—including lesbian, gay, working- class, and African American—through stereotype and caricature, in a society that cares little for those voices. According to Rich, capitalism conspires against those minority voices by making certain books and experiences unavailable to those uninitiated in that experience—making minority voices invisible to the greater public. In order to combat the erasure of these experiences, Rich suggests that we "insist in our art on the depth and complexity of our lives, to keep on creating the account of our lives, in poems and stories and scripts and essays and memoirs that are as rich and strange as we ourselves. Never to bend toward or consent to be rewarded for trivializing ourselves, our people, or each other."

What Rich envisioned as a strategy in 1990 has characterized her literary production for some time. By continually investigating the contradictions of her life, Rich presents to the world not a cardboard stereotype of a lesbian, not an easily categorized vision of the world that surrounds us, but the complex vision of the world written by a Jewish-lesbian-feminist-mother who is "rich and strange" and wonderfully so.

In 1986 Adrienne Rich became the first poet to receive the Ruth Lilly Poetry Prize from the Modern Poetry Association and the American Council for the Arts.

FOR AN OCCUPANT

Did the fox speak to you?
Did the small brush-fires on the hillside
smoke her out?
Were you standing on the porch
not the kitchen porch   the front
one of poured concrete   full in the rising moon
and did she appear   wholly on her own
asking no quarter   wandering by
on impulse   up the drive   and on
into the pine-woods
but were you standing there
at the moment of moon and burnished light
leading your own life   till she caught your eye
asking no charity
but did she speak to you?

Reprinted from *Your Native Land, Your Life*, published by W. W. Norton & Co., 1986.

FOR THE RECORD

Reprinted from *Your Native Land, Your Life,* published by W. W. Norton & Co., 1986.

The clouds and the stars didn't wage this war
the brooks gave no information
if the mountain spewed stones of fire into the river
it was not taking sides
the raindrop faintly swaying under the leaf
had no political opinions

and if here or there a house
filled with backed-up raw sewage
or poisoned those who lived there
with slow fumes, over years
the houses were not at war
nor did the tinned-up buildings

intend to refuse shelter
to homeless old women and roaming children
they had no policy to keep them roaming
or dying, no, the cities were not the problem
the bridges were non-partisan
the freeways burned, but not with hatred

Even the miles of barbed-wire
stretched around crouching temporary huts
designed to keep the unwanted
at a safe distance, out of sight
even the boards that had to absorb
year upon year, so many human sounds

so many depths of vomit, tears
slow-soaking blood
had not offered themselves for this
The trees didn't volunteer to be cut into boards
nor the thorns for tearing flesh
Look around at all of it

and ask whose signature
is stamped on the orders, traced
in the corner of the building plans
Ask where the illiterate, big-bellied
women were, the drunks and crazies,
the ones you fear most of all:
ask where you were.

Poetry

A Change of World, 1951.
Poems, 1951.
The Diamond Cutters, and Other Poems, 1955.
Snapshots of a Daughter-in-Law: Poems, 1954–1962, 1963, revised, 1967.
Necessities of Life, 1966.
Focus, 1967.
Poems Selected and New, 1967.
Leaflets: Poems, 1965–1968, 1969.
The Will to Change: Poems, 1968–1970, 1971.
Diving into the Wreck: Poems, 1971–1972, 1973.
Poems: Selected and New, 1950–1974, 1974.
Adrienne Rich's Poetry: Texts of the Poems, The Poet on Her Work, Reviews and Criticism, edited by Barbara Charlesworth Gelpi and Albert Gelpi, 1975.
Twenty-One Love Poems, 1977.
The Dream of a Common Language: Poems, 1974–1977, 1978.
A Wild Patience Has Taken Me This Far: Poems, 1978–1981, 1981.
Sources, 1983.
The Fact of a Doorframe: Poems Selected and New, 1950–1984, 1984.
Your Native Land, Your Life, 1986.
Time's Power: Poems, 1985–1988, 1989.
An Atlas of the Difficult World: Poems, 1988–1991, 1991.
Collected Early Poems, 1950–1970, 1992.
Adrienne Rich's Poetry and Prose, edited by Barbara Charlesworth Gelpi and Albert J. Gelpi, 1993.

Nonfiction

Of Woman Born: Motherhood as Experience and Institution, 1976.
Women and Honor: Some Notes on Lying (monograph), 1977.
On Lies, Secrets and Silence: Selected Prose, 1966–1978 (includes "Conditions for Work: The Common World of Women" and "'It Is the Lesbian in Us ...'"), 1979.
Compulsory Heterosexuality and Lesbian Existence (monograph), 1981.
Blood, Bread and Poetry: Selected Prose, 1979–1986 (includes "Compulsory Heterosexuality and Lesbian Existence" and "Split at the Root: An Essay on Jewish Identity"), 1986.
What Is Found There: Notebooks on Poetry and Politics, 1993.

Translations

Poems by Ghalib, with Aijaz Ahmad and William Stafford, edited by Aijaz Ahmad, 1969.

Recordings

Adrienne Rich Reading at Stanford, 1973.
A Sign I Was Not Alone, with others, 1978.
Planetarium and *Tracking the Contradictions*, Watershed Series, 1985.

RE-FORMING THE CRYSTAL

I am trying to imagine
how it feels to you
to want a woman
trying to hallucinate
desire
centered in a cock
focused like a burning-glass
desire without discrimination:
to want a woman like a fix

Reprinted from *The Fact of a Doorframe, Poems Selected and New, 1950–1984*, published by W. W. Norton & Co., copyright 1984 by Adrienne Rich.

Desire: yes: the sudden knowledge, like coming out of 'flu, that the body is sexual. Walking in the streets with that knowledge. That evening in the plane from Pittsburgh, fantasizing going to meet you. Walking through the airport blazing with energy and joy. But knowing all along that you were not the source of that energy and joy; you were a man, a stranger, a name, a voice on the telephone, a friend; this desire was mine, this energy my energy; it could be used a hundred ways, and going to meet you could be one of them.

Tonight is a different kind of night.
I sit in the car, racing the engine,
calculating the thinness of the ice.
In my head I am already threading the beltways
that rim this city,
all the roads that used to wander the country
having been lost.
Tonight I understand
my photo on the license is not me,
my
name on the marriage-contract was not mine.
If I remind you of my father's favorite daughter,
look again. The woman
I needed to call my mother
was silenced before I was born.

Tonight if the battery charges I want to take the car out on sheet-ice; I want to understand my fear both of the machine and of the accidents of nature. My desire for you is not trivial; I can compare it with the greatest of those accidents. But the energy it draws on might lead to racing a cold engine, cracking the frozen spiderweb, parachuting into the field of a poem wired with danger, or to a trip through gorges and canyons, into the cratered night of female memory, where delicately and with intense care the chieftainess inscribes upon the ribs of the volcano the name of the one she has chosen.

JANE RULE

"THE SILENCE HAS finally been broken." With these words, Jane Rule ended the introductory chapters to her 1975 book *Lesbian Images* and opened the floodgates of lesbian scholarship. *Lesbian Images* offered biographical sketches, analysis, and criticism of a number of mainstream writers and provided an overview of lesbian-identified writing from the 1930s onward. With the exception of Jeannette Howard Foster's pioneer work, *Sex Variant Women in Literature*, self-published in 1956, a few bibliographies, and an occasional magazine article, Rule's book was the first to offer an awareness of the depth and breadth of contemporary lesbian literature. Written just after the American Psychiatric Association had lifted the stigma of mental illness from homosexuality, but before the advent of women's studies or lesbian studies on campus, Rule's was a trailbreaking study.

Rule's fiction was somewhat troubling to lesbian readers of the 1970s, many of whom had narrowed the scope of their reading to make up for lost time, and although lesbians and gays peopled her books, she did not slide easily into a category for lesbian authors. *This Is Not for You* and *Against the Season*, published before *Lesbian Images*, as well as *Contract with the World*, published afterward, while challenging and genre-defying to the more astute reader, were disappointing to those seeking a quick romantic "fix." Rule's fiction was based on her desire to "speak the truth as I saw it ... to portray people as they really are." Her aim was never to be politically correct or to propagandize; there were homosexuals, heterosexuals, the handicapped, etc., in her work because there were such people in her life. Critic Bonnie Zimmerman notes of Rule: "In a literary sense she is one of the most mainstream of writers ... the least connected to the lesbian feminist or lesbian separatist movement ... universalist in her views." Criticism of her work has since come full circle: a lesbian review of her final novel *After the Fire* pronounced her later work less lyrical and more closely allied with the widely available "pulp lesbian fiction." The independence of vision and striking adherence to Rule's own reality of lesbian/writer, regardless of criticism or censure from virtually all sides, has, with time, enhanced Rule's contribu-

Essay by
MARIE J. KUDA

431

Jane Rule's fiction, she has said, was based on her desire to "speak the truth as I saw it ... to portray people as they really are."

tion to the dissemination of gay and lesbian culture.

Rule's first novel, *Desert of the Heart*, was published in 1964, while she and her lover Helen Sonthoff were living in Vancouver and teaching English at a local university. The women were unprepared for the consequences of publishing a book about a lesbian love affair and Rule soon found herself a figurehead in the Canadian lesbian movement. The novel drew Rule into media prominence again in 1985 after the release of *Desert Hearts*, a film adaptation by Donna Deitch. The film, which won the Jury Prize at the 1986 United States Film Festival, was an underground success and boosted Naiad Press's sales by making *Desert* their version of a best-seller. Naiad Press responded to the popularity of the novel by issuing a second reprint featuring stills from the film on the cover and frontispiece. The renewed media focus on her work introduced Rule to a new generation of lesbian readers. Author and reviewer Lee Lynch found that her goals as a writer changed when she encountered *Desert of the Heart*: "Rule had the magical ability to treat her gay characters as if they could function normally in a world large enough to hold them ... it pushed back even further the walls which squeezed us, sometimes to death. The young dyke writers growing up will be stronger for [Radclyffe] Hall and for Rule, and will create a literature ever freer of doom because of our foremothers."

Considering herself primarily a writer of fiction, Rule was reluctant to accept a commission from Doubleday to write as a lesbian about lesbians. She spent some time weighing the consequences for herself, her partner, and her family before accepting the task of writing *Lesbian Images*. In the book's introduction, she notes that it was her father who helped her decide that the work was indeed necessary in overcoming the perception by readers that lesbianism was not accepted as "one of the faces of love." When the book was released in 1975, nascent lesbian presses like Diana, Daughters, and Naiad Press were still struggling to get off the ground; feminist and lesbian bookstores were just beginning to reach a viable market. So, to the hundreds of women from the United

States and Canada gathered at the second annual Lesbian Writers Conference in Chicago that year, Rule's book and the reissue of Foster's *Sex Variant Women in Literature* burst like twin bombshells. Many shared Rule's insight that being lesbian and a writer were inseparable and, in essence, defined one's politics, most applauded her courage in broaching the mainstream, some criticized her for not being more overt or setting forth their sense of what was "politically correct" in her own fiction. But all hailed *Lesbian Images* as a primer to a "great books" course in lesbian literature.

Rule's selections for *Lesbian Images* are worth noting: included are such notable women writers as Radclyffe Hall, Gertrude Stein, Willa Cather, Vita Sackville-West, Ivy Compton-Burnett, Elizabeth Bowen, Colette, Violette Leduc, Margaret Anderson, Dorothy Baker, and Maureen Duffy. In "Four Decades of Fiction," she covers Alma Routsong, Gale Wilhelm, Djuna Barnes, Elizabeth Cragin, Claire Morgan, Bertha Harris, and Rita Mae Brown. Her nonfiction discussion includes Kate Millett, Jill Johnston, Sidney Abbott, and Barbara Love, as well as Martin and Lyon. Subsequent scholarship would develop the ideas of coding in the work of Cather and Stein, the brutal side of some of Sackville-West's fiction, and other ideas introduced by Rule.

In addition to writing *Lesbian Images* and seven novels, Rule has authored three collections of essays and short fiction. She has also contributed short pieces to the lesbian and gay small press—her short stories have been collected in *Theme for Diverse Instruments* and *Inland Passage;* her essays in *A Hot-Eyed Moderate;* and *Outlander* include works of both genres. In her contribution to the *Index on Censorship,* Rule wrote that her work is still at the mercy of homophobic reviewers, publishing practices, and customs agents in three countries: "No Canadian writer can make a living without reaching the wider audiences for French or English, our two official languages." She has chosen to be published in the United States by Naiad Press and by Pandora Press in England because "Feminist and gay presses are willing to keep books in print long enough to sell by word of mouth.... Only in Canada do I still publish with a mainstream press."

Although Rule's long term reputation and critical acclaim may well be based on her stylistically original fiction, her nonfiction, teaching, and advocacy for lesbian writers have had equal impact on lesbian studies and the creation of a lesbian culture. She has said it best herself: "As a lesbian, I believe it is important to stand up and be counted, to insist on the dignity and joy loving another woman is for me. If that gets in the way of people's reading my books, I have finally to see that it is their problem

American-born Canadian novelist and author of short fiction.

Born: Plainfield, New Jersey, March 28, 1931; immigrated to Canada, 1956; became Canadian citizen.

Education: Mills College, B.A. 1952.

Career: Has held a variety of jobs including typist, teacher of handicapped children, and store clerk. Teacher of English, Concord Academy, Concord, Massachusetts, 1954–56; assistant director, International House, 1958–59, lecturer in English, 1959–70, then visiting lecturer in creative writing, 1973–74, University of British Columbia, Vancouver. Author of column "So's Your Grandmother" in *Body Politic*; contributor of reviews and articles to periodicals and journals, including *Canadian Literature, Chatelaine, Globe and Mail, Housewife, Queen's Quarterly, Redbook,* and *San Francisco Review*.

Recipient: Canadian Authors' Association best novel award and best short story award, both 1978; Gay Academic Union Literature Award, 1978; Fund for Human Dignity award of merit, 1983; Canadian Institute for the Blind's Talking Book of the Year Award, 1991.

Agent: Georges Borchardt, Inc., 136 East 57th Street, New York, New York 10022, U.S.A.

and not mine…. I regret the distorting prejudices that surround me … they will not defeat me, either as a lesbian or a writer."

HIS NOR HERS

"His nor Hers" reprinted from *Inland Passage*, Naiad Press, copyright 1985 by Jane Rule.

The virtue of a reclusive husband is the illusion of freedom he may provide for his wife once the children are old enough for school and social lives of their own. Gillian's husband did not like her to be out as many evening as she was, raising money and/or enthusiasm for one good cause or another. She irritated him also when she was at home, either being far too noisy and playful with their two daughters, already inclined to giggle, or busy at her typewriter clacking out right-minded letters to the editor, to her member of the legislative assembly, to the prime minister himself. But, when she asked him what he wanted her to do, he couldn't say. Gillian suggested that his image of a wife was a warm statue, breathing quietly in the corner of the couch, not even turning her own pages to disturb his reading. It was a far less offensive image to him than it was to her. A quiet presence was what a wife should be, but increasingly he had to settle for a quiet absence.

"Do you know where your daughters are half the time?" he asked her.

"Yes," Gillian answered, for she knew what homes of friends they'd found more hospitable to their taste in music, their interest in their hair, their bursts of high-humoured silliness.

"Well, I don't. I don't know where you are half the time."

"Only because you don't listen."

How could he pay attention through all their mindless morning gossip simply for casually dropped clues to their whereabouts, he wanted to know.

"You can't, darling," Gillian replied. "And if we're all resigned to that, why can't you be?"

Sometimes, when he remembered to, he studied Gillian's clothes to decide whether or not she was dressing appropriately for where she said she was going. Since she inclined to suits without more adornment than a bright scarf at her throat, he thought it only fair to dismiss the idea of her being unfaithful to him. She was cooperative enough when it occurred to him to make love to her, and she had no cause to complain, as some women did, about an overly demanding husband. He had never been suspicious enough to try to check up on her. It would have seemed to him also somehow beneath him. He was not the kind of man to have married a woman he couldn't trust.

He wondered occasionally if he shouldn't have allowed her to take some sort of part-time job, something dignified and clearly low paying to indicate that it was an interest rather than a necessity. It might have used up some of her tireless and tiresome energy and made her more content to stay at home in the evening. But he was not the kind of man to marry a woman who wanted to work, and Gillian had never been forceful in such suggestions.

"It's good for your company image to have a wife active in the community," Gillian reminded him.

Gillian had the taste to do nothing strident, like marching for abortion or peace. She raised money for the art gallery, lobbied for better education for handicapped children, for scholarships for the gifted, and she supported the little theatres. She never asked him for unreasonable donations, nor did she drag him, as so many other husbands were dragged, to the symphony or gallery openings.

"With your interest in the arts, why don't you want to stay at home and read a good book."

"I'm a people person, darling. That's all."

Clearly "people" could not include him, the singular and solitary man that he was. But he had to admit that she never discouraged him from fishing or hunting, even encouraged him to take longer and more expensive sporting holidays than he could make up his mind about for himself since he did not like the idea of being selfish.

JANE **RULE**   435

"You're not selfish. You're a very generous man. Why not occasionally be generous to yourself?"

Away from his wife and daughters, he could stop brooding about them, stop feeling left out of their lives, for which he had no taste to be included. Sometimes he wondered what it would have been like to have a son, but he was even less easy in the company of men if there were no business topic to preoccupy them. He fished and hunted alone. What he would have enjoyed was knowing that Gillian was back at whatever lodge or cabin waiting for him. Yet that sort of wife might complain about being lonely.

Sometimes when Gillian grew impatient with his complaints, she said to him, "You have a good marriage and two lovely children. Why can't you just relax and be satisfied?"

Gillian believed what she said. Long-suffering was not on her list of virtues, nor did she think it should be. She complained neither to her husband nor about him. When she said of him, "He has a difficult temperament; he's reclusive," she was simply describing him to excuse his absence from plays, gallery openings—husbands weren't expected to be on committees. Gillian considered herself as good a wife as her husband could reasonably expect and a good deal better than he might have had.

He did not know that Gillian was not extravagant with his money because she had some of her own. She didn't think of herself as secretive about it so much as keeping her own counsel. There was no need for him to appropriate what was hers as if it were some sort of dowry. She didn't ask him the particulars of his financial life, about which he was also inclined to keep his counsel. Unlike him, she never suspected that he might be unfaithful. She knew that he wasn't. He was far too fastidious a man to be involved in anything he would think of as messy.

Gillian's conscience about him was perfectly clear. She did do good works. She was a good mother. And she knew more clearly than he did that he would be just as irritated with her at home as he was with her for not being there, not because she was an irritating woman but because he was an irritable man.

Gillian did not know how long ago it had first occurred to her that she would one day leave him, after the girls were raised and safely settled. Simply gradually her illusion of freedom made her feel she would one day enjoy the real thing. Gillian would not leave him for anyone else. It would be unfair to involve a third party in divorce. Therefore, whenever a third party became at all pressing about time Gillian did not have, emotional support she could not offer, long before there was any question of commitment, Gillian retreated into being a wife and mother with, yes, some feelings of guilt about the deserted lover but with a sense, too, that it was for the best since she refused to burden any lover with the guilt of feeling responsible for a broken marriage. When Gillian decided to leave, she would deal with the problem of her outraged husband by herself, for outraged she knew he would be, no matter how much he complained about her inadequacies.

"Duplicity" was not the word Gillian would have used to describe her life, perhaps because she could move quite openly with a lover, go out to dinner, go to the theatre without causing a flicker of gossip. She could even invite one home, though she didn't very often, out of loyalty to her husband really because invariably a lover asked, "How can you live with him?" For Gillian it wasn't all that difficult. She knew women who stayed with husbands who drank, who beat them, who didn't pay the bills. Her marriage in comparison was a solid, sane arrangement in which to raise children.

"But he's such an impossible person!" came the protest.

"Aren't we all," Gillian would ask, "one way or another?"

But she liked to avoid such disconnections when she could. Her lovers almost always befriended her daughters, sometimes even became their confidantes. Gillian enjoyed being able to include the girls in her happiness. Sometimes she even took them with her on a holiday with a lover, for their father couldn't abide traveling with children but wouldn't begrudge them the experience. Occasionally, Gillian thought, the girls mourned the loss of a lover even more than she did, but the period between lost love and restored intimate friendship usually didn't last long. By now Gillian had what might almost be described as a community of ex-lovers who had become friends.

With men such an arrangement would not have been possible. If Gillian had been attracted to men, her life might have been full of tension and deceit. As it was, she never had to lie to her husband about whom she was with and only very occasionally about where she was going.

Only once her husband said, "That friend of yours, Joan, I think she's a lesbian."

"She may be," Gillian said lightly, "but she's great, good fun."

Jane Rule in 1975, the year her *Lesbian Images* was published. The book offered biographical sketches and analyses of a number of mainstream writers, as well as an overview of lesbian-identified writing from the 1930s onward.

"Doesn't your own reputation concern you?"

"Of course, but I'm not a bigot, and neither are you."

In fact, Joan was only a good friend. Gillian's taste in women was for the feminine and sensitive. Her husband would never have suspected any of her lovers of being a lesbian. The idea would have offended his whole concept of womanhood. Her lovers might seem to him "flighty" or "neurotic" but never perverse.

It was Gillian's own behavior he would have suspected if he had ever seen her among her ex-lovers, for her bright scarf became an ascot, and she held her cigarette between her teeth when she lighted it. Her laughter was bold, and her eyes were direct and suggestive. Even the way she downed her beer, which she didn't touch at home, would have shocked him.

In this role, her daughters loved her best, for she was full of fun and daring. No matter what they were doing, there was the tension of excitement, which made them prance and whinny. They knew their mother was never like that around father. They associated their mother's mood with themselves away from him rather than with her friends.

Gillian acknowledged the latent eroticism she felt for her daughters and they for her. It was one of the joys of mothering daughters. She would brook no criticism from her friends about it.

"Why should I mind if they grow up to be lesbians?"

But they were both growing up to be even crazier about boys than they were about their mother and her exciting friends. Gillian didn't worry about that either, though it made her sometimes restless, aware of how empty her particular nest would be when they were gone and she had no buffer between her and her irritable and isolated husband. For, though he was critical of the girls, they had grown very good at teasing and cajoling him when it was necessary.

Was it about this time, too, that the pattern of her relationships with other women shifted? Lynn, who had to be called Lynn Number Two or Lynn R.—it had gotten that bad, her friends teased her, such a string of women she'd had—instead of beginning to make unreasonable demands, was simply drifting away, busy when Gillian had a free night, not home at the hour she knew Gillian habitually called. Lynn finally confessed that there was someone else.

Gillian felt both bereft and betrayed. She had never left a lover for someone else, as she wouldn't leave her husband. There was something immoral about inflicting jealous pain.

"Pain is pain," Lynn Number One, who resented this new designation, said to her. "Don't you think I was jealous of your husband?"

"But why would you be?"

"You sleep with him, don't you?"

"Once a month."

"You stay with him."

"The children," Gillian responded automatically.

"Gillian, you've always wanted your cake and to eat it, too. Face it: you're not getting any younger. What was in it for Lynn R.?"

"That's awfully calculating," Gillian said.

She began to drink too much, to get maudlin with old lovers about the past beauty of their relationships, their

Jane Rule with her lover, Helen, on the island of Galiano, British Columbia.

lasting loyalty. (She wasn't speaking to Lynn R.) She often had to be forcibly sobered up before she was sent home, and she was later getting there than she had ever risked, even at the passionate height of an affair. The security of home, which she had never lost sight of in delight, seemed less meaningful to her in sorrow. Before, she could bring all her own nourished happiness in to brighten the gloom. Now, far more particularly miserable than her husband, she could not endure his bleak moods. When he approached her sexually, she turned him harshly away.

"You are *my wife*," he said, more shocked than angry.

Gillian was shocked herself at how without generosity she was for him, how reckless of him. For she let him see how angry and out of control she was. She snatched up her coat and left the house.

She went to a lesbian bar where her friends had sometimes gone, a place too public for the way she arranged her life. There she picked up a young girl, hardly older than her own daughters, and took her to a hotel for the night.

"Won't you even tell me your name?" her young lover pleaded in the morning.

Gillian's terror overcame her remorse. She fled as cruelly as she had from her husband, revolting from what she had done. She was not that kind of woman, to take advantage of a mere child and to compound it with deserting her. If Gillian had had the presence of mind, she would have left money on the dresser.

Arriving home, Gillian expected to have the day to pull herself together and to figure out how to get back from the too far she had gone. Her husband had not gone to work. He sat in his chair in the living-room waiting for her. She put a surprised and guilty hand to her mouth. She had not made up her face, and his eyes were appraising her sternly.

"That is never to happen again," he said, a thought-out new confidence in his voice. "Nor are you ever going to go out in the evening more than one night a week. I have been a patient man, a far too patient man, and I've been taken advantage of."

"I want a divorce," Gillian said in a calm tone that masked hysteria.

"Don't be silly," he said, as if she'd suggested something like a drink before breakfast.

"I'm not being silly. I've come to my senses," Gillian said, first wondering what on earth that phrase meant, then frightened that she knew.

"If you call flinging yourself out of the house in the middle of the night ..."

"Ten o'clock."

"... sensible ..."

"This is a discussion that is now finally over," Gillian said. "Our lawyers can deal with the details."

"Gillian, we have been married for nineteen years. We have two still dependent children. What are you talking about? What's happened to you?"

"Because of the girls, I think you'd better be the one to move out," Gillian said in a practical tone.

"This is *my* house."

"It's *our* house, according to the law."

"I will not tolerate this, Gillian!"

"I suggest you talk it over with your lawyer. That's what I'm going to do," she said and turned to leave the room.

"Gillian!"

Halfway up the stairs, she heard the front door slam, and she sank right there, suddenly too weak to take another step. Though she had entertained the idea of leaving him for years, she had never considered the means of doing so. His lawyer was hers in so far as she had one.

WRITINGS

Novels

Desert of the Heart, 1964.
This Is Not for You, 1970.
Against the Season, 1971.
The Young in One Another's Arms, 1977.
Contract with the World, 1980.
Memory Board, 1987.
After the Fire, 1989.

Short Stories

Theme for Diverse Instruments, 1975.
Inland Passage, and Other Stories, 1985.

Other

Lesbian Images (literary criticism), 1975.
Outlander: Stories and Essays, 1981.
A Hot-Eyed Moderate (essays), 1985.
"Lesbian Literature Need Readers," in *Index on Censorship: International Magazine for Free Expression* (London), October 1990.
"Lesbians and Writers," in *InVersions: Writings by Dykes, Queers, and Lesbians*, 1991.

Adaptations

Desert of the Heart was filmed by Donna Deitch in 1985 and released as *Desert Hearts*.

Legally, she didn't know what "marriage breakdown" was. She did know that humanly hers had, and whatever irrationality and self-destructiveness had led her into this circumstance, there was now no going back.

Slowly Gillian got up and went to the phone in their bedroom. The first call she made was to a locksmith, ordering the locks on all the doors to be changed by four o'clock.

At six o'clock that evening, Gillian and her daughters sat at the dinner table, listening to a pounding fist on the front door, then on the back, not speaking to each other until they heard the slamming of the car door and the starting up of an engine.

"Are you afraid of him, Mother?" her youngest daughter asked timidly.

"I never have been," Gillian said.

"Is it legal?" her oldest daughter asked.

"It will be," Gillian said. "This evening you can play any music you want as loudly as you want, and you can invite your friends over."

But that evening the house was quieter than it would have been if the master of gloom had been home, his forced absence even more palpable than his presence.

Gillian overheard her younger daughter say, "I don't really like Daddy, but I'm used to him."

"He's our father," the older replied, but casually.

Ugly days stretched into ugly weeks in which Gillian often felt a prisoner in her own fortress. She had given up all her committees since her real interest in them had never been strong. They had been little more than a screen behind which she could lead her personal life. Now she had neither a personal life nor a husband to deceive, for he was now nothing but an enemy into whose hands she was determined not to fall. She saw none of the women who had been her intimates for so many years. Any hint of impropriety now would irreparably damage her case in court, leave her not only without a fair financial settlement but even without her daughters.

In the end, her husband behaved as Gillian had counted on him to, not generously but with scrupulous fairness. She could live in the house until the girls left home, at which point it would be sold, the proceeds divided between them. There was generous child support until the girls either reached twenty-one or finished college. For her own support, Gillian was responsible. The money her husband had never known she had made looking for a job less urgent than it should have been for Gillian's state of mind.

"Mother," her oldest daughter finally said to her, "even when Daddy was around, you used to have fun."

"You're right," Gillian said.

"Well, it's time you started having fun again."

It wasn't that simple. Gillian was more than ever at risk, the custody of her daughters the price she could pay for any visibility in the bars. The cohesiveness of her old friends, which she had once prized, excluded her as long as she could not behave as she'd expected others to behave, resigned to loss and open to new adventures of the heart. Gillian simply could not forgive Lynn Number Two her betrayal. There was something else, too. As long as she had been married, the limitations of any other relationship were clear. Now, when she tired of someone—supposing that woman were not as untrustworthy as Lynn Number Two—Gillian could see no way out, no iron-clad and moral excuse for waning interest. Could there be a woman so remarkable as to hold Gillian's interest for the rest of her life? She had never thought of a woman in those terms.

Gillian's husband enjoyed his perfect solitude no more than Gillian enjoyed her freedom. After his outrage had worn itself out, erupting only occasionally at some convenience or familiar object lost to him, he suffered from simple loneliness, which he had no social skills to combat. Even his sporting trips, which he had made sure he could still afford, were not the escapes from domestic irritation which they had been and lost their savor.

His daughters dutifully lunched with him, but he knew he bored them with his complaints, which would be repeated to their mother in a tone not sympathetic to him. He was not even sure what kind of sympathy he was asking for. He had been too deeply humiliated by Gillian's treatment of him to imagine that he wanted her back even on his own terms, which she would never agree to. He wanted back what he could not have, the illusion of Gillian as his wife.

And Gillian also wanted back what she could not have, not her husband, but the illusion of freedom he had given her.

MAY SARTON

IN HER INTRODUCTION to the 1974 edition of Eleanor May Sarton's *Mrs. Stevens Hears the Mermaids Singing*, Carolyn Heilbrun noted that "Sarton's life is a mirror image of the usual American success story. In those wildly famous lives where, Scott Fitzgerald has told us, there are no second acts, the glories and the riches soon betray the writer to madness, impotence, alcohol, literary vendettas.... [F]or Sarton, perhaps uniquely so, considering the accomplishments, there has been little organized acclaim, no academic attention, indifference on the part of the critical establishment.... [S]he has written twenty-seven books and, widely read, is only now beginning to get the critical attention properly due her."

Essay by
MICHAEL BRONSKI

After a single novel and book of poetry published in the 1940s, Sarton's output since 1950 has been prodigious. It was during the 1950s that Sarton's readership started to grow and she became a presence in the literary world (this was especially true of her autobiographical work). By the 1980s—due in part to Heilbrun's efforts and and an increased interest in feminist literary issues—Sarton's work began to receive the academic and critical attention that had earlier eluded it.

In essence, Sarton's writings explore the inner workings of human nature. The author's journals and poems are all detailed examinations of her life, emotions, and fears. At times, Sarton is reticent with regard to the material details of her life—the name of a lover, the exact nature of a fight with a friend—but she is forthcoming about her perceptions and passions. Many of Sarton's novels, such as *Mrs. Stevens Hears the Mermaids Singing* and *The Education of Harriet Hatfield*, feature investigations into personal interior worlds, worlds often similar to the author's own. When *Mrs. Stevens Hears the Mermaids Singing* was published, it was one of the first mainstream novels to deal with an openly lesbian character without any apology or psychoanalytic explanation. Sarton's portrait of Hilary Stevens is complex; although she leads a bisexual life, Stevens states that it is women who have always been her muse, her inspiration. Taken in this light, Sarton's autobiographical character offers a view of lesbianism that is not simply sexual, but the source of artistic creation as well.

May Sarton in 1959.

By contemporary standards, *Mrs. Stevens Hears the Mermaids Singing* seems mild, but the novel's publication eventually cost Sarton her teaching job (largely because she was too closely identified with her character). Although she has spoken frequently about her lesbianism, Sarton has not made the fact overtly central to her work. Despite this reticence, the tensions between the private and the political are very much present in Sarton's work and thought. As the author once indicated in *Paris Review:* "The militant lesbians want me to be militant and I'm just not."

In the *Journal of Homosexuality*, Margaret Cruikshank wrote of Sarton: "Obviously, a writer's persona should not be confused with her real life identity. Nevertheless, the experience of talking to May Sarton helped me understand that excluding her work from my article was a political rather than a literary choice, one that revealed my inability to place her *inside* the lesbian feminist movement. This unstated criterion required that the writer have a particular temperament and emotional history, that she be a certain kind of lesbian. If the critic insists on seeing citizenship papers before admitting writers to Lesbian Nation, she may miss not only women of Sarton's generation, but also others whose independence keeps them from political alignments." The world of solitude that Sarton inhabits is not one of rarified sensibility and platitudes. The emotions in her journals and novels are strongly felt and articulated. Anger comes through especially forcefully and knowingly in fictional accounts such as *As We Are Now*, about the social disregard of the elderly, or *Anger*, about emotional repression in relationships.

Anger also surfaces in Sarton's journals, particularly when she feels that her privacy has been invaded by uninvited outsiders. The solitude of May Sarton's work is a reflection of the privatization of her own life; it also serves as a source of solace. As Cruikshank remarked: "Solitude and independence have not only been natural choices for Sarton; they seem pre-conditions for her art."

Belgian-born American poet, novelist, and writer of nonfiction and children's literature.

Born: Wondelgem, May 3, 1912; brought to the United States in 1916; became a naturalized U.S. citizen in 1924.

Education: Shady Hill School, Cambridge, Massachusetts, and Institute Belge de Culture Française, Brussels, Belgium; graduated from Cambridge High and Latin School, 1929. Apprentice, Eva Le Gallienne's Civic Repertory Theatre, New York City, 1929–34; founder and director, Associated Actors Theatre, New York City, 1934–37; scriptwriter, Overseas Film Unit, New York City, 1941–52; Briggs-Copeland Instructor in English Composition, Harvard University, Cambridge, Massachusetts, 1949–52; lecturer, Bread Loaf Writers' Conference, Middlebury, Vermont, 1951–53; lecturer, Boulder Writers' Conference, Boulder, Colorado, 1954; lecturer in creative writing, Wellesley College, Wellesley, Massachusetts, 1960–64; poet-in-residence, Lindenwood College, St. Charles, Missouri, 1965. Phi Beta Kappa visiting scholar, 1960; visiting lecturer, Agnes Scott College, 1972. Fellow, American Academy of Arts and Sciences.

Recipient: New England Poetry Society Golden Rose Award, 1945; *Poetry* magazine Edward Bland Memorial Prize, 1945; Poetry Society of America Reynolds Lyric Award, 1952; Lucy Martin Donelly fellowship, Bryn Mawr College, 1953–54; Guggenheim fellow in poetry, 1954–55; Johns Hopkins University Poetry Festival Award, 1961; Emily Clark Balch Prize, 1966; National Endowment for the Arts grant, 1966; Sarah Josepha Hale Award, 1972; College of St. Catherine Alexandrine medal, 1975; Deborah Morton Award, Westbrook, 1981; Unitarian Universalist Women's Federation Ministry to Women Award, 1982; Avon/COCOA Pioneer Woman Award, 1983; Human Rights Award, 1985; Fund for Human Dignity Award, 1985; Before Columbus Foundation American Book Award, 1985; University of Maine Maryann Hartman Award, 1986; New England Booksellers Association New England Author Award, 1990. Honorary doctorates from Russell Sage College, 1958, New England College, 1971, Clark University, 1975, Bates College, 1976, Colby College, 1976, University of New Hampshire, 1976, Thomas Starr King School of Religious Leadership, 1976, Nasson College, 1980, University of Maine, 1981, Bowdoin College, 1983, and Goucher College, 1985.

Address: P.O. Box 99, York, Maine 03809, U.S.A.

MUD SEASON

In early spring, so much like a late autumn,
Grey stubble and the empty trees,
We must contend with an unwieldy earth.
In this rebirth that feels so much like dying,
When the bare patches bleed into raw mud,
In rain, in coarsening ooze, we have grown sluggard,
Cold to the marrow with spring's nonarrival:
To hold what we must hold is iron-hard,
And strength is needed for the mere survival.

By dogged labor we must learn to lift
Ourselves and bring a season in;
No one has ever called child-bearing easy,

Poems reprinted from
*Selected Poems of May
Sarton*, edited by Serena
Sue Hilsinger and Lois
Brynes, Norton, 1978.

May Sarton signing books in New York City at Womanbooks.

And this spring-bearing also asks endurance.
We are strained hard within our own becoming,
Forced to learn ways how to renew, restore.
Though we were dazzled once by perfect snow,
What we have not has made us what we are.
Those surface consolations have to go.

In early spring, so much a fall of will,
We struggle through muds of unreason,
We dig deep into caring and con-tention;
The cold unwieldy earth resists the spade.

But we contend to bring a difficult birth
Out from the lack of talent, partial scope,
And every failure of imagination.
Science and art and love still be our hope!
What we are not drives us to consummation.

INVOCATION

Come out of the dark earth
Here where the minerals
Glow in their stone cells
Deeper than seed or birth.

Come under the strong wave
Here where the tug goes
As the tide turns and flows
Below that architrave.

Come into the pure air
Above all heaviness

WRITINGS

Poetry

Encounter in April, 1937.
Inner Landscape, 1938.
The Lion and the Rose, 1948.
The Land of Silence, 1953.
In Time Like Air, 1958.
Cloud, Stone, Suit, Vine, 1961.
A Private Mythology, 1966.
As Does New Hampshire, 1967.
A Grain of Mustard Seed, 1971.
A Durable Fire, 1972.
Collected Poems: 1930–1973, 1974.
Selected Poems, 1978.
Halfway to Silence, 1980.
Letters from Maine: New Poems, 1984.
The Silence Now: New and Uncollected
    Earlier Poems, 1988.

Fiction

The Single Hound, 1938.
The Bridge of Years, 1946.
Shadow of a Man, 1950.
A Shower of Summer Days, 1952.
Faithful Are the Wounds, 1955.
The Fur Person, 1956.
The Birth of a Grandfather, 1957.
The Small Room, 1961.
Joanna and Ulysses, 1963.
Mrs. Stevens Hears the Mermaids Singing,
    introduction by Carolyn Heilbrun,
    1965.
Mrs. Pickthorn and Mr. Hare (fable),
    1966.
The Poet and the Donkey, 1969.
Kinds of Love, 1970.
As We Are Now, 1973.
Punch's Secret (juvenile), 1974.
Crucial Conversations, 1975.
A Walk through the Woods (juvenile),
    1976.
A Reckoning, 1978.
Anger, 1978.
The Magnificent Spinster, 1985.
The Education of Harriet Hatfield, 1989.

Nonfiction

I Knew a Phoenix: Sketches for an
    Autobiography, 1959.
Contributor, The Movement of Poetry,
    1962.
Plant Dreaming Deep (autobiography),
    1968.
Journal of Solitude, 1973.
A World of Light: Portraits and
    Celebrations, 1976.
The House by the Sea, 1977.
Writings on Writing, 1980.
Recovering: A Journal, 1980.
At Seventy: A Journal, 1984.
May Sarton: A Self-Portrait, edited by
    Marita Simpson and Martha
    Wheelock, 1986.
Encore: A Journal of the Eightieth Year,
    1993.

Other

Toscanini: The Hymn of Nations
    (screenplay), 1944.
Valley of the Tennessee (screenplay),
    1944.
Underground River (play), Play Club,
    1947.

Of storm and cloud to this
Light-possessed atmosphere.

Come into, out of, under
The earth, the wave, the air.
Love, touch us everywhere
With primeval candor.

SARAH
SCHULMAN

SINCE THE PUBLICATION of her first novel, *The Sophie Horowitz Story*, in 1984, Sarah Schulman's fiction and essays have provided a constant reminder to writers and readers of the possibilities and responsibilities of lesbian and gay fiction. Throughout all of her writing, Schulman explores the interaction between the nature of art and the reality of politics, examining not only the inherent tensions present there but the inescapable interdependency as well. In Schulman's writing and vision, good, truthful art and politics are inextricably bound together.

Essay by
MICHAEL BRONSKI

Schulman was born in New York City in 1958 into a Jewish, middle-class professional family. From an early age she has been involved in progressive politics and grass roots movements for social change: the women's movement, reproductive rights, lesbian and gay liberation, tenants rights, and most recently, AIDS work and lesbian empowerment. She is a founding member of both ACT-UP and the Lesbian Avengers.

After working for years as a waitress and writing essays, reviews, and news for the lesbian and gay press, she published her first novel, *The Sophie Horowitz Story*, about a lesbian reporter attempting to track down two radical feminist bank robbers who have recently resurfaced after ten years underground. Although Schulman relied upon the detective story genre to move her plot along, the novel is also a meditation on the state of lesbian politics and sexuality, as well as the potential of writing as a tool for social change. In her 1986 novel, *Girls, Visions and Everything* (the title comes from a passage in *On the Road* by Jack Kerouac), Schulman sets the action in a lesbian community on New York's lower East Side. Schulman examines the idea of pursuing personal freedom in a city, and a country, that is becoming increasingly hostile and dysfunctional. The novel begins, "Lila Futuransky always knew she wanted to be an outlaw, but she could never figure out which one. [S]he wanted to be free but couldn't decide what that meant."

All of Schulman's novels take place in Manhattan, and in them the city becomes a microcosm of social ills as well as a metaphor for the political and moral corruptions of the broader culture. Schulman insists on

451

Throughout all of her writing, Sarah Schulman explores the interaction between the nature of art and the reality of politics, examining their inherent tensions as well as their inescapable interdependencies.

exploring the individual's responsibility to her community as well as to the world. In an interview in *Women's Review of Books* she states: "I write about New York City. New York is a very stratified city and your layer of protection determines your sense of responsibility ... because that is the disease of how Americans live, people don't care about something unless it affects them personally. So marginal people know how they live and how the dominant culture lives. Dominant culture people know only how they live. The people who have the most power have the least information and the smallest sense of responsibility."

This view is manifest in Schulman's next three novels. *After Delores* is a lesbian detective *noir* in which an unnamed narrator, obsessed with her ex-lover Delores, stumbles onto a murder. Set in Manhattan's East Village, the plot gives Schulman a chance to satirize various artistic types while considering what it means to be working-poor or homeless in New York. Written in the style of James M. Cain and Dashiell Hammett, *After Delores* examines the role of the isolated individual living in an emotionally and physically dangerous environment.

In *People in Trouble*, Schulman looks at the individual's responsibility to her art as well as collective social problems. *People in Trouble* begins with a quote from Karl Marx: "It is not the consciousness of men that determine their being, but their social being that determine their consciousness." This positions Schulman's idea that political and moral action are inextricably bound up with a clear understanding of material reality. Although *People in Trouble* turns on the romantic triangle of a lesbian, a cross-dressing married woman, and her husband, and is set against the background of urban real estate development, the AIDS crisis, and ACT-UP (called "Justice" here), one of the main themes in the novel is the responsibility of the artist. In her *Women's Review of Books* interview, Schulman states that when she became involved with the art world, "what I found was really appalling to me. I found this group of people who really felt that they were better than other people, more important than other people, and who looked down on other people and didn't feel

American novelist, journalist, playwright, and essayist.

Born: New York City, July 28, 1958.

Education: Hunter College of the City University of New York.

Career: Has held a variety of jobs, including waitress, stagehand, secretary, and teacher. Full-time writer, beginning 1988. Book reviewer, *Advocate* and *New York Times Book Review*.

Memberships: Active in movements for social change: reproductive rights movement, gay and lesbian liberation movement, movement for tenants' rights. Member of ACT-UP, 1987–; founder with Jim Hubbard of the New York Lesbian and Gay Experimental Film Festival, 1986; cofounder of the Lesbian Avengers, 1992.

Recipient: Kitchen Media Bureau video grant, 1982; Fulbright fellow, 1984; American Library Association Gay Book Award, 1988.

---

any responsibility. In fact they felt that the world had a responsibility to them."

In *People in Trouble* Schulman specifically questions the idea that an artist is fulfilling her social responsibility by simply creating art and not partaking in a more active politic. The idea of belonging to—and feeling responsibility for—a group or a community permeates the book. This is a question that Schulman also discusses in the *Women's Review of Books:* "When a straight man says to me 'I don't believe in groups, I'm not a group person,' well, he belongs to the one group that's not called a group. He's unaware of the structure that he's living in. He doesn't feel the responsibility because he feels normal." The idea of the responsibility of the artist in a political world is also addressed in her essay "Why I Fear the Future," in which she quotes W. H. Auden's line, "Not one of my poems ever saved one Jew." She writes at the end of that essay, "Knowing that no large social gains can be won in this period, I still remain politically active. I do this because small victories are meaningful in individual lives. I do this because I don't want to be complicit in a future in which people will die and everyone else will be condemned to vicious banality."

This idea forms the basis for Schulman's novel *Empathy*, in which the main character, Anna O., attempts to make sense of a modern world in which the three mainstays of contemporary thinking—psychoanalysis, communism, and capitalism—are all proven failures. *Empathy* deals with some of the themes of the earlier novels—social responsibility, minoritization, urban decay—but investigates them further through formal invention in an attempt to completely link the personal (and the psychological) with the political. While *People in Trouble* pays tribute to Marx in its epitaph (as well as its analysis), *Empathy* does so to Freud, with Schulman naming two of her characters, Anna O. and Dora, after two of

Freud's most famous cases. Schulman also views the work as a challenge to the false linearity of the "coming-out novel," attempting to address the creation of lesbian identity formally as well as in the content of the novel.

Schulman's fiction addresses the very pertinent question of how we might be able to live responsibly and fruitfully in a politically corrupt world. Her political work with ACT-UP and the Lesbian Avengers, as well as other social action groups, has been a major influence on her writing. Her role as an artist has been guided by her political actions and ideals, and she steadfastly refuses to view "art" and "artists" as separate from or above political concerns.

Sarah Schulman told the Companion:

"The great challenge facing openly lesbian writers whose work is overtly from a lesbian perspective is to end the marginalization of our voice and see our work accepted as American literature and not a special interest novelty act."

GIRLS, VISIONS AND EVERYTHING

Excerpt reprinted from *Girls, Visions and Everything*, Seal Press, copyright 1986 by Sarah Schulman.

When the dust cleared Lila was standing alone on the sidewalk almost giving in to tears. But, priding herself on her good nature and ability to rebound from any situation, she walked back, softly, into the Pyramid Club. Leaning on the bar for a moment to regain her composure, she glanced around the place, to make sure there were no witnesses. Then she saw Emily Harrison sitting quietly on a corner stool looking demure in a neato black lace hat of her own making.

"Hi Emily, I just got mud in my eye. You know what that means? I just got humiliated by a woman. Shit. Want to dance with me?"

It was Thelma Houston singing *Don't Leave Me This Way*. They boogied around a bit, sort of weirdly, until Lila tried to really dance, twirl her and everything. To her surprise, she ended up being twirled instead, since Emily's arms were much stronger than she anticipated. Still, they never did quite get in sync with each other.

"Hey Emily. You feel like talking? I kinda want to talk."

They walked outside, headed towards the Kitsch-Inn where Emily spent every spare moment working on shows. She'd been sleeping there too, on the make-up table, when nothing else was available. It was hot for May, everyone was out on the street. The sky was clear.

"So Lila, what do you want to talk about?" Emily's face was shining in the night light. Lila couldn't look her in the eye, and watched the city instead as they walked along on the sidewalk. Lila felt okay about Emily. She didn't know her very well. They'd only been together over a few joints. It was always a fun conversation which would end very politely as though nothing really important or intimate had gone on. Still, it had occurred to her that Emily had a chameleon's beauty. She was bland in a crowd but somehow mysteriously alluring one on one, if anybody bothered to look.

The first time Lila ever noticed her was in a performance at the Kitsch-Inn. It was a lesbian version of *A Streetcar Named Desire* and Emily was Stella Kowalski. She'd looked exactly like Stella with thin arms in a sleeveless cotton dress, clearly defined neck bones, a few lines in her face. Like she really was pretty, but just a little tired.

"That Stanley," she'd said, and Lila had really believed she was Stella, picturing how her naked legs would wrap around Marlon Brando when he carried her off to make love.

"Stella's not strong," Emily said, sitting on the floor of the Inn, "but she has balance. I'm the same way. I work at a textile factory, always lifting things, working the machinery, and the guys can't figure out where the power comes from. They think it's cute. It turns them on."

Lila understood why. Emily was attractive in a soft way, the kind of pretty that deceived men into thinking they could easily have her because that's what that kind of pretty women are for.

"Lila, do you want to smoke some grass?"

She liked the way Emily said *grass*, an old-fashioned word. They sat and talked about performing and traveling. Then Lila needed cigarettes but was afraid, in a way, to go out, because that might mean the discussion was over. She took the risk anyway, all high and everything, and when she came back, Emily suggested they go to the apartment where she was house-sitting so she could feed the cats.

The walk was misty, quiet. So calm, it had to be a movie set. They were quiet together and Lila liked that. Then Emily babbled things, the kind of things you babble when you're high, and she wasn't embarrassed. Lila liked that too.

"Emily, look at that woman in the gelatti store. The one with her hair dyed black and bleached blonde on top. She's an Italian lesbian named Tina. You lived in Italy, right? You might want to meet her. She's real pretty. Some of my friends told me about her. They're going in for gelatti three times a day just to make conversation. Want to stop and say hi?"

SARAH **SCHULMAN**   455

Novels

The Sophie Horowitz Story, 1984.
Girls, Vision, and Everything, 1986.
After Delores, 1988.
People in Trouble, 1990.
Empathy, 1992.
Rat Bohemia, forthcoming.

Short Stories

"The Penis Story," in *Women on Women*, edited by Joan Nestle and Naomi Holoch, 1990.

Nonfiction

My American History: Lesbian and Gay Life during the Reagan/Bush Years, 1994.

Contributor

The Tribe of Diana: Writings by Jewish Women, edited by Melanie Kaye Kantrowitz and Irena Klepfisz, 1985.
Things that Divide Us, edited by Faith Conlon, Rachel Da Silva, and Barbara Wilson, 1985.

"AIDS and Homelessness: Thousands May Die in the Streets," in *Nation*, 10 April 1989.
"Why I Fear the Future," in *Critical Fictions*, edited by Philomena Mariani, 1991.
"The Surprise of the New: Five Women Writers Who Are Making a Difference," in *Advocate*, 21 May 1991.
"What Ideals Guide Our Actions? Artists, Censorship, and Building Community," in *Out-Look*, winter 1991.
Author of introduction, *Love Bites*, by Della Grace, 1991.
"Is The NEA Good for Gay Art," in *Culture Wars: Documents from the Recent Controversies in the Arts*, edited by Richard Bolton, 1992.
"Special Food," in *Mother Jones*, January–February 1992.
"Getting Normal," in *Mother Jones*, March–April 1992.

Plays

Art Failures, with Robin Epstein (produced New York, 1983).
Whining and Dining, with Robin Epstein (produced New York, 1984).
And coproducer, *When We Were Very Young: Radical Jewish Women on the Lower East Side* (produced New York, 1984).
And coproducer, *The Swashbuckler* (adaptation of story by Lee Lynch; produced New York, 1985).
Epstein on the Beach, with Robin Epstein (three-act; produced New York, 1985).
Hootenanny Night (produced New York, 1986).
Salome/Psychology (produced New York, 1992).
Empathy (produced New York, 1993).
The Group, Guilty with an Explanation, and 1984 (produced New York, 1993).

"No thanks. You can if you want to. I'll wait outside."

Lila was embarrassed again. She had invited someone into her fantasy and they had refused.

"I'm sorry, I guess that sounds sort of coarse. I don't know what I'm talking about. I'm just high. Forget I ever said it."

But Emily saved the moment with a wide smile and Lila felt her body dip into the warm breeze filling the space between them. This was a friend.

In a tenement on East Fourth Street, on the fourth floor, the window overlooked a silent summer street. Some Black men murmuring, someone playing the drums, a lone bicycle. She was a pretty woman in a small apartment on a hot night.

Their talk was full of memories and association, comfortable as old friends, but with the excitement of describing themselves to each other for the first time. Eudora Welty, The Allman Brothers, *Giovanni's Room*, Top Cat, reading Dostoyevsky in high school and finding out there were things to think about in life, like how much control you have and when to take it. About rape, about abortion, about being straight.

"When I lived in Europe I went out with men a few times, but I decided to wait until I met lesbians."

This was a woman who waits.

"I liked being straight," she said, "some of it. But after three months or so I wouldn't want to have sex with them anymore. I would feel repulsed."

"I haven't touched a penis since 1979," Lila told her. "I do have this one friend though, Sal Paradise. He lives in my building. We hang out together. One night, about a year ago, we were up late in my apartment drinking and talking and I felt so close to him that I wanted to reach out and make love with him but he said no."

"And now …?"

"Now we get along fine. What the fuck. People want to sleep with each other at different times for different reasons. It's no secret. It doesn't have to poison everything."

First Emily sat across the floor from Lila and then she sat next to her. Lila brushed some ashes off Emily's leg without thinking. She liked her. She felt like a friend. She wouldn't have minded curling up with her and kissing, but not for romance. She just liked her.

They sat and smoked cigarettes like men do in Hollywood versions of tenement apartments and Lila wondered if Emily was considering kissing her too, or if she was just waiting. Everything felt good and calm. So, Lila, knowing the ways of the grapevine, decided to tell the sad tale of her plan for Helen Hayes, just so Emily wouldn't find out later from someone else. Lila really liked talking to Emily and wanted her to know the truth. She told all the gory details and was genuinely surprised when Emily started laughing out loud.

"You mean you've spent that much time thinking about Helen?"

"Well, it's not like it was the most pressing thing on my mind," answered Lila, a bit defensively. "I just noticed her. Listen, I have lots of crushes all over the place. I just sit back and look at them and think, some of this will come to be and the rest won't, so I'll just enjoy imagining it all for now."

Emily's response was to realize how late it was and how sleepy she was getting, since she had to be at the factory by seven the next morning. Lila put on her shiny shoes and linen jacket and Emily got back to the business of feeding the cats, as if Lila had just stopped by for the rent check, or to deliver a package.

"Come by the Inn and visit."

"I will," Lila said, "I will," and stepped out into the early morning.

RANDY SHILTS

IN SOME WAYS, Randy Shilts set the standard by which other works of gay journalism are to be judged. Beginning with his work as an openly gay journalist during college, he moved quickly into the gay press, coming to San Francisco in 1975 as part of the staff of the *Advocate*. His research for a series of articles on gay public health problems, which appeared until 1978, provided a framework of reference for later assessments of the impact of AIDS. His unique position as a reporter in the mainstream press whose beat was specifically designated as the gay community began in 1977 at KQED-TV. An outgrowth of his free-lance reporting prior to his staff position at the *San Francisco Chronicle*, his writing ranged from book reviews and analytical pieces on movement organizations for major gay and lesbian periodicals, through news reports on the complex politics of the Bay Area gay and lesbian community, and culminating in three major works of contemporary gay social commentary and historiography, *The Mayor of Castro Street: The Life and Times of Harvey Milk, And the Band Played On: Politics, People and the AIDS Epidemic*, and *Conduct Unbecoming: Lesbians and Gays in the U.S. Military*.

Essay by
ROBERT B. MARKS
RIDINGER

　　The Mayor of Castro Street marks the beginning of modern gay and lesbian political biography. Based upon numerous personal interviews and public records, it is the story of the career and assassination of San Francisco Supervisor Harvey Milk, the first openly gay elected public official in the United States. Through the events in Milk's life, Shilts also details the coalescence of gays as a force in San Francisco and California state political life, in particular the campaign against Proposition Six, a legislative initiative aimed at removing homosexual teachers from all California schools. With the exception of *The Crusaders*, a 1972 compilation by Kay Tobin and Randy Wicker of the biographies of prominent activists, *The Mayor of Castro Street* stands as one of the few full-length biographies available on gay and lesbian leaders. It was joined subsequently by such works as Troy Perry's *Don't Be Afraid Anymore* and Mike Hippler's *Matlovich: The Good Soldier*, illustrating the breadth of the developing genre.

Randy Shilts was best known for his investigative reporting in such books as *The Mayor of Castro Street: The Life and Times of Harvey Milk, And the Band Played On: Politics, People and the AIDS Epidemic,* and *Conduct Unbecoming: Lesbians and Gays in the U.S. Military.*

With the appearance of the AIDS epidemic in late 1981, the face of the American gay and lesbian community was altered forever. As the only reporter working for a major city newspaper exclusively assigned to covering the gay and lesbian community in a city that was being devastated by the disease, Shilts was in a unique position to gather information on both the slow progress of medical research on the virus and the federal government's lack of response to the crisis. In his second book, *And the Band Played On,* Shilts initially presents the human faces of the epidemic at the research laboratories of the National Institute of Health, spotlights local clinics in many cities, and discusses the ever-increasing number of confused, frightened, and angry victims. The final section covers the massive demonstration in Washington, D.C., in 1987, by which time more than 20,000 Americans had died of the disease. *And the Band Played On* created the framework of analysis that was later used by works such as James Kinsella's *Covering the Plague: AIDS and the American Media.*

One of the most controversial issues for advocates of equal rights for homosexuals has been the historic position taken by the United States armed services that such persons were unsuitable for military life and were to be summarily discharged if discovered. While several internal studies by various branches and numerous articles in the gay and lesbian press repeatedly called for change, little was done to formally research and document the origins and impact of these policies. The first major works on the subject were Allan Bérubé's *Coming Out under Fire: The History of Gay Men and Women in World War Two* and *Gays in Uniform: The Pentagon's Secret Reports,* both published in 1990. The latter reprinted the full texts of two reports and several memoranda from the Defense Personnel Security Research and Education Center done in 1988 and 1989 on the issue of the suitability of gays and lesbians for military service. Both reports found no substantive grounds for the historic prohibition.

Shilts's third book, *Conduct Unbecoming,* picks up the subject where Bérubé's earlier analysis ended and follows the changing conditions of life for the military's gay cadre from the Vietnam War to Operation Desert Storm. Personal accounts of both enlisted personnel and career officers of both genders form the bulk of the text and illuminate established policy. The book focuses on the situationally flexible ethics of application of the formal ban on homosexuals in the armed forces during periods of exigency—such as Vietnam and the Korean War.

AND THE BAND PLAYED ON

August 1980: Fire Island, New York

Larry Kramer looked across the table toward Enno Poersch. Larry could tell from the edge on Enno's deep, broad voice that he was frantic with concern.

Enno recounted, again, the mysterious diarrhea, vague fatigue, and stubborn rashes that had devastated his lover Nick. Endless tests by countless doctors had found nothing, and the strict health-food regimen to which Nick had adhered religiously for years wasn't doing any good either. Larry was a famous author who seemed to know everybody, Enno thought; he should know something.

"Aren't there hospitals where they specialize in treating bizarre sicknesses?" Enno asked.

Larry remembered when he had met Nick on an all-gay cruise of the Caribbean.

Witty, gregarious, and handsome in a compact Italian way, Nick was a popular cruise staffer. Every day, Nick had sat away from the continuous partying to write long love letters to Enno, and at each port, packets of Enno's romantic missives waited for Nick. They were the kind of lovey-dovey letters that Larry had always wanted, and the pair's love seemed to have lost none of its luster in the eight years since they had met on a sunny Fire Island beach.

As Enno talked about taking Nick from hospital to hospital, Larry imagined Enno, a tall, broad-shouldered lumberjack of a man, cradling the small, wiry Nick in his arms while he carried him up steep, steely stairways to save his life. The image made Larry want to cry, but no, he didn't know anything about hospitals or doctors or what could be ailing Nick.

After Enno excused himself, Larry thought about how strange it was that summer. All that people seemed to talk about were the latest intestinal parasites going around. Dinner conversation often evolved into guys swapping stories about which medications stomped out the stubborn little creatures and whether Flagyl, the preferred antiparasite drug, was really carcinogenic. It was like eavesdropping on a bunch of old ladies sharing arthritis stories on shaded benches in Miami.

Excerpts reprinted from *And the Band Played On*, St. Martin's Press, copyright 1987 by Randy Shilts.

American journalist, biographer, and author of nonfiction.

Born: Davenport, Iowa, August 8, 1951.

Education: University of Oregon, B.S., 1975.

Career: KQED-TV, San Francisco, correspondent for *Newsroom* and City Hall correspondent for *Ten O'Clock News*, 1977–80; KTVU-TV, Oakland, California, reporter, 1979–80; *San Francisco Chronicle*, staff reporter, 1981–87, national correspondent, 1988–94. Contributor of hundreds of articles to *San Francisco Chronicle*. Frequent lecturer at universities, professional association gatherings, and national health organization conferences.

Recipient: American Society of Journalists and Authors' Outstanding Author Award, 1988; Association for Education in Journalism and Mass Communication's Professional Excellence Award, 1988; Bay Area Book Reviewers' Association Award for Nonfiction, 1988; American Medical Writers Association's John P. McGovern Award Lectureship in Medical Writing, 1989; appointed to a Mather Lectureship; named University of Oregon Outstanding Young Alumnus, 1993; Parents and Friends of Lesbians and Gays' Oscar Wilde Award, 1993; California Public Health Association's Outstanding Print Media Award, 1993.

Died: Died of AIDS-related complications in Guerneville, California, February 17, 1994.

Later that night, Larry made his way toward the Ice Palace, where the never-ending Fire Island summer party was in full swing. He walked tentatively through the crowded doorway and saw the "Marlboro Man" saunter languorously through the disco. Larry knew that, intellectually, he could hold his own with anybody in New York, but the sight of Paul Popham, so self-assured in his model-handsome good looks, always left Larry in awe, the way you have to catch your breath after you see a movie star.

At the Y, Larry had told Paul that he had such a naturally well-defined body that he didn't need to work out, and Paul responded with a shy aw-shucks ingenuousness that reminded Larry of Gary Cooper or Jimmy Stewart. At the Ice Palace, the thumping heart of Fire Island nightlife, Larry wondered what it would be like to be Paul, to fit in so well and be accepted in a way Larry, the outsider, had never experienced. No matter where he was, Paul seemed to settle naturally among the beautiful people. On Fire Island, he lived in *the* house with Enno, Nick, and a few other handsome men who made the A-list of every major island party.

This was not Larry's summer to fit in. He hadn't even bothered to buy a house share, slipping to the island for a weekend here or there. He kept a decidedly low profile, but that didn't prevent some nasty moments. The gay man who owned the grocery store had glared at Larry when he was buying an orange juice. "You're trying to ruin the island," the grocer glowered. "I don't understand why you come here."

As the deejay turned up the volume on a Donna Summer song, Larry watched an old friend, another writer, enter the Ice Palace, glance in his direction, and purposefully walk the other way.

The antipathy, Larry Kramer knew, surrounded the book he had written about gay life in New York and on this island. Everything, from its title, *Faggots*, to its graphic descriptions of hedonism on the Greenwich Village–Cherry Grove axis had stirred frenzy among both gay reviewers and the people whose milieu Larry had set out to chronicle. Manhattan's only gay bookstore had banned the novel from its shelves while gay critics had advised readers that its purchase represented an act inimical to the interests of gay liberation.

Randy Shilts, an openly gay reporter in 1977, poses in one of San Francisco's gay bars, where he was filming for a television news story on alcoholism among the city's gay community.

Faggots had explored every dark corner of the subculture that gays had fashioned in the heady days after gay liberation. There were scenes of drug-induced euphoria at the discos, all-night orgies in posh Upper East Side co-ops, and fist-fucking at The Toilet Bowl, one of the many Manhattan sleaze bars where every form of exotic sexuality was explored with gritty abandon. The story climaxed with a weekend of parties and dancing on Fire Island, punctuated by cavorting in the Meat Rack, a stretch of woods that is home to some of the most animated foliage since Birnam Wood marched to Dunsinane.

Against this backdrop, lovers argued about fidelity and the plausibility of having anything resembling a meaningful commitment in the midst of such omnipresent carnality. When the book's protagonist, a Jewish screenwriter–movie producer not unlike Larry Kramer himself, sees his own hopes for love fade, he delivers a tirade that raised many troubling questions.

"Why do faggots have to fuck so fucking much?" Larry had written. "It's as if we don't have anything else to do ... all we do is live in our Ghetto and dance and drug and fuck ... there's a whole world out there! ... as much ours as theirs ... I'm tired of being a New York City–Fire Island faggot, I'm tired of using my body as a faceless thing to lure another faceless thing, I want to love a Person! I want to go out and live in a world with that Person, a Person who loves me, we shouldn't *have* to be faithful!, we should *want* to be faithful! … No relationship in the world could survive the shit we lay on it."

It all needs to change, Larry's protagonist told an unfaithful lover at the book's climax, "before you fuck yourself to death."

The book had proved a sensation, but ever since its publication, Larry had been something of a persona non grata on the island, returning only occasionally to visit friends and observe. It was already past 1:00 a.m. as he watched Paul Popham squire his handsome boyfriend, Jack Nau, back to the dance floor. The beautiful people, at last, were beginning to descend on the Ice Palace. Life on this long spit of sand in the Atlantic, Larry knew, was a regimen of sybaritic sameness.

Afternoons on the beaches were followed by light dinners, perhaps a nap, and then some outrageous party, before adjournment to whatever was the fashionable disco of the season. Of course, nobody got to the Ice Palace before 2:00 a.m., so you'd need some drugs to stay up. Once properly buzzed, it would be hard to get to sleep early, so you'd stop at the Meat Rack after dancing, and then you'd eventually walk home as the sun was rising over the sand. The unchanging ritual made Larry feel old. At forty-five, he didn't have the long nights in him anymore, and he wondered how the other guys could subject themselves to weekends that were more of a burnout than even the hectic pace of life in Manhattan.

At times, Larry Kramer compared the gay life of New York with San Francisco; it was another penchant that irritated the Manhattan gay intelligentsia. Larry had been in San Francisco the day Harvey Milk and Mayor George Moscone were shot, and he had wept the night that 30,000 candles glimmered outside City Hall and speakers talked idealistically of changing the world. He had been amazed to see the governor of California, the entire state supreme court, and scores of other officials at Milk's memorial service. Gays in New York had never achieved such power and respect, he thought, because they seemed more intent on building a better disco than a better social order. Being gay in New York was something you did on weekends, it seemed. During the week everybody went back to their careers and played the game, carefully concealing their sexuality and acting like everything was okay.

Of course, this was not to say that Larry was some crazy gay militant. In fact, he didn't have much use for the gay activist types in New York. The radicals seemed ensconced in rhetoric that was as passé as Chairman Mao. The more respectable gays, who talked earnestly of civil rights, seemed more intent on defending the current gay life-style than on changing it to something more meaningful. Rather than fight for the right to get married, the gay movement was fighting for the prerogative of gays to bump like bunnies.

The community seemed lost, and sometimes Larry felt lost. He had created two hits in his life and those were now behind him. First, after years in the movie business, Larry had written and produced a film based on a D. H. Lawrence novel that everybody agreed could never be made into a movie. *Women in Love* became one of the most acclaimed films of its year, winning an Oscar nomination in screenwriting for Larry and an Academy Award for one of its stars, Glenda Jackson. He had produced other films, but his next big hit as an artist, albeit controversial, was *Faggots*. And now he was fiddling with another novel and typing some screenwriting assignments, but in truth, he felt something like the gay community itself, at sixes and sevens and not really set in any particular direction.

Paul Popham had noticed Larry Kramer at the Ice Palace and thought, briefly, that he ought to give *Faggots* another try. He had managed to read only twenty or thirty pages before he got bored. He had a hard time seeing why anybody would be so deadly serious about being homosexual. Yes, Paul was gay, but it was no more an overwhelming trait than the fact he had been a Green Beret or that he had grown up in Oregon. It just was, and he didn't see any reason to talk about it much. He never felt discriminated against, never pondered suicide, nor wrestled with any guilt about being homosexual. Being gay had, at worst, been only a mild inconvenience, something he had to maneuver around.

None of Paul's private life was anybody else's damn business, he thought. None of it had much to do with politics either. Like a lot of gays on Wall Street, he voted his pocketbook as a registered Republican. This year, he wasn't crazy about the Reaganites, but Carter was a wimp. Come November, Paul had every intention of voting for independent presidential candidate John Anderson, a moderate Republican congressman from Illinois.

Paul scanned the dance floor, taking in the cream of New York gay society, the taut-bodied mustachioed men who were so beautiful you worried they might break if you stared too hard. It all made Paul regret that he hadn't taken better advantage of his share in the beat-up old house on Ocean Walk. Enno had been renting the place for years, and Paul had moved in this year to take the room of his best friend Rick Wellikoff.

Rick had mentioned last September that he had some funny bumps behind his ear. He hadn't wanted to go to the doctor, but Paul talked him into going to the famous dermatologists at New York University, where

Paul was being treated for persistent psoriasis. Both Paul and Rick were stunned when the doctors said Rick had cancer, an unheard-of kind of cancer called Kaposi's sarcoma. It was even stranger when the doctor mentioned that there was another gay man with the same cancer at a nearby hospital. Rick and the second patient, it turned out, even had some mutual friends.

Rick hadn't seemed too sick until lately, and even now it wasn't that he was terribly ill. He just felt dog-tired all the time. Paul thought that maybe Rick's job as a fifth-grade teacher in a rough Brooklyn neighborhood was burning him out, but Rick insisted it was more than that. He quit his job and stayed holed up with his lover in their brownstone on West 78th Street. With a heavy load of work and the bedside visits with Rick, it was all Paul could do to get away for a rare weekend of carefree nights at the Ice Palace and days on friendly Fire Island sands....

July 29, 1981: New York University Medical Center, New York City

Larry Kramer was startled to see David Jackson in Dr. Alvin Friedman-Kien's waiting room. An antique dealer, David was a friendly, nondescript man in his late thirties who sold odds and ends from a shop on Bleecker Street. Larry had come to talk to Friedman-Kien because he was frantic about the new cancer he had read of in *The New York Times*. Friedman-Kien was the doctor who had put together the early KS epidemiology for the CDC. None of his friends seemed that concerned, but Larry had more than a philosophical interest in the subject. He had a history of sexually transmitted diseases not unlike the KS victims he had read about in the paper. So did almost everyone he knew, leading Larry to think this could be something major. Still, the author wasn't prepared to actually run into somebody he knew the moment he arrived at the office of the big expert. David started talking, almost to himself, as if he were trying to straighten everything out in his own mind.

"I was walking the beach at Fire Island and decided to turn over a new leaf," David said. "I was going to eat right and watch my nutrition."

His voice trailed off, and he looked pleadingly toward Larry and told him about seeing these funny purple spots.

"I don't have any friends," David said. "I'm ashamed to tell anybody about this. Will you come and visit me?"

* * *

This was only the tip of the iceberg, Friedman-Kien told Larry Kramer. It was going to get bigger, and studies had to get started right away.

"I don't think anybody's going to do anything about it," the doctor said. "You've got to help. I need money for research. It takes two years to get grants."

Larry had heard of some other guys who had come down with the disease, friends from Fire Island. He promised Friedman-Kien he would get them together in his apartment to try to raise some money.

"What can I do to not get this?" Larry asked, trying to keep the lingering hypochondria out of his voice.

"I know what I'd do if I were a gay man," said Friedman-Kien.

Larry thought it was an odd thing for the doctor to say, but he listened intently for a prescription anyway.

"I'd stop having sex."

* * *

On the way out of Friedman-Kien's office, Larry was jolted to see Donald Krintzman, a fund-raiser for the Joffrey Ballet and the on-again, off-again lover of one of Larry's good friends. He was Friedman-Kien's next appointment.

"Don't tell me you've got it too?" Donald asked.

"No," answered Larry, not sure what to say.

"I've got it," Donald said comfortably. He was just in for blood tests.

Over the next few days, Larry called Donald Krintzman and Larry Mass, a doctor who wrote medical news for the *New York Native*— the city's most important gay publication—as well as Paul Popham, whose best friend, Larry had heard, died of KS last year, to discuss plans for a small fund-raiser at Larry's apartment.

National Cancer Institute, Bethesda, Maryland

When it was introduced a year earlier, most immunologists considered the new Fluorescent Activated Cell Sorter, or FACS, to be one of the most expensive scientific toys ever created. The sorter did by computer what people once did by hand, separating the T-helper lymphocytes from the T-suppressors and then counting them to see if they were in a proper ratio. In a normal person, there were, say, two helper cells for each suppressor, making a normal helper-suppressor ratio of 2:1. This quick counting didn't make the FACS that handy a tool. After all, the subsets of T-lymphocytes themselves had only been recently discovered, and scientists weren't that sure what the lymphocytes did or how significant the ratios were. According to lab chatter, it would be another five to ten years before those mysteries were fathomed. Only then would the expensive white elephant of a cell sorter have any practical value.

Still, Dr. James Goedert was glad the National Cancer Institute had invested the half-million to buy one of the first FACS machines available, because he had a new patient with the same kind of rare skin cancer he had first seen last December. The institute's FACS was so new it hadn't even been used until Goedert ran blood from the two KS patients he was treating. The helper-suppressor ratios were so far off that the lab technicians were suspicious of their results.

On a hunch, Goedert drew blood on fifteen apparently healthy gay men from the Washington area. Half of them, he found, had similar abnormalities in their immune system. The results gave him the kind of sinking feeling one gets watching television footage of an airplane making that gentle arc in the first moments of a crash landing. Whatever was causing these immune problems, Goedert knew, was very widespread. Jim was leaning toward a toxic agent and suspected poppers. He began outlining a study of gay men to test the idea....

August 7, 1981: San Francisco

By early August, there were eighteen cases of gay men suffering from the baffling immune deficiency in the San Francisco Bay Area; two had died.

"No one yet knows the extent of this potential danger, but playing it on the safe side for a few weeks cannot hurt," *The Sentinel*, a local gay paper, editorialized. "Just a few short years ago, the government dropped millions of dollars into research to determine the cause of Legionnaire's disease, which affected relatively few people. No such outpouring of funds has yet been forthcoming to research the how's and why's of KS, a rapidly fatal form of cancer that has claimed far more victims in a very short time than did Legionnaire's disease."

August 11, 1981: 2 Fifth Avenue, New York City

Twilight brought no respite from the humidity as eighty men streamed into Larry Kramer's apartment on the edge of Washington Square. Paul Popham was there with his Fire Island housemate Enno Poersch; KS victim Donald Krintzman came with his lover. The men milled around the apartment, sharing the latest rumors about who was sick and who didn't look well. Larry scanned the crowd and noted, with some relief, that none of the political crazies were there. Present, instead, were la crème de la crème of New York's A-list gay nightlife, the hottest guys you'd see on the island or at the trendiest discos. The conversation abruptly ended when Larry introduced a short balding man who mounted a platform in the center of the comfortable living room.

"We're seeing only the tip of the iceberg," said Dr. Alvin Friedman-Kien in what would become the all-encompassing metaphor for the AIDS epidemic for years to come.

He didn't know what was causing the epidemic, but he knew that the people who got sick had lots of sex partners and a long history of VD. (Larry noticed a lot of the men shift uncomfortably in their Topsiders.) The word needed to get out, Friedman-Kien warned; people needed to take it seriously. The doctor added that he needed money for research—now.

For most of the people in that apartment, the brief stunned silence that followed Friedman-Kien's talk represented the moment between their Before and After. The days of their lives would be counted from this time when they realized that something brutally unexpected had interrupted their plans. For Enno Poersch, this was the moment it dawned on him that the horrible death Nick had suffered seven months ago might be related to Jack Nau's and Rick Wellikoff's illnesses.

When Larry asked for volunteers to work on some larger fund-raisers, Enno stayed behind and so did Paul Popham. Paul had rather prided himself on never getting involved in gay politics, but this was different. Two friends were dead and another was dying. About thirty-five other people stayed behind to organize fund-raising tables at Fire Island for Labor Day weekend. Larry passed the hat for Friedman-Kien's NYU research and collected $6,635. That was just about all the private money that was to be raised to fight the new epidemic for the rest of the year.

Some people left Larry Kramer's apartment angry at Friedman-Kien. When one man asked him how to avoid getting this gay cancer, Friedman-Kien had repeated that he would stop having sex. The gay community didn't need some Moral Majority doctor telling them what to do with their sex lives, somebody fumed. Others suspected that the meeting was simply a furtherance of Larry's well-known distaste for promiscuity.

Still, Larry considered his new cause to be off to a grand start. He spent the next few days writing letters to alert key people to the epidemic. He dropped a note to Calvin Klein, asking for contributions to research, and he dashed off a plea to a closeted gay reporter at *The New York Times* for more coverage. Cases had more than doubled in the month since that first piece in *The Times*, and Larry hadn't seen another word since.

September 4, 1981, Labor Day: Fire Island, New York

"Are you crazy?"

Paul Popham couldn't comprehend what the guy was driving at.

"You're just making a big deal out of nothing," the acquaintance continued, giving Paul another strange look before striding purposefully toward the Donna Summer music pulsating from the Ice Palace.

How could you *not* be concerned, Paul wondered. More than 100 gay men were sick with something, many of them dead, and everybody was acting as though Paul were some major-league party-pooper out to wreck everybody's good time. Paul was downright aggravated. Lord knows, he liked to party too, but this was a time to be serious. He was asking people to put a buck or two in a can, and he was not only ignored but was often treated with unabashed hostility. Guys told him that he was hysterical, or participating in a heterosexual plot to undermine the gay community. At best, the men were apathetic.

The weekend was a disaster from the start. Larry Kramer, Enno Poersch, Paul Popham, and a handful of others had stretched a banner above a card table near the dock where everybody came into The Pines. "Give to Gay Cancer," it read. With some of the money raised at Larry's apartment, they had printed up thousands of copies of a *New York Native* article written by Dr. Larry Mass, another volunteer that weekend, and put them at every doorstep in the island's two gay communities, The Pines and Cherry Grove. To each reprint, they attached slips explaining how people could support Friedman-Kien's research. The small band of organizers figured they'd be able to raise thousands from the 15,000 gay men who had congregated for the last blowout of the '81 season.

They were wrong.

"Leave me alone," was one typical reaction.

"This is a downer," was another.

"What are you talking about?" was about the nicest response they got.

Enno was amazed at all the smart-ass remarks. Larry was dispirited. How do you help a community that doesn't want help? he wondered. For his part, Paul felt a wholly unfamiliar sense of alienation. These are my kind of people, he thought. He knew these faces, had seen them for years dancing at The Saint, strolling around the St. Mark's Baths, sunning on

Biography

The Mayor of Castro Street: The Life and Times of Harvey Milk, 1982.

Nonfiction

And The Band Played On: Politics, People and the AIDS Epidemic, 1987.
Conduct Unbecoming: Lesbians and Gays in the U.S. Military; Vietnam to the Persian Gulf, 1993.

Uncollected Nonfiction

"Talking AIDS to Death?," in *Esquire*, March 1989.

"Is Outing Gays Ethical?," in *New York Times*, 12 April 1990.
"Naming Names," in *Gentleman's Quarterly*, August 1990.
"The Year of the Queer: The Queering of America," in *Advocate*, 1 January 1991.
"Claim You're Gay, Avoid the Draft," in *New York Times*, 7 January 1991.
"The Nasty Business of Outing," in *Los Angeles Times*, 7 August 1991.
"Speak for All, Magic," in *Sports Illustrated*, 18 November 1991.
"Good AIDS, Bad AIDS," in *New York Times*, 10 December 1991.

"What's Fair in Love and War," in *Newsweek*, 1 February 1993.

Adaptations

And The Band Played On: Politics, People and the AIDS Epidemic (television production), 1993.
The Mayor of Castro Street: The Life and Times of Harvey Milk has been optioned for film.
Conduct Unbecoming: Lesbians and Gays in the U.S. Military; Vietnam to the Persian Gulf has been optioned as a television movie.

---

the beach. They were paying $10 to get into the Ice Palace and another $50 or so for the drugs that would keep them up until dawn, not to mention the $4,000 it took to buy this summer's share in a Fire Island house rental. What was a few dollars for scientific research?

The proceeds of the weekend's fund-raising totaled $124: Paul had never thought about how frivolous people could be. He wondered what it would mean for the future, when more people were dying.

* * *

Days after the Labor Day fiasco, Jack Nau died at St. Vincent's Hospital. He hadn't left the institution since he was hospitalized on Independence Day, and he had suffered the excruciating awful demise that dramatically informed doctors of how grisly a disease this gay syndrome was.

Paul Popham felt a certain hollowness when he learned Jack had died. He had loved Jack once, and now, like Rick and Nick, Jack was dead.

Later, it crossed Paul's mind that he'd have to tell Gaetan Dugas about Jack the next time he ran into him....

December 1981: San Francisco

Larry Kramer would maintain that from the start, gay men knew precisely what they needed to do—and not do—to avoid contracting the deadly new syndrome. The problem, he insisted, was in how gay men reacted to this knowledge, not in getting the knowledge out itself. By late

December 1981, Larry was embroiled in controversy over the outspoken role he had assumed in trying to alert New York gays to Kaposi's sarcoma.

"Basically, Kramer is telling us that something we gay men are doing (drugs? kinky sex?) is causing Kaposi's sarcoma," wrote Robert Chesley, a Manhattan gay writer, in one of his several letters attacking Kramer in the *New York Native*. "... Being alarmist is dangerous. We've been told by such experts as there are that it's wrong and too soon to make any assumptions about the cause of Kaposi's sarcoma, but there's another issue here. It is always instructive to look closely at emotionalism, for it so often has a hidden message which is the *real* secret of its appeal. I think the concealed meaning of Kramer's emotionalism is the triumph of guilt: that gay men *deserve* to die for their promiscuity.... Read anything by Kramer closely. I think you'll find that the subtext is always: the wages of gay sin is death.... I am not downplaying the seriousness of Kaposi's sarcoma. But something else is happening here, which is also serious: gay homophobia and anti-eroticism."

After mulling the attack over with his therapist, Larry Kramer responded in kind, indelicately writing that Chesley was a spurned lover who was angry that Larry never wanted to date after their initial tryst. But most of Larry's long response was more to the point.

"... Something we are doing is ticking off the timebomb that is causing the breakdown of immunity in certain bodies, and while it is true that we don't know what it is specifically, isn't it better to be cautious until various suspected causes have been discounted rather than reckless? An individual can choose to continue or cease smoking ... but isn't it stupid to rail against the very presentation of these warnings?

"I am not glorying in death. I am overwhelmed by it. The death of my friends. The death of whatever community there is here in New York. The death of any visible love."

The point-counterpoint between Larry and his critics became such a regular feature in the letters column of the *Native* that one correspondent wrote to sarcastically deny rumors that "Bette Davis has been signed to play the role of Larry Kramer in the film version of 'Letters to the Editor.'"

Meanwhile, Larry was despairing over the lack of any official attention to the epidemic. Half the victims lived in New York City, but Larry's pleas to *The New York Times* for more coverage were unanswered. Even *The Village Voice*, which considered itself the arbiter of all things au courant in Manhattan, had so far failed to run a single story on the gay syndrome. When Larry called Mayor Ed Koch's liaison to the gay community about getting some public health action, the aide assured Larry

"I'll get back to you tomorrow" and was never heard from again. Four months of fund-raising had netted only $11,806.

"Two new cases of KS are being diagnosed in New York each week. One new case is being diagnosed in the United States *each day*. Nothing is being done by the gay community to insist that the straight community, which controls all the purse strings and attention-getting devices, help us," Larry wrote in one of his long *Native* diatribes. "If KS were a new form of cancer attacking straight people, it would be receiving constant media attention, and pressure from every side would be so great upon the cancer- funding institutions that research would be proceeding with great intensity." …

January 12, 1982: 2 Fifth Avenue, New York City

In the meeting at Larry Kramer's apartment, everybody agreed that Paul Popham would be the ideal president of the new organization, Gay Men's Health Crisis, which was geared to raising money for gay cancer research. Some of the more salient reasons were left unspoken. Paul personified the successful Fire Island A-list gays who had never become involved in Manhattan's scruffy gay political scene. He'd help make working on this disease fashionable and something with more status than your typical gay crusade. He was also gorgeous, which would probably help attract volunteers. Unspoken too was the view that Larry Kramer's confrontational style would make him an unsuitable president of the group, even though he had taken a leading role in its organization. His very name was anathema among the crowd they needed to reach if they were to raise substantial funds. Larry had a half-crush on Paul anyway, so he joined the unanimous vote for Paul. After Paul's election, the board of directors of the new Gay Men's Health Crisis was selected, and it included Larry Kramer and Paul's longtime friend and Fire Island housemate, Enno Poersch.

The group had persuaded the Paradise Garage, one of the less popular discos, to hold an April benefit. That, they figured, would give them a chance to raise enough money for research and then they could fold up and get back to their lives. Privately, Paul had made it clear that he did not want his role in the organization to become public knowledge. Nobody at work knew he was gay, he said, and he wanted it to stay that way. Larry bit his tongue. He didn't want to be a scold about this, but Larry privately thought it boded poorly to have a president of the Gay Men's Health Crisis who did not want to say he was a gay man.

ANN ALLEN SHOCKLEY

ANN ALLEN SHOCKLEY put the black lesbian character into twenti-eth-century American literature. Though not without precedent in such early novels as *Young Man with a Horn* and *Home to Harlem*, but without the currency of the socio-political epithet "Black lesbian," the black woman-loving-woman was never a main character in a novel nor even validated as a human being until Shockley wrote her in. Afterwards came others: notably, the title character in Toni Morrison's *Sula* and Celie in Alice Walker's *The Color Purple*. As a unit, Shockley's three principal works that feature black lesbians, *Loving Her*, *The Black and White of It*, and *Say Jesus and Come to Me*, all explore what Rebecca Sue Taylor in *Library Journal* calls "the triple hardship of being female, Black and les-bian," but in the work of Shockley—not to minimize the import—always there is more at issue than gender, sexual expression, and race. Shockley's fictions demonstrate what I called "the paradigm of the considered whole" in "Theme and Portraiture in the Fictions of Ann Allen Shockley." That is, Shockley provides a reader with an all-inclusive view of the single life of a given twentieth-century character by exaggerating the forces that play upon that life.

In *Loving Her*, the major character Renay Johnson is a young black mother, an emerging lesbian, a working-class woman with the aspirations of a classical pianist. If this is not a formula for conflict, add the advent of a first-time sexual and interracial experience with an upper-middle-class white woman, the physical abuse of an alcoholic and ne'er-do-well hus-band, alienation from her mother and friends, and the death of her pre-teen daughter, and one gets the classic Shockley composition.

In *The Black and White of It*, a testy and much-maligned collection of short stories that show black lesbian women in various walks of life from professor to student, slave to singer, senator to mother, and hetero-sexual to bisexual, Shockley stratifies the conditions of black lesbian lives but does not relieve the reader of the impression of the aggravated cir-cumstances of such lives. *The Black and White of It* demonstrates that black lesbian lives, collected over time and played out day to day, are constrained by all the frustration, resentment, joylessness, desperation,

Essay by
SDIANE A. BOGUS

475

and oppression that homophobia and racism leave as byproducts, but the collection declares that to some degree, the moral or ethic code of the black lesbian character also contributes to her pain and unrelieved unhappiness. Within the stories, Shockley demonstrates the contradictions in the lesbian characters' lives by magnifying the moral flaws in the character against the larger and more oppressive social constructs.

One of the short stories in *The Black and White of It*, entitled "Play It but Don't Say It," depicts a cold, grasping black lesbian senator and compulsive eater named Mattie Brown who denies her lesbianism for fear of exposure and for want of power. Like Holly Craft, a singer who marries to hide her homosexuality in "Holly Craft Is Not Gay," and Lynn, the confused femme in "The Play," who, though lesbian, seeks out men (in the presence of her lover) to validate her femininity, Mattie suffers from a lack of pride or self-esteem, from misplaced values, and from the lack of conviction regarding her choices. When Brown is asked by a room of reporters if she "planned to support legislation in favor of homosexuals that would be especially beneficial to the triple jeopardy associated with black lesbians," she responds, "This is not my concern. You see, there are no such black women." Back in the privacy of their room, Mattie's lover and political secretary, who was present at the interview, asks, "For God's sake, what do you think we are?" For this question, she is slapped. Before the story ends, Mattie has gotten rid of her. The story closes with Mattie going "automatically to the kitchen," an ancillary notation about the relationship between pain and food and how women stuff themselves to stuff the pain—a seemingly irrelevant and anticlimactic ending to a typical Shockley composition.

Critics are almost unanimous in their recognition of the defeatism that characterizes the lives of women in *The Black and White of It*. Evelyn White, in a *Backbone* essay, remarked: "These stories ... have certain debilitating effects. They also inspire very crucial questions about lesbian integrity and respect." Further, Karla Jay, writing in *New Women's Times Feminist Review*, stated, "If we can criticize Shockley, it is for the profusion of denial, the profusion of alcohol. We can secretly hope that she presents things out of proportion, but more likely she honestly portrays the oppressive existence of some closeted, self-destructive lesbians whom we have not reached with our movement." But Shockley is not as bleak as all of that. The "paradigm of the considered whole" dictates a balanced view of the lives of lesbians, and although the overall impression of *The Black and White of It* may be bleak, the work contains stories that validate lesbian relationships in the face of oppression, such as "The Mistress and the Slave Girl," a woman-loving-woman story of a plantation owner and her black house–servant during slavery. Quite purposely and purposefully,

American novelist and author of short stories.

Born: Louisville, Kentucky, June 21, 1927.

Education: Fisk University, Nashville, Tennessee, B.A. 1948; Western Reserve University (now Case Western University), Cleveland, Ohio, M.S.L.S. 1959.

Partnerships: Divorced; one son and one daughter.

Career: Assistant librarian, Delaware State College, Dover, 1959-60; assistant librarian, 1960–66, associate librarian, 1966–69, and curator of Negro collection, Maryland State College, Princess Anne (now University of Maryland Eastern Shore); associate librarian and head of special collections, 1969–75, associate librarian for public services, beginning 1975, then associate librarian for special collections, university archivist, and associate professor of library science, Fisk University. Lecturer at University of Maryland, 1968, Jackson State College, 1973, and Vanderbilt University.

Recipient: American Association of University Women short story award, 1962; Fisk University faculty research grant, 1970; University of Maryland Library Administrators Development Institute fellowship, 1974; American Library Association Black Caucus award, 1975; American Library Association Task Force Book Award nomination, 1980; Hatshepsut Award for literature, 1981; Martin Luther King, Jr., Black Author Award, 1982; Susan Koppelman Award, 1988; Outlook Award for outstanding pioneering contribution to lesbian and gay writing, 1990; American Library Association Black Caucus Award for professional achievement, 1992.

Agent: Carole Abel, 160 West 87th Street, 7D, New York, New York 10024, U.S.A.

Address: Fisk University, 17th Avenue North, Nashville, Tennessee 37203, U.S.A.

"Birthday Remembered," "A Special Evening," and "Women in a Southern Time" in this collection serve as counterpoints to the "bleak" portraiture of the lonely spinster professor who takes a student as lover, or the wife who sneaks away to be with her weekend female lover, or the woman in "Love Motion" who fakes orgasm with her husband as she fantasizes about women. Speaking of her work in a letter to Rita Dandridge, her foremost critic and bibliographer, Shockley said, "I consider myself a social[ly] conscious writer." Indeed, her social consciousness is best noted in *Say Jesus and Come to Me.*

In *Say Jesus and Come to Me,* Shockley's intention, she told Dandridge, was to "expose the conservatism and snobbishness of the Black middle class and academicians.... The Black male oppression of women; the superior attitudes and opportunism of some white women towards Black women in the liberation movement, and even to touch the local (Nashville, Tennessee) music scene."

Instead of focusing squarely on "obliterating women's oppression," the ideal espoused by one of the white female feminist characters of the book, Shockley asserts, through main character and lesbian minister Myrtle Black: "I am going to insist on moralistic and humanitarian objectives.... All too frequently they are what get lost in movements." Shockley's work in this satirical book about moral conversion and feminist conviction in the very heterosexual South seems to advocate all her familiar and time-tested themes—the religious and spiritual nature of people and its influence upon their lives, interracial relations, black male and female relations, the psyches of men, and the lives of women, lesbian or otherwise.

I believe in *Say Jesus*, as in all of Shockley's work, her narratives are proof of her own moral idealism. However satiric, cynical, or ridiculing her work may appear, however ambiguous and sketchily developed, there is always a reasonable hope for unity, solidarity, brotherhood, honor, nobility, and honesty among people. Possessor of a forensic rather than a belletristic literary style, Shockley's work provides no great symbols or metaphor, no elements of the beloved black folk tale, but it represents a realistic—though Spartan—whole, a view of lives today that compound the problems and possibilities of being human in twentieth-century America.

A BIRTHDAY REMEMBERED

Reprinted from *The Black and White of It*, Naiad Press, copyright 1987 by Ann Allen Shockley.

"Hello—Aunt El—?"

The familiar voice came over the telephone, young, vivacious, excited—a girlish echo reminding her of the past. "Tobie—"

"Happy birthday!"

"Thank you—" Ellen felt a rush of warmth, pleased that Tobie had remembered. But hadn't Tobie always. Besides, her birthday wasn't difficult to remember, falling on Valentine's Day. *A heart born especially for me*, Jackie used to tease.

"May I come over?"

Now Tobie's voice sounded a little strained. Ellen could visualize the puckers of thin lines forming between her wide-spaced eyes. The tightness in her throat delayed an answer. Why shouldn't she? Then again, why *should* she really want to? Tobie no longer belonged to her—*them*. When Jackie died a year ago, Tobie had to go back to her father. A splintering separation, after all their years of living together, *belonging together*— Tobie, Jackie and herself.

The three of them had survived through the tumultuous stress of trying to make it, ever since Jackie walked out on Roger and came to live with her. Tobie was just five years old—too small and pale for her age, too nervous from the parental arguments.

Roger had been furious, appalled and angry at his wife's leaving him for a woman. Ellen knew it was more an affront to his male ego than los-

FICTION

Novels

Loving Her, 1974.
Say Jesus and Come to Me, 1982.

Short Stories

"Abraham and the Spirit," in *Negro Digest,* July 1950.
"The Picture Prize," in *Negro Digest,* October 1962.
"A Far Off Sound," in *Umbra,* December 1963.
"The Funeral," in *Phylon* (Atlanta), spring 1967.
"The President," in *Freedomways,* fourth quarter 1970.
"Crying for Her Man," in *Liberator,* January–February 1971.
"Is She Relevant?," in *Black World,* January 1971.
"Her Own Thing," in *Black America,* August 1972.
"Ah: The Young Black Poet," in *New Letters* (Kansas City, Missouri), winter 1974.
"The More Things Change," in *Essence* (New York), October 1977.
"A Case of Telemania," in *Azalea,* fall 1978.
"The Black Lesbian in American Literature: An Overview," in *Conditions: Five,* autumn 1979.
The Black and White of It (includes "Play It, but Don't Say It," "Holly Craft Isn't Gay," "Home to Meet the Folks," "A Birthday Remembered," and "A Meeting of the Sapphic Daughters"), 1980.
"Women in a Southern Time," in *Feminary,* 1982.

Contributor

Impressions in Asphalt (anthology), edited by Ruthe T. Sheffey and Eugnia Collier, 1969.
Out of Our Lives: A Selection of Contemporary Black Fiction, edited by Quandra Prettyman Stadler, 1975.
True to Life Adventure Stories, edited by Judy Graham, 1978.

---

ing Jackie. Particularly when it belonged to one who was striving ruthlessly to become a top business executive, amassing along the way all the exterior garnishments that were supposed to go along with it. He had purchased a large, two-story brick colonial house in the suburbs, replete with swimming pool and a paneled country squire station wagon for Jackie to do her errands. When she left him, he had tried to declare her temporarily insane.

Ellen thought that perhaps Jackie *had* been crazy to leave all of that and come to live with her in a cramped apartment on her salary. She wasn't making that much at the time as a staff writer for *Women's Homemaking* magazine's food section. But, somehow, they had made out, until Jackie got a job teaching in an elementary school. Jackie loved children, and had a way with them.

"Hey—Aunt El. You still with me?"

Tobie was waiting for an answer. One could get so involved in the past. "Of course, dear. Please *do* come over," she invited, thinking it wasn't until later she was to have dinner with Harriet. All she had to do was change from her jumpsuit to a dress.

"I'm bringing a friend who I want you to meet. Ok?"

Tobie never had an abundance of friends, only special ones who were close, for that was her way. At first, she and Jackie had mistakenly thought Tobie was ashamed of their relationship—what they were to each other. They knew Tobie was aware of it. How could she not have been. Real love can't be hidden. It inevitably is transmitted through a glance, affectionate touch, strong feelings that show.

ANN ALLEN **SHOCKLEY** 479

Then there was the rainy, cold night in November, one month after Jackie had left him, when Roger came to the apartment, hurling threats, shouting obscenities. He was going to take them to court, declare them perverts, unfit to raise a child. Tobie must have heart the words flung out at them through the paper-thin walls.

"Wonderful, darling. I'll look forward to meeting your—friend."

The phone clicked and Tobie wasn't there anymore. Ellen remained seated on the couch, motionless, as if the remembrance of all that had gone by in ten years had risen like a mist to cover her in sadness. There had not been a divorce because of his man-stubbornness and Jackie's woman-fear for Tobie. When she died, he buried her. She hadn't been allowed to do this one last thing for Jackie. To *be* with her during the last rituals, to hold a fourteen-year-old who was in all but flesh, her daughter too. The next morning after the funeral, Tobie came by to be with her, to cry her tears, sustain her grief. The sorrow shared as one was their solitary entombment for her. Through the passing days, the biting cruelty of it all slowly healed, leaving only the scar tissue. Jackie had been laid to rest in her heart.

Ellen's eyes fell on the array of birthday cards on the coffee table and the vase of red roses that Harriet had sent. Meeting Harriet had helped her to get over the travail of death's cruel separation. Incurable illnesses are like earthquakes—they swallow quickly. It wasn't too bad now. She could look back and recall without too much pain. All it takes is someone to help, someone who cares, and the eraser of time.

The living room was beginning to become shaded with dark-fingered lances of shadows. She reached over and turned on a table lamp. The day was quickly vanishing into the grayness of night. What she should do was get a drink. A good, stiff celebrating birthday martini. After all, she was forty-four years old. Six more years, if still alive, she would reach the half century mark.

She got up and went into the kitchen. There she turned on the light which brought into sharp, garish focus the ultra-modern bright chrome and copper, resembling the spacious kitchens featured in her magazine articles where various culinary talents were exhibited. Thankfully, through her writing skills, she had been able to help make their living better before Jackie passed. She had become editor of the food section and had written a cookbook. Her publisher had assured her that cookbooks always sell, and hers had.

A martini called for gin, vermouth, lemon, and an olive. She got out the glass pitcher and stirrer. Jackie preferred sunrises. She made them for her in the evenings, after the lengthy daily struggles of climbing the ladder together. Jackie had become principal of the school, a model for those beneath her, and an in-school parent for the students. Ellen marveled at how she had blossomed, learning to become independent after being a college trained housewife to Roger. *There's so much to living that I did not know before*, Jackie had told her happily. Yes, indeed, there was a lot to living that neither had known before.

She mixed the drink in the shaker, stirred it slowly and poured some in a glass, topping it with a round green olive with a small red eye-circle. *Here's to you, Ellen Simms, on your birthday!* She lifted the glass in a toast and the drink went down smoothly. Then the doorbell rang. Tobie must have been just around the corner. As soon as she responded, Tobie sang out cheerfully: "Happy birthday to you—happy birthday to you!"

Tobie hugged her and Ellen found her nose pressed into the cold leather of her jacket. Tobie seemed taller. *They do grow*, she mockingly reminded herself, comparing her own short stockiness to Tobie's height.

"A present for you, Aunt El—"

When Tobie thrust the gift into her arms, Ellen protested: "You shouldn't have." The package was neatly store wrapped and tied with a pink ribbon holding a card.

"You know I never forget your birthday, Aunt El—"

At that moment, she saw the boy standing awkwardly behind her. He had a round, friendly face and a mass of dark brown hair parted on the side.

"Hello—" she spoke to him.

"Aunt El—this is Warrick."

"Come in and take off your coats. Would you like some hot cocoa to warm you up? I know it's cold outside." Tobie used to love hot cocoa with a marshmallow floating like a full-grown moon on top. This was her favorite on Sunday mornings when they had a leisurely breakfast together.

"Cocoa—you *know* what I like!" Tobie exclaimed, throwing off her coat and curling up on the sofa.

Ellen watched her, noting the girlishness hadn't gone yet in the transitional adolescent stage. She looked older. Her blonde hair was cut short and bangs covered her forehead. Physically, she looked more like her father with the sharp, angular face, but there was her mother where it counted most, in her warmth and quickness of smile. Did her father know that she was here—with her. Like visiting a widowed parent—eight years of child-rearing, child-caring, child-loving.

"Open your present, Aunt El—"

"All right." First she read the heart shaped card with the fringed edges about Valentine birthdays, and then the scribbled message: *To my one and only, Aunt El, with love, always.* She blinked back the tears and made a fanfare out of unwrapping the gift. It was a big, glossy, illustrated, expensive cookbook of ancient Eastern recipes.

"Thank you, my dear." She leaned over to kiss Tobie's cheek. "It's lovely."

"Tobie saved up a week's salary to buy it—" Warrick announced proudly, settling in the rocker opposite the sofa. His voice was changing, and there was an inflamed red pimple beside his nose. On the front of his red and white pullover sweater were the words Terrence Academy. The right sleeve had a large white T.

"Warrick! Shame on you giving my secrets away," Tobie laughed, playfully chastising him.

"Where are you working?" Ellen asked, hanging their coats in the closet. She couldn't imagine Roger Ewing permitting his teen-aged daughter to work.

"I'm a library page after school at the branch near home. I like to have my *own* money—" she added reflectively.

Ellen hesitated, wondering if she should ask. Don't forget the social amenities. Isn't that what they had taught Tobie throughout the years. "How is your—father?" she asked, the words sounding like cracked dry ice.

"Oh, Dad's ok," she shrugged, kicking off the high wooded wedge platforms with interlacing straps. "His main object in life seems to be to prove how much money he can make and *keep*."

Roger's a miser at heart; he wants every cent I spend accounted for, yet he'll go out and buy something outlandishly showy to prove he's got money, Jackie had commented about him.

Why was it that people happen to be in certain places at the right or wrong time? Like the dinner party she had been assigned to write up for the magazine to describe the elegance of the food, drinks and table setting. There seated next to her was Jackie, looking small, frail and lost among the spirited laughter and inane chitchat of the moneyed. Roger was on her other side, appearing to be thoroughly enjoying himself talking to the big bosomed woman with the glittering necklace and frosted white hair. There was the interest at first sight, hidden hormones clashing while a subtle intuitive knowingness flashed hidden messages about

A History of Public Library Services to Negroes in the South, 1900–1955 (monograph), 1960.

"Does the Negro College Library Need a Special Negro Collection?," in Library Journal, June 1961.

"The Negro Woman in Retrospect: Blueprint for the Future," in Negro History Bulletin (Washington, D.C.), December 1965.

"Tell It Like It Is: A New Criteria for Children's Books in Black and White," in Southeastern Libraries, spring 1970.

A Handbook for the Administration of Special Negro Collections, 1970; as The Administration of Special Black Collections, 1974.

A Manual for the Black Oral History Program, 1971.

"Pauline Elizabeth Hopkins: A Biographical Excursion into Obscurity," in Phylon (Atlanta), spring 1972.

With Sue P. Chandler, Living Black American Authors: A Biographical Directory, 1973.

"American Anti-Slavery Literature: An Overview—1693–1859," in Negro History Bulletin (Washington, D.C.), April–May 1974.

With Veronica E. Tucker, "Black Women Discuss Today's Problems: Men, Families, Societies," in Southern Voices, August–September 1974.

"The New Black Feminists," in Northwest Journal of African and Black American Studies, winter 1974.

"Black Publishers and Black Librarians: A Necessary Union," in Black World, March 1975.

"Joseph S. Cotter, Sr.: Biographical Sketch of a Black Louisville Bard," in College Language Association Journal, March 1975.

"Oral History: A Research Tool for Black History," in Negro History Bulletin (Washington, D.C.), January–February 1978.

"The Black Lesbian in American Literature," in Conditions: Five, autumn 1979.

"Black Lesbian Biography: Lifting the Veil," in Other Black Women, 1982.

Editor

With E. J. Josey, and contributor, Handbook of Black Librarianship, 1977.

Afro-American Women Writers, 1746–1933: An Anthology and Critical Guide, 1988.

Contributor

Black Librarian in America, edited by E. J. Josey. Metuchen, 1970.

Library Lit. 5, edited by Bill Katz and Robert Burgess, 1975.

the clamor of the room. *If only we could decide our own fates, what would life then be?*

"I'll make the cocoa—" she said, retreating to the kitchen.

The martini pitcher was on the counter where she had left it. Immediately she poured another drink. She had been ruminating too much. Stop the past. Drink and be merry. Chase the haunting memories away.

"Aunt El—need any help?"

Tobie came in. She had put her shoes back on and they made a hard noise against the linoleum. The wedges looked like ancient ships, causing her to wonder if they were comfortable. The bell-bottom blue jeans billowed over them like sails. "No—nothing to making cocoa. After all the time of doing it for you—" The reminder slipped out. She wished it hadn't.

Tobie laughed, and the sound made everything all right again. "What do you think of Warrick?" she asked, reaching into the closet for cups and saucers. Everything was known to her in a place that had once been home.

"He seems like a nice—boy." Suppose it had been a girl? People choose who they want. This they had tried to instill in her in their unobtrusive way. "How does you father like him?"

"Dad hasn't met him yet," Tobie said quietly. "I wanted to get *your* opinion *first*. Anyway, Dad stays busy and away so much that we don't have much time to talk. The housekeeper takes care of the house—and me—who, I suppose, goes with the house." She gazed down at the floor, biting her lip, face clouded. "I miss Mom—don't you?"

"Yes—" she replied softly. "But we have to get used to living without loved ones. That time must inevitably come, sooner or later, for somebody."

She turned away, pretending to search the refrigerator so Tobie couldn't see her face. Do something else while waiting for the milk to warm. Prepare sandwiches. Young people were always hungry—feeding growth. She had cold chicken and potato salad left over from last night.

"I thought if *you* liked Warrick, Mom would too. He plays on the basketball team," Tobie continued, watching her slice the chicken and take out the jars of pickles and mustard from the refrigerator.

"Are you—serious about him?" Ellen asked, praying that she wasn't. Not at this stage of youth—almost fifteen.

"Of course not? We're just friends. He's someone to go places and do things with."

"Good!" Ellen exclaimed, feeling an impending burden lifted. "There's plenty of time for the other. You have to go to college and—" she went on hurriedly about those things which normally fall in place for young lives.

Tobie smiled. "I *knew* you were going to say that, Aunt El." Then she looked directly at her, blue eyes locking Ellen's in a vise. "Anyway, someday, if I ever *do* get serious about someone, I hope it will be as wonderful and beautiful as what you and Mom had together."

God, for the first time, it was out in the open! She felt the shock of the words, unexpected, frank—a blessing. "I do too, dear. Like we had." Her hands trembled from the weight of the moment between them. A bridge had transformed Tobie from girl to woman now to her.

"Aunt El, the milk's boiling over!"

"I've lost my cocoa-making expertise," Ellen laughed, snatching the pan off the burner. The milk had boiled into a bubbling white-coated cascade of foam.

THE GAY AND LESBIAN LITERARY COMPANION

When the tray of food was ready, they went back to the living room where Warrick was watching TV. While they ate hungrily, Ellen finished her drink, feeling light, warm and happy.

When the telephone rang, it was like a rude interruption into a special cradle of time. Harriet wanted to know if she would be ready around seven-thirty for dinner. She glanced at her watch. It was just six o'clock. Besides, what was more important to her than this?

Later, Tobie said: "We'd better be going. Warrick's taking me to the movies. Thanks for the treat, Aunt El."

"And, thank *you* for the present. I'm glad you came by to make my birthday a happy one. *Both* of you."

"Nice meeting you, Miss Simms," Warrick said, extending his hand. "Tobie talks about you all the time. Now I can see why!"

She like him. "Come back—anytime."

Tobie kissed her goodbye at the door. When they left, the tears were finally freed—in sadness and happiness too. Tobie was going to make it all right. Jackie would have been proud. They had made good parents.

GERTRUDE STEIN

IN *DEAR SAMMY: Letters from Gertrude Stein and Alice B. Toklas,*
author Samuel M. Steward describes a conversation he had with
Gertrude Stein in 1939 where she suddenly grabs his knee and asks,
"Sammy, do you think that Alice and I are lesbians?" Stein tells Steward
that, even though most of their friends know "all about everything"
regarding her relationship with Toklas and that homosexuals "do all the
good things in all the arts," she wants him not to write about her being a
lesbian until "say twenty years after I die, unless it's found out sooner or
times change."

Much of Stein's writing, as well as her life, exhibits the same interplay of sudden revelation and cryptic secrecy that can be seen in this
episode of Steward's memoirs. Stein wrote some of the most unapologetic
and often frankly erotic accounts of lesbian lives in the early part of this
century, yet she withheld her work from publication and masked its lesbian content through a variety of innovative stylistic disguises. While she
was lionized in her lifetime largely on the strengths of her public persona
and her most accessible book, *The Autobiography of Alice B. Toklas,* scholarship on Stein has enjoyed a huge growth in the second half of the century, in part because so much of her work and her life has remained unex-
plored. In addition, the languages and concepts offered by lesbian, feminist, and postmodernist criticism have created new apertures through
which to approach and discuss her work. Stein spoke of herself as ahead
of her times, and the burgeoning of scholarship about her work and life
seems to indicate she was right.

Times were slow to change in Stein's lifetime, however, and
Steward more than kept his promise to her, delaying publication of his
memoir and collection of letters until 1977. These personal silences
between friends were also reflected in the publishing and criticism of
Stein's work, and it was not until the growth of lesbian and feminist
scholarship, which began during the same time period, that Stein's writing and life began to be examined more on its own merits and in light of
the perspectives her lesbianism might have brought to her writing. Shari
Benstock, for example, writing in *Feminist Issues in Literary Scholarship,*

Essay by
JAYNE RELAFORD
BROWN

487

Gertrude Stein in 1942.

argues that Stein's sexuality was central to the innovations in her writing: "Stein's perverse style has intimate connections to her lesbianism, which is the motivating force for this private language, at odds with any accepted forms of meaning, a language exploring seemingly arbitrary and coincidental links between signifier and signified. Stein's style served as a mask for her lesbian subject matter."

Michael J. Hoffman, in his introduction to *Critical Essays on Gertrude Stein*, describes one of the contributions of Stein's feminist critics as being "to relate Stein's sexual preference to the buried life it led in her writings." Scholars such as Catherine Stimpson, Cynthia Secor, Elizabeth Fifer, and Shari Benstock have engaged themselves in unearthing and explicating the ways Stein's sexuality has been encoded in her work, and demonstrate how understanding the coded sexuality can render Stein's seemingly cryptic style both readable and enjoyable. Among other strategies, these scholars have identified Stein's punning, her plays on gender roles and heterosexual terminology, and parts of her lexicon for lovemaking.

Prior to these relatively recent examinations of the relationship between Stein's life and work, biographical accounts and literary criticism often discussed Stein only in relation to other literary movements or authors; her relationship to cubism and modernism, her influence on such (usually male) authors as Ernest Hemingway and Sherwood Anderson, or stylistic comparisons to James Joyce were more common than examinations of Stein's writing on its own merits. In contrast, Benstock sees Stein as having written from outside the communities of male modernist writers and cubist painters, alienated by virtue of her position not only as a woman, but as a lesbian woman writer. According to Benstock, Stein worked her alienation to her advantage. "By maintaining her separatism," states Benstock, "She created the myth that she was at the center of a literary period whose borders were, in reality, sealed against her."

This myth that Stein created by writing *The Autobiography of Alice B. Toklas* precipitated a storm of both popularity and controversy for her career. The editors of *Transition* hurried to put out the *Testimony against Gertrude Stein* issue in order to "straighten out those points with which we are familiar before the book has had time to assume the character of historic authenticity." Editor Eugene Jolas charged that Stein was in no way "concerned with the shaping of the epoch she attempts to describe." He added that there was "a unanimity of opinion that she had no understanding of what really was happening around her," and quoted Henri Matisse as saying she had presented the epoch "without taste and without relation to reality." On the other hand, the surface accessibility of the narrative, the public's curiosity about the famous persons such as Pablo Picasso and Matisse discussed within its pages, and the clever-

Gertrude Stein with Alice B. Toklas (left) in southeastern France in September, 1944.

ness of the ending where Stein reveals herself, rather than Toklas, as the author of the "autobiography" brought an increased celebrity to Stein. Stein used the narrative voice of "Alice" to portray herself as a founder of twentieth-century literature and "first class genius" in the company of Picasso and Alfred Whitehead (*Selected Writings*). More subtly, she used the autobiography as a means of expressing her relationship as the "husband" of its narrator. "Before I decided to write this book my twenty-five years with Gertrude Stein," writes the Alice-narrator, "I had often said that I would write, The wives of geniuses I have sat with." By placing Stein in one room among the genius-husbands and Alice in another with the wives, Stein wittily establishes both her artistic importance and her important primary relationship.

Ironically, even though Stein's relationship with Toklas has arguably become the most famous lesbian romance in history, their relationship was often erased or portrayed in nonsexual terms during their lifetimes. Toklas was most often referred to as Stein's "secretary," with even friends colluding in the public masquerade. In his introduction and notes to *Bee Time Vine*, Virgil Thomson uses the term to refer to Toklas, also calling her his "chief informant" on matters regarding Stein. During Stein's lifetime, the only more overt allusions to her sexuality came from people trying to use homophobia as a means to denigrate Stein, such as

American poet, playwright, short story writer, novelist, and literary experimentalist.

Born: Allegheny, Pennsylvania, February 3, 1874.

Education: Radcliffe College, Cambridge, Massachusetts; Harvard University, Cambridge, Massachusetts, B.A. 1897; Johns Hopkins Medical School, Baltimore, Maryland, 1897–1901. Lived in Paris.

Partnerships: Companion of Alice B. Toklas, 1907–46.

Career: Contributor to numerous periodicals, including *Psychological Review*, 1896–98, *Transition*, 1927–29, and *Compass*, 1945.

Recipient: Medaille de la Reconnaissance Française, 1922.

Died: Neuilly-sur-Seine, France, July 27, 1946, of cancer.

the authors and artists who contributed to *Transition*'s special issue, *Testimony against Gertrude Stein*, which made references to them as spinsters in "boy scout uniforms" occupying "the family circle [of] two maiden ladies greedy for fame and publicity."

Certainly Stein and Toklas were central to the consistently mixed revelation and disguise of themselves as a couple. Stein and Toklas constantly presented themselves together in public, yet kept their relationship ambiguous. *The Autobiography of Alice B. Toklas* makes it clear that Stein and Toklas live, travel, and plan their lives together, yet their relationship is made the center, rather than the overt content of the book.

More important than the secrecy about Stein's "private life" itself was the fact that a tremendous amount of her writing that could be construed as lesbian was withheld from publication for several decades. Stein's first novel, *Q.E.D.*, the semi-autobiographical story of a lesbian lovers' triangle, was unpublished for almost half a century, because Stein was aware the public was not ready to receive it. In the same conversation with Steward mentioned at the beginning of this essay, Stein explained why she had chosen not to publish *Q.E.D.*, which she had written 35 years earlier. "Well for one thing," she told him, "it was too early to write about such things in our civilization, it was early in the century and everything was puritanical and so it was too soon, maybe not if we were Greek but Greek we weren't."

Q.E.D., which Stein described as "too outspoken for the times even though it was restrained," was finally published in a very limited edition in 1950 under the title *Things As They Are*. To make the story more palatable, or publishable, Stein had much earlier transformed the narrative into heterosexual terms, creating *Three Lives*. Although that book still contained depictions of fierce female attachments, the central

Novels

Three Lives: The Story of The Good Anna, Melanctha and The Gentle Lena, 1909.

Portrait of Mabel Dodge at the Villa Curonia, 1912.

The Making of Americans, Being a History of a Family's Progress, 1925.

A Book Concluding With As a Wife Has a Cow, A Love Story, 1926.

Ida, a Novel, 1941.

Things As They Are: A Novel in Three Parts by Gertrude Stein, Written in 1903, Now Published for the First Time, 1950.

Poetry

Tender Buttons: Objects, Food, Rooms, 1914.

Petits poèmes pour un livre de lecture, translation by Madame la Baronne d'Aiguy, 1944; as The First Reader and Three Plays, 1946.

Two (Hitherto Unpublished) Poems, 1948.

Lifting Belly, edited by Rebecca Mark, 1989.

Plays

Geography and Plays, 1922.

A Village Are You Ready Yet Not Yet A Play In Four Acts, 1928.

Operas and Plays, 1932.

In Savoy; or, This Is for a Very Young Man (A Play of the Resistance in France), 1946.

Last Operas and Plays, edited by Carl Van Vechten, 1949.

Lucretia Borgia: A Play, 1968.

Selected Operas and Plays, edited by John Malcolm Brinnin, 1970.

Collections

Matisse, Picasso, and Gertrude Stein with Two Shorter Stories, 1933.

Selected Writings, edited by Carl Van Vechten, 1949.

Gertrude Stein's America, edited by Gilbert A. Harrison, 1965.

A Primer for the Understanding of Gertrude Stein, edited by Robert Bartlett Haas, 1971.

Fernhurst, Q.E.D., and Other Early Writings, 1971.

The Previously Uncollected Writings of Gertrude Stein, edited by Robert Bartlett Haas, Volume 1: Reflections on the Atomic Bomb, 1973; Volume 2: How Writing Is Written, 1974.

The Yale Gertrude Stein: Selections, 1980.

The Yale Edition of the Unpublished Works of Gertrude Stein

Volume 1: Two: Gertrude Stein and Her Brother, and Other Early Portraits, 1906–1912, edited by Carl Van Vechten, 1951.

Volume 2: Mrs. Reynolds and Five Earlier Novelettes, edited by Carl Van Vechten, 1952.

Volume 3: Bee Time, and Other Pieces 1913–1927, edited by Carl Van Vechten, 1953.

Volume 4: As Fine as Melanctha 1914–1930, edited by Carl Van Vechten, 1954.

Volume 5: Painted Lace, and Other Pieces 1914–1937, edited by Carl Van Vechten, 1955.

Volume 6: Stanzas in Meditation, and Other Poems, edited by Carl Van Vechten, 1956.

Volume 7: Alphabets and Birthdays, edited by Carl Van Vechten, 1957.

Volume 8: A Novel of Thank You, edited by Carl Van Vechten, 1959.

Librettos

Four Saints in Three Acts: An Opera to Be Sung, music by Virgil Thomson (produced Hartford, Connecticut, 1934), 1934.

A Wedding Bouquet: Ballet Music by Lord Berners, 1938.

Capitals, Capitals: Four Men and a Piano, music by Virgil Thomson (produced New York, 1947).

The Mother of Us All, music by Virgil Thomson (produced New York, 1947), 1947.

Preciosilla: For Voice and Piano, G. Schirmer, 1948.

In a Garden: An Opera in One Act, music by Meyer Kupferman, 1951.

Lectures

Lectures in America, 1935.

Narration: Four Lectures, 1935.

Writings and Lectures 1911–1945, edited by Patricia Meyerowitz, 1967; as Look at Me Now and Here I Am: Writings and Lectures, 1971.

Other

Have They Attacked Mary, He Giggled, 1917.

Descriptions of Literature, George Platt Lynes and Adlai Harbeck, 1926.

Composition as Explanation, 1926.

The Elucidation, 1927.

Useful Knowledge, 1928.

An Acquaintance with Description, 1929.

Lucy Church Amiably, 1930; 1969.

Dix Portraits, English with French translations by Georges Hugnet and Virgil Thomson, 1930.

Before the Flowers of Friendship Faded Friendship Faded, Written on a Poem by Georges Hugnet, 1931.

How to Write, 1931.

The Autobiography of Alice B. Toklas, 1933.

Portraits and Prayers, 1934.

The Geographical History of America or the Relation of Human Nature to the Human Mind, 1936.

Is Dead, 1937.

Everybody's Autobiography, 1937.

Picasso, 1939; translated into English by Alice B. Toklas, 1938.

The World Is Round, 1939.

Paris France, 1940.

What Are Masterpieces, 1940; enlarged, 1970.

Wars I Have Seen, 1945.

Brewsie and Willie, 1945.

Four in America, 1947.

Blood on the Dressing Room Floor, 1948.

Motor Automatism, with Leon M. Solomons, 1969.

Gertrude Stein on Picasso, edited by Edward Burns, 1970.

I Am Rose, 1971.

Money, 1973.

Gertrude Stein, by Pablo
Picasso.

relationship was between Melanctha and Jeff Campbell, a male doctor, and the social stigma of their relationship was played out by Melanctha's color and social position, rather than as a lesbian relationship, Stimpson declares in *Critical Inquiry*.

Works like *Q.E.D.*, which described lesbian relationships, and Stein's more explicitly sexual and loving works, such as "Lifting Belly" and "A Sonatina Followed by Another," were among the last to be made available. Stein has "Alice" say in the *Autobiography* that Stein "forgot" about her first novel, but Stimpson notes that even after it was "discovered" Stein chose not to include it in the 1941 Yale catalog of her published and unpublished works, which she helped compile. Toklas, Stein's lifelong companion, lived for many years after Stein's death. Understandably reluctant to have her privacy infringed upon, she finally did publish *Q.E.D.* in a very limited edition. *Q.E.D.* was particularly problematic for Toklas because it chronicled Stein's earlier relationship with May Bookstaver, and Toklas, who spent so much of her last years making sure the archives and publishing of Stein's work was complete, is said to have destroyed Bookstaver's letters to Stein in 1932, according to Stimpson.

Although *Q.E.D.* was the most clearly autobiographical and clearly lesbian in content of Stein's writings, it is the playful erotic dialogues like *Lifting Belly* that often engage the attention of contemporary lesbians. Although the piece attracted little attention when it was first published embedded in *Bee Time Vine*, Naiad Press, a lesbian publishing house, reissued the piece on its own in 1989. The different approaches by the editors of the two volumes indicate how critical time and context are to the understanding of Stein. In the 1953 Yale series, Virgil Thomson introduced the piece by saying, "I do not know the meaning of the title." Euphemistically, he tells his readers that poems such as *Lifting Belly* "reveal their content to persons acquainted with the regions they describe or with their author's domestic life."

In contrast, Rebecca Mark is able to state in her 1989 Naiad Press introduction, "When I read *Lifting Belly* in *The Yale Gertrude Stein*, I was so excited I told everyone I knew about this erotic, lesbian poem." In *Really Reading Gertrude Stein*, lesbian poet and gay cultural historian Judy Grahn predicts that "in future time ... all of her stories will come clear to us as we modern people stand more nearly in the center of who we are."

While Grahn's scenario may seem optimistic, it does seem that as more lesbian scholars and readers emerge "more nearly in the center of who we are," much of Stein's private, cryptic writing has become more accessible. While Stein studies was once confined strictly to the academy, activists like Grahn and Mark have been working to bring her into the lesbian community at large.

Considering the times in which she was writing, part of Stein's greatness as a writer is that she could create language to describe lesbian life and lovemaking. Reading as a contemporary lesbian, Rebecca Mark wonders "how words which rarely mention a body part can make me feel so aroused." "Lifting belly. Are you. Lifting. / Oh dear I said I was tender, fierce and tender. / Do it. What a splendid example of carelessness. / It gives me a great deal of pleasure to say yes. / Why do I always smile. / I don't know. / You are easily pleased. / I am very pleased."

At the end of the twentieth century, the audience Stein predicted may have finally caught up with her. More comfortable with both non-linear narratives and lesbian existence, contemporary readers and scholars "acquainted with the regions" Stein describes are finding many of Stein's writings to be newly negotiable and exceedingly pleasing terrain.

BEFORE THE FLOWERS OF FRIENDSHIP FADED, FRIENDSHIP FADED

I love my love with a v
Because it is like that
I love my love with a b
Because I am beside that
A king.
I love my love with an a
Because she is a queen
I love my love and a a is the best of them
Think well and be a king,
Think more and think again
I love my love with a dress and a hat
I love my love and not with this or with that
I love my love with a y because she is my bride
I love her with a d because she is my love beside
Thank you for being there
Nobody has to care
Thank you for being here
Because you are not there.

And with and without me which is and without she she can be late and then and how and all around we think and found that it is time to cry she and I.

GORE VIDAL

GORE VIDAL is considered by many critics to be one of the most influential American writers of the post-World War II period. Although his work encompasses a wide variety of subjects and ideas, Vidal has gained a certain level of renown for his depiction of homosexual characters and themes. The author's career began with the publication of his first novel, *Williwaw*, in 1946. Written while Vidal was recuperating from a bout of rheumatoid arthritis, *Williwaw* takes place on an Army transport ship against the backdrop of an Artic squall (or "williwaw"). This debut novel—often characterized as "atypical" of Vidal's best work—was hailed by reviewers as being both compelling and finely honed.

It was in his second novel, *In a Yellow Wood*, that Vidal first focused on homosexuality as a thematic device. The story unfolds as a day in the life of Robert Holton, a conventional man who has just returned from the war to a perfunctory job in New York City. During the evening, Holton meets an old friend married to an internationally famous gay artist; eventually, the young clerk accompanies these companions to a gay bar where Holton encounters a number of snobbish, somewhat feminine patrons. While the bar trip is a relatively minor incident in the novel, it serves to illustrate Holton's struggle to reconcile the lure of his ordered life with his desire to embrace the unconventional.

In 1948, Vidal created a stir with his full-length study of a gay man in *The City and the Pillar*. The novel's protagonist, Jim Willard, is a handsome, athletic tennis instructor who projects a very "boy next door" image. Willard's depiction disturbed a number of critics, many of whom felt that the impact of the author's interesting characterization was lost amid thematic generalities and haphazard editing. Still, other voices hailed Vidal's willingness to take a new look at some long-standing stereotypes by presenting a "hero" who was as incapable of love and commitment as many of his fictional heterosexual peers.

Vidal's next five novels were critical and commercial failures. Much of the critics' hostile stance was due to factors such as the author's stylistic experimentation and presentation of complex—and sometimes con-

Gore Vidal in 1987 upon the release of his historical novel *Empire,* which chronicles turn-of-the-century America.

fusing—themes. Even though these works did little to advance Vidal's literary reputation, they nevertheless offered some interesting homosexual plot lines and characters. In *A Season of Comfort,* for example, heterosexual character Bill Giraud is presented as superficially happy and successful. He is haunted, however, by the memory of a sexual dalliance with Jimmy, the high school athletic hero. Later in life, Giraud—who feels that he could never have sex with a man again—decides that this earlier affair was an important, constructive part of his personal development.

In 1954, Vidal decided to seek financial stability by moving to Hollywood, where he wrote film scripts and television dramas. While some critics have found homosexual subtexts in the author's script for *Ben Hur* and his adaption of Tennessee Williams's *Suddenly Last Summer,* this stage in Vidal's career appeared to be more concerned with money-making than making waves. In light of his previous work, Vidal seemed to be burying his "homosexual enfant terrible" image, an effort that was rewarded by favorable critical reaction to works like *Visit to a Small Planet.*

Having established the financial independence he craved, Vidal returned to fiction in 1964 with a formula that led to both critical and popular success, a formula epitomized by the book *Julian.* The story is told as the journal of eccentric fourth-century Roman emperor Julian (with added margin notes and letters by two of the ruler's aging contemporaries). While the main thrust of *Julian* concerns the emperor's observations about his life and times, the novel also serves up a great deal of insouciant and ribald gossip (gossip that often centers around homosexual activities).

In the midst of penning his historical tomes, Vidal created one of his most campy and controversial works. *Myra Breckinridge* offers a colorful central character in the figure of a homosexual male turned female via a sex change operation. As a protagonist, Myra is both fascinating and repellent; she holds forth on a variety of subjects (most notably the connection between sex and power) and engages in all manner of sexual escapades. Through Myra's thoughts and actions, Vidal turned popular and psychoanalytic ideas about gender identity inside out. Many critics found Vidal's open approach to sexuality in modern society refreshing and humorous, while others considered the book's blatant sexuality bor-

THE GAY AND LESBIAN LITERARY COMPANION

American novelist, short story writer, playwright, screenwriter, and essayist. Has also written as Edgar Box.

Born: Eugene Luther Gore Vidal, U.S. Military Academy, West Point, New York, October 3, 1925.

Career: Editor, E. P. Dutton, New York, 1946; lived in Antigua, Guatemala, 1947-49; Democratic Party candidate for Congress in the 29th District of New York, 1960; member of President's Advisory Committee on the Arts, 1961–63; host of television program *Hot Line*, 1964; lived in Italy, 1967–76; cofounder of New Party, 1968-71; cochair of People's Party, 1970–72; ran for nomination as Democratic Party senatorial candidate in California, 1982. Writer and lecturer; appears frequently on television and radio talk shows.

Recipient: Mystery Writers of America Edgar Allan Poe award for television drama, 1955; Screen Writers Annual award nomination and Cannes Critics Prize for screenplay for *The Best Man*, 1964; National Book Critics Circle award for criticism for *The Second American Revolution, and Other Essays*, 1982; named honorary citizen of Ravello, Italy, 1983; Prix Deauville for *Creation*, 1983.

Agent: Owen Laster, William Morris Agency, 1350 Avenue of the Americas, New York, New York 10019, U.S.A.

---

derline pornography. In many respects, a large part Vidal's success with *Myra Breckinridge* was the result of his refusal merely to lecture or to leave difficult issues unresolved.

In his more recent books, such as the controversial mock-history *Live from Golgotha*, Vidal treats all manner of subjects, including homosexuality, in much the same irreverent manner. When looking at these later works—where the depiction of homosexuals and homosexuality seems a natural part of the author's narrative—Vidal's early presentations of homosexuality emerge both prescient and quaint. Perhaps the emphasis on homosexuality as a theme and character device does some disservice to the author, whose body of work is diverse with regard to both theme and characterization. Nevertheless, readers should not overlook Vidal's ground-breaking willingness to take chances with a complex subject at a time when doing so could have meant professional disaster.

LIVE FROM GOLGOTHA

In the beginning was the nightmare, and the knife was with Saint Paul, and the circumcision was a Jewish notion and definitely not mine.

I am Timothy, son of Eunice the Jewess and George the Greek. I am fifteen. I am in the kitchen of my family's home in Lystra. I am lying stark naked on a wooden table. I have golden hyacinthine curls and cornflower-blue, forget-me-not eyes and the largest dick in our part of Asia Minor.

Excerpt from *Live from Golgotha*, Random House, copyright 1992 by Gore Vidal.

GORE **VIDAL**   **497**

Gore Vidal in younger years.

The nightmare always begins the way that it did in actual life. I am surrounded by Jews except for my father, George, and Saint, as I called Saul of Tarsus, better known to the Roman world of which he was born a citizen as Paul. Of course Saint was a Jew to start with, but he ended up as the second- or third-ranking Christian in those days, and by those days I mean some fifty years after the birth of Our Savior, which was—for those who are counting—seventeen years after He was crucified, with a promise to be back in a few days, maybe a week at the outside.

So I was born a couple of years after Our Lord's first departure high atop old Golgotha in suburban Jerusalem. My father converted early to Christianity and then I did, too; it sounded kind of fun and, besides, what else is there to do in a small town like Lystra on a Sunday?

Little did I realize when I became a Christian and met Saint and his friends, that my body—specifically, my whang—was to be a battleground between two warring factions within the infant Christian Church.

It had been Saint's inspired notion that Jesus had come as the messiah for everyone, Gentiles as well as Jews. Most Jews still don't accept this, and of course we pray for them, morning, noon, and night. But the Jews in Jerusalem—like the oily James, kid-brother-of-Our-Lord, and Peter, known as "The Rock" because of the absolute thickness of his head—finally accepted Saint's notion that although the Gentiles were unclean, Jesus was probably too big an enterprise for just the one tribe, and so they allowed Paul to take the Message—"the good news," as we call it—to the Gentiles. Thanks largely to Saint's persuasive preaching and inspired fund-raising, a lot of Gentiles couldn't wait to convert, like my father, George the Greek.

So Saint went sashaying around Asia Minor, setting up churches and generally putting on a great show, aided by the cousins Barnaby and John Mark. But although the Jerusalem Jews liked the money that Saint kept sending back to headquarters, they still couldn't, in their heart of hearts, stomach the Gentiles, and so they refused to eat at the same table with us, since our huge uncut cocks were always on their minds. Finally, things came to a head when Saint took a shine to a young convert and stud named Titus and took him down to Jerusalem for a long weekend of fun. After having drunk too much Babylonian beer, Titus took a leak up against the wall of Fort Antonia, where the Roman troops were stationed. As luck would have it, his snakelike foreskin was duly noted with horror by some loitering Jews, who reported to the rabbinate the presence of a Gentile on the premises a stone's throw from the Temple. The central office then leaned on James, an employee of the Temple, and James told Saint that in the future those goyim who became converted to Jesus must be circumcised. That tore it.

When Saint threatened, there and then, to retire as apostle and fund-raiser, the subject was dropped by the Jerusalem Christians—or Jesists, as they liked to be called—because they were now hooked on the revenues from Asia Minor. Even so, they still kept the heat on Saint personally to show that he had his heart in the right, or kosher, place.

Finally, Saint suggested to John Mark that he undergo a public circumcision in order to convince Jerusalem that Saint was in no way an apostate or self-hating Jew. John Mark split, leaving an opening not only in Saint's office staff but sack, too. As an all-Greek Greek boy who wanted to see the world, I figured that Saint's fussing around with my bod was a small price to pay, or so I thought when I signed on. It wasn't as if there wasn't plenty of me left over for the girls of Lystra. Also, as secretary and gofer, I was pretty good, if not in John Mark's league. The work was never dull. And what a learning experience!

Then came the shock. Saint was denounced by the pillars of the church in Jerusalem: He ate with goyim. He christened goyim. He was having carnal knowledge of a teenage Greek with two centimeters of rose-velvety foreskin, me. This last was only whispered, but it would have been quite enough to get Saint stoned to death by a quorum of Jews anywhere on earth if James were to give the word.

That explains why I am in the nightmare that I can never get out of once it starts. Only this last time when I dreamed it, something unusual happened just before I woke up.

The dream's always the same. I am on my back. The room is chilly. I have goose bumps. All around me are Jews, wearing funny hats. Saint stands beside the table, my joint resting lightly in his hand. Needless to say, between the cold and the approaching mutilation, my fabled weenie has shrunk considerably.

"Let it be reported by all who presently bear witness that Timothy, our youthful brother in Christ, has now, of his own free will, undertaken

Gore Vidal signing a gun control initiative petition in 1982 while campaigning in California for a Democratic senatorial nomination.

to join the elect of the elect through the act of circumcision."

At this point I shut my eyes in the dream, an odd thing to do, since a dreamer's eyes are shut to begin with, but then dreams have their own funny laws. Anyway, I can no longer see Saint's huge staring black eyes set in that round bald head with its fringe of dyed black curls, but I can hear Saint's deep voice as he says, "Mohel, do thy business!"

A rough hand seizes my organ of generation. I feel a sharp pull. Then a burning, the knife ... I scream, and wake up.

But last night I did not wake up as I always do at this point in the dream. Instead, cock afire, voices mumbling all round me in the dark, I had the sense that something was *really* going wrong. For one thing, I was not back in my bed in the bishop's bungalow here in Thessalonika where I am bishop of all Macedonia as well as sometime titular bishop of Ephesus. I was still lying on the kitchen table in my family's house in Lystra. I slowly open my eyes. Salt tears burn the lids.

The room is empty now. I look down at my naked body—my *teenage* body, which means I am still in the dream. My aching joint is swathed in linen like an Egyptian mummy. I am sweating like a horse. I sit up. I swing my legs over the table. I am dizzy. Where is everybody?

Saint is suddenly beside me. "Timmy"—he bats his eyes at me— "how do you feel?"

"Awful," I say. "Why hasn't the dream ended, like it's supposed to?"

"Dream?" He pretends not to know that we're in a dream. He acts as if now—my *now* in Thessalonika—is really and truly *then* in Lystra, our common memories unmediated by sleep and time and all the rest, and I am just coming to, per usual, on the kitchen table.

Carefully, I swing my legs back and forth, aware of the dull ache at the center of my everything. On the window sill, my mother, Eunice, has left the half-skinned remains of a rabbit, a nice touch dream-wise. Flies are devouring the rabbit. Eunice is terrible in the kitchen. I feel sick.

Sitting on the edge of the table, I am as mad as I must have been back then at what had been done to me just so Saint could stay in good with the Jerusalem pillars of salt of the church. Historically, as well as theologically, he should have made a clean break with the Jews then and there, using the preservation of my perfect dong as a perfect pretext. Then he should have preached *only* to the goyim. But I'm afraid that all those years working as a secret agent for Mossad had made Saint even more devious than the Big Fella in the sky had made him in the first place.

"Well, yes, honey bun, this is a dream, natch." Whenever Saint sounds as if he's just gargled in chicken fat, I am immediately on guard. Even at fifteen I knew I was dealing with a con man. "A *recurring* dream, to be precise …"

"No." I am nasty. "It is a recurring *nightmare*…."

Since Saint's eyebrows meet in a straight line when he frowns, one black furry eyebrow seems to be humping the other like a couple of black caterpillars. I must write that down in the book of similes that I am keeping since succumbing to the lure of authorship in first-century A.D. vernacular Greek.

Saint frowns. Caterpillars make love. "Now, Timmy dearest, all of this happened long ago, though it seems like it was only moments ago that you were cut up for God…." Aware he is off and running in the wrong direction, Saint changes course; he poses saintlike before the window. "I am dead and gone to glory." Black transcendent gaze is aimed at dead rabbit.

"When this is a nightmare, yes, you are long since dead, and the nightmare is supposed to end when I wake up in my bed, with Atalanta, my better half…."

"Hallelujah!" Saint cries. "This is no nightmare, Timmy! We're in the big league now. *This is a vision.* There has been a *dispensation.* At last I've been allowed to channel into your recurring nightmare, darling boy, to see how you are—in the pink, obviously, in your rosy teenage succulent pink." He reaches for my right titty. I slap his hand. As a stud, I never had the slightest gender confusion. Anyway, Saint's hand turns out to be just air, though in the nightmare proper it is real enough. Something's going wrong, all right.

"I think I'm going to wake up." I begin to hear Atalanta's heavy breathing beside me in the bed where the nightmare—or vision—is taking place.

"First, a message from our sponsor." Saint is sonorous. "From God in the three sections. Timmy, these are the times that are about to try your soul. Yes, I am now in Heaven on the left-hand side of God, about twenty souls from The Elbow. But I am also, simultaneously, back here in your recurring nightmare—now promoted to vision—with a message…. A

Novels

Williwaw, 1946.

In a Yellow Wood, 1947.

The City and the Pillar, 1949; revised, 1965.

The Season of Comfort, 1949.

A Search for the King: A Twelfth-Century Legend, 1950.

Dark Green, Bright Red, 1950.

The Judgment of Paris, 1953; revised, 1965.

Messiah, 1954; revised, 1965; with introduction by Elizabeth A. Lynn, 1979.

Three: Williwaw; A Thirsty Evil: Seven Short Stories; Julian, the Apostate, 1962.

Julian, 1964; with illustrations by David Whitfield, 1974.

Washington, D.C., 1967.

Myra Breckinridge, 1968; excised edition, 1968.

Two Sisters: A Novel in the Form of a Memoir, 1970.

Burr, 1973; limited edition, 1979.

Myron, 1974.

1876, 1976.

Kalki, 1978; limited edition with illustrations by George H. Jones, 1978.

Creation, 1981.

Duluth, 1983.

Lincoln, 1984; limited edition with illustrations by Thomas B. Allen, 1984.

Myra Breckinridge [and] *Myron*, 1986.

Empire, 1987; limited edition, 1987.

Hollywood: A Novel of America in the 1920s, 1990.

Live from Golgotha, 1992.

Short Stories

A Thirsty Evil: Seven Short Stories (contains "Three Stratagems," "The Robin," "A Moment of Green Laurel," "The Zenner Trophy," "Erlinda and Mr. Coffin," "Pages from an Abandoned Journal," and "The Ladies in the Library"), 1956; limited edition, 1981.

"Pages from an Abandoned Journal," in *The Faber Book of Gay Short Fiction*, edited by Edmund White, 1991.

Mystery Novels (as Edgar Box)

Death in the Fifth Position, 1952; limited edition, 1991.

Death before Bedtime, 1953; limited edition, 1991.

Death Likes It Hot, 1954; 1991.

Three by Box: The Complete Mysteries of Edgar Box (contains *Death in the Fifth Position*; *Death Before Bedtime*; and *Death Likes It Hot*), 1978.

---

message," he repeats. He seems to be programmed, and I ponder for a moment if this is really Saint and not some sort of diabolic vision.

"So what's the message?" The sight of the dead rabbit and all the flies is making me really sick.

"There has been a systematic erasure of the Good News as recorded in the New Testament, which John Mark and the others so carefully assembled in order to record once and for all the Greatest Story Ever Told that *was* told but now is being *untold* thanks to this virus which has attacked the memory banks of every computer on earth as well as in Heaven and limbo, too. We know that it is the work of a single cyberpunk, or Hacker, as he will be known in the future, but why and how Satan has so disposed this man or woman to eliminate the Gospels—my own special good news, too—is a mystery as of this dream."

For me, this was, literally, *nonsense*. "I hear you, Saint. But I don't understand a word you're saying. I mean, *what's* being erased. Let's start with that, OK?"

"The story of Our lord Jesus Christ as told in the three Synoptic Gospels as well as by that creep John." Saint never liked John, who was very much a part of the Jerusalem crowd and close to James.

Plays

Visit to a Small Planet: A Comedy Akin to a Vaudeville (produced on Broadway, 1957), 1957; revised, 1959.

The Best Man: A Play of Politics (produced on Broadway, 1960), 1960; revised, 1977.

On the March to the Sea: A Southron Comedy (adaptation of television play *Honor*; produced Bonn, Germany, 1961).

Three Plays (contains *Visit to a Small Planet: A Comedy Akin to a Vaudeville*; *The Best Man: A Play of Politics*; and *On the March to the Sea: A Southron Comedy*), 1962.

Romulus: A New Comedy (adaptation of work by Freidrich Duerrenmatt; produced on Broadway, 1962), 1962.

Weekend: A Comedy in Two Acts (produced New Haven, Connecticut, and on Broadway, 1968), 1968.

An Evening with Richard Nixon (with others; produced New York, 1972), 1972.

Screenplays

The Catered Affair, 1956.

I Accuse, 1958.

The Scapegoat, with Robert Hamer, 1959.

Suddenly Last Summer, with Tennessee Williams, 1959.

The Best Man (based on play of same title; 1964), published as *The Best Man: A Screen Adaptation of the Original Play*, 1989.

Is Paris Burning?, with Francis Ford Coppola, 1966.

The Last of the Mobile Hotshots, 1970.

Television Plays

Barn Burning, 1954.

Dark Possession, 1954.

Smoke, 1954.

Visit to a Small Planet, 1955.

The Death of Billy the Kid, 1955.

Dr. Jekyll and Mr. Hyde, 1955.

A Sense of Justice, 1955.

Summer Pavilion, 1955.

The Turn of the Screw, 1955.

Stage Door, 1955.

Visit to a Small Planet, and Other Television Plays (contains *Visit to a Small Planet*; *Barn Burning*; *Dark Possession*; *The Death of Billy the Kid*; *A Sense of Justice*; *Smoke*; *Summer Pavilion*; and *The Turn of the Screw*), 1956.

Honor, 1956.

Portrait of a Ballerina, 1956.

The Indestructible Mr. Gore, 1959.

Dear Arthur, 1960.

Dress Gray (adaption of novel by Lucian Truscott), NBC-TV, 1986.

Gore Vidal's "Billy the Kid," TNT, 1989.

Essays

Rocking the Boat, 1962.

Sex, Death, and Money, 1968.

Reflections upon a Sinking Ship, 1969.

Homage to Daniel Shays: Collected Essays, 1952–1972, 1972; as *Collected Essays, 1952–1972*, 1974; as *On Our Own Now*, 1976.

Matters of Fact and of Fiction: Essays, 1973–1976, 1977.

Great American Families, with others, 1977.

Views from a Window: Conversations with Gore Vidal, with Robert J. Stanton, edited by Robert J. Stanton and Gore Vidal, 1980.

The Second American Revolution, and Other Essays, 1982.

Armageddon?; Essays, 1983–1987, 1987.

At Home; Essays, 1982–1988, 1988.

Screening History, 1992.

United States; Essays, 1951–1991, 1992.

Other

Editor, *Best Television Plays*, 1965.

A Conversation with Myself, 1974.

Vidal in Venice, edited by George Armstrong, photographs by Tore Gill, 1985.

Who Owns the U.S.? 1992.

Recordings

An Evening with Richard, Ode Records, 1973.

"How do you 'erase' all those books?" I ask, wondering, first, what's a computer? second, a memory bank? third, a virus?

"This is how." Saint's noncorporeal hand appears to seize my throbbing linen-swathed joint. "Suppose I had channeled in an hour ago, and suppose I had stopped the mohel from circumcising you in what is, for the purposes of the nightmare, your fifteenth year, which always occurs in the fiftieth year since the birth of Our Lord at Las Vegas ..."

"*Where?*"

"At Bethlehem, state of Israel. I misspoke, I fear."

Saint starts to gabble, always a sign he's up to something. Glossolalia—speaking in tongues—was very big back then, particularly when you had nothing to say. "During this vision, I could easily have stopped the circumcision, thus changing my relationship with the Jews and the Greatest Story Now Being Untold. If your foreskin had not been cut off, *they* would have cut me off, as of 50 A.D., and then there would have been no Christian story worth telling, no Crusades, Lourdes, Oral Roberts, Wojtyla. But let us not get sidetracked into what *might* have been when we are stuck with what is happening this very minute in the future. The Gospels are being garbled, those that haven't already vanished, like John Mark's, a wonderful secretary, I still say, loyal as I am to you, with those glorious buns …"

"Shut up, Saint!" I am simultaneously both fifteen-year-old village lout and aging bishop in the midst of a vision-nightmare. "Why is the Hacker garbling the texts and, even if he does, how can all those books vanish?"

"The *why* is as unclear as the *who*. But there is now chaos in the Christian message. Just now, when I misspoke, I was repeating the latest Hacker-inspired blasphemy about Our Lord's birth in Las Vegas, and about his connection with the mob to which former Nevada Senator Laxalt does not— repeat *not*—belong only …"

I am getting a headache. My loins throb. I stand up. My head swims, and the kitchen seems to be going round.

"I'm losing you!" Saint cries. "Before you fade to black, and I to light, remember this: *You* must now tell the Greatest Story Ever to Be Told—by you, alone—Timothy, disciple of me, Saint Paul, and yourself titular bishop of Ephesus and *de facto* bishop of Macedonia, to be martyred in the reign of President Bush, I mean the emperor Domitian—or was it Nerva?— when Greater Israel is in flames…. Write it all down, Timmy, because you are the only witness that the virus cannot get to. You are immune, which means that long after Matt, Mark, Lu-lu, and John-John are just folk memories, there will be only one absolutely true gospel, and that will be according to Saint Timothy! You're all we've got, darling. Because everying written about Our Lord before 96 A.D.—you'll die, my angel, in 97—has been erased or distorted by the computer virus that rushes, nay, implodes the channels of human memory like the myriad photons of Satan, losing quarks to Hell and, worse, to the ultimate black star, that counterforce where all is mirror-reverse and the unknown Hacker at work in the computer is Satan, and Satan's God and you me, Yummy you, Tummy, Timmy, Me … Beware Marvin Wasserstein of General Electric."

During this dreadful spiel, I slowly dissolved out of that kitchen of nearly a half century ago and into my own bed where Atalanta, my helpmeet, has met me, post-nightmare, so many times now in the course of a quarter century of warm mature Christian marriage between two equal-in-Christ, if not in bed, human beings.

I opened my eyes. Atalanta was standing over me, a dishrag in her hand, which she promptly mopped my face with. "You were having a nightmare," she announced. "The usual?"

Heart racing, I took the rag from her and dried the cold sweat from my neck. "The usual," I said. "Only this time Saint came to me in the dream, at the end…."

"How was he?" Atalanta had already lost interest in my nightmare. She was now at the window, looking down on the back courtyard where the maid was hanging up the laundry. Another bright clear day in Macedonia.

"He's put on weight." As usual when I dream of my mutilation, I was aroused. In the old days, I would fall upon my helpmeet, but now I save what is left of my once extraordinary potency for fun and games at the New Star Baths, which, as bishop, I have vowed to shut down as a center of impurity. Happily, our proconsul has shares in the syndicate that owns all the baths in Thessalonika and so, once again, Caesar and Christ must accommodate each other, and I go regularly to the baths for the steam and of course the concerts in season. "He says I am to write down everything because all the Gospels have been destroyed except mine, which isn't written yet."

"Praise God!" Atalanta never listens but then she is, like me, a natural blonde. Of course, she *hears* everything. "How were they all destroyed?"

"A computer virus."

"Oh, yes." Atalanta looked sad. "Yes. I've always been afraid that would happen. Some hacker, just for fun, no doubt, has punched his way into the memory banks and typed out all the secret code numbers and then—presto! no more tapes, Jesus, us. We are such stuff as fax are made on and our little tapes are rounded with a thermal sleep due to Cascade or Fish 6."

"You are talkng in tongues again." But, as I always do when she does, I wrote down, phonetically, the strange words that she had just said.

Lately, Atalanta seems not to know whether or not she has left the everyday world for some waking dream of her own. When I have my non-sense visions—if they are nonsense—I'm asleep, as I was just now with

Saint. But, wide awake and out of nowhere, Atalanta suddenly talks of computer viruses as if she knew what they were.

Now that I am at my desk in the upstairs rumpus room, and Atalanta is off preparing her celebrity auction at the proconsul's palace, I shall follow Saint's advice and begin the Gospel According to Myself with, as we usually do, the Word, after first recording last night's nightmare and this morning's weird message from Atalanta, the house glossolalist.

I shall put in Jesus's genealogy later. Although many gospel writers like to begin with His family, I have always thought genealogy a great bore even when it's one's own. Saint only threw it in because the Jews liked knowing that Jesus came from one of their better families, but, as I once pointed out to Saint, if He really came from God then He wasn't related to anybody human except maybe His mother's extended family. Saint finessed that by saying Jesus was related to *everyone* human as we are all in God's image since we are His children and so on and so forth.

Anyway, I shall skip the begats—Mark did, and his book is far more popular than Matthew's if *Publishers Weekly* in Alexandria is to be trusted. Actually, sales figures are often rigged by rival Christian publishing firms. For instance...

"The men have arrived with the television set." Those were the exact words that the maid said to me as I was sitting at this desk, about to describe Saint Paul's first meeting with our Lord on the eastbound Jerusalem–Damascus freeway.

EDMUND
WHITE

EDMUND WHITE has often said that what interests him as a writer and as a critic is not to see with a "psychological eye," but with a "sociological eye," and yet, as he acknowledged in an interview with Kay Bonetti in the *Missouri Review*, "the philosophical novelist, like Thomas Mann, is someone I tend to loathe and the very concrete novelist who has very few ideas, like Colette, is someone I tend to admire." It is a constant, an abiding base for his work, a taste for the particular, the concrete, which reveals, through its place within a society, the meaning (and range of meanings) of that place. Indeed, if nothing else, it sets his work apart from the two primary forms the American novel has taken in the second half of the twentieth century: the metafictional novel, turning in upon its own technique and concerned with questions of knowability, of uncertainty; and the more conventional and more popular novel of psychological sentiment. White's first novel, *Forgetting Elena*, which has been described as dreamlike—a baroque fantasy—was praised on its publication by such literary luminaries as Vladimir Nabokov, Gore Vidal, and John Ashbery. The intricacy and elaborate quality of its surface style pricks out the equally intricate, nearly hermetic facets of the Fire Island society he describes: feverish, intensely competitive, elegant nearly to the exclusion of any other concern. White explained its attraction to Bonetti: "The idea of writing about a culture that had a surface democracy, but an actual hierarchy, and where morality has been replaced by esthetics … fascinated me. It seemed to be true of how a certain group of highly privileged gay men were living in the seventies."

With his second novel, *Nocturnes for the King of Naples*, White moderated the oblique, apparent fantasy of *Forgetting Elena* and produced a book whose boundaries match those of the visible world, yet whose impulses remain indirect, artistically more concerned with the latent and the suggestive than with the obvious. In *Nocturnes*, in fact, one can witness the modulations between White's two styles, between the elaborate fantasy of *Forgetting Elena* and *Caracole* and the direct, almost plain style of *A Boy's Own Story* and *The Beautiful Room Is Empty*. In his elaborate early style, White's sociological, or rather structuralist, underpinning

Essay by
KEVIN RAY

507

comes clearest, with character and identity dissolving into a meeting and conflicting series of social and linguistic codes. The self is a thing constructed out of bits of the world. "My appearance," his narrator observes in *Nocturnes*, "was composed of allusions to things or people I admired— the slacks from an old gangster movie, the shoes and socks from the athletes I'd watched at school circling the track, the jacket from a veteran whom I'd studied once during a two-hour layover in a bus terminal, the gauzy shirt from a circus barker whose masculinity had become all the more pungent through dandyism." This interplay of elaborate and plain styles is reflected in White's observation of old and new gay styles, which he outlined for *Christopher Street* in 1991. "Whereas," he wrote, "such earlier gay esthetic sensibilities as dandyism or camp had proceeded through indirection and puzzling, deliberately intimidating, reorderings of traditional values, the new esthetic, which I dubbed the Pleasure Machine, was frank, hedonistic, devoid of irony."

All commentators who try to capture what is, at any time, essential about a new culture that is stumbling into being, strive to see their subject as Alexis de Tocqueville saw the new American democracy: as a unique eruption, a severance of past from future. In 1840, concluding *La Democratie en Amerique*, he wrote that "although the revolution that is taking place in the social condition, the laws, the opinions, and the feelings of men is still very far from being terminated, yet its results already admit of no comparison with anything that the world has ever before witnessed.... As the past has ceased to throw its light upon the future, the mind of man wanders in obscurity."

At a time when international gay life has undergone a revolution of its own, accomplishing a profound and startling break with the past, and when the past has "ceased to throw light upon the future"—that is, ceased to be a firm territory from which one may predict what will come—White has attempted to articulate the blind experiment. His attempt comes as gay men in particular, and society more generally, have sought out new relationships to one another, to social institutions, and to conceptions of gender and humanity. *States of Desire: Travels in Gay America*, completed as the decade of radical liberation was ending, and with AIDS not yet on the horizon, provides as close to a poetics as White has given. Reaching out from New York to the West Coast, then drawing back across a continent to where he began, White offers a geography of life rewritten by desire, rewritten as desire. What began as journalism, a travelogue, is appropriated for another purpose and the particular here becomes not simply representative of a place and a mode of life but a link in a chain of understanding. Here, more clearly than he had done before, White draws on work of French theorists—Barthes, Hocquenghem,

Foucault—to insist that the modes of living and desiring he describes reveal people who are engaged in a social critique. At such time, his work is a light thrown onto "the mind of man wander[ing] in obscurity."

Although he had been a prominent and popular gay writer before the publication of *A Boy's Own Story*, and had been admired for the confident craftsmanship of his novels, White was still perhaps best-known, at least in gay circles, as the coauthor of *The Joy of Gay Sex*. But his third novel consolidated his reputation as a writer of fiction, and pushed him immediately to the forefront of that post-Stonewall generation of openly gay writers who in a short time were self-consciously transforming gay writing and publishing. These writers, many of them members of the Violet Quill, a writers' club founded in New York in 1979, broke with earlier generations by electing to identify themselves, explicitly, as gay writers and to take as their subject the rapidly evolving urban gay subcultures that were altering gay and straight life

Edmund White has said that what interests him as a writer and critic is not to see with a "psychological eye," but with a "sociological eye."

alike in America during the 1970s. Writing for *Christopher Street* in the early 1990s, looking back on that time, White noted that in those years "the old polarities that had functioned in an earlier period of gay life (butch/femme, older/younger, richer/poorer) and that had been patterned after borrowed social forms (husband/wife, teacher/student, gentleman/worker) had been rejected in favor of a new tribalism. To be sure, this equality was only apparent ... but on a sweaty disco floor at dawn, surrounded by a congeries of half-nude bodies, the interchangeability of human beings did seem real enough."

The change that AIDS brought to gay life coincided with the emergence of White's more direct mature style, and the elegant sensitivity of *A Boy's Own Story* brought a startling clarity of observation to the three stories he contributed to *The Darker Proof*, a short story collection that also features four pieces by Adam Mars-Jones. Where the earlier fiction drew energy from the sense of being at the center of things, now, without choosing it, that center had grown white hot. Personal history was overtaken by an impersonal history and became an extension of a broad public discourse. In a *Christopher Street* interview with Alfred Corn, White explained that "I was diagnosed early, around '85. The first year-and-a-half I was quite depressed, really ... I stayed at home, and in a way, I was out of touch with friends of mine in America who were ill—which some people thought was just cowardice, as it partly was, but I didn't get much gratification out of that form of cowardice—in other words, facing it and going through it with people is somehow enriching, perhaps, or at least realistic."

It has sometimes been claimed that White flirts with the role of satirist, more in the earlier novels than the later ones, but one must admit in the end that he is no satirist, though a casual humor suffuses his work. Satire requires distance, requires that the purveyor remain both removed from his subject and passionately involved with it, an antagonist, for the satirist is at heart a reformer, outraged by what he sees. White, though briefly touching satire in *Forgetting Elena* and *Nocturnes for the King of Naples*, and glancingly in *States of Desire*, works best from within, as a part of the world he describes. In White one does not find a satirist's rage, nor does one find him standing back from cosmopolitan gay society, surveying, wary. Rather his humor is mild, pervasive, not pointed. In his mature style, irony is diffused by a larger humanity. Beginning with *A Boy's Own Story* and deepening with the stories in *The Darker Proof* and *The Beautiful Room is Empty*, White has returned to the model of Colette, a writer not of ideas, but of concrete lives. His subject is, as it has been from the start, the world, but it is a world apprehended through the observation of his own life. "It's as though I peeled away the fantasy layer, in a style that was extremely ornate and appropriate to that particular vision" he told Bonetti in the *Missouri Review*. "Then I was ready to deal with the painful reality of my youth in a more direct way. If my goal now was to tell the truth, I wasn't going to disguise it with a style that was very rhetorical."

Edmund White told the *Companion:*

"My two direct influences have been contradictory ones—Vladimir Nabokov and Christopher Isherwood. From Nabokov, I acquired a delight in applying a dandy's fastidious standards to everyday American life. Through Isherwood, whose hold on my imagination came to supplant Nabokov's, I learned to admire a sober style and a searching sincerity. I find myself oscillating even now between these two writers, both admirable."

NOCTURNES FOR THE KING OF NAPLES

Can't sleep tonight. I was lying in bed reading the biography of a great man whose genius deserted him. Then I switched off the light and tried to sleep, but I was afraid of something. I got up and made scrambled eggs in the dark, standing there naked and cold, watching the slime from the bowl churn up into gray curds in the pan. They looked like brains on the plate. I ate them and they were delicious, perfumed with tarragon. I poured myself a glass of milk and felt like a good little boy, though the glare from the refrigerator revealed that my body's no longer boyish—odd, troubling reminder. Good boy in a man's body.

I sat by the window on a cold metal chair and looked out at a black building across the way pressing its bulk against the wintry haze, which was bright enough to suggest dawn, though surely that's at least an hour away. The genius who deserted me was you.

A psychiatrist I once knew told me that the unconscious, that irritating retard, can't distinguish between abandoning someone and being abandoned by him. I guess he meant that even though I left you, it's come to seem as though you left me. That rings true. He also said that I was making myself into a "quiet disaster" in order to force you into returning to save me—once again a dimwit stratagem hatched by the unconscious, which doesn't recognize any of the ordinary dimensions such as time, distance, causality or your indifference.

I never kept a diary. I never saved up witty things people told me. I never even bothered to remember my own past, the events that mattered most to me. Nor have I tried to piece things together. I'm a master of the art of pruning, you might say, as though I'd heard that plants should be cut back to make them flourish—except I keep hacking them down to the roots and wonder why they die.

Not all of them do. You're tenacious. Like a tree in paradise heavy with birds.

The leaves hang against the summer sky, real, not stirring, transected by the evening sun; the birds circle and light on its branches weightlessly. You know not to touch me, though I can sense you want to. We're both in jackets and ties, feeling formal after so many days on the beach in swimsuits. I can't be more than … twenty, but I look younger. Everyone says I do except you. You've learned to avoid describing me to myself, since everything you say provides me with another excuse to be vexed. It's a holiday and we've strung lanterns and put out flags along the walkway in honor of the occasion. The decorations, too, lend formality to the evening.

Excerpt reprinted from *Nocturnes for the King of Naples*, St. Martin's Press, copyright 1978 by Edmund White.

EDMUND **WHITE**   511

American novelist, biographer, editor, and educator.

Born: Edmund Valentine White III in Cincinnati, Ohio, January 13, 1940.

Education: University of Michigan, B.A., 1962.

Career: Senior editor, Time, Inc., Book Division, New York City, 1972-73. Assistant professor of writing seminars, Johns Hopkins University, Baltimore, Maryland, 1977–79. Adjunct professor of creative writing, Columbia University School of the Arts, New York City, 1981–83; professor, Brown University, 1990–. Instructor in creative writing at Yale University, New York University, Johns Hopkins University, and George Mason University, Fairfax, Virginia. Executive director of New York Institute for the Humanities, 1981-82. Editor, *Saturday Review* and *Horizon;* contributing editor, *Vogue* and *House and Garden.*

Recipient: University of Michigan Hopwood Awards for fiction and drama, 1961 and 1962; Ingram Merrill grants, 1973 and 1978; Guggenheim fellowship, 1983; American Academy and Institute of Arts and Letters award for fiction, 1983; named Chevalier de l'Ordre des Artes et Lettres, 1993.

Agent: Maxine Groffsky, Maxine Groffsky Literary Agency, 2 Fifth Avenue, New York, New York 10011, U.S.A.

Belle comes toward us across the lawn, smiling, her nose and temples red with today's sunburn. Now she's dressed and has a cardigan over her shoulders. She kisses my cheek, as she did the first time we met, though this evening I catch her darting a glance in your direction the moment she pulls away. Have you told her we're having one of our little disagreements?

Over supper the Captain, the only man who looks natural wearing an ascot (his is yellow with age and the ends hang straight down in crumpled afterthought), neglects my glass and my remarks, which is not like him. And he brings up names I don't know but that you and Belle do. He's excluding me from your old circle, reminding me that there are dozens of people who have admired you for years—tribute-bearers assembled before the throne in their native regalia (gauze leggings over gold pants, woven-feather bodice above a hairless stomach, a short military skirt), their origins so exotic and the precise degree of their vassalage so old and various that only a historian could explain it—but the Captain explains nothing and you're invisible behind the incense rising from the bronze tripod.

All during the festival and the fireworks after supper I avoid you and stay with the Portuguese family who take care of your house. When you catch up with me and ask me where I've been, I say, "It's impolite for couples to stick together."

"Are we still a couple?" you ask.

"Maybe. You should know. You've known so many people whose names I can't even recognize—"

"I don't know *why* the Captain—"

"Why shouldn't he talk about anyone he wants to? Isn't it a little artificial to pretend I'm part of your old gang?"

As we walk out to the end of the dock, our feet sounding a different note on each slat of this crooked xylophone, your hands sketch out several possible replies, none to your satisfaction. From a distance we might look like a patriarch and his heir in our nice summer jackets, out for a stroll on a resort island. That's what a stranger would think. Your friends might say, "They've reconciled. Thank God we didn't let slip anything nasty about the boy while they were quarreling." We stare across the bay toward the lights of a town that rise in a curved band like the crown of a child coming toward us, candles in her hair to celebrate the festival.

The gleam of that bright town in the distance, intensified here and there where a car's headlights shoot out over the waves for a second, fills me with a longing to flee you.

Now, years later, how easy it is to interpret that urge as a loveless boy's fear of a perfect love that came too late, but back then it seemed (my longing to get away) almost metaphysical. In fact I said to you, as we stood on the dock, "Doesn't it ever strike you as strange to be a man rather than a woman, to be here rather than," pointing toward the crown of candles, "there, for instance? Sometimes I want to explode into a million bits, all conscious, and shoot through space and then, I don't know, rain down on everything or, well, yeah, actually catch up with the light rays that bounced off people thousands of years ago. Somewhere out there," my lifted hand was pointing straight up, "Solomon is still threatening to cut the baby in half."

You turn silent and I'm afraid, once again, that I'm boring you. Oh, now, my friend, I can see you loved my enthusiasm but didn't know what to say nor where to begin. So you looked away and I thought you were bored. The hot ingot I had become cooled and hardened.

"Shall we head back?" you asked.

"Go on," I said. "I'll stay in the beach house tonight. I want to play records very loud."

"You can do that—"

"My records. Anyway, I don't want to be anywhere near you tonight."

"Have I done something wrong?"

"Of course not," I said and looked you in the eye and smiled ever so brightly. I was so angry at you, but you climbed in my bedroom window and I relented.

Old friend, you studied me too closely, as though deeper scrutiny would finally reveal my mystery. But there was nothing more to learn, nothing definite in me beyond one surge of emotion after another, all alike and of the same substance, though this one broke early and fanned out timidly across the sand whereas that one broke late, right beside the reef, and shot spray up against the solicitous sky.

On the ferry the next day as we headed back toward the mainland and home, I was caught between regret for the difficult summer and anticipation of the fall. We all sat on the top deck under the sun and even the noisiest holiday-makers grew silent and breathed in the salt breeze.

Once we had docked in that surprisingly vernal inlet, the foliage to the west, where the sun had just set, was already black whereas the trees on the other side were still somberly green. Motionless up to the very moment of our arrival, the branches, once we landed, began to churn and revolve—rides in a somnolent amusement park that function only for the paying visitor. In the taxi to the train station we were jammed in with other vacationers, none of whom we knew, and I was happy to sit scrunched up beside you with one arm around your neck. But I didn't turn to look at you.

Back in the city I had more freedom than on the island, more freedom from the surveillance of your friends. You changed everything to please me. Took down the curtains, rolled up the rugs, stored furniture, painted every stick and surface white—I was in my stark, simple period. Now I've lived so long in hotels I can't imagine caring about my surroundings. They're things to accept, like people, not to change.

One night that fall I brought home a man I'd met during intermission at a theater. We, you and I, had an unspoken rule not against infidelities but against adventures that were conspicuous, intrusive. But nothing pleased and frightened me so much then as to cast aside all our rules.

I set up a little campsite in the kitchen for him and me, that is, I dragged in a brass lamp (one that could be dialed down to near extinction), a scratchy radio and a Chinese red blanket. I bolted the doors and that man and I became drunk and raucous. Once, near dawn, I thought I heard you pacing the hall. Cheap music, cheap wine, fumbling sex with someone who was homely, grateful, not even very clean—what fun and anguish to defile the polished tiles of that kitchen floor beside the room where the maid slept. Just before she was due to awaken I saw my visitor out, though I prolonged the farewell by the front door, whispering and giggling. Lurching about I then restored the lamp to its proper place (my "study" as you called it), threw out the empty bottle and the cigarette ashes and cloaked myself in the red blanket. You were awake and dressed, sitting on the edge of our bed, talking and smiling but inwardly subdued and angry.

"Don't pretend with me!" I said, still drunk. "What are you really feeling?"

"Toward you?"

"Yes, of course, toward me."

You stood and looked out the window at the tree whose leaves were not coloring with autumn, just drying and curling. "This can't go on, can it?"

"What can't?" I wanted the full scene. "What can't go on?"

"I don't need to elaborate," you said and left the room.

The next day as I was walking my bicycle down the hall you stopped me at the door on your way in and invited me to dinner on the following evening. "Okay, maybe," I said casually. After all we lived together.

"Maybe?"

"All right!" I shouted. That was good, wasn't it? We needed to shout, didn't we? "Black tie? White tie? Shall I bring flowers?"

"Eight o'clock. Here." Only when I looked back did I see you watching me with the big brown eyes of a child—the child in a sailor suit you had been and whom I knew from that old photograph in the family album up at the cottage.

I had so much power over you. If I would touch you, as I did once in a while (just a touch, nothing intimate), you'd get excited. I could insist you cancel your social engagements for a week in a row and you would comply, but then that full, powerful life you led away from me would gush in through a crevice I'd neglected and inundate you and, yes, me as well. The telephone would ring, at a restaurant someone would stop by our table, people would drop in, on the street you'd be recognized and friends would draw us away.

You possessed a genius for friendship, a gift you'd refined through energy and intelligence. Your intuition was so keen that you could even sense when a shy person needed to be *ignored*. Yet there was nothing slavish about your politeness. You were cool and, among old friends at least, demanding not of favors, never favors, but of wit, if that means say-

Nonfiction

The Joy of Gay Sex: An Intimate Guide for Gay Men to the Pleasures of a Gay Lifestyle, with Charles Silverstein, 1977.

States of Desire: Travels in Gay America, 1980.

Genet: A Biography, 1993.

Novels

Forgetting Elena, 1973.

Nocturnes for the King of Naples, 1978.

A Boy's Own Story, 1982.

Caracole, 1985.

The Beautiful Room Is Empty, 1988.

Other

Blue Boy in Black (play; produced New York, 1963).

Contributor, *Aphrodisiac* (short stories), 1984.

The Darker Proof: Stories from a Crisis, with Adam Mars-Jones, 1988.

"Back to Mackinac" in *House and Garden* (New York), June 1990.

"Out of the Closet, Onto the Bookshelf: A Prominent Gay Writer Chronicles the Emergence of a New Literature," in *New York Times Magazine*, 16 June 1991.

Editor, and contributor of "Skinned Alive," in *The Faber Book of Gay Short Fiction*, 1991.

---

ing something interesting. I have not, now that you've left me, tried to imitate your style, nor could I; I'm simply carried about from place to place. When I was with you I did try to say interesting things from time to time. Not now. What I've learned is that people will get me home no matter how much I drink and pick me up no matter how little I said or offered the night before. As with possessions, I've given up conversation, but everything still goes on.

We gave a party in honor of an old musician visiting our city. The visit was only a pretext; we scarcely knew the man. Hundreds of guests came. Everyone wanted to meet him. We wanted, I suppose, to show your friends how much we loved each other all over again. I stood at the door and shook hands and told people where to put their coats. Then I passed a tray, which I liked because it gave me an excuse to keep moving. Finally I joined a group and asked our guest of honor to tell me the significance of the red thread in his lapel, and people seemed pleased by the naïveté of my question and the modesty and humor of his answer.

But I couldn't keep it up. Suddenly I was tired and even angry. I rushed to the back of the house and sat on the sooty ledge of the storage room. A few people found me in there and we had, after a while, a band of renegades among the old cans of paint and the tools and firewood. The renegades agreed parties were a terrible bore and they drank a lot and I was quite free to become silent and inch still farther out the window. To me the atmosphere seemed rebellious and one I alone had created. I was very happy until someone asked me, ever so casually, a question. She was a young woman in a black gown. She had lovely breasts and diamonds in her ear lobes, and she wasn't much taller or older than I. "What's it like," she asked, "living with him?" I could tell how much she admired you and envied me. I tore off my tie and jumped off the ledge into the alleyway and ran to the corner with a cocktail shaker in my hand—silver and engraved with your initials entwined in mine. I drank right from the frosted spigot and tossed the empty pitcher in a trash can, but only after I'd lit a match to look at those initials incised in white metal. The engraver had worked cleverly; at first glance the design seemed to be a flourish in a scroll. The letters became apparent only after—ouch! I dropped the pitcher and it made a pathetic clang against the bottom of the trash can.

I ran and ran until I reached a promontory overlooking the city and the river. There I sat on a stone and stared at the cars below as they flowed across the bridge, their lights infusing the water like the blood of an antique senator in a tub. The cool moist earth tried to talk to me but it didn't have a mouth, just something through which it exhaled. Maybe it breathed through its pores. I took off all my clothes and clasped my skinny body, shivering. At my feet lay that little puddle of garments you had bought me. At last I was free of them, the dress shirt, the shoes and socks, the coat and trousers. I studied the watch and its black Roman numerals that circuited through its round ("I," "Aye Aye!," "eye, eye, eye," "ivy") past the ecstatic shriek "VIII" and on to the dignified "X my sign." Now it was 1:30 and the hands said "I vie," as I did with you and your light yoke, your silk shackles. I threw the watch on top of the pile and strode away, still clutching myself, into a chilling fantasy of freedom. For a moment I had the illusion I was walking through a true forest until I came to a metal grille sunk into the ground through which I could see more cars streaking down a tunnel. The warmth and odor of the exhaust filtered up around me and I stood on that grating I know not how long. Could I pry it open and drop onto the shiny roof of a car, crawl to its hood, shrink and turn silver as the ornament breasting the wind? Or slip into a window, surprising a contented family, Dad vigilant and responsible behind the wheel, Mom reading a map by the faint glow of the open glove compartment, the kids and the collie a dim, dozing heap in the back seat?

If I said nothing they might take me home to a bungalow in a development and clothe me and keep me and you would never find me. They might consign me to the back seat and I, too, could become implicated in that tangle of fur, doggy breath, cool hands and cheeks as smooth as glazed fruit, our upturned eyes seeing only the tops of buildings, then trees, then after a while the stars and our ears catching only the murmur of grownups navigating us safely to our beds.

EDMUND **WHITE** 517

OSCAR WILDE

Essay by
KARL BECKSON

Universally acknowledged as the wittiest poet, literary critic, novelist, short story writer, and playwright of the late nineteenth century, Oscar Wilde achieved fame early in life—chiefly the result of his American lecture tour in 1882—but later, at the height of his powers, he suffered subsequent disgrace when he was convicted and imprisoned for homosexual offenses in the most sensational trials of the century. The tragic conclusion of his career was foreshadowed, however, in such a work as *The Picture of Dorian Gray*, which, Wilde said in a letter to Lord Alfred Douglas, secretly contained "the note of Doom that like a purple thread runs through the gold cloth" of his homoerotic novel. In a letter to another friend, Wilde willingly accepted his symbolic "martyrdom," which he believed essential if homosexuals were ever to be accepted by society.

Oscar Fingal O'Flahertie Wills Wilde was born in Dublin on October 16, 1854, the second son of parents prominent in Ireland's cultural and professional life. His father, Dr. William Ralph Wills Wilde, was an internationally well known ear and eye surgeon, the founder of a hospital in 1853, and the author of some 20 books on such subjects as Irish archaeology and antiquarian subjects as well as the 1853 *Aural Surgery*, the standard textbook on the subject. In 1864, Queen Victoria knighted him for his work in directing the medical census in Ireland. Wilde's mother, Lady Wilde (born Jane Francesca Elgee), was prominent in political and literary circles as "Speranza," a pseudonym meaning "hope," designed to inspire Irish nationalists as well as feminists. During her long life, she published many volumes of poems, essays, stories, and collections of folklore.

Wilde received his primary school education at the Portora Royal School in Enniskillen, Ulster, and in October of 1871 he entered Trinity College, Dublin, where he won awards in classical studies. While at Trinity, Wilde was absorbed by Hellenism, which he interpreted as the union of body and soul, as opposed to Christianity, which traditionally denigrated the body in favor of the soul. Hellenism appealed to his homoerotic interests, reenforced by his study of Plato's dialogues, such as

Oscar Wilde is universally acknowledged as the wittiest poet, literary critic, novelist, short story writer, and playwright of the late nineteenth century.

the *Symposium*, which discusses homosexual love between men and between men and boys. In June of 1874, after completing three years at Trinity College, he was awarded a scholarship to attend Magdalen College, Oxford University.

During his years at Oxford, he not only distinguished himself by his extensive learning but also achieved renown for his brilliant talk. In his fourth year, he won the Newdigate Prize for his 1878 poem *Ravenna*, which was published and recited publicly at the Sheldonian Theatre. While at Oxford, he attended the lectures of Walter Pater and John Ruskin, both of whom stressed the experience of art as the key to a full life: Pater urging immersion in intense aesthetic sensations; Ruskin urging the study of great art, which could reveal a world divinely ordered. By surrounding himself with artistic objects, such as blue china and peacock feathers, Wilde assumed the role of an Aesthete. In 1881 he published *Poems*, which revealed his devotion to such poets as Keats, Swinburne, and Rossetti (a devotion, some critics contended, bordering on plagiarism).

By 1881, Punch's cartoons contained a figure resembling Wilde as the arch-Aesthete; as a result, Gilbert and Sullivan's operetta, *Patience*, implied that Wilde was the principal object of this satire of Aestheticism, though Swinburne and Rossetti were also suspected as models for the "fleshly" and "idyllic" poets. The producer of *Patience*, Richard D'Oyly Carte, engaged Wilde to give a series of lectures in America to publicize the production there. For most of 1882, Wilde lectured in the United States and Canada on such topics as the aesthetic movement, house decoration, and nineteenth-century Irish poets. In the early weeks, he appeared on stage in aesthetic costume in imitation of the characters in *Patience:* in knee breeches, velvet jacket, and a sunflower or lily in his buttonhole—dress that provoked charges of "unmanliness." On his return to London, he began reviewing books in various periodicals and newspapers; arranging for the production of his Romantic tragedy *Vera; or the Nihilists* in 1883, which failed in New York; and editing *Woman's World* between 1887 and 1889. In 1884, he married Constance Lloyd, later an author. Two children were born: Cyril in 1885, killed in action in 1915; and Vyvyan in 1886.

In 1888, Wilde published his first volume of fairy tales, *The Happy Prince, and Other Tales*, which reveals prominent homoerotic themes and

Irish-born British poet, playwright, novelist, and short story writer. Also wrote as C.3.3. and Sebastian Melmoth.

Born: Oscar Fingal O'Flahertie Wills Wilde, October 16 (some sources say October 15), 1854 (some sources say 1856) in Dublin.

Education: Trinity College, Dublin, 1871–73; Magdalen College, Oxford, B.A. (first class honors) 1878.

Partnerships: Married Constance Mary Lloyd, May 29, 1884 (died April 7, 1898); two children.

Career: Toured United States and Canada as lecturer, 1882; toured the British Isles as lecturer, 1883–84. Journalist and book reviewer in London, 1884–87; member of editorial staff, *Woman's World* (periodical), London, 1887–89. Prisoner at institutions including Old Baily, Wandsworth Prison, Reading Jail, and Pentonville Prison, 1895–97. Traveler in Switzerland, Italy, and France, under pseudonym Sebastian Melmoth, 1897–1900. Author of such lectures as "Art and the Handicraftsman" and "Lecture to Art Students." Contributor of articles, essays, reviews, and criticism such as "Woman's Dress," "More Radical Ideas Upon Dress Reform," "Sermon in Stones at Bloomsbury," "Mrs. Langtry as Hester Grazebrook," "London Models," "Some Cruelties of Prison Life," "Oscar Wilde on Poets and Poetry," "Slaves of Fashion," " Costume," and "The American Invasion" to periodicals, including *Pall Mall Gazette*, *Dramatic Review*, *Woman's World*, *New York World*, *Court and Society Review*, *English Illustrated Magazine*, London *Daily Chronicle*, *Blackwood's Edinburgh Magazine*, and *Chameleon*. Contributor of poems to periodicals, including *Dublin University Magazine*, *Irish Monthly*, *Kottabos*, *Our Continent*, *In a Good Cause*, *Court and Society Review*, *Art and Letters*, *Centennial Magazine*, *Lady's Pictorial*, and *Burlington*. Translator into English, sometimes under pseudonym Sebastian Melmoth.

Recipient: Oxford Univeristy's Newdigate Prize for Poetry, 1878.

Died: Paris, after a short illness, November 30, 1900; buried in Bagneux Cemetery, Paris; reinterred in 1909 in Père-Lachaise Cemetery (French national cemetery), Paris.

---

fantasies of martyrdom. In "The Happy Prince," a male Swallow fulfills various requests from the statue of the Happy Prince, such as helping the poor by stripping the gold leaf and precious gems from the statue, but when winter comes, the bird refuses to leave the Prince for Egypt. When the Prince kisses the Swallow on the lips, the bird falls dead at his feet. But the power of love—here clearly homoerotic—results in God's elevation of the dead bird and the self-mutilated statue into Paradise.

In the July 1889 issue of *Blackwood's Edinburgh Magazine*, Wilde expressed the theme of homosexual martyrdom in more obvious form in his story "The Portrait of Mr. W. H." Here the quest for the identity of Mr. W. H. (called, in the dedication of Shakespeare's sonnets, as the work's "onlie begetter") involves the effeminate Cyril Graham, who, in school, had always performed female leads in Shakespeare's plays. In order to affirm the truth that the object of Shakespeare's love was Mr. W. H.—Willie Hughes, "some wonderful boy-actor of great beauty"—Cyril kills himself, "the youngest and the most splendid of all the martyrs of literature," as a "sacrifice to the secret of the Sonnets." Such a martyr's

Oscar Wilde with Lord Alfred Douglas in Oxford, around 1893.

death eventually appeals to Cyril's friend, who, when he accepts the theory concerning W. H., threatens suicide but ironically dies not as a martyr but a victim of tuberculosis—a chararacteristic compromise by Wilde on the implicit homoeroticism of the story to avoid critical attacks. In his *Oscar Wilde*, Richard Ellmann remarks that Wilde told the story of Willie Hughes to the statesmen Arthur Balfour and Herbert Asquith, both of whom "advised him not to print it, lest it corrupt English homes."

A portrait—like that in "The Portrait of Mr. W. H."—is also the central symbol of Wilde's most daring work, *The Picture of Dorian Gray*, which appeared in one issue of *Lippincott's Monthly Magazine* in July of 1890. When it appeared in book form in 1891, it contained six additional chapters and a preface delineating the idea of "art for art's sake," the idea that art should be concerned with its own perfection rather than with moral, political, or religious issues.

The homoerotic myth of Narcissus (a small bronze statuette of whom Wilde had on his mantelpiece in his Tite Street home) pervades both character and plot in the novel, which depicts Dorian's narcissistic adoration of his own image in his portrait. Lord Henry Wotton, his mentor, has collected some 17 photographs of the beautiful Dorian, whom he refers to as "a Narcissus," and later, after rejecting the actress Sibyl Vane, who subsequently kills herself, Dorian, "in boyish mockery of Narcissus," kisses or pretends to kiss "those painted lips [of his portrait] that now smiled so cruelly at him."

The painter of the portrait, Basil Hallward, refuses to exhibit it because, as he says, he has put too much of himself into it. Hallward's erotic attraction to Dorian is further dramatized by his own account of their first meeting at a party: "When our eyes met, I felt that I was growing pale. A curious sensation of terror came over me. I knew that I had come face to face with some one whose mere personality was so fascinating that, if I allowed it to do so, it would absorb my whole nature, my whole soul, my very art itself." Later, Hallward confesses to his homoeroticism by remarking that he had never cared for women (a remark that Wilde removed in the second version in an attempt to pacify his critics). Late in the novel, Hallward asks Dorian, who has acquired an unsavory reputation: "Why is your friendship so fatal to young men?" Dorian eventually plunges a knife into the disfigured painting in order to kill this embodiment of conscience, an act that ironically restores it to its original beauty, whereas Dorian is found dead, his hideous body symbolizing his moral decline.

The critical reactions to Wilde's novel, particularly the first version, indicated that many reviewers had grasped its homosexual subtext. The *Daily Chronicle* of June 30, 1890, for example, called it "a tale spawned from the leprous literature of the French *Décadents*—a poisonous book ... [of] effeminate frivolity ... [and] unbridled indulgence in every form of secret and unspeakable vice." In the *Athenaeum* of June 27, 1891, the reviewer of the second version charged that the novel was "unmanly, sickening, vicious" (such terms as "unspeakable vice" and "unmanly" were usually Victorian code words for homosexuality).

In his second volume of tales, the 1891 *A House of Pomegranates*, Wilde later regarded one of the stories, "The Young King," as another foreshadowing of his own tragic destiny. The 16-year-old lad shows "signs of that strange passion for beauty that was destined to have so great an influence over his life." Indeed, the tapestries in his palace depict the "Triumph of Beauty" (for Wilde, beauty—whether in art or in young men and boys—is frequently associated with homoerotic impulses). When the Young King's dreams reveal the suffering of his people who prepare for his coronation, he rejects luxurious raiment, dons peasant clothes, and wears a crown of thorns, associated with Christ's crucifixion, accompanied by transformation and elevation. At the end of the story, no one dares look upon the Young King's face, "for it was like the face of an angel."

Wilde's most notable literary successes occurred in the theater with his four society comedies, beginning with *Lady Windermere's Fan* in 1892. His witty dandies reveal Wilde's own narcissistic impulses, as in *An Ideal Husband* in 1895, in which Lord Goring remarks: "To love oneself is the beginning of a lifelong romance." In his greatest play, *The Importance of Being Earnest* in 1895, Wilde focuses on the comic implications of the double life, as in Jack Worthing's adoption of the name "Ernest" when in town to indulge in pleasure, and in Algernon Moncrieff's invention of a sick friend named "Bunbury," who provides Algernon with an excuse to avoid social obligations. Indeed, Wilde was leading a more daring double life in his homosexual affairs with "renters" (male prostitutes), casual pick-ups, and his own circle of friends, including the young Lord Alfred Douglas, whose father, the Marquess of Queensberry, provoked Wilde into charging him with libel for accusing him of "posing as somdomite" (misspelling the offensive word).

The evidence at the Queensberry trial turned against Wilde, who was himself arrested and convicted in criminal trials held in April and May of 1895 under the notorious Criminal Law Amendment Act of

Poetry

Newdigate Prize Poem: Ravenna, Recited in the Theatre, Oxford, 26 June 1878, 1878.

Poems, 1881; with illustrations by Charles Ricketss, 1892.

The Sphinx, illustrations by Charles Ricketts, 1894; with illustrations by Melvin Leipzig, 1969.

The Ballad of Reading Gaol (as C.3.3., Wilde's prison number), 1896; with illustrations by Frans Masereel, 1978.

The Harlot's House (first published in *The Dramatic Review,* 11 April 1885), illustrations by Althea Gyles, 1904; with illustrations by Daphne Lord, 1967.

Poems in Prose (first published in *Fortnightly Review,* July 1894), 1905; revised as *Prose Poems,* illustrations by Margaret McCord, 1973.

Pan, a Double Villanelle, and *Désespoir, a Sonnet,* 1909.

Remorse: A Study in Saffron, notes by Majl Ewing, 1961.

Serenade, illustrations by Rigby Graham, 1962.

Some Early Poems and Fragments, 1974.

Collected Poetry

The Poems of Oscar Wilde, 1906.

The Poetical Works of Oscar Wilde, Including Poems in Prose, 1908.

The Poetical Works of Oscar Wilde, introduction by Nathan Haskell Dole, 1913.

Panthea, and Other Poems, edited by George Sylvester Viereck, 1925.

The Poems of Oscar Wilde, illustrations by Jean de Bosschere, 1927.

The Harlot's House, and Other Poems, illustrations by John Vasos, 1929.

Poems, selected by Denys Thompson, 1972.

Mervyn Peake, Oscar Wilde: Extracts from the Poems of Oscar Wilde, foreword by Maeve Gilmore, illustrations by Mervyn Peake, 1980.

Plays

Vera; or, The Nihilists: A Drama in Four Acts, produced New York, 1883.

The Duchess of Padua: A Tragedy of the XVI Century, Written in Paris in the XIX Century, produced as *Guido Ferranti: A Tragedy of the XVI Century* on Broadway, 1891; London, 1907.

Salomé: Drame en un acte, produced Paris, 1896; London, 1905; New York, 1906.

Lady Windermere's Fan, produced London, 1892; New York, 1893.

A Woman of No Importance, produced in West End, 1893.

The Importance of Being Earnest: A Trivial Comedy for Serious People, produced London, 1895.

An Ideal Husband, produced in West End and on Broadway, 1895.

A Florentine Tragedy, opening scene by Sturge Moore, produced London, 1906.

For Love of the King: A Burmese Masque, London, Methuen, 1922.

La Sainte Courtisane: Or, The Woman Covered with Jewels.

Collected Plays

The Plays of Oscar Wilde, four volumes, 1905-20.

The Plays of Oscar Wilde, illustrations by Frederic W. Goudy, 1914.

Plays, illustrations by Donia Nachshen, 1931.

Comedies, 1931.

Five Famous Plays, 1952.

Selected Plays, 1954.

Plays, 1961.

Five Plays, 1964.

Plays, 1964.

Five Major Plays, 1970.

Three Plays, 1981.

Wilde: Comedies: A Casebook, edited by William Tydeman, 1982.

Two Society Comedies, 1983.

The Importance of Being Earnest, and Other Plays, 1985.

1885, which stipulated that any homosexual acts committed either in private or in public were punishable by two years at hard labor. Wilde served the specified term principally at Reading Prison, the setting of his most famous poem *The Ballad of Reading Gaol* in 1898, which expresses the mystery of his own self-destructiveness in the famous refrain that "all men kill the thing they love." While in prison, Wilde had written a long autobiographical letter to Douglas (later published as *De Profundis*), which explores his pain and suffering provoked by his relationship with Douglas and with homophobic society at large. Ironically, while defending his own homosexuality, Wilde regards Queensberry as a degenerate Philistine and rejects the view of the Italian criminologist Cesare Lombroso, who regarded homosexuality as a congenital pathology. In the

The Picture of Dorian Gray (novel; originally appeared in *Lippincott's Monthly Magazine*, July 1890). As *The Picture of Dorian Gray: Original Text—1890*, 1964; revised and enlarged, 1891; with introduction by Peter Faulkner, 1976.

Lord Arthur Savile's Crime: A Study of Duty, 1904; as *Lord Arthur Savile's Crime: A Study in Duty*, illustrations by Dorothea Braby, 1954.

The Birthday of the Infanta, 1905; with illustrations by Leonard Lubin, 1979.

The Fisherman and His Soul, 1907; with illustrations by Mallette Dean, 1939.

The Young King [and] *The Star-Child*, 1909.

The Selfish Giant, 1932; with illustrations by Lisbeth Zwerger, 1984; bound with *The Happy Prince*, foreword by Hal W. Trovillion, 1945.

The Happy Prince, foreword by Hal W. Trovillion, illustrations by William J. Goodacre, 1940; bound with *The Selfish Giant*, foreword by Hal W. Trovillion, 1945.

(Presumed author) *Teleny: Or, The Reverse of the Medal* (novel), 1958; as *Teleny: A Novel Attributed to Oscar Wilde*, edited by Winston Leyland, 1984.

The Canterville Ghost, illustrations by Wallace Goldsmith, 1965.

Little Hans, the Devoted Friend, illustrations by Robert Quackenbush, 1969.

The Remarkable Rocket, illustrations by Henry E. Coleman, 1974.

The Star Child, abridged by Jennifer Westwood, illustrations by Fiona French, 1979.

The Nightingale and the Rose, illustrations by Freire Wright and Michael Foreman, 1981.

Collected Fiction

The Happy Prince, and Other Tales, illustrations by Walter Crane and Jacomb Hood, 1888; with illustrations by Rudolph Ruzicks, 1936; bound with *A House of Pomegranates*, preface by John Espey, 1977.

Lord Arthur Savile's Crime, and Other Stories, 1891.

A House of Pomegranates, illustrations by C. H. Shannon, 1891; with illustrations by Jessie M. King, 1915; bound with *The Happy Prince, and Other Tales*, preface by John Espey, 1977.

The Happy Prince, and Other Fairy Tales, 1909; bound with *A House of Pomegranates*, preface by John Espey, 1977.

Fairy Tales, 1913.

The Happy Prince, and Other Stories, illustrations by Spencer Baird Nichols, 1931.

Ben Kutcher's Illustrated Edition of A House of Pomegranates, and the Story of the Nightingale and the Rose, introduction by H. L. Mencken, illustrations by Ben Kutcher, 1918.

The Fisherman and His Soul, and Other Fairy Tales, illustrations by Theodore Nadejen, 1929.

Stories, illustrations by Donia Nachshen, 1931; with introduction by John Guest, 1952.

The Happy Prince, and Other Tales, illustrations by Everett Shinn, 1940.

The Happy Prince: The Complete Fairy Stories of Oscar Wilde, illustrations by Philippe Jullian, 1952; with critical notes by Vyvyan Holland, 1965; as *The Complete Fairy Stories of Oscar Wilde*, 1970; as *The Fairy Stories of Oscar Wilde*, illustrations by Harold Jones, introduction by Naomi Lewis, 1976.

Fairy Tales, illustrations by Charles Mozley, 1960; as *Complete Fairy Tales*, 1961.

The Happy Prince, and Other Stories, introduction by Micheal Mac Liammoir, illustrations by Lars Bo, 1962.

The Picture of Dorian Gray and Selected Stories, foreword by Gerald Weales, 1962.

The Young King, and Other Fairy Tales, introduction by John Updike, illustrations by Sandro Nardini and Enrico Bagnoli, 1962.

The Happy Prince, and Other Stories, illustrations by Peggy Fortnum, 1968.

The Short Stories of Oscar Wilde, introduction by Robert Gorham Davis, illustrations by James Hill, 1968.

Lord Arthur Savile's Crime, and Other Stories, 1973.

Complete Shorter Fiction, edited by Isobel Murray, 1980.

The Birthday of the Infanta, and Other Tales, illustrations by Beni Montresor, 1982.

Oscar Wilde Stories and Fairy Tales, illustrations by Zevi Blum, 1983.

---

process, as Claude J. Summers writes in *Gay Fictions*, Wilde emerges as "Saint Oscar, a kind of Harlequin Christ-figure who transforms his victimization into a martyrdom."

When released in May of 1897, he immediately left England for France, assuming the name of "Sebastian Melmoth," derived from the Christian martyr St. Sebastian and the title of the Gothic 1820 novel *Melmoth the Wanderer* by Wilde's great-uncle, Charles Maturin. Shortly

This portrait was taked by Napoleon Sarony in 1882 at the beginning of
Oscar Wilde's American tour.

The Soul of Man Under Socialism (originally appeared in *Fortnightly Review*, February 1891), published in *The Soul of Man Under Socialism* [by Wilde, and] *The Socialist Ideal—Art* [and] *The Coming Solidarity* [by William Morris and W. C. Owen]), 1892; as *The Soul of Man*, London, 1895; with preface by Robert Ross, 1912.

The Portrait of Mr. W. H. (essay; originally appeared in *Blackwood's Edinburgh Magazine*, July 1889), 1901, revised, 1921; revised again, edited by Vyvyan Holland, 1958.

Phrases and Philosophies for the Use of the Young (originally appeared in *Chameleon*, December 1894), 1902.

The Rise of Historical Criticism, 1905; reprinted, 1978.

De Profundis, with preface by Robert Ross, 1905; enlarged, 1909; with introduction by Frank Harris, 1926; revised, introduction by Vyvyan Holland, 1950; unexpurgated edition published as *De Profundis: Unexpurgated*, introduction by Jacques Barzun, 1964.

Impressions of America (includes lecture text), edited by Stuart Mason, 1906.

Decorative Art in America, edited by Richard Butler Glaenzer, 1906.

The Suppressed Portion of "De Profundis," by Oscar Wilde, Now for the First Time Published by His Literary Executor, 1913.

A Critic in Pall Mall: Being Extracts from Reviews and Miscellanies, 1919.

The Critic as Artist: A Dialogue, 1957.

Collected Nonfiction

Intentions (essays), 1891.

Oscariana: Epigrams (excerpts), compiled by Constance Mary Lloyd Wilde, 1895; revised and enlarged, 1912.

Essays, Criticisms, and Reviews (collection of editorials first published in *Woman's World*, November 1887 to June 1889), 1901.

Sebastian Melmoth (excerpts), 1904.

Epigrams and Aphorisms (excerpts), introduction by George Henry Sargent, 1905.

The Wisdom of Oscar Wilde, selected by Temple Scott, 1906.

Great Thoughts from Oscar Wilde, selected by Stuart Mason, 1912.

Aphorisms of Oscar Wilde, selected and arranged by G. N. Sutton, c. 1914.

The Essays of Oscar Wilde, 1935.

Essays, edited by Hesketh Pearson, 1950; as *The Soul of Man Under Socialism, and Other Essays*, introduction by Philip Rieff, 1970.

Epigrams: An Anthology, compiled by Alvin Redman, introduction by Vyvyan Hollad, 1952; as *The Wit and Humor of Oscar Wilde*, 1959.

Wit and Wisdom, compiled by Cecil Hewetson. 1960; as *Wit and Wisdom of Oscar Wilde*, 1967.

Literary Criticism of Oscar Wilde, edited by Stanley Weintraub, 1968.

The Artist as Critic: Critical Writings of Oscar Wilde, edited by Richard Ellmann, 1969.

The Wit of Oscar Wilde, compiled by Sean McCann, 1969.

Witticisms of Oscar Wilde, compiled by Derek Stanford, 1971.

Wilde Things: The Delicious and Malicious Epigrams of Oscar Wilde, illustrations by Aubrey Beardsley, 1972.

Letters

Wilde v. Whistler: Being an Acrimonious Correspondence on Art between Oscar Wilde and James A. McNeill Whistler (first published in *The Gentle Art of Making Enemies* by Whistler, 1890), 1906.

Letters After Reading, 1921; as *After Reading: Letters of Oscar Wilde to Robert Ross*, 1921.

After Berneval: Letters of Oscar Wilde to Robert Ross, illustrations by Randolph Schwabe, 1922.

Oscar Wilde's Letters to Sarah Bernhardt, edited by Sylvestre Dorian, 1924.

Some Letters from Oscar Wilde to Alfred Douglas, 1892-1897, preface by William Andrews Clark, Jr., notes by Arthur C. Dennison, Jr., and Harrison Post, additional material by A. S. W. Rosenbach, 1924.

Sixteen Letters from Oscar Wilde, edited and notes by John Rothenstein, 1930.

Letters (includes first publication of full text of *De Profundis*), edited by Rupert Hart-Davis, 1962; as *The Letters of Oscar Wilde*, 1962.

Selected Letters of Oscar Wilde, edited by Rupert Hart-Davis, 1979.

Berneval: An Unpublished Letter, notes by Jeremy Mason, 1981.

Oscar Wilde—Graham Hill: A Brief Friendship (letters), notes by Jeremy Mason, 1982.

More Letters of Oscar Wilde, edited by Rupert Hart-Davis, 1985.

---

before his death on November 30, 1900, Wilde wrote to his friend George Ives, a poet and criminologist who had organized a secret order of homosexuals to advance the "Cause": "Yes: I have no doubt we shall win, but the road is long, and red with monstrous martyrdoms. Nothing but the repeal of the Criminal Law Amendment Act would do any good." A

General Omnibus Volumes

Poems by Oscar Wilde, Together with His Lecture on the English Renaissance, 1903.

The Best of Oscar Wilde: Being a Collection of the Best Poems and Prose Extracts of the Writer, collected by Oscar Herrmann, edited by W. W. Massee, illustrations by Frederick Ehrlich, 1905.

Fairy Tales and Poems in Prose, 1918.

Art and Decoration: Being Extracts from Reviews and Miscellanies by Oscar Wilde, 1920.

The Picture of Dorian Gray, The Importance of Being Earnest, The Ballad of Reading Gaol, and Other Works of Oscar Wilde, introduction by Hesketh Pearson, 1930; as *Plays, Prose Writings, and Poems,* 1955; revised, introduction by Isobel Murray, 1975.

The Writings of Oscar Wilde: Poems, Short Stories, Plays, Novels, Fairy Tales, Letters, Dialogues, and Philosophy, 1931.

Poems and Essays, illustrations by Donia Nachshen, 1931.

The Best Known Works of Oscar Wilde, Including the Poems, Novels, Plays, Essays, Fairy Tales and Dialogues, 1931.

The Works of Oscar Wilde, illustrations by Donia Nachshen, 1932.

The Poems and Fairy Tales of Oscar Wilde, 1932.

The Poems of Oscar Wilde, 1935.

The Best Known Works of Oscar Wilde, Including the Poems, Novels, Plays, Essays and Fairy Tales, 1940.

The Portable Oscar Wilde, selected and edited by Richard Aldington, 1946; revised edition selected and edited by Aldington and Stanley Weintraub, 1981.

Selected Works, with Twelve Unpublished Letters, 1946.

Works, edited by G. F. Maine, 1948; new edition, 1963.

Selected Essays and Poems, introduction by Hesketh Pearson, 1954; as *De Profundis, and Other Writings,* 1973.

Poems and Essays, introduction by Kingsley Amis, 1956.

Oscar Wilde: Selections From the Works of Oscar Wilde, edited by Graham Hough, 1960.

Selected Writings, introduction by Richard Ellmann, 1961.

Intentions, and Other Writings, 1961.

Works, introduction by John Gilbert, 1963; as *The Works of Oscar Wilde,* 1977.

De Profundis, notes by Rupert Hart-Davis, additional material by W. H. Auden, 1964.

Selected Writings of Oscar Wilde, edited by Russell Fraser, 1969.

Poems in Prose and the Preface to The Picture of Dorian Gray, 1974.

The Illustrated Oscar Wilde, edited by Roy Gasson, 1977.

The Annotated Oscar Wilde: Poems, Fictions, Plays, Lectures, Essays, and Letters, edited by H. Montgomery Hyde, 1982.

The Picture of Dorian Gray, and Other Writings, edited by Richard Ellmann, 1982.

Complete Works

The Writings of Oscar Wilde (15 volumes), 1907.

Works (15 volumes), edited by Robert Ross, 1908–1910 & 1922; U.S. edition published as *The First Collected Edition of the Works of Oscar Wilde, 1908- 1922,* 15 volumes, 1969.

Second Collected Edition of the Works of Oscar Wilde (14 volumes), edited by Robert Ross, 1909–1912.

The Works of Oscar Wilde (15 volumes), introduction by Richard Le Gallienne, 1909; reprinted as *The Sunflower Edition of the Works of Oscar Wilde,* 1972; as *The Works of Oscar Wilde,* new introduction by Stanley Weintraub, 1980.

Complete Works of Oscar Wilde (10 volumes), edited by Robert Ross, 1921.

The Complete Works of Oscar Wilde (12 volumes), 1923.

Complete Works of Oscar Wilde, introduction by Vyvyan Holland, 1948; new edition, 1966.

---

step in that direction occurred on the 100th anniversary of Wilde's birth when the London County Council authorized a commemorative blue plaque to be placed on his former home on Tite Street. Three years later, the Criminal Law Amendment Act was repealed.

ON THE SALE BY AUCTION OF KEATS' LOVE LETTERS

These are the letters which Endymion wrote
    To one he loved in secret, and apart.
    And now the brawlers of the auction mart
Bargain and bid for each poor blotted note,
Ay! for each separate pulse of passion quote
    The merchant's price. I think they love not art
    Who break the crystal of a poet's heart
That small and sickly eyes may glare and gloat.

Is it not said that many years ago,
    In a far Eastern town, some soldiers ran
    With torches through the midnight, and began
To wrangle for mean raiment, and to throw
    Dice for the garments of a wretched man,
Not knowing the God's wonder, or His woe?

Reprinted from *The Complete Works of Oscar Wilde*, Harper & Row, 1989.

BY THE ARNO

The oleander on the wall
    Grows crimson in the dawning light,
    Though the grey shadows of the night
Lie yet on Florence like a pall.

The dew is bright upon the hill,
    And bright the blossoms overhead,
    But ah! the grasshoppers have fled,
The little Attic song is still.

Only the leaves are gently stirred
    By the soft breathing of the gale,
    And in the almond-scented vale
The lonely nightingale is heard.

The day will make thee silent soon,
    O nightingale sing on for love!
    While yet upon the shadowy grove
Splinter the arrows of the moon.

Reprinted from *The Complete Works of Oscar Wilde*, Harper & Row, 1989.

Before across the silent lawn
In sea-green vest the morning steals,
And to love's frightened eyes reveals
The long white fingers of the dawn

Fast climbing up the eastern sky
To grasp and slay the shuddering night,
All careless of my heart's delight,
Or if the nightingale should die.

IMPRESSION DU MATIN

Reprinted from *The
Complete Works of Oscar
Wilde*, Harper & Row,
1989.

The Thames nocturne of blue and gold
Changed to a Harmony in grey:
A barge with ochre-coloured hay
Dropt from the wharf: and chill and cold

The yellow fog came creeping down
The bridges, till the houses' walls
Seemed changed to shadows and St. Paul's
Loomed like a bubble o'er the town.

Then suddenly arose the clang
of waking life; the streets were stirred
With country waggons: and a bird
Flew to the glistening roofs and sang.

But one pale woman all alone,
The daylight kissing her wan hair,
Loitered beneath the gas lamps' flare,
With lips of flame and heart of stone.

VIRGINIA WOOLF

ADELINE VIRGINIA WOOLF loved women, emotionally and physically. She neither lived nor wrote from a traditional point of view, so to impose a rigid grid of heterosexual interpretation upon her life and her texts is to leave undeveloped their rich homoerotic texture. For many years, Woolf's biographers and scholars did just that, even though relationships with women were central to the author's life and texts. In many critical studies, Woolf's lesbian interactions were interpreted as mere friendships, thus denying their erotic implications. Emphasis on her obsession with her mother, her breakdowns, and her avant-garde lifestyle focused much critical attention on her pathologies, her need for care-taking by others, and her eventual suicide.

Certain facts concerning Woolf's sexuality, in keeping with the bohemian picture of a writer, could not be suppressed—her lesbian liaison with Vita Sackville-West, her close relationships with women throughout her lifetime, her presumed platonic marriage to Leonard Woolf, and the absence of any male romantic figures in her writings. These aspects of her life were employed to depict Woolf as uninterested in a physical relationship, as a child in search of her mother, as a dysfunctional wife, or as an asexual creature. And, because much biographical information about Woolf came from family members or others who had a vested interest in protecting individual reputations, an accurate representation of the author could not emerge.

Woolf's preference for female protectors and confidants is well documented. She declared her love for women openly in a letter written in 1930: "But I am the most passionate about women. Take away my affections and I should be like sea weed out of water; like the shell of a crab, like a husk. All my entrails, light, marrow, juice, pulp would be gone. I should be blown into the first puddle and drown…. It is true that I only want to show off to women. Women alone stir my imagination." Involvements with Madge Vaughan and Violet Dickinson preceded Woolf's best-known relationship, with Vita Sackville-West; a later liaison developed between the author and Dame Ethel Smyth. As Jane Marcus points out in *Virginia Woolf and the Languages of Patriarchy*, in

Essay by
PAMELA J. OLANO

531

Virginia Woolf in 1902.

these friendships Woolf was "never seduced, betrayed, or abandoned."

The experiences of Woolf's personal life are reflected in the complex expression of homoeroticism found in her works. Marcus stresses that "female heterosexuality is most often represented in Woolf's fiction as victimization or colonization." Woolf introduced the homoerotic element in *Mrs. Dalloway* through the relationship of Clarissa Dalloway and Sally Seton, in *Between the Acts* through Miss LaTrobe, the lesbian artist, and in *A Room of One's Own* through the mysterious relationship of the scientists, Chloe and Olivia. Other lesbian narratives can be identified in works such as *To the Lighthouse* (most specifically in the relationship between Lily Briscoe and Mrs. Ramsay), *Orlando* (in the gender metamorphosis of the main character), and *The Pargiters*.

Woolf's inclusion of lesbianism in her texts was sometimes buried beneath one or more heterosexual plots and other times exhibited as a main theme. Homoerotic pairings were often juxtaposed with dysfunctional male/female dyads, and can be read as constructions of alternative relationships— relationships which lie outside of heterosexual structures. Aware of the prohibitions against overt homosexuality during the time in which she lived, Woolf often encoded, or disguised, her lesbian narratives. In a letter to Vita Sackville-West, the author made reference to "Moments of Being: 'Slater's Pins Have No Points,'" a short story with a lesbian subplot. She wrote, "Sixty pounds just received from America for my little Sapphist story of which the Editor has not seen the point, though he's been looking for it in the Adirondacks." Woolf clearly found both irony and delight in the fact that the encoded lesbian narrative remained undiscovered by the American editor.

Woolf was keenly aware of the dangers of being too obviously a sapphist. Citing an early fragment of *A Room of One's Own*, Marcus observes that after the words "Chloe liked Olivia," the author wrote: "The words covered the bottom of the page: the pages had stuck. While fumbling to open them there flashed into my mind the inevitable policeman ... the order to attend the Court; the dreary waiting; the Magistrate coming in with a little bow." These latter references describe Radclyffe Hall's obscenity trial over the novel *The Well of Loneliness*. Banned by English courts, the book significantly affected novelists' freedom to write about lesbianism. At one point, Woolf had planned to testify at the trial; even without this testimony, she was aware of the suit's possible implications.

As Ellen Bayuk Rosenman notes in *Signs: Journal of Women in Culture and Society*, Woolf had no workable cultural definition of lesbianism that bore resemblance to her own same-sex relationships. "No understanding of lesbianism existed that explained her personal relationship with Sackville-West, as private experience and public understandings shared no common ground," Rosenman writes. Neither the depiction of Stephen Gordon in Radclyffe Hall's novel nor the prevailing interpretations of lesbianism by sexologists Havelock Ellis and Richard von Kraft-Ebing seemed appropriate representations of what Woolf experienced. Rosenman concludes that it is not surprising that, under these circumstances, Woolf did not openly—or at times even positively—portray lesbian experience.

In *PMLA*, Sherron Knopp emphasizes Woolf's awareness of the homophobic time in which she lived, as well as the author's disassociation from lesbian definitions of the day. Knopp references a passage from *Orlando* as proof that Woolf understood the penalties for sapphism: "For she was extremely doubtful whether, if the spirit [of the age] had examined the contents of her mind carefully, it would not have found something highly contraband for which she would have had to pay the full fine. She had only escaped by the skin of her teeth." As Knopp alleges, "The examination [that] *Orlando* passes 'by the skin of her teeth' could not be plainer, and *The Well of Loneliness* provided a timely illustration of the 'full fine' one could expect to pay for *not* passing."

Woolf nonetheless continued to inscribe homoerotic desire as she understood it in her works, bringing "buried things to light and [making] one wonder what need there had been to bury them," as she insists in *A Room of One's Own*. Her value to lesbian and gay history, as well as literary production, lies then in her repeated lesbian plots and subplots, and in her personal struggle to express the experiences of her own life in her texts. That Woolf left us a trail of these experiences in her own words, in her diaries and letters, and in her fiction and nonfiction, is evidence of the importance that lesbian relationships had in her life.

A ROOM OF ONE'S OWN

I had come at last, in the course of this rambling, to the shelves which hold books by the living; by women and by men; for there are almost as many books written by women now as by men. Or if that is not yet quite true, if the male is still the voluble sex, it is certainly true that women no longer write novels solely. There are Jane Harrison's books on Greek archaeology; Vernon Lee's books on aesthetics; Gertrude Bell's books on Persia. There are books on all sorts of subjects which a generation ago no woman could have touched. There are poems and plays and criticism; there are histories and biographies, books of travel and books of scholarship and research; there are even a few philosophies and books about science and economics. And though novels predominate, novels themselves may very well have changed from association with books of a different feather. The natural simplicity, the epic age of women's writing, may have gone. Reading and criticism may have given her a wider range, a great subtlety. The impulse towards autobiography may be spent. She may be beginning to use writing as an art, not as a method of self-expression. Among these new novels one might find an answer to several such questions.

I took down one of them at random. It stood at the very end of the shelf, was called *Life's Adventure*, or some such title, by Mary Carmichael, and was published in this very month of October. It seems to be her first book, I said to myself, but one must read it as if it were the last volume in a fairly long series, continuing all those other books that I have been glancing at—Lady Winchilsea's poems and Aphra Behn's plays and the novels of the four great novelists. For books continue each other, in spite of our habit of judging them separately. And I must also consider her—this unknown woman—as the descendant of all those other women whose circumstances I have been glancing at and see what she inherits of their characteristics and restrictions. So, with a sigh, because novels so often provide an anodyne and not an antidote, glide one into torpid slumbers instead of rousing one with a burning brand, I settled down with a notebook and a pencil to make what I could of Mary Carmichael's first novel, *Life's Adventure*.

To begin with, I ran my eye up and down the page. I am going to get the hang of her sentences first, I said, before I load my memory with blue eyes and brown and the relationship that there may be between Chloe and Roger. There will be time for that when I have decided whether she has a pen in her hand or a pickaxe. So I tried a sentence or two on my tongue. Soon it was obvious that something was not quite in order. The smooth gliding of sentence after sentence was interrupted.

THE GAY AND LESBIAN LITERARY COMPANION

British publisher, novelist, essayist, diarist, and author of short fiction.

Born: London, January 25, 1882; daughter of the writer Sir Leslie Stephen. Self-educated.

Partnerships: Married Leonard Woolf in 1912 (died, 1969).

Career: Founder, with brother Thoby Stephen, of *Hyde Park Gate News* (a weekly paper), 1891–95; Morley College, London, England, instructor in English, c. 1905–07; founder and operator of Hogarth Press with husband, beginning 1917. Also wrote essays under name Virginia Stephen.

Recipient: Prix *Feminina* from *Feminina* and *Vie Heureuse* reviews, 1928.

Died: Committed suicide by drowning in the Ouse River, Lewes, Sussex, March 28, 1941.

Something tore, something scratched; a single word here and there flashed its torch in my eyes. She was "unhanding" herself as they say in the old plays. She is like a person striking a match that will not light, I thought. But why, I asked her as if she were present, are Jane Austen's sentences not of the right shape for you? Must they all be scrapped because Emma and Mr Woodhouse are dead? Alas, I sighed, that it should be so. For while Jane Austen breaks from melody to melody as Mozart from song to song, to read this writing was like being out at sea in an open boat. Up one went, down one sank. This terseness, this short-windedness, might mean that she was afraid of something; afraid of being called "sentimental" perhaps; or she remembers that women's writing has been called flowery and so provides a superfluity of thorns; but until I have read a scene with some care, I cannot be sure whether she is being herself or someone else. At any rate, she does not lower one's vitality, I thought, reading more carefully. But she is heaping up too many facts. She will not be able to use half of them in a book of this size. (It was about half the length of *Jane Eyre*.) However, by some means or other she succeeded in getting us all—Roger, Chloe, Olivia, Tony, and Mr Bigham—in a canoe up the river. Wait a moment, I said, leaning back in my chair, I must consider the whole thing more carefully before I go any further.

I am almost sure, I said to myself, that Mary Carmichael is playing a trick on us. For I feel as one feels on a switchback railway when the car, instead of sinking, as one has been led to expect, swerves up again. Mary is tampering with the expected sequence. First she broke the sentence; now she has broken the sequence. Very well, she has every right to do both these things if she does them not for the sake of breaking, but for the sake of creating. Which of the two it is I cannot be sure until she has faced herself with a situation. I will give her every liberty, I said, to choose what that situation shall be; she shall make it of tin cans and old kettles if she likes; but she must convince me that she believes it to be a situation; and then when she has made it she must face it. She must jump. And, determined to do my duty by her as reader if she would do her duty by me as writer, I turned the page and read ... I am sorry to break off so abruptly. Are there no men present? Do you promise me that behind that red curtain over there the figure of Sir Chartres Biron is not concealed? We are all women you assure me? Then I may tell you that the very next words I read were these—"Chloe liked Olivia ..." Do not start. Do not blush. Let us admit in the privacy of our own society that these things sometimes happen. Sometimes women do like women.

"Chloe liked Olivia," I read. And then it struck me how immense a change was there. Chloe liked Olivia perhaps for the first time in literature. Cleopatra did not like Octavia. And how completely *Antony and Cleopatra* would have been altered had she done so! As it is, I thought, letting my mind, I am afraid, wander a little from *Life's Adventure*, the whole thing is simplified, conventionalized, if one dared say it, absurdly. Cleopatra's only feeling about Octavia is one of jealousy. Is she taller than I am? How does she do her hair? The play, perhaps, required no more. But how interesting it would have been if the relationship between the two women had been more complicated. All these relationships between women, I thought, rapidly recalling the splendid gallery of fictitious women, are too simple. So much has been left out, unattempted. And I tried to remember any case in the course of my reading where two women are represented as friends. There is an attempt at it in *Diana of the Crossways*. They are confidantes, of course, in Racine and the Greek tragedies. They are now and then mothers and daughters. But almost without exception they are shown in their relation to men. It was strange to think that all the great women of fiction were, until Jane Austen's day, not only seen by the other sex, but seen only in relation to the other sex. And how small a part of a woman's life is that; and how little can a man know even of that when he observes it through the black or rosy spectacles which sex puts upon his nose. Hence, perhaps, the peculiar nature of woman in fiction; the astonishing extremes of her beauty and horror; her alternations between heavenly goodness and hellish depravity— for so a lover would see her as his love rose or sank, was prosperous or unhappy. This is not so true of the nineteenth-century novelists, of course. Woman becomes much more various and complicated there. Indeed it was the desire to write about women perhaps that led men by degrees to abandon the poetic drama which, with its violence, could make so little use of them, and to devise the novel as a more fitting receptacle. Even so it remains obvious, even in the writing of Proust, that a man is terribly hampered and partial in his knowledge of women, as a woman in her knowledge of men.

Also, I continued, looking down at the page again, it is becoming evident that women, like men, have other interests besides the perennial interests of domesticity. "Chloe liked Olivia. They shared a laboratory together ..." I read on and discovered that these two young women were engaged in mincing liver, which is, it seems, a cure for pernicious anaemia; although one of them was married and had—I think I am right in stating—two small children. Now all that, of course, has had to be left out, and thus the splendid portrait of the fictitious woman is much too simple and much too monotonous. Suppose, for instance, that men were only represented in literature as the lovers of women, and were never the friends of men, soldiers, thinkers, dreamers; how few parts in the plays of Shakespeare could be allotted to them; how literature would suffer! We might perhaps have most of Othello; and a good deal of Antony; but no Caesar, no Brutus, no Hamlet, no Lear, no Jaques—literature would be incredibly impoverished, as indeed literature is impoverished beyond our counting by the doors that have been shut upon women. Married against their will, kept in one room, and to one occupation, how could a dramatist give a full or interesting or truthful account of them? Love was the only possible interpreter. The poet was forced to be passionate or bitter, unless indeed he chose to "hate women", which meant more often than not that he was unattractive to them.

For many years, Woolf's biographers and scholars ignored or lessened the importance of her relationships with women, even though these relationships were central to the author's life and texts.

Now if Chloe likes Olivia and they share a laboratory, which of itself will make their friendship more varied and lasting because it will be less personal; if Mary Carmichael knows how to write, and I was beginning to enjoy some quality in her style; if she has a room to herself, of which I am not quite sure; if she has five hundred a year of her own—but that remains to be proved—then I think that something of great importance has happened.

For if Chloe likes Olivia and Mary Carmichael knows how to express it she will light a torch in that vast chamber where nobody has yet been. It is all half lights and profound shadows like those serpentine caves where one goes with a candle peering up and down, not knowing where one is stepping. And I began to read the book again, and read how Chloe watched Olivia put a jar on a shelf and say how it was time to go home to her children. That is a sight that has never been seen since the world began, I exclaimed. And I watched too, very curiously. For I wanted to see how Mary Carmichael set to work to catch those unrecorded gestures, those unsaid or half-said words, which form themselves, no more palpably than the shadows of moths on the ceiling, when women are alone, unlit by the capricious and coloured light of the other sex. She will need to hold her breath, I said, reading on, if she is to do it; for women are so suspicious of any interest that has not some obvious motive behind it, so terribly accustomed to concealment and suppression, that they are off at the flicker of an eye turned observingly in their direction. The only way for you to do it, I thought, addressing Mary Carmichael as if she were there, would be to talk of something else, looking steadily out of the window, and thus note, not with a pencil in a notebook, but in the shortest of shorthand, in words that are hardly syllabled yet, what happens when Olivia—this organism that has been under the shadow of the rock these million years feels the light fall on it, and sees coming her way a piece of strange food—knowledge, adventure, art. And she reaches out for it, I thought, again raising my eyes from the page, and has to devise some entirely new combination of her resources, so highly developed for other purposes, so as to absorb the new into the old without disturbing the infinitely intricate and elaborate balance of the whole.

But, alas, I had done what I had determined not to do; I had slipped unthinkingly into praise of my own sex. "Highly developed"—"infinitely intricate"—such are undeniably terms of praise, and to praise one's own sex is always suspect, often silly; moreover, in this case, how could one justify it? One could not go to the map and say Columbus discovered America and Columbus was a woman; or take an apple and remark, Newton discovered the laws of gravitation and Newton was a woman; or look into the sky and say aeroplanes are flying overhead and aeroplanes were invented by women. There is no mark on the wall to measure the precise height of women. There are no yard measures, neatly divided into the fractions of an inch, that one can lay against the qualities of a good mother or the devotion of a daughter, or the fidelity of a sister, or the capacity of a housekeeper. Few women even now have been graded at the universities; the great trials of the professions, army and navy, trade, politics, and diplomacy have hardly tested them. They remain even at this moment almost unclassified. But if I want to know all that a human being can tell me about Sir Hawley Butts, for instance, I have only to open Burke or Debrett and I shall find that he took such and such a degree; owns a hall; has an heir; was Secretary to a Board; represented Great Britain in Canada; and has received a certain number of degrees, offices, medals, and other distinctions by which his merits are stamped upon him indelibly. Only Providence can know more about Sir Hawley Butts than that.

When, therefore, I say "highly developed", "infinitely intricate" of women, I am unable to verify my words either in Whitaker, Debrett, or the University Calendar. In this predicament what can I do? And I looked at the bookcase again. There were the biographies: Johnson and Goethe and Carlyle and Sterne and Cowper and Shelley and Voltaire and Browning and many others. And I began thinking of all those great men who have for one reason or another admired, sought out, lived with, confided in, made love to, written of, trusted in, and shown what can only be described as some need of and dependence upon certain persons of the opposite sex. That all these relationships were absolutely Platonic I would not affirm, and Sir William Joynson Hicks would probably deny. But we should wrong these illustrious men very greatly if we insisted that they got nothing from these alliances but comfort, flattery and the pleasures of the body. What they got, it is obvious, was something that their own sex was unable to supply; and it would not be rash, perhaps, to define it further, without quoting the doubtless rhapsodical words of the poets, as some stimulus, some renewal of creative power which is in the gift only of the opposite sex to bestow. He would open the door of drawing-room or nursery, I thought, and find her among her children perhaps, or with a piece of embroidery on her knee—at any rate, the centre of some different order and system of life, and the contrast between this world and his own, which might be the law courts or the House of Commons, would at once refresh and invigorate; and there would follow, even in the simplest talk, such a natural difference of opinion that the dried ideas in him would be fertilized anew; and the sight of her creating in a different medium from his own would so quicken his creative power that insensibly his sterile mind would begin to plot again, and he would find the phrase or the scene which was lacking when he put on his hat to visit her. Every Johnson has his Thrale, and holds fast to her for some such reasons as these, and when the Thrale marries her Italian music master Johnson goes half mad with rage and disgust, not merely that he will miss his pleasant evenings at Streatham, but that the light of his life will be "as if gone out".

And without being Dr Johnson or Goethe or Carlyle or Voltaire, one may feel, though very differently from these great men, the nature of this intricacy and the power of this highly developed creative faculty among women. One goes into the room but the resources of the English language would be much put to the stretch, and whole flights of words would need to wing their way illegitimately into existence before a woman could say what happens when she goes into a room. The rooms

Chalk drawing of Virginia Woolf by Francis Dodd, 1908.

differ so completely; they are calm or thunderous; open on to the sea, or, on the contrary, give on to a prison yard; are hung with washing; or alive with opals and silks; are hard as horsehair or soft as feathers—one has only to go into any room in any street for the whole of that extremely complex force of femininity to fly in one's face. How should it be otherwise? For women have sat indoors all these millions of years, so that by this time the very walls are permeated by their creative force, which has, indeed, so overcharged the capacity of bricks and mortar that it must needs harness itself to pens and brushes and business and politics. But this creative power differs greatly from the creative power of men. And one must conclude that it would be a thousand pities if it were hindered or wasted, for it was won by centuries of the most drastic discipline, and there is nothing to take its place. It would be a thousand pities if women wrote like men, or lived like men, or looked like men, for if two sexes are quite inadequate, considering the vastness and variety of the world, how should we manage with one only? Ought not education to bring out and fortify the differences rather than the similarities? For we have too much likeness as it is, and if an explorer should come back and bring word of other sexes looking through the branches of other trees at other skies, nothing would be of greater service to humanity; and we should have the immense pleasure into the bargain of watching Professor X rush for his measuring-rods to prove himself "superior".

Mary Carmichael, I thought, still hovering at a little distance above the page, will have her work cut out for her merely as an observer. I am afraid indeed that she will be tempted to become, what I think the less interesting branch of the species—the naturalist-novelist, and not the contemplative. There are so many new facts for her to observe. She will not need to limit herself any longer to the respectable houses of the upper middle classes. She will go without kindness or condescension, but in the spirit of fellowship, into those small, scented rooms where sit the courtesan, the harlot, and the lady with the pug dog. There they still sit in the rough and ready-made clothes that the male writer has had perforce to clap upon their shoulders. But Mary Carmichael will have out her scissors and fit them close to every hollow and angle. It will be a curious sight, when it comes, to see these women as they are, but we must wait a little, for Mary Carmichael will still be encumbered with that self-consciousness in the presence of "sin" which is the legacy of our sexual barbarity. She will still wear the shoddy old fetters of class on her feet.

However, the majority of women are neither harlots nor courtesans; nor do they sit clasping pug dogs to dusty velvet all through the summer afternoon. But what do they do then? and there came to my mind's eye one of those long streets somewhere south of the river whose infinite rows are innumerably populated. With the eye of the imagination I saw a very ancient lady crossing the street on the arm of a middle-aged woman, her daughter, perhaps, both so respectably booted and furred that their dressing in the afternoon must be a ritual, and the clothes themselves put away in cupboards with camphor, year after year, throughout the summer months. They cross the road when the lamps are being lit (for the dusk is their favourite hour), as they must have done year after year. The elder is close on eighty; but if one asked her what her life has meant to her, she would say that she remembered the streets lit for the battle of Balaclava, or had heard the guns fire in Hyde Park for the birth of King Edward the Seventh. And if one asked her, longing to pin down the moment with date and season, But what were you doing on 5 April 1868, or 2 November 1875, she would look vague and say that she could remember nothing. For all the dinners are cooked; the plates and cups washed; the children sent to school and gone out into the world. Nothing remains of it all. All has vanished. No biography or history has a word to say about it. And the novels, without meaning to, inevitably lie.

All these infinitely obscure lives remain to be recorded, I said, addressing Mary Carmichael as if she were present; and went on in thought through the streets of London feeling in imagination the pressure of dumbness, the accumulation of unrecorded life, whether from the women at the street corners with their arms akimbo, and the rings embedded in their fat swollen fingers, talking with a gesticulation like the swing of Shakespeare's words; or from the violet-sellers and match-sellers and old crones stationed under doorways; or from drifting girls whose faces, like waves in sun and cloud, signal the coming of men and women and the flickering lights of shop windows. All that you will have to explore, I said to Mary Carmichael, holding your torch firm in your hand. Above all, you must illumine your own soul with its profundities and its shallows, and its vanities and its generosities, and say what your beauty means to you or your plainness, and what is your relation to the ever-changing and turning world of gloves and shoes and stuffs swaying

Novels

The Voyage Out, 1915; revised, 1920.
Night and Day, 1919.
Jacob's Room, 1922.
Mrs. Dalloway, 1925.
To the Lighthouse, 1927.
Orlando: A Biography, 1928.
The Waves, 1931.
The Years, 1937.
Between the Acts, 1941.

Short Stories

Two Stories Written and Printed by Virginia Woolf and L. S. Woolf, 1917; story by Virginia Woolf published separately as *The Mark on the Wall,* 1919.
Kew Gardens, 1919; reprinted, 1969.
Monday or Tuesday, 1919.
A Haunted House, and Other Short Stories, 1943.
The Complete Shorter Fiction of Virginia Woolf, edited by Susan Dick, 1985.

Essays and Criticism

Mr. Bennett and Mrs. Brown, 1924; reprinted, 1977.
The Common Reader, 1925.
A Room of One's Own, 1929.
The Common Reader, Second Series, 1932; as *The Second Common Reader,* 1932.
Three Guineas, 1938.
The Death of the Moth, and Other Essays, 1941.
The Moment, and Other Essays, 1947.
The Captain's Death Bed, and Other Essays, 1950.
Granite and Rainbow, 1958.
Contemporary Writers, 1965.
Collected Essays (four volumes), 1966–67.
The London Scene: Five Essays, 1975.
Moments of Being (autobiographical essays), edited by Jeanne Schulkind, 1976.

Books and Portraits: Some Further Selections from the Literary and Biographical Writings of Virginia Woolf, edited by Mary Lyon, 1977.
Women and Writing, 1979; edited by Michèle Barrett, 1980.
The Essays of Virginia Woolf, edited by Andrew McNeillie, 1986.

The Letters of Virginia Woolf Series

Volume 1: *The Flight of the Mind, 1888–1912,* edited by Nigel Nicolson and Joan Trautmann, Hogarth, 1975; as *The Letters of Virginia Woolf,* Volume 1: *1888–1912,* Harcourt, 1975.
Volume 2: *The Question of Things Happening, 1912–1922,* Hogarth, 1976; as *The Letters of Virginia Woolf,* Volume 2: *1912–1922,* Harcourt, 1976.
Volume 3: *A Change of Perspective, 1923–28,* Hogarth, 1977; as *The Letters of Virginia Woolf,* Volume 3: *1923–1928,* Harcourt, 1978.
Volume 4: *A Reflection of the Other Person, 1929–1931,* Hogarth, 1978; as *The Letters of Virginia Woolf,* Volume 4: *1929–1931,* Harcourt, 1979.
Volume 5: *The Sickle Side of the Moon, 1932–1935,* Hogarth, 1979; as *The Letters of Virginia Woolf,* Volume 5: *1932–1935,* Harcourt, 1979.
Volume 6: *Leave the Letters Till We're Dead, 1936–1941,* Hogarth, 1980; as *The Letters of Virginia Woolf,* Volume 6: *1936–1941,* Harcourt, 1980.

Other Collected Letters

Virginia Woolf and Lytton Strachey: Letters, edited by Leonard Woolf and James Strachey, 1956.
The Hogarth Letters, 1985.

Other

Street Haunting, 1930.
On Being Ill, 1930.
Beau Brummell, 1930.
A Letter to a Young Poet, 1932; reprinted, 1975.
Flush, A Biography, 1933.
Walter Sickert: A Conversation, 1934; reprinted, 1970.
Reviewing, 1939; reprinted, 1969.
Roger Fry: A Biography, 1940.
A Writer's Diary: Being Extracts from the Diary of Virginia Woolf, edited by Leonard Woolf, 1953.
Hours in a Library, 1958.
Nurse Lugton's Golden Thimble, 1966.
Mrs. Dalloway's Party: A Short Sequence, edited by Stella McNichol, 1973.
The Waves: The Two Holograph Drafts, transcribed and edited by John W. Graham, 1976.
Freshwater: A Comedy, edited by Lucio P. Ruotolo, illustrations by Loretta Trezzo, 1976.
The Diary of Virginia Woolf, edited by Anne Olivier Bell, Volume 1: *1915–1919,* Hogarth 1977, Harcourt 1979; Volume 2: *1920–1924,* 1978; Volume 3: *1925–1930,* 1980; Volume 4: *1931–1935,* 1982.
The Pargiters: The Novel-Essay Portion of "The Years," edited by Mitchell A. Leaska, 1977.
Rupert Brooke, 1978.
Virginia Woolf's Reading Notebooks, edited by Brenda R. Silver, 1982.
Melymbrosia: An Early Version of "The Voyage Out," edited by Louise A. DeSalvo, 1982.
The Virginia Woolf Reader, 1984.
A Passionate Apprentice, 1990.
Nurse Lugton's Curtain, 1991.
Paper Darts, 1991.

up and down among the faint scents that come through chemists' bottles down arcades of dress material over a floor of pseudo-marble. For in imagination I had gone into a shop; it was laid with black and white paving; it was hung, astonishingly beautifully, with coloured ribbons. Mary Carmichael might well have a look at that in passing, I thought, for it is a sight that would lend itself to the pen as fittingly as any snowy peak or rocky gorge in the Andes. And there is the girl behind the counter too—I would as soon have her true history as the hundred and fiftieth life of Napoleon or seventieth study of Keats and his use of Miltonic inversion which old Professor Z and his like are now inditing. And then I went on very warily, on the very tips of my toes (so cowardly am I, so afraid of the lash that was once almost laid on my own shoulders), to murmur that she should also learn to laugh, without bitterness, at the vanities—say rather at the peculiarities, for it is a less offensive word—of the other sex. For there is a spot the size of a shilling at the back of the head which one can never see for oneself. It is one of the good offices that sex can discharge for sex—to describe that spot the size of a shilling at the back of the head. Think how much women have profited by the comments of Juvenal; by the criticism of Strindberg. Think with what humanity and brilliancy men, from the earliest ages, have pointed out to women that dark place at the back of the head! And if Mary were very brave and very honest, she would go behind the other sex and tell us what she found there. A true picture of man as a whole can never be painted until a woman has described that spot the size of a shilling. Mr Woodhouse and Mr Casaubon are spots of that size and nature. Not of course that anyone in their senses would counsel her to hold up to scorn and ridicule of set purpose—literature shows the futility of what is written in that spirit. Be truthful, one would say, and the result is bound to be amazingly interesting. Comedy is bound to be enriched. New facts are bound to be discovered.

However, it was high time to lower my eyes to the page again. It would be better, instead of speculating what Mary Carmichael might write and should write, to see what in fact Mary Carmichael did write. So I began to read again. I remembered that I had certain grievances against her. She had broken up Jane Austen's sentence, and thus given me no chance of pluming myself upon my impeccable taste, my fastidious ear. For it was useless to say, "Yes, yes, this is very nice; but Jane Austen wrote much better than you do", when I had to admit that there was no point of likeness between them. Then she had gone further and broken the sequence—the expected order. Perhaps she had done this unconsciously, merely giving things their natural order, as a woman would, if she wrote like a woman. But the effect was somehow baffling; one could not see a wave heaping itself, a crisis coming round the next corner. Therefore I could not plume myself either upon the depths of my feelings and my profound knowledge of the human heart. For whenever I was about to feel the usual things in the usual places, about love, about death, the annoying creature twitched me away, as if the important point were just a little further on. And thus she made it impossible for me to roll out my sonorous phrases about "elemental feelings", the "common stuff of humanity", "the depths of the human heart", and all those other phrases which support us in our belief that, however clever we may be on top, we are very serious, very profound and very humane underneath. She made me feel, on the contrary, that instead of being serious and profound and humane, one might be—and the thought was far less seductive—merely lazy-minded and conventional into the bargain.

But I read on, and noted certain other facts. She was no "genius"—that was evident. She had nothing like the love of Nature, the fiery imagination, the wild poetry, the brilliant wit, the brooding wisdom of her great predecessors, Lady Winchilsea, Charlotte Brontë, Emily Brontë, Jane Austen, and George Eliot; she could not write with the melody and the dignity of Dorothy Osborne—indeed she was no more than a clever girl whose books will no doubt be pulped by the publishers in ten years' time. But, nevertheless, she had certain advantages which women of far greater gift lacked even half a century ago. Men were no longer to her "the opposing faction"; she need not waste her time railing against them; she need not climb on to the roof and ruin her peace of mind longing for travel, experience, and a knowledge of the world and character that were denied her. Fear and hatred were almost gone, or traces of them showed only in a slight exaggeration of the joy of freedom, a tendency to the caustic and satirical, rather than to the romantic, in her treatment of the other sex. Then there could be no doubt that as a novelist she enjoyed some natural advantages of a high order. She had a sensibility that was very wide, eager and free. It responded to an almost imperceptible touch on it. It feasted like a plant newly stood in the air on every sight and sound that came its way. It ranged, too, very subtly and curiously, among almost unknown or unrecorded things; it lighted on small things and showed that perhaps they were not small after all. It brought buried things to light and made one wonder what need there had been to bury them. Awkward though she was and without the unconscious bearing of long descent which makes the least turn of the pen of a Thackeray or a Lamb delightful to the ear, she had—I began to think—mastered the first great lesson; she wrote as a woman, but as a woman who has forgotten that she is a woman, so that her pages were full of that curious sexual quality which comes only when sex is unconscious of itself.

All this was to the good. But no abundance of sensation or fineness of perception would avail unless she could build up out of the fleeting and the personal the lasting edifice which remains unthrown. I had said that I would wait until she faced herself with "a situation". And I meant by that until she proved by summoning, beckoning, and getting together that she was not a skimmer of surfaces merely, but had looked beneath into the depths. Now is the time, she would say to herself at a certain moment, when without doing anything violent I can show the meaning of all this. And she would begin—how unmistakable that quickening is!—beckoning and summoning, and there would rise up in memory, half forgotten, perhaps quite trivial things in other chapters dropped by the way. And she would make their presence felt while someone sewed or smoked a pipe as naturally as possible, and one would feel, as she went on writing, as if one had gone to the top of the world and seen it laid out, very majestically, beneath.

At any rate, she was making the attempt. And as I watched her lengthening out for the test, I saw, but hoped that she did not see, the bishops and the deans, the doctors and the professors, the patriarchs and the pedagogues all at her shouting warning and advice. You can't do this and you shan't do that! Fellows and scholars only allowed on the grass! Ladies not admitted without a letter of introduction! Aspiring and graceful female novelists this way! So they kept at her like the crowd at a fence on the racecourse, and it was her trial to take her fence without looking to right or to left. If you stop to curse you are lost, I said to her; equally, if you stop to laugh. Hesitate or fumble and you are done for. Think only of the jump, I implored her, as if I had put the whole of my money on her back; and she went over it like a bird. But there was fence beyond that and a fence beyond that. Whether she had the staying power I was doubtful, for the clapping and the crying were fraying to the nerves. But she did her best. Considering that Mary Carmichael was no genius, but an unknown girl writing her first novel in a bed-sitting-room, without enough of those desirable things, time, money, and idleness, she did not do so badly, I thought.

Give her another hundred years, I concluded, reading the last chapter— people's noses and bare shoulders showed naked against a starry sky, for someone had twitched the curtain in the drawing-room—give her a room of her own and five hundred a year, let her speak her mind and leave out half that she now puts in, and she will write a better book one of these days. She will be a poet, I said, putting *Life's Adventure*, by Mary Carmichael, at the end of the shelf, in another hundred years' time.

Sources

Dorothy Allison

Interviews

"A Storyteller Out of Hell" by Bo Huston, in *Advocate*, 7 April 1992, 70–72.

"Truth Is Meaner than Fiction" by Lynn Karpen, in *New York Times Book Review*, 5 July 1992, 3.

Critical Sources

Review by George Garrett of *Bastard Out of Carolina*, in *New York Times Book Review*, 5 July 1992, 3.

June Arnold

Interviews

Unpublished and untranscribed conversations with June Arnold by Marie J. Kuda, 1976.

Critical Sources

Review of *The Cook and the Carpenter*, in *Village Voice*, 4 April 1974, 33.

Review of *The Cook and the Carpenter*, in *Ms.*, June 1974, 35.

"Creating a Women's World" by Lois Gould, in *New York Times Magazine*, 2 January 1977, 10–11, 34, 36–38.

Unpublished and untranscribed conversation with Parke Bowman, 1978.

Review of *Applesauce*, in *Washington Post Book World*, 8 January 1978, E4.

Review of *Applesauce*, in *New York Times Book Review*, 15 January 1978, 27.

Review of *Sister Gin*, in *Spectator*, 3 March 1979, 23.

Review by Taffy Cannon of *Baby Houston*, in *Los Angeles Times Book Review*, 19 July 1987.

Review by Eve Ottenberg Stone of *Baby Houston*, in *New York Times Book Review*, 26 July 1987, 10.

"Bringing Up Baby" (review of *Baby Houston*) by Jane Marcus, in *Women's Review of Books*, October 1987, 4.

Review of *Baby Houston*, in *New Directions for Women*, November 1987, 22.

Review by Joyce Maynard of *Baby Houston*, in *Mademoiselle*, December 1987, 70.

The Safe Sea of Women: Lesbian Fiction 1969–1989 by Bonnie Zimmerman, Boston, Beacon Press, 1990.

Review of *Sister Gin*, in *Belles Lettres*, spring 1990, 22.

Unpublished and untranscribed conversation with Beth Dingman, 7 August 1993.

James Baldwin

Interviews

"The Negro in American Culture," in *Cross Currents*, summer 1961, 205-224.

"Disturber of the Peace" by E. Auchincloss and N. Lynch, in *Mademoiselle*, May 1963, 174–175, 199–207.

"At a Crucial Time a Negro Talks Tough: 'There's a Bill Due That Has to be Paid,'" in *Life*, 24 May 1963, 81–86A.

"A Conversation with James Baldwin" by Kenneth B. Clark, in *Freedomways*, summer 1963, 361–368.

"The American Dream and the American Negro" by William F. Buckley, Jr., in *New York Times Magazine*, 7 March 1965, 32–33, 87–89.

"James Baldwin Breaks His Silence," in *Atlas*, March 1967, 47–49.

"James Baldwin ... in Conversation" by Dan Georgakas, in *Black Voices: An Anthology of Afro-American Literature*, edited by Abraham Chapman, New York, New American Library, 1968, 660–668.

"How Can We Get the Black People to Cool It?," in *Esquire*, July 1968, 49-53, 116.

"It's Hard to Be James Baldwin" by Herbert R. Lottman, in *Intellectual Digest*, July 1972, 67–68.

"Why I Left America" with Ida Lewis, in *New Black Voices*, edited by Abraham Chapman, New York, New American Library, 1972, 409–419.

Black Scholar, December 1973–January 1974, 33–42.

"James Baldwin Comes Home" by Jewell Hardy Gresham, in *Essence*, June 1976, 54–55, 80, 82, 85.

"James Baldwin Writing and Talking" by Mel Watkins, in *New York Times Book Review*, 23 September 1979, 35–36.

"James Baldwin: Looking towards the Eighties" by Kalamu ya Salaam, in *Black Collegian*, December/January 1980, 105–110.

Baldwin: Three Interviews by Malcolm King, Wesleyan University Press, 1985.

"Interview with James Baldwin" by David C. Estes, in *New Orleans Review*, fall 1986, 59–64.

Bibliography

Black American Writers: Bibliographical Essays, Volume 2: Richard Wright, Ralph Ellison, James Baldwin, and Amiri Baraka, edited by M. Thomas Inge and others, New York, St. Martin's Press, 1978.

James Baldwin: A Reference Guide, edited by Fred L. and Nancy V. Standley, Boston, G. K. Hall, 1981.

Contemporary Authors Bibliographical Series, Volume 1: *American Novelists*, Detroit, Gale, 1986.

Critical Sources

Saturday Review, 1 December 1956; 1 July 1961; 7 July 1962; 2 February 1963; 2 May 1964; 6 November 1965; 1 June 1968; 5 January 1980.

The Creative Present: Notes on Contemporary Fiction, edited by Nona Balakian and Charles Simmons, New York, Doubleday, 1963.

A World More Attractive: A View of Modern Literature and Politics by Irving Howe, Horizon Press, 1963.

Encounter, August 1963.

Partisan Review, summer 1963.

After Alienation: American Novels in Mid-Century by Marcus Klein, World Publishing, 1964.

Contemporary American Novelists, edited by Harry T. Moore, Southern Illinois University Press, 1964.

Doings and Undoings by Norman Podhoretz, New York, Farrar, Straus, 1964.

The Negro Novel in America by Robert Bone, New Haven, Yale University Press, 1965.

Seasons of Discontent: Dramatic Opinions, 1959–1965 by Robert Brustein, New York, Simon & Schuster, 1965.

Encounter, July 1965.

New York Times Book Review, 12 December 1965; 2 June 1968; 2 May 1976.

The Furious Passage of James Baldwin by Fern Marja Eckman, New York, Evans, 1966.

Black on White: A Critical Survey of Writing by American Negroes by David Littlejohn, New York, Viking, 1966.

Black Voices: An Anthology of Afro-American Literature, edited by Abraham Chapman, New York, New American Library, 1968.

Soul on Ice by Eldridge Cleaver, New York, McGraw-Hill, 1968.

Afro-American Writers by Darwin T. Turner, Appleton, 1970.

The Americans by David Frost, Stein & Day, 1970.

Modern Black Novelists: A Collection of Critical Essays, edited by M. G. Cook, New Jersey, Prentice-Hall, 1971.

The Morning After by Wilfrid Sheed, Farrar, Straus, 1971.

The Politics of Twentieth-Century Novelists by George A. Panichas, Hawthorn, 1971.

James Baldwin: A Critical Study by Stanley Macebuh, New York, Third Press, 1973.

James Baldwin: A Collection of Critical Essays, edited by Kenneth Kinnamon, Englewood Cliffs, New Jersey, Prentice-Hall, 1974.

Black Fiction by Roger Rosenblatt, Boston, Harvard University Press, 1974.

The Dark and Feeling: Black American Writers and Their Work by Clarence Major, Joseph Okpaku, 1974.

The Theme of Identity in the Essays of James Baldwin by Karin Moeller, Acta Universitatis Gotoburgensis, 1975.

The Nature of a Humane Society, edited by H. Ober Hesse, Fortress, 1976.

James Baldwin: A Critical Evaluation, edited by Therman B. O'Daniel, Washington, Howard University Press, 1977.

Squaring Off: Mailer vs. Baldwin by W. J. Weatherby, New York, Mason/Charter, 1977.

Washington Post, 23 September 1979; 15 October 1979; 9 September 1983; 25 September 1983; 14 August 1989.

James Baldwin by Carolyn Wedin Sylvander, New York, Ungar, 1980.

Critical Essays on James Baldwin, edited by Fred L. Standley and Nancy V. Burt, Boston, G. K. Hall, 1981.

Concise Dictionary of American Literary Biography: The New Consciousness, 1941–1968, Detroit, Gale, 1987.

Dictionary of Literary Biography Yearbook: 1987, Detroit, Gale, 1988.

"On James Baldwin (1924–1987)" by Darryl Pinckney, in *New York Review of Books*, 21 January 1988, 8, 10.

"A Memory of James Baldwin" by Mary McCarthy, in *New York Review of Books*, 27 April 1989, 48–49.

"Critical Deviance: Homophobia and the Reception of James Baldwin's Fiction" by Emmanuel Nelson, in *Journal of American Culture*, fall 1991, 91.

The Gay Novel in America, by James Levin, New York, Garland, 1991, 143–45, 302.

"James Baldwin" by Emmanuel S. Nelson, in *Contemporary Gay American Novelists*, Westport, Connecticut, Greenwood Press, 1993, 6–24.

Marie-Clair Blais

Manuscript Collections

National Library of Canada, Ottawa.

Biography

Lily Briscoe: A Self-Portrait by Mary Meigs, Vancouver, Talonbooks, 1981.

Contemporary Authors Autobiography Series, Volume 4. Detroit, Gale, 1986.

Interviews

"L'Insoumise des lettres canadiennes: une entrevue" by Helene Pilotte, in *Chatelaine*, August 1966, 21–23, 51–54.

"Marie-Claire Blais" by Denise Bourdet, in *La Revue de Paris*, February 1967, 129–136.

"Nightmare's Child" by George Russell, in *Weekend Magazine*, 23 October 1976, 11.

"I Am, Simply, a Writer" by John Hofsess, in *Books in Canada*, February 1979, 8–10.

"Les Vingt Années d'écriture de Marie-Claire Blais" by Donald Smith, in *Lettres Québécoises*, winter 1979–80, 51–58.

"Marie-Claire Blais: 'Je veux aller le plus loin possible': une entrevue avec Marie-Claire Blais" by Gilles Marcotte, in *Voix et images* (Montréal), winter 1983, 192–209.

Bibliography

"Bibliographie de Marie-Claire Blais" by Aurélien Boivin, Lucie Robert, and Ruth Major-LaPierre, in *Voix et Images*, winter 1983, 248–95.

Critical Sources

"Marie-Claire Blais" by Edmund Wilson, in his *O Canada: An American's Notes on Canadian Culture*, New York, Farrar, Straus, 1965, 147–57.

"La Thématique de l'aliénation chez Marie-Claire Blais" by Jacques-A. Lamarche, in *Cité Libre* (Montréal), July–August 1966, 27–32.

"L'Espace politique et social dans le roman québécois" by George-André Vachon, in *Recherches Sociographiques*, September–December 1966, 259–279.

"Prix littéraires, *Une Saison dans la vie d'Emmanuel*" by Louis Barjon, in *Etudes*, February 1967, 217–222.

"Marie-Claire Blais et la révolte du roman canadien" by Roger Gillard, in *La Dryade*, summer 1967, 63–80.

"Le Monde étrange de Marie-Claire Blais ou la cage aux fauves" by Gérard-Marie Boivin, in *Culture*, March 1968, 3–17.

"Introduction à l'univers de Marie-Claire Blais" by Michel Brûlé, in *Revue de l'Institut de Sociologie*, 42:3, 1969, 503–513.

"Note sur deux romans de Marie-Claire Blais" by Lucien Goldmann, in *Revue de l'Institut de Sociologie*, 42:3, 1969, republished in Goldmann's *Structures mentales et création culturelle*, Paris, Editions Anthropos, 1970, 401–414.

Marie-Claire Blais by Philip Stratford, Toronto, Forum House, 1971.

"Fiction as Autobiography in Québec: Notes on Pierre Valliéres and Marie-Claire Blais" by James Kraft, in *Novel* (Providence, Rhode Island), autumn 1972, 73–78.

Le Monde perturbé des jeunes dans l'oeuvre romanesque de Marie-Claire Blais: sa vie, son oeuvre, la critique by Thérèse Fabi, Montréal, Editions Agence d'Arc, 1973.

"*Mad Shadows* as Psychological Fiction" by Joan Caldwell, and "The Shattered Glass: Mirror and Illusion in *Mad Shadows*" by Douglas H. Parker, both in *Journal of Canadian Fiction* (Montréal), 2:4, 1973.

"Marie-Claire Blais, French Canadian Naturalist" by L. Clark Keating, in *Romance Notes* (Chapel Hill, North Carolina), Number 15, 1973.

Marie-Claire Blais: le noir et le tendre by Vincent Nadeau, Presses de l'Université de Montréal, 1974.

"La Technique de l'inversion dans les romans de Marie-Claire Blais" by Maroussia Ahmed in *Canadia Modern Language Review* (Toronto), May 1975, 380–86.

"Les Enfants de Grand-mère Antoinette" by Gilles Marcotte, in his *Notre roman à l'imparfait*, Montréal, La Presse, 1976, 93–137.

"The Church in Marie-Claire Blais's *A Season in the Life of Emmanuel*" by Margaret Anderson, in *Sphinx* (Regina, Saskatchewan), Number 7, 1977.

"Saphisme, Mystique et Littérature" by Gabrielle Poulin, in *Lettres Québécoises* (Montréal), 12 November 1978, 6–8.

"Beauty and Madness in Marie-Claire Blais' *La Belle Bête*" by Jennifer Waelti-Walters, in *Journal of Canadian Fiction*, Numbers 25/26, 1979, 186–198.

"Jean Basile, Louky Bersianik, Marie-Claire Blais, Paul Chamberland, Yves Navarre participent pour *le Berdache* à une table ronde: 'Y a-t-il une écriture homosexuelle?'" in *Le Berdache*, November 1979, 25–39.

"La Révolte contre le patriarcat dans l'oeuvre de Marie-Claire Blais" (M.A. thesis) by Victor Tremblay, University of British Columbia, 1980.

"Sur-vivre et sous-vivre: la sexualité dans *Une Saison dans la vie d'Emmanuel*" by Françoise Maccabée-Iqbal, in *Coincidences* (Ottawa), May–December 1980, 85–108.

Lily Briscoe: A Self-Portrait by Mary Meigs, Vancouver, Talon, 1981.

"Marie-Claire Blais' *Une Liaison parisienne:* An Ambiguous Discovery" by Camille R. La Bossière, in *Selecta* (Corvallis, Oregon), Number 2, 1981.

"The Censored Word and the Body Politic: Reconsidering the Fiction of Marie-Claire Blais" by Karen Gould, in *Journal of Popular Culture* (Bowling Green, Ohio), winter 1981, 14–27.

"Textes lesbiens: Language et vision utopique des nouvelles écrivaines du Québec" by Marthe Rosenfeld, in *Le Berdache*, April 1981, 40–44.

The Medusa Head by Mary Meigs, Vancouver, Talon, 1983.

"Un rituel de l'avidité" by Elène Cliché, in *Voix et images* (Montréal), winter 1983, 229–248.

"From Shattered Reflections to Female Bonding: Mirroring in Marie-Claire Blais's *Visions d'Anna*" by Paula Gilbert Lewis, in *Québec Studies*, Number 2, 1984.

"Redefining the Maternal: Women's Relationships in the Fiction of Marie-Claire Blais" by Mary Jean Green, in *Traditionalism, Nationalism and Feminism: Women Writers of Québec*, edited by Paul Gilbert Lewis, Westport, Connecticut, Greenwood, 1985.

L'Oeuvre romanesque de Marie-Claire Blais by Françoise Laurent, Montréal, Fides, 1986.

"Marie-Claire Blais" by Eva-Marie Kröller, in *Dictionary of Literary Biography*, Volume 53: *Canadian Writers since 1960*, Detroit, Gale, 1986.

"L'Art de la fugue dans *Le Loup* de Marie-Claire Blais" by Victor Tremblay, in *French Review* (Champaign, Illinois), May 1986, 911–921.

"Atomized Lives in Limbo: An Analysis of *Mad Shadows* by Marie-Claire Blais" by Coomie S. Vevaina, in *Literary Criterion* (Mysore, India), 22:1, 1987.

"Marie Claire Blais" by Rosemary Lloyd, in *Beyond the Nouveau Roman*, edited by Michael Tilby, New York, Berg, 1990, 123–150.

"The Question of Lesbian Identity in Marie-Claire Blais's Work" by Janine Ricouart, in *Redefining Autobiography in Twentieth-Century Women's Fiction*, edited by Janice Morgan and Colette T. Hall, New York, Garland, 1991, 169–190.

Blanche McCrary Boyd

Critical Sources

"Creating a Women's World" by Lois Gould, in *New York Times Magazine*, 2 January 1977, 10–38.

The Safe Sea of Women: Lesbian Fiction, 1969–1989 by Bonnie Zimmerman, Boston, Beacon Press, 1990.

"The Surprise of the New" by Sarah Schulman, in *Advocate*, 21 May 1991, 90.

Malcolm Boyd

Manuscript Collections

The Malcolm Boyd Collection and Archives at Boston University Library contains Boyd's writings as well as print interviews.

Biography

Contemporary Authors Autobiography Series, Volume 11, Detroit, Gale, 1990, 43–60.

Interviews

"Malcolm Boyd Takes Another Step With Integrity," in *Advocate*, 8 September 1976, 15–16.
Contemporary Authors New Revision Series, Volume 26, Detroit, Gale, 1989, 66–70.
Print interviews are collected at the Malcolm Boyd Collection and Archives at Boston University Library. Boyd has been interviewed more than 3,000 times in print and electronic media.

Marion Zimmer Bradley

Biography

Marion Zimmer Bradley by Rosemarie Arbur, Mercer Island, Washington, Starmont House, 1985.
Twentieth-Century Science Fiction Writers, Chicago, St. James Press, 1986.
Contemporary Authors Autobiography Series, Volume 10, Detroit, Gale, 1989.

Interviews

Publishers Weekly, 30 October 1987, 49–50.

Bibliography

Leigh Brackett, Marion Zimmer Bradley, Anne McCaffrey: A Primary and Secondary Bibliography by Rosemarie Arbur, Boston, G. K. Hall, 1982.

Critical Sources

"Marion Zimmer Bradley" by Laura Murphy, in *Dictionary of Literary Biography*, Volume 8: *Twentieth-Century American Science Fiction Writers*, Detroit, Gale, 1981.
"Recent Feminist Utopias" by Joanna Russ, in *Future Females: A Critical Anthology*, edited by Marleen S. Barr, Bowling Green, Ohio, Bowling Green State University Popular Press, 1981.
"Marion Zimmer Bradley's Ethic of Freedom" by Susan Shwartz, in *The Feminine Eye: Science Fiction and the Women Who Write It*, edited by Tom Staicar, New York, Ungar, 1982.
"Marion Zimmer Bradley," in *The Science Fiction Source Book*, edited by David Wingrove, New York, Van Nostrand Reinhold, 1984.
Women Worldwalkers: New Dimension of Science Fiction and Fantasy, edited by Jane B. Weedman, Lubbock, Texas Tech Press, 1985.
"Marion Zimmer Bradley," in *Anatomy of Wonder: A Critical Guide to Science Fiction*, edited by Neil Barron, third edition, New York, Bowker, 1987.
"Marion Zimmer Bradley," in *Reader's Guide to Twentieth-Century Science Fiction*, compiled and edited by Marilyn Fletcher and James Thorson, Chicago, American Library Association, 1989.

"Heterosexual Plots and Lesbian Subtexts: Toward a Theory of Lesbian Narrative Space" by Marilyn R. Farwell, in *Lesbian Texts and Contexts: Radical Revisions,* edited by Karla Jay and Joanne Glasgow, New York University Press, 1990.

The Gay Novel in America by James Levin, New York, Garland, 1991.

Rita Mae Brown

Interviews

With Carole Horn, in *Washington Post,* 24 October 1977, 1.

With Patricia Holt, in *Publishers Weekly,* 2 October 1978, 16–17.

With Armistead Maupin, in *Interview,* February 1982, 50.

"The Unthinkable Rita Mae Brown Spreads Around a Little 'Southern Discomfort'" by Karen G. Jackovich, in *People,* 26 April 1982, 75– 77.

Contemporary Authors, New Revision Series, Volume 11, Detroit, Gale, 1984.

"Life Without Martina" by Mark Uehling and Nikki Finke Greenberg, in *Newsweek,* 19 August 1985, 9–10.

"Unsinkable Rita Mae Brown" by Jean Carr-Crane, in *Lambda Book Report,* December 1988–January 1989, 4.

Critical Sources

"Poetry Power" by F. Chapman in *Off Our Backs,* April 1972, 27.

"Utopian Vision of the Lesbian Muse" by P. Bennett, in *Gay News,* 24 June 1978, 8.

"Southern Belles Lettres" by A. Denham, in *Nation,* 19 June 1982, 759.

"Rita Mae Brown: Feminist Theorist and Southern Novelist" by Martha Chew, in *Southern Quarterly* (Hattiesburg, Mississippi), fall 1983, 61–80.

Reprinted in *Women Writers of the Contemporary South,* edited by Peggy Whitman Prenshaw, Jackson, University Press of Mississippi, 1984.

"*Rubyfruit Jungle*: Lesbianism, Feminism, and Narcissism" by Leslie Fishbein, in *International Journal of Women's Studies* (Montréal, Québec), March–April 1984, 155–159.

"Questions of Genre and Gender: Contemporary American Versions of the Feminine Picaresque" by James Mandrell, in *Novel,* winter 1987, 149–170.

"Uses of Classical Mythology in Rita Mae Brown's *Southern Discomfort*" by Daniel B. Levine, in *Classical and Modern Literature* (Terre Haute, Indiana), fall 1989, 63–70.

The Safe Sea of Women: Lesbian Fiction, 1969–1989 by Bonnie Zimmerman, Boston, Beacon Press, 1990.

Review by Marilyn Stasio of *Wish You Were Here,* in *New York Times Book Review,* 16 December 1990, 33.

Review by Marilyn Stasio of *Rest in Pieces,* in *New York Times Book Review,* 6 September 1992, 17.

Quentin Crisp

Interviews

"Crisply Quentin: The Naked Civil Servant Turns Survivor-Circuit Celebrity" by Jim
    Bigwood, in *Advocate*, 8 March 1979, 33–35.

"Crisp Thoughts on the Perils of Gay Celebrity," in *Advocate*, 1 October 1985, 8–9.

Mary Daly

Footnotes to "Tidy Reports; Untidy Retorts"

1. Louky Bersianik, *The Euguélionne*, a triptych novel, translated by Gerry Denis,
    Alison Hewitt, Donna Murray, and Martha O'Brien, Victoria, British
    Columbia, Press Porcépic, 1981, 131–132.
2. Jane O'Reilly, "The Death and Life of the ERA," *Boston Globe Magazine*, July 18,
    1982, 21.
3. Virginia Woolf, "Professions for Women," in *The Death of the Moth and Other
    Essays*, New York, Harcourt, Brace & World, 1942; Harvest Books, 1971,
    235–242.
4. John M. Keshishian, M.D., "Anatomy of a Burmese Beauty Secret," *National
    Geographic*, June 1979, 798.
5. John M. Keshishian, M.D., "Anatomy of a Burmese Beauty Secret," *National
    Geographic*, June 1979, 801.
6. John M. Keshishian, M.D., "Anatomy of a Burmese Beauty Secret," *National
    Geographic*, June 1979, 800.
7. John M. Keshishian, M.D., "Anatomy of a Burmese Beauty Secret," *National
    Geographic*, June 1979, 801.

Interviews

"Five Boston-Area Feminists Interviewed," in *Boston Globe*, 13 January 1985, BGM
    12.

Critical Sources

"That Women Be Themselves" by Adrienne Rich, in *New York Times Book Review*,
    11 February 1979, 10.

"The Croning of a Woman" by Rita Mae Brown, in *Washington Post Book World*, 11
    February 1979, F3.

"Taking Off on a Daly Journey" by Erica Smith, in *Herizons*, June 1984, 23–24.

Review of *Pure Lust* by Demaris Wehr, in *New York Times Book Review*, 22 July 1984,
    14.

"Famous Lust Words" by Marilyn Frye, in *Women's Review of Books*, August 1984, 3.

"Mary Daly's *Pure Lust*" by Eileen Manion, in *Canadian Journal*, fall 1985, 134–137.

"Embracing Motherhood: New Feminist Theory" by Heather Jon Maroney, in
    Canadian Journal, winter 1985, 40–64.

"On Political Courage, Witches, and History" (excerpt of keynote address to
    National Women's Political Caucus in Portland, Oregon) by Vermont
    Governor Madeleine M. Kunin, in *Ms.*, November 1987, 84.

"Erratic, Ecstatic, Eccentric" by Julia Penelope, in *Women's Review of Books*, December 1987, 5.

"Chasing through the Wickedary" by Debra Ratterman, in *Off Our Backs*, January 1988, 17.

"What Snools These Mortals Be" by Coral Lansbury, in *New York Times*, 17 January 1988, Section 7, 9.

"BC's Treatment of Feminist-Thinker Daly Protested" by James L. Franklin, in *Boston Globe*, 23 March 1989, 31.

"Snools Deny Daly Tenure: Hags Revolt," in *Off Our Backs*, May 1989, 11.

"Teacher Fights School Over Feminism and Beliefs" by Peter Steinfels, in *New York Times*, 10 May 1989, A31.

Melvin Dixon

Interviews

With Darryl Grant, in *Washington Blade*, 26 April 1991, 43, 52.
With Clarence Bard Cole, in *Christopher Street*, 14:1, 1991, 24–27.

Critical Sources

"Melvin Dixon: Wrestling with Baldwin" by V. R. Peterson, in *Essence*, August, 1991, 42.

Contemporary Gay American Novelists, edited by Emmanuel S. Nelson, Westport, Connecticut, Greenwood Press, 1993.

Andrea Dworkin

Footnotes to "Biological Superiority"

1. Adolf Hitler, *Mein Kampf*, translated by Ralph Manheim, Boston, Houghton Mifflin, 1962, 296.

2. Adolf Hitler, *Mein Kampf*, translated by Ralph Manheim, Boston, Houghton Mifflin, 1962, 442.

3. SuperWomon's ideology is distinguished from lesbian separatism in general (that is, lesbians organizing politically and/or culturally in exclusively female groups) by two articles of dogma: (1) a refusal to have anything to do with women who have anything to do with males, often including women with male children and (2) the absolute belief in the biological superiority of women.

4. Jeremy Noakes and Geoffrey Pridham, editors, *Documents on Nazism 1919–1945*, New York, Viking Press, 1975, 493.

5. George Gilder, *Sexual Suicide*, New York, Quadrangle, 1973.

6. Steven Goldberg, *The Inevitability of Patriarchy*, New York, William Morrow & Company, 1973, 228.

7. Edward O. Wilson, *Sociobiology: The New Synthesis*, Cambridge, Mass., Belknap Press of Harvard University Press, 1975, 573.

8. Virginia Woolf, *A Room of One's Own*, New York, Harcourt, Brace & World, 1957, 115–116.

Interviews

With Elizabeth Wilson, in *Feminist Review*, June 1982, 23–29.
Contemporary Authors New Revision Series, Volume 16, Detroit, Gale, 1985, 98–101.

Critical Sources

"A Grim Parable of Sexual Ideology" by Sherie Posesorski, in *Globe and Mail* (Toronto), 2 August 1986.
"Men As Beasts" by Barbara Amiel, in *Times* (London), 4 June 1987.
"Bitterness and Sexual Aggression" by Naomi Black, in *Globe and Mail* (Toronto), 11 July 1987.
"The Bare-faced Feminist" by Catherine Bennett, in *Times* (London), 18 May 1988, 122.
"Changing My Mind About Andrea Dworkin" by Erica Jong, in *Ms.*, June 1988, 60–64.
"Taking the Lid Off" by Hermione Lee, in *Times Literary Supplement* (London), 3–9 June 1988, 611.
"Street Fighting Feminist" by Lore Dickstein, in *New York Times Book Review*, 29 October 1989, 11.
Review by Brian Morton of *Mercy*, in *Bookseller*, 21 September 1990, 837.
Review by Sarah Kent of *Mercy*, in *Time Out*, 26 September–3 October 1990, 37.
"Powerful Voice Against Violent Oppression of Women" by Brian Morton, in *Glasgow Herald*, 4 October 1990.
"The Return of Carry Nation" by Camille Paglia, in *Playboy*, October 1992, 36.

David B. Feinberg

Biography

"David B. Feinberg" by Jane S. Carducci, in *Contemporary Gay Male Novelists*, edited by Emmanuel S. Nelson, Westport, Connecticut, Greenwood Press, 1992, 122–127.

Interviews

"The Guilt Behind the Book" by Nina Reyes, in *Next* (Boston), 8 March 1989, 36.
"Epidemic of Laughter" by Joel Weinberg, in *Advocate* (Los Angeles), 14 March 1989, 46–47.
"The Inspiration of David Feinberg" by Owen Keenhan, in *Outlines* (Chicago), December 1991, 29.
"Interview" by Jim Provenzano, in *NYQ* (New York), 8 December 1991, 36.

Critical Sources

"When Sex Was All That Mattered" by Catherine Texier, in *New York Times Book Review*, 26 February 1989, 9.
"AIDS—This Side of the Abyss" by Bob Summer, in *Lambda Rising Book Report*, February/March 1989, 10.
"Bounced From the Bar of Life" by Daniel Curzon, in *Los Angeles Times*, 5 March 1989, C21.

"AIDS and the American Novel" by Emmanuel Nelson, in *Journal of American Culture* (Bowling Green, Ohio), spring 1990, 47–53.

"The Further Adventures of B. J. Rosenthal" by Robert Friedman, in *Sentinel*, 21 November 1991, 37.

"Young, Single, and HIV-Positive" by Scott Bradfield, in *New York Times*, 17 November 1991, 11.

"Between the Lines" by Michael Bronski, in *Guide* (Boston), December 1991, 19.

The Gay Novel in America by James Levin, Boston, Garland, 1991.

Katherine V. Forrest

Critical Sources

"Utopia and Ideology in *Daughters of a Coral Dawn* and Contemporary Feminist Utopias" by Holda M. Zaki, in *Women's Studies: An Interdisciplinary Journal*, 14:2.

Elsa Gidlow

Biography

In My Own Way by Alan Watts, Random House, 1973.

"Elsa Gidlow's Sapphic Songs," in *American Poetry-Review* (Philadelphia), January 1978.

"Footprints on the Sands of Time," in *Frontiers*, 4:3, 1979.

Allen Ginsberg

Manuscript Collections

Papers housed in special collections in the Butler Library at Columbia University, and the Humanities Research Center at the University of Texas, Austin.

Biography

A Casebook of the Beat, edited by T. Parkinson, New York, Crowell, 1961.

Howl of the Censor by J. W. Ehrlich, San Carlos, California, Nourse, 1961.

The Sullen Art by David Ossman, New York, Corinth Books, 1963, 87–95.

Mystery of the Universe: Notes on an Interview with Allen Ginsberg by Edward Lucie-Smith, Turret Books, 1965.

Allen Ginsberg in America by Jane Kramer, New York, Random House, 1968, as *Paterfamilias: Allen Ginsberg in America*, London, Gollancz, 1970.

Allen Ginsberg by Thomas F. Merrill, Boston, Twayne, 1969.

Allen Ginsberg in the Sixties by Eric Mottram, Seattle/Brighton, Unicorn Bookshop, 1972.

Ginsberg by Barry Miles, New York, Simon & Schuster, 1989.

Dharma Lion by Michael Schumacher, New York, St. Martin's Press, 1992.

Interviews

With Thomas Clark, in *Writers at Work: The Paris Review Interviews*, third series, New York, Viking, 1967, 279–320.

With Paul Carroll, in *Playboy*, April 1969, 81.

With Alison Colbert, in *Partisan Review*, 38:3, 1971, 289–309.

With John Tytell, in *Partisan Review*, 41:2, 1974, 255–309.

Gay Sunshine Interview: Allen Ginsberg with Allen Young, Bolinas, California, Grey Fox Press, 1974.

With Paul Geneson, in *Chicago Review*, summer 1975, 27–35.

With Paul Portugés, in *Boston University Journal*, 25:1, 1977, 47–59.

Bibliography

"Allen Ginsberg: A Bibliography and Biographical Sketch" by Edward Z. Menkin, in *Thoth*, winter 1967, 35–44.

A Bibliography of Works by Allen Ginsberg by George Dowden, San Francisco, City Lights Books, 1971.

Allen Ginsberg: An Annotated Bibliography 1969–1977 by Michelle P. Kraus, Metuchen, New Jersey, Scarecrow Press, 1980.

Critical Sources

Alone with America: Essays on the Art of Poetry in the United States since 1950 by Richard Howard, New York, Atheneum, 1969, 145–152.

"Allen Ginsberg: Angel Headed Hipster" by George W. Lyon, Jr., in *Journal of Popular Culture*, winter 1969, 391–403.

"The Prophetic Voice of Allen Ginsberg" by Stephen Hahn, in *Prospects: An Annual of American Cultural Studies*, Number 2, 1976, 527–567.

"Allen Ginsberg: The Origins of 'Howl' and 'Kaddish'" by James Breslin, in *Iowa Review*, spring 1977, 82–108.

The Visionary Poetics of Allen Ginsberg by Paul Portugés, Santa Barbara, California, Ross-Erikson, 1978.

"The Survival of Allen Ginsberg" by Mark Shechner, in *Partisan Review*, 46:1, 1979, 105–112.

"Moloch's Poet: A Retrospective Look at Allen Ginsberg's Poetry" by Fred Moramarco, in *American Poetry Review*, September–October 1982, 10–18.

The Post-Moderns: The New American Poetry Revised by D. Allen and G. Butterick, New York, Grove, 1982.

On the Poetry of Allen Ginsberg, edited by Lewis Hyde, Ann Arbor, University of Michigan Press, 1984.

Best Minds: A Tribute to Allen Ginsberg, edited by Bill Morgan and Bob Rosenthal, New York, Lospecchio Press, 1986.

The Portable Beat Reader, edited by Ann Charters, New York, Viking, 1992.

Jewelle Gomez

Interviews

Out/Look, spring 1992, 63–72.

Critical Sources

Keynote address presented at Creating Change Conference in Arlington, Virginia, by Jewelle Gomez, 1991.

"Bold Types" by Barbara Findlen, in *Ms.*, July/August 1991, 87.

"No Either/Or" by Victoria Brownworth, in *Outweek*, 22 May 1991, 54–55.

"Jewelle Gomez and Minnie Bruce Pratt" by Jane Troxell, in *Washington Blade*, 8 November 1991, 42–43.

Review by Robert Morrish of *The Gilda Stories*, in *Multi-Cultural Review*, 1:1, 1992, 549–550.

"A Novelist's Sense of Family" by Esther Ivrem, in *New York Newsday*, 28 July 1992.

Judy Grahn

Interviews

With John Felstiner, in *Women Writers of the West Coast: Speaking of Their Lives and Careers*, edited by Marilyn Yalom, Santa Barbara, California, Capra, 1983.

"Warrior/Dyke" by Judith Beckett, in *Women of Power*, winter/spring 1986.

With Lynne Constantine and Suzanne Scott, in *Belles Lettres*, March/April 1987.

"Lesbian Memory and Creation" by Dell Richards, in *Outlines* (Chicago), August 1988.

Contemporary Authors, Volume 122, Detroit, Gale, 1988.

"The Women-in-Print Movement, Some Beginnings" by Carol Seajay, in *Feminist Bookstore News*, three issues, beginning May/June 1990.

Critical Sources

"Judy Grahn" by Lisa Tipps, in *American Women Writers*, New York, Ungar, 1980.

"Helen of Troy and Female Power" by Lynda Koolish, in *San Francisco Chronicle*, 20 February 1983.

"The Re-Vision of the Muse: Adrienne Rich, Audre Lorde, Judy Grahn, Olga Broumas" by Mary J. Carruthers, in *Hudson Review* (New York), summer 1983, 293–322.

Women Writers of the West Coast: Speaking of Their Lives and Careers edited by Marilyn Yalom, Santa Barbara, California, Capra, 1983.

"In the House of Women" by Michele Aina Barale, in *Women's Review of Books*, October 1985.

Review by Myrna Hughes of *The Queen of Swords*, in *San Francisco Chronicle*, 26 February 1986.

Stealing the Language: The Emergence of Women's Poetry in America by Alicia Suskin Ostriker, Boston, Beacon Press, 1986.

"The Politics of the Refrain in Judy Grahn's *A Woman Is Talking to Death*" by Amitai F. Aviram, in *Women and Language* (Fairfax, Virginia), spring 1987, 38–43.

Feminism and Poetry: Language Experience, Identity in Women's Writing by Jan Montefiore, London and New York, Pandora Press, 1987.

"Uncommon Poetry of a Common Woman" by Margaret Spillane, in *New Haven Independent*, 23 June 1988.

"Judy Grahn's Gynopoetics: *The Queen of Swords*" by Sue Ellen Case, in *Studies in the Literary Imagination* (Atlanta), fall 1988, 47–67.

"*Mundane's World:* How Do We Get There from Here" by Jennie Ruby, in *Off Our Backs*, July 1989.

"Up to the Earth" by Ursula K. Le Guin, in *The Women's Review of Books*, February 1989.

The Safe Sea of Women: Lesbian Fiction, 1969–1989 by Bonnie Zimmerman, Boston, Beacon Press, 1990.

The Reflowering of the Goddess by Gloria Orenstein, Elmsford, New Jersey, Pergamon Press, 1990.

Review by Catharine R. Stimpson of *Really Reading Gertrude Stein*, in *Women's Review of Books*, May 1990, 6.

Review of *Another Mother Tongue*, in *Lambda Book Report*, January 1991, 37.

Review by Karla Jay of *Really Reading Gertrude Stein*, in *American Book Review*, April/May 1991, 22.

"A Mundane Utopia" by Ron Erickson, in *Trumpeter*, winter 1992.

"She Who Is a Tree: Judy Grahn and the Work of a Common Woman" by Alicia Suskin Ostriker, in *Poetry East* (Ann Arbor, Michigan), 1993.

Radclyffe Hall

Biography

The Life of Radclyffe Hall by Lady Una Troubridge, New York, Citadel, 1973.

Radclyffe Hall at the Well of Loneliness: A Sapphic Chronicle by Lovat Dickson, New York, Scribner, 1975.

The Life and Death of Radclyffe Hall by Lady Una Troubridge, London, Jonathan Cape, 1984.

Our Three Selves: A Life of Radclyffe Hall by Michael Baker, London, Hamish Hamilton, k1985.

Critical Sources

"The Personality of Radclyffe Hall" by Clifford Allen, in *Homosexuality and Creative Genius,* edited by Hendrik M. Ruitenbeek, New York, Astor-Honor, 1967, 183–188.

"Radclyffe Hall" in *Lesbian Images* by Jane Rule, New York, Doubleday, 1975, 50–61.

Beyond the Well of Loneliness by Claudia Stillman Franks, Avebury, 1982.

"The Myth of the Mannish Lesbian: Radclyffe Hall and the New Woman" by Esther Newton, in *Hidden from History: Reclaiming the Gay and Lesbian Past,* edited by Martin B. Duberman, Martha Vicinus, and George Chauncey, Jr., New York, New American Library, 1989, 281–293.

Reflecting on the Well of Loneliness by Rebecca O'Rourke, London, Routledge, 1989.

Joseph Hansen

Critical Sources

Poetry News, Calendar & Reviews of Southern California Readings and Publications, November, 1981.

"Joseph Hansen's Anti-Pastoral Crime Fiction," in *Clues: A Journal of Detection* (Bowling Green, Ohio), spring/summer, 1986.
The Gay Novel in America by James Levin, New York, Garland, 1991.

Patricia Highsmith

Critical Sources

Don't Never Forget: Collected Views and Reviews by Brigid Brophy, New York, Holt, 1966.
Mortal Consequences: A History—From the Detective Story to the Crime Novel by Julian Symons, New York, Harper, 1972.
The Gay Novel in America by James Levin, New York, Garland, 1991.

Andrew Holleran

Critical Sources

The Gay Novel by James Levine, New York, Irvington Publishers, 1983.
Gayiety Transigured: Gay Self-Representation in American Literature by David Bergman, Madison, University of Wisconsin Press, 1991.

Christopher Isherwood

Biography

Christopher Isherwood by Carolyn G. Heilbrun, New York, Columbia University Press, 1970.
Isherwood: A Biography of Christopher Isherwood by Jonathan Fryer, London, New English Library, 1977.
Christopher Isherwood: A Critical Biography by Brian Finney, New York, Oxford University Press, 1979.
Christopher Isherwood: A Personal Memoir by John Lehmann, New York, Holt, 1988.

Bibliography

Christopher Isherwood: A Bibliography 1923–1967 by Selmer Westby and Clayton M. Brown, California State College at Los Angeles Foundation, 1968.
"Christopher Isherwood: A Checklist, 1968–1975" by Stathis Orphanis, in *Twentieth-Century Literature*, October 1976, 354–61.
Christopher Isherwood: A Reference Guide by Robert W. Funk, G.K. Hall, 1979.
Christopher Isherwood: A Bibliography of His Personal Papers, edited by James White and William H. White, Montrose, Alabama, Texas Center for Writers Press, 1987.
"A Bibliography of Isherwood" by Cal Gough, in *Lambda News*, August 1991, 29.

Critical Sources

The Modern Novel in Britain and the United States by Walter Allen, New York, Dutton, 1964.

"Insights into Isherwood" by Angus Wilson, in *Observer*, 20 March 1966.

Christopher Isherwood by Carolyn C. Heilbrun ("Columbia Essays on Modern Literature 53"), New York, Columbia University Press, 1970.

"Irony and Style: The Example of Christopher Isherwood" by Alan Wilde, in *Modern Fiction Studies*, winter 1970.

Christopher Isherwood by Alan Wilde ("Twayne's United States Authors Series 173"), New York, Twayne, 1971.

"*Goodbye to Berlin*: Refocusing Isherwood's Camera" by David P. Thomas, in *Contemporary Literature*, winter 1972.

"Christopher Isherwood—A Profile" by Brian Finney, *New Review*, August 1975.

The Auden Generation: Literature and Politics in England in the 1930s by Samuel L. Hynes, London, Bodley Head, 1976.

Christopher Isherwood by Francis King ("Writers and Their Work 240"), Harlow, Essex, Longman, 1976.

"'Camp' and Politics in Isherwood's Berlin Fiction" by Peter Thomas, in *Journal of Modern Literature*, February 1976.

"Sexuality in Isherwood" by Jonathan H. Fryer, in *Twentieth-Century Literature*, October 1976.

"Art, Sex, and Isherwood" by Gore Vidal, in *New York Review of Books*, 9 December 1976, 10–18.

"*Lions and Shadows*" by Hugh Brogan, *Twentieth-Century Literature*, October 1976.

Christopher Isherwood: Myth and Anti-Myth by Paul Piazza, New York, Columbia University Press, 1978.

"Christopher Isherwood: The Novelist as Homosexual" by D. S. Savage, in *Literature and Psychology*, 29:1–2, 1979.

Christopher Isherwood by Claude J. Summers, New York, Ungar, 1980.

"The Secret of Issyvoo" by Stephen Spender, in *Observer*, 12 January 1986.

"Stranger in Paradise" by John Boorman, in *American Film*, October 1986.

Isherwood's Fiction: The Self and Technique by Lisa M. Schwerdt, London, Macmillan, 1989.

Gay Fictions, Wilde to Stonewall: Studies in a Male Homosexual Literary Tradition by Claude J. Summers, New York, Continuum, 1990.

"Not a Single Man: Artist Don Bachardy Pays Tribute to Loves Old and New" by Charlie Scheips, in *Advocate*, 12 March 1991, 62.

"Christopher Isherwood: Hero of Our Time" by Foster Corbin, in *Lambda News*, August 1991, 26–28.

Larry Kramer

Biography

"The Cry of *The Normal Heart*" by Dinitia Smith, in *New York*, 3 June 1985, 42–46.

"Larry Kramer" by Ken Gross, in *People*, 9 July 1990, 72–75.

"The Spent Rage of the Playwright" by Paula Span, in *Washington Post*, 20 October 1992, E-1.

"A Normal Heart" by Otis Stuart, in *Village Voice*, 27 October 1992, 110–112.

"Kramer vs. Kramer" by Michael Shnayerson, in *Vanity Fair*, October 1992, 228–231.

Interviews

"Using Rage to Fight the Plague" by Janice C. Simpson, in *Time*, 5 February 1990, 7–8.

"AIDS Activism" by Marcia Pally, in *Tikkun*, July 1990, 22–24.

"Kramer vs. the World" by Victor Zonana, in *Advocate* (Los Angeles), 1 December 1992, 40–48, and 15 December 1992, 43–48.

With David Nimmons, in *Playboy*, September 1993.

Critical Sources

Review by Paul Berman of *The Normal Heart*, in *Nation*, 11 May 1985, 569–570.

"AIDS on Stage" by Gerald Weales, in *Commonweal*, 12 July 1985, 406–447.

"AIDS Words" by Gregory Kolovakos (review of *Reports from the Holocaust*), in *Nation*, 1 May 1989, 598–602.

"The Literature of AIDS" by Mark Caldwell (review of *The Normal Heart*), in *Dissent*, summer 1990, 342–347.

"Larry Kramer and the Rhetoric of AIDS" by David Bergman, in *Gaiety Transfigured: Gay Self-Representation in American Literature*, Madison, University of Wisconsin Press, 1991, 122–138.

"Reborn with Relevance" by William A. Henry III (review of *The Destiny of Me*), in *Time*, 2 November 1992, 69.

"You Gotta Have Heart" by Jack Kroll (review of *The Destiny of Me*), in *Newsweek*, 2 November 1992, 104.

"AIDS Drama: Displacing Camille" by John M. Clum, in *Acting Gay: Male Homosexuality in Modern Drama*, New York, Columbia UniversityPress, 1992, 39–82.

"AIDS Enters the American Theatre: *As Is* and *The Normal Heart*" by Joel Shatsky, in *AIDS: The Literary Response*, edited by Emmanuel S. Nelson, New York, Twayne, 1992, 131–139.

"Rage and Remembrance: The AIDS Plays" by D. S. Lawson, in *AIDS: The Literary Response*, edited by Emmanuel S. Nelson, New York, Twayne, 1992, 140–154.

"The Gay White Way" by William A. Henry III, in *Time*, 17 May 1993, 62–63.

Tony Kushner

Critical Sources

"An Angel Sat Down at His Table" by Susan Cheever, in *New York Times*, 13 September 1992.

"A Playwright Spreads His Wings" by Hilary de Vries, in *Los Angeles Times*, 25 October 1992, 3, 74–76.

"Avenging Angel" by Tad Friend, in *Vogue*, November 1992, 158–165.

"A Playwright in the Power of 'Angels'" by David Patrick Stearns, in *USA Today*, 12 November 1992, D13.

"Tony Kushner's Paradise Lost" by Arthur Lubow, in *New Yorker*, 30 November 1992, 59–64.

"Kushner Is Soaring with His 'Angels'" by Kevin Kelly, in *Boston Globe*, 14 April 1993, 65.

"On Wings of 'Angels' Epic" by Steve Murray, in *Atlanta Journal and Atlanta Constitution*, 25 April 1993, M1.

"A Broadway Godsend" by Jack Kroll, in *Newsweek*, 10 May 1993, 56–58.

"Tony Kushner: Angels on Broadway" by Cathy Madison, in *Columbia* (New York), spring 1993, 40–41.

"Kushner's *Angels* Ascends to a Pulitzer" by Thomas Vinciguerra, in *Columbia College Today* (New York), spring/summer 1993, 50.

David Leavitt

Interviews

Contemporary Authors, Volume 122, Detroit, Gale, 1988.

With Sam Staggs, in *Publishers Weekly*, 24 August 1990, 47.

Critical Sources

"Domestic Disclosures" (review of *Family Dancing*) by Wendy Lesser, in *New York Times Book Review*, 2 September 1984, 7–8.

"Ordinary Lives Filled with Love and Loss" (review of *Equal Affections*) by Michiko Kakutani, in *New York Times*, 31 January 1985, 16.

"The New Romantics" (review of *Family Dancing*) by Darryl Pinckney, in *New York Review of Books*, 29 May 1986, 30.

Review of *The Lost Language of Cranes*, in *Publishers Weekly*, 8 August, 1986, 55.

"Sexual Politics, Family Secrets" (review of *The Lost Language of Cranes*) by Phillip Lopate, in *New York Times Book Review*, 5 October 1986, 3.

"Gays of Our Lives" (review of *The Lost Language of Cranes*) by Adam Mars-Jones, in *New Republic*, 17 November 1986, 43.

"Post-Counterculture Tristesse" by Carol Iannone, in *Commentary*, February 1987, 57–61.

"Papa and Son" (review of *The Lost Language of Cranes*) by Adrianne Blue, in *New Statesman*, 13 February 1987, 31.

"Fiction Chronicle" (review of *The Lost Language of Cranes*) by Michael Gorra, in *Hudson Review* (New York), spring 1987, 136–148.

"David Leavitt" in *Reasons to Believe: New Voices in American Fiction* by Michael Schumaher, New York, St. Martin's Press, 1988, 175–190.

Review of *Equal Affections*, in *Publishers Weekly*, 18 November 1988, 69.

"David Leavitt's Family Affairs" (review of *Equal Affections*) by Alan Hollinghurst, in *Washington Post Book World*, 22 January 1989, 4.

"Everyone Is Somebody's Child" (review of *Equal Affections*) by Beverly Lowry, in *New York Times Book Review*, 12 February 1989, 7.

"Terminal Addiction" (review of *Equal Affections*) by David Gates, in *Newsweek*, 13 February 1989, 78.

Review of *Equal Affections*, in *People*, 20 February 1989, 27.

Review of *A Place I've Never Been*, in *Publishers Weekly*, 13 July 1990, 40.

"Everybody Loves Somebody Sometime" (review of *A Place I've Never Been*) by Wendy Martin, in *New York Times Book Review*, 26 August 1990, 11.

"Family, Lovers, Loyalty, Betrayal" (review of *A Place I've Never Been*) by James N. Baker, in *Newsweek*, 3 September 1990, 66.

"Aspects of Love" (review of *A Place I've Never Been*) by Jonathan Penner, in *Washington Post Book World*, 7 October 1990, 7.

"Out of the Closet, Onto the Bookshelf" by Edmund White, in *New York Times Magazine*, 16 June 1991, 22.

"David Leavitt" by D. S. Lawson, in *Contemporary Gay American Novelists*, edited by Emmanuel S. Nelson, Westport, Connecticut, Greenwood Press, 1993, 248–253.

Audre Lorde

Interviews

With Anita Cornwell, in *Sinister Wisdom* (Rockland, Maine), fall 1977, 15–21.

With Deborah Wood, in *In the Memory and Spirit of Frances, Zora, and Lorraine: Essays and Interviews on Black Women and Writing*, Washington, D.C., Institute for the Arts and the Humanities, 1979.

With Karla M. Hammond, in *Denver Quarterly*, spring 1981, 10–27.

Bibliography

Modern American Woman Poets by Jean Gould, New York, Dodd, Mead, 1985, 288–296.

Critical Sources

"Broadsides: Good Black Poems, One by One" by Helen Vendler, in *New York Times Book Review*, September 1974, 320–321.

"Nothing Safe: The Poetry of Audre Lorde" by Joan Larkin, in *Margins*, August 1975, 23–25.

"On the Edge of the Estate" by Sandra M. Gilbert, in *Poetry* (Chicago), 104:24, 1977, 296–301.

Review by Gloria Hull of *Between Ourselves*, in *Conditions: One*, 1977, 97–100.

"The Re-Vision of the Muse: Unnaming and Renaming in the Poetry of Audre Lorde, Pat Parker, Sylvia Plath, and Adrienne Rich" by Pamela Annas, in *Hudson Review* (New York), summer 1983, 293–322.

"No More Buried Lives: The Theme of Lesbianism in Lorde, Naylor, Shange, Walker" by Barbara Christian, in *Feminist Issues*, spring 1985, 3–19.

"Audre Lorde" by Irma McClaurin-Allen, in *Dictionary of Literary Biography*, Volume 41: *Afro-American Poets Since 1955*, Detroit, Gale, 1985.

"The Black Woman as Artist and Critic: Four Versions" by Margaret B. MacDowell, in *Kentucky Review* (Lexington), spring 1987, 19–41.

Paula Martinac

Critical Sources

Review by Penny Kaganoff of *Voyages Out 1: Lesbian Short Fiction*, in *Publishers Weekly*, 25 August 1989, 58.

Review by Ray Olson of *Voyages Out 1: Lesbian Short Fiction*, in *Booklist*, 1 October 1989, 262.

Review by Kevin M. Roddy of *Voyages Out 1: Lesbian Short Fiction*, in *Library Journal*, December 1989, 172.

"Sister's Keepers" by Sally S. Eckhoff, in *Village Voice*, 27 March 1990, 77.

"Losing and Finding and Losing Again" by Lynne M. Constantine, in *Belles Lettres* (Gaithersburg, Maryland), spring 1990, 6.

Review by Penny Kaganoff of *Out of Time*, in *Publishers Weekly*, 13 July 1990, 51.

Review of *Out of Time*, in *Kirkus Reviews*, 15 August 1990, 1122.

Review by Rose Fennell of *Out of Time*, in *Lambda Book Report* (Washington, D.C.), October 1990, 44.

Review by Marie J. Kuda of *Out of Time*, in *Booklist*, 1 October 1990, 255.

"Ghost Writing" by Donna Minkowitz, in *Village Voice*, 30 October 1990, 74.

"Paula Martinac Fills in the Pages of Lesbian History" by Liz Galst, in *Advocate*, 4 December 1990, 77.

"Lesbian Fiction Reinventing Itself" by Lynne M. Constantine, in *Belles Lettres* (Gaithersburg, Maryland), spring 1991, 44.

Essay by Penny Perkins, in *Contemporary Lesbian Writers of the United States: A Bio-Bibliographical Critical Sourcebook*, edited by Sandra Pollack and Denise D. Knight, Westport, Connecticut, Greenwood Press, 1993.

Armistead Maupin

Biography

"Travails of the City" by Steve Warren, in *San Francisco Bay Guardian*, 11 October 1989, 24.

"Teller of Tales" by Adam Block, in *Outweek*, 29 October 1989, 42–45.

"Armistead Maupin" by Chuck Allen, in *Frontiers 3*, November 1989, 18–21.

"For Fifteen Years, He's Told Tales of San Francisco" by Richard Dyer, in *Boston Globe*, 20 November 1989, 32.

"Mainstreaming a Cult Classic" by Tony Clifton, in *Newsweek*, 30 November 1989, 77.

"A Gay Novelist Writes of Love and AIDS in his *Tales of the City*" by Kim Hubbard and Vicki Sheff, in *People*, 5 March 1990, 51.

"Out of the Fog" by Micheline Hagan, in *San Francisco Review of Books*, fall 1992, 5–6.

Interviews

"A Talk with Armistead Maupin," in *Publishers Weekly*, 20 March 1987, 53–54.

Contemporary Authors, Volume 130, Detroit, Gale, 1990.

Critical Sources

Review by James P. Degnan of *Tales of the City*, in *Hudson Review*, spring 1980, 146–148.

Review by David Feinberg of *Sure of You*, in *New York Times Book Review*, 22 October 1989, 25–26.

The Gay Novel in America, by James Levin, New York, 1991, 288–289.

"Armistead Maupin" by Barbara Kaplan Bass, in *Contemporary Gay American Novelists*, edited by Emmanuel S. Nelson, Westport, Connecticut, Greenwood Press, 1993, 255–289.

Kate Millett

Interviews

"The Last Interview in This Issue" by Jeff Goldberg, in *UnmuzzledOx*, 4:3, 1977, 132–133.
"Kate Millett" by Mark Blasius, in *Semiotext(e)*, Intervention Series 2: *Loving Children* (New York), summer 1980.

Critical Sources

Review by Jonathan Yardley of *Sexual Politics*, in *New Republic*, 1 August 1970, 26, 30–32.
Review of *Sexual Politics*, in *New York Times Book Review*, 6 September, 1970, 8, 10, 12.
Review by Germaine Greer of *Sexual Politics*, in *Listener* (London), 25 March 1971, 355–356.
Review by Jane Wilson of *Flying*, in *New York Times Book Review*, 23 June 1974, 2–3.
Psychoanalysis and Feminism by Juliet Mitchell, New York, Pantheon Books, 1974.
"The Lady's Not for Spurning" by Annette Kolodny, in *Contemporary Literature*, autumn, 1976, 541–562.
Lesbiana: Book Reviews from the Ladder by Barbara Grier, Tallahassee, Naiad Press, 1976.
Review by Sara Sandborn of *Sita*, in *New York Times Book Review*, 29 May 1977, 13, 20.
Review by Anne Taylor of *The Basement*, in *New Republic*, 7–14 July 1979, 35–36.
Review by Joyce Carol Oates of *The Basement*, in *New York Times Book Review*, 9 September 1979, 14, 24, 26.
"Beyond Ideology: Kate Millett and the Case for Henry Miller," in *Perspectives on Pornography*, edited by Gary Day and Clive Bloom, London, MacMillian, 1988.
Review by Florence King of *The Loony-Bin Trip*, in *Chronicles: A Magazine of American Culture*, June 1990, 43–4.
Review of *The Loony-Bin Trip*, in *New York Times Book Review*, 3 June 1990, 12.
The Safe Sea of Women: Lesbian Fiction, 1969–1989 by Bonnie Zimmerman, Boston, Beacon Press, 1990.

Paul Monette

Manuscript Collections

University of California, Los Angeles Library special collections.

Biography

"Leaving a Legacy for the Gay Community" by Kay Longcope, in *Boston Globe*, 5 March 1990, 30.

Interviews

"A Story of Life in a Time of AIDS" by Bob Sipchen, in *Los Angeles Times*, 13 June 1988, Section 5, 1.

"Paul Monette" by Lisa See, in *Publishers Weekly*, 29 June 1992, 42–43.

Critical Sources

"Dispatches from Aphrodite's War" by William M. Hoffman, in *New York Times*, 11 September 1988, 3.

"Fire and Ice" by Richard Labonte, in *Advocate*, 13 September 1988, 65–66.

"'The Time before the War': AIDS, Memory, and Desire" by John M. Clum, in *American Literature*, 62:2, 1990, 648–667.

Review of *Afterlife* by Christopher Davis, in *Lambda Book Report*, 2:3, 1990, 20–21.

"Paul Monette: A Gay Novelist in Pursuit of the Human Heart" (review of *Afterlife*) by Susan Brownmiller, in *Chicago Tribune*, 11 February 1990, 3.

"An American Romantic" by Eden Ross Lipson, in *New York Times Book Review*, 4 March 1990, 7.

Review by David B. Feinberg of *Afterlife*, in *Outweek*, 4 April 1990, 59.

"Gay Life in the Ruins" (review of *Afterlife*) by John Weir, in *Washington Post*, 26 April 1990, 3.

Review by Judith Viorst of *Afterlife*, in *New York Times Book Review*, 29 April 1990, 7.

Review by Walta Borawski of *Halfway Home*, in *Gay Community News*, 21 April–4 May 1991, 7.

Review by Janice C. Simpson of *Halfway Home*, in *Time*, 6 May 1991, 72.

"No Half Measures" by Maria Maggenti, in *Outweek*, 8 May 1991, 56–58.

Review by K. Orton Williams of *Halfway Home*, in *San Francisco Sentinel*, 9 May 1991, 21.

Review by Marv Shaw of *Halfway Home*, in *Bay Area Reporter*, 23 May 1991.

"All in the Family" by David Kaufman, in *Nation*, 1 July 1991, 21–25, 30.

The Gay Novel in America by James Levin, New York, Garland, 1991.

"Paul Monette" by Michael Lassell, in *Advocate*, 2 June 1992, 34–35.

"A Closet of One's Own" (review of *Becoming a Man*) by Robert Dawidoff, in *Los Angeles Times*, 28 June 1992, 10.

"A Heart Laid Bare" (review of *Becoming a Man*) by Lawrence Biemiller, in *Washington Post*, 21 June 1992, 1.

"Outward Bound" by Maurice Berger, in *Voice*, 30 June 1992, 68.

"Paul Monette" by David Román. in *Contemporary Gay American Novelists*, edited by Emmanuel S. Nelson, Westport, Connecticut, Greenwood Press, 1993.

Lesléa Newman

Interviews

"Hamp Woman Writes of Lesbian Family" by Natalia Munoz, in *Sunday Republican* (Springfield, Massachusetts), 14 January 1990, E2.

"The Jewish Madonna" by Victoria A. Brownworth, in *Lambda Book Report*, November/December 1992, 22.

Critical Sources

"One Step at a Time" (review of *Good Enough to Eat*) by Susanna J. Sturgis, in *Women's Review of Books*, May 1987, 13.

Review by Joanne Jimason of *Heather Has Two Mommies*, in *Belles Lettres*, winter 1991, 59.

"Gay and Lesbian Books for Children," in *Lambda Book Report*, March 1991, 25; *Booklist*, 1992.

"Gay Bibliography Rejected by the New York City Schools," in *Publishers Weekly*, 27 April 1992, 18.

Felice Picano

Manuscript Collections

Beinecke Rare Books and Manuscript Library–American Collection at Yale University.

Biography

Contemporary Authors Autobiography Series, Volume 13, Detroit, Gale, 1991.

Interviews

Lesenlust (Berlin), September 1992.

New York Native, November 1992.

Frontiers, November 1992.

Edge, August 1993.

Playboy (Japan), September 1993.

Esquire (Japan), October 1993.

Critical Sources

The Gay Novel in America by James Levin, New York, Garland, 1991.

"Felice Picano" by Will Meyerhofer, in *Contemporary Gay American Novelists: A Bio-bibliographical Critical Sourcebook*, edited by Emmanuel S. Nelson, Westport, Connecticut, Greenwood Press, 1992.

Manuel Puig

Interviews

"Author and Translator: A Discussion of *Heartbreak Tango*" by Suzanne Jill Levine, in *Translation*, 2:1–2, 1974, 32–41.

With Ronald Christ, in *Partisan Review*, Number 44, 1977, 52–61.

"Manuel Puig at the University of Missouri-Columbia" by Katherine Bouman, in *American Hispanist*, 2:7, 1977, 11–12.

With Ronald Christ, in *Christopher Street*, April 1979, 25–31.

"Betraying a Latin Dream" by Don McPherson, in *Sunday Times* (color supplement), 8 April 1984, 51–52.

"From the Pampas to Hollywood: An Interview with Manuel Puig" (1984) by Reina Roffé, translation by Pamela Carmell, in *Bloomsbury Review*, March–April 1988, 14–15.

"The Art of Fiction CXIV" by Kathleen Wheaton, in *Paris Review*, winter 1989, 128–147.

"Brief Encounter: An Interview with Manuel Puig" (1979) by Jorgelina Corbatta, translated and adapted by Ilan Stavans, in *Review of Contemporary Fiction*, 11:3, 1991, 165–176.

"A Last Interview with Manuel Puig" by Ronald Christ, in *World Literature Today*, 65:4, 1991, 571–578.

Bibliography

"Manuel Puig: Selected Bibliography" by David Draper Clark, in *World Literature Today*, 65:4, 1991, 655–662.

Critical Sources

Suspended Fictions: Reading Novels by Manuel Puig by Lucille Kerr, Urbana, University of Illinois Press, 1987.

The Necessary Dream: A Study of the Novels of Manuel Puig by Pamela Bacarisse, Cardiff, University of Wales Press, 1988.

Review of Contemporary Fiction, 11:3, 1991 (William Gass and Manuel Puig issue).

World Literature Today, 65:4, 1991 (Manuel Puig issue).

Manuel Puig by Jonathan Tittler, Boston, Twayne, 1993.

Adrienne Rich

Biography

"Adrienne Rich" by Anne Newman, in *Dictionary of Literary Biography*, Volume 5: *American Poets since World War II*, Detroit, Gale, 1980.

"Adrienne Rich" by Elizabeth Meese, in *Dictionary of Literary Biography*, Volume 67: *Modern American Critics since 1955*, Detroit, Gale, 1988.

Interviews

With David Montenegro, in *Points of Departure: International Writers on Writing and Politics*, Ann Arbor, University of Michigan Press, 1991, 5–25.

"Adrienne Rich Charts a Difficult World" by David Trinidad, *Advocate*, 31 December 1991, 82–84.

Critical Sources

"Ghostlier Demarcations, Keener Sounds" by Helen Vendler, *Parnassus*, fall/winter 1973.

"On Adrienne Rich: Intelligence and Will" by Robert Boyers, in *Salmagundi*, spring/summer 1973.

"Adrienne Rich: The Poetics of Change" by Albert Gelpi, in *American Poetry Since 1960* edited by Robert B. Shaw, Cheadle, Cheshire, Carcanet Press, 1973.

Adrienne Rich's Poetry: A Norton Critical Edition edited by Barbara Charlesworth Gelpi and Albert Gelpi, New York, Norton, 1975.

Five Temperaments by David Kalstone, New York, Oxford University Press, 1977.

"Adrienne Rich and an Organic Feminist Criticism" by Marilyn R. Farwell, in *College English*, October 1977.

Reconstituting the World: The Poetry and Vision of Adrienne Rich by Judith McDaniel, Argyle, New York, Spinsters Ink, 1979.

"Levertov and Rich: The Later Poems" by Linda W. Wagner, in her *American Modern: Essays in Fiction and Poetry*, Port Washington, New York, Kennikat, 1980.

"All Too Real" by Helen Vendler, in *New York Review of Books*, 17 December 1981.

"The 'I' in Adrienne Rich: Individuation and the Androgyne Archetype" by Betty S. Flowers, in *Theory and Practice of Feminist Literary Criticism* edited by Gabriela Mora and Karen S. Van Hooft, Ypsilanti, Michigan, Bilingual Press, 1982.

"A Poetry of Survival: Unnaming and Renaming in the Poetry of Audre Lorde, Pat Parker, Sylvia Plath, and Adrienne Rich" by Pamela Annas, in *Colby Library Quarterly*, March 1982, 9–25.

"Adrienne Rich: Poet, Mother, Lesbian Feminist, Visionary" by Katherine Arnup, in *Atlantis*, fall/autumn 1982, 97–110.

"Her Cargo: Adrienne Rich and the Common Language" by Alicia Ostriker, in her *Writing Like a Woman*, Ann Arbor, University of Michigan Press, 1983.

"The Re-Vision of the Muse: Adrienne Rich, Audre Lorde, Judy Grahn, Olga Broumas" by Mary J. Carruthers, in *Hudson Review*, summer 1983, 293–322.

An American Triptych: Anne Bradstreet, Emily Dickinson, Adrienne Rich by Wendy Martin, Chapel Hill, University of North Carolina Press, 1984.

Reading Adrienne Rich: Reviews and Re-Visions, 1951–1981, edited by Jane Roberta Cooper, Ann Arbor, University of Michigan Press, 1984.

The Transforming Power of Language: The Poetry of Adrienne Rich by Myriam Diaz-Diocaretz, Utrecht, Hes Publishers, 1984.

Translating Poetic Discourse: Questions on Feminist Strategies in Adrienne Rich by Myriam Diaz-Diocaretz, Amsterdam, John Benjamins, 1985.

"Lingua Materna: The Speech of Female History" by Carol Muske, in *New York Times Book Review*, 20 January 1985.

The Aesthetics of Power: The Poetry of Adrienne Rich by Claire Keyes, Athens and London, University of Georgia Press, 1986.

"Adrienne Rich and Lesbian/Feminist Poetry" by Catharine Stimpson, in *Parnassus*, spring 1986, 249–268.

"'Love for the World and We Are In It': Adrienne Rich's Work of Repair" by Minnie Bruce Pratt, *Lambda Book Report*, November/December 1991.

Jane Rule

Critical Sources

"Jane Rule and the Reviewers" by Judith Niemi, in *Margins*, August 1975, 34–37.

"Strategies for Survival: The Subtle Subversion of Jane Rule" by Marilyn R, Schuster in *Feminist Studies*, fall 1981, 431–450.

"Jane Rule's *Desert* Blooms Anew" by Marie J, Kuda, in *GayLife* (Chicago), 21 November 1985.

"Focus Changes for Golden Rule" by Chris Newport, in *Lambda Book Report*, October/November 1989.

"Cruising the Libraries" by Lee Lynch, in *Lesbian Texts and Contexts*, New York University Press, 1990.

Safe Sea of Women: Lesbian Fiction, 1969–1989 by Bonnie Zimmerman, Boston, Beacon Press, 1990.

May Sarton

Manuscript Collections

Henry W. and Albert A. Berg Collection at the New York Public Library.

Biography

May Sarton: A Biography by Lenora Blouin, Metuchin, New Jersey, Scarecrow Press, 1978.

Bibliography

May Sarton: A Bibliography by Lenora Blouin, Metuchen, New Jersey, Scarecrow Press, 1978.

"A Revised Bibliography" by Lenora Blouin, in *May Sarton: Woman and Poet*, edited by Constance Hunting, Orono, Maine, National Poetry Foundation, 1982, 282–319.

Critical Sources

The Modern American Political Novel: 1900–1960 by Joseph Blotner, Austin, University of Texas Press, 1966.

May Sarton, by Agnes Silbey, Twayne, 1972.

"May Sarton's Women," in *Images of Women in Fiction*, edited by Susan K. Cornillon, Bowling Green University Popular Press, 1972.

Lesbian Images by Jane Rule, Garden City, New York, Doubleday, 1975.

"'Kinds of Love': Love and Friendship in the Novels of May Sarton" by Jane S. Bakerman, in *Critique*, Number 20, 1979.

Dictionary of Literary Biography Yearbook: 1981, Detroit, Gale, 1982.

May Sarton: Woman and Poet, edited by Constance Hunting, Orono, Maine, National Poetry Foundation, 1982.

"A Note on May Sarton" by Margaret Cruikshank, in *Journal of Homosexuality*, May 1986, 153.

"May Sarton" by Constance Hunting, in *Dictionary of Literary Biography*, Volume 48: *American Poets 1880–1945, Second Series*, Detroit, Gale, 1986.

The Gay Novel in America by James Levin, New York, Garland, 1991.

Sarah Schulman

Manuscript Collections

Lesbian Herstory Archives Special Collection.

Interviews

"Sarah Schulman: 'On the Road' to…" by Denise Kulp, in *Off Our Backs*, December 1986, 20.

"Troubled Times" by Andrea Freud Lowenstein, in *Women's Review of Books*, July 1990, 22–23.

"La Chanze," in *Interview*, November 1990, 70.

"It Could Be Verse" by Eileen Myles, in *Interview*, December 1990, 48.

Critical Sources

The Safe Sea of Women: Lesbian Fiction, 1969–1989 by Bonnie Zimmerman, Boston, Beacon Press, 1990.

Randy Shilts

Manuscript Collections

Gay and Lesbian Archives, San Francisco Public Library.

Interviews

With P. Holt, in *Publishers Weekly*, 19 March 1982, 6–7.

Contemporary Authors, Volume 127, Gale, 1989.

Publishers Weekly, 5 January 1990, 22–23.

With Laurie Udesky, in *Progressive*, May 1991, 30.

"AIDS and the Media" by John Katz, in *Rolling Stone*, May 1993, 31–32.

"The Life and Times of Randy Shilts" by Jeff Yarborough, in *Advocate*, 15 June 1993, 32–39.

"The Plutarch of Castro Street" by Mike Weiss, in *West*, 4 July 1993, 8–15.

Critical Sources

"The Making of an Epidemic" by Jim Miller and Pamela Abramson, in *Newsweek*, 19 October 1987, 91.

"Unhealthy Resistance" by Daniel S. Greenberg, in *Nation*, 7 November 1987, 526.

"Plenty of Blame to Go Around" by H. Jack Geiger, in *New York Times Book Review*, 8 November 1987, 9.

"Cries and Whispers of an Epidemic" by Ron Bluestein, in *Advocate*, 24 November 1987, 52–53, 63–67.

"A Brief but Deadly History" by Henry Klingeman, in *National Review*, 4 December 1987, 50–52.

Review by John Stark of *And the Band Played On*, in *People*, 18 January 1988, 16.

"An End to the Silence" by Duncan Campbell, in *New Statesman*, 4 March 1988, 22.

Review by John S. Sullivan of *And the Band Played On*, in *America*, 4 June 1988, 588.

"AIDS without End" by Diane Johnson and John F. Murray, in *New York Review of Books*, 18 August 1988, 57–63.

Review of *And the Band Played On*, in *Progressive*, December 1988, 45.

Review by Joe Wakelee-Lynch of *And the Band Played On*, in *Utne Reader*, January–February 1991, 136.

"A Disease of Society" by Jeffrey Weeks, in *New Statesman*, 26 April 1991, 32.

"Well-Known Author on AIDS Reveals He Has the Disease" by Leah Garchik, in *Detroit Free Press*, 17 February 1993, 3C.

Ann Allen Shockley

Biography

Dictionary of Literary Biography, Volume 33: *Afro-American Fiction Writers after 1955*, Detroit, Gale, 1984, 232–236.

Bibliography

Ann Allen Shockley: An Annotated Primary and Secondary Bibliography by Rita B. Dandridge, New York, Greenwood Press, 1987.

Critical Sources

"Comprehensive Oppression: Lesbians and Race in the Work of Ann Allen Shockley" by Evelyn C. White, in *Backbone 3*, 1979, 38–40.

"Deny, Deny, Deny" (review of *The Black and White of It*) by Karla Jay, in *New Women's Times Feminist Review*, April/May 1981, 17–18.

Review by Rebecca Sue Taylor of *Say Jesus and Come to Me*, in *Library Journal*, 1 May 1982.

Unpublished letter to Rita Dandridge, 29 January 1984.

"Theme and Portraiture in the Fiction of Ann Allen Shockley" (dissertation) by SDiane Bogus, Miami University, 1988.

Gertrude Stein

Manuscript Collections

Beinecke Library, Yale University, New Haven, Connecticut.
Bancroft Library, University of California, Berkeley.
University of Texas, Austin.

Biography

Gertrude Stein: Her Life and Work by Elizabeth Sprigge, New York, Harper, 1957.

The Third Rose: Gertrude Stein and Her World by John Malcolm Brinnin, Boston, Little, Brown, 1959.

Everybody Who Was Anybody: A Biography of Gertrude Stein by Janet Hobhouse, New York, Putnam, 1975.

Interviews

With Robert Bartlett Haas, in *Unclan Review*, summer 1962, 3–11, spring 1963, 40–48, and winter 1964, 44–48.

Bibliography

Gertrude Stein: A Bibliography by Robert A. Wilson, New York, Pheonix Bookshop, 1974.

Critical Sources

Gertrude Stein in Pieces by Richard Bridgeman, New York, Oxford University Press, 1970.

A Primer for the Gradual Understanding of Gertrude Stein, edited by Robert Bartlett Haas, Los Angeles, Black Sparrow Press, 1971.

"The Mind, The Body, and Gertrude Stein" by Catherine R. Stimpson, in *Critical Inquiry*, spring 1977.

"Is Flesh Advisable?: The Interior Theater of Gertrude Stein" by Elizabeth Fifer, in *Signs*, spring 1979.

A Different Language: Gertrude Stein's Experimental Writing by Marianne DeKoven, Madison, University of Wisconsin, 1983.

Critical Essays on Gertrude Stein, edited by Michael J. Hoffman, Boston, G. K. Hall, 1986.

"Beyond the Reaches of Feminist Criticism: A Letter from Paris" by Shari Benstock, in *Feminist Issues in Literary Scholarship*, editedby Shari Benstock, Bloomington, 1987, 7–29.

Testimony Against Gertrude Stein (special issue of *Transition*, February 1935), edited by Eugene Jolas, Servire Press, The Hague.

Gore Vidal

Manuscript Collections

Wisconsin Historical Society, Madison.

Interviews

Fag Rag, winter 1974.

Gay Sunshine, winter 1975.

Views from a Window: Conversations with Gore Vidal, edited by Robert J. Stanton and Gore Vidal, Secaucus, New Jersey, Lyle Stuart, 1980.

"Gore Vidal: The Writer as Citizen" by Claudia Dreifus, in *Progressive*, September 1986, 36.

"Gore Vidal" by Mark Matousek, in *Interview*, June 1987, 92.

"Grandson of a 'Populist Demagogue'" by Herbert Mitgang, in *New York Times Book Review*, 14 June 1987, 42.

"The Rise and Fall of the American Empire" by Alvin P. Sanoff, in *U.S. News and World Report*, 13 July 1987, 62.

"Gore Vidal" by David Sheff, in *Playboy*, December 1987, 51.

"The Chore of Being Gore" by Andrew Kopkind, in *Interview*, June 1988, 62.

"Tug of War" by Colin Wright, in *New Statesman and Society*, 3 November 1989, 43.

"Through the Looking Glass" by Howard Means, in *Washingtonian*, February 1990, 78.

"Mailer and Vidal: The Big Schmooze" by Carole Mallory, in *Esquire*, May 1991, 105.

"'J.F.K.' Is Not What He Had in Mind" by Michael Anderson, in *New York Times Book Review*, 30 August 1992, 27.

Bibliography

Gore Vidal: A Primary and Secondary Bibliography by Robert J. Stanton, Boston, G. K. Hall, 1978.

Critical Sources

"Gore Vidal: The Search for a King" by John W. Aldridge, in his *After the Lost Generation: A Critical Study of the Writers of Two Wars*, New York, McGraw-Hill, 1951, 170–183.

Gore Vidal by Ray Lewis White, Boston, Twayne Publishers, 1968.

The Apostate Angel: A Critical Study of Gore Vidal by Bernard F. Dick, New York, Random House, 1974.

"Gore Vidal" by Robert Graalman, in *Dictionary of Literary Biography*, Volume 6: *American Novelists since World War II*, Detroit, Gale, 1980.

"The Mysteries of Edgar Box (a.k.a. Gore Vidal)" by Earl F. Bargainnier, in *Clues* (Bowling Green, Ohio), spring-summer 1981, 45–42.

"Narrative Patterns in the Novels of Gore Vidal" by David Barton, in *Notes on Contemporary Literature* (Carrollton, Georgia), September 1981, 3–5.

Gore Vidal by Robert F. Kiernan, New York, Ungar, 1982.

"Political Change in America: Perspectives from the Popular Historical Novels of Michener and Vidal" by Samuel M. Hines, Jr., in *Political Mythology and Popular Fiction*, edited by Ernest J. Yanarella and Lee Sigelman, Westport, Connecticut, Greenwood Press, 1988, 81–99.

"Collecting Mystery Fiction: Edgar Box (Gore Vidal)" by Otto Penzler, in *Armchair Detective* (New York), winter 1989, 38.

Gay Fictions, Wilde to Stonewall: Studies in a Male Homosexual Literary Tradition by Claude J. Summers, New York, Continuum, 1990.

"Gore Vidal: A Grandfather's Legacy" by Marvin J. LaHood, in *World Literature Today* (Norman, Oklahoma), summer 1990, 413–417.

The Gay Novel in America by James Levin, New York, Garland, 1991.

"My O My O Myra" by Catherine R. Stimpson, in *New England Review* (Middlebury, Vermont), fall 1991, 102–115.

Gore Vidal: Writer against the Grain edited by Jay Parini, New York, Columbia University Press, 1992.

"Gore's Lore" by Arthur Lubow, in *Vanity Fair*, September 1992, 126.

"A Gadfly in Glorious, Angry Exile" by Martha Duffy, in *Time*, 28 September 1992, 64–66.

"Gore Vidal" by Joel Shatzky, in *Contemporary Gay American Novelists*, edited by Emmanuel S. Nelson, Westport, Connecticut, Greenwood Press, 1993.

Edmund White

Interviews

Library Journal, 15 February 1973.

Alive and Writing: Interviews by Larry McCaffery, University Press of Illinois, 1987, 257–274.

"The Importance of Being: Armistad Maupin and Edmund White" by Walter Kendrick, in *Village Voice*, 28 June 1988, 22.

Paris Review (New York), fall 1988, 47–80.

"An Interview with Edmund White," in *Missouri Review* (Columbia, Missouri), 13:2, 1990, 89–110.

"From Paris to Providence: An Interview with Edmund White" by Alfred Corn, in *Christopher Street* (New York), October 1991, 13.

Critical Sources

"Edmund White" by William Goldstein, in *Publishers Weekly*, 24 September 1982, 6–8.

"Imagining Other Lives" by Leonard Schulman, in *Time*, 30 July 1990.

The Gay Novel in America by James Levin, New York, Garland, 1991.

"Edmund White" by David Bergman, in *Contemporary Gay American Novelists*, edited by Emmanuel S. Nelson, Westport, Connecticut, Greenwood, 1993, 386–394.

Oscar Wilde

Manuscript Collections

William Andrews Clark Memorial Library, University of California, Los Angeles; New York Public Library; Beinecke Library, Yale University; University of Edinburgh Library; Magdalen College, Oxford University.

Biography

The Unrecorded Life of Oscar Wilde by Rupert Croft-Cooke, New York, McKay, 1972.

Oscar Wilde by Sheridan Morley, New York, Holt, Rinehart & Winston, 1976.

Oscar Wilde by Richard Ellmann, London, Hamish Hamilton, 1987, New York, Knopf, 1988.

Bibliography

Bibliography of Oscar Wilde by Stuart Mason, London, Laurie, 1914.

Oscar Wilde: An Annotated Bibliography of Criticism by E. H. Hickhail, London, Macmillan, 1978.

Critical Sources

Oscar Wilde Discovers America by Lloyd Lewis and Henry Justin Smith, 1882, New York, Harcourt, 1936.

The Letters of Oscar Wilde, edited by Rupert Hart-Davis, New York, Harcourt, 1962.

Complete Works of Oscar Wilde, edited by J. B. Foreman, with introduction by Vyvyan Holland, New York, Harper, 1966.

Oscar Wilde: The Critical Heritage, edited by Karl Beckson, London, Routledge and Kegan Paul, 1970.

Oscar Wilde by Richard Ellmann, New York, Knopf, 1988.

Gay Fictions, Wilde to Stonewall: Studies in a Male Homosexual Literary Tradition by Claude J. Summers, New York, Continuum, 1990.

Virginia Woolf

Manuscript Collections

Henry W. and Albert A. Berg Collection of English and American Literature, New York Public Library; Charleston Papers, King's College, Cambridge; Monk's House Papers, University of SussexLibrary; Washington State University's Library at Pullman, Washington; University of Texas at Austin.

Biography

Beginning Again: An Autobiography of the Years 1911 to 1918 by Leonard Woolf, New York, Harcourt, 1964.

All the Way: An Autobiography of the Years 1919 to 1939 by Leonard Woolf, New York, Harcourt, 1967.

The Journey Not the Arrival Matters: An Autobiography of the Years 1939 to 1969 by Leonard Woolf, New York, Harcourt, 1970.

Virginia Woolf: A Biography by Quentin Bell, New York, Harcourt, 1972.

The Jessamy Brides: The Friendship of Virginia Woolf and Vita Sackville West by Joan Trautmann, University Park, Pennsylvania, Pennsylvania State Studies, 1973.

Virginia Woolf and Her World by John Lehmann, New York, Harcourt, 1975.

A Marriage of the Minds by George Spater and Ian Parsons, New York, Harcourt, 1977.

Woman of Letters: A Life of Virginia Woolf, New York, Oxford University Press, 1978.

Virginia Woolf: A Writer's Life by Lyndall Gordon, Oxford, Oxford University Press, 1984.

Virginia Woolf: Life and London; A Biography of Place by Jean Moorcroft Wilson, New York, Norton, 1988.

Bibliography

Virginia Woolf: An Annotated Bibliography of Criticism, by Robin Majumdar, New York and London, Garland, 1976.

A Bibliography of Virginia Woolf by B. J. Kirkpatrick, Oxford, Clarendon Press, 1980.

Critical Sources

The Well of Loneliness by Radclyffe Hall, New York, Covici-Friede, 1928.

Mimesis: The Representation of Reality in Western Literature by Erich Auerbach, translation by Willard R. Trask, Princeton, Princeton University Press, 1953.

Modern Fiction Studies, autumn, 1972 (special Virginia Woolf issue).

Virginia Woolf and the Androgynous Vision by Nancy Topping Bazin, New Brunswick, New Jersey, Rutgers University Press, 1973.

Toward a Recognition of Androgyny by Carol G. Heilbrun, New York, Knopf, 1973.

Portrait of a Marriage by Nigel Nicholson, New York, Anthenaeum, 1973.

Virginia Woolf: A Critical Reading by Avrom Fleishman, Baltimore, Johns Hopkins University Press, 1975.

The Bloomsbury Group: A Collection of Memoirs, Commentary, andCriticism by S. P. Rosenbaum, Toronto, University of Toronto Press, 1975.

Bulletin of the New York Library, winter, 1977 (special Virginia Woolf issue).

Virginia Woolf: Sources of Madness and Art by Jean O. Love, Berkeley and London, University of California Press, 1977.

Bloomsbury: A House of Lions by Leon Edel, Philadelphia and New York, Lippincott, 1979.

Continuing Presences: Virginia Woolf's Use of Literary Allusion by Beverly Ann Schlack, University Park, Pennsylvania State University Press, 1979.

Virginia Woolf: Revaluation and Continuity, edited by Ralph Freedman, Berkeley and London, University of California Press, 1980.

The Absent Father: Virginia Woolf and Walter Pater by Perry Meisel, New Haven and London, Yale University Press, 1980.

Surpassing the Love of Men: Romantic Friendship and Love between Women from the Renaissance to the Present by Lillian Faderman, New York, Morrow, 1981.

New Feminist Essays on Virginia Woolf, edited by Jane Marcus, Lincoln, University of Nebraska Press, 1981.

All That Summer She Was Mad by Stephen Trombley, New York, Continuum, 1982.

Virginia Woolf's Literary Sources and Allusions: A Guide to the Essays by Elizabeth Steele, New York and London, Garland, 1983.

Virginia Woolf: A Guide to Research by Thomas Jackson Rice, New York and London, Garland, 1984.

"Liberty, Sorority, Misogyny," "Taking the Bull by the Udders: Sexual Difference in Virginia Woolf: A Conspiracy Theory," and "Sapphistry: Narration as Lesbian Seduction in *A Room of One's Own*" by Jane Marcus, in *Virginia Woolf and the Languages of Patriarchy*, Bloomington, Indiana University Press, 1987, 75–95, 136–62, and 163–87.

"'If I Saw You Would You Kiss Me?': Sapphism and the Subversiveness of Virginia Woolf's *Orlando*" by Sherron E. Knopp, in *PMLA*, January 1988, 23–34.

Who Killed Virginia Woolf?: A Psychobiography by Alma Halbert Bond, Human Sciences Press, 1989.

Virginia Woolf: The Impact of Childhood Sexual Abuse on Her Life and Work by Louise A. DeSalvo, Boston, Beacon Press, 1989.

"Sexual Identity and *A Room of One's Own*: 'Secret Economies' in Virginia Woolf's Feminist Discourse" by Ellen Bayuk Rosenman, in *Signs: Journal of Women in Culture and Society*, spring 1989, 634– 650.

Index